THE
CAMBRIDGE
MODERN HISTORY

PLANNED BY

THE LATE LORD ACTON LL.D.

REGIUS PROFESSOR OF MODERN HISTORY

EDITED BY

A. W. WARD LITT.D.

G. W. PROTHERO LITT.D.

STANLEY LEATHES M.A.

VOLUME II

THE REFORMATION

New York

THE MACMILLAN COMPANY

LONDON: MACMILLAN & CO., LTD.

1904

Publishing Statement:

This important reprint was made from an old and scarce book.

Therefore, it may have defects such as missing pages, erroneous pagination, blurred pages, missing text, poor pictures, markings, marginalia and other issues beyond our control.

Because this is such an important and rare work, we believe it is best to reproduce this book regardless of its original condition.

Thank you for your understanding and enjoy this unique book!

Part 2

CHAPTER XII

THE CATHOLIC SOUTH

THE great wave of revolution and reconstruction which was passing over northern Europe in the earlier half of the sixteenth century did not leave the south untouched. Though the first actual outbreak occurred beyond the Alps, the feeling to which it gave expression was not merely Teutonic. Many of the causes which led up to it were common to all Western Christendom; some, as for instance the demand for liberty of opinion and free enquiry, were even more characteristic of Italy than of Germany. Accordingly, vigorous attempts arose in many parts of southern Europe to bring about a reformation in the Church — attempts which were by no means a mere echo of the changes in the north. But they never obtained a really strong hold upon the affections of the common people, and never secured the friendship, or even the neutrality, of the civil power; and so, both in Italy and in the Iberian peninsula, their suppression was only a question of time. By the year 1576, when the charges against Bartolomé Carranza were finally adjudicated upon, they were practically at an end. Isolated cases of heresy still occurred, but there was no longer anything like an organised revolt against the doctrinal or disciplinary system of the Papacy.

In tracing the course of the Reform movements of southern Europe we are dealing with forces which became more widely divergent as time went on. Men at first acted together who ultimately found themselves violently opposed to one another; principles were adduced on the same side which proved in time to be sharply contrasted. The old-standing desire to curb the power of the Curia and to vindicate the authority of General Councils over the whole Church joined hands in the earlier stages of the movement with the wider, yet more individualistic, aspirations of the Renaissance. Men who had come under the influence of the new spirit in any of its manifestations were able to work together at first, whether they strove to reconstruct a worn-out theology, or to abolish corrupt practices, or to restore the standard of personal devotion and moral conduct. It was only by degrees that the ascetic, the humanist, and the doctrinal Reformer drifted into relations of antagonism; but this was the position ultimately reached. And a stronger line of division app as time went on. There were some who refused to take any step would separate them from the communion of the Church ; as Carnesecchi expressed it, the Catholic religion was theirs already, and all that they desired was that it should be better preached. Others however felt compelled to withdraw from the fellowship of a corrupt society, still strenuously affirming that by so doing they had in no way departed from the unity of the Church. Of the former, many were influenced by the doctrinal movement in its most extreme forms, and some even died for their opinions without giving way. Of the latter, many recognised that their action could only be justified by the immediate claims of Christian truth. But in spite of individual divergences, here was a real line of division, in southern Europe as in the north.

I

THE REFORMATION IN ITALY

So far as the movement was one of protest against practical abuses, the need for Reform was not less widely felt in Italy than in Germany. Rodrigo Niño, the imperial ambassador to the Doge and Signory, wrote in 1535 that there were few in Venice who were not more Lutheran than Luther himself with regard to such matters as the reform of the clergy and their secular state. Venice was no doubt exceptional, and the state of feeling there was not that of Italy as a whole. Nevertheless, vigorous efforts after practical reform had begun in other parts of Italy long before this. Adrian of Utrecht, Bishop of Tortosa, the friend of Erasmus, and the former tutor of Charles V, ascended the papal throne in 1522 with a firm resolve to set the Church in order, and to begin with his own household. In many ways he seemed well fitted for the task. A student of distinction, his uprightness, personal piety, and strictness of life were known to all men ; and already, as Legate in Spain, he had taken a vigorous part in the reform of the Religious Houses there. But in Rome he proved to be quite helpless. Satisfied with the scholastic theology in which he was so great an adept, he did not understand the questionings which were beginning to stir the minds of others. The Romans had no fellow-feeling for a man who never gave way to anger or to mirth, and to whom the treasures of sculpture in the Vatican were no more than " pagan idols." The scholar who had done so much to foster learning at Louvain was to them only a stranger who knew no Italian, though he spoke Latin very well " for a barbarian." Moreover, the Curia was determined not to be reformed. Thus Adrian achieved nothing ; he died unregretted in 1523, not without the usual suspicion of poison ; and from that time forward every Pope has been an Italian.

But already an important movement had been inaugurated. Just before or shortly after the accession of Adrian VI, a number of earnest-minded men, clergy and laity, had banded themselves together at Rome in the famous "Oratory of Divine Love," to work and pray for the purification of the Church. Their leaders were Giovanni Pietro Caraffa, afterwards Pope Paul IV, and the Count Gaetano da Thiene, who was subsequently canonised. The society consisted of fifty or sixty distinguished men, including amongst others Jacopo Sadoleto, Giammatteo Giberti, Latino Giovenale, Girolamo and Luigi Lippomano, and Giuliano Dati. They held their spiritual exercises in the Church of Santi Silvestro e Dorotea, of which Dati was curate, and consulted together on the evils of the day. In 1524 Gaetano withdrew to form a new Order of Clerks Regular, who were presently joined by Caraffa, and came to be known as Theatines from his see of Theate (Chieti in the Abruzzi); but the original society still continued to meet until it was dispersed by the Sack of Rome in 1527. Many of its former members, including Caraffa and Giberti, met again at Venice, where they came under the influence of the senator Gasparo Contarini. By degrees others were admitted to their consultations, including Gregorio Cortese, the Abbot of San Giorgio Maggiore, Pietro Bembo, and Luigi Priuli, and subsequently Brucioli, the Florentine exile, the learned scholar Marcantonio Flaminio, and the Englishman Reginald Pole. Contarini, still a layman, became from this time forward the leading spirit amongst them.

When the enlightened Alessandro Farnese became Pope as Paul III (1534), he found this group of zealous men ready to his hand. Contarini was made a Cardinal at his first creation, and Sadoleto, Caraffa, and Pole received the purple in the following year. In 1537, when he appointed a commission to suggest measures for the reform of the Church, most of its members were chosen from this quarter, the names being those of Contarini, Caraffa, Sadoleto, Pole, Fregoso, Aleander, Giberti, Cortese, and Tommaso Badia. The fruit of their labours, the famous *Consilium de emendanda Ecclesia*, was unsparing in reprobation of abuses and rich in practical suggestions. But although a few efforts were made to simplify the procedure of the Curia, the forces of inertia proved too strong, and the *Consilium* was little more than a dead letter. In after years it fell into bad odour, partly owing to its damaging admissions, partly because the Lutherans had taken it up. Moreover Caraffa came in time to suspect many of his former associates of heresy; and after he became Pope the work was placed on the *Index Librorum Prohibitorum* of 1559. But, even had it been otherwise received, it could not have stayed the tide. The revolt against abuses had already opened the way to movements of a more destructive character; the new opinions were already making their appearance south of the Alps.

Italy, always a land of popular movements, was in many ways predisposed to welcome the new opinions. Some of them had been foreshadowed there, and revolt against the Papacy was to its peoples no new thing. The Cathari of the north, with their Manichean and anti-trinitarian tendencies, had long died out; but the Waldenses, although by no means so numerous as formerly, were still to be found in the valleys of Piedmont and Calabria. The movements of the sixteenth century in Italy were however entirely unconnected with these, and the impulse as a whole came from without. There is indeed one notable exception. Pietro Speziale of Cittadella finished his great work *De Gratia Dei* in 1542; but he tells us, with obvious sincerity, that he had formulated his theory of Justification and Grace thirty years earlier, before Luther had begun to preach. In the main he agrees with that of Luther, but he resolutely asserts the freedom of the will, and repudiates the Lutheran teaching on this subject; and although he speaks strongly against particular abuses, he does not undervalue the Church system of his day. The old man was thrown into prison in 1543, escaped six years afterwards by the help of two Anabaptists and joined their party, and subsequently made a formal recantation in prison. But Speziale stands alone; and it is clear that the doctrinal revolt as a whole came from the north.

The intercourse between Italy and Germany was very close; and a continual stream of traders and students flowed in both directions. At Venice there was a large Teutonic colony, having its centre in the Fondaco de' Tedeschi. The imperial army which invaded Italy in 1526 contained a large number of Lutherans; and with Georg von Frundsberg's *Landsknechte* there came the scholar Jakob Ziegler, later known in Venice as Luther's lieutenant. The commonwealth of letters ignored national boundaries; and there was a brisk correspondence between Luther and Zwingli and their admirers in Italy. So early as 1519 Luther's works were being sold in Lombardy by Francesco Calvi or Minicio, a bookseller of Pavia, who had procured a stock from Froben at Basel. In the following year, as we learn from a letter of Burchard von Schenk, they were eagerly purchased at Venice; and Marino Sanuto notes in his Diary that a seizure of them had been made at the instance of the patriarch, though not until part of the stock had been disposed of. Writings of Luther, Melanchthon, and others were presently translated into Italian; and being issued anonymously or under fictitious names, they circulated widely. Thus Luther's sermons on the Lord's Prayer appeared anonymously before 1525, and Melanchthon's *Loci Communes* about 1534 under the title *I Principii della Teologia* by "Ippofilo da Terra Nigra"; while other tracts of Luther's were subsequently tacked on to the posthumously issued works of Cardinal Federigo Fregoso.

In ways such as these the opinions of Luther spread, and in a less degree those of Zwingli. There were many who were ready to adopt them, in whole or in part. A hermit who inveighed against "priests and friars" at Venice in 1516 can hardly be called a Lutheran; but Fra Andrea of Ferrara, who preached at Christmas, 1520, at San Marco and in the open air, is expressly said to have "followed the doctrine of Martin Luther." So did a Carmelite friar, Giambattista Pallavicino, who preached at Brescia in Lent, 1527, and others elsewhere. There were three "heretics" at Mirandola in 1524 of whom nothing else is known; but the Florentine physician Girolamo di Bartolommeo Buonagrazia, when proceeded against in 1531, confessed that he had been in correspondence with Luther in 1527, and accepted his doctrine. Nor was Zwingli without supporters. The letters of Egidio della Porta, an Austin friar of Como (a centre of heresy as early as the time of Julius II), prove that he and some of his fellows were ready to leave Italy and throw in their lot with Zwingli in 1525–6. In 1531 a native of Como who had spent three years beyond the Alps was preaching against the current doctrine of the Eucharist. About the same time priests at Como were laying hands on others, who were to administer the Eucharist in both kinds: one of them, Vincenzio Massaro, is said to have taken a fee of fifteen ducats from all whom he ordained. And a letter written in 1530 by Francesco Negri of Bassano, who had fled from a Benedictine House at Padua and joined Zwingli, and who afterwards drifted to Anabaptism, gives the names of many priests in North Italy whom he reckoned as "brethren."

The disaffected were very numerous. According to the ambassador Francesco Contarini, the Lutherans of Germany boasted in 1535 that their sympathisers in Italy alone would make an army sufficient to deliver them from the priests, and that they had enough friends in the monastic orders to intimidate all who were opposed to them. This of course is a violent exaggeration, and in Italy also popular rumour magnified the danger; yet even so it was not slight. The Reforming movement was especially strong in certain well-defined centres, the chief being Venice and its territories, Ferrara, Modena, Naples, and Lucca.

In VENICE, where foreigners were many and toleration was a principle of the State, the Reform soon made its appearance, and before long found a home. Measures of precaution or repression were demanded by the Patriarch on behalf of the Roman Curia; but as late as 1529 the Signory was able to certify that, excepting for the tolerated German conventicles, the city was free from heresy. Soon afterwards however, in a report to Clement VII on the subject, Caraffa mentions, amongst other evils, the fact that many friars had fallen into heresy, and in particular the disciples of "a certain Franciscan now dead." Of these he names Girolamo Galateo, Bartolommeo Fonzio, and Alessandro da Piero di Sacco. The Bishop of Chieti was thereupon commissioned, by a brief of May 9, 1530, to proceed against Galateo; and from this time forward the extirpation of heresy was the ruling passion of his life. He it was who procured from Pope Paul III the bull *Licet ab initio* (July 21, 1542) reorganising the Roman Inquisition on the basis of that of Spain. He was its first head, and in 1555, as Pope Paul IV, he completed the extension of its power over the whole of Italy.

Galateo was already in prison on suspicion of heresy for certain sermons preached "Bible in hand" at Padua; but under the lenient system of the Venetian Inquisition he was soon at liberty. Caraffa now commenced a new process against him; he was found guilty, and sentenced to degradation and death. This led to a contest with the Signory, who delivered him from Caraffa's hands and consigned him to prison. Here he had been for seven years, when, on the intercession of a friendly senator, he was allowed to make his defence in writing. This *Confession* is remarkable. It is Augustinian rather than Lutheran in doctrine. It affirms the doctrine of saving faith without any extravagant depreciation of free-will or of good works; the system of the Church as a whole is defended, and the Pope is "the chief of shepherds." Galateo was allowed out on bail, but directed to amend his *Confession* on some points. He refused to do this, and three years later was cast into prison again, where he died in 1541.

Of Galateo's two companions, Alessandro was already in prison, and is not heard of again. Bartolommeo Fonzio had already incurred the enmity of Caraffa by his advocacy of Henry VIII's divorce; he managed however to clear himself of heresy, and soon left Venice for Germany, where he was employed as a papal agent. But he fell under the suspicion of Aleander and others by his intercourse with the Lutherans; and not without reason, for it was probably he who translated Luther's letter *An den christlichen Adel* into Italian. On retiring from the papal service he was transferred by Clement VII from the Order of Friars Minor to the Third Order of St Francis and permitted to return to Venice; but he was still an object of suspicion, which was not diminished by a little Catechism which he produced. After years of wandering he settled as Padua and opened a school; but it was broken up by order of Caraffa, now Inquisitor-General. Thence he passed to Cittadella, where reformed opinions were widespread, and again began to teach, soon winning the love of the people. But in May, 1558, he was again arrested, by order of the *Dieci*, and condemned after four years' examination for the general unsatisfactoriness of his teaching. He was called upon to abjure but refused; then gave way to persuasion and recanted; then recanted his recantation. At length he was sentenced to death at the stake; the sentence was as usual commuted into one of drowning, and he was cast into the sea on August 4, 1562.

Meanwhile, other teachers were going further in the direction of Lutheranism than Galateo and Fonzio. Giulio della Rovere, an Austin Friar of Milan, got into trouble at Bologna in 1538 for a course of sermons preached there. Three years later he came to Venice, and preached at San Cassiano in Lent, staying in the house of Celio Secondo Curione, of whom more presently. His doctrine was attacked; he abjured, and was sentenced to be imprisoned and then banished. He escaped and fled to the Grisons, where the Reform movement had already

taken root, the main impulse coming from the Swiss Cantons. Here
he ministered, generally at Poschiavo, until his death in 1571. The
Florentine scholar Antonio Brucioli, banished from his own city, had
come to Venice and set up a printing-press. In 1532 (two years before
Luther's German translation was completed) he published his Italian
translation of the whole Bible, based upon Santi Pagnani's learned
Latin version from the original languages; and this he followed up
subsequently by a voluminous commentary. In 1546 he was in the
prisons of the Inquisition, accused of publishing heretical books; and
although it may be doubted whether anything of his could justly be so
described, his troubles at the hands of the Holy Office ended only with
his life. A more striking personality was that of Baldo Lupetino of
Albona in Istria, uncle of the well-known Mattia Vlacich (M. Flacius
Illyricus. He was a conventual Franciscan, and had held the office of
provincial; an acute scholar and a devout man. Accused of preaching
heresy in the Duomo at Cherso, he fell into the hands of the Venetian
Inquisition in 1541; and, although the Lutheran Princes interceded on
his behalf, he was sentenced to imprisonment for life, it being clear from
depositions made then and subsequently that he was a Lutheran. In
1547 he was again in trouble for preaching to his fellow-prisoners, and
was sentenced to be beheaded, his body to be burned, and his ashes to
be cast into the sea " to the honour and glory of Jesus Christ." The
Doge relaxed the sentence; but in 1555 he was again accused, and the
following year he was degraded and drowned.

Nor were disciples lacking. The letters of Aleander, when Nuncio at
Venice, speak of a great religious association of artisans existing there in
1534, the leaders being one Pietro Buonavita of Padua, a carpenter, a
French glover, and several German Lutherans. The two first-mentioned
were taken and imprisoned for life; but Aleander continues to lament the
progress of heresy and the apathy of the Senate. We learn more about
the Reformed in Venetian lands from the letters of Baldassare Altieri of
Aquila in the Abruzzi, a literary adventurer who came to Venice about
1540, served Sir Edmund Hastwell, the English ambassador, till 1548,
and after two years of wandering died at Ferrara in August, 1550. He
acted as a kind of secretary to the Reformed, and wrote on behalf of
" the brethren of the Church of Venice, Vicenza, and Treviso " to Luther,
Bullinger, and others, begging for the good offices of the Lutherans with
the Venetian government. The brethren are, he says, in the sorest need,
and cannot improve their state whilst the Signory allows them no liberty.
They have no public churches; each is a church to himself. There are
plenty of apostles, but none properly called; all is disorder, and false
teachers abound. Nevertheless, they adhere to Luther in doctrine as
against the Sacramentaries, and do not despair, since " God can raise up
new Luthers amongst them." But their appeals were in vain; the
Lutheran Princes had their hands full already, and the Swiss were not

likely to help those who sided with Luther against them. In the end, their associations were broken up. Many were punished, many more gave way; those who were left seem to have gravitated towards anabaptist and speculative views of a very pronounced kind.

It is hard to form a precise idea of the number of the Reformed in Venice, but they were evidently very numerous. Processes for heresy were very common, especially after Giovanni della Casa became Nuncio in 1547, with orders to expedite the work. Of the records which survive many are at Udine; but at Venice alone there still remain over eight hundred processes for Lutheranism between 1547 and 1600, and more than a hundred more for Anabaptism, Calvinism, and other heresies. The greater number are from Venice itself; but Vicenza, Brescia and Cittadella are represented, with a number of smaller places.

FERRARA, long famous for learning and the fine arts, was a centre of hardly less importance, though in quite a different way. Ercole, the son of the reigning Duke Alfonso, had married Renée the daughter of Louis XII of France in 1528, and succeeded his father six years later. Renée had already imbibed the new ideas from her cousin Margaret of Navarre and from her governess Madame de Soubise, poetess and translator of the Psalms. The latter, with the whole of her distinguished family, followed her to Ferrara; and as most of Renée's suite, which included Clément Marot, the poet, were of the same way of thinking, her Court became a rallying-point for the Reformed. From France came the statesman Hubert Languet and the poet Léon Jamet; from Germany the Court physician Johann Sinapius and his brother Kilian, who acted as a tutor to Renée's children. There were also Alberto Lollio and the canon Celio Calagnani, joint founders of the Academy of the *Elevati;* the physician Angelo Manzioli, whose famous *Zodiacus Vitae,* published by him under the pseudonym Marcello Palingenio Stellato, poured ridicule on the monks and clergy; and Fulvio Peregrino Morato, who had preceded Kilian Sinapius in his office but had been banished in 1539, perhaps for Lutheran opinions. He returned to the University in 1539, bringing with him his most famous daughter Olympia Morata, "an infant prodigy who became a distinguished woman." She became an intimate member of Renée's household, corresponded on equal terms with the most learned men of the day, passed through a sceptical phase to devout Lutheranism, and finally, having incurred her patron's anger, married a German physician named Grunthler and accompanied him to his own land. Nor were Renée and Olympia the only well-known women who adopted Reformed views there. Amongst others who did so were Lavinia della Rovere, grand-niece of Pope Julius II, and the Countess Giulia Rangone, a daughter of the House of Bentivoglio. One other resident at the Court must be mentioned — the learned Cretan who took the name of Francesco Porto. He was a man of great caution and reticence, but devoted to the cause of Reform. After studying at Venice and Padua and teaching for ten years at the University of Modena, he came to Ferrara in 1546 to take the place of Kilian Sinapius. The complaints of the Pope led to his expulsion in 1551. He was again with Renée, as her reader, in 1553, but then retired to Venice and ultimately to Geneva.

Hither also at various times came students and others whose lives were in danger elsewhere. Among these was the Piedmontese Celio Secondo Curione, a latitudinarian and a student of the Reformed doctrines from his youth. After several remarkable escapes from capture he fled to Padua, thence (after three years as professor in the University) to Venice, and thence to Ferrara. Through Renée's influence he received a chair at Lucca while Ochino was there, but after a short and troublous stay had to take refuge beyond the Alps. But Ferrara gave shelter to a greater fugitive than any of Italian birth. Early in 1536 Renée was visited by Calvin, who had come to Italy under the assumed name of Espeville. We have no trustworthy account of the visit, but it evidently made the deepest impression upon Renée and her Court. Apparently he celebrated the communion for them in private; certainly he incited them to protest against the accustomed services. In fact, on Holy Saturday (April 14), when the officiating priest in one of the chief churches of Ferrara presented the cross for the veneration of the faithful, one of Renée's choristers, a youth of twenty known as Jehannot or Zanetto, broke out in open blasphemies against what he regarded as idolatry. The incident was probably pre-arranged in order to cause a popular outbreak; but it is clear that the people were scandalised. Under pressure from Rome Ercole took steps to punish the offenders. But he found that the whole suite of his wife were involved; while Renée invoked the French power to protect her servants. The matter dragged on for some months; but at length, as the principal person implicated (probably Calvin himself) escaped from his guards on the road to Bologna, not without suspicion of their connivance, it was allowed to drop.

Henceforward Calvin was Renée's spiritual adviser, and she was in frequent correspondence with him. Under his influence she refused in 1540 to make her confession or to hear mass any longer. This does not seem to have involved an open breach with the Church; there were many more who were equally remiss in their religious duties. Ercole tried to avoid taking action, and winked at her opinions so long as she and her associates avoided giving open scandal. Moreover, when Paul III paid a visit to Ferrara Renée met him on friendly terms, and obtained from him a brief, dated July 5, 1543, by which she was exempted from every jurisdiction but that of the Holy Office. But she disguised her Calvinism less and less, while the activity of the Inquisition was daily increasing; and at length the pressure of the Holy See compelled the Duke to act. In 1554 he applied to the French King for an "able and energetic " teacher for his wife, and the Inquisitor Mathieu Ory was sent. As his exhortations made no impression, she was put on her trial for heresy, and condemned to imprisonment, twenty-four of her servants being likewise sentenced.   But a week afterwards, on September 13, it was announced that she had "abjured and received pardon."   The documents are lost, so that it is hard to say precisely what occurred.   It is certain that Renée made her confession and received the Eucharist, equally so that she was at heart a Calvinist, and went on in her old courses until, after Ercole's death, she retired in 1560 to Montargis and became a protector of the French Huguenots.

Ercole's other capital, MODENA, was equally famous as a centre of learning.   Many of the scholars of the Modenese Academy had long been suspected of heterodoxy, among them being Lodovico Castelvetro, Gabriele Falloppio, the anatomist, and the brothers Grillenzone, who were its founders.   In Advent, 1537, an Austin friar, Serafino of Ferrara, denounced an anonymous book, the *Sommario della Santa Scrittura*, which was being sold in Modena by the bookseller Antonio Gaboldino; but his action only called forth protests.   In 1540 arrived the learned Paolo Ricci, a conventual Franciscan, who had left the cloister, and now, under the assumed name of Lisio Fileno, publicly expounded the Scriptures and denounced the Papacy.   Thus the new opinions gained ground.   The annalist Tassoni (il Vecchio) declares that both men and women disputed everywhere, in the squares, in the shops, in the churches, concerning the faith and the law of Christ, quoting and misquoting the Scriptures and doctors whom they had never read.

Attempts were soon made to put a stop to this.   The *Sommario* was refuted by Ambrogio Catarino and burned at Rome in 1539.   Two years afterwards Ricci was arrested, taken to Ferrara, and made to recant. Other measures were for a time averted by the intercession of Sadoleto, himself a Modenese; he urged that the academicians were loyal to the Roman Church, and should not be molested because they claimed for the learned the right of free enquiry.   The Pope however was still suspicious; and Giovanni de Morone, the Bishop of Modena, then absent on a legation in Germany and himself a friend of Contarini and to the doctrines of Grace, was sent for to reduce this " second Geneva " to order.   It was proposed that suspected persons should sign a formulary of faith, drawn up by Contarini in the plainest possible terms.   After strenuous resistance the signatures were secured, and the matter seemed at an end. But a strong feeling of resentment had sprung up; the Academy was still a hot-bed of disaffection, and preachers of doubtful orthodoxy, such as Bartolommeo della Pergola, were eagerly listened to.

At length Ercole was goaded into taking action throughout his dominions.   A ducal edict of May 24, 1546, was so severe in its provisions that the Modenese Academy promptly dispersed; and in 1548

Fra Girolamo Papino of Lodi was installed as Inquisitor at Ferrara. A poor youth of Faenza, by name Fannio (or Fanino), was soon brought before him, who had fallen into heresy through his perverse interpretation of the Bible. He recanted once through fear, but relapsed, and began preaching throughout Romagna with great success. At length he was arrested at Bagnacavallo, and conveyed to Ferrara. Here his imprisonment was a succession of triumphs. His friends were allowed access to him, and his visitors included Olympia Morata, Lavinia della Rovere, and others, upon whom his cheerfulness and earnestness and his bold predictions made a great impression. After long negotiations between Ferrara and the Holy See, in which Renée herself took part, the order arrived for his execution as a relapsed heretic. It was confirmed by Ercole, and on August 22, 1550, he was strangled and his body cast into the river. His was the second recorded death for religion in Italy, the first being that of Jáime de Enzinas, a Spanish Lutheran and, according to Bucer, an eager disseminator of Lutheranism, who was burned at Rome on March 16, 1547. Another execution followed in 1551, that of a Sicilian priest, Domenico Giorgio, who is described as a "Lutheran and heretic." Minor punishments followed in great numbers; so that Renée was forced to send her Huguenot followers to Mirandola, where under the Count Galeotto Pico they found a place of refuge.

Some years afterwards attention was again called to Modena, where the Reform still prospered. On October 1, 1555, a brief of Paul IV demanded that four of the leaders, Bonifacio and Filippo Valentino (the former of whom was provost of the Cathedral), Lodovico Castelvetro (who had translated the writings of Melanchthon into Italian), and the bookseller Gaboldino, should be arrested and handed over to the Holy Office. Filippo Valentino and Castelvetro, warned in time, made their escape. The others were taken and conveyed to Rome, where Bonifacio recanted; but Gaboldino, on refusing to do so, was condemned to perpetual imprisonment. Four years later Castelvetro, already condemned for contumacy, was persuaded to go to Rome with his brother Giammaria, and stand his trial; but he fled before it was over, was again condemned, and was burned in effigy as a contumacious heretic. The two brothers escaped to Chiavenna, where Lodovico died in 1571, having in 1561 appealed in vain for a hearing before the Council of Trent.

Even this was not the end of heresy in the duchy. The registers of the Inquisition contain long lists of suspects, and not a few condemnations, both at Ferrara and Modena; at Modena indeed, in 1568 alone, thirteen men and one woman perished at the stake.

Very different again was the movement at NAPLES, at any rate in its earlier stages. It centres round one great man, Juan de Valdés, whose position is thus described by Niccolò Balbini, minister of the congregation of Italian refugees at Geneva, in his life of Galeazzo Caracciolo:

"There was at that time in Naples a Spanish gentleman, who having a certain knowledge of evangelical truth and above all of the doctrine of justification, had begun to draw to the new doctrines certain noble-born persons with whom he conversed, refuting the idea of justification by our own deserving, and of the merit of works, and exposing certain superstitions." He adds that the disciples of Valdés "did not cease to frequent the churches, to resort to mass like other people, and to share in the current idolatry." This however gives no idea of his real greatness. Valdés was at once a devout mystic and a born teacher; and having settled in Naples he at once became the leading spirit and the oracle of a wide circle of devout and cultured men and women who submitted themselves wholly to his teaching and guidance.

Born of a noble family at Cuença in new Castile (c. 1500), where his father Ferrando was *corregidor*, he and his twin-brother Alfonso had been educated for the public service. Both were early drawn into sympathy with the protest against abuses, but whilst Alfonso died an "*erasmista*," Juan advanced far beyond this. Alfonso entered the service of the Emperor, and, though an indifferent Latinist, gradually rose to be first secretary. In this capacity he was responsible for several imperial letters which urged the necessity of reform in no gentle terms. But these are not our only index to his opinions. He was a close friend of Erasmus and a student of his writings; and after the Sack of Rome in 1527 he put forth a Dialogue between Lactancio, an imperial courtier, and a certain archdeacon, in which he vindicates the Emperor, and declares the catastrophe to be a judgment upon the sins of the Papacy. Lactancio allows that Luther had fallen into many heresies, but very pertinently says that if they had remedied the things of which he justly complained, instead of excommunicating him, he would never have so lapsed. He calls for a speedy Reformation, that it may be proclaimed to the end of the world how "Jesus Christ built the Church, and the Emperor Charles V restored it." Alfonso follows in the footsteps of Erasmus; and the reader of the *Colloquia* will find little that is new here, unless it be that Alfonso is, as a contemporary said, more Erasmian than Erasmus himself. He was at once attacked, but found many defenders; and Charles himself declared that though he had not read the book, Valdés was a good Christian, who would not write heresies. Accordingly, he was not molested, and ended his life in the Emperor's service early in October, 1532.

Little is known of Juan's early life, excepting that he was for ten years about the Court, apparently under his brother. Towards the end of this period, and just after the *Diálogo de Lactancio* was finished, Juan produced a similar work, the *Diálogo de Mercurio y Caron*, in which Mercury and Charon are made to confer with the souls of the departed as to their religious life and the affairs of the world they have just left. It really consists of two distinct dialogues differing in style and substance, one being mainly political (showing signs of Alfonso's co-operation) and the other mainly religious, although in doctrine it does not go beyond a condemnation of prayers to the Virgin. But they were joined in one, and published with the *Lactancio* in 1529. We next hear of Juan in 1530, at Rome, where he presently became a papal chamberlain under Clement VII, by whom, according to Carnesecchi, he was much beloved. He was at Bologna with the Pope in January, 1533, but soon afterwards removed to Naples, where he remained, excepting for one visit to Rome, till his death in 1541.

At Naples he gave himself up to study, to religious meditation, and to the society of his friends. Between April, 1534, and September, 1536, he produced his *Diálogo de la lengua*, a valuable study of the Spanish tongue, and one of the most beautiful writings of its day. During the next few years he wrote and circulated amongst his friends, in manuscript, his *CX Considerationes* (subsequently translated into English by Nicholas Ferrar), his *Catechism*, *Lac Spirituale*, a large number of short treatises and commentaries, and translations of parts of the Bible from the original languages. His doctrine as contained in these works is certainly not distinctively Lutheran or Calvinist, but that of one whose thoughts turned ever inward rather than outward, a devout evangelical mystic who recommended frequent confession and communion, and had no desire to overturn the ordinances of the Church. His disciples were won by himself rather than by his doctrines; and even the element of his teaching which others seized upon most eagerly — justification by faith only — was not to him what it was to the Lutheran, the corner-stone of his whole system. To him it was the expression of the fact that only by self-abnegation could men receive the divine illumination, and thus conform to the image of God in which they were made. And the tract by means of which this doctrine was most widely diffused in Italy, the famous *Beneficio della morte di Cristo*, which has been called the *Credo* of the Italian Reformed, was not the work of Valdés himself, but of a disciple, the Benedictine monk Benedetto of Mantua, who wrote it in his monastery at the foot of Mount Etna, and at whose request Marcantonio Flaminio revised it and improved the style. It began to be spread broadcast in Italy about 1540, at first in manuscript and then in print, and made a deep impression wherever it went.

The personal influence of Valdés was very great, both amongst those who had known him at the Court of Clement VII and those who now saw him for the first time. In his unprinted life of Paul IV, written early in the seventeenth century, Antonio Caracciolo reckons the number of Valdés' adherents at over three thousand, of whom many were leading men. This is doubtless only a guess, but the number was certainly large. And since at this very time, in 1536, an edict had gone forth in Naples forbidding all commerce with heretics on pain of death and confiscation, it is clear that the many persons of importance in Church and State who took part in his conferences had no idea that their action came under this ban.   Many, and especially the Theatines, regarded him with suspicion ; but that was all.

He and his two chief adherents, Bernardino Ochino and Pietro Martire Vermigli, are styled by Antonio Caracciolo the "Satanic triumvirate."   With them were Marcantonio Flaminio, Pietro Carnesecchi, Galeazzo Caraccioli (nephew of Pope Paul IV), Benedetto Cusano, Marcantonio Magno, Giovanni Mollio, the Franciscan, Jacopo Bonfadio, the historian (burned at Genoa, but probably not for heresy, in 1550), Vittorio Soranzo (afterwards Bishop of Bergamo) and Lattanzio Ragnone of Siena, all of whom were subsequently regarded as heretics.   There were also Pietrantonio di Capua, Archbishop of Otranto (who attended Valdés on his deathbed and always held him in great reverence), the Archbishops of Sorrento and Reggio, the Bishops of Catania, Nola, Policastro, and La Cava (Giovanni Tommaso Sanfelice, imprisoned by Paul IV for over two years on suspicion of heresy), and Giambattista Folengo, a learned monk of Monte Cassino.   With them, too, were the most noble and respected ladies of Naples, Vittoria Colonna, Marchioness of Pescara, her kinswoman Costanza d'Avalos, Duchess of Amalfi, Isabella Manrique of Brisegna, sister-in-law to the Spanish Inquisitor-general of that name, above all Giulia Gonzaga, Duchess of Traietto and Countess of Fondi in her own right.   On the death of her husband she had retired to Fondi, where the fame of her beauty was such that the corsair Khair Eddin Barbarossa attempted to kidnap her for the Sultan. She had now taken up her abode in the convent of San Francesco at Naples, and was much respected for her strict and pious life.   She submitted herself entirely to the guidance of Valdés ; and several of his treatises were written for her benefit.

After his death most of his followers dispersed, and not a few of them were afterwards proceeded against in other parts of Italy.   Those who still remained were led, according to a contemporary writer, by a triumvirate consisting of Donna Giulia, a Benedictine monk named Germano Minadois, and a Spaniard, Sigismundo Miñoz, who was director of the hospital for incurables.   Some presently abandoned the Roman communion.   Galeazzo Caraccioli, for example, visited Germany in the Emperor's service, and learned that it was not enough to accept Justification, but that he must forsake "idolatry" also.   Failing to induce even his own family to accompany him, he went alone to Geneva in March, 1551, where he was well received by Calvin, as was Lattanzio Ragnone, who followed two days later.   He ventured into Italy more than once, and many efforts were made, especially after his uncle became Pope, to recall him ; but they all failed, and he died at Geneva in 1586. Isabella Brisegna also fled, first to Zurich and then to Chiavenna. Some, again, seem to have abandoned their views owing to the preaching of the Jesuit Alfonso Salmeron in 1553 and the following years; and some, as the Austin friar Francesco Romano, recanted under pressure. Others still remained staunch, under the leadership of Giulia, who assisted with her means those who fled, but refused to fly herself. Several were proceeded against and put to death; and at length, in March, 1564, Gian Francesco di Caserta and Giovanni Bernardino di Aversa were beheaded and burned in the market-place. It is probable that only the death of Pius IV in December, 1565, saved Giulia herself from a like fate; as it was, she remained in the convent till her death on April 19, 1566. With her the party came to an end. Meanwhile, however, it had spread elsewhere: between 1541 and 1576 there are over forty trials for Lutheranism in the records which still survive of the Sicilian Inquisition, about half of the culprits, who include not a few parish priests and religious, being put to death. Other heresies had arisen also; the records speak, for instance, of Sacramentaries, Anabaptists, anti-Trinitarians, and those who disbelieved in a future life.

Lucca was the only other place where the movement assumed a really popular form; and here it centres round one man. Pietro Martire Vermigli, born of well-to-do parents at Florence in 1500, had joined the Austin canons at Fiesole in 1516, and learned from them to know his Bible well. He studied Greek and Hebrew at Padua and elsewhere, and being appointed to preach was soon well known throughout Italy. High honours fell to him: he became Abbot of Spoleto, and then Prior of the great house of San Pietro *ad aram* at Naples and Visitor-general of his Order. Here he came into contact with Valdé, began to read the writings of Bucer and others, and lectured on the First Epistle to the Corinthians. He was accused of heresy, and for a time forbidden to preach; but the prohibition was removed by the Pope at the instance of Contarini, Pole, and other friends. In 1541 he left Naples and became Prior of San Frediano at Lucca. This was his opportunity, for the Prior had quasi-episcopal rights over half the city. He gathered about him a body of like-minded scholars, and with them set up a scheme of study which was shared by many of the chief citizens and nobles. He himself expounded St Paul's Epistles and the Psalms. Latin was taught by Paolo Lacizi of Verona, a canon of the Lateran and afterwards Vermigli's colleague at Strassburg; Greek by Count Massimiliano Celso Martinengo, also a canon of the Lateran and subsequently pastor of the Italian congregation at Geneva; and Hebrew by Emanuele Tremelli of Ferrara, a Jew converted by Pole and Flaminio, who afterwards came to England. With them also were Francesco Robortello and Celio Secondo Curione, public professors of letters, and Girolamo Zanchi, afterwards professor of theology at Strassburg. Vermigli himself preached every Sunday to congregations which grew continually; and no small part of the city listened readily when he told them to regard the Eucharist as a mere remembrance of the Passion. This soon became known beyond the walls of Lucca. Vermigli was summoned to the Chapter of his Order at Genoa, and the magistrates of Lucca received a papal injunction to arrest all heretical teachers and send them to Rome. An Austin friar was taken, released by the nobles, and recaptured ; and Vermigli, never a man of much courage, resolved on flight. In August, 1542, he set out for Pisa with two companions ; and "in that city, with certain noble persons, he celebrated the Supper of the Lord with the Christian rite." Thence he wrote to Pole and to the people of Lucca, giving as reasons for his flight the errors and abuses of the pontifical religion and the hatred of his enemies ; after which he went to Switzerland by way of Bologna and Ferrara, and on to Strassburg. He subsequently came to England and was made professor of divinity at Oxford, but returned to Strassburg in 1553, and died at Zurich in 1562. It appears that no fewer than eighteen canons of his house left Lucca within a year, and escaped beyond the Alps. But although the shepherds had fled, the flock did not at once melt away. They were in a measure supported by the senate, which took measures at length to stamp out the heresy, but only under pressure, and as an alternative to the setting up of the Roman Inquisition. In 1545 the senate issued an edict against the "rash persons of both sexes who without any knowledge of Holy Scripture or the sacred canons dare to discuss things concerning the Christian faith as though they were great theologians" ; and by 1551 the last Lucchese Reformers were compelled to fly.

We now turn to leaders of the movement who were not connected with any particular centre. One who was even better known fled at the same time with Vermigli, namely Bernardino Ochino, of Siena. When young he had joined the Friars Observant, and rose to be their Provincial ; but in 1534 he left them for the Capuchins, a stricter body founded some six years before, by whom in 1538 he was chosen Vicar-general. Meanwhile he had begun to preach, was appointed an "apostolic missionary," and was soon recognised as the foremost preacher of the day. His extant sermons hardly account for his fame ; but preaching was at a low ebb, and the strictness of his life added greatly to the effect of his fiery eloquence. At Naples he became a follower of Valdés, as did others of his Order ; including, as he afterwards said, most of the preachers. At Florence he visited Caterina Cibò ; and his conversations with her, put into the shape of *Sette Dialoghi* in 1539, afford clear evidence that he had already rejected much of the current theology. So far, however, he cannot have incurred serious suspicion ; for although his preaching was impugned at Naples in 1536 and 1539, he was re-elected Vicar-general in 1541. The following year came the catastrophe. He was twice cited before the Nuncio at Venice for his sermons, and the second time he was forbidden to preach any more, and went to Verona. Whilst living there, in frequent intercourse with the venerable Bishop Giberti, he received a citation to appear before the newly-founded Roman Inquisition. He set out in August, and on his way through Bologna paid a visit to Contarini, who lay dying there. The accounts of their interview differ; but Ochino gathered that if he went to Rome he would be forced "to deny Christ or be crucified." At Florence he met Vermigli, and resolved forthwith to fly, to throw in his lot with the Swiss Reformers, and to disseminate his doctrine by his pen. He reached Geneva, being then at the age of fifty-five, passing afterwards to Zurich, Augsburg, England, and back to Zurich. But his restless mind could not easily find satisfaction. Before long the Swiss expelled him because of his views on marriage, and he began to turn to the party amongst his compatriots which had abandoned not only the historic system but the historic faith of the Church. As early as September, 1550, a secret Anabaptist meeting had been held at Venice, attended by 60 deputies, which had rejected the divinity of Christ. Many who shared these views had taken refuge amongst the Swiss, including Giorgio Blandrata, formerly physician to Sigismund I of Poland, Niccolò Gallo, Giovanni Paolo Alciati, Matteo Gribaldi, and Valentino Gentile, all of whom fled to Geneva, and Lelio Sozzini, who went to Basel in 1547 and lived there unsuspected till his death in 1562. Calvin at length grew suspicious, and on May 18, 1558, put forth a confession of faith to be signed by all the members of the Italian congregation as a test of orthodoxy. Gribaldi managed to clear himself; Blandrata and Alciati, finding themselves unable to do so, fled to Poland; Gallo and Gentile signed, but afterwards retracted and were proceeded against for heresy: the last-named was ultimately beheaded at Bern, in 1556, as a perjured heretic. After 1558, Poland and Transylvania became the headquarters of this extreme school, which remained the prey of vague and mutually contradictory theories, Arian and Anabaptist, until Fausto Sozzini (1539–1604), the nephew of Lelio, came to Transylvania (1578) and little by little organized a definite "Unitarian Church," the doctrinal manual of which was the Rakovian Catechism. To this party, in its earlier stages, Ochino had made approaches (in his *Dialogi* published in 1563 in Poland); but even the Polish anti-trinitarians thought him unsound; and he died in 1564, forsaken and alone, at Schlackau in Moravia.

Ochino's flight made a great sensation. To Caraffa it suggested the fall of Lucifer. Some attributed it to disappointed ambition, some to a sudden temptation. Vittoria Colonna, hitherto a frequent correspondent, broke with him entirely; but Caterina Cibò, in whose house he had renounced the cowl, appears to have corresponded with him still. In the records of the Roman Inquisition she figures as *doctrix monialium haereticarum*, the nuns being those of St Martha outside Florence. But she does not seem to have been proceeded against, and died at Florence in 1555.

Another man of mark who left the Roman communion was Pierpaolo Vergerio of Capo d'Istria. He had been a lawyer in Venice, entered the service of the Nuncio at the instance of his brother Aurelio, who was secretary to Clement VII, and soon rose to importance. He went to Rome early in 1533, and was sent as Nuncio to Ferdinand of Austria. Two years later he went to invite the German Princes to the Council of Mantua, and had a memorable interview with Luther, whom he describes with characteristic bitterness. In 1536 he received the bishopric of Modrusch, exchanged soon after for that of Capo d'Istria; all the orders being conferred upon him in one day by his brother Giambattista, Bishop of Pola, who at the time of his death was suspected of heresy, and not without reason. Pierpaolo was still a restless and energetic papal agent, distrusted by many, and scheming both for practical reform and for his own aggrandisement. In time a change came over him. During a mission to France he met, and was profoundly impressed by, Margaret of Navarre. Passing into Germany, he consorted much with Melanchthon and others. At the Diet of Worms (1540) he made an oration *De unitate et pace ecclesiae*, in which he urged the necessity for a General Council for the reform of the Church. He allowed that there were grave abuses in the Church, but not that they were any reason for secession; he pointed to the quarrels amongst the Reformed, and urged them to return to " the Body of Christ, who is our consolation and our peace." His survey of the facts is somewhat superficial, but a new tone of charity and earnestness runs through it. He returned to Capo d'Istri to take care of " the little vineyard which God had committed to him"; he visited diligently, preached evangelical doctrine, and reformed practical abuses. He read heretical books in order to confute them; but they only raised doubts in his own mind. Suspicion arose on all sides. Late in 1544 the monks of his diocese, irritated by his strictness, accused him to the Venetian Inquisition, which began a process against him. It was still continuing when the Council of Trent was opened. In February, 1546, he went to the Council and offered his defence; but, although the Cardinal of Mantua warned them not to drive a good Bishop to desperation, they would not hear him or allow him to take his seat, and forbade his return to his diocese. Then he asked for a canonical trial from his fellow-Bishops, but in vain. After this he lost all heart.

The last straw was the case of Francesco Spiera, a lawyer of Cittadella, whose story was long remembered amongst the Reformed. He had incurred suspicion by associating with Speziale and translating the Lord's Prayer into Italian. Being cited by the Inquisition in 1548, he abjured from fear, and repeated his abjuration the following Sunday at Cittadella, against his conscience. Presently, he fell grievously ill, and lay for months under the conviction that he had committed the unpardonable sin by his apostasy. In vain his friends spoke of God's mercy; he met

their exhortations with a hoplessness which was the more terrible
because it was so calm, though broken occasionally by paroxysms of
frenzy. From the investigation made by the Inquisition after his death
it seems likely that some rays of hope dawned upon him towards the
end; but this was unknown to the many who came to see him, and awe
and consternation prevailed amongst them. To Vergerio, who watched
often at his bedside, the warning seemed to be one which he dared not
neglect; he resolved to secede at once, and on December 13, 1548, he
sent his resolve, with an account of the dying Spiera, to Rota, the
Bishop Suffragan of Padua. His deposition and excommunication
followed on July 3, 1549. He fled to the Grisons, and for a time
worked at Poschiavo; in 1553 he passed to Württemberg, where he
remained till his death. He translated parts of the Bible into Slavonic,
and wrote fiery tracts against the Papacy; but to all he appeared a
schemer and a disappointed man: Calvin speaks of him as a " restless
busybody," and Jewel calls him a " crafty knave."

We return now to those who sympathised more or less with the new
views but did not separate from the Church. They were of very different
types. Some, like Michelangelo Buonarotti, were simply men of that
evangelical spirit which easily comes under suspicion when undue stress
is being laid on externals; others, like Falloppio, were bold thinkers who
overstepped the limits of medievalism; others, like Giangiorgio Trissino,
a fugitive for seventeen years who died in the prisons of the Inquisition,
directed their satire against the Papacy only; others really adopted the
Reformed views, like the satiric poet Francesco Berni, whose *Orlando
Innamorato* appears to have been manipulated after his death to disguise
the Lutheran flavour. A better representative of these last is Aonio
Paleario of Veroli, a man of querulous temper but devoutly Christian
life, at once a humanist and a doctrinal Reformer. So early as 1542 he
was accused of heresy at Siena, partly owing to a dispute with a preacher
at Colle, partly on account of his book *Della pienezza, sofficenza, e
satisfazione della passione di Cristo*. But he had friends, and the trial
was stopped without his having to read an oration which he had prepared
in his own defence. He continued to write boldly, and to correspond
with the German and Swiss Reformers. In 1542 or 1543 he unfolded
to them an extraordinary plan for a Council to settle the religious
disputes of the day: all the princes of Europe were to choose holy men,
"entirely free from the suspicion of papal corruption," to the number of
six or seven from each country; and these men, having been consecrated
for the purpose by twelve Bishops, chosen out of their whole number by
the Pope and the hierarchy on account of their holiness of life, were to
act as arbiters and umpires, after hearing the matters in dispute fully
discussed in a perfectly free assembly. Paleario became professor of
belles-lettres at Lucca in 1546, on the nomination of Sadoleto and Bembo,

and in 1555 he went to fill a like office at Milan. Here he was twice proceeded against; in 1559 unsuccessfully in the matter of Purgatory, on the accusation of his former opponent; and again in 1567, when the trial was interrupted by a summons to appear at Rome before the Holy Office itself. He pleaded his age, but ultimately went and stood his trial. His answers on many points were unsatisfactory; but the real ground of his condemnation was his steady assertion that it was unlawful for the Pope to kill heretics, and that, so doing, he could not be the vicar of Christ. He was called upon to make a set abjuration, but refused (June 14, 1570); he was condemned as impenitent in the presence of the Pope himself (June 30); and on July 3 he was strangled and burnt in the Piazza del Castello. The records of the *Misericordia* say that he died penitent. It is probable that this refers to a general statement of penitence, by means of which, with the connivance of the authorities, the punishment of burning alive was frequently avoided. In any case, Aonio died a martyr not so much for his particular opinions as in the cause of liberty of thought itself.

Another who paid the last penalty was Pietro Carnesecchi. Born in 1508 of a noble Florentine family, he was educated in the house of Cardinal Dovizzi at Rome, and entered the papal service. Under Clement VII he became protonotary apostolic, receiving also many rich benefices and a promise of the cardinalate: so great indeed was his influence that it used to be said that he was Pope rather than Clement. But the death of his master removed him from a post which was not really congenial, and he retired into secular life. A visit to Giulia Gonzaga in 1540 brought him into contact again with Valdés, whom he had known at the papal Court. He now took him as his spiritual teacher, and ever afterwards regarded this as the crisis of his life. From this point his history is recorded in the details of the process instituted against him by the Roman Inquisition. After some years of reading heretical books and conferring with heretics at Venice, he was cited to Rome (1546) and put on his trial for heresy. He denied everything, and " fraudulently extorted absolution from the Pope." After a visit to France, where he met many of the Reformers, he returned to Venice (1552 *c.*), and there published some of the works of Valdés. In 1557 a new process was commenced against him; he hid himself, and sentence was pronounced upon him as a refractory heretic. Even this was not final. On the death of Paul IV (1559), the people joyously broke open the prisons of the Inquisition, destroyed the records, and suffered the prisoners (seventy-two " heresiarchs, or rather infernal fiends," says Antonio Caracciolo) to escape. Carnesecchi saw his chance and seized it. His sovereign, Duke Cosimo I, whom he had served as an envoy and councillor of State, took his part; the charges against him were no longer in existence; the new Pope was anxious to relax the severity of his predecessor; and thus, in May, 1561, he was declared innocent. After this he resided at Rome, at Naples, at Florence, always in correspondence with heretics, and for a time with a strong Calvinistic bias, though later his sympathies were Lutheran. The accession of the stern old Inquisitor Ghislieri as Pope Pius V again brought Carnesecchi into danger. Cosimo consented to give him up (being rewarded two years afterwards with the title of Grand Duke); and on July 4, 1566, he was in prison in Rome. The trial was a lengthy one; he fought hard for his life, endeavouring, as was his wont, to resist force by cunning. But it could have only one end. On September 21, 1567, he was handed over to the secular arm, and on October 21, with a friar Giulio Maresio, he was beheaded and burnt.

But the great process against Carnesecchi had an importance apart from the man himself : as it has been said, he is but the secondary figure in it, and its real heroes are the illustrious dead. Carnesecchi was the disciple of Valdés, the friend of Flaminio and Pole ; he had been on terms of intimacy with that body of loyal sons and daughters of the Church of whom mention has been made already, who had striven nobly, through evil report and good report, for its reformation, and who had been hopelessly beaten at the Council of Trent. They had been watched and suspected by the Inquisition ever since ; some indeed had actually suffered at its hands. Most of them were dead before 1566 ; but the pursuit of heresy ceased not at the grave, and those who during their lives were revered as the hope of the Church were impugned as suspects or as actual heretics in the famous process of Carnesecchi. This Catholic minority, for such it really was, grew out of the body of friends who centred round Contarini in Venice ; it was reinforced by many who had sat at the feet of Valdés, or who had travelled in the north. The aim of this party was the reform of the whole ecclesiastical system ; its doctrinal rallying-point was justification by faith in Christ Jesus and not by a man's own works. So far they were at one with Luther. But, realising as they did that this had ever been the doctrine of the Church, they were not impelled, as he was, to deny the reality of free will, to depreciate the fruits of faith, or to eviscerate faith itself by reducing it to an act of intellectual assent, and divorcing it from Christian love which issues in action. "We obtain this blessing of complete and perpetual salvation," wrote Sadoleto to the citizens of Geneva, "by faith alone in God and in Jesus Christ. When I say faith alone, I do not mean, as those inventors of novelties do, a mere credulity and confidence in God, to the exclusion of love and other Christian virtues. This indeed is necessary, and forms the first access which we have to God ; but it is not enough. For we must also bring a mind full of piety towards Almighty God, and desirous of performing whatever is agreeable to Him, by the power of the Holy Spirit." Moreover, loyalty to the Church was with them a fundamental principle.   Many no doubt were in frequent and friendly correspondence with the Reformers ; but it must be borne in mind that the line of division between the Protestant bodies and the Church was very gradually determined, and that men long hoped for a speedy settlement of the existing divisions.   Here again Sadoleto's letter illustrates their position.   He recognises the existing evils in the Church, and will even grant that there are serious doctrinal errors ; but even so, the evils of separation are greater ; and to depart from the unity of the body of Christ is to court destruction.   " Let us enquire and see which of the two is more conducive to our advantage, which is better in itself, and better fitted to obtain the favour of Almighty God : whether to accord with the whole Church, and faithfully observe her decrees and laws and sacraments, or to adhere to men seeking dissension and novelty.   This, dearest brethren, is the place where the road divides : one way leads to life, the other to everlasting death."   The letter is worthy of its occasion: so is the answer which it called forth from Calvin.

The failure of the *Consilium de emendanda Ecclesia*, the death of Clement VII, and the secession of Caraffa, had dashed the reformers' hopes ; but they did not lose heart.   Contarini was still their leader ; and it was probably on this account that he was sent as papal legate to the Colloquy of Ratisbon in 1541, whence he kept up a correspondence with Pole, Morone, and Foscarari, afterwards Bishop of Modena.   For a time all went well, and an agreement was come to, not indeed without great difficulty, upon the point of Justification.   But neither side really trusted the other ; and Contarini himself was jealously suspected by many members of the Curia.   Consequently, the effort (the last real effort to conciliate the reformers) came to nothing ; Contarini returned in deep sadness to Italy, and died the year after at Bologna.   His place as leader of the movement was taken by Reginald Pole, whose house at Viterbo, whither he went as papal governor in 1541, became their headquarters.   Here met together for prayer and study Giberti and Soranzo, the former bishop of Verona, the latter before long of Bergamo, Flaminio, Luigi Priuli, Donato Rullo, Lodovico Beccatello, and others. It was probably Pole's influence which kept Flaminio from seceding to the Lutherans.   Not less was his influence with Vittoria Colonna, to whom he was greatly devoted, and who found in him a wise spiritual guide when many others seemed to have gone astray.   It was he who advised her to believe that we are justified by faith only, and to act as though we were to be justified by our works.

Little by little their hopes faded.   At the Council of Trent, indeed, Pole was one of the Legates, and there were not a few Bishops and theologians who were with him in the matter of Justification.   But it soon became clear that the Council and Curia were against him, and Pole left Trent before the decree on the subject was actually made.   He relapsed into silence, waiting, and advising his friends to wait, for a more convenient season. It seemed as if this had actually come when, in November, 1549, Paul III died. The English Cardinal was beloved by some, respected by all. In the Conclave which followed it long appeared likely that he would be chosen; and the betting outside, based upon information from within, was much in his favour. But his views on Justification robbed him of the tiara. His rival del Monte was chosen, who took the name of Julius III; and Pole once more went into retirement until his mission to England in 1554. The accession of his enemy Caraffa as Paul IV was a still greater blow. Sadoleto's commentary on the Romans and Contarini's book on Justification were declared suspect; Pole ceased to be Legate and was for a time disgraced; Morone was actually imprisoned for heresy, and remained in prison until the death of the Pope in 1559. The Inquisition resumed its activity all over Italy. Although the total extinction of heresy was still long delayed, the end was only a question of time. For the springs were dried up, and no new ones burst forth.

II

SPAIN

Although one of the noblest leaders of the Italian Reform was a Spaniard, the movement never obtained such a hold upon Spain as upon Italy: in part because measures of repression were more promptly and more thoroughly applied—in part, perhaps, because many of the practical abuses had already been abated or removed, while the doctrinal abuses which called forth the protest had not yet prevailed in Spain so largely as elsewhere. Many of the best-known Spanish Reformers lived and died in Flanders or in some other foreign land; and in Spain itself the movement appears to have had little vitality excepting in and about two centres, Valladolid and Seville. Two *autos-de-fé* at Valladolid and two at Seville, of the thorough kind instituted by the Spanish Inquisition, sufficed to break up the Reformed in these centres. Many fugitives escaped and found refuge in Germany, England, or the Low Countries; and the few who remained were gradually swept away by the same drastic methods of the Inquisition.

A reform of the Spanish clergy, regular and secular, had taken place before Luther arose. It had begun, so far as the regulars were concerned, nearly a century before; for example, the Cistercians had been reformed by Fray Martino de Vargas in the time of Pope Eugenius IV, and afterwards Cardinal Mendoza had worked in the same direction. But the chief agent in it was Fray Ximenez de Cisneros of the Order of St Francis, to be better known as Cardinal Ximenez. At the request of Ferdinand and Isabella he drew up a report on the state of all the monasteries of Spain. Thereupon a Bull was sought from Alexander VI in 1494, by which Cisneros was empowered to visit and set in order all the regulars of Spain ; and he inaugurated the most drastic reformation, perhaps, that Religious Houses ever sustained. His action was in general submitted to ; but his own Order, which was the worst of all, resisted strenuously, and obtained a Bull of prohibition against him. On further information the Pope annulled this, and the work went on. The monasteries were disciplined, their " privileges " burned, and their rents and heritages taken away and given to parishes, hospitals, &c. A large number of monks who were scandalous evil-livers, and who seemed irreformable, were deported to Morocco, and the work was complete. With the seculars Cisneros was less successful. But by degrees the regulars reacted healthfully upon them ; Bishops and provincial synods took them in hand ; and the earlier Inquisitors, especially Adrian of Utrecht, did much to put away abuses amongst them. Without doubt, therefore, the moral state of the Spanish clergy in the sixteenth century, especially that of the monks and friars, was immeasurably superior to that of the clergy in any other part of Western Christendom.

Moreover, the purging of the Spanish clergy had been accompanied, or followed, by a revival of learning. Ximenez was a scholar and a munificent patron of scholarship ; and under his fostering care the University of Alcalá had become famous throughout Europe as a centre of theological and humane learning. The Cretan Demetrios Ducas taught Greek ; Alfonso de Zamora, Pablo Coronel, and Alfonso de Alcalá were expert Hebraists ; and amongst other scholars there were the two Vergaras, Lorenzo Balbo, and Alfonso de Nebrija. The greatest monument of the liberality and enterprise of Ximenez was the famous Complutensian Polyglott, which was in preparation at the very time when Erasmus was working at the first edition of his Greek Testament, though it did not begin to appear till 1520.

These facts have no little bearing upon the way in which the writings of Erasmus were received in Spain. To some he was a literary colleague whom they with all the world were proud to honour : to others he was a rival, whose work was to be depreciated wherever possible. Nor was it difficult to do this ; for his satirical writings against clerical abuses really did not apply to Spain. Elsewhere, all good men were agreed in combating the evils against which he wrote. In Spain, the earnestness of his crusade was easily overlooked by those who had not lived abroad ; on the other hand, nowhere was there so keen a scent for heresy. His liberal thought, and his ridicule of religious customs which, however liable to abuse, were in themselves capable of justification, seemed most dangerous to the orthodox Spanish mind ; and only the more large-hearted were able to discern the genuine depth of his piety.

Nowhere, therefore, did Erasmus' writings rouse such feelings as in Spain. Diego Lopez de Stúñiga and Sancho Carranza de Miranda inveighed against him, the former repeatedly, accusing him of bad scholarship, of heresy, of impiety, calling him not only a Lutheran but the standard-bearer and leader of the Lutherans. Erasmus replied, publicly and privately, with comparative moderation; and by degrees the controversy died away. Meanwhile he had many personal friends in Spain, through whose influence some of his writings were translated into Spanish, the first being the *Enchiridion*, which appeared in 1526 or 1527 with a dedication to Manrique the Inquisitor, and bearing his *imprimatur*. Some spoke against it, including Ignatius Loyola, who says that when he read it (in Latin) it relaxed his fervour and made his devotion grow cold; nevertheless it had a wide popularity. This brought its author into still greater prominence; and a contemporary writer says that his name was better known in Spain than in Rotterdam.

Gradually two hostile camps were formed, of *erasmistas* and *anti-erasmistas*. In 1526 the Archdeacon Alfonso Fernandes, the translator of the *Enchiridion*, wrote to Coronel that certain friars were preaching against its author, and suggesting that they should be censured; on the other hand, the friars demanded that certain theses selected from Erasmus' writings should be condemned. In the ecclesiastical *juntas* which met at Valladolid in Lent, 1527, a formal enquiry was begun before Manrique and a body of theologians; but no agreement was reached, and Manrique dissolved the enquiry, leaving things as they were. Alonso Fonseca, Archbishop of Toledo, also took the part of Erasmus; and by the influence of Gattinara and other friends at the Court of Charles V a Bull was obtained from Clement VII imposing silence upon all who spoke or wrote against his writings, which "are contrary to those of Luther." Thus the *erasmistas* had won a complete victory, and for a time had things all their own way. But after the death of Fonseca in 1534 the tide turned. Juan de Vergara and his brother were cited before the Inquisition, accused, says Enzinas, of no crime but favoring Erasmus and his writings; and although they were ultimately acquitted, it was only after years of detention. Fray Alonso de Virués was condemned for depreciating the monastic state and was immured in a convent; but the charges were so preposterous that Charles V, whose chaplain he was, came to his rescue; and the sentence was annulled by the Pope. Mateo Pascual, professor of theology at Alcalá, was less fortunate; he had expressed a doubt as to purgatory in a public discussion, was imprisoned, and his goods were confiscated. Another who fell under suspicion was the great scholar Pedro de Lerma, who had lived at Paris over fifty years, had been dean of the faculty of Theology there, and had returned to Spain as Abbot of Compludo. In 1537 he was called upon to abjure eleven "Erasmian" propositions, one of which seems to have been justification by faith. He forthwith returned to Paris, at the age of over seventy years, accompanied by his nephew Francisco de Enzinas, in whose arms he died not long after.

" Erasmianism " gradually died out in Spain. Elsewhere it either died out, or took a line of its own (as in the case of Juan de Valdés), or became merged in Protestantism. Pedro de Lerma was on the border-line ; his nephews crossed it. Francisco de Enzinas (or Dryander as his name was frequently rendered) was the younger brother of that Jáime who was burnt at Rome in 1547 ; they were sons of rich and noble parents at Burgos, and were educated at Louvain and Paris. On the death of de Lerma Francisco became a matriculated student of Witten-berg University, where there were about that time four other Spanish students, one of whom, Mateo Adriano, was professor of Hebrew and medicine. The young man lived in the house of Melanchthon, becoming so dear to him that he was often spoken of as " Melanchthon's soul "; and it was by his advice that Enzinas translated the New Testament into excel-lent Spanish. Having finished it he went to the Low Countries ; and from this point we are able to follow his steps by means of his *Narrative*. The edicts of Charles V against heresy were being put into force, but he felt safe, as he had many friends. He presented his version to the theolog-ical faculty of Louvain for their *imprimatur ;* but they replied that they had no power to give this, and could not judge of its accuracy. So he him-self published it at Antwerp, with a dedication to the Emperor, in which he defended the translating of the Scriptures (against which, he said, he knew no law) and placed his own version under Charles' protection. On November 23, 1543, he arrived at Brussels to present it in person, and was introduced to the Emperor's presence by the Bishop of Jaen. After a conversation of which Enzinas has left a rather partial account, the Em-peror promised to accept the dedication provided that the version was sat-isfactory ; and it was submitted to his confessor, Fray Pedro de Soto.

Soto was disposed to be friendly, but took the precaution of mak-ing enquiries. The following day he sent for the young man, set be-fore him the dangers of the unguarded reading of the Scriptures, as demonstrated by Alfonso de Castro in his *De Haeresibus*, and added that Enzinas had broken the law by publishing an unlicensed work ; also, that he was still more to blame for consorting with heretics at Wittenberg, and for publishing a heretical book based upon Luther's *De servo arbitrio*. Enzinas answered, reasonably enough, that there was no law in Flanders against translating the Bible, and that if it was wrong to consort with the German doctors, then the Emperor himself and many more were to blame. As to the book, he denied roundly that he had ever published anything but the New Testament, a denial which it is very hard to accept. Ultimately he was committed to prison in Brussels for his civil offence, and thus was saved, evidently by Soto's desire, from the tender mercies of the Spanish Inquisition. There he remained, in easy confinement, until February 1, 1545, when, by the negligence, or more probably connivance, of his gaolers, he escaped and made his way to Wittenberg, and thence to Strassburg, Basel and elsewhere. In disgust at the discords amongst

Protestants, he seriously thought of going to Constantinople to preach the Gospel there; but instead of doing so he married a wife, came to England on Cranmer's invitation, and was made professor of Greek at Cambridge. There he remained for about two years; but in 1549 he returned to the Continent to arrange for the printing of his Spanish versions of the classics, and died at Augsburg on December 30, 1550.

Jáime de Enzinas had remained at Paris for some time after his brother's departure, and whilst there had imbued another Spaniard, Juan Diaz, with his own views. Born at Cuença, the city of the brothers Valdés, Diaz had studied for thirteen years at Paris, becoming proficient in theology and in Hebrew. About 1545 he went to Geneva, and spent some months in Calvin's society. Thence he passed to Strassburg with the brothers Louis and Claud de Senarcleus, the latter of whom, with the help of Enzinas, afterwards wrote his life. At Strassburg the tenets of Calvin were held in some suspicion, and before being admitted to communion Diaz was called upon to show his orthodoxy by making a public profession of faith. At the end of the year the city sent Bucer as its deputy to the second Colloquy of Ratisbon, summoned by Charles V; and by his desire Diaz was sent with him, meanwhile acting also as agent for Cardinal du Bellay, the protector of the Huguenots of France. At Ratisbon in 1546 he had a series of discussions with the Dominican Fray Pedro de Malvenda, whom he had known at Paris; but his account of these is very one-sided, and all that is certain is that neither converted the other. From Ratisbon Diaz went to Neuburg on the Danube. Meanwhile, news of his doings reached his brother Alfonso, who was a lawyer at Pavia. He at once hastened to him in the hope of being able to persuade him to return to the Church, or at least to abandon the society of the Germans. On the advice of Ochino, who was then at Augsburg, Juan refused to do either. Alfonso, maddened with fanaticism and the shame of having a heretic in the family, thereupon compassed his death, and, with an accomplice, cruelly assassinated him at Feld-kirchen on March 27, 1546. The murderers were captured and brought to trial at Innsbruck; but as they were in minor Orders, Soto and others caused the case to be cited to Rome, where the murderers escaped scot-free. Not unnaturally the Protestants regarded Diaz as a martyr, and attributed his death to the direct orders of the ecclesiastical authorities; but though they connived at the escape of the murderers, the act itself was certainly one of private vengeance.

Another Spaniard who adopted the Reformed views about this time was Francisco de San Roman, a rich merchant from Burgos. In 1540, going from Antwerp to Bremen on business, he went by chance into a Lutheran church where Jakob Speng, formerly prior of the Austin canons at Antwerp, was preaching. Although he knew no German, he was attracted by the preacher, stayed at his house, and adopted his views. He at once began to preach and to write in Spanish, with the eagerness of fanaticism and the self-confidence of ignorance. Returning to Flanders, he was arrested and examined; his books were burnt, and he himself was imprisoned. Being released after six months, he went to Louvain, where he met Enzinas, who rebuked him for risking his life uselessly by shrieking like a madman in the market-places, and for impiously taking upon himself to preach without a call from God, and without the requisite gifts or knowledge. The rebuke made no impression. In 1541 he went to Ratisbon and presented himself before Charles, who heard him patiently again and again, but at length ordered his detention as a heretic. He was taken to Spain, handed over to the Inquisition, and burned in an *auto-de-fé* at Valladolid in 1542. His fidelity won him commendation where his rashness and ignorance had failed; and after his death Speng wrote to Enzinas with the tenderest reverence and love for the man whom they had little esteemed while he lived.

Passing over Pedro Nuñez Vela of Ávila, of whom little is known save that in 1548 and again in 1570 he is spoken of as professor of Greek at Lausanne, we turn to Reform movements within Spain itself. Precautions had been taken from 1521 onwards to prevent the diffusion of Lutheran books in Spain. Attempts were not infrequently made to introduce them by sea: in 1524 two casks full were discovered and burnt at Santander, and in the following year Venetian galleys were attempting to land them on the south-eastern shore. But it was neither in Biscay nor in Granada that the storm burst, nor was it caused by the importation of Lutheran books. It began in Seville and in Valladolid then the capital of Spain; and amongst its leaders, even if they were not its founders, were three chaplains of the Emperor, Dr Agustin Cazalla, Dr Constantino Ponce de la Fuente, and Fray Bartolomé Carranza, Archbishop of Toledo and Primate of Spain.

To begin with Seville. A noble gentleman there, Rodrigo de Valer, suddenly turned from a worldly life to one of devotion, studying the Bible till he knew it almost by heart. He also began to inveigh against the corruptions of the Church, preaching in the streets and squares, and even on the Cathedral steps, saying that he was sent by Christ to correct that evil and adulterous generation. He was more than once cited before the Inquisition, but treated with great leniency, partly because he was thought to be insane, partly because he was a *cristiano viejo*, without admixture of Jewish or Moorish blood. At length he was condemned to wear a *sambenito* and to undergo perpetual imprisonment in a convent. There he died about 1550. His life had not been fruitless: he had made many converts, amongst them the canon Juan Gil, of Olvera in Aragon. Gil, or Egidio (as he was also called), had studied with distinction at Alcalá, and was a master of theology of

Siguenza.   About 1537 he obtained the magistral canonry of Seville, which imposed on him the duty of preaching.   At first his preaching had little success.   But he gained new views of truth by his intercourse with Valer, and before long he became famous as a preacher.

But he owed even more to his brother-canon, Constantino Ponce de la Fuente, than to Valer; for he it was who first taught him, in set terms, the doctrine of justification by faith.   Constantino, a native of San Clemente near Cuença, had studied at Alcalá with Gil and a certain Dr Vargas; he was a man of great learning, skilled in Greek and Hebrew, who had probably learnt the doctrine of Justification from books.   In 1533 he had been made a canon of Seville; and although he was not so popular there as Gil, elsewhere his fame was far greater. The three friends now began to work together, Gil being the most active. He and Constantino preached diligently; Vargas expounded the Gospel of St Matthew and the Psalms; and by degrees they gathered a body of adherents to whom they ministered in secret.   For a long while nothing was suspected; in fact, Constantino was chosen by the Emperor to accompany him as his preacher and confessor, and was out of Spain with him from 1548 to 1551, much revered and honoured.   He subsequently came to England with Philip II, and only returned to Seville late in 1555.   During this period he produced a series of books which were then much valued, but were ultimately regarded as heretical.

Meanwhile, the others had been less fortunate.   Gil, indeed, had been nominated by the Emperor for a bishopric in 1550; but soon afterwards he and Vargas were cited before the Inquisition.   Vargas fell ill and died; but Gil was proceeded against vigorously, the charges including the points of Justification, Works, Purgatory, Invocation of Saints, and actual iconoclasm in the Cathedral.   In prison he wrote an apology on Justification which was held to make his case worse; but ultimately, on Sunday, August 21, 1552, he made a public recantation in the Cathedral, extorted, his friends afterwards said, by fraud.   He was sentenced to a year's imprisonment in the castle of Triana near Seville (the headquarters of the Inquisition), with permission to come to the Cathedral fifteen times; he was to fast strictly every Friday, to make his confession monthly, communicating or not as his confessor directed, not to leave Spain, not to say mass for a year, or to exercise other functions for ten years.   Gil however did not modify his views.   In 1555 he visited the Reformed at Valladolid, and died a few days after his return, early in 1556.

The Chapter of Seville had stood by their colleague nobly, although, or perhaps because, their Archbishop, the stern Fernando de Valdés, was at the head of the Inquisition.   They paid Gil a considerable salary whilst he was in prison, and set over his grave in the Cathedral a fine monument; moreover, in spite of great opposition, they elected Constantino magistral canon in his place.   He at once took up his friend's work, and besides preaching began a course of Bible lectures at a school in the city. By degrees he also was suspected by the Inquisition, which frequently summoned him to explain his conduct. When his friends asked him the reason of his frequent visits to Triana, he replied, " They wish to burn me, but as yet they find me too green." As time went on he began to lose heart, and at length, in order to disarm suspicion, resolved to join the newly-arrived Jesuits. But they had been warned, and refused to receive one who would otherwise have been acceptable enough as a recruit.

At length the Inquisition obtained proof of what they had doubtless long suspected : there existed in Seville a sect of considerable size, whose members met together secretly and had their own organisation and services. They had grown up about Gil and Constantino, had increased rapidly, and had obtained copies of the New Testament from abroad through the activity of one of their members. The detection of this society led to the accidental discovery of a large collection of Constantino's writings, in which he had spoken his full mind. He was at once arrested. After a vain denial, he avowed that the books were his, and that they represented his convictions. He was imprisoned in the dungeons of Triana, and died two years afterwards of disease and privation. Meanwhile, the search went on vigorously ; and by degrees all was discovered. From the *Sanctae Inquisitionis artes aliquot detectae*, published under an assumed name in 1567 by a former member of the sect, it appears that more than eight hundred people were proceeded against altogether. They had two centres, the house of Isabel de Baena, " the temple of the new light," the place "where the faithful assembled to hear the Word of God," and the Hieronymite monastery of San Isidro. Led by their prior Garci-Árias, known as *Maestro Blanco* from his white hair, the friars of San Isidro embraced the new views almost to a man, amongst them being the learned Cristóbal de Arellano, Antonio del Corro, and Cipriano de Valera ; they abolished fasts and mortifications, and substituted readings from the Scriptures for the canonical hours. Amongst the lay members of the sect were Juan Ponce de Leon, second son of the Count de Bailén, Juan Gonzales, the physician Cristóbal de Losada, and Fernando de San Juan, rector of the *Colegio de la doctrina ;* above all, there was Julian Hernandez, known to the rest as Julianillo, since he was very small of stature and "no more than skin and bone." But he was a man of fearless courage, and by his means they were able to procure religious books in Spanish, including the New Testament. Juan Perez, the former rector of the *Colegio de la doctrina*, had fled from Spain when Gil was arrested ; in his exile he had prepared a version of the New Testament, which was published at Venice in 1556. By the courage and resourcefulness of Julianillo two great tuns filled with copies were safely smuggled into Seville, despite the watchfulness of the Inquisition.

Little by little the Inquisition got through its work, drawing its net closer and closer about the chief offenders and allowing lesser persons to go free on doing penance. At an *auto-de-fé* celebrated in the Plaza de San Francisco on September 24, 1559, fourteen persons were burnt to death for heresy, including four friars and three women. A large number were sentenced to lesser penalties; and the house of Isabel de Baena, in which they met, was razed to the ground, a " pillar of infamy " being erected on the site. On December 22, 1560, a second *auto* was celebrated at the same place, when eight women, one being a nun, and two men, one of whom was Julianillo, were burnt. Gil, Constantino, and Perez were burnt in effigy, and a number of friars and others were visited with lesser penalties. Some contrived to escape and fled from Spain; and a few single cases of heresy were dealt with in later years. Thus ended the history of the Reform in Seville.

At VALLADOLID the movement had already come to an end, for although it began later than at Seville, it was discovered somewhat earlier. Its founder was Agustin Cazalla, born of rich parents who had lost rank for Judaising. He had studied under Carranza at Valladolid, and afterwards at Alcalá. In 1542 he was made chaplain and preacher to the Emperor, and till 1551 followed the Court. On his return to Spain he was made canon of Salamanca and from that time forward dwelt there or at Valladolid. He became addicted to the Reform either under Carranza's instructions or in Germany, and was confirmed in his views by Carlos de Seso, a nobleman from Italy who had married a Spanish wife and had been made *corregidor* of Toro. Seso had heard of justification in Italy, and became an ardent propagandist; in fact it is clear that Toro, not Valladolid, was the real birthplace of the movement in New Castile. A large number of well-born persons accepted Seso's teaching, including the licentiate Herrezuelo, Fray Domingo de Rojas, many members of the Cazalla family, and many devout ladies; and all who accepted it became teachers themselves. Zamora and Logroño, near which town Seso had a house, were affected by the movement; above all, it found its headquarters in Valladolid, where it soon had a very large following, both of rich and poor. The nuns of the rich House of Belén, outside the city, were largely involved; so were many of the clergy. Meetings and services were held frequently, and the communion administered in the house of Leonor de Vibera, Cazalla's mother.

It is not known how they were discovered, but the arrests were precipitated by the action taken at Zamora, by the Bishop, against Cristóbal de Padilla, steward to the Marquesa de Alcañices, who was preaching the new doctrines there. He was able to warn his friends in the capital, some of whom fled to Navarre, and thence into France. But the greater number were already taken early in June, 1558; the prisons were full; and Valdés the Inquisitor-General was able to report to Charles V, in his retirement at Yuste, that each day brought fresh evidence against them. Moreover, mutual trust was lacking; when under examination, even without torture, they accused one another and endeavoured by all means to exculpate themselves, so that there was no lack of incriminating evidence. The cause was pressed on vigorously, special powers being sought from Rome that it might not be delayed; and an *auto-de-fé*, the first against heresy, was arranged for Trinity Sunday, May 21, 1559, to be held in the Plaza Mayor.

On the appointed day a concourse gathered, the like of which had seldom been seen. After a sermon by the theologian Melchor Cano, the sentences were read out. Fourteen heretics were condemned to death, together with a Portuguese Jew. They were Agustin Cazalla and his brother Francisco (also a priest), his sister and four other women, and seven laymen, including Juan García, a worker in silver of Valladolid, and Anton Asél, a peasant. The bones of Leonor de Vibera were burnt, her house pulled down, and the spot was marked by a "pillar of infamy." Sixteen were reconciled, and sentenced to various terms of imprisonment; thirty-seven were reserved in prison. Of those who suffered, most showed sufficient signs of penitence to be strangled before being burnt, including Cazalla himself. But exhortations were wasted upon the licentiate Herrezuelo, who held to his opinions and was burnt alive.

A second *auto* followed on October 8, in the presence of Philip himself. Seven men and six women were burnt, and five women were imprisoned for life. The former included Fray Domingo de Rojas, Pedro Cazalla, two other priests, a nun of Santa Clara at Valladolid, and four nuns of Belén; of the latter, three were nuns of Belén. Several of those who were burnt were gagged that they might not speak; but Fray Domingo demanded leave to address the King, and said, "Although I die here as a heretic in the opinion of the people, yet I believe in God Almighty, the Father, the Son, and the Holy Ghost, and I believe in the passion of Christ, which alone suffices to save the world, without any other work save the justification of the soul to be with God; and in this faith I believe that I shall be saved." It would seem, however, that only two were burnt alive, Carlos de Seso and Juan Sanchez.

Many isolated cases of heresy are to be found after this, and doubtless the records of others have perished. Leonor de Cisneros, the mother of Herrezuelo, was burnt alive as an obstinate heretic on September 26, 1568; several cases of heresy were dealt with at an *auto-de-fé* at Toledo in 1571, and recent research has found a certain number of other instances elsewhere. As time went on such cases were in increasing proportion of foreign origin. But wherever heresy was discovered it was ruthlessly stamped out. Nor was this merely the work of a few officials. From his retirement at Yuste Charles V adjured his son to carry out the work of repression to the uttermost; and Philip replied that he would do what his father wished and more also. He told Carlos de Seso that if his own son were a heretic, he would himself carry the wood to burn him; and in this, as in most other things, he was a typical Spaniard. The rage against heresy regarded all learning, all evangelical teaching, with suspicion; to speak overmuch of faith or of inward religion might be a disparagement of works and of outward religion. Sooner or later most of the learned men of the day were cited on suspicion of heresy, or, if not actually cited, their actions and words were carefully watched. Fray Luis de Leon, poet and scholar, spent nearly five years in the prisons of the Inquisition whilst his works were being examined; and although he was at length acquitted, his Translation of the Song of Solomon was suppressed, and he again fell under suspicion in 1582. Juan de Ávila, Luis de Granada, even St Teresa, and St John of the Cross were accused; and it is said that Alva himself and Don John of Austria were not above suspicion.

Above all, the Inquisition struck, and not ineffectively, at the highest ecclesiastic in Spain, and brought him low, even to the ground. Bartolomé de Carranza was born in 1503, of a noble family, at Miranda in Navarre, and he entered the Dominican Order at the age of seventeen. In 1523 he was sent to the College of San Gregorio at Valladolid, of which he ultimately became Rector. It is possible that on a visit to Rome in 1539, to attend the Chapter-general of his Order, he met Juan Valdés. As time went on Bartolomé was more and more honoured in Spain for his learning and goodness. In 1545 Charles V sent him as theologian to the Council of Trent, where he won golden opinions. His doctrine of Justification was indeed questioned on one occasion; but he had no difficulty in showing that his words were in harmony with the decree of the Council, and he was vigorous in his treatment of heretical books. In Spain (1553), in England (1554), and in Flanders (1557), he showed himself zealous against heresy; and when, late in the latter year, he was chosen to be Archbishop of Toledo, his own was the single dissentient voice. Having at length accepted the office, he gave himself unreservedly to its duties. But it soon appeared that he was not without enemies. Some of the Bishops were ill-disposed towards him because he rigorously enforced upon them the duty of residence. Valdés, the Inquisitor-General, was jealous of him, perhaps because he himself had aspired to the primatial see. And the great theologian Melchor Cano, of his own order, was a lifelong rival. The two men differed in the whole tone of their minds; Fray Melchor was a thinker of almost mathematical accuracy, while Fray Bartolomé reasoned from the heart.

Under these circumstances very little evidence would suffice for a process for heresy; and Carranza himself, learning that it was in contemplation, wrote repeatedly to the Inquisitors in his own defence. Valdés however had applied to Rome for permission to proceed against him. The brief arrived on April 8, 1559, the King gave his permission in June, and in August Carranza was arrested and imprisoned. The main charges against him were based upon his relations with Cazalla, Domingo de Rojas, and others then under condemnation; upon his writings, especially the *Commentaries on the Catechism*, which he had published at Antwerp just after he became primate; and upon his last interview with Charles V. Of these the first head was by far the most serious. Many of the accused at Valladolid spoke of the way in which he had met their doubts in the early days of the movement; and Rojas in particular, desiring to shelter himself under the aegis of his old master, had in effect implicated him. The evidence showed that he had been in correspondence with Juan Valdés; and it seems clear that at this period his position had been that of the loyal doctrinal Reformers of Italy. Although he had willingly accepted the Tridentine decree on Justification, it does not appear that his doctrinal position ever really changed. His interview with Charles V had been very short, but he was accused of making use of words which savoured of heresy. The *Catecismo* was next examined: and, although some, both of the prelates and of the doctors, had no fault to find, others censured it severely. Melchor Cano in particular found much that was ambiguous, much that was temerarious, much that was even heretical, in the sense in which it was said. Nevertheless, the Tridentine censors had pronounced the book orthodox and had given it their approval.

The process dragged on its slow length, with many delays and many interruptions. At length the case was cited to Rome. On December 5, 1566, Carranza came out of his prison, and a few months afterwards he set out for Italy. Here the question had to be reopened, and the documents re-examined and in many cases translated, which involved a further delay. But it appears that Pius V was convinced of Carranza's innocence; and a decree would probably have been given in his favour had not the Pope died on May 1, 1572. His successor Gregory XIII reopened the case, and sentence was not actually given till April 14, 1576. The Archbishop was declared to have taken many errors and modes of speech from the heretics, on account of which he was " vehemently suspected " of heresy; and he was condemned to abjure sixteen propositions. Having done this, and performed certain penances, he was to be free from all censures, but to be suspended for five years from the exercise of his office, meanwhile dwelling in the house of his Order at Orvieto. The *Catecismo* was prohibited altogether. The decision was severe, but not unjust according to the views of the sixteenth century, which applied the tests of doctrinal orthodoxy to the minutiae of individual opinion. But Carranza was no longer subject to it; for seventeen years in prison had broken his strength. He endeavoured to fulfil his penances, humbly made his profession of faith and received the Eucharist, and expired on May 2, 1576.

Thus ended the Reform in Spain, as it had ended in Italy, uprooted by the intolerant dogmatism which assumed that there was an ascertained answer to every possible theological question, confused right-thinking with accuracy of knowledge, and discerned heresy in every reaction and every independent effort of the human mind. Many of those who had been driven out of Spain continued to work elsewhere. Such were Juan Perez already referred to, Cassiodoro de Reina, and Cipriano Valera, each of whom translated the whole Bible into Spanish, and many more. But without following these further, mention must be made of one great Spanish thinker of the earlier part of the century, who spent most of his life abroad. Miguel Serveto y Reveš was born at Tudela in Navarre about 1511, his family being of Villanueva in Aragon; and he studied at Toulouse. As secretary to Juan de Quintana, the Emperor's confessor, he was with him at Bologna in 1529 and at the Diet of Augsburg in 1530 (where he met Melanchthon, of whose *Loci communes* he became a diligent student), but soon afterwards left his service and went to Basel. In 1531 he published his *De Trinitatis Erroribus*, and in 1552 two *Dialogues* on the Trinity: and the suspicion which he incurred by his views led him to flee to France. Here for the first time he met Calvin, who was his antithesis in every way, being as clear, logical, and narrow in his views as Serveto was the reverse. After acting as proof-reader to Trechsel at Lyons, and producing a remarkable edition of Ptolemy, he went to study medicine at Paris. In this field he greatly distinguished himself, for he appears to have been the first discoverer of the circulation of the blood. After a period of wandering, during which he submitted to rebaptism by the Anabaptists of Charlieu, he came to Vienne, where his old pupil Pierre Palmier was now Archbishop, and remained there till 1553. In 1546–7 he engaged in a violent theological controversy with Calvin; and when at length he published his *Christianismi Restitutio* the letters were added to the book as a kind of appendix. Not unnaturally offended, Calvin meanly accused his adversary, through an intermediary, to the Inquisition, and in April, 1553, both Serveto and the printer of the book were imprisoned. Serveto made his escape, probably by complicity of his gaolers, and was burnt in effigy (June 17). He now resolved to make his way into northern Italy; but by a strange mischance he went by way of Geneva. His arrival was reported to Calvin, who resolved that his enemy should not escape; the blasphemer must die. On October 27, 1553, Serveto was burnt at the stake.

It is difficult to estimate his theological position; for his one follower, Alfonso Ligurio of Tarragona, is now little more than a name. Miguel Serveto stands quite alone, and towers far above other sceptical thinkers of his age. In some ways essentially modern, he is in others essentially medieval. He could not throw in his lot with any party because he held that all existing religions alike were partly right and partly wrong. It is impossible to judge of him by constructing a theological system from his writings; for his mind was analytic and not synthetic, his tenets varied from time to time, and his system was after all but a framework by means of which he endeavoured to hold and to express certain great ideas — creation in the *Logos*, the immanence of God in the universe, and the like. But in his anxiety to correct the rigidity of the theological conceptions of his age he took up a position which often degenerated into the merest shallow negation; and his books on the Trinity are anti-trinitarian, not because of his teaching, but in spite of it. And thus, whilst supplying many elements which were lacking to the religious consciousness of most other men of his age, he obscured them, and marred his own usefulness immeasurably, by alloying them with elements of dogmatic anti-trinitarianism which were never of the essence of his teaching.

III

PORTUGAL

In Portugal the religious revolt never attained serious dimensions : there were a few *erasmistas*, and a number of foreigners were proceeded against for heresy from time to time; but that is all. Nevertheless, the prevalence of heresy was one of the reasons alleged for the founding of the Lisbon Inquisition; and the circumstances under which this took place may well claim attention here.

The social condition of Portugal in the early part of the sixteenth century was not a little remarkable. Great opportunities for acquiring wealth had suddenly been opened to its people by the discovery and colonisation of the Indies. The result was that they flocked abroad as colonists, or else left the country districts in order to engage in commerce at Oporto or Lisbon, which rapidly increased in size. But this had a curious effect upon the rural districts. Before long there were scarcely any peasants, and the few that there were demanded high wages. To supply their place, the landowners began to import huge gangs of negro slaves, who were far cheaper, and could be obtained in any number that was required. But this system had one great disadvantage, so far as the exchequer was concerned. It became increasingly difficult to get the taxes paid; for there was no longer anybody to pay them, the property of the merchants being for the most part not within reach for the purpose. And thus the King, Dom João III (1526–57), found himself in a curious position. He had great hoards of money in the treasury, but there was a continual drain upon them; and there were no means of replenishing them, although he reigned over the richest people in Europe. In a letter to Clement VII dated June 28, 1526, he complains of his poverty, and gives this as his reason for not succouring the King of Hungary in his resistance to the Turks.

Various expedients were adopted in order to replenish the royal treasury. Amongst others, a Bull of 1527 gave the King the right of nominating the heads of all monasteries in his realm, with all the pecuniary advantages which this privilege involved. But Dom João soon found that he could not make much from this source without scandalising his people and incurring the enmity of the Church. There was however a source of revenue, yet untapped, which was not open to this objection : namely, the *novos cristãos*. If he could proceed against them as was done in Spain, a lucrative harvest was ready to hand. Accordingly, early in 1531 the King instructed Bras Neto, his agent in Rome, to apply to the Holy See for a Bull establishing the Inquisition in Portugal on the lines of that of Seville, and urged him to use every means in his power to this end, since it would be for the service of God and of himself, and for the good of his people.

Bras Neto's task proved to be one of considerable difficulty. One Cardinal, the Florentine Lorenzo Pucci, declared roundly that no Inquisition was needed, and that it was only a plan to fleece the Jews ; and his nephew, Antonio, who succeeded him as Cardinal, proved little more tractable. The Jews themselves had always been influential with the Curia, and they resisted strenuously. Bras Neto found that, for his purpose, heresy was a better name to conjure with than Judaism ; and he did not fail to press the necessity for the Inquisition as a safeguard against it. At length he succeeded, and on December 17, 1531, the Bull *Cum ad nihil* was signed, which provided for the inauguration of the Inquisition at Lisbon. The reasons given were that some of the *novos cristãos* were returning to the rites of their Jewish forefathers, that certain Christians were Judaising, and that others were following "the Lutheran and other damnable heresies and errors" or practising magical arts. These reasons were, as Herculano has said, "in part false, in part misleading, and in part ridiculous": there were no Lutherans in Portugal ; the *novos cristãos* had as yet given no trouble there ; and the Christians of Portugal were no more inclined to Judaism, and less inclined to magic, than those of other parts of Europe. But the allegations had served their purpose. On January 13, 1532, a brief was dispatched to Frey Diogo da Silva, the King's confessor, expediting the Bull and nominating him as Inquisitor-General; and it looked as if the question was ended. As a matter of fact it was hardly begun. For now began a series of intrigues and counter-intrigues on the matter, now one side getting the best of it and now the other. The brave knight Duarte de Paz, who was the agent for the Jews, worked for them with a zeal and vigour restrained only by the fact that he was a Portuguese subject. The King more than once procured laws which placed the Jews at the mercy of his subjects, and then had to withdraw them. Money, promises, threats, were freely expended on both sides. Herculano calculates that between February, 1531, when the matter was first opened, and July, 1547, when it was finally settled, over two million *cruzados* (or nearly £300,000) were paid by the King to the Papacy, without counting gifts to individual Cardinals. And since the Jews disbursed money even more freely, it is clear that one party at any rate was the gainer by the negotiations.

To trace the changes in detail. On October 17, 1532, a brief was issued suspending the Bull of December 17, 1531. On April 7, 1533, this was followed up by a Bull which divided the *novos cristãos* into two classes, those who had received baptism by compulsion and those who had been baptized voluntarily or in infancy : the former are not bound to observe the laws of the Church, the latter are, but their past failures are condoned. The King was very angry at this amnesty and directed his agents to suggest various alternatives, one being that the Jews should be shipped to Africa so as to be interposed between Christians and Moors. But Clement VII did not waver. On April 2, 1534, he dispatched a dignified brief to Dom João, saying that he was not bound to give reasons for his action, but that he would do so as an act of grace ; and he proceeded to give his reasons with admirable clearness. Not long afterwards he died. His successor Paul III seemed more tractable at first. But he would not withdraw the pardon, even when Dom João threatened to renounce the papal obedience like the King of England. At length however, at the desire of Charles V, Paul agreed to the setting-up of the Inquisition ; and it was again provided for by a Bull of May 23, 1536. But the matter did not end here, and it was not until July 16, 1547, that the precise extent of the amnesty was settled and the Inquisition finally established.

Even when it was established it had very little to do with heresy properly so called. A few writings, for instance those of Antonio Pereira Marramaque, who insisted upon the duty of translating the Bible, were placed on the Portuguese Index ; but it was far more largely concerned with foreign works than with those of natives. A considerable number of foreign students or traders came under its influence ; for instance, the Scottish poet George Buchanan (1548 *c.*) and the Englishmen William Gardiner and Mark Burgess. Even the records of the foreign Church at Geneva, so largely recruited from Spain and Italy, only supply some five or six Portuguese names. So that Damião de Goes remains the one Portuguese heretic of distinction during this period.

Damião was born about 1501 of a noble family, went to Antwerp about 1523, and spent six years there in study. Then he travelled in the north, and returned by way of Germany, passing through Münster to Freiburg, where he stayed some months with Erasmus, and had long conferences with him. After this he was in Italy from 1534 to 1538, with one short interval, during which he came to Basel to tend Erasmus, who died in his arms on the night of July 11–12, 1536. In 1537, at the desire of Sadoleto, he began a correspondence with the Reformers at

Wittenberg, in the hope of bringing them back to the Church. He was at Louvain in 1538, and after fighting on the side of Flanders and being for two years a prisoner of war, he at length returned to Portugal in 1545. He was almost immediately denounced to the Inquisition, but as the charges were vague and the Inquisitor-General his friend, he was set free, and soon after was appointed royal archivist and historiographer. In 1550 a second denunciation was made by Simão Rodrigues, a Jesuit who had known him in Italy ; it was more precise and therefore more dangerous, but although he was vehemently suspected the charges fell through. More than twenty years later, however, the charges were again disinterred. He was brought before the judge Diogo da Fonseca, on April 4, 1571, and remanded ; and the old man of seventy remained in prison for twenty months while the charges were being investigated. He frankly confessed that he had been remiss in the performance of his religious duties, and that he had held certain points of doctrine which were then held by many great theologians, and were only subsequently made unlawful by the Council of Trent. This, he said, was between 1531 and 1537 ; and against it he set more than thirty years of blameless life. Nevertheless, he was sentenced to perpetual imprisonment. Here the King interfered, commuted the punishment, and sent him on December 16, 1572, to perform his penance in the monastery of Batalha. We do not know when he returned to his own home ; but he died there not long afterwards of an accident — a judgment, as people said.

Such then was the work of the Portuguese Inquisition during this period in its relation to heresy. It was founded for reasons ostensibly religious, but actually fiscal ; and although when once established it made Protestantism impossible in Portugal, there is nothing to suggest that the movement for Reform would have found many adherents there had there been no Inquisition.

CHAPTER XIII

HENRY VIII
1519-1547

ON his election to the Empire Charles became a much greater potentate in the eyes of all, and, as he was also the Queen of England's nephew, there were manifest reasons for England to desire his friendship. On the other hand, the close alliance of France, which Wolsey had twice succeeded in securing, however beneficial to England, was exceedingly unpopular. It had scarcely been contracted when efforts were made to undermine it ; and soon a strong party at Court, headed by the Queen herself, endeavoured to prevent the French interview, which had been arranged for April 1, 1519, from taking effect. The new Emperor, equally desirous to counteract, if he could not prevent, the meeting, agreed to visit England on his way from Spain to Germany. Matters, however, had to be arranged beforehand, and though the anti-French party contrived to put off the visit to Francis till June, 1520, it was only in April of that year that the imperial ambassador in England succeeded in concluding a specific treaty. It was settled that the Emperor should, if possible, land at Sandwich in May just before the King went to France, or, if he failed to do so, should have a meeting with Henry at Gravelines after the French interview. He actually landed on May 26, at Dover, barely in time for a very hurried visit. Next day, which happened to be Whitsunday, the King conducted him to Canterbury, where he was introduced to the Queen, his aunt, and attended service in the Cathedral. On the 31st he had to embark again for Flanders, in order that Henry might fulfil his engagement with Francis. But a further meeting at Gravelines after the French interview was promised.

Wolsey meanwhile had taken care that this French interview should not be a failure. A great deal of negotiation, indeed, had been found necessary ; but Francis, to facilitate matters, at last put all the arrangements under Wolsey's control, so that they advanced rapidly. The King crossed from Calais to Dover the same day that the Emperor embarked from Sandwich. At Guines on June 6 he signed a treaty of which the counterpart was signed by Francis the same day at Ardres, partly bearing on the prospective marriage of Mary and the Dauphin, partly framed to secure French intervention in disputes with Scotland in a form which should give England satisfaction. The interview took place on the 7th, in a spot between the English castle of Guines and the French castle of Ardres. The scene, magnificent beyond all precedent, even in that age of glitter, was called, from the splendour of the tents and apparel, the Field of Cloth of Gold; and the mutual visits and festivities continued till the 24th, when the two Kings separated.

Nothing could have appeared more cordial, and the world was for some time under the impression that the alliance between England and France was now more firmly knit than ever. And yet, immediately afterwards, the King with Queen Catharine proceeded by agreement to another meeting with the Emperor at Gravelines, which took place on July 10. On the 14th at Calais a secret treaty was signed, binding both Henry and the Emperor to make no further arrangements with France giving effect either to the marriage of the Dauphin with Mary or to that of Charles himself with the French King's daughter Charlotte—a match to which he was bound by the Treaty of Noyon. Indeed, there is no doubt that in their secret conferences both at Canterbury and at Calais, the project had been discussed of setting aside agreements with France by both parties and marrying the Emperor to the Princess Mary. Of these perfidious compacts Francis was, of course, not directly informed; but he was not to be persuaded that the two meetings with the Emperor, before and after the interview, were mere matters of courtesy. He felt, however, that it would be impolitic to display resentment. The Emperor was crowned at Aachen on October 23.

In April, 1521, the Duke of Buckingham was summoned from Gloucestershire to the King's presence, and on his arrival in London was charged with treason. Information had been given against him of various incautious expressions tending to show that, being of the blood of Lancaster, he had some expectation of succeeding to the Crown, the fulfilment of which events might hasten; also, that, should he succeed, Wolsey and Sir Thomas Lovel would be beheaded; and further, that if he had been arrested on an occasion when the King had been displeased with him, he would have tried, as his father had with Richard III, to get access to the King's presence and would then have stabbed him. That this testimony was strongly coloured by malice, there is little doubt. But the Duke had a formal trial before the Duke of Norfolk as High Steward, and was found guilty by seventeen of his peers. He was beheaded on Tower Hill on May 17, to the general regret of the people.

At this time Francis I had stirred up war against the Emperor, who was already perplexed with a rebellion in Spain, while occupied in Germany with Luther and the Diet of Worms. Charles, hard pressed, was willing to accept Henry's mediation, and the French, after some reverses for which their early success had not prepared them, were glad to accept it also. But the Imperialists changed their tone with the change of fortune, and demanded Henry's aid by the treaty of London against the aggressor. Wolsey was sent to Calais to hear deputies of both sides and adjust the differences. On opening the conference, he found the Imperialists intractable; they had no power to treat, only to demand aid of England. But Wolsey, they said, might visit the Emperor himself, who was then at Bruges, to discuss matters. This strange proceeding, as State-papers show, had been certainly planned between Wolsey and the Imperialists beforehand; and the Cardinal suspended the conference, making plausible excuses to the French, while he went to the Emperor at Bruges and concluded with him a secret treaty against France on August 25. It would seem, however, that the terms of this treaty were the subject of prolonged discussion before it was concluded; and Wolsey, instead of being only eight days absent from Calais, as he told the Frenchmen he would be, was away for nearly three weeks. He had successfully contended, among other things, that if a suspension of hostilities could be obtained in the meantime, England should not be bound to declare war against France till March, 1523. On his return to Calais he laboured hard to bring about this suspension, but in vain. The capture of Fuenterrabia by the French in October, and their refusal to restore it, or even to put it into the hands of England for a time as security, finally wrecked the conference, and Wolsey returned to England in November. His health had given way at times during these proceedings, and he was certainly disappointed at the result. But he was rewarded by the King with the abbey of St Alban's in addition to his other preferments.

Pope Leo X died on December 2 following. Charles V had promised Wolsey at Bruges that on the first vacancy of the papal chair he would do his best to make him Pope, and the King sent Pace to Rome to help to procure his election. The Emperor wrote to Wolsey that he had not forgotten his promise, but he certainly did not keep it, and in January, 1522, Adrian VI was elected. It may be doubted whether Wolsey was much disappointed; but he knew now what reliance to place on a promise of Charles V. On February 2 he and the papal ambassador presented to the King the deceased Pope's Bull bestowing upon him the title of Defender of the Faith, in acknowledgment of the service he had done the Church by writing a book against Luther.

Henry had been more eager to take part with the Emperor than Wolsey thought prudent. Charles now required a loan and claimed from Henry fulfilment of a promise of the pay of 3000 men in the Netherlands. He was already in Henry's debt; but Wolsey was disposed to allow him a further advance of 100,000 crowns on condition that the

King should not be called on to declare openly against Francis till the money was refunded. This did not suit Charles at all, and he hastened on another visit which he was to pay to Henry on his way back to Spain, and arrived at Dover again in 1522 on May 26 — the very day of his landing there two years before. He was feasted and entertained even more than he cared for at Greenwich, London, and Windsor, at which last place on June 19 he bound himself by a new treaty to marry Mary when she had completed her twelfth year. But he secured a further loan of 50,000 crowns, and had the satisfaction, during his stay, of seeing Henry committed to immediate war with France by an open declaration of hostility, which the English herald Clarencieux made to Francis at Lyons on May 29. On July 2 a further treaty was concluded for the conduct of the war, and on the 6th the Emperor sailed from Southampton. Just before his departure he gave Wolsey a patent for a pension of 2500 ducats on vacant bishoprics in Spain, and guaranteed him the continuance of another pension which Francis had hitherto paid him in recompense for the bishopric of Tournay, that city having surrendered to the Imperialists on December 1. But Spanish pensions were commonly in arrear, and that charged on the Spanish bishoprics was only in lieu of one specifically charged on the see of Badajoz, which the Emperor had already granted to Wolsey in 1520. Nor was Charles at all ready at any time, when called upon, to pay his debts to the King himself.

It was no surprise to Francis when England declared war against him. As a means of keeping Henry in check, he had again let Albany find his way to Scotland while the Calais conferences were still going on in 1521. He pretended that he had not connived at Albany's escape, and he made a show of urging him to return; but he meant to make use of him in Scotland. Albany, on his arrival, desired of Henry a prolongation of the truce between the two kingdoms, in which France should be included. Evidently France was so impoverished by taxation that she would have been glad to stave off war by any means. But Henry would hear nothing about prolonging the truce while Albany was in Scotland; and he wrote to the Estates of that country in January, 1522, not to allow him to remain there, seeing that he had escaped from France surreptitiously and his presence was not even safe for their King. This was just what Henry had told them before; but it was a stranger plea to urge than formerly; for this time Queen Margaret, James V's own mother, had solicited Albany's return. She, indeed, had found it hard to live amid a factious nobility, especially as she had been neglected by her own husband, from whom she was now seeking a divorce. But Henry had small regard for his sister's good name, and insinuated that it was Albany who had tried to separate her from her husband, with the intention of marrying her himself. Such a charge was scarcely even plausible, for Albany had a wife then living, with whom, as he told the

English herald, he was perfectly satisfied. The Estates of Scotland made a very temperate but firm reply, saying they were prepared to live and die with their Governor, while both Margaret and Albany repelled the shameful insinuations against them, certainly not with greater vehemence than the case deserved. Henry then sent a fleet to the Firth of Forth, and some raids into Scotland took place, in which Kelso was partly burned.

As to France, so soon after the declaration of war as the wind would serve and bad victualling arrangements permit, a force under the Earl of Surrey as Lord Admiral sailed from Southampton, and on July 1 sacked and burned the town of Morlaix in Britanny, setting fire to the shipping in the harbour. It then returned with a rich booty to the Solent ; for the merchants of Morlaix had stores of linen cloths. There was also some desultory fighting about Calais and Boulogne ; but nothing noteworthy was done till September, when Surrey, now the commander of an invading force, in co-operation with an imperial army, burned and destroyed with great barbarity a number of places in Picardy. Hesdin also was besieged, and the town much injured ; but it was found difficult to assault the castle, and the besiegers withdrew. The season was wet, the artillery difficult to move, and the understanding between the allies not altogether satisfactory. Surrey's empty victories won him great applause in England ; but he returned to Calais in October.

Meantime the Scots had created some alarm. In May, for want of French support, Albany had been on the point of withdrawing from the country and letting peace be made, when some slender succours came ; moreover, the English raids called for retribution. Albany advanced to the borders at the head of a very numerous army, intending to invade England on September 2. Though the design was known even in July, when the Earl of Shrewsbury was appointed lieutenant-general of an army to be sent against Scotland, the borders were ill prepared to resist, and Carlisle, against which Albany's great host was directed, was defenceless. But Lord Dacre, Warden of the Marches, was equal to the emergency. Towards the close of August he sent secret messages to Albany, which led to negotiations, though he acknowledged that he had no powers to treat ; and he appealed to Margaret to use her influence for peace, which would become more hopeless than ever between the kingdoms if arrangements were not made at once. He effectually concealed the weakness of his own position, and caused the enemy to waste time till, at length, on September 11, Albany agreed with him for one month's abstinence from war, and disbanded his army. Wolsey was much relieved, and Dacre was thanked for his astuteness. It was in vain, now, that Albany in further negotiations pressed for the comprehension of France ; and he sailed again for that country in October, leaving a Council of Regency in Scotland, and promising to return in the following August.

Much money was wanted for the French war. Wolsey had not only levied from the City of London a loan of £20,000, but afterwards, on August 20, had sent for the mayor and chief citizens to inform them that commissioners were appointed over all the country to swear every man to the value of his moveable property, of which it was thought that everyone should give a tenth; and though some had already contributed to the loan as much as a fifth of their goods, they were told that the loan would only be allowed as part of the tenth to be exacted from the whole city. Nor was even this enough; for Parliament, which had not met for more than seven years, was called in April, 1523, expressly for further supplies. A subsidy of £800,000 was demanded, for which the Commons were asked to impose a property tax of four shillings in the pound on every man's goods and lands. Sir Thomas More, who was elected Speaker, backed up the demand, but it was resisted as impossible. There was not coin, it was said, out of the King's hands in all the realm to pay it. Cardinal Wolsey came down to the House, and would have discussed the matter; but the Commons pleaded their privileges, and he contented himself with setting before them evidences of the increased prosperity of the country, and withdrew. After long debate a grant was made of two shillings in the pound, payable in two years, on every man's lands or goods who was worth £20, with smaller rates on men of inferior means. But Wolsey insisted that this was not enough, and ultimately further grants were made of one shilling in the pound on landed property, to be paid in three years, and one shilling in the pound on goods, to be paid in the fourth year. The amount was unprecedented. The Parliament sat continuously, except for a break at Whitsuntide, till August 13, when it was dissolved. The clergy were also taxed at the same time through their convocations, that of Canterbury meeting at first at St Paul's, and that of York under Wolsey at Westminster; an attempt of Wolsey to induce them to resolve themselves into a single national synod failed. They were permitted to vote their money in the usual way; and, after much opposition, a grant was made of half a year's revenue from all benefices, payable in five years.

The war, which had languished somewhat since Surrey's invasion of France, was now renewed with greater vigour. In August the Duke of Suffolk was appointed Captain-general of a new invading army — a larger one, it was said, than had sailed from England for a hundred years. France was not only in great poverty but was now isolated. Scotland could not help her, and her old ally, Venice, had turned against her, not being allowed to remain neutral. Moreover, Henry was calculating on the disaffection of the Duke of Bourbon, with whom both he and the Emperor had been for some time secretly in communication. In September the Duke's sudden defection took Francis by surprise, and compelled him to desist from conducting personally a new expedition into Italy. Meanwhile Suffolk, having crossed the Channel, was joined by a considerable force under Count van Buren, not, however, well provided with waggons and means of transport, while France was harassed elsewhere by the Imperialists. But the invading armies were weakened by divided counsels ; a plan of besieging Boulogne was given up, and the allies only devastated Picardy, took Bray by assault, and compelled Ancre and Montdidier to surrender. It was reported in England that Suffolk was on his way to Paris, and, that he might have the means to follow up his advantages, commissions were issued .on November 2 to press all over England for what was called an " anticipation," that is to say, for payment by those possessed of £40 in lands or goods of the first assessment of the subsidy, before the term when it was legally due. The money was gathered in. But before the month of November was out, Buren had disbanded his forces, and Suffolk had returned to Calais. A severe frost had produced intense suffering, and it was found impossible to preserve discipline. The King had determined to send over Lord Mountjoy with reinforcements ; but, before he could be sent, the English troops had taken their own way home through Flanders, and many of them shipped at Antwerp, Sluys, and Nieuport.

Meantime, though later than he promised, eluding English efforts to intercept him, Albany had again crossed the sea to Scotland. During all the time of his absence Henry had persistently tried to undermine his influence and weaken the Scotch alliance with France. For this it was not difficult to make further use of Margaret, who, in the hope of seeing her old authority restored, was soon persuaded once more to desert Albany. A truce had been arranged with the lords without reference to him, and Albany in France took serious alarm at rumours that Henry had been negotiating to keep him permanently out of Scotland with the suggestion of marrying James to the Princess Mary. But the truce was allowed to expire in February, when Surrey was appointed lieutenant-general of the army against Scotland, and under his direction the Marquis of Dorset, who was appointed Warden of the East Marches, invaded Teviotdale in April, 1523. A series of further invasions was kept up all through the summer, and, just when Albany returned in September, Surrey succeeded in laying Jedburgh in ashes — till then a great fortified town more populous than Berwick. He met, however, with a most obstinate resistance, and was thrown on the defensive when Albany, immediately on his arrival, prepared to invade in his turn. Knowing the weakness of Berwick and the strength of Albany's reinforcements, Surrey was seriously alarmed. But Wolsey had reason for believing his fears to be exaggerated, as the event proved them to be. Encumbered by heavy artillery Albany moved slowly, and at last laid siege to Wark Castle on November 1. The fortress seemed in real danger, the outer works being actually won ; but the garrison made a gallant defence, and next day, as Surrey was coming to the rescue, Albany suddenly gave up the siege, and returned to Edinburgh.

His mysterious retreat was branded by the English as a shameful flight, and satirised in contemptuous verse by Skelton, the poet laureate. But the truth seems to be that several of the Scotch lords deprecated a policy of invasion as being only in the interest of France. Albany's influence was clearly on the wane; for next year he met a Parliament in May, and again obtained leave for a brief visit to France on the understanding that if he did not return in August his authority was at an end. He left immediately and never returned again.

Meanwhile, on the death of Adrian VI in September, 1523, Charles V again promised with the same insincerity as before to advance Wolsey's candidature for the papacy as advantageous alike to England and himself. But on November 19 Giuliano de' Medici, a great friend of both princes, was elected as Clement VII. He soon after confirmed for life Wolsey's legatine authority, which at first had been only temporary but had been prolonged from time to time.

In 1524 the war made little progress after February, when the Emperor recovered Fuenterrabia; all parties were exhausted. But little came of the mission of a Nuncio (Nicholas von Schomberg, Archbishop of Capua), whom the Pope sent to France, Spain, and England successively to mediate a peace. Negotiations went on with Bourbon on the part both of the Emperor and Henry for a joint attack on France. But the King and Wolsey had long suspected the Emperor's sincerity, and were determined that there should be either peace or war in earnest. Bourbon invaded Provence, and laid siege to Marseilles; whereupon orders were issued in England, September 10, to prepare for a royal invasion in aid of the Duke. The siege of Marseilles, in itself, was entirely in the Emperor's interest; no English army crossed the Channel, and Bourbon was forced to abandon the enterprise.

Henry, in the meantime, had been feeling his way to a separate peace with France, in case the Emperor showed himself remiss in fulfilling his engagements. In June a Genoese merchant, Giovanni Joachino Passano, came over to London, as if on ordinary business. He was soon known to be an agent of Louise of Savoy, the French King's mother, who had been left Regent in her son's absence. His stay in England was unpopular with the English, but his secret negotiations with Wolsey were disavowed, and in January, 1525, another French agent, Brinon, President of Rouen, joined him in London.

Francis, seeing how matters lay, made a sudden descent into Italy and recovered Milan, which he had lost in the spring. But the protracted siege of Pavia ended with the defeat and capture of the French King, which seemed to throw everything into the Emperor's hands, and it was not likely that he would share with his allies the fruits of his victory. Wolsey, however, had been ordering matters so as to secure his master's interests, whether the French should succeed or fail in Italy ; and just before the news of the battle reached England he had taken a most extraordinary step to cover his communications with the French agent.   A watchman arrested one night a messenger of de Praet, the Imperial ambassador, as a suspicious character.   His letters were taken and brought to Wolsey, who first opened and read them, then sent for the ambassador and upbraided him for the terms (very un-complimentary, certainly, to himself) in which he had dared to write to his own sovereign.   The King himself followed this up by a letter to the Emperor, desiring him to punish de Praet as a mischief-maker trying to disturb the cordiality between them ; and Charles, afraid to alienate Henry, made only a mild remonstrance against the insult.

Just after this occurrence, and before news had yet arrived of the great event at Pavia, an important embassy came over from Flanders, from the Emperor's aunt, Margaret of Savoy.   The situation in Italy was then so doubtful, and the Imperial forces there so distressed for want of means, that England was to be urged to send a large army over sea to create a diversion by a new joint attack on the North of France. Another request was, that the Princess Mary and her dowry might be given up to them at once, or sent over as early as possible in anticipation of the time appointed by the treaty.   The first point Wolsey was willing to concede, if assured of sufficient co-operation from Flanders ; but the conditions he required were declared by the Flemings to be quite im-possible in the exhausted condition of the country.   The second demand looked strange enough, and Wolsey asked what adequate hostages they could give for a young Princess who was the treasure of the kingdom. Would they meanwhile put some of their fortified towns into the King's hands ?   This, too, the ambassadors said, could not be thought of ; and the embassy had made little progress when, on March 9, the news from Pavia reached London.   The King professed delight at the Emperor's victory ; bonfires were lighted, wine flowed freely for everyone in the streets, and on Sunday the 12th a solemn mass was celebrated by Wolsey at St Paul's.

The Cardinal then, at the request of the Flemings, dismissed Brinon and Passano, and strongly urged that now was the time for both allies to put forth all their strength.   They might completely conquer France between them, and Henry, meeting the Emperor in Paris, would accompany him to Rome for his coronation.   The scheme, of course, was preposterous ; but the proposal of it to the Emperor by the English ambassadors in Spain wrung from him the confession that he had no money to carry on the war, with other admissions besides, which proved clearly that he was really seeking to break off his engagement to the Princess Mary, and was bent on a more advantageous match with Isabella of Portugal.   Thus England was to obtain nothing in return for all her loans to the Emperor ; but the Emperor, as it soon appeared,

meant to make his own terms with his prisoner, and keep to himself
entirely the profits of a joint war; in which, indeed, English aid had
profited him little.

Meanwhile the victory at Pavia was declared in England to be a
great opportunity for the King to recover his rights in France by
conducting a new invasion; in aid of which commissions were issued
to levy further contributions, called an "Amicable Grant," though
some instalments of the parliamentary subsidy had still to be received.
As commissioner for the City of London, Wolsey called the Lord Mayor
and Aldermen before him, telling them that he and the Archbishop of
Canterbury had each given a third part of their revenues, and urging
that persons of over £50 income might well contribute a sixth of
their goods according to their own valuation made in 1522. At this
there was very natural discontent, the more so as many had incurred
serious losses since that date; but the matter was pressed both in London
and in the country. The demand was generally resisted. At Reading
the people would only give a twelfth. In Suffolk the Duke of Suffolk
persuaded them to give a sixth; but the clothiers said it would compel
them to discharge their men, and a serious rising took place. At last,
instead of a forced demand, Wolsey persuaded the King to be content
with a voluntary "benevolence." But a new objection was raised that
benevolences were illegal by an Act of Richard III; and ultimately
the King had to give up the demand altogether, and to pardon the
insurgents.

Wolsey told the citizens that the demand was abandoned because the
French King's capture had disposed him to make suit to England for an
honourable peace; for if the King had not crossed the sea (he alleged)
the money would have been returned, and now it would probably not be
required. But until peace was actually concluded, they must still hold
themselves prepared to make further sacrifices. Thus did Wolsey smooth
the way for a policy of peace with France, which he was now actively
pursuing. Passano, who had not ceased to hold indirect communication with him, again appeared in London in June, no longer as a
secret agent, but as an accredited ambassador from Louise of Savoy, now
ennobled with the title of the Seigneur de Vaulx. He concluded with
Wolsey a forty days' truce; but the Flemings immediately concluded one
for five months with France, and the truce concluded by de Vaulx was
prolonged to December 1 by Brinon, who soon followed him again to
England with a commission to both for a more lasting treaty. The
terms required by Wolsey were hard; but demands made at first for a
cession of Ardres or Boulogne were given up, and the old payments
exacted from France were increased to a capital sum of 2,000,000 crowns
payable at the rate of 100,000 crowns a year. After long discussions
with Wolsey, a set of five treaties was signed at his palace of the Moor
in Hertfordshire on August 30, the most important being a league for

mutual defence, in which Henry bound himself to use his influence with the Emperor to induce him to set Francis at liberty on reasonable conditions. At the request of the Frenchmen peace was proclaimed a week later (September 6).

The Pope, the Venetians, and other Italian Powers who dreaded the overwhelming ascendancy of the Emperor, were glad of this arrangement between France and England. But it had little effect on the Emperor's conduct towards his prisoner, who by this time had been conveyed to Madrid. His sister Margaret, Duchess of Alençon, came to Spain to treat for his liberation; but the conditions demanded by the Emperor were such as she had no power to grant. The chief difficulty concerned the cession of Burgundy. But Francis fell dangerously ill, and on his recovery he agreed to concede even this for the sake of liberty. On January 14, 1526, he signed the Treaty of Madrid, with all its onerous terms, including, among other things, the promise to refund the sum of 500,000 crowns due from the Emperor to Henry.

England had been unable to do anything to mitigate the severity of the conditions. Henry, indeed, had sent a new ambassador, Dr Edward Lee, to Spain with that object; but it was easy to prevent either him or his colleagues from effectually interfering with the negotiations. After the treaty was signed, however, Francis told them that he was grateful to Henry above all princes living for not having invaded France, and that Henry should know his secret mind upon some things as soon as he had returned to his realm. What he meant by this we may imagine from the sequel.

The preponderance in Europe which seemed to be secured to Charles by the Treaty of Madrid alarmed not only the King of England. It was generally believed, however, that Francis, on regaining his liberty, neither would nor could allow himself to be bound by provisions to which he had no right to assent without consulting the Estates of his realm and the duchy of Burgundy. The Italian Powers accordingly looked anxiously to Francis, and, on account of Francis, not less anxiously to Henry.

England was strong, and even stronger than she had been. The only active pretender to Henry's throne, Richard de la Pole, self-styled Duke of Suffolk, " White Rose " as his followers called him, had been slain at the battle of Pavia fighting for Francis. Moreover the Duke of Albany had left Scotland for the last time (he accompanied Francis to Italy and, but for the event of Pavia, would have gone on to Naples); so that the French party in Scotland was overpowered, and though there were changes enough in that country none of them were injurious to English interests. Henry was powerful, and no prince was held in higher esteem. Special gifts had been conferred upon him by three successive Popes,—a golden rose by Julius II, a sword and cap by Leo X (besides the title of Defender of the Faith), and another golden rose by Clement VII. He was also still highly popular at home; for his subjects did not impute their heavy taxation to him. One thing indeed he did at this time, which was disagreeable to his own Queen. He had a bastard son six years old, whom in June, 1525, he created Duke of Richmond, assigning him at the same time a special household and lands as if for a legitimate Prince. But this, apparently, did not greatly abate his popularity; and it seems to have been partly to conciliate public opinion that Wolsey, in that year, handed over to the King the magnificent palace he had built at Hampton Court as too grand to belong to a subject.

It was on March 17, 1526, that Francis was released and reached Bayonne. That same day he took the English Ambassador Tayler in his arms, expressing warm gratitude to Henry, and soon after he dispatched de Vaulx once more to England with his ratifications of the Treaties of the Moor. On May 22, after Francis had reached Cognac, ambassadors of the Pope, the Venetians, and the Duke of Milan made an alliance with the French King against the Emperor.

Henry, who had confirmed his own treaty with Francis at Greenwich on April 29, was not a party to this League of Cognac; but he was strongly solicited to join it by the Italian Powers. Indeed, a special place was reserved for him in the treaty itself as Protector and Conservator of the alliance if he chose to join it, with a principality in Naples as an additional attraction. But he and Wolsey only dallied with the confederates, insisting on various modifications of the treaty, while the others were already committed to hostilities in Italy. Meanwhile the confederacy moved on to its ruin, which was completed at the Sack of Rome.

Francis naturally desired to obtain from the Emperor the best terms he could for redeeming his sons. Wolsey, however, had from the first endeavoured to keep him from any kind of agreement, assuring him that he was in no wise bound by the Treaty of Madrid, and hinting that a match with the Princess Mary would be more suitable for him than one with the Emperor's sister Eleanor, whom by that treaty he had engaged to marry. And though the bait did not take immediately — for Francis, as his own ministers said, was ready to marry the Emperor's mule to recover his sons — the Emperor still insisted on such intolerable conditions that Francis at last desired an offensive alliance with England by which he might either dictate terms or redeem his sons by war. An embassy with this view headed by de Grammont, Bishop of Tarbes, came to England in February, 1527. The ambassadors were long in negotiation with Wolsey, who insisted first on a new treaty of perpetual peace, with a heavy tribute from France, and after all his demands were conceded coolly told them that, if the Emperor would not release the Princes without Francis marrying Eleanor, the King recommended him to do so. Three treaties were at last signed on April 30, and, after the Bishop of

Tarbes had gone back to France and returned again, another was concluded on May 29, for maintaining a joint army in Italy. But there were still matters to be settled, for which Henry desired a personal interview with Francis. This the French did not favour, but said that Wolsey would be welcome in France as his master's representative; and Francis himself wrote that he would go to Picardy to meet him.

The King is said to have alleged later,—though there is no sufficient proof of the truth of the story,—that, during this embassy the Bishop of Tarbes had expressed a doubt concerning the Princess Mary's legitimacy, as her mother Catharine had been the wife of Prince Arthur, her father's brother. It was the King himself who was now contemplating a divorce on this plea, although no one yet knew it. As a first step, in May he allowed himself to be cited in private before Wolsey as Legate and called upon to justify his marriage. Nothing came of this proceeding, except that on June 22 Henry shocked his wife by telling her that they must part company, as he found by the opinion of divines and lawyers that they had been living in sin. He desired her, however, to keep the matter secret for the present; and Wolsey, on his way to France, persuaded both Archbishop Warham and Bishop Fisher that the King was only trying to answer objections raised by the Bishop of Tarbes.

Wolsey himself, however, did not know all the King's mind upon the subject when, after landing at Calais in July, he proceeded through France with a more magnificent train than ever, not as ambassador but as his King's lieutenant, to a meeting with Francis at Amiens. On this matter he believed he was commissioned, not only to hint that Catharine would be divorced, but also to put forward a project for marrying the King to Renée, daughter of Louis XII. This would, of course, have knit firmer the bond between Henry and Francis against the Emperor, who was Catharine's nephew. But in France he was instructed to keep back "the King's secret matter," or only to intimate it very vaguely; and during the whole of his stay there, which extended to two months and a half, he did not venture to say anything definite upon the subject.

Another matter, however, helped to strengthen the case for a union against the Emperor. A month before Wolsey crossed the Channel, news had reached England that Rome had been sacked, and the Pope shut up in the Castle of St Angelo. At Canterbury Wolsey ordered a litany to be sung for the imprisoned Pope, but considered how he could best utilise the incident for the King's advantage. At Amiens on August 18, three new treaties were made, which Henry and Francis ratified forthwith; and among other things it was settled that Mary should be married to the Duke of Orleans instead of to Francis, and that no brief or Bull should be received during the Pope's imprisonment, but that whatever should be determined by the clergy of England and France in the meantime should be valid. It was also agreed what terms should be demanded of the Emperor by the two Kings; and meanwhile an English detachment under Sir Robert Jerningham was sent to join the French commander Lautrec in an Italian expedition for the Pope's delivery.

Before Wolsey returned from France he had made the discovery that the King's real object in seeking a divorce had not been imparted to him, and that Henry was pursuing it independently. It was not a French princess whom Henry designed to place in Catharine's room, but one Anne Boleyn, daughter of Sir Thomas Boleyn, a simple knight, who had only been created a viscount (by the title of Rochford) in 1525. The elder sister of this lady had already been seduced by the King, but she herself had resisted till she was assured of the Crown, and Henry persuaded himself that all that was required for his marriage with Anne Boleyn was a dispensation for a case of near affinity created by illicit intercourse with her sister. For he did not, in this first phase of the question, maintain, as he afterwards did, that cases like that of Catharine could not be dispensed for at all. He maintained that the dispensation procured for his marriage with Catharine was technically insufficient, and that the marriage was consequently *ipso facto* invalid.

He accordingly, while Wolsey was still in France, dispatched Dr Knight, his secretary, to Italy on pretences that did not satisfy the Cardinal; and Knight performed his mission with great dexterity according to his instructions. He arrived at Rome while the Pope was still in confinement, and though it was hopeless to procure an interview, found means to convey to him the draft dispensation desired by the King, and obtained a promise that it should be passed when he was at liberty. Not long after the Pope escaped to Orvieto, where Knight obtained from him, in effect, a document such as he was instructed to ask for. But unfortunately it was absolutely useless for the King's purpose until he should be declared free of his first marriage; and Knight's mission had no effect except to open the eyes of the Pope and Cardinals to Henry's real object.

Meanwhile, France and England having become the closest possible allies, the two sovereigns elected each other into their respective Orders of St Michael and the Garter; and their heralds Guienne and Clarencieux jointly declared war upon the Emperor at Burgos on January 22, 1528. On this the English merchants in Spain were arrested, and it was rumoured that the heralds were arrested also; in return for which Wolsey actually imprisoned for a time the Imperial Ambassador Mendoza. This war was extremely unpopular in England. A French alliance, indeed, was generally hateful, especially against the Emperor, who was regarded as a natural ally. The mart for English wools was removed from Antwerp to Calais; trade was interrupted both with the Low Countries and Spain; and this, added to the effect of bad harvests at home, produced severe distress. Cloth lay on the merchants' hands unsaleable, and the clothiers of the Eastern Counties were obliged to discharge their spinners, carders, and "tuckers." The state of matters became, in fact, intolerable, and a commercial truce was arranged with Flanders from the beginning of May to the end of February following.

The expedition of Lautrec and Jerningham in Italy, very successful in the spring, proved completely disastrous in the following summer. Plague carried off the two commanders, and the defection of Andrea Doria completed the ruin of the allied forces.

After Knight's failure Wolsey addressed himself to the real difficulty in attaining the King's object, and dispatched his secretary Stephen Gardiner with Edward Foxe to persuade the Pope to send a Legate commissioned jointly with Wolsey to try in England the question whether the dispensation to marry Catharine was sufficient. The commission desired was a decretal one, setting forth the law by which judgment should proceed, and leaving the judges to ascertain the facts and pass judgment without appeal. This was resisted as unusual, and the ambassadors were obliged to be satisfied with a general commission, which Foxe took home to England, believing it to be equally efficacious. His report seems to have convinced the King and Anne Boleyn that their object was as good as gained. But Wolsey saw that the commission was insufficient, and he instructed Gardiner to press again by every possible means for a decretal commission, even though it should be secret and not to be employed in the process; otherwise his power over Henry was gone and utter ruin hung over him as having deceived the King about the Pope's willingness to oblige him. Urged in this way, the Pope with very great reluctance gave for Wolsey's sake precisely what was asked for — a secret decretal commission, not to be used in the process, but only to be shown to the King and Wolsey, and then to be destroyed. He also gave a secret promise in writing not to revoke the commission which was not to be used. This secret commission was entrusted to Campeggio, the legate sent to England as Wolsey's colleague to try the cause, with strict injunctions not to let it go out of his hands.

Campeggio suffered severely from gout, and his progress to England was slow and tedious. He reached London on October 7, prostrated by illness; but he had the full command of the business, and Wolsey found, to his dismay, that he had no means of taking it out of his hands. Moreover, Campeggio had promised the Pope before leaving not to give sentence without reference to him. He tried first to dissuade the King from the trial; then to induce the Queen to accept an honourable release by entering a convent. Both attempts he found hopeless. The Queen was as determined as the King, and was supported by general sympathy out of doors, the women, particularly, cheering her wherever she went.

On November 8 the King declared to the Lord Mayor and Aldermen at Bridewell the reasons for his conduct, imputing, as before, to the French ambassadors the first doubts of his marriage. But before matters had come to a trial Catharine showed Campeggio a document which seemed to make the validity of the marriage unimpeachable. It was a copy of a brief preserved in Spain, by which Julius II had given, at the earnest request of Queen Isabella, a full dispensation for the marriage, assuming that the previous marriage with Arthur had really been consummated. The King and Wolsey were seriously perplexed. They put forth reasons for believing the brief to be a forgery, and urged the Queen herself, as if in her own interest, to write to the Emperor to send it to England. The object, however, was too plain; and though, under positive compulsion, she did write as requested, her messenger, as soon as he reached Spain, took care to inform the Emperor that she had written against her will.

The King was now living under one roof with Anne Boleyn, having given her a fine suite of apartments next to his own at Greenwich, and was quite infatuated in his passion, only awaiting an authoritative pronouncement that should allow him to marry. Early in February, 1529, his prospects seemed to be changed by a false report of the death of Clement VII; but the Pope, after being really very ill, recovered slowly in the spring, and was no sooner again fit for business than he was pestered by English agents with demands to declare the brief in Spain a forgery. The attempt to discredit the brief, however, was at last abandoned; and the King and Wolsey determined to commence the trial and push it on as fast as possible, for fear of some arrest of the proceedings. Good reasons had already been given at Rome by the Imperial ambassador for revocation of the cause; but the Pope declined to interfere with the hearing before the Legates.

The Court was formally opened accordingly at Blackfriars on May 31, when citations were issued to the King and Queen to appear on June 18. On that day the Queen appeared in person before the Legates, and objected to their jurisdiction. This objection being considered, on the 21st the Legates pronounced themselves to be competent judges; whereupon the Queen intimated an appeal to the Pope and withdrew, after some touching words addressed to the King in Court. Being called again and refusing to return, she was pronounced contumacious, and the trial went on. But an incident at the fifth sitting, which was on the 28th, astonished everyone. John Fisher, Bishop of Rochester — a lover of books, who commonly avoided public life — said that the King at a former sitting had professed justice to be his only aim, and had invited everyone who could throw light upon the subject to relieve his scruples. He therefore felt bound in duty to show the conclusion which he had reached after two years' careful study; which was that the marriage was indissoluble by any authority, divine or human, and he presented a book which he had composed on the subject. He was followed by Standish, Bishop of St Asaph, and Dr Ligham, Dean of the Arches, who maintained the same view.

The Legates remonstrated, rather mildly, that Fisher was pronouncing in a cause which was not committed to him ; and the King composed, but probably did not deliver, a very angry speech in reply addressed to the judges. The Court went on, taking evidence chiefly about the circumstances of Prince Arthur's marriage, till July 23, when Campeggio prorogued it to October 1. Shortly afterwards arrived an intimation that the cause was " advoked " to Rome and all further proceedings must be prosecuted there. This the Imperialists had procured on the Queen's demand for justice, which the Pope could not resist, and Henry saw that it was a death-blow to his expectations.

The fall of Wolsey was now inevitable. From the first the business of the divorce had been a source of intense anxiety to him, knowing as he did that, if he failed to give the King satisfaction, his ruin would be easily achieved by the leading lords who had been so long excluded from the King's counsels. And now that the failure was complete he was visibly out of favour. But the King was too well aware of his value not to desire his advice about many things, even now ; and there was one matter in particular in which his guiding hand had scarcely completed his work. The King, indeed, had intended to send him to Cambray to assist in a European settlement if the trial could have been got over soon enough ; but Bishop Tunstall and Sir Thomas More were sent in his place. By the Treaty of Cambray, signed on August 5, the state of war between Francis and the Emperor was ended, the conditions of the Treaty of Madrid were at length modified, and Francis was permitted to redeem his sons without parting with Burgundy. It was undoubtedly the Emperor's fear of England that secured these favourable conditions for France, and France had in return to take upon herself all the Emperor's liabilities to Henry. The English also made their own separate treaties at Cambray both with the Emperor and with Francis.

But through the influence of Anne Boleyn Wolsey was presently excluded from the King's presence, and ultimately he found himself cut off from all communication with his sovereign. On October 9, the first day of Michaelmas term, he took his seat as Chancellor for the last time in Westminster Hall. That day an indictment was preferred against him in the King's Bench, and the 30th of the same month was appointed for his trial. But meanwhile he was made to surrender the Great Seal and to execute a curious deed, in which he confessed the *praemunire* of which he was afterwards found guilty, and desired the King to take all his land and property in part compensation for his offences. This he did, not because the *praemunire* was just, but only in the hope of avoiding a parliamentary impeachment ; which nevertheless was brought forward in the House of Lords, but was thrown out in the Commons by the exertions of his dependent, Thomas Cromwell.

For a new Parliament had been called, after an interval of six years, and the session had been opened by Sir Thomas More, who had just been appointed Lord Chancellor in Wolsey's place. The elections had been unduly influenced, and the Commons were so subservient that one of their Acts was expressly to release the King from repayment of the forced loan — for which, as may be imagined, they incurred general ill-will. They also sent up a host of bills to the Lords, attacking abuses connected with probates, mortuaries, and other matters of spiritual jurisdiction, and also against clerical pluralities, and non-residence. Bishop Fisher thought it right to protest in the House of Lords against the spirit and tendency of such legislation ; and because he had pointed to the example of Bohemia as a kingdom ruined by lack of faith, the Speaker and thirty of the Commons were deputed to complain to the King that Fisher seemed to regard them as no better than Turks and infidels. It may be suspected that they were prompted ; for Henry was certainly glad of the opportunity of calling on the Bishop to explain himself.

On the breaking up of the Legatine Court the King had been just about to give up further pursuit of a divorce as hopeless ; and in that belief he had sought to get the cause superseded at Rome that he might not be summoned out of his own realm. But in August, when he visited Waltham Abbey in a progress, he was told of a suggestion made by one Thomas Cranmer, a private tutor who had been there just before (having been driven from Cambridge by an epidemic), that he might still get warrant enough for treating his marriage as invalid by procuring a number of opinions to that effect from English and foreign universities. He at once caught at the idea, and relied on the friendship of Francis to procure what he wanted on the other side of the Channel.

In the beginning of the year 1530, when the Emperor had gone to Bologna to be crowned by the Pope, Anne Boleyn's father, who had recently been created Earl of Wiltshire, and Dr Stokesley, Bishop elect of London, were sent thither with a commission to treat for a universal peace and a general alliance against the Turk. That was the pretext ; and no doubt aid against the Turks would then have been particularly valuable to the Emperor, seeing that they had got fast hold of Hungary, and had quite recently besieged Vienna. But the main object was to explain to Charles with great show of cordiality, now that the two sovereigns were friends again, the manifold arguments against the validity of Henry's marriage with his aunt. And with this purpose in view, Stokesley on his way through France strove to quicken the process of getting opinions from French universities. The decisions even of the English universities were only obtained in March and April, under what pressure it is needless to say. The mere purpose of the proceedings raised the indignation of the women at Oxford, who pelted with stones Bishop Longland, the Chancellor, and his companion, when they came to obtain the seal of the University. No wonder, therefore, that when Wiltshire arrived at Bologna in March no French university had been induced to pronounce a judgment. His mission, in truth, was anything but a success, and it is hard to see that much could have been expected of it. For the Pope, just before his coming, had issued a Bull, dated March 7, committing the King's cause to Capisucchi, Auditor of the Rota ; which after his arrival was followed by another on the 21st, forbidding all ecclesiastical judges or lawyers from speaking or writing against the validity of the marriage. Worse still, Wiltshire's presence gave opportunity to serve him, as Henry's representative, with a summons for his master to appear in person or by deputy before the tribunal at Rome. The Pope, however, offered to suspend the cause till September, if Henry would take no further step till then ; and the King accepted the offer. ✔

Wolsey, meanwhile, had been living at Esher, in a house belonging to him as Bishop of Winchester, whither on his disgrace he was ordered to withdraw. But his enemies, fearing lest the King should again employ his services, were anxious that he should be sent to his other and more remote northern diocese ; and an arrangement was made in February, 1530, by which he received a general pardon, resigning to the King for a sum of ready money the bishopric of Winchester and the Abbey of St Alban's, while the possessions of his archbishopric of York were restored to him. He began his journey north early in Lent, paused at Peterborough over Easter, and spent the summer at Southwell, a seat of the Archbishops of York, where he was intensely mortified to learn that the King had determined to dissolve two Colleges, the one at Ipswich and the other at Oxford, of which he had brought about the establishment with great labour and cost. For this object, as early as 1524, he had procured Bulls to dissolve certain small monasteries and apply their revenues to his new foundations ; and the obloquy he had incurred from other causes was certainly increased by the dissolution of those Houses. Indeed in 1525 a riot took place at Bayham in Sussex, where a company in disguise restored, though only for a few days, the extruded Canons. The Ipswich College was suppressed by the King. At Oxford, however, the buildings had advanced too far to be stopped and the work was completed on a less magnificent design. After Wolsey's death the King called it " King Henry VIII's College." It is now known as Christ Church.

In the autumn Wolsey moved further north, and, reaching Cawood by the beginning of November, at length hoped to be installed in his own Cathedral of York on the 7th. But on the 4th he was visited by the Earl of Northumberland, who suddenly notified to him his arrest on a charge of treason. His Italian physician Agostini had been bribed by the Duke of Norfolk to betray secret communications which he had held with the French Ambassador de Vaulx, and the charge was added that he had urged the Pope to excommunicate the King and so cause an insurrection. Unconscious of this, he was conducted to Sheffield, where, at the Earl of Shrewsbury's house, he was alarmed to learn that Sir

William Kingston had been dispatched to bring him up to London. As Sir William was Constable of the Tower, Wolsey now perceived that his execution was intended; and sheer terror brought on an illness, of which he died on the way at Leicester.

So passed away the great Cardinal, the animating spirit of whose whole career is expressed in the sad words he uttered at the last, that if he had served God as diligently as he had served the King, He would not have given him over in his grey hairs. Conspicuous beyond all other victims of royal ingratitude, he had strained every nerve to make his sovereign great, wealthy, and powerful. His devotion to the King had undoubtedly interfered with his spiritual duties as a Churchman; it was not until his fall that he was able to give any care to his episcopal function. The new career, so soon terminated, showed another and a more amiable side in his character. That he might have been happy if unmolested, even when stripped of power, there is little reason to doubt. Yet his was a soul that loved grandeur and display, magnificent in building and in schemes for education; he was ambitious, no doubt, and it might be high-handed, as the agent of a despotic master, but with nothing mean or sordid in his character. And something of ambition might surely be condoned in one whose favour the greatest princes of Europe were eager to secure. For with a penetrating glance he saw through all their different aims and devices. The glamour of external greatness never imposed upon him; and, whatever bribes or tributes might be offered to himself, his splendid political abilities were devoted with single-minded aim to the service of his King and country. He raised England from the rank of a second-rate Power among the nations. His faults, indeed, are not to be denied. Impure as a priest and unscrupulous in many ways as a statesman, he was only a conspicuous example in these things of a prevailing moral corruption. But his great public services, fruitful in their consequences even under the perverse influences which succeeded him, would have produced yet nobler results for his country, if his policy had been left without interference.

Meanwhile, the King had fallen on a new device to force the Pope's hand. A meeting of notable persons was called on June 12, to draw up a joint address to his Holiness, urging him to decide the cause in Henry's favour, lest they should be driven to take the matter into their own hands. To obtain subscriptions to this the nobles were separately dealt with, and the document was sent down into the country to obtain the signatures and seals of peers and prelates, among others of Wolsey at Southwell. It was finally dispatched on July 13; and Clement, though he might well have felt indignant at this attempt to influence his judicial decision by threats, made on September 27 a remarkably temperate reply. He had, moreover, a few months before, sent to England a Nuncio named Nicholas del Burgo to smooth matters; and the prospect of justice to Catharine was not improved by this perpetual dallying.

Bishop Fisher, however, was most assiduous in writing books to support her cause — so much so that Archbishop Warham, awed by the King's authority, called him to his house one day, and earnestly, but in vain, besought him to retract.

Nevertheless inhibitions came from Rome which, it was believed, made the King at one time really think of putting away Anne Boleyn. This was at the beginning of the year 1531. But he recovered heart when repeated briefs seemed only to grow weaker; and, conscious of his power at home, he sought to attain his object by breaking down the independence of the clergy, from the whole body of whom he contrived to extort, not only a heavy fine for a *praemunire* which they were held to have incurred by submitting to the legatine jurisdiction of Wolsey, but also an acknowledgment of his being "Supreme Head" of the Church of England. This title was only conceded to him by the Convocation of Canterbury after a three days' debate, when it was carried at last by an artifice, and with the modifying words "so far as the law of Christ allows." Nor was it without protest that the northern clergy were brought to the same acknowledgment. This encroachment on their liberties made the clergy of the south regret their pecuniary grant; but they were altogether helpless, though in the end of August their assessment led to a riotous attack on the Bishop of London's palace at St Paul's.

Parliament had met on January 15, and was kept sitting into March without doing anything material. All the members were anxious to go home, and the Queen's friends easily got leave. On March 30 it was prorogued for Easter, when Sir Thomas More as Chancellor, though utterly sick of an office which he had unwillingly accepted even with the assurance that his own convictions would be respected, found himself obliged to declare to the Commons, in order that they might check ill reports in the country, the conscientious motives by which the King said he had been induced to seek a divorce, and the opinions obtained in his favour from the greatest universities in Christendom. What effect this had in allaying popular indignation at the King's proceedings is very doubtful. A strange occurrence in February in Bishop Fisher's household had produced a most unpleasant impression. A number of the servants fell ill, and two of them died. It was found that the cook had put poison in some pottage, of which happily the Bishop himself had not tasted; but it was generally believed his life had been aimed at by Anne Boleyn's friends. The King, however, was very angry; and, to avert suspicion, caused the Parliament to pass an *ex post facto* law, which was at once put in force, visiting the crime of poisoning with the hideous penalty of being boiled alive.

At Rome the cause hardly made any progress. Henry in fact, though he would not appear there, either personally or by proxy, employed agents to delay it, especially a lawyer named Sir Edward Carne, called his *excusator*, who, without showing any commission from him, argued that he should not be summoned out of his realm. In his protest to that effect Henry had the support of Francis I, who urged that the cause might at least be tried at Cambray, and procured a decision for the King from the University of Orleans that he could not be compelled to appear at Rome. And though the process actually began in June, it was soon suspended for the Roman holidays from July to October, when the *excusator* at length produced a commission, and the question about giving him a hearing next occupied the Court. In November this was refused until he should produce a power from the King to stand to the trial; but he managed afterwards to get the question further discussed, and, in point of fact, the whole of the following year was wasted before the principal cause was reached.

Meanwhile, Catharine suffered more and more from the delay of justice. On May 31 she had to endure a conference with about thirty of the leading peers, accompanied by Bishops Stokesley and Longland and other clergymen, who were sent by the King to remonstrate with her on the scandal she had caused by his being cited to Rome. In July she was ordered to remain at Windsor while the King went about hunting with Anne Boleyn; and, when the Queen sent a message after him regretting that he had not bid her farewell, he sent her word in reply that he was offended with her on account of the citation. After that they never met again. She was ordered to withdraw to the Moor in Hertfordshire, and afterwards to Easthampstead. But even then she was not free from deputations; for another came to her at the Moor in October, to urge her once more to allow her cause to be decided in England. But it was in vain they plied her with arguments, which she answered with equal gentleness and firmness. As she came to understand the King's mind, she was more resolved than ever to have her cause decided at Rome.

And Rome was at last really moved in her behalf. Slow as he was to take action, Clement was compelled, on January 25, 1532, to send the King a brief of reproof for his desertion of Catharine and cohabitation with Anne Boleyn. But Henry induced the Parliament, now assembled for a new session, to pass a bill, — which he told the Nuncio was passed against his will by the Commons out of their great hatred to the Pope — for abolishing the payment of First-fruits to Rome. This Act, however, it was left in the King's power to suspend till the Pope met his wishes; and how little the Commons acted spontaneously in such matters may be seen by what speedily followed. On March 18 the Speaker and a deputation of that body waited on the King to complain of a number of grievances to which the laity were subjected by "the Prelates and Ordinaries," and which they desired the King would remedy. But with this petition they at the same time begged for a dissolution of Parliament, considering the excessive cost they had sustained by long attendance.

The King replied that their second request was inconsistent with their first. They must wait for the answer of the Ordinaries to their complaints, and meanwhile he desired their assent to a very unpopular bill about wardships, which he had persuaded the Lords to pass. But he could not get the Commons to agree to it.

Parliament was prorogued for ten days at Easter. On Easter Day (March 31), William Peto, Provincial of the Grey Friars, preached before the King at Greenwich a sermon in which he pointed out how Kings were encouraged in evil by false counsellors. After the sermon, being called to a private interview, Peto further warned the King that he was endangering his Crown, as both small and great disapproved of his designs. The King dissembled his ill-will and licensed Peto to leave the kingdom on his duties; after which he caused Dr Richard Curwen, a chaplain of his own, to preach in the same place a sermon of an opposite tenor. In this Curwin not only contradicted what Peto had said in the pulpit, but added that he wished Peto were there to answer him; on which the Warden of the convent, Henry Elstowe, at once answered him in Peto's place. Peto was then recalled by the King, who asked him to deprive the Warden; but he refused, and both he and Elstowe were committed to prison.

When Parliament met again in April the Commons were solicited for aid in the fortification of the Scotch frontier. They objected to the expense; and two members said boldly that the Borders were secure enough, if the King would only take back his Queen and live in peace with the Emperor; for without foreign aid the Scots could do no harm. On the 30th the King sent for the Speaker and others of the Commons, and delivered to them the answer of the Ordinaries to their complaints, which he said he did not think would satisfy them, but he would leave them to consider it, and would himself be an indifferent judge between them. In such strange fashion did he declare his impartiality. On May 11 he sent for them again, and said that he had discovered that the clergy were but half his subjects, since the Bishops at their consecration took an oath at variance with the one they took to him. After some references to and fro the final result was the famous "Submission of the Clergy" agreed to on May 15, and presented to the King at Westminster on the following day. Hereby they agreed to enact no new ordinances without royal licence and to submit to a Committee of sixteen persons, one half laymen and one half clerics, the question as to what ordinances should be annulled as inconsistent with God's laws and those of the realm.

On that same day Sir Thomas More, who had done his best to prevent these innovations, surrendered his office of Chancellor, from which he had long sought in vain to be released. To fill his place in some respects, Thomas Audeley, the Speaker, was at first appointed Keeper of the Great Seal, but in the following January received the full title and office of Lord Chancellor.

Henry's way was now tolerably clear, and on June 23, 1532, he made a secret alliance with Francis I for mutual aid against the Emperor when it should be required. Francis for his part delighted in the belief that to gratify an insane passion Henry had put himself completely in his hands. Henry, however, was really using him to ward off excommunication; which, if pronounced, Francis informed the Pope he would resent as deeply as Henry himself. And, to give greater effect to the threat, Henry persuaded him to an interview, the only professed object of which — the concerting of measures against the Turk — was not only seen to be a pretence, but was meant to be seen through. It took place in October between Calais and Boulogne, with much less pomp than the Field of Cloth of Gold twelve years before. But the various meetings lasted over a week, and made an effective demonstration; and to counteract this the Emperor arranged a meeting with the Pope, which took place at Bologna in December. Anne Boleyn, of course, crossed with Henry to the meetings with Francis, who was found ready to dance with her. She had been created Marchioness of Pembroke on September 1, and Imperialists were relieved to find that Henry had not yet married her. Clement was compelled to warn the King by another brief on November 15 to put her away on pain of excommunication.

Towards the close of the year the Earl of Northumberland invaded the Scotch border, and a state of war continued between the two countries for some months, but led to no great results.

Another event favoured Henry's aims. Archbishop Warham, who had striven hard to maintain the old privileges of the clergy, died in August. Henry at once proposed to name as his successor Thomas Cranmer, who had been so useful in suggesting the appeal to the universities. He had lately sent him as ambassador to the Emperor with secret messages to the German Princes to gain their alliance against their sovereign. This intrigue was ineffectual, but he accompanied the Emperor to Vienna, and then to Mantua, where in November he received his recall with a view to his approaching elevation. In February, 1533, bulls for his promotion were demanded of the Pope, who was then still at Bologna in frequent conference with the Emperor, and were obtained free of payment of First-fruits by the suggestion that the King, if favourably dealt with, had it in his power to cancel the Act against First-fruits generally.

But before this, on January 25, Henry had secretly married Anne Boleyn, and, knowing her to be with child, was preparing to have her openly proclaimed as Queen. To guard against consequences, however, he first obtained from Convocation opinions against the Pope's dispensing power in cases similar to that of Catharine, and then from Parliament an Act making appeals to Rome high treason. On Easter Eve, April 12, Anne went to mass in great state and was publicly named Queen. No sentence had yet been given by any Court to release the King from his marriage with Catharine; but on Good Friday the new Archbishop wrote to him (of course by desire) a very humble request that he would allow him to determine that weighty cause which had remained so long undecided. The King willingly gave him a commission to try it; and the Archbishop cited him and Catharine to appear before him at Dunstable — a place carefully selected as being conveniently out of the way. There, on May 23, sentence was given of the nullity of the King's first marriage; and five days later at Lambeth a very secret enquiry was held before Thomas Cromwell and others as to the validity of the King's marriage with Anne Boleyn. Of course it was pronounced valid, though the very date of the event was uncertain, and all the details were kept a profound secret. Anne was crowned at Westminster on Whitsunday, June 1, with all due state, but with no appearance of popular enthusiasm. Then another deputation was sent to Catharine, now at Ampthill, to inform her that she was no longer Queen and must henceforth bear the name of Princess Dowager; but she refused to submit to such a degradation.

Sentence of excommunication was pronounced against Henry at Rome on July 11; but even now he was allowed until the end of September to set himself right, before the sentence should be declared openly, by taking back his wife and putting away Anne Boleyn. This troubled his ally Francis more than himself; for the Pope was coming to France for an interview at which he hoped to make Henry's peace. This interview, indeed, had been planned with Henry's own approval, the policy then being to make the Pope feel that he must look to France and England to save him from the necessity of holding a General Council at the Emperor's bidding. But Henry now completely changed his tone and endeavoured to dissuade Francis from meeting the Pope at all; — which, however, Francis was bent on doing, in order to arrange the marriage, which afterwards took place, of his son Henry, Duke of Orleans, with the Pope's niece, Catharine de' Medici. He met the Pope at Marseilles in October; but, while they were both there still in November, Dr Edmund Bonner, a skilful agent of the King, who had followed Clement from Rome, intimated to his Holiness an appeal on Henry's behalf to the next General Council against the sentence of excommunication. Next month the King's Council at home came to a resolution that the Pope should henceforth be designated merely "Bishop of Rome"; and during the following year written acknowledgments were extorted from Bishops, abbeys, priories, and parochial clergy all over the kingdom that the Roman pontiff had no more authority than any foreign Bishop.

The policy which the King had now been pursuing for four successive years had been inspired by Thomas Cromwell, who, as we have seen, had been in Wolsey's service. He was a man of humble origin, who, after a roving youth spent in Italy and elsewhere, had risen by the use of his wits, and since his master's fall had now been for three years a Privy

Councillor. In 1534 he was made the King's chief secretary, and a few months later Master of the Rolls. But even in August, 1533, he had directed Cranmer as Archbishop to examine one Elizabeth Barton, commonly called the Nun of Canterbury, or the Holy Maid of Kent, who had long professed to have visions and trances. Afterwards he examined her himself, and committed her and a number of her friends to prison. She had uttered fearful warnings to the King in the case of his marrying Anne Boleyn; and efforts were made to prove that she had been encouraged by Catharine's friends. It was even sought to implicate Catharine herself but no case could be made out against her. The charge was more plausible against Bishop Fisher, who had certainly communicated with her in previous years, but only in order to test her pretentions, which found wide credit, even with people of high standing. His name, and at first that of Sir Thomas More likewise, were included in a bill of attainder against the Nun's adherents; but Sir Thomas entirely cleared himself, and the charge against the Bishop amounted only to misprision. Ultimately the Nun and six others were attainted of treason and afterwards executed at Tyburn, while the Bishop and five more were found guilty of misprision of treason, and were sentenced to forfeiture of goods.

On March 23, 1534, the Pope pronounced Henry's marriage with Catharine valid, while Parliament in England was passing an Act of Succession in favour of Anne Boleyn's issue. Her daughter, Elizabeth, had been born in September, 1533. Orders were circulated throughout the kingdom to arrest preachers who maintained the Pope's authority, and to put the country in a state of defence in case the Emperor should attempt invasion. The King's subjects generally were required to swear to the Act of Succession; and those who refused were sent to the Tower, Sir Thomas More and Bishop Fisher among the first. Then, to prevent inconvenient preaching, the different Orders of Friars were placed under two Provincials appointed by the King. But the Grey Friars Observants declined the articles proposed to them by these Visitors as contrary to their obedience to the Pope; whereupon some were sent to the Tower, and soon afterwards the whole Order was suppressed.

It was fortunate for Henry that on May 11, this year, he was able to make a peace with his nephew, James V, which relieved him from the danger of a papal interdict being executed by means of an invasion from Scotland. Just about the same time William, Lord Dacres, who for nine years past had ruled the West Marches as his father had done before him, was committed to the Tower on a charge of treason, arising, apparently, out of border feuds. He was tried in July, and, strange to say, acquitted, for such a result of an indictment was then quite unheard of. And the joy of the people at the event was all the greater because it was known that Anne Boleyn had been using her influence against him as one who sympathised with Catharine.

But a more serious danger now appeared in Ireland. Gerald, Earl of Kildare, the Lord Deputy, who had used the King's artillery for his own castles, had been summoned to England in 1533, but delays ensued, and he only arrived in London in the spring of 1534, suffering from a wound that he had received in an encounter, and not likely to live long. He was not at first imprisoned, and efforts were made to lure his son, Lord Thomas Fitzgerald, over to England. But the young man (deceived, it is said, by a false report of his father's execution) rebelled, declaring that he upheld the Pope's cause and that the King's adherents were accursed. He murdered Archbishop Allen of Dublin, the Chancellor of Ireland (July 28), as he was endeavouring to sail for England, and became for a short time virtual ruler of the country, which he ordered all the English to quit on pain of death. Piers Butler, Earl of Ossory, however, made a stand for the King at Waterford, and Lord Thomas was compelled to raise the siege laid by him to Dublin, when Sir William Skeffington, appointed a second time as Lord Deputy, arrived from Wales in October; after which matters began to mend.

In England, to complete the work of the year, Parliament met in November, and passed, among other legislation, Acts for confirming the King's title as Supreme Head of the Church, for granting him the first-fruits and tenths before paid to the Pope, and for attainting More and Fisher of misprision and the Earl of Kildare of treason. But Parliament passed measures at dictation, and several of the chief lords of England were in secret communication with the imperial ambassador Chapuys to urge the Emperor to invade England.

Cromwell was now appointed the King's Vicar-General in spiritual things, and in the spring of 1535 the Act of Supremacy began to be put into execution. An oath to the succession of Anne Boleyn's issue had already been extorted in the previous year from the monks of the Charter House, which some of them seem not to have taken until after a significant visit from one of the London Sheriffs. But now they were required to swear to the supremacy in derogation of the Pope's authority. Prior Houghton, with two other Priors of the Order who had lately come up to London, approached Cromwell at the Rolls in the hope of obtaining some mitigation of the terms required; but unconditional acknowledgment of the King's supremacy was insisted on. All three refused, and repeated their refusal a few days later in the Tower. They were tried in April, together with Dr Reynolds of the Brigettine Monastery of Sion, who, having been also committed to the Tower, had joined in their refusal; and all received sentence together. With them also were condemned, for a private conversation about the King's tyranny and licentiousness, John Hale, vicar of Isleworth, and a young priest named Robert Feron; but the latter had his pardon after sentence, having turned King's evidence. All the others were hanged at Tyburn on May 4, with even more than the usual barbarities.

Next came the turn of Bishop Fisher and Sir Thomas More, who with three fellow-prisoners, Dr Wilson, Abell, and Fetherstone, priests lately most intimate in the Royal household, were warned that they must swear to the Statutes both of Succession and Supremacy. All declined to do so. Six weeks were given them to consider the matter; and visits were paid by Cromwell and other councillors to More and Fisher in the Tower to shake their constancy; but all in vain. Fisher denied that the King was Supreme Head of the Church of England; More said he would not meddle with such questions. Fisher was condemned on June 17, and was beheaded on Tower Hill on the 22nd. The King was all the more resolved on his death because the Pope had made him a Cardinal on May 20. On July 1 More was brought up for trial on a complex indictment, one article of which showed that he did not, like Fisher, expressly repudiate the King's ecclesiastical supremacy, but only kept silence when questioned about it. He made, as might be expected, an admirable defence, but in vain; and after his condemnation he declared frankly as to the statute that it was against his conscience, as he could never find, in all his studies, that a temporal lord ought to be head of the spiritualty. He was sentenced to undergo a traitor's death at Tyburn; but it was commuted by the King to simple decapitation on Tower Hill, where he suffered on July 6.

These executions filled the world with horror, both at home and abroad. The Emperor Charles V is said to have declared that he would rather have lost the best city in his dominions than such a councillor as Sir Thomas More. In Italy More was vehemently lamented, and men related with admiration the touching devotion of his daughter, Margaret Roper, who broke through the guards to embrace him on his way to the Tower. He was indeed a man to inspire affection far beyond his own family circle. Full of domestic feeling, yet no less full of incomparable wit and humour, dragged into the service of the Court against his will on account of his high legal abilities and intellectual gifts, he had refused to yield one inch to solicitations against the cause of right and conscience. A true saint without a touch of austerity, save that which he practised on himself in secret, he lived in the world as one who understood it perfectly, with a breadth of view and an innate cheerfulness of temper which no external terrors could depress. Of a mind altogether healthy, he was not beguiled by superstition or corrupted by gifts, but held his course straight on. Brought up in the household of Cardinal Morton, he had early devoted himself to learning, and became the special friend of Erasmus. His learning was entirely without pedantry, even as his humour was without gall. He loved men, he loved animals, he loved mechanism, and every influence that tended to humanise or advance society. He had served his King in diplomatic missions with an ability that was fully appreciated, and as Lord Chancellor with an integrity that was noted as altogether exceptional. But his very probity had made him at last an obstacle in the King's path, and he was sacrificed.

The three priests who had refused to acknowledge the Supremacy were retained in confinement. Two years later Dr Wilson received a pardon. The other two remained steadfast during five years' imprisonment, and were executed in 1540.

Pope Paul III, who had conferred the hat upon Fisher (he had succeeded Clement VII in the previous year), would have issued a Bull to deprive Henry of his kingdom; but, owing to the mutual jealousies of the Emperor and Francis I, there was no sovereign who dared to execute the sentence. Henry, moreover, had been scheming for years with the citizens of Lübeck to fill the throne of Denmark with one who would unite with him and the Northern Powers of Europe against both Pope and Emperor; and, though his plan was a failure, the Danes elected a Lutheran King (Christian III), ill-pleasing to Charles V. Further, the English King was seeking to conclude a league with the German Protestants, and his intrigues gave the Emperor some anxiety.

During the latter half of 1535 the Bishops in England were inhibited from visiting their dioceses pending a royal visitation of the whole kingdom, while Cromwell sent out special Visitors for the monasteries, who with remarkable celerity traversed the greater part of the country in a very few months and sent private reports of gross immoralities, alleged to have been discovered in a number of the Houses they visited. It is impossible, for many reasons, to attach much credit to these reports, or to think highly of the character of the Visitors. The object was seen when Parliament met again in February, 1536, and passed, as the principal measure of the session, an Act for the dissolution of such monasteries as had not revenues of £200 a year. It was passed, as tradition in the next generation reported, under very strong pressure, and certainly, as the preamble shows, on the King's own statement of the results of the visitation. These, it was said, proved that the smaller monasteries were given to vicious living, while the larger were better regulated; though in truth the Visitors had reported abominations quite as flagrant in the latter as in the former.

Meanwhile, in January, Catharine of Aragon had died at Kimbolton. On hearing of the event Henry could not help exclaiming, "God be praised! We are now free from fear of war." If Catharine had lived, the Bull of privation might even yet have been launched when the Emperor arrived at Rome in the spring; but the King calculated truly. The Court and Anne Boleyn wore mourning for Catharine. But Anne's own fate was near at hand; for Henry had long since grown tired of her, and could not make men respect her. He now said that he had been induced to marry her by witchcraft. In the course of the month she miscarried. On May Day there was a tournament at Greenwich, during which the King suddenly left her and went to Westminster. Next day she was apprehended and taken to the Tower. One Mark Smeton, Groom of the Chamber, had been arrested and examined beforehand, and afterwards her brother George, Lord Rochford, and three other courtiers were likewise placed in the Tower. Anne was charged with acts of adultery with them all. She protested her innocence, though she acknowledged some familiarities. On the 15th she and her brother were condemned, and the latter suffered two days later with the four other supposed paramours. On the 17th a secret enquiry was conducted by persons learned in the canon law, after which Cranmer pronounced her marriage with the King invalid. On the 19th she was beheaded on Tower Green.

For some time before her arrest the King had been secretly talking of matrimony with Jane, daughter of Sir John Seymour, of Wolfhall, Wiltshire. On the very day of Anne's execution Cranmer gave the King a dispensation for this new match, and on the next day the couple were secretly betrothed. On Ascension Day, however (May 25), the King wore white as a widower in mourning; and it was not till Whitsunday, June 4, that Jane was openly produced as Queen, having been married the week before.

Parliament had been dissolved not long before Anne Boleyn's arrest. It was the same Parliament which had been summoned at Wolsey's fall, and it had lasted for six years and a half. A new Parliament was called, and met on June 8, to pass, among other things, a new Act of Succession in favour of Jane Seymour's issue, disinheriting that of both the two former Queens. The Princess Mary, though her chief enemy was now dead, was not restored to favour until, to make life bearable, she had signed without reading an abject submission, acknowledging the King's laws by which she herself was a bastard. Shortly afterwards died the Duke of Richmond, the King's natural son, who was believed to have been destined by Henry to succeed him on the throne in case of failure of issue by Jane Seymour; for he had procured a clause in the Succession Act enabling him in that contingency to dispose of the Crown by will. Another Act passed was for the attainder of Lord Thomas Howard, brother of the Duke of Norfolk, who had presumed to contract marriage with the King's niece, Lady Margaret Douglas. He died in the Tower next year. At this time also the office of Lord Privy Seal was taken from Anne Boleyn's father, the Earl of Wiltshire, and given to Cromwell.

In July there was a meeting of Convocation, over which Dr Petre presided as deputy to Cromwell, the King's Vicar-General. Since Cranmer had been raised to the Primacy several other Bishops favourable to the new principle of Royal Supremacy had been appointed, including Latimer of Worcester; and, as the King was hoping to strengthen his position by an alliance with the German Protestants, it was important to set forth by authority a formulary of the faith as acknowledged by the Church of England. This was done in Ten Articles not greatly at variance with the beliefs hitherto received, though dissuading the use of the term Purgatory, and omitting all notice of four out of the Seven Sacraments. This omission of course attracted some observation. But as to their positive contents Cardinal Pole himself found little fault with these Articles, his main objection being to the authority by which they were set forth. They were printed as " Articles devised by the King's Highness to stablish Christian quietness and unity among us."

The legislation of past years had created much popular discontent, which was now increased by the dissolution of the monasteries. In the north rumours were spread that the King would appropriate all the Church plate; and when the Commissioners for levying a subsidy came to Caistor, in Lincolnshire, just after two small neighbouring monasteries had been suppressed, the people banded together to resist them. The Commissioners made a hasty retreat, but some of them were captured and compelled by the rebels to swear to be true to the King and to take their side. The insurgents likewise sent up two messengers to Windsor to lay their grievances before their sovereign. The answer returned by Henry was rough in the extreme, and he sent a force under the Duke of Suffolk to quell the rising, preparing himself to follow with another, which was to muster at Ampthill. The muster, however, was countermanded on news that the rebels were ready to submit; but Lincolnshire was scarcely quiet when a more formidable rising began in Yorkshire, called the Pilgrimage of Grace. A lawyer named Robert Aske caused a muster on Skipwith Moor, at which the men swore to be faithful to the King and preserve the Church from spoil; for here, as in Lincolnshire, men desired to combine loyalty with religion, which they believed to be in danger from the rule of Cromwell and such Bishops as Cranmer and Latimer. Aske and his friends got possession of York. They took an oath of adhesion from the Mayor and commons at Doncaster. They replaced the expelled monks in their monasteries. Pomfret Castle was delivered up to them by Lord Darcy as too weak to hold out, though the Archbishop of York had taken refuge with him there; and a herald named Lancaster, sent thither by the Earl of Shrewsbury, was forbidden by Aske to read the King's proclamation, though he fell on his knees and begged leave to execute his commission.

The Duke of Norfolk, sent by the King to put down the rising, joined the Earl of Shrewsbury and others in the Midlands, and sent an address to the rebels, offering them the choice of battle or submission. But on reaching Doncaster he found that the movement had assumed such dimensions that a conflict would have been disastrous; and accordingly he made an agreement there with the rebels (October 27) and arranged for a general truce in the north, while Sir Ralph Ellerker and Robert Bowes were sent up to the King to ask for an answer to

the demands of the insurgents.   Henry wrote a temporising reply, but
detained the messengers for some time on the excuse of various sinister
rumours.   Conferences were arranged in December at Pomfret and
Doncaster, and a general pardon was proclaimed at the latter place.
Hereupon the King, putting a smooth face on matters, wrote to Aske to
come up and confer with him frankly ; and, though not without misgivings
in spite of his safe conduct, Aske came and seems to have been won over
by royal affability.   Early in January (1537) he returned to Yorkshire
and did his best to allay disquiet, declaring that the King was every way
gracious and had approved the general pardon, — that he was sending
Norfolk once more into the north, and that grievances would be
discussed at a free Parliament at York, where also the Queen would
be crowned.

But the pardon had been already ill received at Kendal, in Westmorland, where the people said they had done no wrong ; and grave
suspicions were aroused in Yorkshire that the King was fortifying Hull
and Scarborough.   One John Hallom was taken in an attempt to
surprise Hull, and Sir Francis Bigod made an equally futile effort to
march on Scarborough.   Bigod fled and was afterwards captured near
Carlisle, where he had joined himself to a new rising provoked by the
King's use of border thieves to keep the country down.   The Duke
of Norfolk, when he came back, went first to Carlisle, where he proceeded
by martial law against seventy-four of the insurgents and terrified the
country with savage executions.   He then went on to Durham and
York, where he endeavoured to learn who were chiefly responsible for
the demands made and conceded at Doncaster.   He got Aske into his
hands and sent him up to the King ; while the Earls of Sussex and
Derby reduced Lancashire to submission by hanging the Abbots of
Whalley and Sawley and one or two monks, and securing the surrender
of the Abbey of Furness.

The King's principal danger was past ; but meanwhile his anxieties
abroad had increased.   One thing was in his favour, that during the whole
of 1536 the Emperor and Francis I were at war, and neither of them wished
to interfere with him.   But the Pope was trying to make peace between
them ; and having created Reginald Pole a Cardinal in December,
he gave him on February 7 a commission as Legate to bring about
Henry's return to his obedience to Rome.   Pole was a grandson of the
Duke of Clarence, brother of Edward IV ; and his mother, the Countess
of Salisbury, was a sister of that Earl of Warwick who was put to death
by Henry VII.   At the beginning of his reign Henry VIII wished to
atone for his father's wrong, and Reginald Pole, showing a great love of
letters, was educated at the King's expense at Oxford and Padua.   For
this Pole was certainly most grateful ; but he did not approve Henry's
later policy and obtained leave to go abroad again. Pressed by the King for
a statement of his views as to the Royal Supremacy, he had written a

treatise intended for the King's own eye, severely censuring his policy and the cruelty with which he had enforced it. The King was exasperated at this, and still more at Pole's being made a Cardinal. But it was now his duty to go to England, or as near it as he could, and publish the papal censures against Henry; for which an opportunity was offered by the presence of James V at Paris, where, on January 1, 1537, he married the French King's daughter Madeleine. There were many indications, indeed, that the English would welcome a Scotch invasion if Henry did not mend his ways. But Francis did not dare to receive at his Court a papal Legate denounced by Henry as a traitor, whose surrender he claimed by treaty; and Maria of Hungary, the Regent of the Netherlands, also warned Pole not to come near her, but to seek refuge with the Cardinal of Liège. Pole's mission was consequently a complete failure.

And now Henry, having reduced the whole of the north country to subjection, left unfulfilled his promise of a free Parliament at York. On Norfolk's return he instituted a Council to govern the north—at first under Bishop Tunstall of Durham, afterwards under Holgate, Bishop of Llandaff. Meanwhile a Council of divines met in London to supply some omissions in the King's book of Articles issued in the previous year; and the result was the publication of a treatise entitled *The Institution of a Christian Man*, which the King allowed to go forth as a manual of doctrine agreed upon by the Bishops, without giving it the express sanction of a work which had been examined by himself. It was accordingly called "the Bishops' Book." Five years later, a considerably revised edition of it, which had really been examined by the King, was issued under the title of *A Necessary Doctrine for any Christian Man*, and was commonly called "the King's Book." In both these treatises the old number of seven Sacraments was acknowledged, and the doctrine concerning each of them was defined.

On October 12 the Queen gave birth to a son (the future Edward VI) at Hampton Court. She died twelve days after. Three months previously James V also had lost his newly-wedded Queen Madeleine.

In the following year (1538) the suppression of the monasteries was carried further. Several of the Abbots and priors were induced to make formal surrenders, which were often, no doubt, voluntary in one sense, since pensions were more acceptable than visitations. The King's agents were likewise zealous in putting down images, pilgrimages, and superstitions. A wonder-working crucifix at Boxley in Kent was destroyed; and a solemn enquiry was held into the nature of a venerated relic, the "Blood of Hailes," reputed to be the blood of our Lord.

Meanwhile the dissolution of the monasteries was quickened by information for treason against the heads of Houses who rejected the Royal Supremacy. The Prior of Lenton in Nottinghamshire, and the Abbot of Woburn were both executed. All friars were compelled to put aside their habits, and their Houses were confiscated. These proceedings were not relaxed in view of danger from abroad, when the King heard of the ten years' truce made in June between the Emperor and Francis. In September the magnificent shrine of St Thomas at Canterbury was robbed of all its treasures, and the relics which had been the object of so many pilgrimages were burned. Henry's wrath was stimulated against the Saint who had brought a King of England low. The news of this outrage excited peculiar horror at Rome; but all the Pope could do was to reissue (December 17) the Bull of Excommunication already published in 1535, with additions setting forth the King's new enormities, and to attempt to procure its proclamation at least at Dieppe and Boulogne, or in Scotland or Ireland.

But Henry anticipated the danger which threatened him. At the end of August Cardinal Pole's brother Sir Geoffrey was arrested; and, questions having been put to him concerning his communications over sea, the fear of torture wrung from him information which was thought to implicate his other brother Lord Montague and the Marquis of Exeter. These two noblemen were accordingly lodged in the Tower on November 4. Exeter would be next in succession if the King died without lawful issue, and Montague was the lineal heir of Clarence. The Marchioness of Exeter and the Countess of Salisbury, Montague's mother, were also closely examined. The two noblemen were tried for treason and beheaded on December 9, others who were found guilty along with them being hanged and quartered at Tyburn. Sir Geoffrey received a pardon on January 4, in consideration of his unwilling disclosures. On the other hand, Sir Nicholas Carew, who was arrested on December 31, was found guilty of treason in February, 1539, mainly for conversations with the Marquis of Exeter, and was beheaded on Tower Hill on March 3.

The Pope, however, was now encouraged by the better understanding between the Emperor and Francis to send Cardinal Pole on a new mission to those two sovereigns to induce them to forbid commercial intercourse with England; and David Beton was at the same time made a Cardinal with a view to his publishing in Scotland the Bull of Excommunication against Henry. Pole travelled by land to Spain, and on February 15 was received by the Emperor at Toledo in spite of the remonstrances of the English ambassador, Sir Thomas Wyatt. Yet his arrival did not seem agreeable to the Emperor, who declined to do as the Pope desired; and Pole returned to Carpentras, where he stayed with his friend Sadoleto till he received an answer to a message that he sent to Francis. But the French King was only willing to prohibit intercourse with England on condition that the Emperor would do the same; and Pole's second legation bore no more practical fruit than the first had done.

Henry was nevertheless seriously alarmed. Orders were given for the construction and repair of fortifications on the coasts, and general musters were held. The people, believing in the national danger, were zealous for the defence of the country. Parliament was called together in April, and occupied itself mainly in passing what was called the Act of the Six Articles for enforcing religious unity. This was an answer to the taunts that the English were heretics, and that the Pope's excommunication was well deserved. By this severe enactment denial of transubstantiation involved death by fire and confiscation of goods, no abjuration being allowed in bar of execution; and it was further declared felony to maintain, either that Communion in both kinds was necessary, or that priests or any man or woman who had vowed chastity or widowhood might marry, or that private masses were not laudable, or that auricular confession was not expedient. But for all these offences except the denial of transubstantiation, a first conviction was visited merely with imprisonment and confiscation; a second was punished capitally. There was also passed a great Act of Attainder against not only Exeter and Montague, but the Countess of Salisbury and a large number of other persons, some of whom were alive — for the most part refugees abroad — and some had been condemned and executed in recent years for treason. But the danger seemed even to increase in the latter part of the year, when the Emperor, on the invitation of Francis, passed through France on his way to the Low Countries, and was hospitably entertained in Paris.

In this crisis Henry sought security by arranging a new marriage for himself with Anne, sister of William, Duke of Cleves, who by his pretensions to Gelders was a thorn in the side of the Emperor, and had, besides, family and other ties with the Protestant Princes of Germany. With these, moreover, Henry had for some time been cultivating a good understanding and had given them great hopes in the previous years of a religious union against both Pope and Emperor. And though the Germans were sadly disappointed by the passing of the Act of the Six Articles, against which they strongly remonstrated, the political support of England was too valuable to be hastily rejected.

In November proceedings for treason were taken against the two great Abbots of Reading and Colchester; and against the Abbot of Glastonbury for felony; all three were executed. These trials were certainly irregular, and the treasons seem to have consisted merely of private conversations disapproving of Royal Supremacy and of the King's proceedings. But the unwillingness of these Abbots to surrender was perhaps their chief crime, and a rush of surrenders followed, so that very soon not a single monastery was left.

In the last days of December Anne of Cleves crossed from Calais to Deal, from which she went that day to Dover and on by stages through Canterbury to Rochester, where she remained all New Year's Day, 1540. Here she received a surprise visit from the King, who came incognito and made himself known to her; as he afterwards stated, he was disappointed as to her beauty, though he had secured beforehand her portrait painted by Holbein.   He returned to Greenwich and received his bride publicly in Greenwich Park on January 3.   The wedding took place on the 6th.

Just six months later this marriage was declared null, but for the present no one doubted its validity.   Believing that it would bring favour to the new German theology, Dr Barnes and two other preachers of what was called the New Learning, were indiscreetly bold at Paul's Cross; but what school of opinion would prevail was for some time uncertain.   Parliament met on April 12, and under the management of Cromwell, who on the 17th was created Earl of Essex, did its best still further to enrich the Crown.   The great Military Order of St John of Jerusalem was suppressed and its endowments were confiscated; a heavy subsidy was also voted, payable by instalments in four years. But, these things being secured, a great change took place.   On June 10 Cromwell was arrested at the Council table and committed to the Tower, where he was questioned about the circumstances of the King's marriage, and forced to make written statements to serve as evidence for its dissolution.   But nothing was yet known on the subject when the two Houses of Parliament, acting on a hint, prayed that the validity of his marriage might be inquired into by Convocation.   This was done, and after various depositions had been read to show that the King had never given his " inward consent " to his own public act, a sentence of nullity was pronounced.

This removed at once any fear of a misunderstanding with the Emperor, while it disappointed Francis and the Duke of Cleves. Anne herself, however, consented to the separation and was provided for in England, admitting that she remained a maid.   A month later it was announced that the King had married Catharine Howard, niece of the Duke of Norfolk, who was prayed for as Queen on August 15. Meanwhile, July 9, a Bill of Attainder was passed against Cromwell in Parliament on account of various acts, some of which were regarded as treasonable and some heretical, among the latter being his support of Dr Barnes.   He was beheaded on Tower Hill on July 28.   Two days later Dr Barnes, and with him Jerome and Garrard, the two other clergymen who had preached at Paul's Cross in the spring, were burned as heretics at Smithfield; while three of the Old Learning who had been attainted in Parliament were hanged at the same place as traitors.

It would be a mistake to say that Cromwell entirely directed the policy of England during the years of his ascendancy; for, as he told Cardinal Pole, he himself considered it the very height of statesmanship to endeavour to discern what was in the King's own mind and set himself zealously to follow it out.   And this, indeed, is the explanation of his whole policy. He laboured to satisfy the King; yet at times he mistook the King's intention, and had the mortification occasionally to see the King himself deliberately upset all that he had been endeavouring to establish, or even to incur the King's heavy displeasure. He maintained his position by pure obsequiousness, and there was no kind of cruelty or tyranny of which he declined to be the agent. Seldom have vast and multifarious interests been so completely under the control of a statesman so unscrupulous. He was continually open to bribes and was guilty of many acts of simony. No doubt there was something engaging in his personality to men who like himself could take the world as it came. His early wanderings had given him a knowledge of men which, combined with a first-rate capacity for business, had paved his way to fortune. They had also given him cultivated tastes and an acquaintance with Italian literature which few Englishmen possessed in his day. It was from a study of the great work of Machiavelli, at a time when it was still in manuscript, that he derived those political principles which guided him through his whole career.

For more than a year the King was highly satisfied with his fifth wife. In other matters he was not yet at ease. He had now no such convenient tool as Cromwell, and, distrusting most of his remaining ministers, stood in fear of a new insurrection. In April, 1541, a conspiracy was detected in Yorkshire to kill Holgate, Bishop of Llandaff, whom he had appointed President of the North, and take possession of Pomfret Castle. Though called a rebellion by chroniclers, the design was suppressed before it came to a head, and the conspirators were executed, some in London and some at York. It was clear that the north of England was in a dangerous state, and Henry thought it advisable to go thither in person with a force of 4000 or 5000 horse. First, however, he determined to clear the Tower of inconvenient prisoners. The aged Countess of Salisbury, who had been attainted in Parliament without a trial two years before, was beheaded in the Tower on May 28. Lord Leonard Grey was tried on June 25, and executed on the 28th for conduct considered treasonable when he was Lieutenant of Ireland.

The King left London for the north on June 30; but his progress was impeded by storms and floods, so that he only reached Lincoln on August 9. On entering Yorkshire he was met by the country gentlemen; and those of them who had taken part in the rebellion of 1536–7, including Edward Lee, Archbishop of York, made their submission to him kneeling, with large gifts of money and thanks for his pardon. The like submission and gifts had been made to him in Lincolnshire. He delayed his arrival at York till the middle of September, expecting (as he afterwards gave out) a visit there from James V. But as the Scottish King made no sign of coming, he left on the 27th on his return southward. By the beginning of November he was again at Hampton Court, when secret information was revealed to him through Cranmer. The Queen, it was found, had before her marriage to him been too intimate with more than one person ; and it was alleged that even during the royal progress in Lincolnshire she had secret meetings with a paramour. The supposed accomplices of her guilt were executed ; and, Parliament having met in January, 1542, an Act of Attainder was passed against the Queen, who on February 13 was beheaded within the Tower. She steadfastly denied any misconduct since her marriage ; and her fate has been thought to have been the result of political intrigue.

For about a year and a half the King remained a widower. Meanwhile it should be noted that, having obtained from Parliament in 1539 powers for the creation of new bishoprics, during the next three years he applied a portion of the confiscated property of the monasteries to the endowment of six new sees ; one of which, Westminster, was dissolved in the following reign, but the other five, after some vicissitudes, are in existence at the present day. Here also may be mentioned the publication of an Authorised English Bible, which was first issued and ordered to be read in churches as early as 1536.

In March, 1542, Henry began pressing his richer subjects for a loan; which, though little hope was entertained of repayment, was generally granted, in the expectation that the money would be used in a war against France. But, though Francis and the Emperor were on the verge of war, and the former really invaded the latter's dominions in July, England remained neutral for nearly a whole year after. Henry's design was first to get Scotland completely into his power.

A brief account seems desirable at this point of the course of events in Scotland. At the time of Albany's final withdrawal from the kingdom in the early summer of 1524, James V was only twelve years old, and should have remained still for some time under tutelage. But the circumstances were peculiar. Albany had not relinquished his claims upon the government, but had left behind him a garrison at Dunbar, and his cause was still upheld by James Beton, Archbishop of St Andrews, and Gawin Dunbar, Bishop of Aberdeen. His party, however, had really collapsed, and in July Queen Margaret caused her son to be declared of age by a Council at Holyrood, at which most of the Scotch lords swore fealty. There seemed then to be a very general feeling for an agreement with England, especially as the lords were encouraged to believe that their King would be allowed to marry the Princess Mary, notwithstanding her engagement to the Emperor ; from which, as Wolsey secretly informed Margaret, Henry intended to induce Charles to release her.

Unfortunately, the plans of the King and Wolsey included the reconciliation of Margaret to her husband Angus, who, after being for two years a refugee in France, came to England just as Albany returned, and was bent on going back to his own country. Margaret would not hear of being reconciled to him — all the less as she had now bestowed her affections on young Henry Stewart, second son of Lord Evandale, whom she had made Lord Treasurer; and both she and Arran, the great rival of Angus, declared that if the latter were allowed to cross the border, negotiation with England was at an end. Angus, however, made his way to Scotland, and, together with the Earl of Lennox and some other gentlemen, scaled the town walls of Edinburgh at four o'clock on a November morning; after which they opened the gates to their companies, and, when it was day, proclaimed at the Cross that they came as loyal subjects objecting to evil councillors about the King. But, as the Castle opened fire upon him, Angus found it prudent in the evening to quit the town and retire to Dalkeith; and that same night Margaret took her son with her from Holyrood into the Castle for security. She then dispatched in his name an embassy to England; which, being received at Greenwich just before Christmas, proposed a peace, with the marriage of James to Mary, and returned with an encouraging reply. But Angus had been meanwhile making friends with Archbishop Beton and others who were displeased with the Queen's exclusiveness; and, when the lords came to Edinburgh for a Parliament in February, 1525, they compelled her to bring her son out of the Castle to the Tolbooth, where a Council was appointed to carry on the government; and the summonses of treason against Angus and his friends were declared untrue.

Margaret next sent a secret message to Albany asking for French support; but the time was unlucky, for the date of her messenger's instructions was just two days before the battle of Pavia. Indeed from this time the French were generally very cautious about interfering in Scotch affairs without the consent of Henry, who was always a possible ally against the Emperor, or might be a very dangerous enemy. And Henry not only favoured Angus, but remonstrated strongly with his sister on her efforts to procure a divorce from him. Angus thus had full control of affairs for three years, during which the young King was jealously guarded, and all important offices were filled by his relatives. It was a time when none could prevail against a Douglas. But Margaret obtained from Rome a divorce from Angus and married Henry Stewart, who was afterwards created Lord Methven; and her son, after repeated efforts had been made for his liberation, escaped to Stirling Castle in June, 1528. In a few months Angus and his brother Sir George Douglas were driven to take refuge in England, where, to James' great grief, they were well received by Henry.

James had no desire to quarrel with his uncle, but the intrigues of Angus, together with border raids, brought about the hostilities which we have noticed in 1532, when the Earl of Northumberland invaded the East Marches as far as the neighbourhood of Dunbar. By the mediation of Francis peace negotiations were opened next year at Newcastle, and in

May, 1534, peace was concluded in London. Henry then sent to his nephew the Order of the Garter and afterwards endeavoured, but without success, to draw him into his own policy in religion against the Pope. Henry might well desire this ; for his own conduct had raised the political importance of Scotland among the nations. The Emperor courted James' friendship, and the Pope sent him a consecrated sword and hat, meaning to take away Henry's title of Defender of the Faith and bestow it upon the Scottish King. Scotland, moreover, was an asylum for persons who disliked Henry's measures against the Church ; and there was a serious possibility of an invasion from Scotland to drive Henry from the throne if he would not make his peace with Rome.

In 1536 James went to France under engagement to marry Mary of Bourbon, daughter of the Duke of Vendôme ; but the lady did not please him, and he actually married Madeleine, eldest daughter of Francis I, at Paris in January, 1537. He took her with him to Scotland ; but she died in the following July. Next year he married Mary, eldest daughter of the Duke of Guise and widow of the Duke of Longueville. Thus he was still strongly bound to France ; but France remained on good terms with England, and James had no desire to disturb the existing tranquillity. In 1541 died two infant Princes to whom Mary had given birth, and also James' mother Margaret, the Queen Dowager. Another child was expected in 1542, the year at which we have now arrived, when Henry, as we have said, was scheming to get Scotland completely under his power.

In the spring Sir Thomas Wharton, Deputy Warden of the West Marches, submitted to the King and his Council a proposal to kidnap James while he was somewhere near Dumfries, and to bring him to Henry. The project, however, was disapproved as dangerous and sure to be attended with scandal if it failed. In July the outbreak of war between Francis and the Emperor cut off Scotland from any hope of aid from France against English aggression ; and, while James was anxious for a conference between commissioners of both realms to put down border raids, Sir Robert Bowes was sent down to the border and arranged with Angus an invasion of Teviotdale. It took place on August 24, when the English burned several places ; but on their return they were caught in an ambuscade at Hadden Rig, Sir Robert Bowes and most of the leaders being taken prisoners. Angus, however, escaped.

That very day, in total ignorance of this reverse in the north, the Privy Council were making preparations for a more considerable invasion under Norfolk. The news of Bowes' defeat made Englishmen all the more eager to avenge it. But James had done nothing to provoke war. His ambassador was still in the English Court, desiring a passport for a larger embassy to treat of peace ; and, though he hardly met with due civility, a meeting was at length arranged, which took place at York in September between commissioners on both sides. But musters were made at the same time all over England ; and, as Henry would accept no terms, without free delivery of the prisoners taken by the Scots and renunciation of their alliance with France, the result was war. After it was begun Henry published a manifesto in his own justification, in which James was reproached with having shown ingratitude for the protection afforded to him in his early years, by declining to meet Henry at York. The English King also revived the old claim of superiority over Scotland.

The Duke of Norfolk crossed the border in October, and burned Kelso and laid waste the neighbouring country, but was obliged to return to Berwick in eight days for lack of victuals. An army suddenly raised by James was only able to skirmish with the invaders and harass their retreat. James would have pursued them further to revenge the injury; but the nobles objected, and he returned to Edinburgh. He was warned not to risk his life, being childless, in dangerous expeditions. But in November he passed secretly to the West Borders as far as Lochmaben, and directed Lord Maxwell, the Warden there, with the Earls of Cassillis and Glencairn and other lords, to invade England near the Solway. They entered the Debateable Land by night, in numbers reckoned at about 17,000, and burned some places on the Esk before daybreak on November 24. But Wharton at Carlisle, having got notice of the project, sallied out first with a small company to reconnoitre; and when others, following, brought up his numbers to about 2000, he crossed the Leven in view of the enemy. The Scots, believing that the Duke of Norfolk had come upon them, began to withdraw, discharging ordnance to cover their retreat, which they could only effect by fording the Esk with a moss on their left hand. But the retreat soon became a rout. Many were drowned in the Esk; only twenty were slain, and about 1200 prisoners were taken, including two Earls and five Barons. Deeply mortified with this disgraceful defeat, James withdrew to Edinburgh and then to Falkland, where he remained, ill and dejected, while news was brought him that his Queen at Linlithgow had borne him a daughter on December 8. He had no comfort in the news, and died on the 14th.

The child was Mary Stewart, who thus became Queen when only a week old. On hearing of her father's death, Henry liberated the Solway Moss prisoners from the Tower, and called his pensioners, the Earl of Angus and his brother, to a conference with them, proposing a treaty between the two kingdoms, with provisions for the future marriage of Prince Edward with the new-born babe, who was to be brought up in England till she reached marriageable age. Having given pledges to promote this design, the Scotch lords were allowed to return to their country, for which they set out on New Year's Day, 1543, honoured with great gifts upon their departure. Meanwhile Cardinal Beton had claimed the government of Scotland under an alleged will of the deceased King; but, this being treated as a forgery, the claims of the Earl of Arran, as next in the succession, were admitted by the nobles, and Beton was thrown into prison. Hereupon the Cardinal laid the kingdom

under interdict. Nevertheless Arran called a Parliament, which met at
Edinburgh on March 12, and in the main favoured Henry's policy; for
the marriage in itself was generally approved, the Douglases were restored
to their estates, and, the influence of Beton being excluded, an Act was
passed to permit the use of English Bibles. But the English King's
demand for the control of the young Queen during her childhood was
absolutely refused, as likewise was another for the surrender of fortresses
in Scotland ; and a little later, Sir George Douglas being sent up with
the Earl of Glencairn for an adjustment, Henry agreed that the royal
child should remain in Scotland till she was ten years old, sufficient
hostages meanwhile remaining for her at the English Court. To this,
in effect, the Scotch lords were brought, though with difficulty, to consent in the beginning of June ; and by the efforts of Glencairn and Sir
George Douglas two treaties were concluded at Greenwich on July 1, for
peace and for the marriage.

This arrangement offered a fair show of an international settlement ;
but there were secret articles, apart from the treaty, which Henry was
getting his friends in Scotland to sign, and by which he hoped to keep
the government of the country entirely in his power. Meanwhile,
however, Cardinal Beton had been released from prison on April 10 ;
Matthew, Earl of Lennox, who had just come from France (son of that
Earl who had entered Edinburgh with Angus in 1524), sought to supplant Arran both as Governor and in the succession to the Crown ; and
Argyle and Bothwell joined the party to protect the rights of the Queen
Dowager and the independence of the country.

Meanwhile Henry, having obtained another heavy subsidy from
Parliament, had concluded, on February 11, a secret treaty with the
Emperor against France, which was still unavowed when confirmed, first
by the Emperor in Spain, March 31, and then by Henry at Hampton
Court on Trinity Sunday, May 20. But joint demands were formulated
to be made of Francis by heralds of the Emperor and Henry at once.
Francis, however, refused passports to the heralds to enter his country
and the demands were intimated in London to the French ambassador.
Then on July 7 Sir John Wallop was appointed commander of a
detachment which joined the Emperor at the siege of Landrecies ;
where, however, the joint efforts of the allies, though prolonged for
months, proved a total failure.

Just after Wallop's departure the King, on July 12, married his
sixth and last wife, Catharine Parr. England won little glory from
the campaign abroad, though, strengthened by Henry's alliance, the
Emperor was able in September to bring the Duke of Cleves into
subjection.

Open war with France rendered Henry's designs on Scotland more
difficult. To secure the aid of Arran he had made him the most
splendid offers — that he should have the Princess Elizabeth as a bride

for his son, and that he should himself be King of Scotland beyond the Forth. But Arran could not easily withstand the growing feeling of suspicion against England ; and, though he ratified the treaty with Henry at Holyrood on August 25, in presence of a number of the nobility, he had even before that date resigned the charge of the infant Queen and her mother to the Cardinal and his friends. He then sought a meeting and reconciliaton with the Cardinal at Falkirk, where he abjured his Protestant heresies. Immediately afterwards, on September 9, they crowned the child at Stirling as Queen. Henry's anger was intense. But the feeling of the Scots against England was still more aggravated by the discovery that some Scotch merchant-ships, whose safety ought to have been secured by the treaty, had been arrested at an English port on the plea that they were carrying victuals to France. Henry, moreover, let the two months expire within which he should have ratified the treaty ; so that the Scots justly felt they had been deluded. Early in October a French fleet arrived at Dumbarton with money to oppose the designs of England. With it also came a French ambassador, La Brossé, and a papal Legate, Cardinal Grimani. But the Earl of Lennox at once intercepted the money, and, to maintain his opposition to Arran, left the party of France and joined that of Henry.

In September, while professing peace with Scotland, Henry had meditated a further outrage by an invasion under the Duke of Suffolk ; but this was wisely forborne. The Scottish people were already deeply incensed ; and the English ambassador, Sir Ralph Sadler, had to leave Edinburgh for his own safety, and take refuge in Angus' Castle of Tantallon. In December the Scotch Parliament met, declared the treaties with England no longer binding, and renewed the old league with France. Henry immediately sent a herald to Scotland with a threatening and reproachful message to be read to the Estates. It was received by the Governor after the Parliament had been dissolved. It apparently helped to bring about a formal agreement which Angus and Lennox made with him on January 13, 1544, and in which the Earls of Cassillis and Glencairn likewise took part, all promising to unite against the old enemy England. But the same lords presently asked England's aid to support them in their own country; and a treaty was signed at Carlisle on May 17, by Glencairn and by the Bishop of Caithness in behalf of Lennox, binding them to procure Henry's appointment as Protector of Scotland, to put the chief fortresses of the country into his hands, and, if possible, to get possession of the young Queen's person, and convey her to England. Lennox was then to have the regency of Scotland and to marry Henry's niece, Margaret Douglas. This marriage actually took place in the following summer ; and Darnley was born of it next year.

But already at the beginning of the same month of May a fleet of 200 sail under John Dudley, Viscount Lisle, had appeared in the

Firth of Forth and landed an army under the Earl of Hertford. The Earl first captured Leith, then burned Edinburgh and Leith also, and re-embarked in less than a fortnight, leaving a detachment to return to Berwick by land, which likewise wasted and burned everything on its way. Having thus dealt an effective blow at Scotland, which was followed up in the summer and autumn by continual ravages of the border, with destruction of towns and villages on a scale quite unprecedented, Henry crossed, on July 14, to the siege of Boulogne, which was formed before his arrival. It had been agreed, after some disputes, that this time the Emperor and the King should operate against the common enemy separately and join their forces at Paris. The siege of Boulogne, which was very protracted, was not quite in accordance with this plan. The Emperor advanced into the heart of France, and captured St Dizier after a six weeks' siege; but, in default of active support from his ally, on September 18 he made a separate peace with Francis at Crépy, and England was left to carry on the war alone. Boulogne had capitulated on September 14. Another siege — that of Montreuil — was abandoned, in which Count van Buren had been engaged with the Duke of Norfolk. The King crossed again to Dover on the 30th. In October, after the failure of a French attempt to recover Boulogne by surprise, conferences took place at Calais through the mediation of the Emperor; but peace could not be established, as the French insisted on the restoration of Boulogne, and the English on a promise to render no further assistance to the Scots.

The league between Henry and the Emperor had been hollow from the first; nor had it then been easily adjusted, the objects of the allies being entirely different. Henry had foreseen, long before he entered on it, that his Scottish policy would involve a war with France; the Emperor desired, if he could not drive the Turks out of Hungary, at least to break up the shameful alliance between them and the French King. The Pope meanwhile was urging both the Emperor and Francis to peace, so that a General Council might meet to put down heresy — that of England most of all; and now that peace was made, the Council was appointed to meet at Trent in March, 1545.

England being thus isolated, her resources were now put to a severe strain. Henry had already, at the beginning of the year 1544, been absolved by Parliament from repayment of the forced loan he had levied two years before, and it was not in this year that he began to debase the currency. On May 16, however, he issued a proclamation "enhancing" gold and silver, that is, raising the rate of the coins to prevent their being exported; for the quality of the English coinage, at this date, was still high, and it was consequently in much demand in other countries. But before another twelvemonth had expired, a debased currency was issued, which was afterwards lowered still further. Meanwhile, in June of this year a loan was obtained from the City of London by the mortgage of some Crown lands, and in January, 1545, a new benevolence was demanded for the wars of France and Scotland.

For the subjugation of the latter country Henry had relied chiefly on the aid of the Douglases and of the Scotch heretics, who hated Cardinal Beton and desired the overthrow of the monasteries and the Church. But the Douglases were double-dealers, and, since Hertford's burning of Edinburgh, when the Governor released them from confinement to serve against the common enemy, they had shown so much loyalty to their country that they were absolved from attainder by the Scottish Parliament in December. The King on this gave ear to a project of Sir Ralph Evers and Brian Layton for subduing the domains of the Douglases, together with the whole country south of Forth. In February, 1545, accordingly, Evers and Layton raided the Scotch border in the usual fashion as far as Melrose, where they wrecked the Abbey and violated the tombs of the Douglases. Angus and Arran, however, met them at Ancrum Moor near Jedburgh and with greatly inferior numbers routed the English host, taking prisoners the leaders and some hundreds of their followers.

The war between France and England still went on, but was attended with little advantage to either side. Marshal du Biez formed the siege of Boulogne in January; but as England commanded the sea it was ineffectual; and, though renewed efforts were made in the summer, they were equally fruitless.

The French, indeed, collected a great fleet under Annebaut and entered the Solent, where a squadron drawn up at Portsmouth was unable for some time to attack them for lack of wind. In preparing for action, moreover, the English lost a fine vessel, the *Mary Rose*, which heeled over by accident and sank before the King's eyes, almost all her crew being drowned. The French, on the other hand, would have attacked the fleet at Portsmouth harbour, but could not approach with safety; and though they overran part of the Isle of Wight they were soon driven out. They were then carried eastward off the Sussex coast, which they attacked with little effect, and after an indecisive action in the Channel, ending at nightfall, they retired to their own coast. The siege of Boulogne was then abandoned, and in September Lord Lisle landed in Normandy and burned Tréport; but sickness had broken out in the fleet and it returned.

That same September the Earl of Hertford invaded the Scotch Marches, took Kelso, Home, Melrose, and Dryburgh, and even outdid previous works of destruction. Between the 8th and the 23rd of the month he demolished seven monasteries, sixteen castles, towers, or "piles," five market-towns, 243 villages, thirteen mills, and three hospitals.

In November Parliament met and, besides granting the King a new and heavy subsidy, put at his disposal the property of all hospitals, colleges, and chantries to meet the cost of the wars. Oxford and Cambridge took alarm, but received assurances that they should be spared; there were limits, evidently, that even Henry would not exceed. There was also a heresy bill brought forward in the House of Lords, which after much discussion was read no less than five times and then passed unanimously; but apparently it was rejected in the Commons, for it did not become law. On Christmas Eve the King in person prorogued Parliament and is recorded to have delivered a remarkable speech, in which he referred to the prevalent disputes about religion and urged more charity and forbearance.

In the autumn there had seemed to be a prospect of peace with France. For peace the French were anxious if Henry could be induced to give up Boulogne. The Emperor offered his services as mediator; but a conference at Brussels led to no result, because, though the whole English Council was in favour of the surrender, Henry himself was firmly opposed to it. The Emperor was not greatly distressed by the failure, but sought to renew and strengthen his treaty with England, as the unexpected death of the Duke of Orleans at this time upset some arrangements in the Peace of Crépy, and he was determined on keeping Milan to himself. Another set of mediators also offered their services — the German Protestants, who, though quite alienated from Henry for years past by the Act of the Six Articles and the divorce from Anne of Cleves, were alarmed by the near approach of the General Council summoned to meet at Trent, which did in fact open its first session in December. Anxious to discredit the Council, it was important for them to make peace between England and France, and in November they sent deputies to a Conference at Calais, which, though continued into the next month, proved as ineffectual as that at Brussels.

Direct negotiations, however, took place between English and French commissioners in May, 1546, with the result that peace was finally concluded at Campe, between Ardres and Guines, on June 7, on conditions severe enough for Francis, binding him to pay all the old pensions due to England and a further sum of 2,000,000 crowns for war expenses at the end of eight years. Boulogne was to be retained in Henry's hands till all was paid; but some points were left to be adjusted later on; and Henry agreed to the comprehension of the Scots, provided they would be bound by the treaties of 1543.

Meanwhile he had just achieved one great object in Scotland, which he had been clandestinely pursuing for years in order to get a more complete command of the country. This was the murder of Cardinal Beton. He was aided by factions, political and religious, within the country; for the Cardinal had caused one George Wishart to be burned as a heretic in front of his Castle at St Andrews on March 2, and Wishart's friends swore to revenge his death. Early in the morning of May 29 a party of them entered the Castle when the drawbridge was down to admit workmen, struck down the porter and threw him into the foss, then forced the door of the Cardinal's chamber, killed him and hung out his body over the walls. The event caused Angus, Maxwell, and others to renounce the English alliance and strengthen the Governor's hands against the insurgents. But the Castle of St Andrews was a strong fortress and could not be starved out, as the English, in whose interest it was really held, had the command of the sea. Towards the close of the year the persons chiefly implicated in the murder escaped to London, and those within made a capitulation with the besiegers that they would surrender as soon as an absolution came from Rome for the guilty parties. But this was a mere policy to draw off the besieging forces, for England had no intention of losing its hold on St Andrews.

The state of the King's health was now becoming critical, and in the prospect of a minority there was some speculation as to who should have the rule of his successor. By virtue of his birth Norfolk seemed highly eligible, and it appears that his son the Earl of Surrey (the poet) not only spoke of this privately, but had a shield painted with an alteration in his coat-of-arms suitable only for an heir-apparent to the Crown, which he kept secret from all but his father and his sister the Countess of Richmond. The matter, however, became known, and he and his father were both arrested on December 12, and committed to the Tower. Norfolk signed a confession of guilt on January 12, 1547. Next day Surrey was tried at the Guildhall, and he was executed on the 19th. Against Norfolk a Bill of Attainder was passed in Parliament, and only awaited the royal assent, for which a commission was drawn on the 27th; but the King died that night, and the Duke was saved.

The reign of Henry VIII has left deeper marks on succeeding ages than any other reign in English history. Nothing is more extraordinary than that within less than a century after Fortescue had written in praise of the Constitution and Laws of England, a despotism so complete should have been set up in that very country. But it was a despotism really built upon the forms of the constitution and due mainly to the remarkable ability of the unscrupulous King himself, who was careful to disturb nothing that did not really stand in his way. The enigma, in fact, becomes quite intelligible, when we consider how much weight the constitution itself allowed to the personal views of a very able sovereign. England was but a country of limited extent, without colonies or even dependencies except Ireland, or any continental possession save Calais. To frame a policy for such a nation required little more than one good diplomatic head, and when that head was the King's there was not much chance of controlling him. Henry VIII was really a monarch of consummate ability, who, if his course had not been misdirected by passion and selfishness, would have left a name behind him as the very founder of England's greatness. Not only was his judgment strong and clear, but he knew well how to select advisers. To talk of parliamentary control is out of the question. The King called Parliament only when he wanted money, or when he wished despotic measures passed with a semblance of popular sanction. But the forms of Parliamentary legislation and control were kept up; and thus, with weaker Kings and a more effective popular sentiment, the ancient assembly afterwards proved able to recover all and more than all its former authority.

The old nobility were the King's natural advisers; the Commons could scarcely as yet be called a real power in the State. But the old nobility were reduced in numbers, and were no match for him in intelligence. They were superseded, moreover, in the end, by a new nobility created by himself out of the middle classes. Meanwhile, he took counsel both of noblemen and of commoners just as suited himself, and he soon found out who served him best. Early in the reign he made large use of churchmen, such as Warham, Fox, Wolsey, Pace, and Gardiner; for churchmen were generally men of greater penetration than ordinary lay agents of the Crown. A perceptible change took place in this matter, when with Cromwell's aid he compelled the Church to acknowledge Royal Supremacy and disown the Pope's authority. The churchmen then promoted were only those who fell in with the new policy and who, occupied in enforcing it on the clergy, were not capable of much service in framing Acts of State or assisting in secular government. For in truth this great ecclesiastical revolution was that which completed and consolidated the fabric of Henry's despotism. If among the laity he had neither lord nor commoner who durst withstand him, there were churchmen like some of the Observant Friars who actually spoke out against the public scandal which he was creating by repudiating his lawful wife; and the King felt, truly enough, that if he was to have his way, the voice of the Church must be either silenced or perverted. So the central authority of Christendom was no longer to determine what was right or wrong. In England the Church must be under Royal Supremacy.

To this decisive breach with Rome Henry himself was driven with some reluctance; for no King was at first more devoted to the Church or more desirous to stand well in the opinion of his own subjects. Nor could it be said that the Church's yoke was a painful one to mighty potentates like him. But wilfulness and obstinacy were very strong features of Henry's character. Whatever he did he must never appear to retract; and he had so frequently threatened the Pope with the withdrawal of his allegiance in case he would not grant him his divorce that at last he felt bound to make good what he had threatened. For the first time in history Europe beheld a great prince deliberately withdraw himself and his subjects from the spiritual domain of Rome, and enforce by the severest penalties the repudiation of papal authority. For the first time also Europe realised how weak the Papacy had become when it was proved unable to punish such aggression. Foreign nations were scandalised, but no foreign prince could afford lightly to quarrel with England. Henry was considered an enemy of Christianity much as was the Turk, but the prospect of a crusade against him, though at times it looked fairly probable, always vanished in the end. Foreign princes were too suspicious of each other to act together in this, and Henry himself, by his own wary policy, contrived to ward off the danger. He was anxious to show that the faith of Christendom was maintained as firmly within his kingdom as ever. He made Cranmer a sort of insular Pope, and insisted on respect being paid to his decrees — especially in reference to his own numerous marriages and divorces. But, beyond the suspension of the canon law and the complete subjugation of the clergy to the civil power, he was not anxious to make vital changes in religion ; and both doctrine and ritual remained in his day nearly unaltered. The innovations actually made consisted in little more than the authorisation of an English Bible, the publication of some formularies to which little objection could be taken, and — what has not been mentioned above — the first use of an English Litany. For though as yet there was no English prayer-book, a Litany in the common tongue was ordered in 1544 when the King was about to embark for France.

The Authorised English Bible was undoubtedly a new force in the religious history of England. Wiclif's Bible had preceded it by more than a century, and there had been earlier translations still. But Wiclif's attempt to popularise the Scriptures in an English form had been disapproved of by the Church, which considered the clergy as the special custodians and interpreters of Holy Writ, without whose guidance it could too easily be perverted and misconstrued. This was the feeling which inspired the constitution of Archbishop Arundel in 1408, forbidding the use of any translation which had not been approved by the diocesan of the place or by some provincial council. In days when the sacred writings were only multiplied by copyists, translations of particular books of Scripture, or even of the whole, might be episcopally authorised, if good in themselves, as luxuries for private use, without apparent prejudice to the faith. But Wiclif's version was regarded as a deliberate attempt to vulgarise a literature of peculiar sanctity which required careful exposition by men of learning. The vernacular Bible, however, was prized by many laymen, even in the fifteenth century, and certainly influenced not a little the religious thought of the period ; for, in opposition to the special claims of the Church, the Lollards set up a theory that Scripture was the only true authority for any religious observances and that no special learning was required to interpret it, the true meaning of Holy Writ being always revealed to men of real humility of mind. This was also the idea of Tyndale, who, encouraged by a London merchant, went abroad and printed for importation into

England a translation he had made of the New Testament, not from the Latin Vulgate, like Wiclif's, but from the original Greek text ; his aim being, as he said himself, to make a ploughboy know the Scriptures even better than a divine.

The invention of printing gave Tyndale's translation an immense advantage over its predecessors. It was smuggled into England and found no lack of purchasers, who were obliged to keep it in secrecy. But every effort was used by authority to put it down. Copies were bought up by the Bishops in the hope that the whole impression would be suppressed ; and there was more than one burning of the books in St Paul's Churchyard. But the effect was only to encourage Tyndale to print off further copies and extend the scope of his labours ; for he went on to translate some books of the Old Testament from the Hebrew. And in England, though his New Testament was denounced as erroneous and heretical (no doubt the language in many parts tended to discredit Church authority), yet the obvious thought presented itself that the best way to counteract the poison of an erroneous version would be the issue of one that was accurate and scholarly. So in June, 1530, when a royal proclamation was issued for the suppression of Tyndale's and other heretical books, it was intimated that, though translation of the Scriptures was not in itself a necessary thing, yet, if corrupt translations were meanwhile laid aside and the people forsook mischievous opinions, the King intended hereafter to have those writings translated into English " by great, learned, and Catholic persons."

A few years later, Cromwell having become Vicegerent in spiritual matters, Miles Coverdale under his secret patronage brought out in October, 1535, a complete English Bible, not, like Tyndale's, translated from the Greek and Hebrew, but, as the title-page announced, from the " Dutch " (meaning the German) and Latin — in fact, an English version of the Vulgate amended by comparison with the German Bible of Luther. This work, however, though dedicated to the King, was not issued by authority ; and though Cromwell's injunctions of 1536 required every church to be supplied within a twelvemonth with a whole Bible " in Latin and also in English," the direction could not have been obeyed. In 1537 appeared Matthew's Bible which was really made up of Tyndale's version of the New Testament and of the Old Testament as far as the Second Book of Chronicles, the other Books of the Old Testament being supplied from Coverdale with alterations. Its origin would not have pleased the Bishops, but the facts were concealed ; and, a copy being submitted to Cranmer, he wrote to Cromwell that he thought it should be licensed till the Bishops could set forth a better, which he did not expect they would ever do. The King approved ; Grafton and Whitchurch, the printers, were allowed to sell it ; and its sale was forced upon the clergy by new injunctions from Cromwell in 1538. Another and more luxurious edition, however, was called for, and Grafton went to Paris to see it printed, with Coverdale's aid as corrector, on the best of paper with the best typographic art of the day. This work was far advanced when it was stopped by the French Inquisition; but Coverdale and Grafton succeeded in conveying away the presses, type, and a company of French compositors, by whose aid the work was finished in London in April, 1539.

That edition was known as "the Great Bible." It was issued by the King's authority and Cromwell's; but the clergy were by means pleased with the translation, which they severely censured in Convocation in 1542, two years after Cromwell's death. They appointed committees of the best Hebrew and Greek scholars to revise it; but the King sent a message through Cranmer forbidding them to proceed, as he intended to submit the work to the two Universities. This was simply a false pretence to stop revision; for a patent was immediately granted to Anthony Marlar, giving to him instead of Grafton, who was now in disgrace, the sole right of printing the Bible for four years. The Great Bible continued to be used in churches, and six were set up in St Paul's Cathedral for general use.

These were the principal translations issued in Henry VIII's time; and authority being given for their use, those, who maintained the old Lollard theory that the Bible could be safely interpreted without the aid of a priesthood, were encouraged in their opposition to the Church. This theory was clearly gaining in strength during the latter part of Henry's reign and its adherents became still more numerous in that of his son. Men founded their convictions on an infallible book, were confident in their own judgments, and died by hundreds under Mary for beliefs that were only exceptionally held in the beginning of her father's reign. The pure delight in the sacred literature itself inspired many with enthusiasm; and among other results we find the musician Marbeck, who knew no Latin, compiling a Concordance to the English Bible, and the heroic Anne Askew, when examined for heresy, full of scriptural texts and references in defending herself.

These cases, and especially the last, deserve more than a passing mention. Some account has been already given of martyrdoms, both for refusal to acknowledge the Royal Supremacy and for doctrines of a novel kind. But the results of the severe Act of the Six Articles have not as yet been touched upon. They were not, in truth, so appalling as might have been expected. The presentments at first were quashed, and new regulations were made about procedure, which, with further modifications passed by Statute, considerably abated the terrors of the Act. But in 1543, just after the King's marriage with Catharine Parr, four men of Windsor were found guilty of heresy, of whom three were burned at the Castle, and one was pardoned. The man pardoned was John Marbeck, the celebrated musician just referred to, who possibly owed his escape in part to his musical talents; for he was organist of St George's Chapel. Yet it does not seem that he had really transgressed the law in anything; and Bishop Wakeman of Hereford, at his examination, said with reference to his Concordance, "This man hath been better occupied than a great sort of our priests."

In 1546 the victims of the Six Articles seem to have been more numerous, and the chief sufferer was a zealous lady separated from her husband, and known by her maiden name of Anne Askew. She and three others were tried at the Guildhall for heresy, and confessed opinions about the Sacrament for which they were all condemned to the stake. Two of her fellows next day (one of them, Shaxton, had been Bishop of Salisbury) yielded to the exhortations of Bishops Bonner and Heath, and were saved on being reconciled to the Church; but Anne was resolute, and would not be persuaded even by the Council, before whom she disputed for two days when they evidently wished to save her, answering continually in language borrowed from Scripture. She was committed to Newgate and afterwards to the Tower, where she was racked some time before she was burnt at Smithfield. Suspicions seem to have been entertained that she was supported in her heresies by some of the ladies about Queen Catharine Parr, and she was tortured to reveal her confederates; but she denied that she had any. The story of her examination and torture written by her own hand and printed abroad for the English market, certainly added new force to the coming revolution.

There was indeed another great change bearing on religion and social life, though not much on doctrine or ritual — the dissolution of the monasteries. Its immediate effect was to produce a vast amount of suffering. It is true that a considerable number of the monks and nuns received pensions, but very many were turned out of the houses which had been their homes and wandered about in search of means to live. Even at the first suppression Chapuys was told that, what with monks, nuns, and dependents on monasteries, there must have been 20,000 persons cast adrift; and though this was evidently a vague and probably exaggerated estimate, it indicates at least very widespread wretchedness and discomfort. More permanent results, however, arose out of the prodigious transfer of property, affecting, as it is supposed, about a third of the land of England. It has been doubted whether the monks had been easy landlords; but when the monastic lands were confiscated and sold to a host of greedy courtiers the change was severely felt. The lands were all let at higher rents, and the newly-erected Court "for the Augmentation of the Crown Revenues" did its best to justify its title. Moreover, the purchasers, in order to make the most of their new acquisitions, began to enclose commons where poor tenants had been accustomed to graze their cattle; the tenants sold the beasts which they could not feed, and the cost of living in a few years advanced very seriously. This was one of the main causes of Ket's rebellion in the following reign.

Meanwhile, all over the country men beheld with sadness a host of deserted buildings with ruined walls, where formerly rich and poor used to receive hospitality on their travels ; where gentlemen could obtain loans on easy terms or deposit precious documents, as in places more secure than their own homes ; where the needy always found relief and shelter, and where spiritual wants were attended to no less than physical. The blank was felt particularly in solitary and mountainous districts, where the monks had assisted travellers, often commercial travellers and " baggers of corn," whose services were most useful to the country side, with men and horses to pursue their journeys in safety. " Also the abbeys," said Aske, " was one of the beauties of this realm to all men and strangers passing through the same; all gentlemen much succoured in their needs with money, their younger sons there succoured, and in nunneries their daughters brought up in virtue, and also their evidences (*i.e.* title-deeds) and money left to the uses of infants in abbeys' hands — always sure there. And such abbeys as were near the danger of seabanks great maintainers of seawalls and dykes, maintainers and builders of bridges and highways [and] such other things for the commonwealth."

What arts and industries disappeared or were driven into other channels on the fall of the monasteries is a matter for reflexion. Rural labour, of course, still went on where it was necessary for the support of life ; but some arts, formerly brought to high perfection in monastic seclusion, were either paralysed for a time or migrated into the towns. Sculpture, embroidery, clockmaking, bellfounding, were among these ; and it is needless to speak of what literature owes to the transcribers of manuscripts and the composers of monastic chronicles. True, monasticism had long been on the decline before it was swept away, and monastic chronicles were already, one might say, things of the past ; but it was in monasteries also that the first printing-presses were set up, and the art which superseded that of the transcriber was cherished by the same influence. Finally, the education of the people was largely due to the convent schools ; and there is no doubt that it suffered very severely not only from the suppression of the monasteries, but perhaps even more from the confiscation of chantries which began at the end of the reign, for the chantry priest was often the local schoolmaster. Nor did the boasted educational foundations of Edward VI do much to redress the wrong, for in truth his schools were old schools refounded with poorer endowments.

Still more did the higher education of the country suffer ; for the monasteries had been in the habit of sending up scholars to the universities and often maintained some of their own junior members there to complete their education. After the Suppression, consequently, university studies went gradually to decay, and few men studied for degrees. In the six years from 1542 to 1548 only 191 students were admitted bachelors of arts at Cambridge and only 173 at Oxford. The foundation of Regius Professorships at Oxford and Cambridge was a slight compensation. The dispersion of valuable monastic libraries, moreover, was to some extent counteracted by the efforts of Leland, the antiquary, in his tour through England to preserve some of their choicest treasures for the King.

Altogether, no such sweeping changes had been known for centuries. As regards the land some of the results may have been in the end for good. Better husbandry and new modes of farming, no doubt, succeeded in developing more fully the resources of the soil. A check, too, was doubtless placed on indiscriminate charity. But problems were raised which were new in kind. At the beginning of the reign the chief evils felt were depopulation, vagrancy, and thieves. Economic laws, of course, were not understood ; and attempts were made by legislation to prevent husbandmen's dwellings being thrown down by landlords, who found it profitable to devote arable land to pasture to increase the growth of wool. The frequent repetition of these Acts only shows how ineffective they were in practice ; and in the beginning of the seventeenth century they had become so complicated that Coke rejoiced at their repeal. But the evils of vagrancy and poverty assumed new forms. The precise effect of the fall of the monasteries upon pauperism is not altogether easy to estimate ; but the statement of Chapuys removes all doubt that it was the immediate cause of bitter penury. The evidence of the Statute-book on this point requires careful interpretation ; for it was only in a later age that law was invoked to do the duty of charity. Down to the middle of Henry VIII's reign repeated Acts had been passed for the punishment of sturdy beggars and vagabonds : but it gradually came to be perceived that this problem could not be dealt with apart from relief of the deserving poor. In 1536 the same session of Parliament which dissolved the smaller monasteries passed an Act for the systematic maintenance of paupers by charitable collections ; and, in the first year of Edward VI, Parliament for the first time attempted to deal with the two problems together, with penalties of atrocious severity against vagabonds. But severity was futile ; the Act was speedily repealed, and under Elizabeth a regular system of Poor Law relief was established.

From the beginning of his reign Henry had been profuse in his expenditure. His tastes were luxurious and he gratified them to a large extent at the cost of others. He made Wolsey present him with Hampton Court ; after the Cardinal's fall he took York Place and called it Whitehall ; he purchased from Eton College the Hospital of St James, made it into a palace, and laid out St James' Park ; he built Nonsuch and made another large park in the neighbourhood. Before he had been many years King, the enormous wealth left him by his father must have been nearly all dissipated. Yet the subsidies he required from Parliament were very moderate till 1523, when, as we have seen, unprecedented taxation was imposed for the French war in addition to a forced loan, from repayment of which he was absolved by the legislature in the year of Wolsey's fall. Then in a few years followed the pillage of the monasteries, while throughout the reign there were numerous attainders involving large confiscations. In addition to this immense booty came further subsidies, a further forced loan for a new war with France, and a new release by Parliament from the duty of repayment. Finally, to relieve an exhausted exchequer, the King was driven to the expedient of debasing the currency. In 1542 a gold coinage was issued of 23 carats fine and 1 carat of alloy, with a silver coinage of 10 oz. pure silver to 2 oz. of alloy. In 1544 the gold was still 23 carats fine, but the silver was only 9 oz. to 3 oz. of alloy. In 1545 the gold was 22 carats and the silver 6 oz. to 6 oz. of alloy. In 1546 the gold was only 20 carats and the silver 4 oz. to 8 oz. of alloy. This rapid deterioration of the money, though it brought a profit to the King in the last year of £5. 2*s*. in the coinage of every pound weight of gold, and of £4. 4*s*. on every pound weight of silver, produced, of course, the most serious consequences to the public. Apart from this, no doubt, prices must soon have been affected by the quantity of silver and gold poured into Europe from Mexican and Peruvian mines. But the great issue of base money in this and the following reign produced a complete derangement of commerce and untold inconvenience, not only by the sudden alteration of values but by the want of confidence which it everywhere inspired. Not till the reign of Queen Elizabeth could a remedy be effectually applied to so great an evil.

The King's high-handed proceedings, alike as regards the Church, the monasteries, and the coinage, lowered the moral tone of the whole community. Men lost faith in their religion. Greedy courtiers sprang up eager for grants of abbey lands. A new nobility was raised out of the money-getting middle classes, and a host of placemen enriched themselves by continual peculation. Covetousness and fraud reigned in the highest places.

Yet "there is some soul of goodness in things evil," and the same policy that under Henry VIII destroyed the autonomy of the Church and suppressed the monasteries made him seek not only to unify his kingdom but to bring together the British Islands under one single rule. England, itself, no doubt, was a united country at his accession, but its cohesion was not perfect. Wales and the north country beyond Trent each required somewhat special government; and Ireland, of course, was a problem by itself. Yet no serious perplexities had grown up when in 1525 the King sent his bastard son, the Duke of Richmond, into Yorkshire, with a Council to govern the north, and his daughter Mary, with another Council, to hold a Court on the borders of Wales for the settlement of disputes in that country without reference to the Courts at Westminster. This arrangement was soon set aside when

Mary's legitimacy was questioned, and the disaffection of Rice ap Griffith, whose father and grandfather had governed Wales for Henry VII, was undoubtedly connected with the Divorce question. A little later a new Council for the Marches was set up under Roland Lee, whom the King appointed Bishop of Coventry and Lichfield; and by several successive Acts of Parliament Wales itself was divided into shires, and the administration of justice in the principality assimilated to that which prevailed in England, only with a Great Sessions held twice a year in every county instead of quarterly assizes. The admission of twenty-seven members for Welsh constituencies to the English Parliament completed the union of the principality with the kingdom.

Of a similar tendency was an Act of the King's 27th year, by which the old prerogatives of counties palatine were abolished, and the sole power of appointing justices or pardoning offences over the whole kingdom restored to the Crown. Of the beneficial results of these changes it is impossible to doubt, especially in Wales, where " gentlemen thieves " had been a good deal too influential. The north of England was less easily coerced, and after the severe measures taken by Norfolk to put down the rebellion a new Council of the North was established, first under Bishop Tunstall of Durham, afterwards under Bishop Holgate of Llandaff. This Council which, like that of Wales, was abolished by the Long Parliament in 1641, was undoubtedly without parliamentary authority; it acted merely by the deputed authority of the Crown. Yet its acts could scarcely have been felt as extremely tyrannical after the submission of the whole country in 1537, renewed to the King himself when he went thither in 1541.

In Ireland the King's policy was after many years wonderfully successful. Early in the reign he had allowed the Earl of Kildare, as Lord Deputy, to manage everything, to treat his own enemies as the King's and appropriate their confiscated lands. This, however, could not last, and in 1520 the Earl of Surrey was sent over as Deputy, who with the aid of Sir Piers Butler set about reducing the land to subjection. He made a good beginning and handed over the work to Sir Piers; but the feud between the Geraldines and the Butlers made government impossible. Kildare was restored for a time, but, as we have seen, had to be recalled, whereupon his son, becoming the Pope's champion, almost wrested for a time the whole government of Ireland from the King. But before many years the Geraldines were completely crushed, and young Kildare and his five uncles were hanged at Tyburn. Lord Leonard Grey's government, however, was complained of; he was recalled and sent to the block. It was under his successor, St Leger, that real progress was at last made. Without attempting distant expeditions he endeavoured first of all to make the Pale secure, and by and by induced the Irish chieftains to submit, accepting titles from the King and renouncing the Pope's spiritual authority. The triumph was completed by the passing of Acts both in the Irish and in the English Parliament by which the King's style was altered to "King" instead of "lord" of Ireland. The new style was proclaimed in England on January 23, 1542. When Irish chieftains sat in a Dublin Parliament as earls and barons, with the quondam head of the Irish knights of St John as Viscount Clontarf, a great step had evidently been taken towards conciliation. In 1542 it was announced that Ireland was actually at peace; and, although this state of matters did not continue, the end of the reign was comparatively untroubled.

Thus Henry, notwithstanding his defiance of the Pope, was wonderfully successful in making himself secure at home. Abroad he had warded off the danger of any attempt at invasion to enforce the papal excommunication by continually fomenting the mutual jealousies of the two leading princes on the Continent. The time came, however, when, neutrality being no longer possible, he prepared to throw in his lot with the Emperor against France; and it was in view of a war with France, as we have seen, that he attempted, just when Ireland had been pacified, to get Scotland completely under his power — a task which proved too much both for him and for his successor.

Naturally, the navy and the defence of the coast occupied much of this King's attention. From the earliest years of his reign, indeed, Henry took much interest in his ships. Trinity House owes its origin to a guild founded by royal licence at Deptford Strand before he had been four years upon the throne. Earlier still, when the *Regent* was burned in 1512, he immediately set about the building of the *Great Harry*, on board of which he received a grand array of ambassadors and Bishops when it was dedicated in June, 1514. She was the largest vessel then afloat, and her sailing qualities were no less admirable than her bulk. In 1522 Admiral Fitzwilliam reported that she outsailed all the ships of the fleet except the unfortunate *Mary Rose*. The Royal Navy consisted commonly of about thirty or forty sail, but it could always be augmented from merchant-ships, or ships which were private property; though it was reported by Marillac in 1540 that there were only seven or eight vessels besides the King's which were of more than 400 or 500 tons burden. Henry's solicitude about his ships was further shown on the sinking of the *Mary Rose* before his eyes in 1545. Next year, for the first time, a Navy Board was established.

The importance of the command of the sea was shown in two instances at the end of the reign, when the French besieged the English in Boulogne, and when the Scotch government attempted to besiege Henry's friends, the murderers of Cardinal Beton, in St Andrews. The hold which Henry thus had both on France and Scotland was important for his own protection; and the foundation of England's greatness as a world-power may be traced to a tyrant's strenuous efforts to defend his own position. Of less permanent importance in this way were the numerous fortifications he raised upon the coast. He built Sandgate Castle in Kent, Camber Castle near Rye, and fortifications at Cowes, Calshot, and Hurst upon the Solent, and a number of other places besides.

As to his army, for the most part he was not very well served. The policy of his father had been to prohibit by law the large retinues formerly maintained by the nobles to prevent the renewal of civil war.

The result was that, when troops were needed for active service abroad, the nobles had no personal following, but, being each bound by indenture to bring so many soldiers into the field, hired men for the occasion at specific wages. In consequence they were raw and ill-disciplined; and their extraordinary revolt under Dorset in Spain in 1512 was almost paralleled in 1523, when Suffolk, partly by the weather and partly by the insubordination of his followers, was compelled to disband his army and return to Calais. After that date there was no great fighting for nearly twenty years, when the King again became involved both with France and with Scotland. In this French war he supplemented his own forces by engaging German mercenaries who demanded exorbitant pay and cheated him besides. He also detained in England with the Emperor's leave two Spanish noblemen of great distinction, and took a number of their countrymen into his service, who were delighted with his liberality. The increase of English influence abroad during this reign was in fact due rather to the personal qualities of the King, and to the skilful use which he made of European complications, than to the number or excellence of the troops at his command.

CHAPTER XIV

THE REFORMATION UNDER EDWARD VI

"WOE unto thee, O land," said the Preacher, "when thy king is a child." The truth of his words did not recommend them to the Parliament of Edward VI ; and, when Dr John Story quoted them in his protest against the first Act of Uniformity, he was sent to expiate his boldness in the Tower. Yet he had all the precedents in English history on his side. Disaster and civil strife had attended the nonage of Henry III and Edward III, of Richard II and Henry VI ; and the evils inseparable from the rule of a child had culminated in the murder of Edward V. When, in 1547, a sixth Edward ascended the throne, the signs were few of a break in the uniform ill-fortune of royal minorities. Abroad, Paul III was scheming to recover the allegiance of the schismatic realm ; the Emperor was slowly crushing England's natural allies in Germany ; France was watching her opportunity to seize Boulogne ; and England herself was committed to a hazardous design on Scotland. At home, there was a religious revolution half-accomplished and a social revolution in ferment ; evicted tenants and ejected monks infested the land, centres of disorder and raw material for revolt ; the treasury was empty, the kingdom in debt, the coinage debased. In place of the old nobility of blood stood a new peerage raised on the ruins and debauched by the spoils of the Church, and created to be docile tools in the work of revolution. The royal authority, having undermined every other support of the political fabric, now passed to a Council torn by rival ambitions and conflicting creeds, robbed of royal prestige, and unbridled by the heavy hand that had taught it to serve but not to direct.

Henry VIII died at Whitehall in the early morning of Friday, January 28, 1547. Through the night his brother-in-law, the Earl of Hertford, and his secretary, Sir William Paget, had discussed in the gallery of the palace arrangements for the coming reign. Hertford then started to bring his nephew, the young King, from Hatfield, while Henry's death remained a secret. It was announced to Parliament and Edward was proclaimed early on the following Monday morning. In the afternoon he arrived in London, and an hour or so later the

474

Council met in the Tower. Its composition had been determined on St Stephen's Day, five weeks before, when Henry, acting on an authority specially granted him by Parliament, had drawn up a will, the genuineness of which was not disputed until the possibility of a Stewart succession drew attention to the obstacles it placed in their way to the throne. But the arrangements made in the will for the regency destroyed the balance of parties existing in Henry's later years. Norfolk had been sent to the Tower, and from the sixteen executors, who were to constitute Edward's Privy Council, Bishops Gardiner and Thirlby were expressly excluded. To the eleven, who had previously been of Henry's Council, five were added; two were the Chief Justices, Montagu and Bromley, but the other three, Denny, Herbert, and North, were all inclined towards religious change. Besides the sixteen executors Henry nominated twelve assistants, who were only to be called in when the others thought fit. Unless, in defiance of the testimony of those present when Henry drew up his will, that selection is to be regarded as due to the intrigues of the Reformers, it would seem that Henry deliberately sought to smooth the way for the Reformation by handing over the government to a Council committed to its principles. Not half a dozen of its members could be trusted to offer the least resistance to religious change; and, when the Council assembled in the Tower on that Monday afternoon, it only met to register a foregone conclusion.

Henry had been given no authority to nominate a Protector; but such a step was in accord with precedent and with general expectation, and one at least of the few conservatives on the Council thought that the appointment of Hertford to the protectorate afforded the best guarantee for the good government and security of the realm. He was uncle to the King, a successful general, and a popular favourite; and, though his peerage was but ten years old, it was older than any other that the Council could boast. He was to act only on the advice of his co-executors; but there was apparently no opposition to his appointment as Protector of the realm and Governor of the King's person. On the following day the young King and the peers gave their assent. Five days later Paget produced a list of promotions in the peerage which he said Henry had intended to make. Hertford became Duke of Somerset, and Lord High Treasurer and Earl Marshal in succession to Norfolk; Lisle became Earl of Warwick, and Wriothesley Earl of Southampton; Essex was made Marquis of Northampton, and baronies were conferred on Sir Thomas Seymour, Rich, and Sheffield.

Half of Henry's alleged intentions were not fulfilled, a strong argument in favour of their genuineness; Russell and St John had to wait for their promised earldoms, and seven others for their baronies, nor would Paget have then selected Wriothesley for promotion. For scarcely was Edward crowned (February 20) and Henry buried, when the Lord-Chancellor fell from power. He had been peculiarly identified with the reactionary policy of Henry's later years; and his ambition and ability inspired his colleagues with a distrust which increased when it was found that, in order to devote more time to politics, he had, without obtaining a warrant from the Council, issued a commission for the transaction of Chancery business during his absence. A complaint was at once lodged by the common lawyers, ever jealous of the Chancery side, and the judges unanimously declared that Southampton had forfeited the Chancellorship.

A more important change ensued. Doubts of the validity of a dead King's commission had already led the Chancellor to seek reappointment at the hands of his living sovereign, and the rest of the Council now followed suit. On March 13 Edward VI nominated a new Council of twenty-six. It consisted of the sixteen executors, except Somerset and Southampton, and the twelve assistants named by Henry VIII; but they now held office, not in virtue of their appointment by Henry's will, but of their commission from the boy-King. At the same time the Protector received a fresh commission. He was no longer bound to act by the advice of his colleagues; he was empowered to summon such councillors as he thought convenient, and to add to their numbers at will. No longer the first among equals, he became King in everything but name and prestige; and the attempt of Henry VIII to regulate the government after his death had, like that of every King before him, completely broken down.

Few rulers of England have been more remarkable than the Protector into whose hands thus passed the despotic power of the Tudors. Many have been more successful, many more skilled in the arts of government; but it is doubtful whether any have seen further into the future, or have been more strongly possessed of ideas which they have been unable to carry out. He was born before his time, a seer of visions and a dreamer of dreams. He dreamt of the union of England and Scotland, each retaining its local autonomy, as one empire of Great Britain, "having the sea for a wall, mutual love for a defence, and no need in peace to be ashamed or in war to be afraid of any worldly power." Running himself the universal race for wealth, he yet held it to be his special office and duty to hear poor men's complaints, to redress their wrongs, and to relieve their oppression. He strove to stay the economic revolution which was accumulating vast estates in the hands of the few, and turning the many into landless labourers or homeless vagrants; but his only success was an Act of Parliament whereby he gave his tenants legal security against eviction by himself. Bred in an arbitrary Court and entrusted with despotic power, he cast aside the weapons wherewith the Tudors worked their will and sought to govern on a basis of civil liberty and religious toleration. He abstained from interference in elections to Parliament or in its freedom of debate, and from all attempts to pack or intimidate juries. He believed that the strength of a King lay not in the severity of his laws or the rigour of his penalties, but in the affections of his people; and not one instance of death or torture for religion stains the brief and troubled annals of his rule.

The absolutism, which came in with the new monarchy and was perfected by Cromwell, was relaxed; and the first Parliament summoned by the Protector (November 4, 1547) effected a complete revolution in the spirit of the laws. Nearly all the treasons created since 1352 were swept away, and many of the felonies. It was, indeed, still treason to deny the Royal Supremacy by writing, printing, overt deed or act; but it was no longer treason to do so by "open preaching, express words or sayings." Benefit of clergy and right of sanctuary were restored; wives of attainted persons were permitted to recover their dower; accusations of treason were to be preferred within thirty days of the offence; no one was to be condemned unless he confessed or was accused by two sufficient and lawful witnesses; and Proclamations were no longer to have the force of law. The heresy laws, the Act of Six Articles, all the prohibitions against printing the Scriptures in English, against reading, preaching, teaching, or expounding the Scriptures, "and all and every other act or acts of Parliament concerning doctrine or matters of religion" were erased from the Statute-book.

The main result of this new-found liberty was to give fresh impetus to the Reformation in England. The Act of Six Articles, with all its ferocious penalties, had failed to cure diversities of opinion; and the controversies of which Henry complained to his Parliament in 1545 now broke out with redoubled fury. Among a people unused to freedom and inflamed by religious passions, liberty naturally degenerated into licence. The tongues of the divines were loosed; and they filled the land with a Babel of voices. Each did what was right in his own eyes, and every parish church became the scene of religious experiment. Exiles from abroad flocked to partake in the work and to propagate the doctrines they had imbibed at their respective Meccas. Some came from Lutheran cities in Germany, some from Geneva, and some from Zwinglian Zurich. In their path followed a host of foreign divines, some invited by Cranmer to form a sort of ecumenical council for the purification of the Anglican Church, some fleeing from the wrath of Charles V or from the perils of civil war. From Strassburg came in 1547 Pietro Martire Vermigli, better known as Peter Martyr, a native of Florence and an ex-Augustinian, and Emmanuel Tremellius the Hebraist, a Jew of Ferrara; and from Augsburg came Bernardino Ochino, a native of Siena, once a Franciscan and then a Capuchin. In 1548 John à Lasco (Laski), a Polish noble, and his disciple, Charles Utenhove, a native of Ghent, followed from Emden; and in 1549 Martin Bucer and Paul Fagius fled hither from Strassburg. Jean Véron, a Frenchman from Sens, had been in England eleven years, but celebrated the era of liberty by publishing in 1547 a violent attack on the Mass. Most of these were Zwinglians; and even among the Lutherans many soon inclined towards the doctrine of the Swiss Reformers. Of the humbler immigrants who came to teach or to trade, not a few were Anabaptists, Socinians, and heretics of every hue; and England became, in the words of one horrified politician, the harbour for all infidelity.

The clamour raised by the advent of this foreign legion has somewhat obscured the comparative insignificance of its influence on the development of the English Church. The continental Reformers came too late to affect the moderate changes introduced during Somerset's protectorate, and even the Second Prayer-book of Edward VI owed less to their persuasions than has often been supposed. England never became Lutheran, Zwinglian, or Calvinistic; and she would have resented dictation from Wittenberg, Zurich, or Geneva as keenly as she did from Rome, had the authority of Luther, Zwingli, or Calvin ever attained the proportions of that of the Roman Pontiff. Each indeed had his adherents in England, but their influence was never more than sectional, and failed to turn the course of the English Reformation into any foreign channel.

In so far as the English Reformers sought spiritual inspiration from other than primitive sources, there can be no doubt that, difficult as it would be to adduce documentary evidence for the statement, they, consciously or unconsciously, derived this inspiration from Wiclif. Like them, he appealed to the State to remedy abuses in the Church, attacked ecclesiastical endowments, and gradually receded from the Catholic doctrine of the Mass. The Reformation in England was divergent in origin, method, and aim from all the phases of the movement abroad; it left the English Church without a counterpart in Europe, — so insular in character that no subsequent attempt at union with any foreign Church has ever come within measurable distance of success. It was in its main aspect practical and not doctrinal; it concerned itself less with dogma than with conduct, and its favourite author was Erasmus, not because he preached any distinctive theology, but because he lashed the evil practices of the Church. Englishmen are little subject to the bondage of logic or abstract ideas, and they began their Reformation, not with the enunciation of any new truth, but with an attack upon the clerical exaction of excessive probate dues. No dogma played in England the part that Predestination or Justification by Faith played in Europe. There arose a master of prophetic invective in Latimer and a master of liturgics in Cranmer, but no one meet to be compared with the great religious thinkers of the world. Hence the influence of English Reformers on foreign Churches was even less than that of foreign divines in England. Anglicans never sought to proselytise other Christian Churches, nor England to wage other than defensive wars of religion; in Ireland and Scotland, which appear to afford exceptions, the religious motive was always subordinate to a political end.

The Reformation in England was mainly a domestic affair, a national protest against national grievances rather than part of a cosmopolitan movement towards doctrinal change. It originated in political exigencies, local and not universal in import; and was the work of Kings and statesmen, whose minds were absorbed in national problems, rather than of divines whose faces were set towards the purification of the universal Church. It was an ecclesiastical counterpart of the growth of nationalities at the expense of the medieval ideal of the unity of the civilised world. Its effect was to make the Church in England the Church of England, a national Church, recognising as its head the English King, using in its services the English tongue, limited in its jurisdiction to the English Courts, and fenced about with a uniformity imposed by the English legislature. This nationalisation of the Church had one other effect: it brought to a sudden end the medieval struggle between Church and State. The Church had only been enabled to wage that conflict on equal terms by the support it received as an integral part of the visible Church on earth; and when that support was withdrawn it sank at once into a position of dependence upon the State. From the time of the submission of the clergy to Henry VIII there has been no instance of the English Church successfully challenging the supreme authority of the State.

It was mainly on these lines, laid down by Henry VIII, that the Reformation continued under Edward VI. The papal jurisdiction was no more; the use of English had been partially introduced into the services of the Church; the Scriptures had been translated; steps had been taken in the direction of uniformity, doctrinal and liturgical; and something had been done to remove medieval accretions, such as the worship of images, and to restore religion to what Reformers considered its primitive purity. That Henry intended his so-called "settlement" to be final is an assumption at variance with some of the evidence; for he had entrusted his son's education exclusively to men of the New Learning, he had given the same party an overwhelming preponderance in the Council of Regency, and according to Cranmer he was bent in the last few months of his life upon a scheme for pulling down roods suppressing the ringing of bells and turning the Mass into a Communion. Cranmer himself had for some years been engaged upon a reform of the Church services which developed into the First Book of Common Prayer, and the real break in religious policy came, not at the accession of Edward VI, but after the fall of Somerset and the expulsion of the Catholics from the Council. The statute procured by Henry VIII from Parliament, which enabled his son, on coming of age, to annul all Acts passed during his minority, was probably due to an overweening sense of the importance of the kingly office; but, although it was repealed in Edward's first year, it inevitably strengthened the natural doubts of the competence of the Council to exercise an ecclesiastical supremacy vested in the King. No government, however, could afford to countenance such a suicidal theory; and the Council had constitutional right on its side when it insisted that the authority of the King, whether in ecclesiastical or civil matters, was the same whatever his age might be, and refused to consider the minority as a bar to further prosecution of the Reformation.

No doubt, they were led in the same direction, some by conviction and some by the desire, as Sir William Petre expressed it, "to fish again in the tempestuous seas of this world for gain and wicked mammon." But there was also popular pressure behind them. Zeal and energy, if not numbers, were on the side of religious change, and the Council found it necessary to restrain rather than stimulate the ardour of the Reformers. One of its first acts was to bind over the wardens and curate of St Martin's, Ironmonger Lane, to restore images which they had "contrary to the King's doctrine and order" removed from their church. Six months later the Council was only prevented from directing a general replacement of images illegally destroyed by a fear of the controversy such a step would arouse; and it had no hesitation in punishing the destroyers. In November, 1547, it sought by Proclamation to stay the rough treatment which priests suffered at the hands of London serving-men and apprentices, and sent round commissioners to take an inventory of church goods in order to prevent the extensive embezzlement practised by local magnates. Early in the following year Proclamations were issued denouncing unauthorised innovations, silencing preachers who urged them, and prohibiting flesh-eating in Lent. In April, 1548, the ecclesiastical authorities were straitly charged to take legal proceedings against those who, encouraged by the lax views prevalent on marriage, were guilty of such "insolent and unlawful acts" as putting away one wife and marrying another. The Marquis of Northampton was himself summoned before the Council and summarily ordered to separate from the lady he called his second wife. Similarly the first Statute of the reign was directed not against the Catholics, but against reckless Reformers; it sought to restrain all who impugned or spoke unreverently of the Sacrament of the altar; the right of the clergy to tithe was reaffirmed, and the Canon Law as to precontracts and sanctuary, abolished by Henry VIII, was restored. It was no wonder that the clergy thought the moment opportune for the recovery of their position as an Estate of the realm, and petitioned that ecclesiastical laws should be submitted to their approval, or that they should be readmitted to their lost representation in the House of Commons.

These measures illustrate alike the practical conservatism of Somerset's government and the impracticability of the theoretical toleration to which he inclined. His dislike of coercion occasionally got the better of his regard for his own proclamations, as when he released Thomas Hancock from his sureties taken for unlicensed preaching. But he soon realised that the government could not abdicate its ecclesiastical functions, least of all in the early days of the Royal Supremacy, when the Bishops and Cranmer especially looked to the State for guidance. Personally he leaned to the New Learning, and, like most Englishmen, he was Erastian in his view of the relations between Church and State and somewhat prejudiced against sacerdotalism. Yet, in spite of the fact that after his death he was regarded as a martyr by the French Reformed Church, he cannot any more than the English Reformation be labelled Lutheran, Zwinglian, or Calvinist; and, when he found it incumbent upon him to take some line in ecclesiastical politics, he chose one of comparative moderation and probably the line of least resistance. The Royal Supremacy was perhaps somewhat nakedly asserted when, at the commencement of the reign, Bishops renewed their commissions to exercise spiritual jurisdiction, and when in the first session of Parliament the form of episcopal election was exchanged for direct nomination by royal letters patent. But the former practice had been enforced, and the latter suggested, in the reign of Henry VIII, and Somerset secured a great deal more episcopal co-operation than did either Northumberland or Elizabeth. Convocation demanded, unanimously in one case and by a large majority in the other, the administration of the Sacrament in both kinds and liberty for the clergy to marry; and a majority of the Bishops in the House of Lords voted for all the ecclesiastical bills passed during his protectorate. Only Gardiner and Bonner offered any resistance to the Visitation of 1547; and it must be concluded, either that Somerset's religious changes accorded with the preponderant clerical opinion, or that clerical subservience surpassed the compliance of laymen.

The responsibility for these changes cannot be apportioned with any exactness. Probably Gardiner was not far from the mark, when he implied that Cranmer and not the Protector was the innovating spirit; and the comparative caution with which the Reformers at first proceeded was as much due to Somerset's restraining influence as the violence of their later course was to the simulated zeal of Warwick. Cranmer's influence with the Council was greater than it had been with Henry VIII; to him it was left to work out the details of the movement, and the first step taken in the new reign was the Archbishop's issue of the Book of Homilies for which he had failed to obtain the sanction of King and Convocation five years before. Their main features were a comparative neglect of the Sacraments and the exclusion of charity as a means of salvation. Gardiner attacked the Book on these grounds; and, possibly out of deference to his protest, the saving power of charity was affirmed in the Council's injunctions to the royal visitors a few months later.

The Homilies were followed by Nicholas Udall's edition of the Paraphrase of Erasmus that had been prepared under Henry VIII, and was now intended, partly no doubt as a solvent of old ideas, but partly as a corrective of the extreme Protestant versions of Tyndall and Coverdale, which, now that Henry's prohibition was relaxed, recovered

their vogue. The substitution of English for Latin in the services of
the Church was gradually carried out in the Chapel Royal as an example
to the rest of the kingdom. Compline was sung in English on Easter
Monday, 1547 ; the sermon was preached, and the *Te Deum* sung, in
English on September 18 to celebrate Pinkie ; and at the opening of
Parliament on November 4, the *Gloria in Excelsis*, the Creed, and
the *Agnus* were all sung in English. Simultaneously, Sternhold, a
gentleman of the Court, was composing his metrical version of the
Psalms in English, which was designed to supplant the " lewd " ballads
of the people and in fact eventually made " psalm-singing " a characteristic of advanced ecclesiastical Reformers.

The general Visitation in the summer and autumn of 1547 was
mainly concerned with reforming practical abuses, with attempts to
compel the wider use of English in services, the removal of images
that were abused, and a full recognition of the Supremacy of the
boy-King. In November and December Convocation recommended the
administration of the Sacrament in both kinds, and liberty for priests
to marry ; but the latter change did not receive parliamentary sanction
until the following year. The bill against " unreverent " speaking of the
Sacrament was, by skilful parliamentary strategy which seems to have
been due to Somerset, combined with one for its administration in both
kinds, the motive being obviously to induce Catholics to vote for it for
the sake of the first part, and Reformers for the sake of the second. The
Chantries Bill was in the main a renewal of the Act of 1545 ; but its
object was now declared to be the endowment of education, and not the
defence of the realm ; and the reason alleged for suppression was the
encouragement that chantries gave to superstition and not their appro-
priation by private persons. Such opposition as this bill encountered was
due less to theological objections than to the reluctance of corporations
to surrender any part of their revenues ; and Gardiner subsequently
expressed his concurrence in the measure. Its effect on gilds was to
convert such of their revenues as had previously been devoted to obits
and masses into a rent paid to the Crown ; but a bill, which was introduced a year later and passed the House of Commons, to carry out the
intentions of founding schools alleged in the Chantries Act, disappeared
after its first reading in the House of Lords on February 18, 1549.

Immediately after the prorogation in January, 1548, questions were
addressed to the Bishops as to the best form of Communion service ; the
answers varied, some being in favour of the exclusive use of English, some
of the exclusive use of Latin. The form actually adopted approaches
most nearly to Tunstall's recommendation, a compromise whereby Latin
was retained for the essential part of the Mass, while certain prayers in
English were adopted. This new Order for Communion was issued in
March, 1548, a Proclamation ordering its use after Easter was prefixed,
and in a rubric all " varying of any rite or ceremony in the Mass " was

forbidden. A more decided innovation was made in February, when by Proclamation the Council ordered the removal of all images, under the impression that this drastic measure would cause less disturbance than the widespread contentions as to whether the images were abused or not. Ashes and palms and candles on Candlemas Day had been forbidden in January; and soon afterwards a Proclamation was issued against the practice of creeping to the cross on Good Friday and the use of holy bread and holy water. These prohibitions had been contemplated under Henry VIII; they met with guarded approval from Gardiner; and they were comparatively slight concessions to the Reformers in a Proclamation, the main purpose of which was to check unauthorised innovations. The Council also sought to remove a fruitful cause of tumult by forbidding the clergy to preach outside their own cures without a special licence. How far this bore hardly on the Catholics depends upon the proportion of Catholics to Reformers among the beneficed clergy; but it is fairly obvious that it was directed against the two extremes, the ejected monks on the one hand and the itinerant "hot-gospellers" on the other.

These measures were temporary expedients designed to preserve some sort of quiet, pending the production of the one "uniform and godly" order of service towards which the Church had been moving ever since the break with Rome. The assertion of the national character of the English Church necessarily involved an attempt at uniformity in its services. The legislation of 1547 seemed to imply unlimited religious liberty, and to leave the settlement of religious controversy to public discussion; but it was not possible to carry out a reformation solely by means of discussion. Local option, too, was alien to the centralising government of the Tudors, and, unchecked, might well have precipitated a Thirty Years' War in England. Uniformity, however, was not the end which the government had in view, so much as the means to ensure peace and quietness. Somerset was less anxious to obliterate the liturgical variations between one parish and another, than to check the contention between Catholics and Reformers which made every parish the scene of disorder and strife; and the only way he perceived of effecting this object was to draw up one uniform order, a compromise and a standard which all might be persuaded or compelled to observe. Nor was the idea of uniformity a novel one. There were various Uses in medieval England, those of York, Hereford, Lincoln, and Sarum; but the divergence between these forms of service was slight, and before the Reformation the Sarum Use seems to have prevailed over the greater part of the kingdom.

As regards doctrine, the several formularies issued by Henry VIII accustomed men to the idea that the teaching of the Church of England should be uniform and something different from that of either Catholic or Reformed Churches on the Continent. Nor was it only in the eyes of antipapalists that some reformation of Church service books seemed necessary.   The reformed Breviary of Cardinal Quignon, dedicated in 1535 to Paul III, anticipated many of the changes which Cranmer made in the ancient Use.   In Catholic as well as in Protestant churches the medieval services were simplified and shortened, partly in view of the busier life of the sixteenth century, and partly to allow more time for preaching and reading the Scriptures.

Thus Cranmer was only following the general tendency when, in 1543, he obtained Henry's consent to the examination and reformation of the Church service books.   For some years he laboured at this task; but what stage he had reached in 1547 when Convocation demanded the production of his work is not clear.   That demand was refused; and it was not until September, 1548, that the final stage in the evolution of the First Book of Common Prayer was commenced.   Its development remains shrouded in obscurity.   There is no trace of any formal commission to execute the task, of the composition of the revising body, or of the place where it carried on its work.   Cranmer without doubt took the principal part, and once at least he called other divines to help him at Windsor; but it is unsafe to assume that the revisers continued to sit there, or indeed that there was any definite body of revisers at all. Probably about the end of October most of the Bishops were invited to subscribe to the completed book; but it seems to have undergone further alteration without their consent, and there is not sufficient evidence to show that it was submitted to Convocation.   In December, it was in the House of Lords the subject of an animated debate in which Cranmer, Ridley, and Sir Thomas Smith defended, and Tunstall, Bonner, Thirlby, and Heath attacked, the way in which it treated the doctrine of the Mass.

Cranmer himself had already advanced beyond the point of view adopted in the First Book of Common Prayer.   In the autumn of 1548 Bullinger's correspondents had rejoiced over the Archbishop's abandonment of Lutheran views; but the doctrine assumed, if not affirmed, in the new Book seemed to them to constitute " a marvellous recantation."   The First Book of Common Prayer bore, indeed, little resemblance to the service books of the Zwinglian and Calvinistic Churches. Its affinity with Lutheran liturgies was more marked, because the Anglican and Lutheran revisers made the ancient Uses of the Church their groundwork, while the other Reformed churches sought to obliterate as far as possible all traces of the Mass.   It is the most conservative of all the liturgies of the Reformation; its authors wished to build upon, and not to destroy, the past; and the materials on which they worked were almost exclusively the Sarum Use and the Breviary of Cardinal Quignon.   Whatever intention they may have had of denying the supplemental character of the sacrifice of the Mass was studiously veiled by the retention of Roman terminology in a somewhat equivocal sense; room was to be made, if possible, for both interpretations; the sacrifice might be regarded as real and absolute, or merely as commemorative and analogical. The "abominable canon" was removed because it shut the door on all but the Roman doctrine of the Mass, and the design of the government was to open the door to the New Learning without definitely closing it on the Old.

The intention was to make the uniform order tolerable to as many as was possible, and the result was a cautious and tentative compromise, a sort of Anglican *Interim*, which was more successful than its German counterpart. The penalties attached to its non-observance by the First Act of Uniformity were milder than those imposed by any of the subsequent Acts, and they were limited to the clergy. Neither in the First Act of Uniformity nor in the First Book of Common Prayer is there any attempt to impose a doctrinal test or dogmatic unity. All that was enforced was a uniformity of service; and even here considerable latitude was allowed in details like vestments and ritual. A few months later a licensed preacher declared at St Paul's, that faith was not to be "coacted," but that every man might believe as he would. Doctrinal unity was in fact incompatible with that appeal to private judgment which was the essence of the Reformation, and Somerset's government was wise in limiting its efforts to securing an outward and limited uniformity.

Even this was sufficiently difficult. Eager Reformers began at once to agitate for the removal of those parts of the Book of Common Prayer which earned Gardiner's commendation, while Catholics resented its departure from the standard of orthodoxy set up by the Six Articles. Religious liberty was in itself distasteful to the majority; and zealots on either side were less angered by the persecution of themselves than by the toleration of their enemies. Dislike of the new service book was keenest in the west, where the men of Cornwall spoke no English and could not understand an English service book; they knew little Latin, but they were accustomed to the phrases of the ancient Use, and men tolerate the incomprehensible more easily than the unfamiliar. So they rose in July, 1549, and demanded the restoration of the old service, the old ceremonies, the old images, and the ancient monastic endowments. They asked that the Sacrament should be administered to laymen in one kind and only at Easter — a strange demand in the mouths of those who maintained the supreme importance of the sacramental system — and that all who refused to worship it should suffer death as heretics; the Bibles were to be called in again, and Cardinal Pole was to be made first or second in the King's Council.

On the whole the Protector's religious policy was accompanied by singularly little persecution; and the instances quoted by Roman Catholic writers date almost without exception from the period after his fall. The Princess Mary flatly refused to obey the new law; and after some remonstrance Somerset granted her permission to hear Mass privately in her own house. Gardiner was more of an opportunist than Mary; probably he thought that his opposition would be the more effective for being less indiscriminate. But it was no less deliberate, and in the early and effective days of the Royal Supremacy, when Bishops were regarded as ecclesiastical sheriffs, their resistance to authority was as little tolerated as that of the soldier or the civil servant would be now. Gardiner was sent to the Fleet, but he was treated by Somerset with what was considered excessive lenience ; and in January, 1548, he was, by the King's general pardon, released. He returned to his diocese, and preached obedience to the Council on the ground that to suffer evil was a Christian's duty. The reason was scarcely pleasing to the government, and on June 29 he was ordered to preach a sermon at Whitehall declaring the supreme ecclesiastical authority of the young King during his minority ; at the same time he was forbidden to deal with the doctrines that were in dispute. On neither point did he give satisfaction, and on the following day he was sent to the Tower. Bonner was sent to the Marshalsea for a similar reason. He had protested against the visitation of 1547, but withdrew his protest, and after a few weeks in the Fleet remained at liberty until September, 1549. He was then accused of not enforcing the new Book of Common Prayer and was ordered to uphold the ecclesiastical authority of the King in a sermon at St Paul's ; on his failure to do so he was imprisoned and deprived by Cranmer of his bishopric ; and at the same time his chaplain Feckenham was sent to the Tower. These, however, are practically the only instances of religious persecution exercised during Somerset's protectorate.

This comparative moderation, while consonant with the Protector's own inclination, was also rendered advisable by the critical condition of England's relations with foreign powers. Any violent breach with Catholicism, any bitter persecution of its adherents, would have turned into open enmity the lukewarm friendship of Charles V, precipitated that hostile coalition of Catholic Europe for which the Pope and Cardinal Pole were intriguing, and rendered impossible the union with Scotland on which the Tudors had set their hearts. For this reason Somerset declined (March, 1547) the proffered alliance of the German Protestant Princes ; and, to strengthen his position, he began negotiations for a treaty with France, and discussed the possibility of a marriage between the Princess Elizabeth and a member of the French royal family. The treaty was on the point of ratification when the death of Francis I (March 31) produced a revolution in French policy. The new King, Henry II, had, when Dauphin, proclaimed his intention of demanding the immediate retrocession of Boulogne ; but his designs were not confined to the expulsion of the English from France. He also dreamt of a union with Scotland. Through Diane de Poitiers the Guise influence was strong at Paris ; through Mary de Guise, the Queen Regent of Scotland, it was almost as powerful at Edinburgh ; and England was menaced with a *pacte de famille* more threatening than that of the Bourbons two centuries later. Even Francis had considered a scheme

for marrying the infant Queen of Scots to a French Prince ; and, while
Henry VIII in his last days had been organising a new invasion of
Scotland, the French King had been equally busy with preparations for
the defence of his ancient allies.

Henry II of France changed a defensive into an offensive policy ; and,
in taking up the Scottish policy urged upon him by Henry VIII, Somerset
was seeking, not merely to carry out one of the most cherished of Tudor
aims, but to ward off a danger which now presented itself in more
menacing guise than ever before.   There might be doubts as to the
policy of pressing the union with Scotland at that juncture — there could
be none as to the overwhelming and immediate necessity of preventing
a union between Scotland and France ; and Gardiner's advice, to let
the Scots be Scots until the King of England came of age, would have
been fatal unless he could guarantee a similar abstinence during the
same period on the part of Henry II.   Somerset, however, pursued
methods different from those of Henry VIII.   He abandoned alike the
feudal claim to suzerainty over Scotland and the claim to sovereignty
which Henry had asserted in 1542 ; he refrained from offensive references to James V as a " pretensed king " ; he endeavoured to persuade
the Scots that union was as much the interest of Scotland as of
England ; and all he required was the fulfilment of the treaty which the
Scots themselves had made in 1543.   His efforts were vain ; encouraged
by French aid in men, money, and ships, the Scottish government refused
to negotiate, and stirred up trouble in Ireland.   In September, 1547, the
Protector crossed the border, and on the 10th he won the crushing
victory of Pinkie Cleugh.   The result was to place the Lowlands at
England's mercy ; and, thinking he had shown the futility of resistance,
Somerset attempted to complete the work by conciliation.

During the winter he put forward some remarkable suggestions for
the Union between England and Scotland.   He proposed to abolish the
names of English and Scots associated with centuries of strife, and to
" take again the old indifferent name of Britons."   The United Kingdom
was to be known as the Empire, and its sovereign as the Emperor of
Great Britain.   There was to be no forfeiture of lands or of liberty,
but freedom of trade and of marriage.   Scotland was to retain her local
autonomy, and the children of her Queen were to rule over England.
Never in the history of the two realms had such liberal terms been
offered, but reason, which might have counselled acceptance, was no
match for pride, prejudice, and vested interests.   Care was taken that
these proposals should not reach the mass of the Scottish people.   Most
of the nobility were in receipt of French pensions ; and the influence of the
Church was energetically thrown into the scale against accommodation
with a schismatic enemy.   It was only among the peasantry, where
Protestantism had made some way, that the Union with England was
popular ; and that influence was more than counterbalanced by the

presence of French soldiery in the streets of Edinburgh and in most of the strongholds of Scotland. The seizure of Haddington in April, 1548, secured for a year the English control of the Lowlands; but it did not prevent the young Queen's transportation to France, where she was at once betrothed to the Dauphin. This step provoked Somerset in October to revive once more England's feudal claims over Scotland, and to hint that the English King had a voice in the marriage of his vassal. But the Guises could afford to laugh at threats, since they knew that the internal condition of England in 1549 prevented the threats being backed by adequate force in Scotland or in France. In both kingdoms they became more aggressive; they were in communication with rebels in Ireland, and in January, 1549, a French emissary was sent to England to see if Thomas Seymour's conspiracy might be fanned into civil war.

Thomas Seymour, the only one of the Protector's brothers who showed any aptitude or inclination for public life, had served with distinction on sea and land under Henry VIII. He had commanded a fleet in the Channel in 1545, had been made master of the Ordnance, and had wooed Catharine Parr before she became Henry's sixth wife. A few days before the end of the late reign he was sworn of the Privy Council; and on Edward's accession he was made Baron Seymour and Lord High Admiral. These dignities seemed to him poor compared with his brother's, and he thought he ought to be governor of the King's person. After unsuccessful attempts to secure the hands of the Princess Mary, the Princess Elizabeth, and Anne of Cleves, he married Catharine Parr without consulting his colleagues; and before her death he renewed his advances to the Princess Elizabeth. He refused the command of the fleet during the Pinkie campaign, and stayed at home to create a party for himself in the country. He suffered pirates to prey on the trade of the Channel, and himself received a share of their ill-gotten goods; he made a corrupt bargain with Sir William Sharington, who provided him with money by tampering with the Bristol mint, and he began to store arms and ammunition in various strongholds which he acquired for the purpose. The disclosure of Sharington's frauds (January, 1549) brought Seymour's plots to light. After many examinations, in which Warwick and Southampton took a leading part, a bill of attainder against the Admiral was introduced into Parliament; it passed, with a few dissentients, in the House of Commons, and unanimously in the House of Lords, and on March 20 Seymour was executed. The sentence was probably just, but the Protector paid dearly for his weakness in allowing it to be carried out. His enemies, such as Warwick and Southampton, who seem to have been the prime movers in Seymour's ruin, perceived more clearly than Somerset, how fatally his brother's death would undermine his own position and alienate popular favour in the struggle on which he had now embarked in the cause of the poor against the great majority of the Council and of the ruling classes in England.

This struggle was fought over the Protector's attitude towards the momentous social revolution of the sixteenth century, a movement which lay at the root of most of the internal difficulties of Tudor governments, and vitally affected the history of the reign of Edward VI. It was in effect the breaking up of the foundations upon which society had been based for five hundred years, the substitution of competition for custom as the regulating principle of the relations between the various classes of the community.

Social organisation in medieval times was essentially conservative; custom was the characteristic sanction to which appeal was universally made. Land, in the eyes of its military feudal lord, was valuable less as a source of money than as a source of men; it was not rent but service that he required, and he was seldom tempted to reduce his service-roll in order to swell his rèvenues. But the Black Death and the Peasants' Revolt, co-operating with more silent and gradual causes, weakened the mutual bonds of interest between landlord and tenant, while the extension of commerce produced a wealthy class which slowly gained admission into governing circles and established itself on the land. To these new landlords land was mainly an investment; they applied to it the principles they practised in trade; and sought to extract from it not men but money. They soon found that the *petite culture* of feudal times was not the most profitable use to which land could be turned; and they began the practice known as "engrossing," of which complaint was made as early as 1484 in the Lord Chancellor's speech to Parliament. Their method was to buy up several holdings, which they did not lease to so many yeomen, but consolidated, leaving the old homesteads to decay; the former tenants became either vagabonds or landless labourers, who boarded with their masters and were precluded by their position from marrying and raising families. Similarly the new landed gentry sought to turn their vague and disputed rights over common lands into palpable means of revenue. Sometimes with and often without the consent of the commoners, they proceeded to enclose vast stretches of land with a view to converting it either to tillage or to pasture. The latter proved to be the more remunerative, owing to the great development of the wool-market in the Netherlands; and it was calculated that the lord, who converted open arable land into enclosed pasture land, thereby doubled his income.

Yet another method of extracting the utmost monetary value from the land was the raising of rents; it had rarely occurred to the un-commercial feudal lord to interfere with the ancient service or rent which his tenants paid for their lands, but respect for immemorial custom counted for little against the retired trader's habit of demanding the highest price for his goods. The direct result of these tendencies was to pauperise a large section of the community, though the aggregate wealth of the whole was increased. The English yeomen, who had supplied the backbone of English armies and the great majority of students at English Universities, were depressed into vagabonds or hired labourers. As indirect results, schools and universities declined ; and foreign mercenaries took the place of English soldiers ; for " shepherds," wrote a contemporary, " be but ill archers."

These evils had not passed without notice from statesmen and writers in the previous reign. Wolsey, inspired perhaps by Sir Thomas More, had in 1517 made a vigorous effort to check enclosures ; and More himself had sympathetically pourtrayed the grievances of the population in the pages of his *Utopia*. Later in the reign of Henry VIII remedial measures had been warmly urged by conservatives like Thomas Lupset and Thomas Starkey, and by more radical thinkers like Brynkelow and Robert Crowley. But the King and his ministers were absorbed in the task of averting foreign complications and effecting a religious revolution, while courtiers and ordinary members of Parliament were not concerned to check a movement from which they reaped substantial profit. After the accession of Edward VI the constant aggravation of the evil and the sympathy it was known to evoke in high quarters brought the question more prominently forward. The Protector himself denounced with more warmth than prudence the misdeeds of new lords " sprung from the dunghill." Latimer inveighed against them in eloquent sermons preached at Court ; Scory told the young King that his subjects had become " more like the slavery and peasantry of France than the ancient and godly yeomanry of England." Cranmer, Lever, and other reforming divines held similar opinions, but the most earnest and active member of the party, which came to be known as the " Commonwealth's men," was John Hales, whose *Discourse of the Common Weal* is one of the most informing documents of the age.

The existence of this party alarmed the official class, but the Protector more or less openly adopted its social programme ; and it was doubtless with his connivance that various remedial measures were introduced into Parliament in December, 1547. One bill " for bringing up poor men's children " was apparently based on a suggestion made by Brynkelow in the previous reign that a certain number of the poorest children in each town should be brought up at the expense of the community ; another bill sought to give farmers and lessees security of tenure ; and a third provided against the decay of tillage and husbandry. None of these bills got beyond a second reading, and the only measure which found favour with Parliament was an Act which provided that a weekly collection in churches should be made for the impotent poor, and that confirmed vagabonds might be sold into slavery.

The failure of Parliament to find adequate remedies was the signal for agrarian disturbances in Hertfordshire and other counties in the spring of 1548 ; and the Protector, moved thereto by divers supplications, some of which are extant, now determined to take action independently of Parliament.   On the first of June he issued a Proclamation, in which he referred to the "insatiable greediness" of those by whose means "houses were decayed, parishes diminished, the force of the realm weakened, and Christian people eaten up and devoured of brute beasts and driven from their houses by sheep and bullocks." Commissioners were appointed to enquire into the extent of enclosures made since 1485 and the failure of previous legislation to check them, and to make returns of those who broke the law.

The commissioners, of whom Hales was the chief, encountered an organised and stubborn resistance from those on whose conduct they were to report.   With a view to disarming opposition, the presentment of offenders was postponed, until evidence should have been collected to form the basis of measures to be laid before Parliament ; and subsequently Hales obtained from the Protector a general pardon of the offenders presented by the commission.   Both measures failed to mollify the gentry, who resolutely set themselves to burke the enquiry.   They packed the juries with their own servants ; they threatened to evict tenants who gave evidence against them, and even had them indicted at the assizes.   Other means taken to conceal the truth were the ploughing up of one furrow in a holding enclosed to pasture, the whole being then returned as arable land, and the placing of a couple of oxen with a flock of sheep and passing off the sheep-run as land devoted to fatting beasts.   Under these circumstances it was with difficulty that the commissioners could get to work at all ; and only those commissions on which Hales sat appear to have made any return.   The opposition was next transferred to the Houses of Parliament.   In November, 1548, Hales introduced various bills for maintaining tillage and husbandry, for restoring tenements which had been suffered to decay, and for checking the growth of sheep-farms.   An Act was passed remitting the payment of fee-farms for three years in order that the proceeds might be devoted to finding work for the unemployed ; and a tax of twopence was imposed on every sheep kept in pasture.   But the more important bills were received with open hostility ; and after acrimonious debates they were all rejected either by the Lords or by the Commons.

This result is not surprising, for the statute of 1430 had limited parliamentary representation, so far as the agricultural districts were concerned, to the landed gentry ; and there are frequent complaints of the time that the representation of the boroughs had also fallen mainly into the hands of capitalists, who, by engrossing household property and monopolising trade, were providing the poorer townsfolk with grievances similar to those of the country folk.   Nor was there a masterful Tudor to overawe resistance.   The government was divided, for Somerset's adoption of the peasants' cause had driven the majority of the Council into secret opposition.   Warwick seized the opportunity.   Hitherto there had been no apparent differences between him and Somerset ; but now his park was ploughed up as an illegal enclosure, and he fiercely attacked Hales as the cause of the agrarian discontent. Other members of the government, including even his ally Paget, remonstrated with the Protector, but without effect, except to stiffen his back and confirm him in his course. Fresh instructions were issued to the commissioners in 1549; and, having failed to obtain relief for the poor by legislation, Somerset resorted to the arbitrary expedient of erecting a sort of Court of Requests, which sat in his own house under Cecil's presidency to hear any complaint that poor suitors might bring against their oppressors.

Measures like these were of little avail to avert the dangers Somerset feared. Parliament had scarcely disposed of his bills, when the resentment of the peasants found vent in open revolt. The flame was kindled first in Somersetshire; thence it spread eastwards into Wilts and Gloucestershire, southwards into Dorset and Hampshire and northwards into Berks and the shires of Oxford and Buckingham. Surrey remained in a state of "quavering quiet"; but Kent felt the general impulse. Far in the west Cornwall and Devon rose; and in the east the men of Norfolk captured Norwich and established a "commonwealth" on Mousehold Hill, where Robert Ket, albeit himself a landlord of ancient family, laid down the law, and no rich man did what he liked with his own. The civil war, which the French king had hoped to evoke from Seymour's conspiracy, seemed to have come at last, and with it the opportunity of France. On August 8, 1549, at Whitehall Palace, the French ambassador made a formal declaration of war.

The successful Chauvinist policy of the French government would have precipitated a conflict long before but for the efforts of the English to avoid it. Henry II had begun his reign by breaking off the negotiations for an alliance with England, and declining to ratify the arrangement which the English and French commissioners had drawn up for the delimitation of the Boulonnais. But a variety of circumstances induced him to modify for a time his martial ardour, and restrict his hostility to a policy of pin-pricks administered to the English in their French possessions. The complete defeat of the German Princes at Mühlberg (April, 1547) made Henry anxious as to the direction in which the Emperor would turn his victorious arms; and the route of the Scots at Pinkie five months later inspired a wholesome respect for English power. Then, in 1548, Guienne broke out in revolt against the *gabelle*, and clamoured for the privileges it had once enjoyed under its English kings. Charles V, moreover, although he disliked the religious changes in England and declined to take any active part against the Scots, gave the French to understand that he considered the Scots his enemies. Somerset, meanwhile, did his best to keep on friendly terms with Charles, and sought to mitigate his dislike of the First Act of Uniformity by granting the Princess Mary a dispensation to hear mass in private. Unless the Emperor's attention was absorbed elsewhere, a French attack on England might provoke an imperial onslaught on France.

Still, the endless bickerings with France about Boulogne were very exasperating; and eventually the Protector offered to restore it at once for the sum stipulated in the treaty of 1546, if France would further the marriage between Edward VI and Mary, Queen of Scots. That, however, was the last thing to which the Guises would consent; the preservation of their influence in Scotland was at that moment the mainspring of their action and the chief cause of the quarrel with England. The only condition on which they would keep the peace was the abandonment of Scotland to their designs, and that condition the Protector refused to the last to grant. Before the end of June, 1549, the French had assumed so threatening an attitude that Somerset sent Paget to Charles V with proposals for the marriage of the Princess Mary with the Infante John of Portugal, for the delivery of Boulogne into the Emperor's hands, and for a joint invasion of France by Imperial and English armies. This embassy seems to have alarmed Henry II, and he at once appointed commissioners to settle the disputes in the Boulonnais. The Protector thereupon forbade Paget to proceed with the negotiations for a joint invasion. The Emperor at the same time, doubtful of the value of England's alliance in her present disturbed condition, and immersed in anxieties of his own, declined to undertake the burden of Boulogne, or to knit any closer his ties with England. This refusal encouraged the French king to begin hostilities. He had collected an army on the borders of the Boulonnais; and in August it crossed the frontier. Ambleteuse (Newhaven) was captured through treachery; Blackness was taken by assault; Boulogneberg was dismantled and abandoned by the English; and the French forces sat down to besiege Boulogne.

The success of the French was mainly due to England's domestic troubles. Levies which had been raised for service in France were diverted to Devon or Norfolk. Fortunately, both these revolts were crushed before the war with France had lasted a fortnight. The rising in the west, for which religion had furnished a pretext and enclosures the material, died away after the fight at the Barns of Crediton, and the relief of Exeter by Russell on August 9. The eastern rebels, who were stirred solely by social grievances, caused more alarm; and a suspicion lest the Princess Mary should be at their back gave some of the Council sleepless nights. The Marquis of Northampton was driven out of Norwich, and the restraint and orderliness of the rebels' proceedings secured them a good deal of sympathy in East Anglia. Warwick, however, to whom the command was now entrusted, was a soldier of real ability, and with the help of Italian and Spanish mercenaries he routed the insurgents on August 26 at the battle of Dussindale, near Mousehold Hill. His victory made Warwick the hero of the gentlemen of England.   He had always opposed the Protector's agrarian schemes, and he was now in a position to profit by their failure.

The revolts had placed Somerset in a predicament from which a modern minister would have sought refuge in resignation.   His sympathy with the insurgents weakened his action against them ; and his readiness to pardon and reluctance to proscribe exasperated most of his colleagues.   He was still obstinate in his assertion of the essential justice of the rebels' complaints, and was believed to be planning for the approaching meeting of Parliament more radical measures of redress than had yet been laid before it.   Paget wrote in alarm lest far-reaching projects should be rashly adopted which required ten years' deliberation ; and other officials made Cecil the recipient of fearful warnings against the designs of the "Commonwealth's men."   The Council and the governing classes generally were in no mood for measures of conciliation, and disasters abroad and disorders at home afforded a good pretext for removing the man to whom it was convenient to ascribe them.

The malcontents found an excellent party-leader in Warwick ; few men in English history have shown a greater capacity for subtle intrigue or smaller respect for principle.   A brilliant soldier, a skilful diplomatist, and an accomplished man of the world, he was described at the time as the modern Alcibiades.   No one could better turn to his own purposes the passions and interests of others, or throw away his tools with less compunction when they had served his end.   Masking profound ambitions under the guise of the utmost deference to his colleagues, he never at the time of his greatest influence attempted to claim a position of formal superiority.   Afterwards, when he was practically ruler of England, he sat only fourth in the order of precedence at the Council-board ; and content with the substance of power, he eschewed such titles as Protector of the Realm or Governor of the King's person.

In the general feeling of discontent he had little difficulty in uniting various sections in an attack on the Protector.   The public at large were put in mind of Somerset's ill-success abroad ; the landed gentry needed no reminder of his attempts to check their enclosures.   Protestant zealots recalled his slackness in dealing with Mass-priests, and Catholics hated his Prayer Book.   Hopes were held out to all ; Gardiner in the Tower expected his release ; Bonner appealed against his deprivation ; and Southampton made sure of being restored to the woolsack.   Privy Councillors had private griefs as well as public grounds to allege ; the Protector had usurped his position in defiance of Henry's will ; he had neglected their advice and browbeaten them when they remonstrated ; he consulted and enriched only his chosen friends ; Somerset House was erected, but Warwick's parks were ploughed up.

It was at Warwick's and Southampton's houses in Holborn that the plot against the Protector was hatched in September, 1549 ; and the immediate excuse for his deposition appears to have been the abandonment,

after a brave defence, of Haddington, the chief English stronghold
in Scotland (September 14). Somerset had left Westminster on the
12th with the King and removed to Hampton Court; Cranmer, Paget,
St John, the two Secretaries of State, Petre and Sir Thomas Smith,
and the Protector's own Secretary, Cecil, remained with him till the
beginning of October; but the rest of the Council secretly gathered in
London and collected their retainers. The aldermen of the City were
on their side, but the apprentices and poorer classes generally adhered
to the Protector. One of Warwick's methods of enlisting the support
of the army was to send their captains to Somerset with petitions
for higher pay than he knew the Protector could grant. The Duke
apparently suspected nothing, unless suspicion be traced in the "matter
of importance" to which he referred in his letter of the 27th, urging
Russell and Herbert to hasten their return from the west. But by the
3rd or 4th of October rumours of what was happening reached him.
On the latter day that "crafty fox Shebna," as Knox called St John,
deserted to his colleagues in London, and secured the Tower by dis-
placing Somerset's friends. On the 6th Somerset sent Petre to demand
an explanation of the Council's conduct; but Petre did not return.

The Protector now thought of raising the masses against the classes.
Handbills were distributed inciting the commons to rise in his defence;
extortioners and "great masters" were conspiring, they were told, against
the Protector because he had procured the peasants their pardon. On
the night of the 6th he hurried the King to Windsor for the sake of
greater security. But either he repented of his efforts to stir a social
war, or he saw that they would be futile; for in a letter to the Council
on the 7th he offered to submit upon reasonable conditions drawn up by
representatives of both parties. The Council in London delayed their
answer until they had heard from Russell and Herbert, to whom both
parties had appealed for help. The commanders of the western army
were at Wilton, and their action would decide the issue of peace or war.
They promptly strengthened their forces, and moved up to Andover.
There they found the country in a general uproar; five or six thousand
men from the neighbouring counties were preparing to march to Somerset's aid. But Russell and Herbert were disgusted with the Protector's inflammatory appeals to the turbulent commons; they threw
the whole weight of their influence on the Council's side, and succeeded
in quieting the commotion, reporting their measures to both the rival
factions.

On receipt of this intelligence the Lords in London brushed aside
the conciliatory pleas of the King, Cranmer, Paget, and Smith, and took
steps to effect the Protector's arrest. They were aided by treacherous
advice from Paget, who purchased his own immunity at the expense of his
colleagues. In accordance probably with Paget's suggestions, Sir Philip
Hoby was sent to Windsor on the 10th with solemn promises from the

Council that the Duke should suffer no loss in lands, goods, or honours, and that his adherents should not be deprived of their offices. On the delivery of this message Paget fell on his knees before the Protector, and, with tears in his eyes, besought him to avail himself of the Council's merciful disposition. The others, relieved of their apprehensions, wept for joy and counselled submission. Somerset then gave way; and, through the "diligent travail" of Cranmer and Paget, his servants were removed from attendance on the King's person. When this measure had been effected, the Council no longer considered itself bound to observe the promises by which it had induced the Protector and his adherents to submit. Wingfield, St Leger, and Williams were sent with an armed force to arrest them all except Cranmer and Paget. On the 12th the whole Council went down to Windsor to complete the revolution. Somerset was conveyed to London, paraded as a prisoner through the streets, and shut up in the Tower; Smith was deprived of the secretary-ship, expelled from the Council, and also sent to the Tower; and a like fate befell the rest of those who had remained faithful to the Protector. Of the victors, Warwick resumed the office of Lord High Admiral, which had been vacant since Seymour's attainder; Dr Nicholas Wotton, who was also Dean of Canterbury and of York, succeeded Smith as Secretary; and Paget received a peerage in reward for his services. The distri-bution of the more important offices was deferred until it was settled which section of the Protector's opponents was to have the upper hand in the new government. For the present it was advisable to meet Parliament with as united a front as possible, in order to secure its sanction for the Protector's deposition, and its reversal of so much of his policy as both sections agreed in detesting.

On the broader aspects of that policy there was not much difference of opinion. Most people of influence distrusted that liberty on which Somerset set so much store. Sir John Mason, for instance, an able and educated politician, described his repeal of Henry VIII's laws concerning verbal treason as the worst act done in that generation; and in accordance with this view a bill was introduced declaring it felony to preach and hold "divers" opinions. Differences about the definition of the offence apparently caused this bill to fail; but measures sufficiently drastic were passed to stifle any opposition to the new government. Ministers sought to perpetuate their tenure of office by making it high treason for anyone to attempt to turn them out. That tremendous penalty, the heaviest known to the law, had hitherto been reserved for offences against the sacrosanct persons of royalty; it was now employed to protect those who wielded royal authority. It became high treason for twelve or more persons to meet with the object of killing or even imprisoning a member of the Privy Council—an unparalleled enactment which, had it been retrospective, would have rendered the Privy Council itself liable to a charge of treason for its action against the Protector. The same clause

imposed the same penalty upon persons assembling for the purpose of
"altering the laws"; and the Act also omitted the safeguards Somerset
had provided against the abuse of such treason laws as he had left on
the Statute-book; it contained no clause limiting the time within which
charges of treason were to be preferred or requiring the evidence of
two witnesses.

The fact that this Act did not pass until it had been read six times
in the Commons and six times in the Lords may indicate that it
encountered considerable opposition; but there was probably little hesitation in reversing the Protector's agrarian policy. Parliament was not
indeed content with that; it met (November 4, 1549) in a spirit of
exasperation and revenge, and it went back, not only upon the radical
proposals of Somerset, but also upon the whole tenour of Tudor land
legislation. Enclosures had been forbidden again and again; they were
now expressly declared to be legal; and Parliament enacted that lords
of the manor might "approve themselves of their wastes, woods, and
pastures notwithstanding the gainsaying and contradiction of their
tenants." In order that the process might be without let or hindrance,
it was made treason for forty, and felony for twelve, persons to meet for
the purpose of breaking down any enclosure or enforcing any right of
way; to summon such an assembly or incite to such an act was also
felony; and any copyholder refusing to help in repressing it forfeited
his copyhold for life. The same penalty was attached to hunting in
any enclosure and to assembling with the object of abating rents or the
price of corn; but the prohibition against capitalists conspiring to raise
prices was repealed, and so were the taxes which Somerset had imposed
on sheep and woollen cloths. The masses had risen against the classes,
and the classes took their revenge.

This, however, was not the kind of reaction most desired by the
Catholics who, led by Southampton, had assisted Warwick to overthrow
Somerset. Southampton was moved by private-grudges, but he also
desired a return to Catholic usages or at least a pause in the process of
change; and for a time it seemed that his party might prevail. "Those
cruel beasts, the Romanists," wrote one evangelical divine, were already
beginning to triumph, to revive the Mass, and to threaten faithful servants
of Christ with the fate of the fallen Duke. They were, said another,
struggling earnestly for their kingdom, and even Parliament felt it
necessary to denounce rumours that the old Latin service and superstitious uses would be restored. Southampton was one of the six lords to
whose charge the person of the King was specially entrusted; the Earl
of Arundel was another, and Southwell reappeared at the Council-
board. Bonner had been deprived by Cranmer in September; but no
steps were taken to find a successor, and the decision might yet be
reversed. Gardiner petitioned for release, while Hooper thought himself in the greatest peril.

So the balance trembled.   But Southampton was no match for " that most faithful and intrepid soldier of Christ," as Hooper styled Warwick. " England," he went on, "cannot do without him."   Neither could the Earl afford to discard such zealous adherents as the Reformers ; in them he found his main support.   They compared him with Moses and Joshua, and described him and Dorset as " the two most shining lights of the Church of England."   They believed that Somerset had been deposed for his slackness in the cause of religious persecution ; Warwick resolved to run no such risk.   The tendency towards religious change, which Henry VIII had failed to stop, was still strong, and Warwick threw himself into the stream.   Privately he seems, if he believed in anything, to have favoured Catholic doctrines ; and the consciousness of his insincerity made him all the louder in his professions of Protestant zeal, and all the more eager to push to extremes the principles of the Reformers. He became, in Hooper's words, " a most holy and fearless instrument of the Word of God."

But this policy could not be combined with the conciliation of Catholics ; and the coalition which had driven Somerset from power fell asunder, as soon as its immediate object had been achieved, and it was called upon to formulate a policy of its own.   Southampton ceased to attend the Council after October ; and Parliament, which had completely reversed the Protector's liberal and social programme, effected almost as great a change in the methods and aims of his religious policy.   The direction may have been the same, but it is pure assumption to suppose that the Protector would have gone so far as his successors or employed the same violence to attain his ends.   The difference in character between the two administrators was vividly illustrated in the session of Parliament which began a month after the change.   Under Somerset there had always been a good attendance of Bishops, and a majority of them had voted for all his religious proposals ; at the opening of the first session after his fall there were only nine Bishops, and a majority of them voted against two of the three measures of ecclesiastical importance passed during its course.   One was the Act for the destruction of all service books other than the Book of Common Prayer and Henry's Primer ; and the other was a renewal of the provision for the reform of Canon Law.   A majority of Bishops voted for the bill appointing a commission to draw up a new Ordinal ; but, when they complained that their jurisdiction was despised and drafted a bill for its restoration, the measure was rejected.

The prorogation of Parliament (February, 1550) was followed by the final overthrow of the Catholic party and the complete establishment of Warwick's control over the government.   He had already begun to pack the Council, which had remained practically unchanged since Henry's death, by adding to it five of his own adherents.   Southampton was now expelled from the Council, Arundel was deprived of his office of Lord Chamberlain, and Southwell was sent to the Tower.   The offices vacated by the Catholic lords and Somerset's party were distributed among Warwick's friends. St John became Earl of Wiltshire and Lord High Treasurer; Warwick succeeded him as Lord Great Master of the Household and President of the Council; and Northampton succeeded Warwick as Great Chamberlain of England. Arundel's office of Chamberlain of the Household was conferred on Wentworth, and Paget's Comptrollership on Wingfield; Russell was created Earl of Bedford, and Herbert was made President of the Council of Wales.

The new government now felt firm in the saddle, and it proceeded to turn its attention to foreign affairs. His failure abroad had been the chief ostensible reason for Somerset's downfall; but his successors had done nothing to redeem their implied promise of amendment. In spite of the fact that the agrarian insurrections — the immediate cause of the Protector's reverses in France and Scotland — had been suppressed, and large bodies of troops thus set free for service elsewhere, not a place had been recaptured in France, and in Scotland nearly all the English strongholds fell during the winter into the enemy's hands. The Council preferred peace to an attempt to retrieve their fortunes by war; and early in 1550 Warwick made secret overtures to Henry II. The French pushed their advantage to the uttermost; and the peace concluded in March was the most ignominious treaty signed by England during the century.

Boulogne, which was to have been restored four years later for 800,000 crowns, was surrendered for half that sum. All English strongholds in Scotland were to be given up without compensation; England bound itself to make no war on that country unless fresh grounds of offence were given, and condoned the marriage of Mary to the Dauphin of France. The net result was the abandonment of the whole Tudor policy towards Scotland, the destruction of English influence across the Border, and the establishment of French control in Edinburgh. Henry II began to speak of himself as King of Scotland; it was as much subject to him, he said, as France itself; and he boasted that by this peace he had now added to these two realms a third, namely England, of whose King, subjects, and resources he had such absolute disposal that the three might be reckoned as one kingdom of which he was King. To make himself yet more secure, he began a policy of active, though secret, intervention in Ireland. Had he succeeded in this, he would really have held England in the hollow of his hand; had a son been born to Mary Stewart and Francis II, England might even have become a French province. Fortunately, the accession of Mary Tudor broke the French ring which girt England round about; but it was certainly not Warwick's merit that England was delivered from perhaps the most pressing foreign danger with which she was ever threatened.

While, however, the policy which Warwick adopted involved a reversal of the time-honoured Burgundian alliance and a criminal neglect of England's ultimate interests, its immediate effects were undeniably advantageous to the government. It was at once relieved from the pressure of war on two fronts, and an intolerable drain on the exchequer was stopped. Security from foreign interference afforded an excuse for reducing expenditure on armaments and military forces, and even for seriously impairing the effective strength of the navy, the creation of which had been Henry VIII's least questionable achievement; and the Council was left free to pursue its religious policy, even to the persecution of the Princess Mary, without fear of interruption from her cousin the Emperor. The alliance of England, Scotland, and France was a combination which Charles could not afford to attack, more particularly when the league between Henry II, Maurice of Saxony, and the reviving Protestant Princes in Germany gave him more than enough to do to defend himself. France, the persecutor of heresy at home, lent her support to the English government while it pursued its campaign against Roman doctrine, just as she had countenanced Henry VIII while he was uprooting the Roman jurisdiction.

The path of the government was thus made easy abroad; but at home it was crowded with difficulties. The diversity of religious opinion, which Henry VIII's severity had only checked and Somerset's lenience had encouraged, grew ever more marked. The New Learning was, in the absence of effective opposition, carrying all before it in the large cities; and the more trenchantly a preacher denounced the old doctrines, the greater were the crowds which gathered to hear him. The favourite divine in London was Hooper, who went far beyond anything which the Council had yet done or at present intended. Between twenty and thirty editions of the Bible had appeared since the beginning of the reign, and nearly all were made vehicles, by their annotations, of attacks on Catholic dogma. Altars, images, painted glass windows became the object of a popular violence which the Council was unable, even if it was willing, to restrain; and the parochial clergy indulged in a ritual lawlessness which the Bishops encouraged or checked according to their own individual preferences. That the majority of the nation disliked both these changes and their method may perhaps be assumed, but the men of the Old Learning made little stand against the men of the New. In a revolution the first advantage generally lies with the aggressors. The Catholics had not been rallied, nor the Counter-Reformation organised, and their natural leaders had been silenced for their opposition to the government. But there were deeper causes at work; the Catholic Church had latterly denied to the laity any voice in the determination of Catholic doctrine; but now the laity had been called in to decide. Discussion had descended from Court and from senate into the street, where only one of the parties was adequately equipped for the contest. Catholics still were content to do as they had been taught and to leave the matter to the clergy; they were ill fitted to cope with antagonists who regarded theology as a matter for private judgment, and had by study of the Scriptures to some extent prepared themselves for its exercise. The authority of the Church, to which Catholics bowed, had suffered many rude shocks; and in the appeal to the Scriptures they were no match for the zeal and conviction of their opponents.

Under the circumstances it might seem that the Council would have done well to resort to some of Henry VIII's methods for enforcing uniformity; and indeed both parties agreed in demanding greater rigour. But they could not agree on the question to whom the rigour should be applied; their contentions indirectly tended towards the emancipation of conscience from the control of authority, though such a solution seemed shocking alike to those who believed in the Royal and to those who believed in the Papal Supremacy. There was no course open to the government that would have satisfied all contemporary or modern critics. England was in the throes of a revolution in which no government could have maintained perfect order or avoided all persecution. The Council's policy lacked the extreme moderation and humanity of Somerset's rule, but it averted open disruption, and did so at the cost of less rigour than characterised the rule of Henry VIII, of Mary, or of Elizabeth.

At one end of the religious scale Joan Bocher, whom Somerset had left in prison after her condemnation by the ecclesiastical Courts in the hope that she might be converted, was burnt in May, 1550; and a year later another heretic, George van Paris, suffered a similar fate. Against Roman Catholics the penalties of the first Act of Uniformity now began to be enforced; but they were limited to clerical offenders and of these there seem to have been comparatively few. Dr Cole was expelled from the Wardenship of New College, and Dr Morwen, President of Corpus Christi, Oxford, was sent for a time to the Fleet; two divines, Crispin and Moreman, who had been implicated in the Cornish rebellion, were confined in the Tower; two of Gardiner's chaplains, Seton and Watson, are said to have been subjected to some restraint; four others, John Boxall, afterwards Queen Mary's Secretary, William Rastell, More's nephew, Nicholas Harpsfield and Dr Richard Smith, whose recantations were as numerous as his apologies for the Catholic faith, fled to Flanders; and these, with Cardinal Pole, whose attainder was not reversed, make up the list of those who are said by Roman martyrologists to have suffered for their belief in the reign of Edward VI. To them, however, must be added five or six Bishops, who were deposed. Bonner was the only Bishop deprived in 1550, but in the following year Gardiner, Heath of Worcester, Day of Chichester, and Voysey of Exeter all vacated their sees, and Tunstall of Durham was sent to the Tower. Their places were filled with zealous Reformers; Coverdale became Bishop of Exeter, Ridley succeeded Bonner at London, and Ponet took Ridley's see; Ponet was soon transferred to Gardiner's seat at Winchester, and Scory supplied the place left vacant by Ponet, but was almost at once translated to Day's bishopric at Chichester. Warwick wished to enthrone John Knox at Rochester as a whetstone to Cranmer, but the Scottish Reformer proved ungrateful; and Rochester, which had seen five Bishops in as many years, remained vacant to the end of the reign.

The most remarkable of these creations and translations, which were made by letters patent, was perhaps the elevation of Hooper to the see of Gloucester. Hooper had, after a course of Zwinglian theology at Zurich, become chaplain to the Protector on the eve of his fall; but he found a more powerful friend in Warwick, who made him Lent preacher at Court in February, 1550. He was one of those zealous and guileless Reformers in whom Warwick found his choicest instruments; he combined fervent denunciations of the evils of the times with extravagant admiration for the man in whom they were most strikingly personified; and, as soon as his Lenten sermons were finished, he was offered the see of Gloucester. He declined it from scruples about the new Ordinal, the oath invoking the Saints, and the episcopal vestments. After a nine months' controversy, in which the whole bench of Bishops, with Bucer and Martyr, were arrayed against him and only John à Lasco and Micronius appeared on his side, and after some weeks' confinement in the Fleet, Hooper allowed himself to be consecrated. The simultaneous vacancy of Worcester enabled the Council to sweep away one of Henry VIII's new bishoprics by uniting it with Gloucester; and another was abolished by the translation of Thirlby from Westminster to Norwich, and the reunion of the former see with London.

These episcopal changes afforded scope for another sort of ecclesiastical spoliation; most of the new Bishops were compelled to alienate some of their manors to courtiers as the price of their elevation; and Ponet went so far as to surrender all his lands in return for a fixed stipend of two thousand marks. These lands were for the most part distributed among Warwick's adherents; and no small portion of the chantry endowments and much Church plate found its way to the same destination. Somerset had issued a commission in 1547 for taking a general inventory of Church goods in order to prevent the private embezzling which was so common just before and during the course of the Reformation; and this measure was supplemented by various orders to particular persons or corporations to restore such plate and ornaments as they had appropriated. But it may be doubted whether these prohibitions were very effectual; and after Somerset's fall private and public spoliation went on rapidly until it culminated (March, 1551) in a comprehensive seizure by the government of all such Church plate as remained unappropriated.

The confiscation of chantry lands followed a similar course. The first charge upon them was the support of the displaced chantry priests, whose pensions in 1549 amounted to a sum equivalent to between two and three hundred thousand pounds in modern currency. The next was stated to be "the erecting of Grammar schools to the education of youth in virtue and godliness, the further augmenting of the Universities, and better provision for the poor and needy." But the bill introduced into Parliament in 1549 "for the making of schools" failed to pass the House of Lords; and the "further order" designed by the Protector was inevitably postponed. Meanwhile the confiscated chantry lands afforded tempting facilities for the satisfaction of the King's immediate needs. In 1548-9 some five thousand pounds' worth were sold and the proceeds devoted to the defence of the realm. But less legitimate practices soon obtained; the chantry lands were regarded as the last dish in the last course of the feast provided by the wealth of the Church, and the importunity of courtiers correspondingly increased. Grants as well as sales became common; the recipients, with few exceptions, repudiated the obligation to provide for schools out of their newly-won lands; and the fortunes of many private families were raised on funds intended for national education. A few schools were founded by private benefactors, and it is probable that education gained on the whole by its emancipation from the control of the Church. But it was not until the closing years of the reign that the government made a serious endeavour to secure the adequate maintenance of those schools whose foundations had been shaken by the abolition of chantries; and Edward VI's services to education consisted principally in assigning a fixed annual pension to schools whose endowments of much greater potential value had been appropriated.

These proceedings, like the other religious changes made during 1550 and 1551, were effected by the action of the Council, of individual Bishops, or of private persons; for Parliament, which Warwick distrusted, did not meet between February, 1550, and January, 1552. But some of the Council's measures were based upon legislation passed in the session of 1549-50; such were the wholesale destruction of old service books which wrought particular havoc among the libraries of Oxford and Cambridge, and the compilation and execution of the new Ordinal, which was published in March and brought into use in April, 1550. By it a number of ceremonies hitherto used at ordinations were discontinued; and it embodied a clause which has been divergently interpreted both as abolishing and as retaining all the minor orders beneath that of deacon. Ridley signalised his elevation to the see of London by a severe visitation of his diocese, and by reducing the altars in St Paul's and elsewhere to the status and estimation of "the Lord's tables." Corpus Christi Day and many Saints' days ceased to be observed partly because they savoured of popery, and partly because the cessation of work impeded the acquisition of wealth. Cranmer, Bucer, and Martyr wer   the Prayer Book, and the Council wa   the Princess Mary to relinquish her private masses, when suddenly in the autumn of 1551 the nation was startled by the news of another Court revolution.

Somerset, after his submission and deposition from the Protectorate, had been released from the Tower on February 6, 1550. In April he was readmitted to the Privy Council ; and in May he was made a gentleman of the privy chamber and received back such of his lands as had not already been sold. The Duke's easy-going nature induced him readily to forgive the indignities he had suffered at Warwick's hands ; and in June, 1550, the reconciliation went so far that a marriage was concluded between the Duke's daughter and Warwick's eldest son, Lord Lisle. From this time Somerset, to all appearance, took an active part in the government. But it was clear that he only existed on sufferance, as a dependant of the Earl of Warwick. The situation was too galling to last long. The Duke was allowed no free access to his royal nephew ; he was excluded from the innermost secrets of the ruling faction, and was often dependent for knowledge of the government's plans on such information as he could extract from attendants on the King ; he was not only opposed to almost every principle on which Warwick acted, but was personally an obstacle to the achievement of the designs which the Earl was beginning to cherish. He was thus, unless he was willing to be Warwick's tool, forced to become the centre of active or passive resistance — the leader of the opposition, in so far as Tudor practice tolerated such a personage. Within three months of his readmission to the Council he was exerting himself to procure the release of Gardiner, of the Earl of Arundel, and of other prisoners in the Tower ; and, while Warwick was absent, Somerset was strong enough to obtain the Council's promotion or restoration of several of his adherents. He attempted to prevent the withdrawal of the Princess Mary's licence to hear mass, and sought so far as he could to restore a friendly feeling between England and the Emperor. In these efforts he found considerable support among the moderate party ; and the spiritless conduct of foreign affairs by the new government, coupled with the harshness of its domestic administration, made many regret the Protector's deposition. Before the session of 1549–50 broke up, a movement was initiated for his restoration ; the project was defeated by a prorogation, but it was resolved to renew it as soon as Parliament met again, and this was one of the reasons why Parliament was not summoned till after Somerset's death.

Warwick viewed the Duke's conduct with anger, which increased as his own growing unpopularity made Somerset appear more and more formidable ; and before the end of September, 1551, Warwick had elaborated a comprehensive scheme for the further advancement of himself and his faction and for the total ruin of Somerset and the opposition. Cecil, the ablest of the ex-Protector's friends, had ingratiated himself with Warwick by his zeal against Gardiner at the time when Somerset was endeavouring to procure his release, and in September, 1550, he had been sworn one of the two Secretaries of State; a year later (October 4, 1551) he occurs among the list of Warwick's supporters marked out for promotion. Warwick himself was created Duke of Northumberland; Grey, Marquis of Dorset, became Duke of Suffolk; Wiltshire Marquis of Winchester; Herbert Earl of Pembroke; while knighthoods were bestowed on Cecil, Sidney (Warwick's son-in-law), Henry Dudley (his kinsman), and Henry Neville. On the 16th Somerset and his friends, including Lord Grey de Wilton, the Earl of Arundel, and a dozen others, were arrested and sent to the Tower; Paget had been sequestered a fortnight earlier, to get him out of the way.

The real cause and occasion of this sudden *coup d'état* are still obscure. It is probable that foreign affairs had more to do with the matter than appears on the surface. The Constable of France, when informed of it, suggested that Charles V and the Princess Mary were probably at Somerset's back, and offered to send French troops to Northumberland's aid; it is quite as likely that Henry II was at the bottom of Northumberland's action. Somerset had, since the days when he served in the Emperor's suite, been an imperialist; and Charles V, who still professed a personal friendship for him, would have welcomed his return to power in place of the Francophil administration, which had just (June, 1551) put the seal on its foreign policy by negotiating a marriage between Edward VI and Henry II's daughter, Elizabeth. The dispute with the Emperor concerning the treatment of the Princess Mary was at its height; and it is possible that plot and counterplot were in essence a struggle between French and Imperial influence in England. In any case the stories told to the young King and published abroad were obviously false; Edward was informed that his uncle had plotted the murder of Northumberland, Northampton, and Pembroke, the seizure of the Crown and other measures against himself, to which the young King's knowledge of the fate of Edward V would give a sinister interpretation; the people of London were informed that he meant to destroy the city.

The plot was said to have been hatched in April, 1551; but the first hint of its existence was conveyed to the government in a private conversation between Northumberland and Sir Thomas Palmer on October 4, long after the conspiracy, if it ever was real, had been abandoned. Palmer, who was one of the accomplices, was nevertheless left at liberty for a fortnight; he was never put upon his trial, and, when Somerset was finally disposed of, he became Northumberland's right-hand man; finally, he confessed before his death that his accusation had been invented at Northumberland's instigation. The Earl of Arundel, who, according to Northumberland's theory, had been the principal accomplice in Somerset's felony, was subsequently readmitted to the Council, became Lord Steward of the Household to Mary and to Elizabeth, and

Chancellor of the University of Oxford. Paget, at whose house the intended assassination was to have taken place, was never brought into Court ; neither was Lord Grey, another accomplice, who was afterwards made captain of Guines "as amends" for the unjust charge. To the minor conspirators a very simple principle was applied quite irrespective of their guilt : if they implicated Somerset, they were released without trial; if they persisted in asserting their own and his innocence they were executed. But, in spite of all Northumberland's efforts, no confirmation was obtained of Palmer's main charge. Scores of witnesses were imprisoned in the Tower and put to torture ; but the story of the intended assassination was so baseless that the charge did not appear in any one of the five indictments returned against Somerset, and was not so much as alluded to in the examinations of the Duke himself and his chief adherents.

Meanwhile, stringent measures were taken to prevent disturbance. The creation of Lords-Lieutenant put local administration and the local militia into the hands of Northumberland's friends, and provided him with an instrument akin to Cromwell's Major-generals. London was overawed by the newly-organised bands of *gens d'armes ;* and an effort was made to appease one source of dissatisfaction by proclaiming a new and purified coinage. Parliament, which was to have met in November, was further prorogued ; and Northumberland's control of the government was strengthened by a decision that the King's order (he was just fourteen) should be absolutely valid without the counter-signature of a single member of the Council. Lord-Chancellor Rich resigned soon after in alarm at this violent measure, and he consequently took no part in Somerset's trial. The tribunal consisted of twenty-six out of forty-seven peers ; among them were Northumberland, Northampton, and Pembroke, who were really parties in the case. They had already acted practically as accusers, had drawn up the charges, and examined the witnesses ; they now assumed the function of judges, and after their verdict determined whether it should be executed or not.

The trial took place on December 1 at Westminster Hall ; the charges were practically two, one of treason in conspiring to imprison a Privy Councillor, and one of felony in inciting to an unlawful assembly. Both these offences depended upon the atrocious statute which, passed in the panic of reaction after Somerset's fall, was to expire with the next session of Parliament — a further reason for its prorogation. In another respect the trial would not have been possible under any other Act ; for that Act removed the previous limitation of thirty days within which accusations must be preferred, and five months had elapsed between Somerset's alleged offences and Palmer's accusation. Nevertheless the charge of treason broke down, and the government boasted of its magnanimity in condemning the prisoner to death only for felony. There was as little evidence for that offence as for the other, and the sum of the ex-Protector's guilt appears to have been this : he had spoken to one or two friends of the advisability of arresting Northumberland, Northampton, and Pembroke, calling a Parliament, and demanding an account of their evil government.

Somerset was sent back to the Tower amid extravagant demonstrations of joy by the people, who thought he had been acquitted. He remained there seven weeks, and there was a general expectation that no further steps would be taken against him. Parliament, however, was to meet on January 23, and it was certain that a movement in Somerset's favour would be made. Northumberland had endeavoured to strengthen his faction in the Commons by forcing his nominees on vacant constituencies; but his hold on Parliament remained nevertheless weaker than that of his rival, and it was therefore determined to get rid of Somerset once and for all. An order of the King drawn up on January 18 for the trial of Somerset's accomplices, was, before its submission to the Council on the following day, transformed by erasures and interlineations into an order for the Duke's execution. No record of the proceedings was entered in the Council's register; but Cecil, with a view to future contingencies, secured the King's memorandum and inscribed on the back of it the names of the Councillors who were present. Somerset's execution took place at sunrise on the 22nd; in spite of elaborate precautions a riot nearly broke out, but the Duke made no effort to turn to account the popular sympathy. He had resigned himself to his fate, and died with exemplary courage and dignity.

Parliament met on the following day, and it soon proved that Northumberland had been wise in his generation. Parliament could not restore Somerset to life, but it could at least ensure that no one should again be condemned by similar methods. It rejected a new treason bill designed to supply the place of the former expiring Act, and passed another providing that accusations must be made within three months of the offence, and that the prisoner must be confronted with two witnesses to his crime. The House of Commons also refused to pass a bill of attainder against Tunstall, Bishop of Durham, who had been imprisoned on a vague charge remotely connected with Somerset's pretended plots. His bishopric was, however, marked out for spoliation, and a few months later Tunstall was deprived by a civil Court. Parliament was more complaisant in religious matters, and passed the Second Act of Uniformity, besides another Act removing from the marriage of priests the stigma hitherto attaching to the practice as being only a licensed evil. The Second Act of Uniformity extended the scope of religious persecution by imposing penalties for recusancy upon laymen; if they neglected to attend common prayer on Sundays and holidays, they were to be subject to ecclesiastical censures and excommunication; if they attended any but the authorised form of worship, they were liable to six months' imprisonment for the first offence, a year's imprisonment for the second, and lifelong imprisonment for the third.

This Second Act of Uniformity also imposed a Second Book of Common Prayer. The First Book of Common Prayer had scarcely received the sanction of Parliament in 1549, when it began to be attacked as a halting makeshift by the Reformers. The fact that Gardiner expressed a modified approval of it was enough to condemn it in their eyes, and in the Second Book those parts which had won Gardiner's approval were carefully eliminated or revised. The Prayer Book of 1549 was elaborately examined by Bucer and more superficially by Peter Martyr; but the changes actually made were rather on lines indicated by Cranmer in his controversy with Gardiner than on those suggested by Bucer; and the actual revision was done by the Archbishop, assisted at times by Ridley. There is no proof that Convocation was consulted in the matter, nor is there any evidence that the Book underwent modification in its passage through Parliament. The net result was to minimise the possibility of such Catholic interpretations as had been placed on the earlier Book; in particular the Communion Office was radically altered until it approached very nearly to the Zwinglian idea of a commemorative rite. The celebrated Black Rubric, explaining away the significance of the ceremony of kneeling at Communion, was inserted on the Council's authority after the Act had been passed by Parliament. Two other ecclesiastical measures of importance were the *Reformatio legum ecclesiasticarum* and the compilation of the Forty-two Articles. The Articles of Religion, originally drawn up by Cranmer, were revised at the Council's direction and did not receive the royal signature until June, 1553, while Parliament in the same year refused its sanction to the Book of Canon Law prepared by the commissioners; lay objections to spiritual jurisdiction were the same, whether it was exercised by Catholic or by Protestant prelates.

The extensive reduction of Church ritual effected by the Second Act of Uniformity rendered superfluous a large quantity of Church property, and for its seizure by the Crown the government's financial embarrassments supplied an obvious motive. The subsidies granted in 1549–50, the money paid for the restitution of Boulogne, profits made by the debasement of the coinage, and other sources, had enabled Northumberland to tide over the Parliament of 1552, without demanding from it any further financial aid. But these sources were now exhausted, and in the ensuing summer the final gleanings from the Church were gathered in. Such chantry lands as had not been sold or granted away were now disposed of; all unnecessary church ornaments were appropriated; the lands of the dissolved bishoprics and attainted conspirators were placed on the market; church bells were taken down, organs were removed, and lead was stripped off the roofs. When these means failed, the heroic measure was proposed of demanding an account from all Crown officers of moneys received during the last twenty years. Still there was a deficit; and in the winter Northumberland was reduced to appealing to Parliament.

By this time his government had become so unpopular that he shrank from meeting a really representative assembly, and had recourse to an expedient which has been misrepresented as the normal practice of Tudor times. There had already been isolated instances of the exercise of government influence to force particular candidates on constituencies; but the Parliament of March, 1553, was the only one in the sixteenth century that can fairly be described as nominated by the government; and Renard, when discussing the question of a Parliament in the following August, asked Charles V whether he thought it advisable to have a general Parliament or merely an assembly of "notables" summoned after the manner introduced by Northumberland. A circular appears to have been sent round ordering the electors to return the members nominated by the Council. Even this measure was not considered sufficient to ensure a properly subservient House of Commons; and at the same time eleven new boroughs returning twenty-two members were created, principally in Cornwall, where Crown influence was supreme. The process of packing had already been applied to the Privy Council, more than half of which, as it existed in 1553, had been nominated since Northumberland's accession to power. To this Parliament the Duke represented his financial needs as exclusively due to the maladministration of the Protector, who had been deposed three and a half years before; and a subsidy was granted which was not, however, to be paid for two years. Acts were also passed with a view to checking fiscal abuses; but Northumberland again met with some traces of independence in the Commons, and Parliament was dissolved on March 31, having sat for barely a month.

The ground was fast slipping from under Northumberland's feet, and the Nemesis which had long dogged his steps was drawing perceptibly nearer. Zimri had no peace, and from the time of Somerset's fall never a month passed without some symptom of popular discontent. In October, 1551, a rumour spread that a coinage was being minted at Dudley Castle stamped with Northumberland's badge, the bear and ragged staff, and in 1552 he was widely believed to be aiming at the Crown. Even some of his favourite preachers began to denounce him in thinly veiled terms from the pulpit. No longer a Moses or Joshua, he was not obscurely likened to Ahitophel. His only support was the young King, over whose mind he had established complete dominion; and Edward VI was now slowly dying before his eyes. The consequences to himself of a demise of the Crown were only too clear; his ambition had led him into so many crimes and had made him so many enemies that his life was secure only so long as he controlled the government and prevented the administration of justice. There was no room for repentance; he could expect no mercy when his foes were once in a position to bring him to book. The accession of Mary would almost inevitably be followed by his own attainder ; and the prospect drove him to make one last desperate bid for life and for power.

There were other temptations which led him to stake his all on a single throw. No immediate interference need be feared from abroad. Scotland, now little more than a province of France, had no desire to see a half-Spanish princess on the English throne, and France was even more reluctant to witness the transference of England's resources to the hands of Charles V. The Emperor was fully occupied with the French war, and Mary had nothing on which to rely except the temper of England. Northumberland's endeavour to alter the Succession might well seem worth the making. He could appeal to the fact that no woman had sat on the English throne, and that the only attempt to place one there had been followed by civil war. Margaret Beaufort had been excluded in favour of her son ; and in the reign of Henry VIII there were not wanting those who preferred the claim of an illegitimate son to that of a legitimate daughter. He could also play upon the dread of religious reaction and of foreign domination which would ensue if Mary succeeded and, as she probably would, married an alien. The Netherlands, Hungary, and Bohemia had all by marriage been brought under Habsburg rule and with disastrous consequences ; might not England be reserved for a similar fate ? Some of these objections applied also to the Princess Elizabeth, but not all, and Northumberland would have stood a better chance of success had he selected as his candidate the daughter of Anne Boleyn. But such a solution would not necessarily have meant a continuance of his own supremacy, and that was the vital point.

Hence the Duke had recourse to a plan which was hopelessly illegal, illogical, unpopular, and unconstitutional. Edward VI was induced to settle the Crown on Lady Jane Grey, the grand-daughter of Henry VIII's sister, Mary, Duchess of Suffolk ; she was married to Northumberland's fourth son, Guilford Dudley, and Dudley was to receive the Crown matrimonial, and thus mitigate the objections to a female sovereign. The arrangement was illegal, because Edward VI had not been empowered by law, as Henry had, to leave the Crown by will ; and any attempt to alter the Succession established by Parliament and by Henry's will was treason. It was illogical, because, even supposing that Henry's will could be set aside and his two daughters excluded as illegitimate, the next claimant was Mary, Queen of Scots, the grand-daughter of Henry's elder sister Margaret. Moreover, if the Suffolk line was adopted, the proper heir was Lady Jane's mother, the wife of Henry Grey, Duke of Suffolk. There was thus little to recommend the King's "device" except the arbitrary will of Northumberland, who in May, 1553, endeavoured to implicate his chief supporters in the plot by a series of dynastic marriages. His daughter Catharine was given to Lord Hastings ; Lady Jane's sister Catharine to Pembroke's son, Lord Herbert ; and Lady Jane's cousin

Margaret Clifford (another possible claimant) to Northumberland's brother Andrew. The news of these arrangements confirmed the popular suspicions of the Duke's designs, and during the month of June foreign ambassadors in London were kept pretty well informed of the progress of the plot. The reluctant consent of the Council was obtained by a promise that Parliament should be summoned at once to confirm the settlement; and on June 11 the judges were ordered to draw up letters patent embodying the young King's wishes. They resisted at first, but Edward's urgent commands, Northumberland's violence, and a pardon under the Great Seal for their action at length extorted compliance. On the 21st the Council with some open protests and many mental reservations signed the letters patent. The Tower had been secured; troops had been hastily raised; and the fleet had been manned. Every precaution that fear could inspire had been taken when the last male Tudor died on July 6 at Greenwich; nothing remained but for the nation to declare, through such channels as were still left open, its verdict on the claims of Mary and the Duke of Northumberland's rule.

CHAPTER XV

PHILIP AND MARY

THE contention of religious parties amid which the reign of Mary commenced — the legacy of the preceding reign — still further weakened the royal authority at home, while it materially lowered England in the estimation of the great Powers abroad. The Protector Somerset had failed to accomplish the design to which he had devoted his best energies, that of Union with Scotland, whereby the United Kingdom should assert its position as the leading Protestant State in Europe. The innate cruelty of Northumberland's nature, as seen in the merciless malignity with which he brought his rival to the scaffold, and carried out the reversal of his policy, had caused him to be regarded with aversion by the great majority of his countrymen ; while the humiliating circumstances under which peace had been concluded both with France and with Scotland had revealed alike the financial and the moral weakness of the nation. Not only had the rulers of the country themselves ceased to be actuated by a statesmanlike and definite foreign policy, but the leading Powers on the Continent had gradually come to regard England from a different point of view. The revenue of the English Crown was but a fraction of that which Henry II of France or Charles V could raise. And by degrees the country whose King, a generation before, had hurled defiance at Rome and treated on equal terms with Spain and France, had come to be looked upon by these latter Powers as one whose government and people were alike fickle and untrustworthy, and whose policy vacillated and rulers changed so often as to render its alliance a matter scarcely deserving serious diplomatic effort, its annexation far from impracticable. But whether that annexation would have to be effected by diplomacy or by force, by a matrimonial alliance or by actual conquest, was still uncertain. Such, however, was the alternative that chiefly engaged the thoughts of the representatives of the great continental Powers during the reign of Mary.

When we turn to consider the instruments who served their diplomacy in England, it must be admitted that the envoys of both France and Spain were well fitted to represent their respective sovereigns. The bad faith and cynical inconsistency of Henry II reappeared in the mischievous intrigues and shameless mendacity of Antoine de Noailles. The astute and wary policy of the Emperor was not inadequately reproduced by the energetic and adroit, although sometimes too impetuous, Simon Renard. On the Venetian envoys, Giacomo Soranzo and Giovanni Michiel, it devolved carefully to observe rather than to seek to guide events; and the latter, although designated an imperialist by de Noailles, appears to have preserved a studiously impartial attitude; while the accuracy of his information was such that the French ambassador did not scruple to avail himself of the dishonesty of Michiel's secretary, Antonio Mazza, to purchase clandestinely much of the intelligence transmitted to the Doge of Venice by his envoy.

In the selection of her representatives at the foregoing Courts, Mary, on the other hand, does not appear to have been unduly biassed by personal predilections. Thirlby, Bishop of Norwich, afterwards stood high in her favour; but when, in April, 1553, he was for the second time accredited ambassador to the Emperor, it was under the auspices of Northumberland. Expediency alone can have suggested that Nicholas Wotton and Peter Vannes, both of whom had taken an active part in the proceedings connected with the divorce of Catharine of Aragon, should be retained at their posts, — the one in Paris, the other in Venice. Wotton's loyalty to his new sovereign, his ability and courage, were alike unquestionable; and when, in 1555–7, Mary's throne was threatened by the machinations of the English exiles, it was to his vigilance and dexterity that the English government was mainly indebted for its earliest information of the conspirators' intentions. At Venice, Peter Vannes discharged his duties as ambassador with commendable discretion and assiduity, although, at one critical juncture, he did not escape the reproach of excessive caution. But as a native of Lucca, and one who had been collector of the papal taxes in England, who had filled the post of Latin secretary to Wolsey, King Henry and King Edward in succession, and who had been employed on more than one important diplomatic mission, he offered a combination of qualifications which it would have been difficult to match. Although he was nearly sixty years of age, his energies showed no decline; and Mary herself could suggest no one more fit to be her representative at the Venetian Court.

The 6th of July, the day of Edward's death, had not passed away before the Council were apprised of the event; but it was decided that the fact should be kept strictly secret until the necessary measures had been taken for securing the succession of the Lady Jane Grey. In pursuance of this decision, Howard (the Lord Admiral), the Marquis of Westminster (the Lord Treasurer), and the Earl of Shrewsbury forthwith placed a strong garrison in the Tower; while the civic authorities were summoned to appear, through their representatives, before the Council at Greenwich. The Lord Mayor, together with "six aldermen, as many merchants of the staple and as many merchant adventurers," accordingly repaired thither, when the late monarch's decease was made known to them, and the letters patent, whereby he had devised the Succession to the House of Suffolk, were laid before them. These they were called upon to sign, and also to take an oath of allegiance to Queen Jane. They were, however, charged to divulge nothing, but quietly to take whatever measures they might deem requisite for the preservation of order in the City, and to procure the acquiescence of the citizens in the succession of their new sovereign; and, at three o'clock in the afternoon of Monday (the 10th), Jane was conveyed by water to the Tower, where she was formally received as Queen. At five o'clock, public proclamation was made both of Edward's death and of the fact that by his decree "the Lady Jane and her heirs male " were to be his recognised successors. Printed copies of the document which the late King had executed were at the same, time circulated among the people, in order to make clear the grounds on which the claim of the new Queen rested.

In the meantime, two days before her brother's death, Mary, apprised of the hopeless nature of his illness, had effected her escape by night from Hunsdon to her palace at Kenninghall, an ancient structure, formerly belonging to the Dukes of Norfolk, which had been bestowed on her by Henry on the attainder of the actual Duke. The Princess had formerly been accustomed to hold her Court there; but the buildings were ill adapted for defence, and on the 11th she quitted Kenninghall for Framlingham in Suffolk. Framlingham, another of the seats of the Howards, was situated in the district where Northumberland's ruthless suppression of the rebellion of 1549 was still fresh in the memories of the population; and the strength and position of the castle surmounted by lofty towers and on the margin of a wide expanse of water, made it an excellent rallying-point for Mary's supporters. Moreover, being distant but a few miles from the coast, it offered facilities for escape to the Continent, should such a necessity arise. Within less than forty-eight hours it had become known to Northumberland in London, that the Earl of Bath, Sir Thomas Wharton, Sir John Mordaunt, Sir William Drury, Sir Henry Bedingfield (formerly the custodian of Mary's mother at Kimbolton), along with other noblemen and gentlemen, some of them at the head of a considerable body of retainers, were gathering at Framlingham. The Council, on assembling at the Tower on the 12th, had already decided that it was expedient for the security of the realm, that Mary should forthwith be brought to London; and Suffolk was, in the first instance, designated for the task of giving effect to their decision. Jane, however, overcome by a sense of responsibility and by nervous apprehension, entreated that her father might be permitted " to tarry at home to keep her company "; and Northumberland was accordingly called upon to proceed on the perilous errand. The terror which his name was likely to inspire, and his reputation as "the best manne of war in the realme," might be looked upon as justifying his selection. But on the other hand it was also notorious that throughout the eastern counties his name was held in execration as that of the man who had brought Somerset to the scaffold; and the rumour was already spreading widely that he had, by foul play, precipitated the death of the young King. The wishes of the Council were, however, too strongly urged for him to be able to decline the errand; and the following day was devoted to making ready for the expedition and to the arming of a sufficient retinue. When the Lords of the Council assembled at dinner, Northumberland availed himself of the opportunity to deliver an harangue in which he adverted to the perils awaiting him and his followers, and commended the families of the latter to the care of his audience. He further reminded those who listened, that to "the originall grounde" on which their policy rested — "the preferment of Goddes Word and the feare of papestry's re-entrance" — there was now added the new oath of allegiance, which bound them to support the Queen's cause, and he adjured them to be faithful to their vow.

On Friday, July 14, he set out with his forces through the streets of London; but the absence of all sympathy on the part of the populace either with him or his errand was only too apparent. He himself, as he passed along Shoreditch, was heard to exclaim: "The people press to see us, but not one sayeth 'God speed ye!'" Under the belief that Mary's change of residence to Framlingham was simply designed to facilitate her escape to Flanders, he had some days before given orders that ships carrying picked crews to the number of two thousand men should be stationed off the Norfolk coast to intercept her passage. The spirits of Mary's supporters at this crisis were far from high; nor was Charles at Brussels by any means sanguine in his niece's cause. His instructions, transmitted on June 23 to his ambassadors extraordinary to the English Court while they were still at Calais, were drawn up in contemplation of the crisis which seemed likely to arise on Edward's death, which was even then regarded as imminent. On their arrival in London they were forthwith to obtain, if possible, an interview with the young King; and precise directions were given with respect to their attitude towards Northumberland and the Council. In the event of Edward's death, Mary's best policy, Charles considered, would be her betrothal to one of her own countrymen; — the machinations of France would thus be effectually counteracted, the mistrust of Northumberland and his party would be disarmed. It would be well also to come as soon as might be to a general understanding with the Council; a result which, the imperial adviser considered, might be attained by Mary's undertaking to introduce no innovations either in the administration of civil affairs or in religion, and at the same time concluding a kind of amnesty with those actually in office, — "patiently waiting until God should vouchsafe the opportunity of restoring everything by peaceful means." His envoys were also enjoined to give his niece all possible assistance and advice in connexion with any obligations she might enter into with the Council and any pledges she might give.

Edward's death, followed within a week by that of Maurice of Saxony from a wound received in the battle of Sievershausen, materially modified the aspect of affairs. On the Continent, Charles was now able to concentrate his efforts on the conflict with France; while in England the remarkable change in Mary's prospects constrained both Catholic and Protestant writers to recognise in results so rapidly attained an express intervention of Providence.

The first report transmitted to Charles by his ambassadors after their arrival in London conveyed the tidings of Edward's death, and of Northumberland's occupation of the Tower as champion of the cause of the Lady Jane Grey. It further stated that Mary, after taking counsel with her confidants, had been proclaimed Queen at Framlingham, a course adopted under the belief that large numbers would thus be encouraged openly to declare themselves in her favour. In the opinion of Renard himself, however, she was committing herself to a line of action which, considering the resources at Northumberland's command, the support which he was regularly receiving from France, and the actual complications in continental affairs, must be pronounced hopeless. Charles in his reply (July 11, 1553) advised his envoys to content themselves for the present with watching the situation; but he suggested that, if Northumberland persisted in his opposition to Mary's claims, it might be well to endeavour to persuade those English peers who favoured the Catholic cause to make such a demonstration as might serve to render the Duke more amenable to reason. Renard's misgivings were, however, soon modified by further and more accurate intelligence; and in a letter to Prince Philip he was able to report that Paget had resumed his seat in the Council, in whose policy a complete change had taken place. Then came news that on July 19, while the rebel leaders were marching from Cambridge to attack the castle at Framlingham, Mary had been proclaimed on Tower Hill by Suffolk himself, and again at Paul's Cross, and that he had at the same time given orders that the insignia of royalty should be removed from his daughter's chambers. The diarist at his post in the Tower and the imperial ambassadors in the City concur in describing the demonstrations which followed as characterised by remarkable enthusiasm, — the bonfires and roaring cannon, the pealing bells and sonorous long-disused organs, the profuse largesses, — all offering a marked contrast to the apathy and silence with which the proclamation of Jane had been received. The Council now sent off official information of the event to Mary, who was at the same time advised not to disarm her forces until Northumberland's submission or defeat was beyond doubt. Three days later Renard was able to report that the proclamation had everywhere been so favourably received that Mary might now be regarded as secure in her position " as true and hereditary Queen of England, without difficulty, doubt, or impediment."

While events were progressing thus rapidly in London Northumberland, accompanied by the Marquis of Northampton and Lord Grey, had arrived on the evening of Saturday, July 15, at Cambridge. Here he rested for the Sunday, and as both Lord High Steward and Chancellor of the University was hospitably entertained by the academic authorities. On the Monday he set out for Bury St Edmunds, expecting to be joined at Newmarket by the reinforcements from the capital. These however failed to appear, while defections from his own ranks became numerous; and he now learned that the crews of the ships sent to intercept Mary's passage, had, on arriving at Yarmouth, declared for her, and their captains had followed their example. On the 18th, accordingly, Northumberland set out on his return from Bury to Cambridge, where at five o'clock on the evening of the 20th, the news having arrived that Mary had been proclaimed in London, he himself also proclaimed her in the market-place; and, as the tears ran down his face, ejaculated that he knew her to be a merciful woman. An hour later he received an order from the Council. It was signed by Cranmer, Goodrich (Bishop of Ely and Lord Chancellor), the Marquis of Winchester, the Duke of Suffolk, and the Earls of Pembroke, Bedford, and Shrewsbury, and directed him forthwith to disarm and disband his army, but not himself to return to London until the royal pleasure was known. If he would thus " shew himselfe like a good quiet subject," the missive went on to say, " wee will then continue as we have begun, as humble suters to our Soueraigne Lady the Queenes Highnesse, for him and his and for our selves."

The Cambridge authorities now hastened to send congratulatory letters to Framlingham; while Gardiner, the former Chancellor of the University, was re-elected to that office. In the letter announcing his re-election he was urged to restore to the Schools their former freedom and " to annul the lawless laws which held their consciences in bondage." The Constable de Montmorency, writing (July 24) to Lord Howard, the governor of Calais, promised that he would himself conduct all the forces at his disposal to protect that town, should the Emperor, taking advantage of the crisis, seek to occupy it. But five days later Noailles was able to report to the Duke of Orleans that troops, cavalry and footsoldiers, had rallied to Mary's support to the number of between 35,000 and 40,000 men—all inspired with unprecedented enthusiasm and asking for no pay, but voluntarily contributing money, plate, and rings from their own slender resources. At Framlingham there were now to be seen, besides Mary's avowed supporters, numerous nobles and gentlemen, confessing their disloyalty and asking for pardon. In most cases these petitions received a favourable response. Cecil, who could plead that he had signed the Instrument of Succession under compulsion, was restored to favour although not to office. But the Dudleys, both Robert and Ambrose, and about a hundred other leading commoners, among whom was Sir Thomas Wyatt, remained for a time under arrest. On July 27 the two Lord Chief Justices, Sir Roger Cholmeley and Sir Edward Montagu, were committed to the Tower, where, on the following day, they were joined by the Duke of Suffolk and Sir John Cheke, and, before the end of the month, by Northumberland and his Duchess, with their eldest son (the Earl of Warwick), Guilford Dudley, and the Lady Jane.

On July 29 Henry at Compiègne signed the credentials of the Sieur Antoine de Noailles as ambassador to Mary; and two days later it was intimated to Nicholas Wotton, Pickering, and Chaloner that the Queen desired to retain them in their posts as her representatives at the French Court. Early in August, Cardinal Pole, in his monastic retirement at Maguzzano on the Lago di Garda, received from Julius III his appointment as papal Legate to England, with instructions to visit both the Imperial and the French Court on his journey thither.

For the present Mary determined to be guided mainly by the advice of her cousin the Emperor, a decision the wisdom of which was clearly attested by subsequent events as well as by the letters, numerous and lengthy, which Charles addressed to his envoys at her Court in connexion with each important question as it arose. From the first he advised that the Queen should scrupulously avoid appearing to set herself in opposition to the prejudices and feelings of her people, and should above all things endeavour to appear "*une bonne Anglaise.*" It was from France alone, he considered, that she had reason to apprehend much danger; although Scotland, as subservient to French policy, also required to be carefully watched. The French envoys had just presented their credentials to Courtenay, and, as a well-known sympathiser with the Italian Reformers, he was regarded by the Emperor with especial mistrust. It was rumoured that the young nobleman was making advances to Elizabeth. Such an alliance, Charles pointed out, was fraught with danger and must, if possible, be prevented. The Princess' attitude in relation to the new doctrines also required to be carefully observed. As for the rebels, let exemplary punishment be inflicted on the leaders, and the rest be treated with clemency. The Lady Jane doubtless deserved death, but it might be well for the present simply to keep her in close custody, where she would be unable to hold communication with traitors. Finally, Mary was advised to get the finances in good order, so as to have funds ready for any emergency, and, more especially, to exercise a vigilant control over the expenditure of the secret service money.

Counsel of a very different nature came from Italy, where Cardinal Pole's fervid enthusiasm as a would-be reformer of religious discipline in England was prudently held in check alike by Emperor and Pope. His letters at this period, while conceived in a spirit of unselfish devotion to the interests of Catholicism, attest the unpractical character of the writer and the influences of the monastic seclusion in which he had lately sought refuge. Early in August, Gian Francesco Commendone, the papal chamberlain, and Penning, one of Pole's confidants, were sent expressly, the one from Brussels, the other from Rome, in order more accurately to gauge both the royal intentions and popular feeling. It was only after considerable delay that they succeeded in gaining admission to Mary's presence, when her own language held out so little hope of her being able at once to adopt a decisive policy that Commendone forthwith set out on his return journey. Penning, however, remained until the Coronation, and was then sent back to Pole with a letter from the Queen. In a letter to the Queen, dated August 13, the Cardinal had already enunciated his views of Mary's position and responsibilities. Heresy was the source of all evil; unbridled passion had led her father first to divorce himself from his wedded wife, and next to separate from his mother the Church and to disobey her spiritual Head. Mary had already reaped a reward for her loyalty to the true faith in her astonishing triumph over her rebel subjects. If ever the interposition of Divine Providence in human affairs had been clearly apparent, it was in the recent crisis in England. He hopes that the character of her rule will make manifest her consciousness of this fact, and he is especially anxious to be informed as to her real sentiments. When once admitted to her presence, he relies on being able to convince her that her crown and the welfare of the nation alike depend on obedience to the Church. In her reply, Mary expressed her heartfelt grief at being, as yet, unable to disclose her secret wishes, but intimated that, as soon as it was in her power, she hoped to carry them into effective execution. Pole, however, could see no advantage in delay, holding that it was especially desirable that he should himself be near at hand "to assist the Queen's good intentions"; demurring at the same time to the proposal that the Pope should forthwith "exempt England from every interdict and censure," on the ground that so momentous a decision would more fitly be considered by himself on his arrival.

All that Julius III and the Emperor could do was to contrive that a counsellor of so much distinction and of so small discretion should be kept back as long as possible from the arena where his influence was likely to prove most disastrous. By the Pontiff, Pole was designated *legatus pro pace* and instructed to visit on his journey to England both the Imperial and the French Court, with the view of bringing about, if possible, an understanding between Charles and Henry. By the Emperor, the audience which the Cardinal asked for at Brussels was deferred, under various pretexts, until January, 1554. As early however as October 2, Pole had arrived at Trent, where we find him writing to Courtenay and extolling the negative virtues which had adorned his captivity in the Tower, little surmising on what a career his cousin had already embarked, to the ruin alike of his health and his fortunes.

During these critical days Elizabeth had remained in seclusion at Hatfield, preserving an attitude of studied neutrality. But on July 29 she entered London with a large train of followers and took up her residence at Somerset House. Five days later, the Queen made her triumphal entry into the City in the evening, and was joined at Aldgate by her sister, the two riding side by side through the streets amid the acclamations of the populace. Mary, following the usual practice of royalty prior to coronation, now proceeded to occupy the State apartments in the Tower. At the Great Gate, the Duke of Norfolk, Bishop Gardiner, the Duchess of Somerset, and the youthful Courtenay awaited her arrival, all in a kneeling posture, and were by her command formally restored to liberty. Jane, on the other hand, found herself a prisoner, and was consigned to the custody of the new governor, Sir John Brydges. Gardiner was sworn a member of the Privy Council, and, on August 23, appointed Lord High Chancellor. On the 8th of the same month the funeral service for the late King was held in Westminster Abbey, being conducted by Cranmer and according to the Protestant ritual. Mary, however, commanded that a requiem mass should also be celebrated in the Tower, which she strongly pressed Elizabeth to attend. The Princess did not comply; but by her regular attendance at Court gave evidence of her desire to conciliate her sister as far as possible, and six weeks later was to be seen hearing mass in her company. Her compliance, however, as Noailles himself admits, was generally regarded as dictated by fear rather than principle.

It soon however became evident that the recognition of the Legate and the contemplated resumption of relations with the Roman See were measures which would be attended with far greater difficulties than the restoration of the ancient worship. Even Gardiner, whose general sympathy with such designs there can be no reason for doubting, felt himself bound, like the Emperor, to counsel the greatest caution and deliberation. The nobles and country gentry, enriched by those monastic and Church lands which they would be called upon to restore, the Bishops whose deposition was regarded as imminent, alike represented vested interests which could hardly be assailed without danger. In a proclamation issued August 18, Mary announced, accordingly, her intention of deferring various questions of policy until Parliament, summoned to assemble on October 5, could be consulted. But in the meantime certain measures which did not appear to admit of being thus postponed were carried into effect. Of some sixty rebels denounced as traitors seven were convicted of high treason; but of these three only — Northumberland, Sir John Gates, and Sir Thomas Palmer — actually suffered the extreme penalty. Gardiner himself is said to have interceded on behalf of the Duke, who, buoyed up by the hope that the royal clemency would be extended to him on the scaffold itself, there acknowledged the justice of his sentence and made a complete renunciation of Protestantism, even going so far as to attribute the intestine strife and the miseries, which for so many years had troubled alike England and Germany, to the defection of those realms from the true faith. The Roman ritual was not as yet formally restored as obligatory on all loyal subjects, but in her private chapel Mary heard mass. The Protestant Bishops were deposed ; and an injunction was issued that none of the clergy should preach without the royal licence, while any member of that body was to be liable to suspension if his conduct proved unsatisfactory. Gardiner, Bonner, Heath, and Day were reinstated in their respective sees of Winchester, London, Worcester, and Chichester. The see of Durham, which Northumberland had suppressed, appropriating its ample revenues to his own use, was restored, and Cuthbert Tunstall installed as Bishop. On August 29 Gardiner received instructions himself to select and appoint capable preachers who were to be sent to discharge their functions throughout the country.

Not a few of the more eminent preachers among the Reformers, foreseeing the storm, had already fled to the Continent ; but a certain number still remained, such as Latimer and John Bradford, openly to call in question the prerogatives which the Queen still arrogated to herself as Head of the Church. Foremost, however, among those who refused to flee was Archbishop Cranmer, who at his palace in Lambeth confronted the reactionary tendencies around him with an intrepidity which marked him out for general observation. Already obnoxious, owing to his complicity in the diversion of the Succession to the Crown, he was by his open denunciation of the restoration of the Mass, which he declared to involve " many horrible blasphemies," exposed to the charge of open resistance to the royal authority. On September 8 he was summoned before the Council to answer for the publication of the Declaration in which he had given expression to his views. His defence, if such it could be termed, was rightly regarded as evasive. He pleaded that Scory, the deprived Bishop of Chichester, had published the Declaration without his formal authorisation, though he admitted that it had been his intention to give it. He was accordingly committed to the Tower, where Ridley, who had publicly proclaimed the illegitimacy of both Mary and Elizabeth, had already been a prisoner for two months. Latimer's committal appears to have taken place about the same time ; and, early in October, Cranmer was followed by his brother Primate, Archbishop Holgate. The latter was now more than seventy years of age, and chiefly obnoxious on account of the persistent energy with which he assailed all that reflected the Roman ritual and ornamentation in the churches.

On October 1 Mary was crowned in Westminster Abbey — the procession from the Tower and the entire ceremonial being marked by much splendour and by a revival of all the features and details which belonged to such ceremonies in medieval times. The whole Court also now resumed the brilliant attire and costly adornments of the reign of Henry VIII. On the 5th of the month Mary's first Parliament assembled. The Council, out of deference to the royal wishes, had contemplated measures which would have reversed all the anti-papal enactments of both the preceding reigns. But here the Commons assumed a decisive attitude ; and it was eventually determined that the question of restoring the lands and other property, which had been wrested from the Church and the suppressed monasteries, should not be considered, and that, with respect to the supremacy in matters of religion, legislation should go back no further than to the commencement of Edward's reign. Whatever appeared to favour papal authority was, as Mary in a letter to Pole herself admitted, regarded with suspicion. On the other hand, much was done to propitiate the new sovereign. A bill was at once brought in legalising the marriage of Catharine of Aragon and abolishing all disabilities attaching to the profession of the old faith. The opposition of the Protestant party in the House caused a certain delay ; but after an interval of three days the ministers brought in two bills : the one affirming the legality of Catharine's marriage without adverting to the papal decision ; the other rescinding the legislation affecting religious worship and the Church during the reign of the late King. The retrospective force of the latter bill went, however, no further — the ecclesiastical supremacy of the Crown being still tacitly admitted. But, on the other hand, it involved the renunciation of the chief results of Cranmer's efforts during the preceding reign — the Reformed Liturgy, the First and Second Books of Common Prayer, the administration of the Sacrament in both kinds, and the recognition of a married clergy — and was consequently not allowed to pass without considerable opposition. But its opponents, although representing nearly a third of the Lower House, did not deem it prudent to press the question to a division, and in the Upper House no resistance was offered.

It was manifest that conclusions so incompatible — the recognition of Mary as Head of the Church in England and the tacit assumption of the Papal Supremacy — represented a temporising policy which was not likely to secure the permanent support of either party. Cardinal Pole declared himself profoundly dissatisfied : the Divine favour had recently been conspicuously shown in that outburst of loyal feeling which had secured Mary's succession, and sovereign and people alike were bound by gratitude forthwith to seek reconciliation with the Holy See and to afford its Legate an honourable reception. The Emperor and Gardiner, on the other hand, still counselled caution, and more especially patience in awaiting the results of a gradual re-establishment of that Roman ritual which early association and religious sentiment endeared to the hearts of a majority of the population. In common with many of her subjects, the Queen herself firmly believed that nothing would more effectually contribute to the desired end than the prospect of a Catholic heir to the throne; and, although in her thirty-seventh year and in infirm health, she consequently regarded her own marriage as a duty to the State. But even if personal predilection was to be sacrificed on the altar of duty, her choice of a husband was a matter involving anxious consideration amid the conflicting claims of the national welfare and of the Catholic faith. In its broadest phase, the question lay between a native of her own country and a foreigner. The nation undoubtedly wished to see her married to one of her own nobles; it is equally certain that Mary's devout attachment to the interests of the Roman Church inclined her to look abroad. In the course of the year following upon her accession report singled out three supposed claimants for her hand, of whom one was sixteen years her senior, the other two each about ten years her junior.

There is no evidence that Reginald Pole ever aspired to marry Mary, or that she, in turn, ever regarded him in any other light than that of a much valued friend and counsellor. The personal graces and touching experiences of Edward Courtenay might well recommend him to a woman's sympathies. He was the son of Edward Courtenay, Marquis of Exeter, who had been executed in 1539 for his share in the conspiracy in favour of Reginald Pole, and was thus the great-grandson of Edward IV. Mary herself had just freed him from an imprisonment of nearly fifteen years and had created him Earl of Devonshire, while at her coronation he was selected to bear the sword before her. His mother, the Marchioness of Exeter, one of Mary's dearest friends, was now one of her ladies in waiting. His long isolation from society and neglected education had however ill qualified him to play a part in politics, while the fascinations which surrounded him in his newly acquired freedom proved too potent for his self-control, and his wild debaucheries became the scandal of the capital. Whatever influence Pole might have been able to exert would probably have favoured Courtenay's claims. As a boy, both he and his brother Geoffrey had received much kindness from the Marquis of Exeter, the young Earl's father — favours which Geoffrey had ill repaid by bearing evidence which brought the Marquis to the scaffold — and Pole's own mother, the Countess of Salisbury, prior to her tragic execution, had shared the captivity of the Marchioness. But Courtenay's indiscretions soon rendered the efforts of his best friends nugatory. It now became known that his conduct had completely lost him Mary's favour, and he was next heard of as conspiring against his would-be benefactress.

To a fairly impartial observer it might well have seemed that the arguments for and against the Spanish marriage were of nearly equal force. Certain political advantages were obvious, and as Renard pointed out to the Queen herself it would afford the necessary counterbalance to the matrimonial alliance which already existed between France and Scotland; while the national antipathy to Spaniards, having its origin in commercial rivalry, could hardly be supposed to extend to a great prince like Philip. On the other hand it would be necessary to obtain the papal dispensation; for Mary and Philip were within the degrees of consanguinity forbidden by the Canon Law. There also appeared to be considerable danger as regarded the Succession; for if Mary died without issue, as seemed highly probable, it was difficult to foresee what claims her husband might not advance. Such were the circumstances in which Gardiner, who had formed a regard for Courtenay when they were prisoners together, had, in the first instance, suggested that the Queen should marry the young English noble, and that Elizabeth should be excluded from the Succession; while Paget, who had just received back his Garter, thought it best that Mary's choice should be left free, but that she should recognise Elizabeth as her presumptive successor. The great majority of the nobles and gentry, whether Catholic or Protestant, were divided and perplexed by the opposing considerations of the danger of a foreign yoke, the hope of seeing an hereditary faith restored, and the necessity which might yet ensue of being called upon to surrender those former possessions of the Church which constituted, in many cases, the present holder's chief wealth.

A selection which would draw closer the ties between England and Spain was naturally regarded with jealousy by the French monarch, and Noailles was instructed to use every effort to avert it. He accordingly plied his arguments and persuasions with untiring assiduity in every direction, and so far succeeded that the Commons were prevailed upon to vote an Address to the Crown, in which, while urging upon Mary the desirability of marriage, they also advised that her choice should be restricted to the peerage of her own realm. A week later Renard had an audience of the Queen, at which he made the offer from Charles himself of Philip's hand. Mary had previously made careful enquiry of the ambassador himself respecting the Prince's habits and natural disposition, and, after a short time had been allowed to elapse for apparent deliberation, intimated her acceptance of the offer.

Such were the circumstances in which, on November 17, the Commons presented the above-mentioned Address. The customary mode of procedure required that Gardiner, as Chancellor, should be the royal mouthpiece in reply. But Mary, rising from her throne, herself gave answer, and did so, if we may credit Renard, in terms of some asperity, repudiating the right of the Commons to control her decision, and declaring that Elizabeth, who was illegitimate, should never be her successor. Early in December it was rumoured that Courtenay was making advances to Elizabeth, and that Noailles was playing the part of go-between. Elizabeth, accordingly, deemed it prudent to request her sister's permission to retire to her seat at Ashridge in Hertfordshire;

and her application was granted by Mary with every demonstration of cordial affection.

The triumph of the imperialist party seemed complete ; and Noailles was fain to report to Henry that Mary seemed more Spanish than English in her sympathies. The Chancellor himself, now that Courtenay's chances appeared to be at an end, came forward as a supporter of the match with Spain, and proceeded to take a foremost part in the negotiations with respect to the various questions, direct and collateral, which such an alliance involved — the marriage treaty itself, the provisions in case of issue, and those in case of failure. On January 2, 1554, Count Egmont and other plenipotentiaries appeared in London, duly empowered to make the final arrangements. Courtenay himself gave them official welcome at Tower Hill, and conducted them to Westminster. On the 14th Gardiner read aloud in the presence chamber the articles which had been agreed upon, and pointed out the political advantages which would result from such an alliance. The articles, originally extending over thirteen pages, had been expanded to twenty-two, and represented the labours of ten commissioners — those co-operating with Renard, the Counts Egmont and Lalaing, de Courrières, and Philip Nigri ; those appointed by the Queen, Gardiner, Arundel, Paget, Sir Robert Rochester, and Petre. As finally agreed upon, the treaty must be held highly creditable to Gardiner's sagacity and ability ; and when, eighteen years afterwards, the marriage of Elizabeth with the Duke of Anjou was in contemplation, it served as the model for that which was then to be drawn up. It has however been pointed out as a somewhat suspicious feature that the concessions were all on the imperial side. If, indeed, treaties could bind, Philip stood hand-tied in his relations to England. While nominally sharing the government with the Queen, he was pledged scrupulously to respect the laws, privileges, and customs of the realm ; he was to settle on her a jointure of £60,000 ; their offspring were to succeed them in England in conformity with the traditional rights, and might also succeed to the territories in Burgundy and Flanders ; and, in the event of Philip's son, Don Carlos, dying without issue, this right of succession was to extend to Spain, Milan, and the Two Sicilies. Should Mary's marriage be unfruitful, Philip's connexion with England was to cease at her death. Under no pretext was England to be made participant in the war between the Emperor and France.

In the meantime Cardinal Pole's arrival in Brussels had been retarded by a long and involuntary stay at the university town of Dillingen, the residence of the Bishop of Augsburg ; while his endeavours to carry on his correspondence with Mary had been frustrated, their messengers having been stopped on each side of the Channel. It was with difficulty that she had conveyed to him the simple intimation that, as matters then stood, his appearance in England as the legate of the Holy See might prove disastrous to the cause which they both had nearest at heart.   But at length, making his way with nervous haste through the plague-smitten towns of Germany, he was able, through the good offices of Fray de Soto, who held a chair of divinity at Dillingen, to present himself at the imperial Court, where he arrived in January, 1554 ; and Mary's marriage with Philip being by this time virtually decided, his reception was both cordial and splendid.   The assurances which he received from Charles and his ministers were indeed so flattering, that he even ventured to hope that his mission as a peace-maker might yet be crowned with success.   But, long before the Cardinal could present himself at the French Court, a fresh crisis had supervened in England.

Here the belief was fast gaining ground that the realm was destined to become a dependency of Spain ; while in France it was no less firmly believed that Philip's marriage would be made the opportunity for the subjugation of Scotland.   Henry, placing no reliance on Mary's pacific assurances, deemed it advisable to send troops into that country, while Wotton, convinced that war was imminent, petitioned to be recalled. That Elizabeth should marry Courtenay and supplant her sister on the throne, now seemed to be the issue most favourable to French interests ; and while Henry's ambassadors at the English Court did their best to foment the growing suspicion of Spain, the monarch himself strove to spread the rumour of a fresh rising in England.   Writing to his envoy in Venice, he gave him the earliest intelligence of a rising in Kent ; and on February 18 Peter Vannes, writing to Mary, enclosed a copy of Henry's letter : according to the intelligence he had received from Noailles, Henry added, it was almost certain that all England would imitate the example thus set and "prefer to die in battle rather than become subject to a foreign Prince."   As early as Christmas, the conspirators, assembling in London, had concerted a general rising, which, however, was not to take place until March 18.

Their plans, however, had been suspected ; and Gardiner, having wrung from the weak and faithless Courtenay a full confession of the plot, had taken prompt measures for its repression.   The ringleaders, who were thus anticipated in their designs nearly two months before the time agreed upon for carrying them into execution, flew recklessly to arms.   Suffolk and Sir James Croft, each seeking to raise his tenantry — the one in Warwickshire, the other in Wales — were both arrested and consigned to the Tower before the second week in February had passed.   In Devonshire, towards the close of January, local feeling appears to have led a certain number of the gentry to make a demonstration in Courtenay's favour, Sir Peter Carew, who had been sheriff of the county, being foremost among them.   His family, however, were unpopular and commanded but little influence, and the other leaders, after vainly awaiting Courtenay's promised appearance at Exeter, suddenly dispersed in panic.   Carew fled to Paris and thence to Venice, where his adventurous and turbulent career was nearly brought

to a conclusion by bravos whom Peter Vannes was accused of having
hired to assassinate him.

The chief danger arose in Kent, where Sir Thomas Wyatt, a bold
and skilful leader, succeeded in collecting a considerable force at
Rochester, which was shortly after augmented by 2000 men who had
deserted from the standard of Lord Abergavenny near Wrotham Heath.
This gathering was the response to a proclamation which he had
previously (January 25) issued at Maidstone, in which Mary's supporters
were denounced as aiming at the perpetual servitude of her most
loving subjects. Englishmen were adjured to rise in defence of liberty
and the commonwealth, while intimation was given that aid was on
its way from France. With Noailles Wyatt appears actually to have
been in correspondence. The Council were divided as to the course
which should be pursued and distracted by mutual recriminations; while
they also evinced no alacrity in taking measures for the raising of troops.
Mary, whom Renard dissuaded from quitting the capital, exhibited on
the other hand a courage and resolution which roused the loyal feeling
of all around her. While part of the City Guard at once set out to
meet the insurgents, the Corporation proceeded to arm an additional
force of 500 men to follow in their track. As they approached Rochester
Bridge, the Duke of Norfolk, by whom they were commanded, sent
forward a herald to proclaim that "all such as wolde desyst their
purpose shuld have frank and free pardon." On February 1 the Queen
herself appeared at a gathering of the citizens in the Guildhall and
delivered a speech which excited general enthusiasm. Wyatt, she said,
had demanded to be entrusted with the care of her person, the keeping
of the Tower, and the placing of her counsellors; she was convinced that
her loyal subjects would never consent that such confidence should be
placed in so vile a traitor. As for her marriage, the conspirators were
simply making it "a Spanish cloak to cover their pretended purpose
against our religion." The Council had pronounced her marriage expedient "both for the wealth of the realm and also of you, our subjects";
should the nobility and the Commons deem it otherwise, she was willing
"to abstain from marriage while she lived." Her courage and out-
spokenness produced a considerable effect; for two days later Noailles
sent word that the populace, who had been reported to be meditating
an attack on the palace and the consignment of Mary herself into
Wyatt's hands, were actively occupied with putting the City into a state
of defence and had mustered to the number of 25,000 armed men.
To whoever should succeed in making Wyatt a prisoner and bringing
him before the Council, a reward of an annuity of one hundred pounds
was held out, payable in perpetuity to himself and his descendants.

At this juncture Wyatt appeared in Southwark, but his army
amounted only to some 7000 men; no force had arrived from France,
while the royal army was daily receiving reinforcements. The

contemporary chronicler has described in graphic narrative the incidents of the final episode:—Wyatt's arrival at Hyde Park Corner ; the fierce fighting that ensued as he pressed on to the City ; the flight of the cowardly Courtenay ; Lord Howard's resolute refusal to open Lud Gate ; Wyatt's consequent retreat in the direction of Charing Cross, and surrender at Temple Bar. The number of those slain in the fighting was about forty ; fifty of the conspirators were afterwards hanged, the rest were allowed to betake themselves to their homes.

Mary's former clemency had been censured by Charles ; and the Queen herself, justifiably incensed at the manner in which that clemency had been requited, was determined not to err again in the same direction. Gardiner, preaching in her presence on February 11, exhorted her now to have mercy on the commonwealth, "the conservation of which required that hurtful members should be cut off." On the following day the tragedy of the execution of the Lady Jane and Lord Guilford Dudley took place on Tower Hill. Of Suffolk's duplicity and entire want of good faith there could be no doubt, while his known sympathy with the Continental Reformers filled up the measure of his offence ; and his execution followed about a week later. Wyatt and Suffolk's wealthy and ambitious brother, Lord Thomas Grey, suffered the same fate in the following April. On the same day that the executions commenced Courtenay again found himself a prisoner in the Tower ; here he was confronted with Wyatt, who directly accused him of complicity in the rebellion, and for a time his fate seemed doubtful. A few weeks later, however, he was removed to Fotheringay ; and a year after he was released on parole, on condition that he quitted the kingdom, when he selected Padua as the place of his retirement. The last of the rebels to suffer was William Thomas, Clerk of the Council under Edward VI, whose execution took place on May 18. According to the statement of Wyatt in his confession before the Commission, Thomas had been the first to suggest the assassination of Mary. In the Tower he attempted suicide ; and no detail of ignominy was omitted at his execution.

From each victim an endeavour was made to extort evidence which might assist the authorities in tracing the conspiracy to its suspected origin, and the investigations were consequently lengthened. Charles, although he still counselled caution and deliberation in dealing with matters of religion, urged promptitude in the punishment of the conspirators, so that Mary, "while taking such measures as seemed requisite for her own security in regard to Elizabeth and Courtenay," might the sooner be able to exercise clemency towards those whom she designed to spare, and thus reassure the great majority. The Emperor, indeed, found her procrastination so inexplicable that he was inclined to attribute it to a desire on the part of Gardiner to protect Courtenay. At the commencement of the outbreak Mary had summoned Elizabeth back to Court, where a closer surveillance could be maintained over her movements. The Princess deferred compliance under the plea of illness ; but on February 22 she arrived in a litter at St James'. Here she remained, a virtual prisoner, until March 18, when the order was given for her removal to the Tower. Thence, on May 18, she was removed to Woodstock, where she continued to reside until the following April, under the custody of Sir Henry Bedingfield, closely watched and deprived of writing materials, but allowed to have service performed according to the English ritual. After the conspiracy had been crushed Charles strongly urged that the Princess should be executed, on the ground of her connivance at Wyatt's plans. Wyatt himself, indeed, in his last words on the scaffold, completely and emphatically exonerated her. It was asserted, however, that there was documentary evidence of her guilt, but that it was destroyed by Gardiner, to whose exertions she was, at this crisis, probably indebted for her life.

The gain to the imperial power which would accrue from the marriage between Mary and Philip had been regarded by Venice with an apprehension scarcely less than that of France ; and it was an ascertained fact that a Venetian carrack, anchored at the mouth of the Thames, had supplied Wyatt with arms and a cannon. Suspicion fell upon Soranzo ; but on being interrogated before the Council he stoutly denied all knowledge of the transaction, although complaints against him continued to be urged, and the charge itself was formally preferred by Vargas in Venice. On March 27, accordingly, Soranzo's letters of recall were drawn up, and Giovanni Michiel was appointed his successor. On May 22 the latter arrived in England. It probably attests his impartiality in the discharge of his functions that, both by Renard and Noailles, he was subsequently reproached as favouring the opposite party. He appears in reality to have conducted himself throughout with discretion and probity ; and, while gaining the esteem of the most discerning judges with whom he came in contact in England, he continued to command the undiminished confidence of the Venetian Council.

In March, Pole had arrived at St Denis, and shortly after had an audience of the King, by whom he was received with marked cordiality. The question of Mary's marriage was naturally one on which the expression of his views was invited ; and he was unable to conceal his personal conviction that, Courtenay's political career having now terminated, it would be better that the Queen of England should remain unmarried. In any case, he admitted that her marriage with Philip appeared to him undesirable. That such was his opinion soon became known at the imperial Court ; and, on his return to Brussels in April, he not only received a sharp rebuke from the Emperor, but shortly after learned that Charles had urged in Rome the desirability of his recall. He continued, however, to reside in the monastery of Diligam, near Brussels ; for Pope Julius could not but feel that his presence as Legate in England would soon be indispensable. But for the present the fact that his attainder by Parliament was still unreversed, and the evident expediency of reassuring those who now held the alienated Church lands as to his intentions with regard to their restitution, sufficed to justify a slight further delay.

In the meantime, the reaction which ensued after the insurrection had been suppressed had enabled Mary to make known her policy, and to carry it into effect with less reserve. In March, Egmont returned from Brussels, and in his presence and that of the Earl of Pembroke the Queen formally betrothed herself to Philip. Every effort was now made to diffuse throughout the country the belief that the marriage would prove conducive to the stability of the realm and to the increase of its prestige. Wotton, writing to Noailles from Paris, pointed out, at some length, that the involved alliance with Spain was England's indispensable rejoinder to the danger which menaced her through the conjunction of France with Scotland; while he further maintained that it was as a means of defence against this ominous combination that Charles desired to bring about a union between England and Flanders, between the House of Tudor and that of Habsburg; as for the intention with which France credited him, — the subjugation of the country and the disarming of its population, — such designs had no place in the imperial breast. In support of these views he adduced the fact that large numbers of the English malcontents were daily arriving in France, seeking service under Henry, "in order to carry on the war against the Emperor by sea."

The assembling of Mary's second Parliament (April 2, 1554) at Westminster also served, from the contrast it presented to its predecessor, to emphasise a new departure in public affairs. Not more than seventy of the members of the former House reappeared in the new; and the entire body evinced a spirit of far more ready compliance with the royal wishes. The leading members accepted gratefully the pensions which Mary, aided by the imperial liberality, was able to offer them; and the marriage bill, as it came down from the Upper House, received a ready assent. The necessity for discussion, indeed, was diminished by the fact that the conditions already agreed upon between Charles and Gardiner were now restated with explanatory clauses to obviate misinterpretation. It was also expressly stipulated that the royal match should not in any way "derogate from the league recently concluded between the Queen and the King of France, but that the peace between the English and the French should remain firm and inviolate." Some opposition was offered, however, to the proposal to repeal the two Acts for the dissolution of the bishopric of Durham, the measure being carried by a majority of only 81 in a House of 321.

Her main objects thus attained, Mary dismissed Parliament on May 5; and for the next two months her energies and attention were mainly concentrated on the preparations for the reception of Philip, who arrived from Corunna in Southampton Water on July 20. He was escorted

on the voyage by 150 vessels, carrying a splendid retinue and treasure
in bullion amounting to half-a-million of English money. The marriage
ceremony, performed by Gardiner, took place in the Cathedral Church
of his own diocese of Winchester. At the conclusion, proclamation
was made of the future style of Philip and his bride, — "King and
Queen of England, France, Naples, Jerusalem, and Ireland, Defenders
of the Faith, Princes of Spain and Castile, Archdukes of Austria,
Dukes of Milan, Burgundy, and Brabant, Counts of Habsburg, Flanders,
and Tyrol." Their public entry into London took place towards the
close of August; and the capital now became thronged with Spaniards,
among whom priests and friars formed a considerable element. The
regularity with which Philip attended mass and observed the other
offices of his Church was necessarily construed into evidence of his designs for the restoration of the Roman worship; nor can it be doubted
that both to him and Mary this appeared as the paramount object com-
manding their attention.

Among the royal advisers Gardiner and Paget, by virtue of both
experience and ability, assumed the foremost place. Neither, however,
could be said to be recommended by consistency of principle in his
past career; they had, at more than one juncture, been rivals and
even bitter enemies, and they still differed widely in their policy and
aims. While Gardiner, who aspired to a dictatorship in the Council,
insisted on immediate and coercive measures against heresy, Paget,
although admitting that the re-establishment of the ancient faith
was essential to a satisfactory adjustment of the affairs of the realm,
demurred to what he termed methods of "fire and blood." In their
perplexity the two sovereigns appear alike to have come to the conclusion that it might be well to take counsel with advisers who, by
their remoteness from the theatre of recent events, might be better
able to take a dispassionate view. Foremost among these stood Reginald Pole, who, as Legate, had already, in the preceding April, at Mary's
request, nominated six more Bishops to fill the vacant sees, — White,
to Lincoln; Bourne, to Bath; Morgan, to St David's; Brooks, to
Gloucester; Cotes, to Chester; Griffith, to Rochester. In a highly
characteristic letter the Legate himself now appealed to King Philip to
admit him, as the Vicar of Christ, "at that door at which he had so long
knocked in vain." A precedent afforded by the records of Gardiner's own
see of Winchester was at the same time opportunely brought forward as
a solution of the difficulty caused by Pole's still unreversed attainder.
In the fifteenth century, when the proctor of the English Crown appealed
against the exercise of the legatine functions with which Martin V had
invested Cardinal Beaufort, at that time also Bishop of Winchester, it
had been suggested that Beaufort might act *tanquam cardinalis* although
not *tanquam legatus*. It was now ruled that Pole might be admitted
into the realm as a Cardinal Ambassador although not as Legate;

while the apprehensions which this decision might have aroused were to a great extent dissipated when it was known that he had obtained from the Pontiff powers whereby he would be able to grant to all holders of monastic and collegiate lands the right of continuing in possession.

On November 20 Pole landed at Dover, and proceeded thence by Canterbury and Rochester to Gravesend. Here he was presented with two documents which finally cleared away all impediments from his path : the first, an Act of Parliament, passed ten days before, reversing his attainder ; the second, letters patent brought by the Bishop of Durham, empowering him to exercise without restraint his functions as Legate. His progress from Gravesend to Whitehall, accordingly, resembled a triumphal procession, and on his arrival in the capital he was greeted with special honour by Philip and Mary. Writs, in which the title of "Supreme Head" was discarded, were forthwith issued for a third Parliament, to meet on November 12 ; and on the 27th the Legate delivered before the assembled members a Declaration, couched in highly figurative language, explanatory of the circumstances under which he had been sent, of the object of his coming, and of the powers with which he had been invested. At the conclusion of his address he was formally thanked by Gardiner, and after he had quitted the assembly the Chancellor declared that he had spoken as one inspired. On the following day the question was put to both Houses, whether England should return to the obedience of the Apostolic See? The affirmative was carried without a dissentient among the Peers, and with but two in the Commons. On St Andrew's Day, Pole, on bended knee before Mary, presented her with the Supplication of the two Houses, "that they might receive absolution, and be readmitted into the body of the Holy Catholic Church, under the Pope, the Supreme Head thereof." After further formalities, and intercession made by King and Queen on behalf of the Houses, Pole pronounced the absolution and received the petitioners, by his authority as Legate, "again into the unity of our Mother the Holy Church."

The legislation of the two preceding reigns in all that related to the authority of the Roman see was now rescinded ; and on Advent Sunday Gardiner, at Paul's Cross, in the presence of the King and the Legate, called upon the nation to rouse itself from the slumbers and delusions of the past years and to return to the true fold, while he himself at the same time abjured the doctrine set forth in his *De Vera Obedientia* and declared his unreserved submission to the papal power.

Another Supplication, and one of very different tenour, now issued from within those prison walls where the chief leaders of the Reformers were confined. It detailed the hardships to which they were subjected ; claimed that the accusations brought against them should be distinctly stated, in order that they might be heard in their own defence ; and, since it was as heretics that they had been singled out for imprisonment, they

urged that "heresy" should be legally defined. Parliament's response to
this appeal was the re-enactment of three ancient statutes formerly in
force against Lollardism. The measure passed rapidly through both
Houses, the only opposition which it encountered proceeding from the
Lords, where some objection was urged to the restoration of the old
episcopal jurisdiction, while the penalties enacted were pronounced
excessive. As the result of this legislation, John Rogers (the protomartyr of the reign) died at the stake in the following February; and
a series of like tragical scenes followed, in which the sufferings of the
martyrs and the fortitude with which they were endured, combined
to produce a widespread impression. So marked, indeed, was the
popular sympathy, that Renard felt bound to suggest to Philip the
employment of less extreme measures, "otherwise the heretics would
take occasion to assert that the means employed by the Church to
bring back perverts to the fold were, not teaching and example, but
cruel punishments." He further advised that Pole should, from time
to time, have audience of the Council and be consulted by them with
regard to the penalties to be enforced. Unfortunately, neither Gardiner
nor Pole was inclined from previous experience to advocate a lenient
course. The former was especially anxious to give proof of the sincerity of his recent repudiation of his former tenets; the latter was
scarcely less desirous of showing that under a gentle demeanour he
was capable of cherishing a strong purpose. Five years before, when
his merits as a candidate for the tiara were under discussion at the
Conclave, it had been urged against Pole that when at Viterbo he had
been wanting in the requisite severity towards obstinate heretics; and
he had himself always claimed to have inclined to mercy when assisting
at the conferences of the Council of Trent. But he was especially
anxious at this time to leave no occasion for a similar reproach in
England, and his discharge of his functions during the remainder of
the reign cannot be regarded as lenient; although in Convocation, as
late as January, 1555, he admonished the Bishops to use gentleness
in their endeavours towards the reclaiming of heretics.

For the merciless severities which ensued, the violence of the more
intolerant Reformers also afforded a partial extenuation; and it is
now generally admitted that the part played by Bonner was not that
attributed to him by Foxe, of a cruel bigot who exulted in sending
his victims to the stake. The number of those put to death in his
diocese of London was undoubtedly disproportionately large, but this
would seem to have been more the result of the strength of the Reforming
element in the capital and in Essex than to the employment of exceptional rigour; while the evidence also shows that he himself dealt
patiently with many of the Protestants, and did his best to induce them
to renounce what he conscientiously believed to be their errors.

In the course of 1555 events abroad brought about a further

modification of the relations of England with the Holy See. In February an embassy had been sent to Julius III, to make known to him the unreserved submission of the English Parliament. The ambassadors proceeded leisurely on their journey, and while still on the way were met by the tidings of the Pontiff's death, which had taken place on March 23. Charles forthwith sent an urgent request to Pole to repair to Rome, in order to support the imperial interests in the new election. The Cardinal, however, sought to be excused, on the ground that the negotiations for peace were even of yet greater importance for the welfare of Christendom. His friend, Cardinal Alessandro Farnese, hastened from Avignon to Rome, in order to support his claims in the Conclave; but Pole himself seemed, according to Michiel, without any personal ambition at this crisis. The efforts of France were forestalled by the election of Cardinal Corvini; but, before another three weeks had elapsed, Marcellus II himself was no more.

This second opportunity seemed both to Mary and to Gardiner one that should not be disregarded, and Pole's claims were now strongly urged; even Noailles admitted that no election was more likely to bring peace to Christendom, nor could he conceive of any other Pontiff who would hold the balance with such equal impartiality between France and the Empire. Again, however, the Italian party triumphed; and even Pole himself may have questioned the wisdom of his abstention when Gian Pietro Caraffa (now in his eightieth year) succeeded as Paul IV to the papal chair. The house of Caraffa was Neapolitan and had long been on friendly terms with France, while it cherished a corresponding hereditary enmity towards Spain. Paul could remember Italy in the days of her freedom, and his hatred of the Spanish domination had been intensified by not unfrequent collisions with the imperial representatives in the Neapolitan territory, and not least by the strenuous efforts they had made to defeat his election to the Archbishopric of Naples. The bestowal of Milan and the crown of Italy on Philip, on his betrothal to Mary, had still further roused Caraffa's ire. Paul, indeed, did not scruple to accuse Charles of dealing leniently with heretics in order to show his aversion from the Roman policy. Before the year 1555 closed he had concluded a secret treaty with France, which had for its special object the expulsion of the imperialist forces from the Italian peninsula. Charles, when informed by the Nuncio of the election, blandly observed that he could well remember, when himself a boy of fourteen, hearing the new Pope sing mass at Brussels. Michiel, however, to whom Philip at Hampton Court communicated the intelligence, could perceive that neither the King himself nor those "Spanish gentlemen" with whom he found the opportunity of conversing at Richmond were pleased, and says plainly: "They by no means approve of this election." In the same letter (June 6) he informs the Doge, that "Her Majesty expects and hopes during this week to comfort the realm by an auspicious delivery";

although he adds that this is earlier than the ladies of the bedchamber anticipate.

On Hampton Court, whither, some two months before, Sir Henry Bedingfield had conducted the Princess Elizabeth, the main interest of the English nation now became concentrated; and probably no period in her whole life was marked by more torturing doubt and anxiety. Her days passed in almost complete solitude; Gardiner, the Earl of Arundel, and other members of the Council were her only visitors; the object of their visits, as she soon became painfully aware, being to draw from her some unguarded expression which might be construed into an admission of her complicity in the insurrection. Their design, however, was baffled by her indignant and persistent denials; and when, early in July, Mary accorded her captive an interview, Elizabeth again, and in yet stronger language, asseverated her entire innocence. A visit from the King, addressing her with respectful demeanour and kindly words, encouraged while it somewhat mystified her; but before another ten days had passed away the sagacious Princess could easily interpret the change of purpose which his bearing had then indicated.

It now became known that Mary had been under a complete delusion, and that there would probably be no offspring from the royal marriage. Elizabeth's supporters at once took heart again, as they realised the change which had supervened in regard to her future prospects. They appeared in London in high spirits and large numbers, so comporting themselves, indeed, that the Council, in alarm, ordered the more prominent among them to retire to their estates, as suspected heretics and leagued with rebels. But Elizabeth herself was set at liberty and sought again her former seclusion at Ashridge; and, as Mary slowly awoke from her fond dream of maternity, Philip, freed from the obligation which had detained him at her side, began to advert to continental politics and to plead that the affairs of the Continent demanded his personal supervision abroad. Before, however, quitting his island kingdom, he deemed it necessary to advise his consort with respect to the treatment of Elizabeth during his absence — advice which differed materially from that given by his father. It was no longer suggested that political exigencies might call for the sacrifice of a sister's life. On the contrary, Mary was now recommended to extend all possible indulgence to the Princess, and the changed conditions of Elizabeth's existence became obvious even to the public at large: nor did intelligent observers require to be reminded that the daughter of Anne Boleyn was the only barrier to the succession of Mary Stewart, the betrothed of the French monarch, to the throne of England.

But round the present occupant of that throne the clouds were gathering more darkly than before, and Mary's temper and health were visibly affected by the wanton imputations directed against both herself and Philip. Among the Spanish party, not a little chagrined at the royal disillusionment, there were those who represented the young King as the victim of a designing woman, and who affected to believe that Mary's pretended pregnancy was a mere device to detain her husband by her side.   The Council, on the other hand, had to listen to allegations which asserted that the King, despairing of a lineal succession, was meditating a *coup de main*, by bringing over large bodies of Spanish troops and occupying the harbours and ports, and thus realising the long-suspected design of the Habsburg, — the reduction of England to a dependency of Spain.   Both Charles and Philip, again, became aware that with Mary's vanished hopes a considerable advantage in their negotiations with France had also disappeared; and the malicious exultation of Noailles knew no bounds.   Rarely in the annals of royalty in England had satire and ridicule been at once so rancorous and so unmerited.   The haughty Habsburg, acutely sensitive, under a seemingly impassive exterior, to all that affected his personal dignity, determined to quit the country, and, in obedience to his father's behest, to devote himself to the affairs of those vast possessions which he was soon to be called upon to rule.   On August 28, 1555, Philip sailed for the Low Countries.

The incidents which preceded his departure are described in detail by Michiel.   Before embarking, the King summoned the lords of the Council to the Council Chamber, and there handed them a series of suggestions for the government of the realm during his absence, together with a list of names of those whom he deemed most eligible for the conduct of affairs.   If we may credit the Venetian envoy, the judgment and ability displayed in this document excited the approval and admiration of all who perused it.   At Greenwich, where Philip embarked, he took leave of Mary at the head of the staircase of their apartments; the Queen maintaining her self-possession until he was gone, and then giving way to uncontrollable grief.   Pole, whom the King had designated as her chief counsellor, was indeed now the only adviser to whom she could turn with any confidence, and her sense of loneliness and desertion was intense.   The Cardinal, touched by her pitiable condition, compiled a short prayer for her use during her husband's absence.

The departure of Philip was, however, perfectly justified by the pressing state of affairs at the imperial Court, whither he had already received more than one urgent summons from his father.   Charles' health was giving way, and, although only in his fifty-sixth year, he was already contemplating retirement to "our kingdoms of Spain," there "to pass the rest of our life in repose and tranquillity."   But before this could be, it was imperative that he should make the necessary dispositions for the succession in his own imperial domains; while he also aspired to arrange, if possible, for the regal succession in England. Although no reasonable hope of issue from his   ge could
   r be entertained, the astute Emperor would no   oject

of securing the English Crown to his own House without a final effort; and he now proposed that the Princess Elizabeth should be betrothed to his nephew, the Archduke Ferdinand. But in return for the accession of territory and influence that would thus accrue to the Austrian branch, he insisted that Philip should receive for Italy the title of "Vicar of the Empire," implying the delegation of the supreme imperial power. The objections of Ferdinand prevented the public execution of this stipulation, which was however later secretly carried out. For a time, indeed, it was currently reported that Ferdinand's succession to the Empire itself was in jeopardy; a coolness arose between the two brothers; and when on October 25, 1555, Charles made a formal surrender at Brussels of his Flemish provinces to his son, neither the King of the Romans nor his son Maximilian appeared in the august assemblage. The ceremony took place in the Town Hall of the capital, where Charles, taking his seat on his throne, with Philip on his right hand and Mary, the late Regent of the Low Countries, on his left, and surrounded by his nobles and ministers of State and the delegates of the provinces, formally ceded to his son, the "King of England and of Naples," the entire surrounding territories — "the duchies, marquisates, principalities, counties, baronies, lordships, villages, castles, and fortresses therein, together with all the royalties."

It can scarcely be deemed surprising if, amid these new and vast responsibilities, Philip's insular kingdom and its lonely Queen might seem at times forgotten; or that Charles, whose design it had been to set out for Spain as soon as possible, found his departure unavoidably retarded until the year 1556 was far advanced. But in the February of that year the Truce of Vaucelles ended for a time the hostilities with France, Henry thereby retaining possession of the entire territories of the Duke of Savoy. With his habitual want of good faith, however, the French monarch did not scruple, whenever an opportunity presented itself, still secretly to foment insurrection against both Philip and Mary in their respective domains.

At length, on August 9, the Emperor finally quitted Brussels, and embarked, a month later, for Spain. His departure was pathetically deprecated and deplored by Mary, who, now guided almost solely by Pole, had during the previous year been directing her main efforts to the suppression of heresy within her realm.

The entire number of those who thus suffered during her reign was less than 400, — a number which appears small when contrasted with the thousands who had already died in a like cause in Provence, or who were destined to do so in the Low Countries. But the social eminence, high character, and personal popularity of not a few of the English martyrs, unalloyed, as in many cases these qualities were, with political disaffection, served to invest their fate with a peculiar interest in the eyes of their fellow-countrymen, — an interest which Foxe's *Book of Martyrs*, chained to the "eagle brass" of many a parish church, did much to perpetuate. The prominence thus secured for that partial record was the means of winning for its contents an amount of attention from later historical writers greatly in excess of its actual merits. It needed, however, neither misrepresentation nor partisanship to gain for many of the martyrs of Mary's reign the deep sympathy of observant contemporaries. John Rogers, once a prebendary of St Paul's and lecturer on divinity, followed to the stake by his wife and children, nerved by their exhortations, and expiring unmoved and unshaken before their gaze, — the reasonable defence and legally strong position of Robert Ferrar, the former Bishop of St David's, — the transparent honesty and scholarly acumen of John Bradford, — the fine qualities and youthful heroism of Thomas Hawkes (whom Bonner himself would gladly have screened), — all commanded sympathy and were entirely dissociated from that political discontent which undoubtedly called for prompt and stern repression.

With regard however to the three distinguished martyrs, who died at Oxford, there was a wide difference. In proportion to their eminence had been their offence as contumacious offenders. Cranmer, as signatory to the late King's will and thereby participant in the diversion of the Succession as well as in the actual plot on behalf of the Lady Jane, had two years before been condemned to suffer the penalty of high treason. And although the extreme penalty had been remitted, the sentence had carried with it the forfeiture of his archbishopric, and he remained a prisoner in the Tower. His captivity was shared by Ridley and Latimer, of whom the former had been scarcely less conspicuous in his support of the Lady Jane, while the latter, as far back as the reign of Henry, had been, for a time, a prisoner within the same walls, denounced as active in "moving tumults in the State." Had it not been for Wyatt's conspiracy they would probably have regained their freedom; but with that experience Mary came to the conclusion that her past clemency had been a mistaken policy, and in conjunction with Pole she now resolved to show no leniency to those convicted of heretical doctrine. Such a mode of procedure was convenient when compared with prosecutions for treason, as at once less costly, more expeditious, and allowing the use of evidence afforded by the culprits themselves. It was also certain that not one of the three distinguished ecclesiastics would have ventured to deny that heresy was an offence which called for the severest penalties. Cranmer, in conjunction with his chaplain Ridley, had pronounced sentence in 1549 on Joan Bocher, and in doing so had been perfectly aware that her condemnation involved her death by burning at the hands of the secular power. Ridley in his notable sermon at Paul's Cross in 1553 had denounced Mary as a usurper, not on the ground of the illegality of her succession but as one altogether intractable in matters of "truth, faith and obedience." Latimer, when Bishop of

Worcester, had expressed his unreserved approval of a sentence whereby a number of Anabaptists perished at the stake ; and, on the occasion when Friar Forest met with a like fate for denying the supremacy claimed by Henry VIII, had preached against the papal claims to spiritual jurisdiction in England. Accordingly, just as the Reformers had resorted to political rebellion in order to bring about the downfall of theological error, so the Crown now sought to punish political disaffection on the grounds of religious heresy. The power which invoked the law could also enforce its own definition of the offence.

The Reformers had however frequently complained that they suffered persecution as heretics, while the exact nature of their offence remained itself undefined. It was accordingly resolved that no doubt should be suffered to remain in the cases of Latimer, Cranmer, and Ridley : — out of their own mouths should their condemnation be justified. Such was the design with which, in March, 1554, they were brought from the Tower to Oxford, and there called upon to defend, in a formal disputation, their doctrine respecting the Mass. Nor would it have been easy to take exception to the right of these three eminent men to represent the tenets of their party. The first had been Bishop of Worcester in the reign of Henry ; the second had filled the see of Canterbury for more than twenty years ; the third had been Bishop of London, and in that capacity had assisted at the deprivation of Bonner (his predecessor, and now his successor), and also at that of Gardiner. All three again had filled positions of importance in their University of Cambridge, and were presumed to be masters of dialectical disputation ; just as their opponents, who were eleven in number, had been selected from the two Universities. Latimer, however, was now in his seventieth year, and it was no reflexion on his courage that he declined an ordeal in which quickness of apprehension and a ready memory were essentials. The disputation was, however, vigorously maintained by Cranmer and Ridley in conflict with their numerous antagonists. But they did so only to be pronounced defeated ; and after proceedings which extended over six days, they were recommitted to "Bocardo," as the common gaol was designated (in allusion to a logical position from which a disputant finds it impossible to extricate himself). The condemnation involved the assumption that doctrines of faith and practice were amenable to the decisions of casuistry rather than to the teaching of Scripture, and was therefore contrary to the principles of the more advanced Reformers.

The captives succeeded in corresponding with each other and coming to an understanding with respect to a declaration of their distinctive tenets (May, 1554). Among other leading divines then suffering imprisonment were three of the Bishops created in Edward's reign,— John Hooper of Exeter, Robert Ferrar of St David's, and Miles Coverdale of Exeter, and well-known Reformers, such as Rowland Taylor, John Philpot, John Bradford, and Edward Crome. But none of these were comparable for learning, dialectical capacity, and intellectual acumen with the three Bishops whose doctrines already stood condemned ; and, when the other Reformers learnt that they were to be called upon to face a similar ordeal, they anticipated such a requirement by an intimation that they would not consent to engage in a formal disputation but were willing to set forth their views and defend them in writing.

They also explained what their leading tenets were :— the acceptance of the doctrine of Justification by Faith alone, the repudiation of the doctrines of Purgatory and transubstantiation, together with the adoration of the Host, clerical celibacy, and Latin services. They, however, professed unqualified loyalty to the Queen and deprecated all conspiracies against her authority. With respect to this manifesto no action appears to have been taken ; but the petitioners were still detained in captivity, and before the year closed Parliament enacted afresh the ancient laws against Lollardism, including Archbishop Arundel's notorious statute *de haeretico comburendo*, all of which had been abolished by Somerset. Conscious of the net which was being drawn around them, and that their heresy was becoming a question of life or death, the captives instructed John Bradford to draw up in their name a new Declaration, couched however in far from conciliatory terms. As against the newly enacted laws of Richard II and his two successors, they appealed to Parliament to re-enact the "many godly laws touching the true religion of Christ" set forth in the two preceding reigns "by two most noble Kings"; laws which, they affirmed, had been passed only after much discussion among the doctors of Cambridge and Oxford, and with the cordial and full assent of the whole realm. Not a single parish in England, they declared, was desirous of a return to "the Romish superstitions and vain service" which had recently been introduced. They maintained that the homilies and services adopted during King Edward's reign were truly Catholic, and were ready to prove them so ; or, if they failed in this, to give their bodies to be burned as the Lollard laws prescribed.

The Parliament to which the petitioners appealed gave no response to their supplication, although a spirit of reaction is distinctly discernible in the Commons during this session. That body had shown a marked disinclination to re-enact the laws against Lollardism ; and although it had consented to annul the ecclesiastical legislation of Henry VIII, so far as this affected the papal prerogatives and authority, it had confirmed institutions and individuals alike in their possession of the property which Henry had wrested from the Church. In the event, again, of the royal marriage being blessed with offspring, Philip had been appointed Regent, should he survive his consort ; but his regency was to last only so long as the minority of their child, and was to carry with it the obligation to reside in England. And finally, it was decided that the articles of the marriage treaty were to continue in full force, while the proposal that Philip himself should be honoured with a solemn coronation was rejected. Altogether, there had been much to remind the King of certain essential differences between monarchy in Spain and monarchy in England. And when on January 16, 1555, the dissolution of Parliament took place, Noailles could note, with malicious satisfaction, the smallness of the retinue which accompanied the sovereigns to the House of Lords and the dissatisfaction shown in the House itself by both Mary and her consort.

After a painful and ignominious imprisonment extending over more than two years, the three Bishops found themselves in September, 1555, again seated in the Divinity School at Oxford, awaiting their trial for the heresies of which they had already been convicted. The conduct of the proceedings was entrusted to a Commission appointed by the Legate; and Cranmer, the first who was formally summoned, stood with his head covered, pleading at the outset that he had sworn never to admit the authority of the Bishop of Rome in England, and at the same time refusing to recognise that of the Bishop of Gloucester, who had been appointed to preside over the proceedings, as his lawful judge. Fresh charges, among them his marriage, were now brought against him; he was then cited, as a Metropolitan, to appear within eighty days in Rome to answer all accusations, and was finally consigned again to Bocardo. Ridley and Latimer were to be more summarily dealt with. Pole, indeed, sent Fray de Soto, who had been appointed to fill the Hebrew chair at Oxford in the absence of Richard Bruern, to argue with them. But it was of no avail; and both perished at the same stake, "to light," as Latimer himself there expressed it, "such a candle in England as should never be put out." Cranmer, who, from a tower above his prison chamber, witnessed their dying agonies, showed less resolution; and when Fray de Garcia, the newly appointed Regius Professor of Divinity, was sent to ply him with further arguments, he wavered, and admitted that even the papal supremacy, now that it had been recognised by King, Queen, and Parliament, appeared to him in a new light. He was at last induced to sign a recantation, declaratory of his submission to the Pope as Supreme Head of the Catholic Church, and to the reigning sovereigns of his country and their laws. His formal degradation, however, which took place on February 14, opened his eyes to the fact that he had no mercy to look for at the hands of the papal delegates; and as his crozier was wrested from his grasp, and the mock vestments which symbolised his whole ecclesiastical career were successively removed from his person, and the pallium taken away, he resisted forcibly, at the same time producing from his sleeve a document in which he formally appealed from Paul IV to the next General Council. Prior to this ceremony he had for a few weeks been consigned to the care of the Dean of Christchurch and had lived in the enjoyment of every comfort; but he was now once more consigned to Bocardo. There, the terror of death came back, and he was induced to transcribe and sign other recantations. Eventually, however, in the Church of St Mary, on the day appointed for his execution, when a full and complete declaration of his penitence which should edify the religious world was expected, he astonished his audience by a complete disavowal of all his previous recantations, which were no less than six in number; and, when he was led forth to die, his vacillation in the prison was forgotten in his heroism at the stake. Suffering, ostensibly, as a heretic, Cranmer really expiated by his death the share which he had taken in procuring Henry's first divorce.

To the reactionary feelings which were discernible in Mary's third Parliament the martyrdoms that had taken place between February and October, 1555, had lent no slight additional strength; while those of Ridley and Latimer, only a few days before the assembling of her fourth Parliament on October 21, must have been especially fresh in men's memories. The attention of the new House was first invited to the needs of the royal exchequer, and Gardiner, as Chancellor, exerted all his powers to induce the assembly to grant a substantial subsidy. His demands were acceded to, although not without some opposition; and the gift of a million pounds — the payment of which, in the case of the laity, was to be extended over two years, in that of the clergy, over four — gave promise of effective relief; the latter body, if we may credit Pole, accepting their share of the burden with exemplary cheerfulness. To Mary, however, this satisfactory result must have appeared dearly purchased, involving as it did the loss of her Chancellor. In urging upon Parliament the necessities of the realm, Gardiner's oratorical efforts, combined with the dropsy from which he was suffering, brought on complete exhaustion; and although he sufficiently recovered to admit not only of his removal from Whitehall to Winchester House, but even of his presence at the Cabinet Councils which the ministers came from Greenwich to attend, it soon became apparent that his days were numbered. On November 12 he died. The reports which gained credit among his enemies, of his penitence and self-reproach in his last hours, have been shown by circumstantial evidence to be fabrications. Michiel, one of the least prejudiced, as he was certainly one of the most competent, observers, recalls the late Chancellor's untiring energy, wide practical knowledge, keen insight into character, and consummate tact, and represents his loss as irreparable; an estimate which the undisguised joy of the French party at the event seems only to confirm. The great prelate was ultimately laid to rest in his own Cathedral, to which he had bequeathed a third of his private fortune, and where his chantry chapel, in the Renaissance style, still preserves his memory.

On the day preceding Gardiner's death a bill was read in the House of Lords whereby the Crown surrendered into the hands of the Roman Pontiff the first-fruits and tenths of all ecclesiastical benefices — for "the discharge of our conscience," as Mary subsequently expressed it in a

series of instructions which she placed in the hands of Pole. But the
bill when it came down to the Commons at once gave rise to a warm
discussion, and was eventually carried against an ominous minority of
126. Six days later (December 9), Mary dissolved Parliament; and two
years elapsed before it met again.

In the meantime the royal purpose was becoming more inexorable
and pronounced. In the communications to Pole, above referred to,
Mary gave it as her opinion that it would "be well to inflict punishment" on those "who choose by their false doctrine to deceive simple
persons." It was, however, her express desire that no one should be
burnt in London "save in the presence of some member of the Council,"
and that during such executions some "good and pious sermons should
be preached." It was probably under the belief that Pole's better
nature would exert a certain influence, that Philip, when he departed
for the Low Countries, had advised Mary to take the Cardinal for her
chief counsellor. But firmness was never one of Pole's virtues, and when
confronted by a stronger will, in conjunction with that more practical
knowledge of men and affairs in which he was notoriously deficient, he
deferred to the judgment of others and reluctantly acquiesced in a
policy which he himself would never have originated. But he still at
times vacillated; and, as we have already noted, would recommend the
Bishops to have recourse to gentle methods in their endeavours to
reclaim heretics; while in August, 1556, he succeeded in setting free
no less than twenty prisoners whom Bonner had condemned to the
stake. It was possibly in anticipation of his resignation of the office
of *legatus a latere* that Pole aspired to succeed Gardiner as Privy Seal,
for the incompatibility of the two offices was obvious; the seal was
ultimately, at Philip's suggestion, bestowed on Lord Paget, who, as
a layman and a statesman of known tolerance in religious questions,
succeeded on January 29, 1556. The Chancellorship was not bestowed
on Thirlby, now Bishop of Ely, who had been discharging its duties as
deputy and whose claims were favoured by Mary — his known Catholic
sympathies rendering it inadvisable, even in the eyes of Philip, to
continue him in the office; and on January 1, the Great Seal was
conferred on Heath, Archbishop of York. Pole, however, succeeded
Gardiner as Chancellor of the University of Cambridge; and on March 22,
1556, the day after Cranmer was burnt at Oxford, he was consecrated
to the Archbishopric of Canterbury.

Under his auspices, and with the aid of the royal munificence, several
of the foundations which had been swept away by Mary's father in his
anger at their contumacious resistance to his arbitrary decrees now
rose again. The Grey Friars reappeared at Greenwich, the Carthusians
gathered once more in their splendid monastery at Sheen, the Brigettines
reassembled at Sion; while Feckenham, abandoning his deanery at
St Paul's, made his solemn entry into Westminster as Abbot of a body

of Benedictine monks who took the places of the expelled canons. Parliament had ceased from troubling; and, with the false teachers silenced, the heretical books suppressed, the authority of the ecclesiastical courts re-established, the new Primate might almost flatter himself that the ideal conditions contemplated in his *Reformatio Angliae* had become an accomplished reality. The denunciation of the Dudley conspiracy rudely dispelled this pleasing vision. On Easter Eve, April 4, 1556, official intelligence was received of a new plot, having for its aim the seizing of Mary's person and her deposition, in order to make way for Elizabeth, who was to marry, not Ferdinand, but Courtenay ; — a name still potent to conjure with, although the unfortunate nobleman was himself unambitious of the honour and then nearing his end, which came to him in the following September near Padua.

The plot itself, in its origin, was not suggestive of any very deep or widespread agencies, being the outcome of a series of meetings among some country gentlemen in Oxfordshire and Berkshire, — Sir Anthony Kingston, Sir Nicholas Throckmorton (a friend of Courtenay's, who had already been pardoned for complicity in Wyatt's rebellion), Sir Henry Peckham, and Sir Henry Dudley, a relative of the late Duke of Northumberland. Further evidence, however, obtained at a considerable interval, implicated not only Noailles, the ambassador, with whom Dudley was in correspondence, but also Henry, at whose Court Dudley had been received and his proposals favourably considered, and finally Elizabeth herself. The fact that, in the preceding February, Charles and Philip had concluded at Vaucelles a truce with Henry, which was to last for five years and included important concessions to France, showed the faithlessness of the French monarch. Henry, however, advised the conspirators to defer the execution of their plans, and to their disregard of this advice the collapse of the whole scheme appears to have been mainly attributable.

Among the arrests made in England were those of two members of Elizabeth's own household ; of these a son of Sir Edmund Peckham (one of Mary's staunchest supporters) turned King's evidence and his testimony chiefly implicated Elizabeth. Again, however, Philip exerted his influence for her protection, while the Princess asseverated her innocence. It was at this juncture, May 25, that Noailles himself requested to be recalled ; he had indeed some fear of being arrested by order of the Privy Council. His place at the English Court was temporarily taken by a brother, a councillor of the *Parlement* of Bordeaux ; and it was not until November 2 that Soranzo was able to report the arrival of the more distinguished brother, François, the protonotary, and Bishop of Acqs or Dax, in the same capacity. To François de Noailles Elizabeth confided her design of seeking an asylum in France ; he however strongly dissuaded her from such a step, suggesting that her best policy would be to remain in England. In after years the

Bishop of Acqs was wont to boast that Elizabeth was indebted to him for her crown.

Lord Clinton had been instructed to make a formal protest at the French Court against the countenance which Henry afforded to the English malcontents: but his remonstrance only drew from the King the splenetic observation that they were so numerous that they "filled not only France but the whole of Italy." In the Italian peninsula, indeed, Philip now found himself involved in relations far from amicable with the reigning Pontiff. Caraffa's aggressive nature did not dispose him to judge charitably of others, while he was believed by Philip to harbour designs against his Neapolitan kingdom. The Pope was especially indignant when he heard of the Truce of Vaucelles; and, when in June, 1556, despatches were intercepted at Terracina sent from the Spanish envoy in Rome to Alva, Philip's viceroy in Naples, describing the defenceless condition of the papal territory, his suspicions became certainty. In the ensuing month his nephew, Cardinal Caraffa, arrived in Paris to concert measures with Henry for expelling the Spaniard altogether from Italy. The personal ambition of the Guises favoured the Pontiff's projects, and war was ultimately resolved on. Paul cited both Charles and Philip before him as vassals who had been unfaithful to their feudal obligations, pronounced the latter deprived of his kingdom of Sicily, and detained the Spanish envoy a prisoner at St Angelo. Alva issued a counter manifesto and conducted his army into the papal territory, while late in December the Duke of Guise in turn made a rejoinder by crossing the Alps at the head of a considerable force.

Such was broadly the political situation in Europe when the year 1557 opened; England appearing leagued with Spain, on the one hand, against France aided by the temporal power of the Roman Pontiff on the other; while Englishmen in turn were divided between sympathy with those of their countrymen who had fled from persecution, and resentment at the manner in which they had deserted to the common foe.

At Calais and throughout the English Pale the exiles were now discovered to be concerting with the native Huguenot element the surrender to Henry of two important fortresses, those of Guines and Hames (between Guines and Calais),—a design which was defeated only by its timely discovery. It was at this juncture that Philip crossed over to Dover and from thence proceeded to Greenwich, where Mary was residing. Two days later the royal pair passed through London to Whitehall amid the acclamations of the citizens. The King's stay extended over nearly four months (March 18–July 3), and to the majority his visit appeared singularly opportune. The immediate object of his visit—to induce Mary to join him in his impending war with France—was one in favour of which his arguments might well appear irresistible. The Duke of Guise had already overrun his Neapolitan territory; and it seemed probable that the King of France would shortly conquer, if not vigorously opposed, all that was still English within the limits of his realm. Again, and for the last time, Pole found himself involved in relations of difficulty with the House of Habsburg; and he was under the necessity of privately explaining by letter to Philip that diplomatic etiquette forbade that the Legate of the Holy Father should meet his master's declared enemy; whereupon he withdrew quietly to Canterbury. In April, however, his embarrassment received an unlooked-for solution, by Paul's peremptory recall of his Legates from the whole of Philip's dominions; and when King and Queen joined in urging that the actual condition of England made the presence of a Legate exceptionally necessary, the Pope at first sought to evade compliance by offering to appoint a *legatus natus* and to attach the office to the Archbishopric of Canterbury Eventually, however, in a Consistory convened on June 14, he appointed William Peto, Mary's former confessor; thus substituting, as Phillips, Pole's biographer, indignantly expresses it, a begging friar for the royally descended Cardinal! At the same time, the merciless Pontiff cruelly wounded his former Legate's sensitive spirit by insinuating that he was a heretic. Pole expostulated in an *Apology*, extending over eighty folio pages, vindicatory of his whole career; but Paul never revoked the imputation, which darkened the Cardinal's remaining days.

While, in the meantime, Philip and his Queen were concerting measures with the Council, tidings arrived which imparted fresh force to the Pope's representations. On April 24 Thomas Stafford, a nephew of Pole and a grandson of the last Duke of Buckingham, had set sail with two ships from Dieppe and, having landed unopposed on the Yorkshire coast, had seized Scarborough Castle. Thence he issued a proclamation, announcing that he had come to deliver England from the tyranny of the foreigner and to defeat "the most devilish devices" of Mary. The rebellion, if such it could be termed, — for Stafford's appeal met with but slight response, — was speedily suppressed, Wotton's vigilance having given the government early intimation of his sailing; and its leader with a few of his personal adherents were captured by the Earl of Westmorland and sent to London. Stafford was found guilty of high treason, and suffered the punishment of a traitor at Tyburn (May 28). Henry, who designated Stafford as "that fool" and repudiated all knowledge of his mad undertaking, had probably full information of what was intended; and on June 7 war with France was declared. Affecting to regard this step as simply further evidence of "the Queen of England's submission to her husband's will," Henry at once ordered his ambassador at her Court to present his letters of recall, but François de Noailles had already been dismissed by Mary. On his way back to Paris, the latter stayed at Calais and made a careful survey of the fortifications; the ruinous condition of the outer wall more especially attracted his attention; and on his arrival in the capital and being admitted to an interview with the King, he expressed his belief that a sudden attack made by an adequate force on that ancient seaport would carry all before it.

Before Philip quitted England he received the gratifying intelligence that Alva's Fabian tactics had been successful against Guise, and that he had been finally driven from the Neapolitan territory. The mortification of Paul was equally intense, for he had scrupled at nothing to bring about an opposite result: had suggested to Solyman a descent on the Two Sicilies, and had brought over mercenaries from Protestant Germany, — and all this in order to defeat the forces of the eldest son of the Church! When the Duke of Guise appeared to present his letters of recall the Pope's fury passed all bounds of decorum: "You have done little for your King, less for the Church, and for your own honour nothing." Such were Paul's parting words, although he little deemed how complete and how lasting the failure of the French intervention was to prove, and that the Habsburg rule was destined to remain unshaken, alike in the north and south of the Italian land, until the war of the Spanish Succession.

On his return to Brussels Philip was accompanied by Michiel Surian, who had been appointed ambassador to his Court, and the Venetian Republic henceforth maintained no resident envoy in England. Of English affairs it had recently received the elaborate "Report" drawn up by Giovanni Michiel, and presented to the Doge and Senate in the preceding May. The King's first attention was now directed to the war with France, to which he addressed himself with unwonted energy. The signal victory of his arms at St Quentin, achieved mainly by a powerful division of Spanish cavalry, was attended by the capture of Montmorency, the French general, and the dispersion, with great slaughter, of his entire army; and three weeks later, St Quentin, which barred the road to Paris, was surrendered by Coligny. The news was received with great rejoicings in London, where a solemn *Te Deum* was sung; and Pole, at Mary's request, conveyed her congratulations to her husband. The conclusion of his letter is noteworthy: "We are anxiously expecting news of some good agreement with his Holiness, which may our Lord God deign to grant." With the Colonna already at the gates of Rome, even Paul himself now became aware that to yield was inevitable. Rarely however has the victor used his success with greater consideration for the vanquished. When Naples and its territory had been brought back to submission, Alva repaired to Rome, and, escorted by the papal guard into the Pontiff's presence-chamber, there fell upon his knees, imploring pardon for having dared, even at the command of his temporal sovereign, to bear arms against the Church, and was formally absolved. And again in London there were bonfires and illuminations in celebration of a peace, — the peace thus effected between Philip and the Papacy.

Although Mary is described by Michiel in his "Report" as friendly to the Scotch, the aid which she afforded Philip in his war with France almost necessarily involved hostilities with the former nation, in whose midst Mary of Lorraine, as Regent, had been for some time past installing her countrymen in official posts with undisguised partiality. The betrothal of the Queen of Scots to the Dauphin and the intimate relations which the Regent had throughout maintained with the French Court, served still further to strengthen the political alliance between the two countries. It was consequently no surprise when, in October, 1547, it became known in London that the Regent had built a fortress to prevent English forces from marching to the relief of Berwick; that Scottish troops were ravaging the country south of the Tweed; that there had been a massacre of some English troops which had ventured to land in the Orkneys; and that a battle between the forces of the two nations on the frontier was regarded as imminent. The intelligence of the great disaster sustained by the French arms at St Quentin gave pause, however, to the Scottish ardour. A council was convened in the church at Eckford, where the expediency of continuing the war was discussed, the decision being in the negative. The invading force was consequently disbanded, having achieved little more than the distraction, for a short time, of the attention of England from the war with France, and a certain addition to her military expenses. On April 24, 1558, the marriage of Mary Queen of Scots with the Dauphin was celebrated with great splendour in Notre Dame; and to not a few it seemed that France, by a less costly process than armed conquest, had effected a virtual annexation of Scotland. In the following November the National Council, assembled at the Palace of Holyrood, decided to confer on the King-Dauphin (as Francis was now termed in Paris) the Crown matrimonial.

At nearly the same time that François de Noailles' account of the neglected condition of Calais was communicated to Henry, Michiel, in his "Report," had described the town as an almost impregnable fortress, garrisoned by 500 soldiers and by a troop of 50 horse. Writing on January 4, 1558, he had to inform the Doge and Council of Ten that the capture of Calais was imminent; two days later, Lord Wentworth, notwithstanding his gallant defence, was compelled to surrender to the Duke of Guise, the only condition that he could obtain being that the lives of the inhabitants and of the garrison were to be spared. They were allowed, however, to take nothing with them, the soldiery giving up their arms, the citizens all their worldly possessions. A fortnight later the garrisons of Guines and Hames also surrendered, although on somewhat less humiliating terms. The expelled population of Calais betook themselves mostly to England, where their destitute and homeless condition served still further to increase the widespread indignation at the supineness and stupidity, as well as the suspected treachery, whereby the last stronghold of English power in France had been irrevocably lost.

Early in the year Mary again became a prey to the delusion that she was about to become a mother, and Philip was at once informed. He affected to entertain no misgiving, and before the end of January the Count de Feria, who had married Jane Dormer, one of the Queen's maids of honour, was sent over to convey the King's congratulations. England was already known to the new ambassador, who now assumed a foremost place among the royal counsellors. De Feria, however, had conceived a thorough contempt alike for English institutions and the English character. He had been instructed especially to urge two important measures — the equipment of a fleet for the defence of the coasts and the enrolment of an army to guard the Scotch marches; and he was unable to comprehend the slowness of the process by which the necessary supplies were eventually raised, when he also noted the apparent affluence and well-being of London and the surrounding districts. Like Antoine de Noailles before him, he pronounced the English character to be singularly changeable and wanting in firmness of purpose. His surprise, however, must be interpreted as illustrating rather the relative comfort in which the population lived, as compared with the invariably scanty fare and wretched huts of the people in Spain. Otherwise, the prevalence of ague fever, — an epidemic which raged with terrible fatality in the summer and autumn of the years 1557 and 1558, — together with the dearness of corn, the languishing state of trade and agriculture, and the heaviness of taxation, contributed to render the general condition of the country depressing in the extreme; while the popular dissatisfaction became further intensified, when it was known that Philip was employing the new marine exclusively for his own purposes.

The disappointment and chagrin which weighed on Mary's spirits during the last few months of her life were deepened by her increasing ill health; and her morbid condition both of mind and body appeared to not a few to be finding expression in the revival of religious persecution. But the recurrence of secret meetings, open manifestations of fierce discontent, together with the malevolence which assailed Spaniards even in the streets of the capital, may be accepted as affording a sufficient explanation of the renewed severities which marked the administration of Bonner's Court, where treason and heresy had become almost synonymous. Although, however, opinion may differ with respect to the degree and character of the chief influences in operation, it is undeniable that feelings of aversion on the part of the people from foreign rule and papal authority, and of sullen resentment at the humiliation of the English name and the squandering of the national resources, were alike becoming intensified, when, in the early morning of November 17, Mary of England passed away, to be followed a few hours later by Archbishop Pole — both eminent examples of the inadequacy of deep convictions and pious motives to guide the State aright.

CHAPTER XVI

THE ANGLICAN SETTLEMENT AND THE
SCOTTISH REFORMATION

WHEN at the beginning of 1560 there was a new Pope, pledged to convoke the Council for a third time and to stem and repel the tide of heresy, the latest disaster that met his eye was no mere relapse of England followed by a lapse of Scotland; for what was shaping itself in the northern seas already looked ominously like a Protestant Great Britain. Two small Catholic Powers traditionally at war with each other, the one a satellite of the Habsburg luminary, the other a satellite of France, seemed to be fusing themselves in one Power that might be very great: great perhaps for good, but more probably for evil. "Earnest embracing of religion," wrote a Scottish to an English statesman, "will join us straitly together." The religion that William Maitland meant when he sent these words to Sir William Cecil was not the religion of Pius IV and the General Council.

Suddenly all farsighted eyes had turned to a backward country. Eyes at Rome and eyes at Geneva were fixed on Scotland, and, the further they could peer into the future, the more eager must have been their gaze. And still we look intently at that wonderful scene, the Scotland of Mary Stewart and John Knox: not merely because it is such glorious tragedy, but also because it is such modern history. The fate of the Protestant Reformation was being decided, and the creed of unborn millions in undiscovered lands was being determined. This we see — all too plainly perhaps — if we read the books that year by year men still are writing of Queen Mary and her surroundings. The patient analysis of those love letters in the casket may yet be perturbed by thoughts about religion. Nor is the religious the only interest. A new nation, a British nation, was in the making.

We offer no excuse for having as yet said little of Scotland. Called upon to play for some years a foremost part in the great drama, her entry upon the stage of modern history is late and sudden. In such phrases there must indeed be some untruth, for history is not drama. The annals of Scotland may be so written that the story will be

continuous enough. We may see the explosion of 1559 as the effect
of causes that had long been at work. We might chronicle the remote
beginnings of heresy and the first glimmers of the New Learning. All
those signs of the times that we have seen elsewhere in capital letters we
might see here in minuscule. Also, it would not escape us that, though
in the days of Luther and Calvin resistance to the English and their
obstinately impolitic claim of suzerainty still seemed the vital thread
of Scottish national existence, inherited enmity was being enfeebled,
partly by the multiplying perfidies of venal nobles and the increasing
wealth of their paymasters, and partly also by the accumulating proofs
that in the new age a Scotland which lived only to help France and
hamper England would herself be a poor little Power among the
nations : doomed, not only to occasional Floddens and Pinkies, but to
continuous misery, anarchy, and obscurity.

All this deserves, and finds, full treatment at the hands of the
historians of Scotland. They will also sufficiently warn us that the
events of 1560 leave a great deal unchanged. Faith may be changed ;
works are much what they were, especially the works of the magnates.
The blood-feud is no less a blood-feud because one family calls itself
Catholic and another calls itself Protestant. The " band " is no less a
" band " because it is styled a " Covenant " and makes free with holy
names. A King shall be kidnapped, and a King shall be murdered, as of
old : — it is the custom of the country. What is new is that farsighted
men all Europe over, not only at London and at Paris, but at Rome and
at Geneva, should take interest in these barbarous deeds, this customary
turmoil.

Continuity there had been and to spare. In that mournful procession of the five Jameses there is no break (1406–1542). The last of
them is engaged in the old task, and failing as his forebears failed. It is
)picturesque ; sometimes it is heroic ; often it is pathetic ; but it is never
modern. Modern history sees it as a funeral procession burying a dead
time, and we are silent while it passes. In a few sentences we make our
way towards the momentous years.)

Scotland had been slow to emerge from the Middle Age. A country
which of all others demanded strong and steady government had been
plagued by a series of infant Kings and contested Regencies. In the
sixteenth century its barons still belonged to the twelfth, despite a thin
veneer of French manners. Its institutions were rudimentary ; its
Parliaments were feudal assemblies. Since the close of the War of
Independence there had been hardly anything that could properly be
called constitutional growth. Sometimes there was a little imitation of
England and sometimes a little imitation of France, the King appearing
as a more or less radical reformer. But the King died young, leaving
an infant son, and his feudatories had no desire for reformation. The

Scottish monarchy, if monarchy it may be called, was indeed strictly limited; but the limits were set much rather by the power of certain noble families and their numerous retainers than by an assembly of Estates expressing the constant will of an organised community. The prelates, lords, and represented boroughs formed but one Chamber. Attempts to induce the lesser tenants-in-chief to choose representatives who would resemble the English knights of the shire had been abortive, and a bad habit prevailed of delegating the work of a Parliament to a committee known as "the Lords of the Articles." Normally the assembly of Estates was but the registrar of foregone conclusions. In troublous times (and the times were often troublous) the faction that was in power would hold a Parliament, and the other faction would prudently abstain from attendance. When in 1560 an unusually full, free, and important Parliament was held for the reformation of religion, an elementary question concerning the right of the minor barons to sit and vote was still debatable, and for many years afterwards those who desire to see the true contribution of Scotland to the history of representative institutions will look, not to the blighted and stunted conclave of the three Estates with its titular Bishops and Abbots commendatory, but to the fresh and vigorous Assembly of the Presbyterian Church.

Steady taxation and all that it implies had been out of the question. The Scots were ready to fight for their King, unless they happened to be fighting against him; but they would not provide him with a revenue adequate for the maintenance of public order. He was expected "to live of his own" in medieval fashion, and his own was not enough to raise him high above his barons. Moreover, Douglases and Hamiltons and others, hereditary sheriffs and possessors of "regalities," were slow to forget that these crowned stewards of Scotland were no better than themselves. What had "come with a lass" might "go with a lass," and was in no wise mysterious. We shall see Queen Mary, widow of a King of France, giving her hand first to a Lennox-Stewart whose mother is a Douglas and then to a Hepburn, while the heir presumptive to the throne is the head of the Hamiltons. We shall see Queen Elizabeth having trouble with northern earls, with Percies and Nevilles, who set up an altar which she had cast down, and belike would have cast down an altar which she had set up; but their power to disturb England was as nothing to the power of disturbing Scotland which was exercised by those near neighbours and like-minded fellows of theirs who joined the bellicose Congregation of Jesus Christ. And even in the briefest sketch we must not omit to notice that, as beyond England lay Scotland, so beyond the historic Scotland lay the unhistoric land of "the savages." The very means that had been taken by Scottish Kings to make Scotsmen of these "red-shanks" and to bring these savages within the pale of history had raised up new feudatories of almost royal rank and of more than baronial turbulence. Thenceforward, the King would have to reckon, not only with an Albany, an Angus, and an Arran, but also with an Argyll and with a Huntly. When we see these things we think of the dark age : of Charles the Simple and Rolf the Pirate.

Neither valorous feats of arms which overtaxed a people's strength nor a superabundance of earls and barons should conceal from us the nakedness of the land. It is more than probable that in the middle of the sixteenth century the whole of the Scottish nation, including untamable Highlanders, was not too large to be commodiously housed in the Glasgow of to-day. Life was short, and death was violent. It is true that many hopeful signs of increasing prosperity and enlightenment are visible in the days of James IV (1488–1513). But those days ended at Flodden. The flowers of the forest were once more mown down. The hand went back upon the dial towards poverty and barbarity. An aptitude for letters we may see. Of a brief springtime of song Scotland may fairly boast, for as yet no icy wind was blowing from Geneva. Universities we may see : more universities indeed than the country could well support. By a memorable, if futile, Act of Parliament James IV attempted to drive the sons of the gentry into the grammar-schools. But an all-pervading lack of wealth and of the habits that make for wealth was an impediment to every good endeavour. The printing press had been in no hurry to reach England (1477) ; but thirty years more elapsed before it entered Scotland. An aptitude for jurisprudence we might infer from subsequent history ; but it is matter of inference. Of lawyers who were not ecclesiastics, of temporal lawyers comparable to the professionally learned justices and serjeants of England, we can hardly read a word. When at length James V founded the College of Justice (1532), half the seats in it, and indeed one more, were allotted to the clergy, and in later days foreign science was imported from the continental universities to supply the deficiencies of an undeveloped system. Scotland had been no place for lawyers, and the temporal law that might be had there, though it came of an excellent stock, had for the more part been of the bookless kind. And as with jurisprudence, so with statesmanship. The Scottish statesman who was not a Bishop was a man of a new kind when Lethington began his correspondence with Cecil ; for, even if we employ a medieval standard, we can hardly attribute statecraft or policy to the Albanys and Anguses and Arrans.

In this poor and sparsely peopled country the Church was wealthy ; the clergy were numerous, laic, and lazy. The names of " dumb dogs " and " idle bellies " which the new preachers fixed upon them had not been unearned. Nowhere else was there a seed-plot better prepared for revolutionary ideas of a religious sort. Nowhere else would an intelligible Bible be a newer book, or a sermon kindle stranger fires. Nowhere else would the pious champions of the Catholic faith be compelled to say so much that was evil of those who should have been their pastors. Abuses which had been superficial and sporadic in England were widely spread and deeply rooted in the northern kingdom. In particular, the commendation of ecclesiastical benefices to laymen, to babies, had become a matter of course. The Lord James Stewart, the King's base-born son, who at the critical moment is Prior of St Andrews and sits in Parliament as a member of the spiritual Estate, is a typical figure. The corslet had "clattered" beneath the Archbishop's cassock, and when Bishops and Abbots lie among the dead on Flodden field they have done no less but no more than their duty. We say that the Scottish Church was rich, and so it nominally was, for the kirk-lands were broad ; but when the Protestant ministers, much to their own disappointment, had to be content with a very small fraction of the old ecclesiastical revenues, they had probably secured a larger share than had for a long time past been devoted to any purpose more spiritual than the sustentation of royal, episcopal, and baronial families. We exclaim against the greedy nobles whose lust for the kirk-lands is one of the operative forces in the history of the Scottish Reformation. They might have said that they were only rearranging on a reasonable and modern basis what had long been for practical purposes the property of their class. Their doings send back our thoughts to far-off Carolingian days, when the "benefice" became the hereditary fief. To the King it was, no doubt, convenient that the power of those nobles who would leave heirs should be balanced by the power of other nobles, called prelates, whose children would not be legitimate. But such a system could not be stable, and might at any time provoke an overwhelming outcry for its destruction, if ever one bold man raised his voice against it. Men who are not themselves very moral can feel genuine indignation when they detect immorality among those who, though no worse than themselves, pretend to superior holiness. Prelates, and even primates of Scotland, who were bastards and the begetters of bastards, were the principal forerunners and coadjutors of John Knox ; and unfortunately they were debarred by professional rules from pleading that they, or the best among them, were in truth the respectable husbands of virtuous wives.

Lollardy too there had been, and in some corners of the land it had never been thoroughly extirpated. Also there had been a little burning, but far from enough to accustom the Scots to the sight of a heretic tortured by the flames. Then the German leaven began to work, and from 1528 onwards a few Lutherans were burnt. The protomartyr was Patrick Hamilton, the young and well-born Abbot of Ferne. Like many another Scottish youth he had been at the University of Paris. Afterwards he had made a pilgrimage, if not to Wittenberg, at all events to Marburg. It is characteristic of time and place that historians have to consider whether a feud between Douglases and Hamiltons counts for nothing in his martyrdom. " The reek of Patrick Hamilton," we are told, infected many ; and we can well believe it.   The College of St Leonard was tainted with humanism and new theology.   Young men fled from Scotland and made fame elsewhere.   Such were Alexander Aless, who as Alesius became the friend of Melanchthon, and John Macalpine, who as Machabaeus professed divinity at Copenhagen. Such also was George Buchanan, the humanist and the Calvinist, the tutor and the calumniator of Queen Mary.   And we see the Wedderburns who are teaching Scotsmen to sing ballads of a novel kind, "good and godly ballads," but such as priests are loth to hear.   And we see Sir David Lindsay, the herald, the poet, the King's friend, scourging the lives and sometimes the beliefs of the clergy with verses which rich and poor will know by heart.   In short, there was combustible material lying about in large quantities, and sparks were flying.

But the day of revolt was long delayed.   What held in check the rebellious and even the Reforming forces, was the best of Scottish traditions, the undying distrust of an England which claimed an overlordship; and in the days of Henry VIII no wholesomer tradition could there be. His father had schemed for amity by way of matrimonial alliance, and Margaret Tudor had become the wife and mother of Scottish Kings. It was plain that in the age of great monarchies England would be feeble so long as she had a hostile Scotland behind her.   But the Tudor would not see that he could not annex Scotland, or that a merely annexed Scotland would still be the old enemy.   Just as in the days of the Great Schism England had acknowledged one, and Scotland the other, of the rival Popes, so in the new days of a greater schism James V became the better Catholic because his bullying uncle had broken with Rome.   As was natural for a King of Scots, he leant upon the support of the clergy, and thereby he offended his barons.   They failed him in his hour of need.   After the shameful rout at Solway Moss, he turned his face to the wall and died, a worn-out desperate man at the age of thirty years (December 14, 1542).

His wife, Mary of Lorraine, the sister of those Guises who were to be all-powerful in France, had just borne him a daughter : she was the ill-fated Mary Stewart (December 8, 1542).   Once more, a baby was to be crowned in Scotland.   Next to her in hereditary succession stood a remote cousin, the head of the House of Hamilton, James Earl of Arran, the Châtelherault of after times.   But his right depended on the validity of a divorce which some might call in question ; and Matthew Stewart, Earl of Lennox, had pretensions.   At the head of the Scottish clergy stood the able, though dissolute, Archbishop of St Andrews, Cardinal David Beton.   For a moment it seemed as if a Reformed religion, or some northern version of Henricanism, was to have its chance.   The nobles chose Arran for Regent ; many of them envied the clergy ; many were in Henry's pay.   Arran for a while inclined towards England ; he kept heretical chaplains ; a Parliament, in spite of clerical protest, declared that the Bible might be read in the vulgar tongue. Beton had been imprisoned ; a charge of falsifying the late King's will had been brought against him. Henry's opportunity had come : the little Queen was to be wedded to Edward Tudor. But Henry was the worst of unionists. He bribed, but he also blustered, and let all men see that Scotland must be his by foul means if not by fair. A treaty was signed (July 1, 1543) ; but within six months (December 11) it was repudiated by the Scots. Meanwhile the feeble Arran, under pressure of an interdict, had reconciled himself with Beton and had abjured his heresies. The old league with France was re-established. Henry then sent fleet and army. Edinburgh was burnt (May, 1544). The Lowlands were ravaged with pitiless ferocity. The Scottish resistance was feeble. There were many traitors. The powerful Douglases played a double part. Lennox was for the English, and was rewarded with the hand of Henry's niece, Margaret Douglas. But Scotland could not be annexed, the precious child could not be captured, and Henry could not yet procure the murder of the Cardinal.

Patriotism and Catholicism were now all one. Not but that there were Protestants. One George Wishart, who had been in Switzerland and at Cambridge, was preaching the Gospel, and some (but this is no better than a guess) would identify him with a Wishart who was plotting Beton's murder. He had powerful protectors, and among his disciples was a man of middle age, born in 1505, who as yet had done nothing memorable ; he was priest, notary, private tutor ; his name was John Knox. Wishart was arrested, tried and burnt for heresy (March 2, 1546). Thereupon a band of assassins burst into the castle of St Andrews and slew Beton (May 29, 1546). The leaders were well-born men, Leslies, Kirkaldys, Melvilles. Their motives were various. Ancient feuds and hopes of English gold were mingled with hatred for a " bloody butcher of the saints of God." They held the castle and the town. The ruffianly and the godly flocked in. There was a strange mixture of debauchery and gospel in the St Andrews of those days. John Knox appeared there and was " called " to preach to the congregation ; reluctantly (so he says) he accepted the call. The Regent had laid siege, but had failed. At length came French ships with requisite artillery. The besieged capitulated (July, 1547) ; they were to be taken to France and there liberated. John Knox was shipped off with the rest, and was kept in the galleys for nineteen months, to meditate on faith that justifies.

Meanwhile Henry of England had died (January 28, 1547) ; but the Protector Somerset was bent on marrying his boy King to the girl Queen. He had excellent projects in his head. He could speak of a time when England and Scotland would be absorbed and forgotten in Great Britain ; but the French also were busy around Mary Stewart. So he led an army northwards, and fought the battle of Pinkie (September 10,

1547). No more decisive defeat could have been inflicted on the Scottish host and the Britannic idea. Other events called Somerset home. The Scots could always be crushed in the field, but Scotland could not be annexed. Then came help from the good friend France, in the shape of French, German, and Italian troops; the English employed Germans and Spaniards. A Parliament decided to accept a French proposal (July, 1548): the Queen of Scots should marry, not the English King, but young Francis the Dauphin, and meantime should be placed out of harm's way. She was shipped off at Dumbarton, and landed in Britanny (August 13, 1548) to pass a happy girlhood in a lettered and luxurious Court. The war was prosecuted with a bloodthirst new in the savage annals of the borders; it was a war fought by mercenary Almains. When peace was signed in 1550, England had gained nothing, and upon the surface (though only upon the surface) Scotland was as Catholic as ever it had been, grateful to France, bitterly resentful against heretical England.

During the struggle Mary of Lorraine had borne herself bravely; she appeared as the guiding spirit of a national resistance. She or her advising kinsfolk were soon to make, though in less brutal sort, the mistake that Henry VIII had made, and this time it was to be irretrievable. During a visit to France (September, 1550–October, 1551) she schemed with her brothers and the French King. She was to take Arran's place as Regent; he had been compensated with the duchy (no empty title) of Châtelherault, and his eldest son (who now becomes the Arran of our story) was to command the French King's Scots guard. The arrangement was not perfected until 1554, for "the second person in the kingdom" was loth to relax his hold on a land of which he might soon be King; but the French influence was strong, and he yielded. Mary of Lorraine was no bad ruler for Scotland; but still the Scots could not help seeing that she was ruling in the interest of a foreign Power. Moreover, there had been a change in the religious environment: Mary Tudor had become Queen of England (July 6, 1553). John Knox, who after his sojourn in the French galleys had been one of King Edward's select preachers and had narrowly escaped the bishopric of Rochester, was fleeing to Geneva; and thence he went to Frankfort, there to quarrel with his fellow exile Dr Cox over the Book of Common Prayer. In Scotland Catholicism had been closely allied with patriotism; but when England became Catholic, Protestant preachers found refuge in Scotland. The King of France was cherishing the intrigues of English heretics against the Spanish Queen; Mary of Lorraine was no fanatic, and her policy was incompatible with stern repression. She was trying to make Scotland more securely French; the task was delicate; and she needed the support of nobles who had little love for the clergy. A few high offices were given to Frenchmen; a few French soldiers were kept in the fortresses; they were few, but enough to scatter whole hosts of undrilled Scots. An attempt to impose a tax for the support of troops was resisted, and the barons showed a strange reluctance to fight the English. At length the time came for the Queen's marriage (April 24, 1558). The Scottish statesmen had laboriously drawn a treaty which should guard the independence of their realm and the rights of the House of Hamilton. This was signed; but a few days earlier Mary Stewart had set her hand to other documents which purported to convey Scotland for good and all to the King of France. We may find excuses for the girl; but, if treason can be committed by a sovereign, she was a traitor. She had treated Scotland as a chattel. The act was secret; but the Scots guessed much and were uneasy.

In the meantime Calvinism, for it was Calvinism now, was spreading. After the quarrels at Frankfort, Knox had gone back to Geneva and had sat at the master's feet. In 1555 he returned to Scotland, no mere preacher, but an organiser also. He went through the country, and " Churches" of the new order sprang into being where he went. Powerful nobles began to listen, such as Lord Lorne, who was soon to be Earl of Argyll, and the Queen's bastard brother, the Lord James Stewart, who was to be Earl of Moray and Regent. And politicians listened also, such as William Maitland, the young laird of Lethington. Knox was summoned before an ecclesiastical Court (May 15, 1556); but apparently at the last moment the hearts of the clergy failed them, and the prosecution was abandoned. It was evident that he had powerful supporters, especially the Earl of Glencairn. Moreover the natural leader of the clergy, John Hamilton, the Primate of Scotland, was a bastard brother of Châtelherault and, as a Hamilton, looked with suspicion on the French policy of Mary of Lorraine, so that the chiefs of Church and State were not united. However, Knox had no mind for martyrdom; and so, after sending to the Regent an admonitory letter, which she cast aside with scornful words, he again departed for Geneva (July, 1556). Then the Bishops summoned him once more; but only his effigy could be burnt.

The preaching went on. In the last days of 1557 the first " Covenant" was signed. " The Congregation of Jesus Christ," of which Argyll, Glencairn, and other great men were members, stood out in undisguised hostility to that " congregation of Satan" which styled itself the Catholic Church. They demanded that King Edward's Prayer Book (which was good enough for them if not for their absent inspirer) should be read in all the churches. The Regent was perplexed; the French marriage had not yet been secured; but she did not prevent the prelates from burning one Walter Milne, who was over eighty years of age (April, 1558). He was the last of the Protestant martyrs; they had not been numerous, even when judged by the modest English standard; fanaticism was not among the many faults of the Scottish prelates; but for this reason his cruel death made the deeper mark. On St Giles' day (September 1) in 1558 that Saint's statue was being carried through

the town of Edinburgh, of which he was the patron. Under the eyes of
the Regent the priests were rabbled and the idol was smashed in pieces.
It was plain that the next year would be stormy; and at this crisis the
face of England was once more changed.

A few weeks later Henry Percy, brother of the Earl of Northumberland, was talking with the Duke of Châtelherault. God, said the
Englishman, has sent you a true and Christian religion. We are on the
point of receiving the same boon. Why should you and we be enemies —
we who are hardly out of our servitude to Spain; you who are being
brought into servitude by France? The liberties of Scotland are in
jeopardy and the rights of the Hamiltons. Might we not unite in the
maintenance of God's Word and national independence? This is the
ideal which springs to light in the last months of 1558 : — deliverance
from the toils of foreign potentates; amity between two sister nations;
union in a pure religion. The Duke himself was a waverer; his duchy
lay in France; he is the Antoine de Bourbon of Scottish history; but
his son the Earl of Arran had lately installed a Protestant preacher at
Châtelherault and was in correspondence with Calvin. Percy reported
this interview to an English lady who had once been offered to the Duke
as a bride for Arran and had just become Queen Elizabeth.

Mary, Queen of England and Spain, died on the 17th of November,
1558. The young woman at Hatfield, who knew that her sister's days
were numbered, had made the great choice. Ever since May it had
been clear that she would soon be Queen. The Catholics doubted and
feared, but had no other candidate; King Philip was hopeful. So
Elizabeth was prepared. William Cecil was to be her secretary, and
England was to be Protestant. Her choice may surprise us. When a
few months later she is told by the Bishop of Aquila that she has been
imprudent, he seems for once to be telling the truth.

Had there been no religious dissension, her title to the throne would
hardly have been contested among Englishmen. To say nothing of her
father's will, she had an unrepealed statute in her favour. Divines
and lawyers might indeed have found it difficult to maintain her legitimate birth. Parliament had lately declared that her father was lawfully
married to Catharine of Aragon, and with this good Catholics would
agree. But there was another scandal, of which good Protestants might
take account. Elizabeth's godfather, the Henrican Archbishop and
Protestant martyr, had adjudged that Henry was never married to Anne
Boleyn. His reasons died with him; but something bad, something
nameless, might be guessed. It is sometimes said that Elizabeth's
birth condemned her to be Protestant or bastard. But it would be
truer to say that, had she cared much about legitimacy, she would have
made her peace with Rome. Hints came to her thence, that the plenitude of power can set these little matters straight for the benefit of well-

disposed princes; and in papal eyes Cranmer's sentence would have been a prejudice in her favour. But pure legitimism, the legitimism of the divine entail, was yet in its infancy, and neither Protestant nor Catholic was bound to deny that a statute of the realm may set a bastard on the throne of William the Conqueror. For the people at large it would be enough that the Lady Elizabeth was the only living descendant of old King Henry, and that beyond her lay civil war. The thin stream of Tudor blood was running dry. Henry's will (but its validity might be questioned) had postponed the issue of his elder to that of his younger sister: in other words, the House of Scotland to the House of Suffolk. Mary Stewart was born in Scotland; she could not have inherited an acre of English land, and it was highly doubtful whether English law would give the crown to an alien who was the child of two aliens. Neither her grandmother's second marriage, namely that with Archibald Douglas (whence sprang Lady Lennox and her son Lord Darnley), nor the marriage of Mary Tudor with Charles Brandon (whence sprang Greys and Stanleys) was beyond reproach; — few marriages were beyond reproach in those days of loose morals and conniving law. John Knox at Geneva had, to Calvin's regret, just blown a first blast of the trumpet against the monstrous regiment of women, and unfortunately, though the tone was new, the tune was not. The Scottish gospeller could only repeat the biblical and other arguments that had been used a century ago by that Lancastrian sage, Chief Justice Fortescue. No woman had sat upon the English throne, save Mary, and she (it might be said) was a statutory Queen. Many people thought that next in right to Elizabeth stood Henry Hastings, who was no Tudor but a Yorkist; and already in 1565 Philip of Spain was thinking of his own descent from Edward III. Thus Elizabeth's statutory title stood between England and wars of the roses which would also be wars of religion.

At this moment, however, she put a difference of creed between herself and the Dauphiness. It may be that in any case Henry II of France, who was in want of arguments for the retention of Calais, would have disputed Elizabeth's legitimacy; it was said that he had been prepared to dispute the legitimacy of her Catholic sister. But had Elizabeth been Catholic, the French and Scottish claim to her throne would have merely been an enemy's insult: an insult to England, a challenge to Spain. As it was, Henry might lay a strong case before the Pope and the Catholic world: Elizabeth was bastard and heretic to boot, and at this moment Paul IV was questioning Ferdinand's election to the Empire because some of his Electors were Lutherans. That heretics are not to rule was no new principle; the Counts of Toulouse had felt its edge in the old Albigensian days.

After the fall of Calais in January (1558) England was panic-stricken. The French were coming; the Scots were coming; Danes and Hanseats were coming. German troops were being hastily hired to protect

Northumberland. Philip's envoy, the Count of Feria, saw incompetence everywhere. The nobles held aloof, while some aged clergymen tried to conduct a war. He hardly dared to think what would happen if a few French ships touched the shore. Since then, there had been some improvement. No invader had landed, and Guise's capture of Thionville had been balanced by Egmont's victory at Gravelines. Shortly before Mary's death negotiations for a peace were begun at Cercamp; the outline of the scheme was a restoration of conquests. But Calais stopped the way. The French could not surrender that prize, and they were the more constant in their determination because the King of Spain would not much longer be King of England, and an isolated England would have no conquest to restore. When Elizabeth became Queen, Calais was not yet lost; that was the worst of it. Both Kings were weary of the war; behind both yawned gulfs of debt and heresy. But the ruler of the Netherlands was deeply concerned in the recovery of Calais — perhaps more materially, though less sentimentally, than were the English. Feria has reported the profound remark that when Calais was captured many Englishmen ceased to go to church. A Protestant Elizabeth might have to sign away the last memorial of old glories; and that would not fill the churches. Philip, it might be plain, would not suffer the French to invade England through Scotland; but the tie between Spain and an heretical England would be the coolest selfishness, the King's mind would be distracted between his faith and his policy, and if he were compelled to save England from the French, he certainly would not save England for the English.

True that for Protestant eyes there was light on the horizon. Anyone could see that there would be religious troubles in France and Scotland. Geneva was active, and Rome seemed to be doting. That summer the psalms had gone up loudly from the Pré-aux-Clercs, and a Châtillon had been arrested. That autumn St Giles of Edinburgh had lain prostrate in the mud. Expectant heirs and royal cadets, Bourbons and Hamiltons, were wavering; Maximilian was listening to an enlightened pastor; France, Scotland, the Empire, might some day fall to evangelical lords. Good news came from Poland, Bohemia, and Hungary; it was even rumoured that the Pope would at last succeed in shaking Philip's faith. Still, the black fact of the moment was that Philip and Henry were making peace in order that they might crush their respective heretics. And England's military weakness was patent to all. Her soldiers and captains were disgracefully old-fashioned, and what gunpowder she had was imported from the Netherlands. "To make a lewd comparison," said an Englishman, "England is as a bone thrown between two dogs." Was this bone to display an irritating activity of its own, merely because the two dogs seemed for the moment to be equal and opposite? To more than one mind came the same thought: "They will make a Piedmont of England."

Within the country the prospect was dubious. The people were discontented: defeat and shame, pestilence and famine, had lately been their lot. A new experiment would be welcome; but it would miserably fail were it not speedily successful. No doubt, the fires in Smithfield had harmed the Catholic cause by confirming the faith and exasperating the passions of the Protestants. No doubt, the Spanish marriage was detested. But we may overestimate the dislike of persecution and the dislike of Spain. No considerable body of Englishmen would deny that obstinate heretics should be burnt. There was no need for Elizabeth to marry Philip or bring Spaniards into the land; but the Spanish alliance, the old Anglo-Burgundian alliance, was highly valued: it meant safety and trade and occasional victories over the hereditary foe. Moreover, the English Reformers were without a chief; beyond Elizabeth they had no pretender to the throne; they had no apostle, no prophet; they were scattered over Europe and had been quarrelling, Knoxians against Coxians, in their foreign abodes. Edward's reign had worn the gloss off the new theology. We may indeed be sure that, had Elizabeth adhered to the old faith, she must have quelled plots and rebellions or herself been quelled. We look at Scotland, France, and the Netherlands, and, it may be, infer that the storm would have overwhelmed her. Perhaps we forget how largely the tempests that we see elsewhere were due to the momentous choice that she made for England. It must probably be allowed that most of the young men of brains and energy who grew to manhood under Mary were lapsing from Catholicism, and that the educated women were falling faster and further. London too, Bonner's London, was Protestant, and London might be worth an abolished Mass. But when, after some years of fortunate and dexterous government, we see how strong is the old creed, how dangerous is Mary Stewart as its champion, we cannot feel sure that Elizabeth chose the path which was, or which seemed to be, the safest.

Of her own opinions she told strange tales. Puzzled by her shifty discourse, a Spanish envoy once suggested atheism. When a legal settlement had been made, it was her pleasure, and perhaps her duty, to explain that her religion was that of all sensible people. The difference between the various versions of Christianity "*n'estoit que bagatelle.*" So she agreed with the Pope, except about some details; she cherished the Augsburg confession, or something very like it; she was at one, or nearly at one, with the Huguenots. She may have promised her sister (but this is not proved) to make no change in religion; at any rate she had gone to mass without much ado. Nevertheless it is not unlikely that at the critical time her conduct was swayed rather by her religious beliefs or disbeliefs than by any close calculation of loss and gain. She had not her father's taste for theology; she was neither prig like her brother nor zealot like her sister; but she had been taught from the first to contemn the Pope, and during Edward's reign she had been highly educated in the newest doctrines. John Hooper, the father of the Puritans, had admired her displays of argumentative divinity. More than one Catholic who spoke with her in later days was struck by her ignorance of Catholic verity. The Bishop of Aquila traced her phrases to "the heretic Italian friars." He seems to have been thinking of Vermigli and Ochino, and there may have been some little truth in his guess. Once she said that she liked Italian ways and manners better than any other, and sometimes seemed to herself half Italian. Her eyes filled with tears over Peter Martyr's congratulations. She had talked predestination with Fra Bernardino and had translated one of his sermons; the Puritans were persuaded that if she would listen to no one else, she would listen to him. All this might have meant little; but then she had suffered in the good cause. She had been bullied into going to mass; she had been imprisoned; she had nearly been excluded from the throne; some ardent Catholics had sought her life; and her suspected heresies had been at least a part of her offending. It would have been base to disappoint all those who had prayed for her and plotted for her, and pleasant it was when from many lands came letters which hailed her as the miraculously preserved champion of the truth. She had a text ready for the bearer of the good news: "This is the Lord's doing and it is marvellous in our eyes."

One point was clear. The Henrican Anglo-Catholicism was dead and buried. It died with Henry and was interred by Stephen Gardiner. In distant days its spirit might arise from the tomb; but not yet. The Count of Feria and Bishop Tunstall were at needless pains to explain to the young Queen that she was favouring "Lutherans and Zwinglians," whom her father would have burnt. But in 1558 nothing was to be gained by mere schism. Her fellow sovereigns, more especially her brother-in-law, could have taught her that a prince might enjoy all the advantages of spotless orthodoxy and yet keep the Pope at arm's length. Many Englishmen hated "popery"; but by this time the core of the popery that they hated was no longer the Papacy, but the idolatrous Mass. The choice lay between Catholicism with its Pope and the creed for which Cranmer and Ridley died. It could scarcely be hoped that the Bishops would yield an inch. Very shame, if no worthier motive, would keep them true to the newly restored supremacy of Rome. Happily for Elizabeth, they were few and feeble. Reginald Pole had hardly outlived Mary, and for one reason or another had made no haste in filling vacant sees;—Feria thought that the "accursed Cardinal" had French designs. And death had been and still was busy. Only sixteen instead of twenty-six Bishops were entitled to attend the critical Parliament, and only eleven with the Abbot of Westminster were present. Their constancy in the day of trial makes them respectable; but not one of them was a leader of men. The ablest of them had been Henry's ministers and therefore could be taunted as renegades.

A story which came from a good quarter bade us see Elizabeth announcing to the Pope her accession to the throne, and not rejecting Catholicism until Paul IV declared that England was a papal fief and she an usurping bastard. Now, Caraffa was capable of any imprudence and just at this moment seemed bent on reviving the claims of medieval Pontiffs, in order that he might drive a long-suffering Emperor into the arms of the Lutherans. But it is certain now that in the matter of courtesy Elizabeth, not Paul, was the offender. She ignored his existence. Edward Carne was living at Rome as Mary's ambassador. He received no letters of credence from the new Queen, and on the 1st of February, 1559, she told him to come home as she had nothing for him to do. Meanwhile the French were thinking to obtain a Bull against her; they hoped that at all events Paul would not allow her to marry her dead sister's husband. At Christmastide (1558), when she was making a scene in her chapel over the elevation of the Host, the Pope was talking kindly of her to the French ambassador, would not promise to refuse a dispensation, but could not believe that another Englishwoman would want to marry a detestable Spaniard. A little later he knew more about her and detained Carne (a not unwilling prisoner) at Rome (March 27), not because she was base-born, but because she had revolted from the Holy See. He had just taken occasion to declare in a Bull that princes guilty of heresy are deprived of all lawful power by the mere fact of their guilt (February 15). This edict, though it may have been mainly aimed at Ferdinand's three Protestant Electors, was a salutary warning for Elizabeth and Anthony and Maximilian; but no names were named. Philip had influence enough to balk the French intrigue and protect his sister-in-law from a direct anathema. The Spaniard may in Paul's eyes have been somewhat worse than a heretic; but the quarrel with the other Habsburg, and then the sudden attack upon his own scandalous nephews, were enough to consume the few remaining days of the fierce old man. He has much to answer for; but it was no insult from him that made Elizabeth a Protestant.

No time was lost. Mary's death (November 17, 1558) dissolved a Parliament. Heath, Archbishop of York and Chancellor of the realm, dismissed it, and with loyal words proclaimed the new Queen. Within three weeks (December 5) writs went out for a new Parliament. Elizabeth was going to exact conformity to a statutory religion. For the moment the statutory religion was the Roman Catholic, and she would have taken a false step if in the name of some higher law she had annulled or ignored the Marian statutes. At once she forbade innovations and thus disappointed the French, who hoped for a turbulent revolution. A new and happy *et caetera* was introduced into the royal style and seemed to hint, without naming, a Headship of the Church. Every change pointed one way. Some of the old Councillors were retained, but the new Councillors were Protestants. William Cecil, then aged thirty-eight, had been Somerset's and was to be Elizabeth's secretary. Like her he had gone to mass, but no Catholic doubted that he was a sad heretic. The Great Seal, resigned by Heath, was given to Nicholas Bacon. He and Cecil had married sisters who were godly ladies of the new sort. The imprisoned heretics were bailed, and the refugees flocked back from Frankfort, Zurich and Geneva. Hardly was Mary dead, before one Bishop was arrested for an inopportune sermon (November 27). Another preached at her funeral (December 13) and praised her for rejecting that title which Elizabeth had not yet assumed ; he too was put under restraint. Mary's chief mourner was not her sister, but appropriately enough, the Lady Lennox who was to have supplanted Elizabeth. No Bishop preached the funeral sermon for Charles V, and what good could be said of that Catholic Caesar was said by the Protestant Dr Bill (December 24). The new Queen was artist to the finger-tips. The English Bible was rapturously kissed ; the Tower could not be re-entered without uplifted eyes and thankful words ; her hand (it was a pretty hand) shrank, so folk said, from Bonner's lips. Christmas day was chosen for a more decisive scene. The Bishop who was to say mass in her presence was told not to elevate the Host. He would not obey ; so after the Gospel out went Elizabeth ; she could no longer witness that idolatry. Three weeks later (January 15) she was crowned while Calvin was dedicating to her his comments on Isaiah. What happened at the coronation is obscure. The Bishops, it seems, swore fealty in the accustomed manner; the Epistle and Gospel were read in English ; it is said that the celebrant was one of the Queen's chaplains and that he did not elevate the Host ; it is said that she did not communicate ; she was anointed by the Bishop of Carlisle, whose rank would not have entitled him to this office, had not others refused it. At length the day came for a Parliament (January 25). A mass was said at Westminster early in the morning. At a later hour the Queen approached the Abbey with her choir singing in English. The last of the Abbots came to meet her with monks and candles. "Away with those torches," she exclaimed ; " we can see well enough !" And then Edward's tutor, Dr Cox, late of Frankfort, preached ; and he preached, it is said, for an hour and a half, the peers all standing.

The negotiations between Spain, England and France had been brought to a pause by Mary's death, but were to be resumed after a brief interval, during which Elizabeth was to make up her mind. Some outwardly amicable letters passed between her and Henry II. She tried to play the part of the pure-bred Englishwoman, who should not suffer for the sins of the Spanish Mary. But the French were not to be coaxed out of Calais, and she knew that they were seeking a papal Bull against her. It became plain that she must not detach herself from Spain and that, even with Philip's help, Calais could only be obtained after another war, for which England was shamefully unready. Then, in the middle of January, came through Feria the expected offer of Philip's hand. Elizabeth seemed to hesitate, had doubts about the Pope's dispensing power and so forth; but in the end said that she did not mean to marry, and added that she was a heretic. Philip, it seems, was relieved by the refusal; he had laboriously explained to his ambassador that his proposal was a sacrifice laid upon the altar of the Catholic faith. He had hopes, which were encouraged in England, that one of his Austrian cousins, Ferdinand or Charles, would succeed where he had failed, secure England for orthodoxy, and protect the Netherlands from the ill example that an heretical England would set.

Meanwhile the great Treaty of Cateau-Cambrésis was in the making. Elizabeth tried to retain Philip's self-interested support; and she retained it. Without substantial aid from England, he would not fight for Calais; she would have to sign it away; but so earnest had he been in this matter that the French covenanted to restore the treasured town after eight years and further to pay half-a-million of crowns by way of penalty in case they broke their promise. No one supposed that they would keep it; still they had consented to make the retention of Calais a just cause for war, and Elizabeth could plausibly say that some remnants of honour had been saved. But the clouds collected once more. New differences broke out among the negotiators, who had half a world to regulate, and, before the intricate settlement could be completed, a marriage had been arranged between Philip and one of Henry's daughters. Elizabeth of France, not Elizabeth of England, was to be the bride. The conjunction was ominous for heretics.

From the first days of February to the first days of April the negotiations had been pending. Meanwhile in England little had been accomplished. It had become plain that the clergy in possession (but there was another and expectant clergy out of possession) would not yield. The Convocation of Canterbury met when Parliament met, and the Lower House declared for transubstantiation, the sacrifice of the Mass, and the Roman supremacy; also it idly protested that laymen were not to meddle with faith, worship, or discipline (February 17, 1559). The Bishops were staunch; the English Church by its constitutional organs refused to reform itself; the Reformation would be an unprecedented state-stroke. Probably the assembled Commons were willing to strike. The influence of the Crown had been used on the Protestant side; but Cecil had hardly gathered the reins in his hand, and the government's control over the electoral machinery must have been unusually weak. Our statistics are imperfect, but the number of knights and burgesses who, having served in 1558, were again returned in 1559 was not abnormally small, and with the House of 1558 Mary had been well content. Also we may see at Westminster not a few men who soon afterwards are "hinderers of true religion" or at best only "faint professors"; but probably the nation at large was not unwilling that

Elizabeth should make her experiment. A few creations and restorations of peerages strengthened the Protestant element among the lords. The Earl of Bedford and Lord Clinton appeared as proxies for many absent peers, and, of all the lords, Bedford (Francis Russell) was the most decisively committed to radical reform. The Howards were for the Queen, their cousin; the young Duke of Norfolk, England's one duke, was at this time ardently Protestant, and in the next year was shocked at the sight of undestroyed altars.

Money was cheerfully voted. The Queen was asked to choose a husband, and professed her wish to die a maid. She may have meant what she said, but assuredly did not mean that it should be believed. A prudently phrased statute announced that she was "lawfully descended and come of the blood royal"; another declared her capable of inheriting from her divorced and attainted mother; the painful past was veiled in general words. There was little difficulty about a resumption of those tenths and first-fruits which Mary had abandoned. Round the question of ecclesiastical supremacy the battle raged, and it raged for two months and more (February 9 to April 29). Seemingly the Queen's ministers carried through the Lower House a bill which went the full Henrican length in its Caesaro-papalism and its severity. Upon pain of a traitor's death, everyone was to swear that Elizabeth was the Supreme Head of the Church of England. In the Upper House, to which the bill came on the 27th of February, the Bishops had to oppose a measure which would leave the lives of all open Romanists at the mercy of the government. Few though they were, the dozen prelates could still do much in a House where there were rarely more than thirty temporal lords, and probably Cecil had asked for more than he wanted. On the 18th of March the project had taken a far milder form; forfeiture of office and benefice was to be the punishment of those who would not swear. Against this more lenient measure only two temporal lords protested; but a Catholic says that other "good Christians" were feigning to be ill. The bill went back to the Commons; then back with amendments to the Lords, who read it thrice on the 22nd. Easter fell on the 26th, and it had been hoped that by that time Parliament would have finished its work. Very little had been done; doctrine and worship had hardly been touched. Apparently an attempt to change the services of the Church had been made, had met with resistance, and had been abandoned.

Elizabeth was in advance of the law and beckoned the nation forward. During that Lent the Court sermon had been the only sermon, the preacher Scory or Sandys, Grindal or Cox. A papist's excited fancy saw a congregation of five thousand and heard extravagant blasphemy. On Easter day the Queen received the Communion in both kinds; the news ran over Europe; Antoine de Bourbon on the same day had done the like at Pau; Mary of Lorraine had marked that festival for the return of all Scots to the Catholic worship. The colloquy of Westminster follows. There was to be a trial by battle in the Abbey between chosen champions of the two faiths. Its outcome might make us suspect that a trap was laid by the Protestants. But it is by no means certain that the challenge came from their side, and the Spanish ambassador took some credit for arranging the combat. The colloquy of Westminster stands midway between that of Worms (1557) and that of Poissy (1561). The Catholics were wont to get the better in these feats of arms, because, so soon as Christ's presence in the Eucharist was mentioned, the Protestants fell a-fighting among themselves. Apparently on this occasion the rules of the debate were settled by Heath and Bacon. The Great Seal had passed from an amiable to an abler keeper. The men of the Old Learning were to defend the use of Latin in the services of the Church, to deny that a "particular Church" can change rites and ceremonies and to maintain the propitiatory sacrifice of the Mass. Their first two theses would bring them into conflict with national feeling; and at the third point they would be exposed to the united force of Lutherans and Helvetians, for the sacrifice, and not the presence, was to be debated. It was a less advantage for the Reformers that their adversaries were to speak first, for there was to be no extemporary argument but only a reading of written dissertations. In the choir of the Abbey, before Council, Lords, Commons and multitude, the combatants took their places on Friday, the 31st of March. At once the Catholics began to except against the rules that they were required to observe. Dr Cole, however, maintained their first proposition and Dr Horne read the Protestant essay. The Reformers were well content with that day's work and the applause that followed. On Monday the second question was to be handled. Of what happened we have no impartial account; we do not know what had passed between Heath and Bacon, or whether the Catholic doctors were taken by surprise. Howbeit, they chose the worst course; they wrangled about procedure and refused to continue the debate. Apparently they were out of heart and leaderless. Two of the Bishops were forthwith imprisoned by the Council for intemperate words, and thus the Catholic party in the House of Lords was seriously weakened at a critical moment. Moreover, the inference that men do not break off a debate with preliminary objections when they are confident of success in the main issue, though it is not always just, is always natural.

The next day Parliament resumed its work. Meanwhile, Elizabeth had at length decided that she would not assume the Henrican title, though assuredly she had meant that it should be, as it had been, offered to her. Women should keep silence in the churches; so there was difficulty about a "dumb head." She had managed to get a little credit from Philip's envoy and a little from zealous Calvinists by saying that she would not be Head of the Church, and she could then tell appropriate persons that she scorned a style which the Pope had polluted. So Cecil had to go to the Commons and explain that there must be a new bill and new oath. He met with some opposition, for there were who held that the Queen was Supreme Head *iure divino*. Ultimately a phrase was fashioned which declared that she was the only Supreme Governor of the realm as well in all spiritual or ecclesiastical things or causes as in temporal, and that no foreign prince or prelate had any ecclesiastical or spiritual authority within her dominions. However, among other statutes of Henry VIII, one was revived which proclaims that the King is Head of the Church, and that by the word of God all ecclesiastical jurisdiction flows from him. Catholics suspected that Elizabeth's husband would be head of the Church, if not head of his wife, and saw the old title concealed behind the new *et caetera*. Protestant lawyers said that she could take the title whenever she pleased. Sensible men saw that, having the substance, she could afford to waive the irritating name. On the 14th of April the bill was before the Lords. There were renewed debates and more changes; and the famous Act of Supremacy was not finally secured until the 29th.

In the last days of an unusually long session a bill for the Uniformity of Religion went rapidly through both Houses (April 18–28). The services prescribed in a certain Book of Common Prayer, and none other, were to be lawful. The embryonic history of this measure is obscure. An informal committee of Protestant divines seems to have been appointed by the Queen to prepare a book. It has been thought that as the basis of their labours they took the Second Book of Edward VI, but desired a further simplification of ceremonies. On the other hand, there are some signs that Cecil and the Queen thought that the Second Book, which had hardly been introduced before it was abrogated, had already gone far enough or too far in the abolition of accustomed rites. All this, however, is very uncertain. Our guess may be that, when men were weary of the prolonged debate over the Supremacy and its continuance was becoming a national danger (for violent speeches had been made), the Queen's advisers took the short course of proposing the Book of 1552 with very few changes. At such a moment relief might be found in what could be called a mere act of restoration, and the Edwardian Book, however unfamiliar, was already ennobled by the blood of martyrs. There are signs of haste, or of divided counsels, for the new Book when it came from the press differed in some little, but not trivial, matters from that which Parliament had expressly sanctioned. The changes sanctioned by Parliament were few. An offensive phrase about the Bishop of Rome's "detestable enormities" was expunged, apparently by the House of Lords. An addition from older sources was made to the words that accompany the delivery of bread and wine to the communicant, whereby a charge of the purest Zwinglianism might be obviated. At the moment it was of importance to Elizabeth that she should assure the German Princes that her religion was

Augustan ; for they feared, and not without cause, that it was Helvetian.
A certain "black rubric" which had never formed part of the statutory
book fell away ; it would have offended Lutherans ; we have reason to
believe that it had been inserted in order to meet the scruples of John
Knox. Of what was done in the matter of ornaments by the statute,
by the rubrics of the Book and by "injunctions" that the Queen
promptly issued, it would be impossible to speak fairly without a
lengthy quotation of documents, the import of which became in the
nineteenth century a theme of prolonged and inconclusive disputation. It
must here suffice that there are few signs of any of the clergymen who
accepted the Prayer Book either having worn or having desired to wear
in the ordinary churches — there was at times a little more splendour in
cathedrals — any ecclesiastical robe except the surplice. But, to return
to Elizabeth's Parliament, we have it on fairly good authority that nine
temporal lords, including the Treasurer (the Marquis of Winchester),
and nine prelates (two Bishops were in gaol) voted against the bill, and
that it was only carried by three votes. Unfortunately at an exciting
moment there is a gap, perhaps a significant gap, in the official record,
and we cease to know what lords were present in the House. But about
thirty temporal peers had lately been in attendance, and so we may infer
that some of them were inclined neither to alter the religion of England
nor yet to oppose the Queen. On the 5th of May, the Bishops were
fighting in vain for the renovated monasteries. On the 8th, Parliament
was dissolved.

At a moment of strain and peril a wonderfully durable settlement
had been made. There is cause for thinking that the Queen's advisers
had been compelled to abandon considerable parts of a lengthy programme ; but the great lines had been drawn and were permanent.
For this reason they can hardly be described in words that are both
just and few ; but perhaps we may make a summary of those points
which were the most important to the men of 1559. A radical change
in doctrine, worship and discipline has been made by Queen and Parliament against the will of prelates and ecclesiastical Councils. The
legislative power of the Convocations is once more subjected to royal
control. The derivation of episcopal from royal jurisdiction has been
once more asserted in the words of Henry VIII. Appeal from the Courts
of the Church lies to royal delegates who may be laymen. What might
fairly be called a plenitude of ecclesiastical jurisdiction of the corrective
sort can be, and at once is, committed to delegates who constitute what
is soon known as the Court of High Commission and strongly resembles
the consistory of a German Prince. Obstinate heresy is still a capital
crime ; but practically the Bishops have little power of forcing heretics
to stand a trial, and, unless Parliament and Convocation otherwise ordain,
only the wilder sectaries will be in danger of burning. There is no
"liberty of cult." The Prayer Book prescribes the only lawful form of

common worship. The clergyman who adopts any other, even in a private chapel, commits a crime ; so does he who procures this aberration from conformity. Everyone must go to church on Sunday and bide prayer and preaching or forfeit twelve pence to the use of the poor. Much also can be done to ensure conformity by excommunication which has imprisonment behind it. The papal authority is abolished. Clergy and office-holders can be required to swear that it is naught ; if they refuse the oath, they lose office and benefice. If anyone advisedly maintains that authority, he forfeits his goods ; on a third conviction he is a traitor. The service book is not such as will satisfy all ardent Reformers ; but their foreign fathers in the faith think it not intolerable, and the glad news goes out that the Mass is abolished. The word "Protestant," which is rapidly spreading from Germany, comes as a welcome name. In the view of an officially inspired apologist of the Elizabethan settlement, those who are not Papists are Protestants.

The requisite laws had been made, but whether they would take effect was very uncertain. The new oath was not tendered to the judges ; and some of them were decided Romanists. Nor was the validity of the statutes unquestioned, for it was by no means so plain as it now is that an Act against which the spiritual Lords have voted in a body may still be an Act of the three Estates. Gradually in the summer and autumn the Bishops were called upon to swear ; they refused and were deprived. It is not certain that the one weak brother, Kitchin of Llandaff, actually swore the oath, though he promised to exact it from others. Futile hopes seem to have been entertained that Tunstall and Heath would at least take part in the consecration of their Protestant successors. Such successors were nominated by the Queen ; but to make Bishops of them was not easy. Apparently a government bill dealing with this matter had come to naught. Probably the Queen's advisers had intended to abolish the canonical election ; they procured its abolition in Ireland on the ground that it was inconsistent with the Royal Supremacy ; but for some cause or another the English Parliament had restored that grotesque Henrican device, the compulsory election of a royal nominee. By a personal interview Elizabeth secured the conversion of the dean of the two metropolitan churches, that pliant old diplomat Nicholas Wotton. When sees and benefices were rapidly falling vacant, his adhesion was of great importance if all was to be done in an orderly way.

But given the election, there must still be confirmation and consecration ; statute required it. The coöperation of four " Bishops " would be necessary if Matthew Parker was to sit where Reginald Pole had sat. Four men in episcopal Orders might be found : for instance, William Barlow, of whose Protestant religion there could be no doubt, since Albert of Prussia had lately attested it ; but these men would not be in possession of English sees. Moreover, it seems to have been doubted whether the Edwardian Ordinal had been revived as part of the **Edwardian Prayer Book**. Cecil was puzzled, but equal to the occasion. In a document redolent of the papal chancery Elizabeth "supplied" all "defects," and at length on the 17th of December, in the chapel at **Lambeth**, Parker was consecrated with Edwardian rites by Barlow, Scory, Coverdale and Hodgkin. The story of a simpler ceremony at the Nag's Head tavern was not concocted until long afterwards ; it should have for pendants a Protestant fable which told of a dramatic scene between Elizabeth and the Catholic prelates, and an Anglican fable which strove to suggest that the Prayer Book was sanctioned by a synod of Bishops and clergy. A large number of deans and canons followed the example set by the Bishops. Of their inferiors hardly more than two hundred, so it seems, were deprived for refusing the oath. The royal commissioners treated the hesitating priests with patient forbearance ; and the meaning of the oath was minimised by an ably worded Proclamation. We may conjecture that many of those who swore expected another turn of the always turning wheel. However, Elizabeth succeeded in finding creditable occupants for the vacant dignities ; of Parker and some of his suffragans more than this might be said. The new service was introduced without exciting disturbances ; the altars and roods were pulled down, tables were purchased, and a coat of whitewash veiled the pictured saints from view. Among the laity there was much despondent indifference. Within a dozen years there had been four great changes in worship, and no good had come of it all. For some time afterwards there are many country gentlemen whom the Bishops describe as " indifferent in religion." Would the Queen's Church secure them and their children ? That question could not be answered by one who looked only at England. From the first, Elizabeth and Cecil, who were entering into their long partnership, had looked abroad.

The month of May, 1559, which saw the ratification of the Treaty of Cateau-Cambrésis, is a grand month in the annals of the heresy which was to be destroyed. A hideous act of faith at Valladolid may show us that Catholicism is safe in Spain ; but the English Parliament ends its work, a French Reformed Church shapes itself in the synod of Paris, and Scotland bursts into flame. In 1558 we saw it glowing. Mary of Guise was temporising ; she had not yet obtained the crown matrimonial for the Dauphin. In the winter Parliament she had her way ; the crown was to be (but never was) carried to her son-in-law. His father had just ceased his intrigues with English Protestants, and was making peace in order that he might be busy among the Protestants of France. The Regent of Scotland was given to understand that the time for tolerance was past. In March, 1559, the Scottish prelates followed the example of their English brethren and uttered their *Non possumus*. They proposed remedy many an indefensible abuse, but to new beliefs there o be no concession. The Queen-mother fixed Easter day for the return of all men to the Catholic worship. The order was disregarded. On the 10th of May the more notorious of the preachers were to answer at Stirling for their misdeeds. They collected at Perth, with Protestant lords around them. At this moment Elizabeth's best friend sprang into the arena. John Knox had been fuming at Dieppe. Elizabeth, enraged at his ill-timed "blast," denied him a safe conduct. François Morel, too, the French Reformer, implored Calvin to keep this fire-brand out of England lest all should be spoilt. But if Knox chose to revisit his native land that was no affair of Elizabeth's, and he was predestinated to win for Calvinism the most durable of its triumphs. He landed in Scotland on the 2nd of May and was at Perth by the 11th. Then there was a sermon; a stone was thrown; an image was broken, and the churches of St Johnston were wrecked. Before the end of the month there were two armed hosts in the field. There were more sermons, and where Knox preached the idols fell and monks and nuns were turned adrift. There were futile negotiations and disregarded truces. At the head of the belligerent Congregation rode Glencairn, Argyll, and Lord James. Châtelherault was still with the Regent; and she had a small force of disciplined Frenchmen. At the end of July a temporary truce was made at Leith. The Congregation could bring a numerous host (of the medieval sort) into the field, but could not keep it there. However, as the power of the French soldiers was displayed, the revolutionary movement became more and more national. The strife, if it was between Catholic and Calvinist, was also a strife for the delivery of Scotland from a foreign army. None the less there was a revolt. Thenceforth, Calvinism often appears as a rebellious religion. This, however, is its first appearance in that character. Calvin had long been a power in the world of Reformed theology, and his death (1564) was not far distant; but in 1559 the Count of Feria was at pains to tell King Philip that "this Calvin is a Frenchman and a great heretic" (March 19). Knox, when he preached "the rascal multitude" into iconoclastic fury, was setting an example to *Gueux* and Huguenots. What would Elizabeth think of it?

Throughout the winter and spring Englishmen and Scots, who had been dragged into war by their foreign masters, had been meeting on the border and talking first of armistice and then of peace. Already in January Maitland of Lethington had a strong desire to speak with Sir William Cecil and since then had been twice in London. He was the Regent's Secretary, conforming in religion as Cecil had conformed; but it is likely that the core of such creed as he had was unionism. The news that came from Scotland in May can hardly have surprised the English Secretary. "Some great consequences must needs follow"; this was his quiet comment (May 26). Diplomatic relations with France had just been resumed. Nicholas Throckmorton, one of those able men who begin to collect around Elizabeth, had gone to reside there as her ambassador, had gone to "practise" there and exacerbate the "garboils" there. One of the first bits of news that he sends home is that Arran has been summoned to Court from Poitou, where he has been Calvinising, has disobeyed the summons and cannot be found (May 30). The Guises connect Arran's disappearance with Throckmorton's advent; and who shall say that they are wrong? In June Cecil heard from the border that the Scottish lords were devising how this young man could be brought home and married "you know where." "You have a Queen," said a Scot to Throckmorton, "and we our Prince the Earl of Arran, marriable both, and the chief upholders of God's religion." Arran might soon be King of Scotland. The Dauphiness, who at the French Court was being called Queen of England, did not look as if she were long for this world: Throckmorton noted her swoons. Arran had escaped to Geneva. Early in July Elizabeth was busy, and so was Calvin, over the transmission of this invaluable youth to the quarter where he could best serve God and the English Queen. Petitions for aid had come from Scotland. Cecil foresaw what would happen: the Protestants were to be helped "first with promises, next with money, and last with arms" (July 8). But to go beyond the first stage was hazardous. The late King of England was only a few miles off with his fleet and veteran troops; he was being married by proxy to a French Princess; he had thoughts of enticing Catharine Grey out of England, in order that he might have another candidate for the throne, if it were necessary to depose the disobedient Elizabeth. And could Elizabeth openly support these rebels? In the answer to that question lay the rare importance of Arran. The Scottish uproar must become a constitutional movement directed by a prince of the blood royal against a French attempt to deprive a nation of its independence. Cecil explained to Calvin that if true religion is to be supported it must first convert great noblemen (June 22).

Then the danger from France seemed to increase. There was a mischance at a tournament and Henry II was dead (July 10). The next news was that "the House of Guise ruleth" (July 13). In truth, this was good news. Elizabeth's adversary was no longer an united France. The Lorrainers were not France; their enemies told them that they were not French. But the Duke and Cardinal were ruling France; they came to power as the uncles of the young King's wife, and soon there might be a boy born who would be Valois-Tudor-Stewart-Guise. A Guise was ruling Scotland also, and the rebellion against her was hanging fire. So early in August Cecil's second stage was reached, and Ralph Sadler was carrying three thousand pounds to the border. He knew his Scotland; Henry VIII had sent him there on a fool's errand; there would be better management this time. In the same month Philip turned his back on the Netherlands, never to see them more. Thenceforth, he would be the secluded King of a distant country. Also, Paul IV died, and for four

months the Roman Church had no supreme governor. The Supreme
Governor of the English Church could breathe more freely. She kept
her St Bartholomew (August 24). There was burning in Bartlemy Fair,
burning in Smithfield — but only of wooden roods and Maries and Johns
and such-like popish gear. "It is done of purpose to confirm the
Scottish revolt" : such was a guess made at Brussels (September 2) ; and
it may have been right, for there was little of the natural iconoclast in
Elizabeth. A few days later (August 29) Arran was safely and secretly
in her presence, and thence was smuggled into Scotland. Probably she
took his measure ; he was not quite sane, but would be useful. Soon
afterwards Philip's ambassador knew that she was fomenting tumults
in Scotland through "a heretic preacher called Knox." That was
unkindly said, but not substantially untrue. Early in October "the
Congregation" began once more to take an armed shape. Châtelherault,
that unstable "second person," had been brought over by his impetuous
son. The French troops in Scotland had been reinforced ; the struggle
was between Scot and Frenchman. So, to the horror of Bishops-elect
(whose consecration had not yet been managed), the table in Elizabeth's
chapel began to look like an altar with cross and candles. "She will
not favour the Scots in their religion," said Gilles de Noailles, the French
ambassador. "She is afraid," said the Cardinal of Lorraine. "She is
going to marry the Archduke Charles, who is coming here in disguise,"
said many people. Surely she wished that just those comments should
be made ; and so Dr Cox, by this time elect of Ely, had to stomach
cross and candles as best he might.

The host of the Congregation arrived at Edinburgh ; a manifesto
declared that the Regent was deposed (October 21). She and the
French were fortifying Leith ; the castle was held by the neutral Lord
Erskine. But once more the extemporised army began to melt away.
Treasure sent by Elizabeth was captured by a border ruffian, James
Hepburn, Earl of Bothwell, who was to play a part in coming tragedies.
The insurgents fled from Edinburgh (November 6). In negotiation
with Cecil, Knox was showing the worldly wisdom that underlay his
Hebraic frenzies ; he knew the weak side of his fellow-countrymen ;
without more aid from England, the movement would fail. Knox,
however, was not presentable at Court ; Lethington was. The Regent's
Secretary had left her and had carried to the opposite camp the state-
craft that it sorely needed. He saw a bright prospect for his native
land and took the road to London. Cecil's third stage was at hand.
There were long debates in the English Council ; there were "Philipians"
in it, and all that passed there was soon known at the French embassy.
The Queen was irresolute ; even Bacon was for delay ; but, though some
French ships had been wrecked, others were ready, and the danger to
Scotland, and through Scotland to England, was very grave. At length
Cecil and Lethington won their cause. An army under the Duke of

Norfolk was to be raised and placed on the border. Large supplies of arms had been imported from the dominions of the Catholic King. Bargains for professed soldiers were struck with German princes. William Winter, Master of the Ordnance, was to take fourteen ships to the Forth. He might "as of his own hand" pick a quarrel with the French; but there was to be no avowed war (December 16). On the morrow Dr Parker was consecrated. He had been properly shocked by Knox's doings. "God keep us from such visitation as Knox hath attempted in Scotland: the people to be orderers of things!" (November 6). If in that autumn the people of Scotland had not ordered things in a summary way, Dr Parker's tenure of the archiepiscopate might have been precarious. A few days later and there was once more a Pope (December 25): this time a sane Pope, Pius IV, who would have to deplore the loss, not only of England, but of Scotland also. God of His mercy, said Lethington, had removed that difference of religion.

/ Once more the waves were kind to Elizabeth.⎫ They repulsed the Marquis of Elbeuf (René of Lorraine), and suffered Winter to pass. All the news that came from France was good. It told of unwillingness that national treasure should be spent in the cause of the Guises, of a dearth of recruits for Scotland, of heretics burnt and heretics rescued, of factions in religion fomented by the great. Something was very wrong in France, for envoys came thence with soft words. "Strike now," was Throckmorton's counsel; "they only seek to gain time." So a pact was signed at Berwick (February 27, 1560) between Norfolk and the Scottish lords who acted on behalf of "the second person of the realm of Scotland." Elizabeth took Scotland, its liberties, its nobility, its expectant heir under her protection, and the French were to be expelled. On second thoughts nothing was published about "the profession of Christ's true religion." Every French envoy spoke softer than the last. Mary Stewart had assumed the arms of England because she was proud of being Elizabeth's cousin. The title of Queen of England was taken to annoy, not Elizabeth, but Mary Tudor. All this meant the Tumult of Amboise (March 14-20). Behind that strange essay in rebellion, behind la Renaudie, men have seen Condé, and behind Condé two dim figures, Jean Calvin and the English Queen. Calvin's acquittal seems deserved. The profession of Christ's true religion was not to be advanced by so ill laid a plot. But a very ill laid plot might cripple France at this critical moment, and, before we absolve Elizabeth, we wish to know why a certain Tremaine was sent to Britanny, where the plotters were gathering, and whether Chantonnay, Granvelle's brother, was right in saying that la Renaudie had been at the English Court. Certain it is that Throckmorton had intrigued with Anthony of Navarre, with the Vidame of Chartres, with every enemy of the Guises; he was an apt pupil in the school that Renard and Noailles had founded in England. A little later (May 23) messages from Condé to the Queen were going round by Strassburg ; and in June Tremaine brought from France a scheme which would put Breton or Norman towns into English hands : a scheme from which Cecil as yet recoiled as from "a bottomless pit."

Be all this as it may, the tumult of Amboise fell pat into Cecil's scheme, and on the 29th of March Lord Grey crossed the border with English troops.   The Scottish affair then takes this shape : — A small but disciplined force of Frenchmen in the fortified town of Leith ; the Regent in Edinburgh Castle, which is held by the neutral Erskine ; English ships in the Forth ; an English and Scottish army before Leith ; very few Scots openly siding with the Queen-mother ; the French seeking to gain time.   We hasten to the end.   An assault failed, but hunger was doing its work.   The Regent died on the 11th of June ; even stern Protestants have a good word for the gallant woman.   Cecil went into Scotland to negotiate with French plenipotentiaries.   He wrung from them the Treaty of Edinburgh, which was signed on the 6th of July.   The French troops were to quit Scotland.   The French King and Queen were never thereafter to use the arms and style of England.   Compensation for the insult to her title was to be awarded to Elizabeth by arbitrators or the King of Spain.   A pact concluded between Francis and Mary on the one hand and their Scottish subjects on the other was to be observed. That pact itself was humiliating.   There was to be pardon for the insurgents ; there were to be but six score French soldiers in the land ; a Scottish Council was to be appointed : — in a word, Scotland was to be for the Scots.   But the lowest point was touched when the observance of this pact between sovereign and rebels was made a term in the treaty between England and France.   Cecil and famine were inexorable.   We had to sign, said the French commissioners, or four thousand brave men would have perished before our eyes and Scotland would have been utterly lost.

And so the French troops were deported from Scotland and the English army came home from a splendid exploit.   The military display, it is true, had not been creditable ; there had been disunion, if no worse, among the captains ; there had been peculation, desertion, sheer cowardice.   All the martial glory goes to the brave besieged.   But for the first time an English army marched out of Scotland leaving gratitude behind.   Perhaps the truest victory that England had won was won over herself.   Not a word had been publicly said of that old suzerainty ; no spoil had been taken, not a town detained.   Knox included in his liturgy a prayer that there might nevermore be war between Scotland and England, and that prayer has been fulfilled.   There have been wars between British factions, but never another truly national war between the two nations.   Elizabeth in her first two years " had done what none of her ancestors could do, for by the occasion of her religion she had obtained the amity of Scotland, and thus had God blemished the fame of the great men of the world through the doings of a weak woman " : — such was the judgment of a daughter of France and a mother in the Protestant Israel, of Renée, the venerable Duchess of Ferrara.   Another observer, Hubert Languet, said that the English were so proud of the conversion of Scotland that they were recovering their old insolence and would be the very people to defy the imminent Council at Trent.   The tone of Catholic correspondence changes : the Elizabeth who was merely rushing to her ruin, will now set all Europe alight in her downward course.   That young woman's conduct, when we now examine it, will not seem heroic.   As was often to happen in coming years, she had been pursuing two policies at once, and she was ready to fall back upon an Austrian marriage if the Scottish revolt miscarried.   But this was not what men saw at the time.   What was seen was that she and Cecil had played and won a masterly game ; and Englishmen must have felt that the change of religion coincided with a transfer of power from incapable to capable hands.

All this had been done, not only without Spanish help, but (so a patriot might say) in defiance of Spain.   To discover Philip's intentions had been difficult, and in truth he had been of two minds.   Elizabeth was setting the worst of examples.   Say what she would, she was encouraging a Protestant revolt against a Catholic King.   She was doing this in sight, and with the hardly concealed applause, of the Netherlanders ; a friar who dared to preach against her at Antwerp went in fear of his life ; whole families of Flemings were already taking refuge in England.   Philip's new French wife was coming home to him ; his mother-in-law, Catharine de' Medici, implored him to stop Elizabeth from "playing the fool."   He had in some kind made himself responsible for the religious affairs of England, by assuring the Pope that all would yet be well.   But the intense dread of France, the outcome of long wars, could not be eradicated, and was reasonable enough.   He dared not let the French subdue Scotland and threaten England on both sides.   Moreover he was for the moment miserably poor ; Margaret of Parma, his Regent in the Netherlands, had hardly a crown for current expenses, and the Estates would grant nothing.   So in public he scolded and lectured Elizabeth, while in private he hinted that what she was doing should be done quickly.   The French, too, though they asked his aid, hardly wished him to fulfil his promise of sending troops to Scotland.   Then his navy was defeated by the opportune Turk (May 11) ; and the Spaniards suspected that the French, if guiltless of, were not displeased at, the disaster.

This was not all.   The Pope also had been humiliated.   The conciliatory Pius IV had not long been on the throne before he sent to Elizabeth a courteous letter (May 5, 1560).   Vincent Parpaglia, the Abbot of San Solutore at Turin, once the secretary of Cardinal Pole, was to carry it to her as Nuncio.   She was to lend him her ear, and a strong hint was given to her that she could be legitimated.   When she heard that the Nuncio was coming, she was perhaps a little frightened ; the choice between recantation and the anathema seemed to lie before her ; so she talked catholically with the Spanish ambassador. But Philip, when he heard the news, was seriously offended. He saw a French intrigue, and the diplomatic machinery of the Spanish monarchy was set in motion to procure the recall of the Nuncio. All manner of reasons could be given to the Pope to induce a cancellation of his rash act. Pius was convinced or overawed. Margaret of Parma stopped Parpaglia at Brussels. How to extricate the Pope from the adventure without loss of dignity was then the difficult question. Happily it could be said that Pole's secretary was personally distasteful to Philip, who had once imprisoned Parpaglia as a French spy. So at Brussels he enjoyed himself for some months, then announced to Elizabeth that after all he was not coming to her, and in the friendliest way sent her some Italian gossip (September 8). He said that he should go back by Germany, and, when he turned aside to France, Margaret of Parma knew what to think : namely, that there had been a French plot to precipitate a collision between Pius and Elizabeth. At the French Court the disappointed Nuncio "made a very lewd discourse of the Queen, her religion and proceedings." As to Elizabeth, she had answered this first papal approach by throwing the Catholic Bishops into prison. And then, it is to be feared that she, or someone on her behalf, told how the Pope had offered to confirm her Book of Common Prayer, if only she would fall down and worship him.

In August, 1560, a Parliament met at Edinburgh, to do for Scotland what the English Parliament had done in 1559. The Pope's authority was rejected, and the Mass was abolished. Upon a third conviction the sayer or hearer of mass was to be put to death. A Confession of Faith had been rapidly compiled by Knox and his fellow preachers ; it is said that Lethington toned down asperities. "To see it pass in such sort as it did" surprised Elizabeth's envoy Randolph. The Scot was not yet a born theologian. Lethington hinted that further amendments could be made if Elizabeth desired them (September 13), and she made bold to tell the Lutheran princes that Scotland had received "the same religion that is used in Almaine" (December 30). The Reforming preachers were few, but the few earnest Catholics were cowed. "This people of a later calling," as an English preacher called the Scots, had not known the disappointment of a young Josiah's reign, and heard the word with gladness. There were wide differences, however, between the proceedings of the two Parliaments. The English problem was comparatively simple. Long before 1559 the English Church had been relieved of superfluous riches; there was only a modest after-math for the Elizabethan scythe. In Scotland the kirk-lands were broad, and were held by prelates or quasi-prelates who were turning Protestant or were closely related to Lords of the Congregation. Catholic or Calvinist, the possessor meant to keep a tight grip on the land. The Bishops could be forbidden to say mass; some of them had no desire to be troubled with that or any other duty; but the decent Anglican process, which substitutes an Edmund Grindal for an Edmund Bonner, could not be imitated. The Scottish lords, had they wished it, could not have thrust an ecclesiastical supremacy upon their Catholic Queen; but to enrich the Crown was not their mind. The new preachers naturally desired something like that proprietary continuity which had been preserved in England: the patrimony of the Church should sustain the new religion. They soon discovered that this was "a devout imagination." They had to construct an ecclesiastical polity on new lines, and they set to work upon a Book of Discipline. Elementary questions touching the relation between Church and State were left open. Even the proceedings of the August Parliament were of doubtful validity. Contrary to wont, a hundred or more of the "minor barons" had formed a part of the assembly. Also, it was by no means clear that the compact signed by the French envoys authorised a Parliament to assemble and do what it pleased in matters of religion.

An excuse had been given to the French for a refusal to ratify the treaty with England. That treaty confirmed a convention which the Scots were already breaking. Another part of the great project was not to be fulfilled. Elizabeth was not going to marry Arran, though the Estates of Scotland begged this of her and set an united kingdom of Great Britain and Ireland before her eyes. Perhaps it was well that Arran was crazy; otherwise there might have been a premature enterprise. A King of Scots who was husband of the English Queen would have been hateful in England; Scotland was not prepared for English methods of government; and Elizabeth had troubles enough to face without barbaric blood feuds and a Book of Discipline. She had gained a great advantage. Sudden as had been the conversion of Scotland, it was permanent. Beneath all that was fortuitous and all that was despicable, there was a moral revolt. "It is almost miraculous," wrote Randolph in the June of 1560, "to see how the word of God takes place in Scotland. They are better willing to receive discipline than in any country I ever was in. Upon Sunday before noon and after there were at the sermons that confessed their offences and repented their lives before the congregation. Cecil and Dr Wotton were present. . . . They think to see next Sunday Lady Stonehouse, by whom the Archbishop of St Andrews has had, without shame, five or six children, openly repent herself." Elizabeth, the deliverer of Scotland, had built an external buttress for her English Church. If now and then Knox "gave her cross and candles a wipe," he none the less prayed for her and everlasting friendship. They did not love each other; but she had saved his Scottish Reformation, and he had saved her Anglican Settlement.

Then, at the end of this full year, there was a sudden change in France. Francis II died (December 5, 1560); Mary was a childless widow;

the Guises were only the uncles of a dowager. A mere boy, Charles IX, was King; power had passed to his mother, Catharine de' Medici and the Bourbons. They had no interest in Mary's claim on England, and, to say the least, were not fanatical Catholics. After some hesitation Mary resolved to return to Scotland. She had hoped for the hand of Philip's son, Don Carlos; but her mother-in-law had foiled her. The kingdom that had been conveyed to the Valois was not to be transferred to the Habsburg, and a niece of the Guises was not to seat herself upon the throne of Spain. The Scottish nobles were not averse to Mary's return, as Elizabeth would not marry Arran and there was thus no longer any fear that Scotland would be merged in France. Mary was profuse of kind words; she won Lord James to her side, and even Lethington was given to understand that he could make his peace. The treaty with England she would not confirm; she would wait until she could consult the Scottish Estates. Elizabeth regarded this as a dangerous insult. Her title to the Crown had been challenged, and the challenge was not withdrawn. Mary's request for a safe-conduct through England was rejected. Orders were given for stopping the ship that bore her towards Scotland, but apparently were cancelled at the last minute. She landed at Leith on the 19th of August, 1561. The long duel between the two Queens began. The story of it must be told elsewhere; but here we may notice that for some years the affairs of Scotland were favourable to the Elizabethan religion. Mary issued a proclamation (August 25, 1561) strikingly similar to that which came from Elizabeth on the first day of her reign. "The state of religion" which Mary "found publicly and universally standing at her home-coming was to be maintained until altered by her and the Estates of the realm." But she and the Estates were not at one, and her religious position was that of a barely tolerated nonconformist. Lord James and Lethington were her chief advisers, and her first military adventure was a successful contest with turbulent but Catholic Gordons. Also it pleased her to hold out hopes that she might accept Elizabeth's religion, if her claim to be Elizabeth's heir presumptive were conceded. The ratification of the treaty she still refused, asserting (a late afterthought) that some words in it might deprive her of her right to succeed Elizabeth if Elizabeth left no issue. She desired to meet Elizabeth; Elizabeth desired to meet her; and the Scottish Catholics said that Mary would not return as "a true Christian woman" from the projected interview. Her uncles were out of power. It was the time of the colloquy of Poissy (September, 1561); it was rumoured that Theodore Beza was converting the Duke of Guise, who talked pleasantly with Throckmorton about the English law of inheritance. The Cardinal of Lorraine publicly flirted with Lutheranism. Elizabeth learnt that her cross and candles marked her off from mere Calvinian Huguenots, though she kept in close touch with Condé and the Admiral. Moreover, the English Catholics were slow to look to

Scotland for a deliverer; the alien's right to inherit was very dubious; they looked rather to young Darnley, who was born in England and by English law was an Englishman and the son of an English mother. So the Elizabethan religion had a fair chance of striking root before the General Council could do its work.

The invitation to the General Council came, and was flatly refused (May 5, 1561). At this point we must turn for one moment to an obscure and romantic episode. From the first days of her reign the English Queen had shown marked favour to her master of the horse, Lord Robert Dudley—a young man, handsome and accomplished, ambitious and unprincipled; the son of that Duke of Northumberland who set Jane Grey on the throne and died as a traitor. Dudley was a married man, but lived apart from his wife, Amy, the daughter of Sir John Robsart. Gossip said that he would kill her and marry the Queen. On the 8th of September, 1560, when he was with the Queen at Windsor, his wife's corpse was found with broken neck at the foot of a staircase in Cumnor Hall. Some people said at once that he had procured her death; and that story was soon being told in all the Courts of Europe; but we have no proof that it was generally believed in England after a coroner's jury had given a verdict which, whatever may have been its terms, exculpated the husband. Dudley (the Leicester of after times) had throughout his life many bitter enemies; but none of them, so far as we know, ever mentioned any evidence of his guilt that a modern English judge would dream of leaving to a jury. We should see merely the unscrupulous character of the husband and the violent, opportune and not easily explicable death of the wife, were it not for a letter that the Spanish ambassador wrote to Margaret of Parma. That letter was not sent until its writer knew of Amy's death (which he mentioned in a postscript), but it professed to tell of what had passed between him, the Queen and Cecil at some earlier, but not precisely defined, moment of time. It suggests (as we read it) that Elizabeth knew that Dudley was about to kill his wife. Cecil, it asserts, desired the ambassador to intervene and reduce his mistress to the path of virtue. Those who are inclined to place faith in this wonderful tale about a truly wonderful Cecil, will do well to remember that a postscript is sometimes composed before any part of the letter is written, and that Alvaro de la Quadra, Bishop of Aquila, was suspected by the acute Throckmorton of taking the pay of the Guises. At that moment the rulers of France were refusing ratification of the Edinburgh treaty, and were much concerned that Philip should withdraw his support from Elizabeth. The practical upshot of the letter is that Elizabeth has plunged into an abyss of infamy, will probably be deposed in favour of the Protestant Earl of Huntingdon (Henry Hastings), and will be imprisoned with her favourite. The sagacity of the man who wrote this can hardly be saved, except at the expense of his honesty. Howbeit, Elizabeth, whether she loved Dudley or no (and this will never be known) behaved as if she had thoughts of marrying him, and showed little regard for what was said of his crime. One reading of her character, and perhaps the best, makes her heartless and nearly sexless, but for that reason indecorously desirous of appearing to the world as both the subject and the object of amorous passions. Also she was being pestered to marry the Archduke Charles, who would not come to be looked at, or Arran who had been looked at and rejected. Then (January, 1561) there was an intrigue between the Bishop of Aquila and the suspected murderer. Philip was to favour the Queen's marriage with the self-made widower, and the parties to this unholy union were thenceforth to be good Catholics, or at any rate were to subject themselves and the realm to the authority of the General Council.

There was superabundant falsehood on all sides. Quadra, Dudley, Cecil and Elizabeth, were all of them experts in mendacity, and the exact truth we are not likely to know when they tell the story. But the outcome of it all was that a papal Nuncio, the Abbot Martinengo, coming this time with Philip's full approval, arrived at Brussels with every reason to believe that Elizabeth would favourably listen to the invitation that he was bringing, and then, at the last moment, he learnt that he might not cross the Channel. There are signs that Cecil had difficulty in bringing about this result. Something stood in his way. He had to stimulate the English Bishops into protest, and to discover a little popish plot (there was always one to be discovered) at the right moment. It is conceivable that Dudley and Quadra had for a while ensnared the Queen with hopes of a secure reign and an easy life. It is quite as likely that she was employing them as unconscious agents to keep the Catholics quiet, while important negotiations were pending in France and Germany. That she seriously thought of sending envoys to the Council is by no means improbable; and some stout Protestants held that this was the proper course. But while Quadra and Dudley were concocting their plot, she kept in close alliance with foreign Protestants. Arrangements for a reply to the Pope were discussed with the German Protestant Princes at Naumburg (January, 1561); and strenuous endeavours were made through the puritanic Earl of Bedford to dissuade the French from participation in the Tridentine assembly. The end of it was that the English refusal was especially emphatic, and given in such a manner as to be a rebuff not only to Rome but to Spain. An irritating reference to a recent precedent did not mend matters: King Philip and Queen Mary had repulsed a Nuncio. Another reason could be given. In Ireland the Elizabethan religion, which had been introduced there by Act of Parliament, was not making way. In August, 1560, the Pope, who had already taken upon himself to dispose of two Irish bishoprics, sent to Ireland David Wolfe, a Jesuit priest, and conferred large powers upon him. He seems to have slipped over secretly from Britanny, where he had lain hid.   Elizabeth could say, and probably with truth, that his proceedings were hostile to her right and title.   As to a Council, of course she was all for a real and true, a "free and general" Council; all Protestants were; but with the papistical affair at Trent she would have nothing to do.   Pius had thought better of her; her lover's crypto-Catholicism had been talked of in high places.

The papal Legate at the French Court, the Cardinal of Ferrara, had some hope of succeeding where others had failed: "not as Legate of Rome or the Cardinal of Ferrara, but as Hippolito d'Este," an Italian gentleman devoted to Her Grace's service.   There were pleasant letters; cross and candles were commended; she was asked to retain them "even as it were for the Cardinal of Ferrara's pleasure"; but hardly had the Council been re-opened at Trent (January 18, 1562) than Elizabeth was allying herself with the Huguenots and endeavouring to form a Protestant league in Germany.   The dream of a France that would peacefully lapse from the Roman obedience was broken at Vassy (March 1, 1562), and the First War of Religion began.   In April Sechelles came to England as Condé's envoy and was accredited by Hotman to Cecil.   The danger to England was explained by the Queen's Secretary:—The crown of France would be in the hands of the Guisians; the King of Spain would help them; the Queen of Scots would marry Don Carlos; the Council would condemn the Protestants and give their dominions to a Catholic invader (July 20).   On the other hand, Calais, Dieppe, or Havre, "perhaps all three," might be Elizabeth's, so some thought; indeed "all Picardy, Normandy, and Gascony might belong to England again."   The Queen had been thinking of such possibilities; already in June, 1560, an offer of "certain towns in Britanny and Normandy" had been made to her.   She hesitated long, but yielded, and on the 20th of September, 1562, concluded the Treaty of Hampton Court with the Prince of Condé.   She was to help with money and men and hold Havre, Dieppe, and Rouen until Calais was restored.   It was a questionable step; but Philip was interfering on the Catholic side, and Calais was covetable.   Of course she was not at war with Charles IX; far from it; she was bent on delivering the poor lad and his mother from his rebellious subjects, who were also "her inveterate enemies," the Guises. Of religion she said as little as possible; but the Church of which she was the Supreme Governor affirmed in prayer that the Gallican Catholics were enemies of God's Eternal Word, and that the Calvinists were perse-cuted for the profession of God's Holy Name.   The expedition to Havre failed disastrously.   After the battle of Dreux (December 19, 1562) and the edict of Amboise (March 19, 1563), all parties in France united to expel the invader.   The Earl of Warwick (Ambrose Dudley) and his plague-stricken army were compelled to evacuate Havre after a stubborn resistance (July 28), and the recovery of Calais was further off than ever.   Elizabeth had played with the fire once too often.   She never after this thought

well of Huguenots; and friendship with the ruling powers of France
became the central feature of her resolutely pacific policy. However,
when at the beginning of 1563 she met her Second Parliament, and the
Reformed Church of England held its first Council, all was going well.
Since October an English army had once more been holding a French
town; a foolhardy plot devised by some young nephews of Cardinal
Pole had been opportunely discovered, and the French and Spanish
ambassadors were supposed to have had a hand in it. Some notes of
Cecil's suggest effective parliamentary rhetoric:

1559 The religion of Christ restored. Foreign authority rejected . . . 1560 The
French at the request of the Scots, partly by force, partly by agreement, sent back
to France, and Scotland set free from the servitude of the pope. 1561 The
debased copper and brass coinage replaced by gold and silver. England, formerly
unarmed, supplied more abundantly than any other country with arms, munitions
and artillery. 1562 The tottering Church of Christ in France succoured . . .

The Queen, it is true, was tormenting her faithful subjects by playing fast and loose with all her many wooers, and by disallowing all talk
of what would happen at her death. It was a policy that few women
could have maintained, but was sagacious and successful. It made men
pray that her days might be long; for, when compared with her sister's,
they were good days, and when they were over there would be civil
war. We hear the preacher : — " How was this our realm then pestered
with strangers, strange gods, strange languages, strange religion, strange
coin! And now how peaceably rid of them all!" So there was no
difficulty about a supply of money, and another turn might be given to
the screw of conformity. Some new classes of persons, members of the
House of Commons, lawyers, schoolmasters, were to take the oath of
Supremacy; a first refusal was to bring imprisonment and forfeiture, a
second death. The temporal lords procured their own exemption on
the ground that the Queen was "otherwise sufficiently assured" of their
loyalty. That might be so, but she was also sufficiently assured of a
majority in the Upper House, for there sat in it four-and-twenty
spiritual Lords of her own nomination.

The Spanish ambassador reported (January 14, 1563) that at the
opening of this Parliament, the preacher, Nowell, Dean of St Paul's,
urged the Queen " to kill the caged wolves," thereby being meant the
Marian Bishops. Nowell's sermon is extant, and says too much about
the duty of slaying the ungodly. Hitherto the Reformers, the men to
whom Cranmer and Ridley were dear friends and honoured masters, had
shown an admirable self-restraint. A few savage words had been said,
but they had not all come from one side. Christopher Goodman desired
that " the bloody Bishops" should be slain; but he had been kept out
of England as a dangerous fanatic. Dr John Story, in open Parliament,
had gloried in his own cruelty, and had regretted that in Mary's day
the axe had not been laid to the root of the tree. At a time when

letters from the Netherlands, France or Spain were always telling of burnt Protestants, nobody was burnt in England and very few people lay in prison for conscience' sake. The deprived Bishops seem to have been left at large until Parpaglia's mission ; then they were sent to gaol. Probably they could be lawfully imprisoned as contumacious excommunicates. Martinengo's advent induced Cecil to clap his hand on a few "mass-mongers," and on some laymen who had held office under Mary. But in these years of horror it is a small matter if a score of Catholics are kept in that Tower where Elizabeth was lately confined ; and her preachers had some right to speak of an unexampled clemency.

Rightly or wrongly, but very naturally, there was one man especially odious to the Protestants. When the statute of 1563 was passed, it was said among the Catholics that Bonner would soon be done to death, and the oath that he had already refused was tendered to him a second time by Horne the occupant of the see of Winchester. The tender was only valid if Horne was "Bishop of the diocese." Bonner, who, it is said, had the aid of Plowden, the most famous pleader of the time, threatened to raise the fundamental question whether Horne and his fellows were lawful Bishops. He was prepared to dispute the validity of the statutes of 1559 : to dispute the validity of the quasi-papal power of " supplying defects " which the Queen had assumed : to attack the very heart of the new order of things. Elizabeth, however, was not to be hurried into violence. The proceedings against him were stayed ; her Bishops were compelled to petition the Parliament of 1566 for a declaration that they were lawful Bishops ; their prayer was not granted except with the proviso that none of their past acts touching life and property were to be thereby validated ; and eleven out of some thirty-five temporal Lords were for leaving Dr Parker and his suffragans in their uncomfortably dubious position. Elizabeth allowed Lords and Commons to discuss and confirm her letters patent ; she was allowing all to see that no Catholic who refrained from plots need fear anything worse than twelve-penny fines ; but she had not yet been excommunicated and deposed.

A project for excommunication and deposition was sent to Trent from Louvain, where the Catholic exiles from England congregated. Like Knox and Goodman in Mary's reign, those who had fled from persecution were already setting themselves to exasperate the persecutor. The plan that found favour with them in 1563 involved the action of the Emperor's son, the Archduke Charles. He was to marry Mary Stewart (who, however, had set her heart on a grander match), and then he was to execute the papal ban. Englishmen, it was said, would never again accept as King the heir to the throne of Spain ; but his Austrian kinsman would be an unexceptionable candidate or conqueror. The papal Legates at Trent consulted the Emperor, who told his ambassadors that if the Council wished to make itself ridiculous, it had better depose Elizabeth ; he and his would have nothing to do with this absurd and dangerous scheme (June 19). Soon afterwards he was allowing his son's marriage, not with the Catholic Mary, but with the heretical Elizabeth, to be once more discussed, and the negotiations for this union were being conducted by the eminently Lutheran Duke of Württemberg, who apparently thought that pure religion would be the gainer if a Habsburg, Ferdinand's son and Maximilian's brother, became King of a Protestant England. Philip too, though he had no wish to quarrel with his uncle, began seriously to think that, in the interest of the Catholic faith and the Catholic King, Mary Stewart was right in preferring the Spanish to the Austrian Charles; and at the same time he was being assured from Rome that it was respect for him which had prevented Pius from bringing Elizabeth's case before the assembled Fathers. She was protected from the anathema, which in 1563 might have been a serious matter, by conflicting policies of the worldliest sort. The only member of the English episcopate who was at Trent, the fugitive Marian Bishop of St Asaph, might do his worst; but the safe course for ecclesiastical power was to make a beginning with Jeanne d'Albret and wait to see whether any good would come of the sentence. Ferdinand, however, begged Elizabeth to take pity on the imprisoned prelates, and she quartered most of them upon their Protestant successors. The English Catholics learnt from the Pope, whom they consulted through the Spanish ambassadors at London and Rome, that they ought not to attend the English churches (October, 1562). As a matter of expediency this was a questionable decision. It is clear that the zealous Romanists over-estimated the number of those Englishmen whose preference for the old creed could be blown into flame. The State religion was beginning to capture the neutral nucleus of the nation, and the irreconcilable Catholics were compelled to appear as a Spanish party secretly corresponding with the Pope through Quadra and Vargas.

Simultaneously with the Parliament a Convocation of the province of Canterbury was held (January 12, 1563), and its acts may be said to complete the great outlines of the Anglican settlement. A delicate task lay before the theologians: no other than that of producing a confession of faith. Happily in this case also a restoration was possible. In the last months of Edward's reign a set of forty-two Articles had been published; in the main they were the work of Cranmer. In 1563 Parker laid a revised version of them before the assembled clergy, and, when a few more changes had been made, they took durable shape and received the royal assent. A little more alteration at a later day made them the famous "Thirty-nine Articles." To all seeming the leaders of English theological thought were remarkably unanimous.

A dangerous point had been passed. Just at the moment when the Roman Church was demonstrating on a grand scale its power of defining dogma, its adversaries were becoming always less hopeful of

Protestant unanimity. In particular, as Elizabeth was often hearing from Germany, the dispute about the Lord's Supper was not to be composed, and a quarrel among divines was rapidly becoming a cause of quarrel among Princes. Well intentioned attempts to construct elastic phrases had done more harm than good, and it was questionable whether the Religious Peace would comprehend the Calvinising Palsgrave. As causes of political union and discord, all other questions of theology were at this moment of comparatively small importance ; the line which would divide the major part of the Protestant world into two camps, to be known as Lutheran and Calvinist, was being drawn by theories of the Holy Supper. It is usual and for the great purposes of history it is right to class the Knoxian Church of Scotland as Calvinian, though about Predestination its Confession of Faith is as reticent as are the English Articles. Had it been possible for the English Church to leave untouched the hotly controverted question, the Queen would have been best pleased. She knew that at Hamburg, Westphal, a champion of militant Lutheranism, "never ceased in open pulpit to rail upon England and spared not the chiefest magistrates" ; it was he who had denounced the Marian exiles as "the devil's martyrs." Since the first moment of her reign Christopher of Württemberg and Peter Paul Vergerio had been endeavouring to secure her for the Lutheran faith. Jewel, who was to be the Anglican apologist, heard with alarm of the advances made by the ex-Bishop of Capo d'Istria ; and the godly Duke had been pained at learning that no less than twenty-seven of the Edwardian Articles swerved from the Augustan standard. Very lately he had urged the Queen to stand fast for a Real Presence. Now, Lutheranism was by this time politically respectable. When there was talk of a Bull against Elizabeth, the Emperor asked how a distinction was to be made between her and the Lutheran Princes, and could take for granted that no Pope with his wits about him would fulminate a sentence against those pillars of the Empire, Augustus of Saxony and Joachim of Brandenburg. When a few years later (1570) a Pope did depose Elizabeth, he was careful to accuse her of participation in "the impious mysteries of Calvin," by which, no doubt, he meant the *Cène*. But though the Augustan might be the safer creed, she would not wish to separate herself from the Huguenots or the Scots, and could have little hope of obtaining from her Bishops a declaration that would satisfy the critical mind of the good Christopher. Concessions were made to him at points where little was at stake ; words were taken from his own Württemberg Confession. When the perilous spot was reached, the English divines framed an Article which, as long experience has shown, can be signed by men who hold different opinions ; but a charge of deliberate ambiguity could not fairly be brought against the Anglican fathers. In the light of the then current controversy we may indeed see some desire to give no needless offence to Lutherans, and apparently the Queen

suppressed until 1571 a phrase which would certainly have repelled
them; but, even when this phrase was omitted, Beza would have
approved the formula, and it would have given greater satisfaction at
Geneva and Heidelberg than at Jena or Tübingen. A papistical controversialist tried to insert a wedge which would separate a Lutheran
Parker from an Helvetic Grindal; but we find Parker hoping that
Calvin, or, if not Calvin, then Vermigli will lead the Reformers at
Poissy, and the only English Bishop to whom Lutheran leanings can
be safely attributed held aloof from his colleagues and was for a while
excommunicate. It was left for Elizabeth herself to suggest by cross
and candles that (as her German correspondents put it) she was living
"according to the divine light, that is, the Confession of Augsburg,"
while someone assured the Queen of Navarre that these obnoxious
symbols had been removed from the royal chapel. As to "the sacrifices
of masses," there could be no doubt. The anathema of Trent was
frankly encountered by "blasphemous fable." Elizabeth knew that
her French ambassador remained ostentatiously seated when the Host
was elevated, for "reverencing the sacrament was contrary to the usages
established by law in England."

Another rock was avoided. Ever since 1532 there had been in the
air a project for an authoritative statement of English Canon Law. In
Edward's day that project took the shape of a book (*Reformatio Legum
Ecclesiasticarum*) of which Cranmer and Peter Martyr were the chief
authors, but which had not received the King's sanction when death took
him. During Elizabeth's first years we hear of it again; but nothing
decisive was done. The draft code that has come down to us has
every fault that it could have. In particular, its list of heresies is
terribly severe, and apparently (but this has been doubted) the obstinate
heretic is to go the way that Cranmer went: not only the Romanists
but some at least of the Lutherans might have been relinquished to
the secular arm. Howbeit, the scheme fell through. Under a statute
of Henry VIII so much of the old Canon Law as was not contrariant nor
repugnant to the Word of God or to Acts of the English Parliament
was to be administered by the Courts of the English Church. Practically
this meant, that the officials of the Bishops had a fairly free hand in
declaring law as they went along. They were civilians; the academic
study of the Canon Law had been prohibited; they were not in the least
likely to contest the right of the temporal legislature to regulate
spiritual affairs. And the hands of the Queen's ecclesiastical commissioners were free indeed. Large as were the powers with which
she could entrust them by virtue of the Act of Supremacy, she pro-
fessedly gave them yet larger powers, for they might punish offenders
by fine and imprisonment, and this the old Courts of the Church could
not do. A constitutional question of the first magnitude was to arise
at this point. But during the early years of the reign the commissioners

seem to be chiefly employed in depriving papists of their benefices, and this was lawful work.

But while there was an agreeable harmony in dogma and little controversy over polity, the quarrel about ceremonies had begun. In the Convocation of 1563, resolutions, which would have left the posture of the communicants to the discretion of the Bishops and would have abolished the observance of Saints' days, the sign of the cross in baptism and the use of organs, were rejected in the Lower House by the smallest of majorities. It was notorious that some of the Bishops favoured only the simplest rites ; five deans and a dozen archdeacons petitioned against the modest surplice. But for its Supreme Governor, the English Church would in all likelihood have carried its own purgation far beyond the degree that had been fixed by the secular legislature. To the Queen, however, it was of the first importance that there should be no more changes before the face of the Tridentine enemy, and also that her occasional professions of Augustan principles should have some visible support. The Bishops, though at first with some reluctance, decided to enforce the existing law ; and in course of time conservative sentiment began to collect around the rubrics of the Prayer Book. However, there were some men who were not to be pacified. The "Vestiarian controversy" broke out. Those who strove for a worship purified from all taint of popery (and who therefore were known as "Puritans") "scrupled" the cap and gown that were to be worn by the clergy in daily life, and "scrupled" the surplice that was to be worn in church. Already in 1565 resistance and punishment had begun. At Oxford the Dean of Christ Church was deprived, and young gentlemen at Cambridge discarded the rags of the Roman Antichrist.

In the next year the London clergy were recalcitrant. The Spanish ambassador improved the occasion. In reply, Elizabeth told him that the disobedient ministers were "not natives of the country, but Scotsmen, whom she had ordered to be punished." Literal truth she was not telling, and yet there was truth of a sort in her words. From this time onwards, the historian of the English Church must be often thinking of Scotland, and the historian of the Scottish Church must keep England ever in view. Two kingdoms are drifting together, first towards a "personal" and then towards a "real" Union ; but two Churches are drifting apart into dissension and antagonism. The attractions and repulsions that are involved in this process fill a large page in the annals of Britain ; they have become plain to all in the age of the Bishops' Wars and the Westminster Assembly ; but they are visible much earlier. The attempt to Scoticise the English Church, which failed in 1660, and the attempt to Anglicise the Scottish Church, which failed in 1688, each of these had its century.

For a while there is uncertainty. At one moment Maitland is sure that the two kingdoms have one religion ; at another (March, 1563) he can tell the Bishop of Aquila that there are great differences; but undoubtedly in 1560 the prevailing belief was that the Protestants of England and Scotland were substantially at one; and, many as were to be the disputes between them, they remained substantially at one for the greatest of all purposes until there was no fear that either realm would revert to Rome. From the first the Reforming movement in the northern kingdom had been in many ways an English movement. Then in 1560 Reformation and national deliverance had been effected simultaneously by the aid of English gold and English arms. John Knox was a Scot of Scots, and none but a Scot could have done what he did; but, had he died in 1558 at the age of fifty-three, his name would have occurred rather in English than in Scottish books, and he might have disputed with Hooper the honour of being the progenitor of the English Puritans. The congregation at Geneva for which he compiled his Prayer Book was not Scottish but English. His Catholic adversaries in Scotland said that he could not write good Scots. Some of his principal lieutenants were Englishmen or closely connected with England. John Willock, while he was " Superintendent " (Knoxian Bishop) of Glasgow, was also parson of Loughborough. " Mr. Goodman of England " had professed divinity at Oxford, and after his career in Scotland was an English archdeacon, though a troublesome Puritan. John Craig had been tutor in an English family, and, instead of talking honest Scots, would " knap suddrone." But further, Knox had signed the English Articles of 1553, and is plausibly supposed to have modified their wording. A Catholic controversialist of Mary's day said that " a runagate Scot " had procured that the adoration of Christ in the Sacrament should be put out of the English Prayer Book. To that book in 1559 Knox had strong objections; he detested ceremonies; the Coxian party at Frankfort had played him a sorry trick and he had just cause of resentment; but there was nothing doctrinally wrong with the Book. It was used in Scotland. In 1560 a Frenchman whom Randolph took to church in Glasgow, and who had previously been in Elizabeth's chapel, saw great differences, but heard few, for the prayers of the English Book were said. Not until some years later did " the Book of Geneva " (Knox's liturgy) become the fixed standard of worship for the Scottish Church. The objection to all prescript prayers is of later date and some say that it passes from England into Scotland. This Genevan Use had been adopted by the chaplain of Elizabeth's forces at Havre, and, though he was bidden to discontinue it, he was forthwith appointed to the deanery of Durham. A Puritan movement in England there was likely to be in any case. The arguments of both parties were already prepared. The Leipzig *Interim*, the work of the Elector Maurice, had given rise to a similar quarrel among the Lutherans, between Flacians on the one side and Philipians on the other, over those rites and ornaments which were " indifferent " in themselves, but had, as some thought, been soiled by superstition.   The English exiles who returned from Zurich and Geneva would dislike cap, gown, and surplice ; but their foreign mentors counselled submission; Bullinger was large-minded, and Calvin was politic.   Scotland, however, was very near, and in Scotland this first phase of Puritanism was in its proper place.   So long as Mary reigned there and plotted there, the Protestant was hardly an established religion ; and, had Knox been the coolest of schemers, he would have endeavoured to emphasise every difference between the old worship and the new.   It was not for him to make light of *adiaphora ;* it was for him to keep Protestant ardour at fever heat.   Maitland, who was a cool schemer, made apology to Cecil for Knox's vehemence: " as things are fallen out, it will serve to good purpose."   And yet it is fairly certain that Knox dissuaded English Puritans from secession.   In his eyes the Coxian Church of England might be an erring sister, but still was a twin sister, of the Knoxian Church of Scotland.

Elizabeth's resistance to the Puritan demands was politic.   The more Protestant a man was, the more secure would be his loyalty if Rome were aggressive.   It was for her to appeal to the "neutral in religion" and those " faint professors " of whom her Bishops saw too many.   It is not perhaps very likely that surplices and square caps won to her side many of those who cared much for the old creed. Not the simplest and most ignorant papist, says Whitgift to the Puritans, could mistake the Communion for the Mass: the Mass has been banished from England as from Scotland: we are full as well Reformed as are the Scots.   But Elizabeth feared frequent changes, was glad to appear as a merely moderate Reformer, and meant to keep the clergy well in hand.   Moreover, in Catholic circles her cross and candles produced a good impression.   When she reproved Dean Nowell for inveighing against such things, this was soon known to Cardinal Borromeo, and he was not despondent (April 21, 1565).   Even her dislike for a married clergy, which seems to have been the outcome of an indiscriminating misogyny, was favourably noticed.   It encouraged the hope that she might repent, and for some time Rome was unwilling to quench this plausibly smoking flax.   But her part was difficult.   The Puritans could complain that they were worse treated than Spanish, French, and Dutch refugees, whose presence in England she liberally encouraged.   Casiodoro de Reyna, Nicolas des Gallars, and Utenhove, though the Bishop of London was their legal " superintendent," were allowed a liberty that was denied to Humphry and Sampson; there was one welcome for Mrs Matthew Parker and another for Madame la Cardinale.

The controversy of the sixties over rites and clothes led to the controversy of the seventies over polity, until at length Presbyterianism and Episcopalianism stood arrayed against each other.   But the process was gradual.   We must not think that Calvin had formulated a Presbyterian system, which could be imported ready-made from Geneva to

Britain. In what is popularly called Presbyterianism there are various elements. One is the existence of certain presbyters or elders, who are not pastors or ministers of the Word, but who take a larger or smaller part in the government of the Church. This element may properly be called Calvinian, though the idea of some such eldership had occurred to other Reformers. Speculations touching the earliest history of the Christian Church were combined with a desire to interest the laity in a rigorous ecclesiastical discipline. But Calvin worked with the materials that were ready to his hand and was far too wary to raise polity to the rank of dogma. The Genevan Church was essentially civic or municipal; its Consistory is very much like a committee of a town council. This could not be the model for a Church of France or of Scotland, which would contain many particular congregations or churches. Granted that these particular Churches will be governed by elders, very little has yet been decided : we may have the loosest federation of autonomous units, or the strictest subordination of the parts to some assembly which is or represents the whole. Slowly and empirically, the problem was solved with somewhat different results in France, Scotland, and the Low Countries. As we have said, the month which saw Knox land in Scotland saw a French Church taking shape in a national Synod that was being secretly held at Paris. Already Frenchmen are setting an example for constituent assemblies and written constitutions. Knox, who had been edifying the Church of Dieppe—that Dieppe which was soon to pass into Elizabeth's hands—stood in the full current of the French movement ; but, like his teacher, he had no iron system to impose. Each particular congregation would have elders besides a pastor ; there would be some general assembly of the whole Church ; but Knox was not an ecclesiastical jurist. The *First Book of Discipline* (1560) decides wonderfully little ; even the structure of the General Assembly is nebulous ; and, as a matter of fact, all righteous noblemen seem to be welcome therein. It gradually gives itself a constitution, and, while a similar process is at work in France, other jurisdictional and governmental organs are developed, until kirk-session, presbytery, synod and assembly form a concentric system of Courts and councils of which Rome herself might be proud. But much of this belongs to a later time ; in Scotland it is not Knoxian but Melvillian.

A mere demand for some ruling elders for the particular Churches was not likely to excite enthusiasm or antagonism. England knew that plan. The curious Church of foreign refugees, organised in the London of Edward VI's days under the presidency of John Laski, had elders. Cranmer took great interest in what he probably regarded as a fruitful experiment, and the Knoxian Church has some traits which, so good critics think, tell less of Geneva than of the Polish but cosmopolitan nobleman. Dr Horne, Elizabeth's Bishop of Winchester, had been the pastor of a Presbyterian flock of English refugees at Frankfort. With a portion of that flock he had quarrelled, not for being Presbyterian, but because the Presbyterianism of this precocious conventicle was already taking that acutely democratic and distinctly uncalvinian form, in which the elders are the annually elected officers of a congregation which keeps both minister and elders well under control. Among Englishmen a drift towards Congregationalism appears almost as soon as the ruling elder.

The enthusiasm and antagonism were awakened by a different cry: it was not a call for presbyters, but a call for "parity," for an equality among all the ministers of God's Word, and consequently for an abolition of all "prelacy." As a battle cry this is hardly Calvinian; nor is it Knoxian; it is first audible at Cambridge. The premisses, it is true, lay ready to the hand of anyone who chose to combine them. The major was that Protestant principle which refers us to the primitive Church. The minor was a proposition familiar to the Middle Age:—originally there was no difference between the *presbyter* and the *episcopus*. Every student of the Canon Law knew the doctrine that the prelacy of Bishops is founded, not on divine command, but on a "custom of the Church." When the Puritan said that the episcopal jurisdiction was of popish origin, he agreed with Laynez and the Pope; at least, as had been amply shown at Trent, the divine right of Bishops was a matter over which Catholic doctors could quarrel bitterly. But the great Reformers had been chary of their words about ecclesiastical polity; there were many possibilities to be considered, and the decision would rest with Princes or civic Councils. The defenders of Anglican episcopacy occasionally told the Puritan that he was not a good Calvinist, and even Beza could hardly be brought by British pressure to a sufficiently dogmatic denunciation of prelacy. As to Knox, it is clear that, though he thought the English dioceses too large, he had no radical objection to such prelacy as existed in England. Moreover, the Church that he organised in Scotland was prelatic, and there is but little proof that he regarded its prelatic constitution as a concession to merely temporary needs. The word "bishop" was avoided (in Scotland there still were lawful Bishops of another creed); but over the "dioceses" stand "superintendents" (the title comes from Germany), who, though strictly accountable to the general assembly, are distinctly the rulers of the diocesan clergy. Between superintendent and minister there is no "parity"; the one may command, the other must obey. The theory that valid orders can be conferred by none but a Bishop, Knox would, no doubt, have denied; but some at all events of the contemporary English Bishops would have joined him in the denial.

Apparently Thomas Cartwright, a young professor of divinity at Cambridge, spoke the word (1570) that had not yet been spoken in Scotland. Cambridge was seething with Puritanism; the Bishops had been putting the vestiarian law in force; and the French Church had declared for parity. "There ought to be an equality": presbyter and Bishop were once all one. But if the demand for parity was first heard south of the Tweed, it was soon echoed back by Scotland; and thenceforth the English Puritan was often looking northward. In Scotland much had been left unsettled. From August, 1561, to May, 1568, Mary Stewart is there; Rizzio and Darnley, Bothwell and Moray, Lethington and Knox, are on the stage; and we hold our breath while the tragedy is played. We forget the background of unsolved questions and uncertain law. Is the one lawful religion the Catholic or the Protestant? Are there two established Churches, or is one Church established and another endowed? There is an *interim:* or rather, an armed truce. The Queen had not confirmed the statutes of 1560, though mass-mongers were occasionally imprisoned. Nothing decisive had been done in the matter of tithes and kirk-lands and advowsons. The Protestant ministers and super-intendents were receiving small stipends which were charged upon the ecclesiastical revenues; but the Bishops and Abbots, some of whom were Protestant ministers, had not been ousted from their temporalities or their seats in Parliament, and, as vacancies occurred, the bishoprics were con-ferred upon new occupants, some of whom were Catholics. The General Assembly might meet twice a year; but John Hamilton still went to Parliament as a reverend father in God and primate of Scotland. If Mary had succeeded in re-establishing Catholicism, we should probably have said that it had never been disestablished. And when she had been deposed and a Parliament held in her son's name had acknowledged the Knoxian Church to be " the immaculate spouse of Christ," much was still unsettled. What was to be done with the bishoprics and abbacies and with the revenues and seats in Parliament that were involved there-with? Grave questions of civil and ecclesiastical polity were open, and a large mass of wealth went a-begging or illustrated the beatitude of possession. Then in the seventies we on the one hand see an attempt to Anglicise the Church by giving it Bishops, who will sit in Parliament and be somewhat more prelatic than were Knox's superintendents, and on the other hand we hear a swelling cry for parity.

To many a Scot prelacy will always suggest another word of evil sound: to wit, Erastianism. The link is Anglican. The name of the professor of medicine at Heidelberg—it was Thomas Lüber, or in Greek Erastus—won a fame or infamy in Britain that has been denied to it elsewhere. And in some sort this is fair, for it was an English Puritan who called him into the field; and after his death his manuscript book was brought to England and there for the first time printed. His Prince, the Elector Palatine Frederick III, was introducing into his dominions, in the place of the Lutheranism which had prevailed there, the theology that flowed from Zurich and Geneva; images were being destroyed and altars were giving place to tables. This, as Elizabeth knew when the Thirty Nine Articles lay before her, was a very serious change; it

strained to breaking-point the professed unanimity of the Protestant
Princes.   Theology, however, was one thing, Church-polity another;
and for all the Genevan rigours Frederick was not yet prepared.   But
to Heidelberg for a doctor's degree came an English Puritan, George
Withers, and he stirred up strife there by urging the necessity of a
discipline exercised by pastor and elders (June, 1568).   Erastus answered him by declaring that excommunication has no warrant in the
Word of God; and further that, when the Prince is a Christian, there
is no need for a corrective jurisdiction which is not that of the State,
but that of the Church.   This sowed dissension between Zurich and
Geneva: between Bullinger, the friend of the English Bishops, and Beza,
the oracle of the Puritans.   Controversy in England began to nibble
at the Royal Supremacy; and in Scotland the relation between the
State (which until 1567 had a papistical head) and the Knoxian Church,
was of necessity highly indeterminate.   Knox had written sentences
which, in our rough British use of the term, were Erastian enough;
and a great deal of history might have been changed, had he found
in Scotland a pious prince or even a pious princess, a Josiah or even
a Deborah.   As it fell out, the Scottish Church aspired to, and at times
attained, a truly medieval independence.   Andrew Melvill's strain of
language has been compared with that of Gregory VII; so has Thomas
Cartwright's; but the Scottish Church had an opportunity of resuming
ancient claims which was denied to the English.   In 1572 an oath was
imposed in Scotland; the model was English; but important words
were changed.   The King of Scots is " Supreme Governor of this realm
as well in things temporal as in the conservation and purgation of
religion."   The Queen of England is " Supreme Governor of this realm
as well in all spiritual or ecclesiastical things or causes as temporal."
The greater continuity of ecclesiastical history is not wholly on one
side of the border.   The charge of popery was soon retorted against
the Puritans by the Elizabethan divines and their Helvetian advisers:—
Your new presbyter in his lust for an usurped dominion is but too like
old priest.

In controversy with the Puritans the Elizabethan religion gradually
assumed an air of moderation which had hardly belonged to it from the
first; it looked like a compromise between an old faith and a new.   It is
true that from the beginning of her reign Elizabeth distrusted Calvin;
and when she swore that she never read his books she may have sworn
the truth.   That blast of the trumpet had repelled her.   Not only had
" the regiment of women" been attacked, but Knox and Goodman had
advocated a divine right of rebellion against idolatrous Princes.   Calvin
might protest his innocence; but still this dangerous stuff came from his
Geneva.   Afterwards, however, he took an opportunity of being service-
able to the Queen in the matter of a book which spoke ill of her father
and mother.   Then a pretty message went to him and he was bidden to

feel assured of her favour (September 18, 1561).   Moreover, in German history Elizabeth appears as espousing the cause of oppressed Calvinists against the oppressing Lutherans.   Still as time went on, when the Huguenots, as she said, had broken faith with her about Havre and Calais, and the attack on "her officers," the Bishops, was being made in the name of the Genevan discipline, her dislike of Geneva, its works, and its ways, steadily grew.   Though in the region of pure theology Calvin's influence increased apace in England and Scotland after his death, and Whitgift, the stern repressor of the Puritans, was a remorseless predestinarian, still the Bishops saw, albeit with regret, that they had two frontiers to defend, and that they could not devote all their energy to the confutation of the Louvainists.

Then some severed, or half-severed, bonds were spliced.   Parker was a lover of history, and it was pleasant to sit in the chair of Augustine, seeing to editions of Ælfric's Homilies and the Chronicles of Matthew Paris.   But the work was slowly done, and foreigners took a good share in it.   Hadrian Saravia, who defended English episcopacy against Beza, was a refugee, half Spaniard, half Fleming.   Pierre Baron of Cambridge, who headed a movement against Calvin's doctrine of the divine decrees, was another Frenchman, another pupil of the law-school of Bourges. And it is to be remembered that at Elizabeth's accession the Genevan was not the only model for a radically Reformed Church.   The fame of Zwingli's Zurich had hardly yet been eclipsed, and for many years the relation between the Anglican and Tigurine Churches was close and cordial.   A better example of a purely spiritual power could hardly be found than the influence that was exercised in England by Zwingli's successor Henry Bullinger.   Bishops and Puritans argue their causes before him as if he were the judge.   So late as 1586 English clergymen are required to peruse his immortal *Decades*.   There was some gratitude in the case.   A silver cup with verses on it had spoken Elizabeth's thanks for the hospitality that he had shown to Englishmen.   But that was not all; he sympathised with Elizabeth and her Bishops and her Erastianism.   He condemned "the English fool" who broke the peace of the Palatinate by a demand for the Genevan discipline.   When the cry was that the congregation should elect its minister, the Puritan could be told how in an admirably reformed republic Protestant pastors were still chosen by patrons who might be papists, even by a Bishop of Constance who might be the Pope's own nephew and a Cardinal to boot, for a Christian magistracy would see that this patronage was not abused. And then when the bad day came and the Pope hurled his thunderbolt, it was to Bullinger that the English Bishops looked for a learned defence of their Queen and their creed.   Modestly, but willingly, he undertook the task: none the less willingly perhaps, because Pius V had seen fit to couple Elizabeth's name with Calvin's, and this was a controversialist's trick which Zurich could expose.   Bullinger knew all the

Puritan woes and did not like surplices; he knew and much disliked the "semi-popery" of Lutheran Germany; but in his eyes the Church of England was no half-way house. As to Elizabeth, he saw her as no lukewarm friend of true religion, but as a virgin-queen beloved of God, whose wisdom and clemency, whose felicity and dexterity were a marvel and a model for all Christian Princes (March 12, 1572).

The felicity and dexterity are not to be denied. The Elizabethan religion which satisfied Bullinger was satisfying many other people also; for (to say nothing of intrinsic merits or defects) it appeared as part and parcel of a general amelioration. It was allied with honest money, cheap and capable government, national independence, and a reviving national pride. The long Terror was overpast, at least for a while; the flow of noble blood was stayed; the axe rusted at the Tower. The long Elizabethan peace was beginning (1563), while France was ravaged by civil war, and while more than half the Scots looked to the English Queen as the defender of their faith. One Spaniard complains that these heretics have not their due share of troubles (November, 1562); another, that they are waxing fat upon the spoil of the Indies (August, 1565). The England into which Francis Bacon was born in 1561 and William Shakespeare in 1564 was already unlike the England that was ruled by the Queen of Spain.

CHAPTER XVII

THE SCANDINAVIAN NORTH

THE Scandinavian nations had entered somewhat late into the general stream of European history, and, at the beginning of the sixteenth century, were still not a little behind the rest of Western Europe in civilisation. But they were early brought into contact with the Reformation movement, and nowhere were its effects more generally felt or more far-reaching. In order to see to what extent this was the case, some attention must be paid to their earlier history.

It was not till the tenth century that Denmark, Norway, and Sweden began to exist as single monarchies; and it was under their early Kings that Christianity, first introduced some time previously, came to be the religion of all their people. From this time forward, although they were frequently devastated and rent asunder by internal warfare, the three kingdoms may be said to have taken their part, each in its own way, in European history. The Swedes, pressed by their heathen neighbours to the north and north-east, were at first unable to make much headway. The Norwegians, fully occupied by their activities beyond the seas, in Iceland, in parts of Scotland and Ireland, and even in far-away Greenland, never acquired much strength at home. Denmark was usually the most powerful kingdom of the three. Under the Kings of the Estridsen line the Danes vindicated their independence of the Empire, and conquered large territories from the heathen Wends and Esthonians on the shores of the Baltic; in fact, there was a time, under Valdemar the Victorious (1204–41), when the Baltic was to all intents and purposes a Danish lake. But the capture and imprisonment of Valdemar by Count Henry of Schwerin gave a blow to their power from which it never recovered. The increasing influence of the Teutonic knights and the Livonian knights of the sword on the one hand, and the rapid advance of Sweden under its Folkung dynasty on the other, still further shattered it. The Danes were further hampered by the commercial and naval rivalry of the Hanseatic League, and by frequent border warfare with the duchy of Holstein. Altogether, it looked for a time as though Sweden must take the place of Denmark as the chief power of the north. But although the Swedes gradually extended their sway over Dalecarlia and Finland, their further extension was prevented by the advance of the Russians of Novgorod to the shores of the Gulf of Finland ; and thus the peoples of the north were once more thrown back upon themselves.

After several unsuccessful attempts at dynastic union, the three kingdoms were at length united. In 1363 Valdemar III (Atterdag) of Denmark had given his daughter Margaret in marriage to Hakon of Norway. On his death in 1375 Margaret's son Olaf became King of Denmark. Five years later, on the death of his own father, Olaf succeeded to the crown of Norway ; and Margaret became the real ruler of both realms in the name of her son. About the same time she laid claim to the crown of Sweden in right of her late husband Hakon ; and, although the claim was at first very shadowy, it became formidable when the Swedish nobles espoused her cause. The King, Albert of Mecklenburg, was defeated and made prisoner at the battle of Falköping ; and the Treaty of Lindholm (1393) left her undisputed mistress of Sweden. Thus the three realms were united under Queen Margaret, for her son Olaf had died in 1387. The personal union before long became a constitutional one. In 1397 Margaret caused her grand-nephew Erik to be crowned King at Kalmar ; and on that occasion there was concluded, by nobles representing the three kingdoms, the famous Union of Kalmar, by which Sweden, Norway, and Denmark were declared to be for ever united under one King, each retaining its own laws and customs. But the Union was not regularly promulgated or made widely known, its terms were vague and indefinite, and they opened up more questions than they solved. It was provided that a son of the reigning King should be chosen if possible ; but nothing was said as to the method by which the three kingdoms were to participate in the election. It was provided that all should take up arms against the general enemy ; but no reference was made to the carrying out of projects which concerned one of the three only. It is plain that nothing but pressing common interests or a strong ruler could render such an agreement permanent, and this was precisely what was wanting. On the one hand, Erik and his successors really ruled in the interests of Denmark ; on the other, the condition of Sweden, practically one of anarchy, made any settled government well-nigh impossible. Revolts were of frequent occurrence, and before long the Danish governors were driven out, and Karl Knudson, the leader of the higher nobility, became administrator (*Riksføreståndare*) of Sweden. On the accession of the House of Oldenburg to the throne of Denmark in 1448, Karl Knudson was proclaimed King of Sweden, and soon afterwards of Norway also. Christian I soon regained his hold over the latter realm ; but from this time forward the Danish Kings were seldom able to make good their claims over Sweden, which continued to be ruled by Swedish administrators until

1520, when the death of Sten Sture the younger placed Sweden for the moment entirely in the hands of Christian II of Denmark. On the other hand, the Oldenburg line had gained ground elsewhere. In 1460 Christian I was chosen as Duke of Schleswig and Count of Holstein. But the great revolt of the Ditmarsch peasants, ending in the destruction of the Danish army, with two Counts of Oldenburg and the flower of the Schleswig-Holstein nobility, in 1500, further weakened the Danish throne, and indirectly helped to break up the Union of Kalmar.

The general effect of the changes which had taken place in the Scandinavian kingdom since the twelfth century had been to strengthen the power of the nobles at the expense of the King and the *bönder* or free peasants. Neither in Denmark nor in Sweden was there a law of heredity; and every election was secured at the cost of a "capitulation" which involved a certain weakening of the royal prerogative. In order to obviate the evils of a disputed succession, the Kings frequently attempted to secure an election in their own lifetime and left large appanages to their younger sons: with the result that the effort to transform these personal fiefs into hereditary possessions often led to civil wars, and still further weakened the Crown. Under pressure from the nobles the royal castles were step by step demolished everywhere, and the royal domain was gradually encroached upon. The *Rigsraad*, or Council of State, consisting entirely of the nobles and the higher clergy, altogether supplanted the ancient assemblies of the people as the final legislative authority. In Sweden King Albert (Count of Mecklenburg) was little more than the President of this Council. Even in Denmark things were not much better; and they did not improve. Under the Oldenburg Kings the Court was German rather than Danish, and its influence was none the greater on that account. Nor, owing to the privileges of the Hanseatic towns, was there a great merchant class, to act as a counterpoise to the nobles. And as for the *bönder*, formerly the most important class of all, their condition was pitiable indeed. By degrees their rights were encroached upon, till, from free and noble-born small proprietors, they became mere peasants. In Denmark they were at length compelled to have recourse to the practice of commendation, which ended, in the latter part of the fifteenth century, in a widespread system of serfage.

The power of the clergy had grown *pari passu* with that of the nobles. Down to the twelfth century, indeed, the Scandinavian Bishops were only suffragans of the see of Bremen. It was not till 1104 that the see of Lund, in the Danish province of Skaane, was raised to metropolitical rank, with jurisdiction over all the bishoprics of the three kingdoms; and it was only in 1152 that the famous mission took place of the Cardinal of Albano, Nicholas Breakspeare (afterwards Pope Adrian IV), which gave to the northern Churches their permanent character. Under his guidance Nidaros (Trondhjem) was made the metropolitical see of Norway, and soon afterwards Upsala was raised to a similar position in Sweden; the payment of *Roma skat* was introduced, and the ecclesiastical system of the northern nations was remodelled on the lines which prevailed at the time in other parts of Western Christendom; though it was not till 1250 that a papal Bull took the choice of the Bishops from the people and gave it to the Chapters. From this time forward the power and the riches of the clergy had rapidly increased. They held large fiefs in all three countries; it is said that more than half of Denmark was in the hands of the Bishops, and Copenhagen itself was built on a fief of the Bishop of Roskilde. Their possessions, like those of the nobles, were exempt from taxation, nor were they liable to the same restrictions with regard to trade as the people at large. With some conspicuous exceptions, they were not less opposed to the Kings than were the nobles; quarrels respecting clerical immunities were frequent, and they generally ended in the infliction of ecclesiastical censures, followed by the surrender of the King at discretion and the payment of an indemnity. As a rule, the higher clergy had been trained abroad, and were not less foreign in feeling and sympathies than the Court itself. Owing partly to difficulties in securing confirmation at Rome, partly to the exaggerated importance that was attached to their civil and constitutional functions, Bishops elect frequently remained unconsecrated for years, their spiritual functions being carried out by others. Naturally, abuses were far from uncommon amongst them, and there was not much love lost between them and the people at large. Indeed, the success of the Reformation, both in Denmark and in Sweden, was largely due to the fact that it put an end to the power of the clergy and despoiled them of their possessions.

I. THE REFORMATION IN DENMARK

The accession of Christian II in 1513 marks the beginning of a new era. A man of great natural gifts but violent passions, his father had given him an education which at once developed his love for the people and his self-love, and at the same time made him one of the most learned monarchs of the day. He was sent to Norway to put down a rebellion in 1502, and as regent there he received his apprenticeship in government during a series of turbulent years. His marriage in 1515 with Isabella, sister of the future Emperor Charles V, obtained for him an influence in Europe such as for centuries no other King of Denmark had enjoyed. But he was cruel and treacherous, both by nature and of deliberate policy. These characteristics had already shown themselves in Norway: they were present throughout his reign, and after ten years they helped to drive him from his beloved Denmark. Thus, although he introduced many notable changes, he himself was overthrown by the reaction to which they gave rise ; and they were only carried out in their entirety by others after his downfall.

Christian had himself reconquered Norway for his father : at his own accession he found Sweden practically independent. On the death of the administrator Svante Sture in 1512 the *Rigsraad* had chosen the old Erik Trolle in his place and had decided in favour of union with Denmark. But a popular party led by Hemming Gadd, the Bishop of Linkœping, had risen against him and set up Sten Sture the younger in his stead ; who, being a wise and statesmanlike leader, soon obtained the upper hand. There was still a strong party opposed to him however, under the leadership of Gustaf, the son of Erik Trolle and Archbishop of Upsala. In the course of the civil war which followed Gustaf was besieged in his castle of Stækeborg near Stockholm. He at once appealed to the Danes for help ; and his assailants were excommunicated by Archbishop Berger of Lund, by virtue of the authority which he claimed as Primate of Scandinavia. Thereupon Sten Sture and the *Rigsraad* resolved that Trolle should be no longer recognised as Archbishop, and that he should be imprisoned and his castle razed to the ground. Gustaf at once appealed to Pope Leo X, who approved the excommunication of Sten Sture and called upon Christian to enforce it. From 1517 onwards, therefore, Christian was endeavouring by negotiation or otherwise to take possession of Sweden. At first he had little success, excepting that in 1518, after an attack on Stockholm which failed of its object, he suggested an interview with Sten Sture, demanded hostages for his own safety, and then carried them off to Denmark, Bishop Gadd and a young man named Gustaf Eriksson among them. In the following year he returned to Sweden with a large army of mercenaries. On January 18, 1520, Sten Sture was defeated in a battle fought on the ice on Lake Åsunden and so severely wounded that he died some weeks after. A second battle before Upsala left all Sweden in Gustaf's hands except Stockholm, which was valiantly defended by Sten Sture's widow, Christina Gyllenstjerna ; and the promise of a general amnesty made in Christian's name by his general, Otte Krumpen, together with the persuasions of Gadd, who had gone over to the King's side, at length prevailed upon her to open the gates. Christian entered Stockholm, and was crowned King of Sweden on Sunday, November 4, 1520.

The event that followed is the blackest in Christian's life. On the Wednesday, during the coronation festivities, the Swedish magnates and the authorities of Stockholm were suddenly summoned into the citadel. Then Diederik Slaghoek, a Westphalian follower of the King's, and Jens Andersen, surnamed Beldenak, the Bishop of Odense, stood forth in the name of Gustaf Trolle and demanded reparation for the wrongs which, as they alleged, had been inflicted on him. Christian at once called for the names of those who had signed the act of deposition and committed them to prison ; the only exceptions being Bishop Brask of Linkœping, who had signed under protest, and another Bishop who now joined himself with Trolle as accuser. The following day, November 8, at nine o'clock, they were brought before a Court of twelve ecclesiastics, one of whom was Trolle, who thus became a judge in his own cause. The single question was put to them by Beldenak, whether men who had raised their hands against the Pope and the Holy Roman Church were not heretics? They could give but one answer. Thereupon they were told that they had condemned themselves, and were declared guilty of notorious heresy. On the very same day, at noon, they were brought forth into the market-place and there beheaded one by one before the eyes of the citizens. The Bishops of Strengnæs and Skara were the first to suffer; they were followed by the rest of the signatories, amongst whom was the father of Gustaf Eriksson, afterwards King of Sweden; and these by others of the principal nobles and citizens, who showed their sympathy too plainly, until the square ran with blood. A spectator counted more than ninety corpses before the day was done; and the ghastly work was not confined to one time or place. The bodies lay where they had fallen for three days, after which they were conveyed outside the town and burnt; the bodies of Sten Sture and of his young son, born since his excommunication, being exhumed and thrown upon the pyre. It was hoped that this terrible deed, which is known as the Stockholm bath of blood (*Stockholms Blodbad*), had secured Sweden to the Danes; as a matter of fact, as it has been said, the Union of Kalmar was drowned in it for ever. Fierce revolts broke out everywhere, and before long Sweden was independent under its own King Gustavus.

Christian was a more successful ruler at home than he had been in Sweden. He was well aware of the evils under which Denmark was groaning, and was resolved to provide a remedy. As the price of his election to the Crown he had been compelled to accept not only the conditions which had bound his father, but others even more onerous. One of these gave the judicial power entirely into the hands of the magnates; another nullified the royal right of conferring nobility; the last of all provided that if he broke his agreement in any particular, "then shall all the inhabitants of the kingdom faithfully resist the same without loss of honour and without in any wise by so doing breaking their oath of fealty to us." But from the first Christian treated his "capitulation" as a dead letter, and endeavoured in every way to increase the power of the burghers and the peasants. Himself brought up in the household of a burgher, Hans Metzenheim, surnamed Bogbinder, he surrounded himself with advisers of ignoble and often of foreign birth: Sigbrit, the mother of his beautiful Dutch mistress Dyveke, Diederik Slaghök, who has been mentioned already, a Malmö merchant named Hans Mikkelsen, and many more. Mother Sigbrit, as she was called, a woman of great capacity, was his chief counsellor in all fiscal and commercial matters. By her advice he disregarded the *Rigsraad* altogether, subjected the higher orders to taxation, and violated all their most cherished privileges. Nor was it otherwise with the clergy, who soon found that in him they had a master. He levied from them by arbitrary and lawless methods the money which he really needed, but could not obtain in any legal way; Beldenak in particular was fleeced unmercifully. Meanwhile he skilfully availed himself of the jealousy between them and the nobles, who could not forget that many of them, including Archbishop Berger and Bishop Beldenak, were not nobly born, in order to overturn the power of both. For the time it seemed as if he had succeeded; and two great collections of laws, the so-called Secular and Ecclesiastical Code, which he put forth in 1521 and 1522 on his own authority, without submitting them to the *Rigsraad*, might seem to have marked the downfall of the aristocratic power. But in little more than a year they had been publicly burned and their author was a fugitive.

But Christian's work was not merely destructive. The people at large found in him a careful and wise ruler, who scrutinised every detail of civil life and government and was never weary of working for their good. His reforms of municipal government were at once elaborate and rigorous. He built great ships and put down piracy; he made wise treaties with foreign Powers. He extended commercial privileges to his burghers, and restricted those of the Hanseatic towns, endeavouring to make Copenhagen the centre of the Baltic trade; and with this object in view he encouraged Dutch merchants to found houses there, and extended a warm welcome to the rich banking-house of the Fuggers. He brought Flemish gardeners to Denmark in order that they might teach his people horticulture, and established them in the little island of Amager, where their descendants are to this day. He abolished the old "strand rights" and rights of wreck, and decreed that all possible assistance should be given to ships in peril and to shipwrecked mariners; and when the Jutland Bishops remonstrated with him, saying that there was nothing in the Bible against wrecking, Christian answered, "Let the lord-prelates go back and study the eighth commandment." He caused uniform weights and measures to be used throughout his dominions; he took steps for the improvement of the public roads, and made the first attempt at the creation of a postal system. He abolished the worst evils of serfage, and made provision for the punishment of cruel masters. His laws on behalf of morals and of public order are enlightened and wise; he abolished the death penalty for witchcraft; he founded a system for the relief of the sick. He did his utmost for the encouragement of learning. The University of Copenhagen, authorised by Pope Martin V in 1419, actually founded by Christian I in 1478 with three professors only, of law, theology, and medicine, first became important under Christian II. He founded a Carmelite House in Copenhagen, which was to maintain a graduate in divinity who should lecture daily in the

University; and the famous Paul Eliae or Eliaesen (Povel Helgesen), a student of Erasmus' writings and of Luther's earlier works, and an earnest seeker after Catholic reform, who has been not inaptly styled the Colet of Denmark, came from Elsinore to be the first head lecturer. Christian directed that schools should be opened for the poor throughout his dominions; he exerted himself to provide better school-books; he actually went so far as to enact that education should be compulsory for the burghers of Copenhagen and all the other large towns of Denmark.

Meanwhile Christian had been turning his attention to matters strictly ecclesiastical. Here too it cannot be said that he was anything but an opportunist, and it would be superfluous to credit him with any very pronounced convictions in favour of the Reformed doctrines; but there is no reason to doubt the earnestness with which he set to work to correct practical abuses. As early as 1517 there had come to Denmark a papal envoy named Giovanni Angelo Arcimboldo, afterwards Arch-bishop of Milan, with a commission to sell Indulgences, the right to act under which he purchased from the King for 1100 *gulden*. It was just at the time when Christian was engaged in negotiations with Sweden; and he resolved to make use of Arcimboldo as an intermediary. Soon however he discovered that the envoy, apparently in pursuance of secret instructions from the Pope, was negotiating independently with Sten Sture. Arcimboldo managed to escape to Lübeck with part of his booty; but the King at once gave orders for the seizure of what was left, and found himself in possession of a rich harvest in money and in kind. That this action did not involve any breach with the existing eccle-siastical system is plain from the fact that the victims of the terrible "Stockholm bath of blood" were put to death by Christian, not as traitors to the King, but as rebels against the Holy See.

But he had already gone further than this. In 1519 he wrote to his maternal uncle, Frederick of Saxony, begging him to send to the University of Copenhagen a theologian of the school of Luther and Carlstadt. Frederick sent Martin Reinhard, who arrived at Copenhagen late in 1520, and began preaching in the church of St Nicholas. But Reinhard unfortunately knew no Danish, and his sermons had to be interpreted, it is said by Paul Eliaesen. The effect was not happy: the sermons lost much of their force, and the preacher's gestures, divorced from his words, seemed grotesque and meaningless. At the next carnival the canons of St Mary's took advantage of the fact by dressing up a child and setting him to imitate the preacher. What was more serious, Paul began to find that he had no sympathy with Luther's developed position. Mocked by the people and bereft of his interpreter, Reinhard was sent back to Germany. Christian now endeavoured to attract Luther himself; and, although this proved impossible, Carlstadt came for a short visit. But the Edict of Worms (May, 1521), which placed Luther and his followers under the ban of the Empire, was a hint too significant to be neglected, and for a time no more is heard of foreign preachers in Copenhagen.

Within Denmark itself, however, things were not standing still; and Christian's codes of laws, already referred to, were full of bold provisions for ecclesiastical reform. The monasteries were again subjected to episcopal visitation. Clerical non-residence, which, partly owing to local difficulties, was commoner in Norway and Denmark than elsewhere, was stringently forbidden. To make an end of the ignorant "priest-readers" (*laese-praester*) of whom the Danish Church was full, no candidate for holy Orders was to be ordained unless he had studied at the University and had shown that he understood and could explain "the Holy Gospel and epistle" in Danish. The clergy were not to acquire landed property or to receive inheritances, "at least unless they will follow the precept of St Paul, who in his First Epistle to Timothy counsels them to be the husband of one wife, and will live in the holy state of matrimony as their ancestors did." The state which the Bishops were accustomed to keep up was forbidden: in journeying "they shall ride or travel in their litters, that the people may know them from other doctors; but they shall not be preceded by fife and drum to the mockery of holy Church." The spiritual Courts were no longer to have cognisance of questions of property. Most radical change of all, a new supreme tribunal was to be set up at Roskilde, by royal authority alone, consisting of "four doctors or masters well learned in ecclesiastical and imperial law," the decisions of which, as well ecclesiastical as civil, were to be final, the appeal to the Pope being abolished.

But Christian's new code never came into operation. His position was already one of great difficulty, and the toils were fast closing round him. He was in bad odour at Rome, partly on account of his attempted reforms, partly because of the three Bishops whom he had slain in Sweden; for Hemming Gadd had been put to death not long after the massacre of Stockholm, in spite of his loyalty to the King. This last matter was arranged without much difficulty. The Nuncio Giovanni Francesco di Potenza, whom Leo X had sent to Denmark, declared Christian innocent and found a scapegoat in Diederik Slaghoek, now Archbishop elect of Lund. For this and other crimes he was condemned to death, and burnt on January 22, 1522. But there were other difficulties which could not be met in this way. The citizens of Lübeck had declared war, and were soon devastating Bornholm and threatening Copenhagen. Christian was embroiled in a hopeless contest in Sweden. He had offended his father's brother, Frederick of Schleswig-Holstein, by obtaining the investiture of the duchy at the hands of Charles V, which he now abandoned by the Treaty of Bordesholm (August). And now, when everything was against him abroad, the seething discontent at home came to a head. Late in 1522 the nobles of Sjælland broke out

in open rebellion. To meet this, Christian gathered together an army
of peasants, and summoned a council of nobles (*Herredag*) to meet at
Kallundborg. The nobles and bishops from Jutland failed to put in an
appearance, alleging that the wind and time of year made it impossible.
Thereupon he summoned them and the representatives of the commons
to meet in a national assembly (*Riksdag*) at Aarhuus.

But it was too late : the Jutlanders had already assembled at Viborg,
renounced their allegiance to him, and proclaimed Frederick King,
putting forth at the same time a statement of grievances (March, 1523).
A letter in which they communicated the news to Christian reached him
early in the following month. The case was far from desperate. Norway
had not declared against him ; most of the islands were still his, and
many of the chief citadels ; the peasants were devoted to him, and so
were many excellent leaders, chief amongst them being the brave
Admiral Sören Norby. But Christian had lost heart. Every day
some renounced their allegiance, and an alliance which Frederick had
contracted with Sweden and Lübeck filled him with alarm. On April 13
he left his capital and embarked for Flanders with his young Queen and
his three little children, and spent the next nine years in exile, often
under great hardships. He continued vigorously to dispute Frederick's
throne, but without success, in spite of the fact that he invoked the aid
of his powerful brother-in-law, and at length, late in 1529, was formally
reconciled to the Roman communion. Two years later he desired to
enter into communication with Frederick, and gave himself into the
hands of his uncle's commander, Knud Gyldenstjerne, on a safe-conduct.
But in spite of this he was thrown into the dungeons of Sönderborg,
where he remained for seventeen years, part of the time with no
companion but a half-witted Norwegian dwarf; and he only left
Sönderborg for a less rigorous captivity elsewhere, which endured till
his death in 1559.

Frederick's new position was no happy one. For years his dominions
were torn asunder by civil war ; and Christian was still recognised as the
lawful King by the Pope, the Emperor, and the Lutherans. The new
King owed everything to those who had elected him, and concession was
naturally the order of the day. To Norway he granted that henceforward it should be a free elective monarchy, as Denmark and Sweden
were. To the nobles he made even greater concessions than Christian II
had made at his coronation, promising amongst other things that none
but noble-born Danes should be appointed to bishoprics in future;
whilst as regards the Church he bound himself "not to permit any
heretic, Luther's disciple or any other, to preach or teach, either openly
or publicly, against the holy faith, against the most holy father the
Pope or the Church of Rome." This last promise was more than once
repeated subsequently, in return for subsidies granted by the clergy ; but
both parties must soon have come to realise that a change was coming

whether they would or no. And although the actual settlement did
not take place till after his death, the reign of Frederick I saw the real
overthrow of the Church in Denmark.

Although the causes which brought this about were political rather
than religious, they were not entirely so, and there were already not a
few in Denmark who were propagating the new doctrines. Paul Eliaesen
had indeed found himself unable to go the whole length with the
Lutherans, and before long received from them the nickname of Paul
Turncoat (Povel *Vendekaabe*) for his alleged instability. But Paul was
neither a coward nor a renegade : he is almost the only representative in
the north of that class of earnest and enlightened men who desired
reform, both practical and doctrinal, without any general loosening of
the ecclesiastical system. It is true that after Christian II turned him
out of his lectureship in 1522 a rich canonry was founded for him by
Bishop Lage Urne of Roskilde, the duties of which were to teach in the
University and preach to the people. But he had lost his former office
in consequence of a bold public denunciation of the King's cruelty; and
he was not more flexible in the hands of Frederick I in 1526, when that
monarch tried to make him a Lutheran propagandist. Yet, although
he refused to throw in his lot with the extremists, and became more
decided in his opposition to them as their action became more decided,
he never ceased to inveigh against the corruptions of the old order. He
translated selected tracts by Luther into Danish, and asserted many of
his earlier theses, even whilst he condemned that teacher's later actions ;
and his last effort at peace-making, his *Christian Reconciliation and
Accord*, written about 1534, is an earnest plea for peace on the basis
of the historic system of the Church, with the services in Danish,
communion in both kinds, marriage of the clergy and the like.

But although Paul could go no further than this, there were many
of his disciples who went much farther. Chief amongst them was
Hans Tausen, known as the "Danish Luther." The son of a peasant
of Fyen (b. 1494) he had joined the Johannite priory of Antvorskov,
where his abilities soon won recognition and he was sent abroad. After
studying and lecturing at Rostock he was nominated professor of
theology at Copenhagen; but his Prior, willing to see him still better
equipped, sent him abroad again, and he now studied at Cologne and
Louvain. Thence he passed to Wittenberg (1523), where he was listening
to Luther's teaching with avidity when the alarmed Prior summoned him
home in 1524 and imprisoned him. After a time he was transferred to
the Johannite house at Viborg, in order that the Prior there, the learned
Peder Jensen, might show him the error of his ways. He soon won
Jensen's confidence, and was permitted to preach to the people after
vespers. His preaching created a great sensation, but soon caused the
prior to admonish and warn him ; so one day, at the end of his sermon,
Tausen threw himself upon the protection of his hearers, left the

monastery, and took up his abode in the house of one of the chief citizens.

Here he was joined by Jörgen Sadolin, who had studied with him under Luther, and whose sister he presently married ; and the two continued their irregular preaching under the eye, and in spite of the prohibition of, the Bishop, Jörgen Friis. The same kind of thing was going on at Malmö, where under the protection of the Burgomaster, Jörgen Kok "the moneyer" (*mönter*), one Klaus Mortensen the cooper (*tændebinder*) had begun preaching in the open air, until the people rose and insisted that one of the churches should be placed at their disposal. And the movement was spreading elsewhere. In 1524 there was printed a Danish version of the New Testament, which is commonly attributed to Hans Mikkelsen, formerly Burgomaster of Malmö, now a fugitive with the dethroned King, and which may be in part his work. It was imported into Denmark in very large quantities, and was largely read by the people in spite of episcopal prohibition, until its place was taken five years later by a far better version. This was the work of the gentle Christian Pedersen, known as the father of Danish literature. He had been a canon of Lund, but followed Christian II into exile, and became a convinced Lutheran; he returned to Denmark in 1531, and spent the rest of his life, till his death in 1554, in literary work for the cause of the Reform.

Such was the state of religion in Denmark when the struggle began which led to the overthrow of the Danish Church. In May, 1525, the nobles complained to Frederick I that the see of Lund had been overlong vacant : they pointed out that the Archbishop of Lund was "the gate and bulwark between Denmark and Sweden, as the Duke of Schleswig is between Denmark and Germany," and begged the King "no longer to allow that the Church in this land should be thus dealt with." The circumstances were peculiar. On the death of Archbishop Berger in 1519, the Chapter had elected their Dean, Aage Sparre ; the King had nominated Jörgen Skodborg ; and Leo X, to the great indignation of the Danes, tried to appoint a young Italian by provision. All three were set aside, and Diederik Slaghök was elected instead; but after his death there was a deadlock. Frederick now attempted to put an end to this by negotiation with the Pope. At first he seemed to have succeeded ; Clement VII apparently accepted the nomination of Skodborg, and confirmed it. But what had happened in reality was that Skodborg had been induced to buy out his Italian rival, and by so doing had recognised his claim. Frederick was furious at finding that he had been tricked. On August 19, 1526, he published a rescript by which he repudiated the appointment of Skodborg and (with the consent of the *Rigsraad*) confirmed the election of Aage Sparre, saving however Skodborg's right of appeal to the King and the *Rigsraad*. The accustomed fees for the confirmation were paid to the King instead of the Pope.

This momentous act had consequences greater, probably, than those who took part in it anticipated. The procedure in question was accepted at the *Herredag* at Odense in December, 1526, not without careful stipulations for the safeguarding of ecclesiastical liberties; and from this time forward no Danish Bishop sought papal confirmation. As other sees fell vacant they were filled in the same way, confirmation being given by the King; but in each case the Bishop elect remained unconsecrated, such purely episcopal functions as were required being performed by one or other of the retired Bishops or those who, like the Bishop of Greenland, had never proceeded to their dioceses. Meanwhile Frederick was rapidly carried in the direction of further change. His son Christian, Duke of Schleswig, was already a convinced Lutheran; and in 1525 Albert of Brandenburg, the head of the Teutonic Order, renounced Catholicism and as Duke of Prussia became a suitor for the hand of Christian's daughter. The prospect of a strong Protestant alliance finally decided the question. Frederick, who had already shown Lutheran inclinations, from this time forward did his utmost to propagate the new views throughout his dominions. Naturally, not a few of his courtiers went with him; and in particular Mogens Gjœ, the high steward of Denmark, became an ardent Reformer.

His son Christian had already shown the way in Schleswig and Holstein. A Lutheran preacher named Hermann Tast had been working at Husum since 1522, and under his influence and that of other German preachers whom Christian had brought in as his chaplains, the new views were spreading everywhere. Early in 1526 Christian attacked Bishop Munk of Ribe, telling him that he ought to provide his diocese with married priests who could preach the Gospel. The Bishop temperately replied that the Gospel was already preached, and that, with regard to the marriage of the clergy, "when the Holy Church throughout Christendom adopts it, we will do the same." From this time forward Christian took matters into his own hands, and drew up a new Lutheran order which he imposed on the duchies; four clergymen who would not accept it were deprived, and the Duke's chaplains ordained others in their places. At Flensburg in 1529, after a disputation between Tast and the Anabaptist Melchior Hofmann, the doctrines of the Sacramentaries and Anabaptists were abjured; and the system was complete when Bugenhagen gave them a Lutheran "Bishop" in 1541, and the Danish ritual came into use in 1542. In Denmark Christian's Reforming tendencies were the cause of his never being acknowledged by the *Rigsraad* as successor to the throne during his father's lifetime.

Frederick followed his son's lead by nominating Tausen and others as his chaplains, thus at once exempting them from episcopal control and giving them protection. The plan was of course not unknown before, but it was so effective that it caused the Bishops no little alarm. At the

Herredag of 1526 they remonstrated against any preacher being licensed excepting with their consent, and "in such wise that he preach God's Word." Frederick was discreetly silent on the former point, and answered as to the latter that he never commissioned them to preach anything else ; so the practice went on unchecked. Soon it produced its effect in a wide-spread defection, which so alarmed the Bishops that they endeavoured to secure the presence in Denmark of Eck or Cochlaeus, or some other champion of orthodoxy, in order that the doctrinal question might be thoroughly thrashed out. But this proved to be impossible, and they were thrown back on their own resources, and resolved to fight it out on the constitutional grounds with which alone they were familiar.

At the *Herredag* at Odense in August, 1527, they demanded that the people should be compelled to pay the tithes and other dues, which were now being refused on all sides. This was granted, in return for concessions to the nobles ; as was also the claim that they should be supported in the exercise of Church discipline. But when they went on to protest against the propagation of the new doctrines and the protection of the preachers, Frederick replied that faith is free, and that each man must follow his conscience ; that he was lord of men's bodies and of their goods, but not of their souls ; and that every man must so fashion himself in religion as he will answer for it to God at the Last Day. He would no longer issue letters of protection to preachers ; but if anyone molested those who were preaching what was godly and Christian, he would both protect and punish. He further suggested that the religious question should be decided by a national assembly convoked for the purpose ; but this sug-gestion was at once repudiated by nobles and Bishops alike. He managed however to estrange the nobles from the Bishops by supporting their attacks on ecclesiastical property ; and thus the ecclesiastical movement went on vigorously. In some places the old order was overturned alto-gether ; at Viborg for instance even the Cathedral came into the hands of the Lutherans in 1529, and at Copenhagen, whither the King had summoned Tausen, they soon had the upper hand. Meanwhile, the Bishops seemed incapable of taking the only measures that could have been of any use. Preaching was almost in abeyance on their side ; and in many places there were services only two or three times a year, and large numbers of country benefices were left entirely vacant. In 1530 for instance the sixteen extensive parishes of the diocese of Aarhuus had only two priests between them.

In 1530 the contest advanced a stage further. Preparations were being made in Germany for the Diet of Augsburg, which, it was hoped, would put an end to the religious controversy ; and it seemed to the Bishops that the same happy result might be looked for in Denmark, if the Lutheran leaders could be made to appear before the King and the magnates. Twenty-one of them were accordingly cited to appear at Copenhagen before the *Herredag*, the Bishops taking care also to secure the help

of Paul Eliaesen and of two German theologians, one of whom was Dr
Stageführ of Cologne. The session was opened, and several days were
spent in accusations against the preachers as heretics. When the time
came for his reply, Tausen suddenly produced a confession of faith in
forty-three articles, which he and his fellows allotted among themselves
and publicly defended day after day before great multitudes of excited
people, in the Church of the Holy Spirit.

At first the Bishops only reminded the King of his oath to put down
heresy; but finding that this had no effect either upon him or upon the
assembly, they drew up twenty-seven articles against the preachers and
asked that their opponents might be kept under restraint till the whole
matter was decided. Tausen and his followers replied with an *apologia*,
also in twenty-seven articles, in which they made a violent attack upon
the whole Church system. But here the matter ended; the disputation
which had been projected never took place because of a disagreement as
to the language in which it was to be held. The Bishops asked that it
should be in Latin, so that their German advocates might take part; the
preachers insisted upon Danish, not only as the language best understood
by the assembly, but because their whole appeal was to the common
people. Naturally, the popular voice was on their side. There were
loud outcries in Copenhagen against the Bishops and still more against
the German doctors; and when Frederick dismissed the assembly, enjoin-
ing peace upon both parties, there could be no question that the Bishops
had lost their case. They were disheartened in many ways: the ablest
of their number, Lage Urne of Roskilde, was dead; Jörgen Friis of
Viborg had been excommunicated, rather gratuitously, by the Pope;
Beldenak had been deprived of his civil rights for disrespect to the Crown,
and soon afterwards resigned; and his successor Knud Gyldenstjerne,
the same who brought the dethroned Christian to Copenhagen, had so far
thrown in his lot with the Lutheran movement as to make Sadolin a
kind of coadjutor in his diocese, where he translated Luther's *Shorter
Catechism* into Danish and issued it to the clergy to be used as a manual
of instruction. On all hands the Lutherans were gaining ground. In
some places there were iconoclastic outbreaks, though both now and
throughout the period they were surprisingly few; and to this day many
of the Danish churches contain their ancient altar-tables and reredoses,
and the clergy wear the old copes. But everywhere the Reform pro-
gressed, until Elsinore was almost the only stronghold of Catholicism.

At this point however there came a period of disorder, caused by the
death of Frederick I at Gottorp in Schleswig. The effect of Frederick's
concessions to the nobles had been to divide the country into a series of
semi-independent local governments; and nobles, Bishops, and people
alike realised that they had everything to gain or to lose under the new
King. Under these circumstances conflict was inevitable. No sooner
had the Estates come together than the Bishops demanded that the

religious question should be dealt with. This was distasteful to many of the lay nobles; but in return for concessions they gave way, and it was resolved that the old order should be in all respects upheld, saving for actual abuses, that the Mass should be restored wherever it had been abolished, and that nobody should preach without the consent of the Bishop. Thus all the innovations introduced since the *Herreday* of Odense in 1527 were swept away. The Estates next proceeded to the election of a successor to the Crown. The late King, Frederick I, had left two sons, Christian of Schleswig-Holstein and his half-brother Hans. Most of the nobles favoured the former, whilst the Bishops placed all their hopes in the latter, who was a mere child and might still be kept from Lutheranism. Failing to come to an agreement, they resolved to postpone the election for a year; whereupon Mogens Gjœ and others left Denmark and endeavoured to persuade Christian to claim the crown by force. This he refused to do. But his self-restraint was of little use, for within a year civil war had broken out. The towns, smarting under the curtailment of their privileges at the hands of the lay nobles and of their religious liberties at those of the Bishops, began to look back longingly to the days of King Christian II, and soon broke out in revolt. The Burgomasters of Copenhagen and Malmö, who were at the head of the movement, made common cause with the democracy of Lübeck, whose forces took the field under Count Christopher of Oldenburg in order to place the imprisoned Christian II once more on the throne. Such at least was the avowed object of the so-called Count's War (*Grevefeide*); but behind these were plans of another kind; for the people of Lübeck, under their determined leader Wullenwever and his admiral Meyer, had only thrown in their lot with the Danish towns in order to get Denmark into their own hands and so to restore the old supremacy of the Hanseatic League in the north.

Christopher directed his forces towards Sjælland, and disembarked at Skovshoved on June 23, 1534. Copenhagen opened its gates to him, and Malmö soon drove out the garrison which had been placed there to overawe it; and before long the islands had all overthrown their oppressors, often with great ferocity, and proclaimed Christian II. Freedom of worship was at once restored. Bishop Roennov of Roskilde was deprived and his see given to the aged Gustaf Trolle, formerly of Upsala; and on Roennov offering a bribe of 10,000 marks in order to retain possession of the See, Trolle was transferred to Fyen, in the place of Gyldenstjerne, who was likewise ejected. From the islands Christopher turned his attention to the mainland. One of his lieutenants was sent to Jutland, where the peasants quickly gathered round him. The nobles at once marched against them, but were routed in the outskirts of Aalborg; and thus the greater part of Jutland once more owned Christian II's sway. But the turning-point of the war was already come. In the face of so great dangers the Estates had sought an alliance with King Gustavus of Sweden, and another with Duke Christian of Schleswig-Holstein; by the terms of the latter, Christian was to unite with them against the common enemy, and differences were to be settled afterwards. He observed the terms loyally; but first the nobles of Jylland and then those of Fyen elected him their King; and at length, in an assembly held at Ry, near Skanderborg, the nobles and Bishops of the mainland united in proclaiming him.

Whether as ally or as King, everything depended upon him and his power. As Duke of Schleswig he made peace with Lübeck, thus becoming free to use his army elsewhere. Then he dispatched his best general, Hans Ranzau, against the peasants of Jutland, who shut themselves up in Aalborg. Ranzau took the town by assault, and crushed the rising in Jutland by putting the enemy to the sword, sparing none but women and children. Thence he passed into Fyen, and inflicted a crushing defeat upon the main body of Christopher's army on the hill of Öxnebjerg, near Ässens, in which Gustaf Trolle was mortally wounded. Meanwhile, Gustavus had invaded Skaane and Jylland, where his mere presence was enough to restore heart to the nobles, who had only given in their allegiance to Count Christopher through necessity. The Danish admiral Peder Skram (*Danmarks Vovehals*) attacked and defeated the great Lübeck fleet near Bornholm, thus regaining command of the sea; and Ranzau's army being thereupon transported to Sjælland, Copenhagen was invested by land and by sea. These disasters occasioned great disorders at Lübeck: Wullenwever and Meyer having in vain attempted to retrieve their fortunes by sending forth a new commander, Albert of Mecklenburg, were themselves removed from power, and Lübeck made its peace with Denmark. Gradually all resistance died away: Malmö opened its gates on April 2, 1536, Copenhagen surrendered at discretion on July 29, and on August 6 Christian III entered his capital in triumph. Soon after the victory of Ässens Norway had acknowledged his sway.

The accession of Christian, as the Bishops well knew, meant their downfall; and it was only actual necessity which had compelled them to accept him. Before the outbreak of the Count's War it had seemed that their cause might yet triumph: Tausen himself had been proceeded against and silenced, their own authority was restored, they had even reopened communications with Rome, which had been met, however, with chilling reserve. Now, all was lost. Christian III was a determined foe of the old order and had long ago expressed his intention of uprooting it. Nor were they long kept in suspense. On August 11 Christian consulted with his commanders, who agreed that the Bishops should be "pinioned." At four o'clock the following morning three of them were brought as prisoners into the castle. Four hours afterwards the King called together the lay members of the *Rigsraad*, and proposed that the Bishops should be deprived of their share in the government of the realm and that their possessions should be forfeited to the Crown.

They not only consented willingly, but also voted that their spiritual power should no longer be recognised, unless it should be approved by a general council of the Danish Church; and the remaining Bishops were forthwith sought out and arrested. This vote of the *Rigsraad* was approved by a national assembly (*Rigsdaag* or *Thing*) at Copenhagen, in which however the nobles took the chief part, which solemnly declared, on October 30, 1536, that they wished to keep the holy Gospel and no longer to have Bishops, and that the goods of the Church ought to be given up to the Crown in order to lighten the taxation of the people. Thus fell the Danish Bishops, as the result partly of the jealousy roused in the nobles by their greed of temporal power, partly of the fanatical Lutheranism of Christian III. They were not badly treated. The *Raad* of August 12 had decided that they were to be set at liberty and adequately supported, on condition of their promising to remain quiet; Roennov indeed continued in prison till his death in 1544, but the rest were set free, and two of them, Gyldenstjerne and Ove Bilde, ultimately conformed to the new order.

Christian now turned to Luther for help; and as the services of Melanchthon were not obtainable, Jakob Bugenhagen, who had already organised the Reform in Pomerania, was sent in July, 1537, to accomplish the same work in Denmark. He was first called upon to crown Christian and his wife, by a usurpation of the ancient privilege of the Archbishops of Lund. Then the King nominated seven Superintendents, who were to take the place of the ancient Bishops, and who soon became known by their name. On September 2, Bugenhagen, himself no more than a presbyter, laid hands on them; and thus, by a deliberate innovation, the new Danish ministry was constituted. Of the persons chosen all were Danes, with the unfortunate exception of Wandel, a German who knew no Danish, and who had to be accompanied about his diocese by an interpreter. The most important of them was Peder Plade (Palladius), who had studied at Wittenberg, and became Bishop of Sjælland, and whose *Visitatsbog* gives us the most graphic picture that we possess of the internal life of the new Church. Tausen was so far discredited as to be for the time overlooked, though subsequently, on the death of Wandel, he became Bishop of Ribe.

On the same day (September 2) was published the new Church Ordinance (*Kirkeordinantsen*), which had been prepared by the Danish theologians and approved by Luther. It was subsequently sanctioned by the Assembly of Odense in 1539, and became, with additions made at various later synods (1540–55), the fundamental law of the Danish Church. The Bishops were to have under them a number of provosts or deans rural; and both alike were to be chosen by delegates of the clergy, who in turn were chosen by the people or their representatives, saving the rights of the nobles in some places; all being finally subject to the King's approval. These provisions, however, remained practically inoperative, so far as episcopal elections were concerned. In each diocese there were to be two diocesan officers (*Stiftslensmænd*) who administered the confiscated Church property (or so much of it as had not fallen into the hands of the nobles) in the name of the King, and with the Bishops supervised the finances of the churches, hospitals, and schools, and confirmed the election of the lower clergy. These latter continued to hold their share of the tithe, to which the nobles still refused to contribute; the episcopal tithe, however, was confiscated and largely used for good works. The University, which had fallen into decay, was greatly enlarged; ecclesiastical revenues were applied to the support of men of merit and learning and the plans of Christian II with regard to education were at length carried out. A liturgy was compiled, and a new translation of the Bible from the original tongues was set on foot. For the rest, changes were made gradually, and there was at first little disorder. The Augsburg Confession was ultimately adopted with certain modifications, and Tausen's Confession of 1530 was dropped; on the other hand, the Formula of Concord was never accepted by the Danish Church. The monastic houses and Cathedral Chapters were not at once abolished, though their members were free to depart. The Chapter of Roskilde was engaged in a formal disputation with Palladius and others as late as December, 1543; this and most of the other Chapters only ceased to exist as the canons died out; and the convent of women at Maribö was not suppressed till 1621. Unfortunately, in other respects a very different temper prevailed as time went on. In 1551 Christian was compelled to issue an edict forbidding the nobles to treat the children of ministers as serfs. The power and influence of the nobles were, however, considerably increased under his rule, the downfall of clerical authority contributing largely to this result. The adherents of the Roman communion were treated with no little severity; and the Pole John Laski, when he left England at the commencement of Queen Mary's reign, found that there was no toleration in Denmark for such heretics as himself and his followers. Nevertheless, in spite of many drawbacks, the Reformation brought with it a distinct advance in civilisation; and, when Christian III died on New Year's Day, 1559, Denmark was in a more settled condition than it had been since the days of Queen Margaret, whilst trade and learning flourished as they had never done before.

II. THE REFORMATION IN NORWAY AND ICELAND

The same thing could hardly be said with regard to the result of the changes in Norway and Iceland, where the ecclesiastical Order had been much less unpopular, and probably less in need of reform, than in Denmark. In fact, it cannot be said that in either case any popular movement for Reformation existed. As regards Norway, Frederick I had made the same promises to uphold the Church and to put down Lutherans which he had made in Denmark; and his change of opinion was followed by the same results in both countries. In 1528 there came to Bergen a Lutheran preacher named Antonius, who seems to have devoted himself mainly to the German residents. Next year he was followed by two others, Hermann Fresze and Jens Viborg, who bore royal letters of protection similar to those which had been given to Tausen, and perhaps one or two more in other places. Meanwhile a systematic spoliation began of the religious houses and churches in Bergen. In 1528 the Nonnesæter cloister was secularised and given over as his residence to Vincent Lunge, the commander of the royal citadel (*Bergenhus*). Soon afterwards, the Dominican priory was destroyed by fire, apparently with the connivance of Lunge and the prior Jens Mortenssön, who are said to have divided the spoil; and the chapel royal was pillaged. But these were nothing compared with the outrageous proceedings of Eske Bilde, who replaced Lunge in 1529, and became known as the *Kirkebryder*, from his activity in destroying churches. About the citadel of Bergen stood a group of the richest and most venerable churches in Norway, together with the palace of the Archbishops of Trondhjem and the canons' houses. On the pretext (for it seems to have been no more) that they interfered with the effective character of the fortress, Frederick ordered an attack to be made on these. One by one they were destroyed, and their treasures removed to Denmark; and at length, in May, 1531, the ancient cathedral itself was demolished. This was done in pursuance of a bargain made some three months before with the Bishop of Bergen, Olaf Thorkildssön, by which he was to receive in exchange for his palace and cathedral the great monastery of Munkeliv, formerly Benedictine, now Brigittine, on the further side of the harbour. These proceedings naturally gave courage to the disaffected; the Lutherans now seized upon the Church of St Cross (*Kors Kirke*), whilst the German merchants intruded their minister Antonius in the Church of St Halvard, and another in the Maria Kirke.

Whether Archbishop Olaf Engelbrektssön of Trondhjem would have been able to do anything to stay the hand of the destroyer is perhaps doubtful, for his own diocese was not a little troubled by the same kind of thing; but as a matter of fact it was only when the work was complete that his suffragan of Bergen told him what was being done. Archbishop Olaf was already none too well disposed towards King Frederick. In 1523, whilst on his way to Rome to be consecrated, he had gone to Malines, where the exiled Christian II (who might still have claimed to be the legal King of Norway) then resided, and had sworn allegiance to him. On his way home the Archbishop had visited Copenhagen, and had done homage to Frederick I; nor does he seem to have flinched from his allegiance. But the spoliations in Norway now made him feel that the Church would be safer under Christian, or at any rate that they could get on better without Frederick. He was by no means the only man in Norway who held this view; and Christian himself was at this very time seeking an opportunity of invading Norway. Before long it came. The Bishops and the Danish nobles in Norway were summoned to a *Herredag* to meet in Copenhagen in June, 1531; the Archbishop, being provided with a good excuse in a great fire which devastated Trondhjem and almost destroyed the cathedral, remained behind. On November 5 Christian reached the Norwegian coast with a fleet of twenty-five ships and a considerable army, and the next day he issued a proclamation to the people of Norway in which he put himself forward as their deliverer, and summoned them to gather round him at Oslo. The Archbishop accepted and proclaimed him, as did the Bishops, but in a somewhat lukewarm fashion; and Christian dissipated his energies and wasted his opportunity to such an extent that the following year he was compelled to make overtures to his uncle, which, as we have seen, ended in his imprisonment. Frederick was far too wise to push matters to an extremity, and the Bishops were glad to purchase their safety by paying him fines; but two monasteries which had given help to Christian were secularised, and Knud Gyldenstjerne carried off no small amount of Church plunder to Denmark.

The death of Frederick I and the wars which followed once more plunged Norway into disorder. The Archbishop was at the head of the Norwegian Council, and had he only known his own mind, it is possible that he might have chosen his own King, or even secured the independence of Norway. But he hesitated until Duke Christian had won his first victories, and then it was too late. In May, 1535, the Bishops of Oslo and Hamar, together with the chief nobles of the south, signed a manifesto by which they accepted Christian III as King, provided that he would promise to be faithful to the ancient laws of Norway; and they sent this to the Archbishop and the northern lords for their signature. By this time Olaf was beginning to recognise the fact that anything was better than a Lutheran King; and just then he received a letter from the Emperor urging him to support the claims of Frederick, the Count Palatine, who was about to marry the daughter of the imprisoned Christian II. He therefore temporised in the hope that matters might settle themselves. Soon, however, there came two emissaries of Duke Christian to Norway with instructions to press forward his cause, whereupon the members of his party decided to go northwards to Trondhjem. They arrived towards the end of December, 1535, and a Council was at once summoned, at which were present the Bishops, the chief Danish nobles in Norway, and a considerable number of the *bönder* of the northern provinces. Vincent Lunge, the chief adherent of Duke Christian, at once demanded that he should be elected

King, and that Norway should forthwith pay *skat* to him. To this it was answered, reasonably enough, that no election could be complete until the person chosen should have promised to observe the laws and customs of Norway, and that not till then was *skat* due. The *bönder* now withdrew and held a hasty consultation with the Archbishop, from which, probably roused by his words, they rushed in fury to the house of Vincent Lunge and slew him. Some of the other leaders barely escaped with their lives, and these were at once arrested and imprisoned by Olaf. There followed a short and ill-judged attempt on the part of Olaf to get the upper hand in Norway; but his party was less strong than he had supposed, and before long practically the whole land was subject to Christian, and Olaf was seeking terms. Presently losing all hope, the Archbishop collected all the treasure upon which he could lay his hands, together with the archives of the kingdom, and set sail for the Netherlands on April 1, 1537. He died at Lierre, in Brabant, on March 7 of the following year.

His departure left the way open for Christian III, who almost immediately took possession. He had already taken steps both to avenge himself and to put an end to what had long been a serious danger to his realm. By the third article of his "capitulation," made in the *Rigsdaag* at Copenhagen in October, 1536, he vowed that the kingdom of Norway should "hereafter be and remain under the Crown of Denmark, and not hereafter be or be called a separate kingdom, but a dependency of the kingdom of Denmark." Thus Norway lost its ancient liberties at a stroke. After this, although the "Recess" on religion which had been put forth at the same time (ratifying the changes which had already been made) said nothing of Norway, it was inevitable that the Norwegian Church should fall after the example of her sister of Denmark. One by one the Bishops were turned out, with two exceptions. Hans Reff, the Bishop of Oslo, a man of easy convictions, soon succeeded in convincing the King of his conversion to Lutheranism, and was reinstated in charge not only of Oslo, but of Hamar, where he remained till his death in 1545. Gebel Pedersson, the Bishop elect of Bergen, a man of far nobler character, had become a convinced Lutheran : in 1537 he went to Denmark, where Bugenhagen laid hands on him, and returned to take charge as Bishop of Bergen and Stavanger. For the rest, little or none of the care which was taken in Denmark to supply teachers, preachers, and schools, was extended to Norway. The under-manning of the Bishoprics was typical of what went on elsewhere. In large numbers of country places the old clergy were left till they died; at their death their places were left unoccupied. The few Lutheran pastors who were sent to Norway were unacquainted with the ancient Norse language, which was still, to a large extent, used in country places. Their attempts to obtain possession of the tithes led to frequent disputes which often ended in bloodshed ; and on the whole the Reformation caused as much harm to the social condition of the people in Norway, for half a century at any rate, as it did good in Denmark.

In ICELAND things were even worse. At first, indeed, there seemed to be hope of a conservative reformation ; for Bishop Gisser Einarsen of Skalholt, who had been educated in Germany, began making changes on the lines of those in Denmark, though without overturning the ancient ministry ; and an Icelandic version of the New Testament, printed in 1540, found plenty of readers. But when a formal attempt was made to introduce the Danish ecclesiastical system, there came a violent reaction. In 1548 Bishop Jon Aresen, of Holum, and Œgmund, the ex-Bishop of Skalholt, placed themselves at the head of what rapidly grew into a revolt against the Danish power. And although the former was taken prisoner in 1551 by David Gudmundarsen, and executed as a traitor, together with his two sons, his followers long strove to avenge his death. It was not till 1554 that they were put down, and the Reformation imposed by force on Iceland.

III. THE REFORMATION IN SWEDEN

We now return to trace the fortunes of SWEDEN, where, as we have seen, the massacre of Stockholm had decided the fate of the Danish rule. But if the Swedish War of Independence was already inevitable, in its actual course it was the work of one man, the young Gustaf Eriksson, known to later ages as Gustavus Vasa from the fascine or sheaf (*vasa*) which was the badge of the family. Born in 1496 at Lindholm, he had studied from 1509 to 1514 at Upsala, after which he entered the service of the younger Sten Sture and fought under him against the Danes. Given as a hostage to Christian II in 1518 and carried away treacherously to Denmark, he had broken his parole in September of the following year and made his way to Lübeck, whence after some months he was allowed to proceed to Sweden, and landed near Kalmar on May 31, 1519. He spent the summer as a fugitive in the south, till the news of the massacre reached him and he fled to his own remote province of Dalecarlia. Here, after enduring many hardships and having many narrow escapes, he found himself early in 1521 at the head of a sufficient force of dalesmen to raise the standard of revolt. From this time forward it was never lowered until the whole country was in his hands and the Danes had been driven out. The first success of the insurgents was the capture of the town, though not of the citadel, of Vesterås. Upsala fell not long afterwards, and within little more than a year most of the Danish garrisons had been invested. Thanks to the undisciplined character of his troops two attacks upon Stockholm failed ; and the same thing occurred elsewhere. But Christian's own throne was insecure ; and when once the power of Denmark was divided it could only be a question of time. On June 20, 1523, Gustavus entered Stockholm, and by July 7 the last Danish garrison in Sweden, that of Kalmar, had capitulated. Meanwhile Gustavus was no longer merely the leader of a band of insurgents. On July 14, 1522, he was able to issue a proclamation as the recognised commander of five provinces. An assembly at Vadstena on August 24 is said to have offered him the crown, which he refused, accepting however the office of Administrator, and adding that it would be time enough to choose a King when they had driven the foe out of the land. A general diet, so-called, met at Strengnäs on May 27, 1523. It is not clear whether the few magnates who still survived were summoned, but the diet nominated a new *Riksråd*, and then, on June 7, proceeded to elect Gustavus as King of Sweden.

The new King's position was no easy one. Although he had been duly elected he had little power ; the peasants who were his strongest supporters were impatient of control, and the older nobles looked on him with jealousy, and almost with contempt. Sweden was so devastated by the war as to be practically bankrupt ; the fields lay fallow, the mines were unworked, and many of the cities, Stockholm in particular, were desolated. The Swedish possessions in Finland were still in the enemy's hands ; and the only ally of the Swedes, the city of Lübeck, had helped them in pursuance of its own schemes of aggrandisement, and was now claiming large sums of money in return for advances made and aid given during the course of the struggle. To appease them, the diet of Strengnäs had granted to Lübeck, Danzig, and their allies a monopoly of Swedish commerce; but ambassadors still followed Gustavus wherever he went, and urged the speedy payment of the account. To eke out the scarcity of money, Gustavus, like most of the kings of his day and to an even greater extent, had adopted the plan of debasing the coinage ; but the effect was to inspire distrust, and before long he was compelled to circulate his *klippings* at a greatly depreciated rate.

He was at the end of his resources, and the only remedy seemed to be to turn to the Church, which was still as wealthy as ever. The Bishops as a whole were not unfriendly. Johan Brask, Bishop of Linkœping, an astute and far-seeing patriot, had early thrown in his lot on the winning side with Gustavus ; the Danish Bishops of Strengnäs and Skara had been replaced by Bishops elect who were favourable to him, and the vacant sees of Vesterås, Åbo, and Upsala (from the last-named of which Gustaf Trolle had fled) were likely to be filled in the same way. Moreover, Gustavus himself was just then in good odour in Rome. He had indeed been accused of heresy by Christian II in 1521 ; and his sojourn at and alliance with Lübeck lent colour to the charge. But his cause found a staunch defender in the famous Joannes Magni (Johan Magnusson), a Swedish scholar and canon of Linkœping who had lived away from his country for seventeen years without losing any of his interest in its affairs. He had studied at Louvain under Adrian of Utrecht, a man very likeminded with himself; and in 1522 his old master, now Pope Adrian VI, sent him as Legate to Sweden. He arrived whilst the Diet of Strengnäs was in session, was warmly welcomed, and in turn spoke very warmly with regard to Gustavus, and seemed to look favourably on his plans for restoring efficiency to the Church. So much pleased with him was the new *Riksräd* that it addressed a letter to the Pope begging that he and the Bishops might be empowered to set to work at once. To this request no answer was ever made, but soon afterwards the Canons of Upsala chose Joannes to be their Archbishop.

Under these circumstances Gustavus, after having already in 1522 claimed an aid from the clergy, made in 1523 an urgent demand for money upon Bishop Brask, and issued a proclamation calling upon all the monasteries and churches to send him, as a loan, such church vessels and such money as could be spared, the amount which each diocese or monastery was expected to provide being stated in a schedule. The result was not satisfactory. The demands of the Lübeck ambassadors were indeed met, but the forced loan caused no little irritation in Sweden, and gave mortal offence at Rome. A letter from Adrian VI was presently received, saying nothing about the confirmation of the Bishops elect for which Gustavus had asked, and insisting on the restoration of Archbishop Trolle. The King wrote back in no measured terms, refusing to restore him; and in November 2, 1523, in demanding confirmation for the Bishop elect of Åbo, he threatened that if it was refused they would do without it, and that he himself would carry out the reformation of the Church. "Let not your Holiness imagine," he concludes, "that we shall allow foreigners to rule the Church in Sweden." These were plain words, and they appear to have had some effect. Early in 1524 the new Pope granted confirmation to Peter Magnusson, the Legate's brother, Bishop elect of Vesterås (in place of the former elect Peter Jakobsson or Sunnenvæder, removed for disloyalty); and thus on Rogation Day there was consecrated, in Rome, the Bishop from whom the whole of the later Swedish episcopate derived its succession.

Meanwhile Gustavus' position was not growing easier. Soon after his accession a war for the recovery of Finland had greatly taxed his resources. This was followed by an expedition against the "robbers' stronghold" of Sören Norby in the island of Gottland, which was rendered difficult by the ill-concealed jealousy of Denmark and Lübeck, and became a positive danger when Bernhard von Mehlen, the German knight to whom Gustavus had given the command of the expedition, turned traitor and endeavoured by means of it to reconquer Sweden for Christian II. Nor were things better at home. The further demand for money which he was forced to make upon clergy and people alike gave rise to serious discontent. When Peter Sunnenvæder was removed from Vesterås for disaffection, as has been mentioned above, he fled to

Dalecarlia, together with Knud, the Provost of Vesterås, at one time Archbishop elect of Upsala, who had also been turned out, and there they raised the standard of revolt. One plot followed another, now on behalf of Christian II, now on behalf of one of the Stures, and again, early in 1527, on behalf of a pretender to their name. Gustavus found no great difficulty in suppressing them, and generally took severe measures of reprisal; but he could not prevent their recurrence. An entire readjustment of burdens, as between the clergy, the nobles, and the people at large, was plainly needed; and when the King convoked the general Diet of Vesterås to meet in June, 1527, it was with the deliberate intention of taking action in the matter.

But it was no longer merely or chiefly a question of money; during the last few years Lutheranism had made great strides in Sweden, and the whole status of the Swedish Church was now at issue. The first preachers of the new opinions were Olaus and Laurentius Petri (Olaf and Lars Petersson, b. 1497 and 1499), the sons of a blacksmith at Örebro, who had sent them to study at Wittenberg with no idea of the consequences which were likely to follow. On their return to Sweden in 1519, Olaus went to Strengnäs, where, as master of the Chapter school, he soon acquired a great influence over the Archdeacon, Laurentius Andreae (Lars Andersson, 1482–1552). For a time his teaching aroused no suspicion, and his sermons preached at the diet of Strengnäs made a great impression; but he had already roused the suspicions of Bishop Brask, who accused him of heresy in a letter dated May 7, 1523, and from this time forward was constantly urging Gustavus to take action against him. At first the King seemed to agree, though he urged that persuasion was a better remedy than force. But the inducements to take the other side were very strong; and before long, partly from interest and partly from conviction, he had decided to give his support to the new preachers, still protesting however that he desired to reform and not to overthrow the Church.

In the summer of 1524 he summoned Olaus Petri to Stockholm as city clerk, sent his brother to Upsala as professor of theology, and made Laurentius Andreae, already his Chancellor, Archdeacon of Upsala. The advancing wave was checked for a moment in the autumn, when the iconoclastic excesses brought about at Stockholm by two Dutch Anabaptists, Knipperdolling and Melchior Rink, caused a reaction of popular feeling and drew from Gustavus a stern condemnation. At Christmas, however, a discussion held in the royal palace between Olaus Petri and Peter Galle, a champion of the old order, on the subject of the sufficiency of Scripture, once more gave them confidence; and in February, 1525, Olaus publicly set the rules of the Church at defiance by marrying a wife. A few months afterwards Gustavus directed Archbishop Magni to set on foot the translation of the Bible into Swedish. The work was actually planned out and the books allotted to different translators; but, apparently owing to the opposition of Brask, it was never carried out; and the vacant place was in part filled by a version of the New Testament, mainly the work of Andreae, which appeared in 1526, followed subsequently, in 1540–1, by a much better translation of the whole Bible, which was edited and largely made by Laurentius Petri. In the same year (1526) Gustavus sent a series of doctrinal articles to the prelates, intending to use their replies as the basis for a second and more exhaustive theological disputation; and although this plan fell through owing to the natural reluctance of some of the persons concerned to submit their faith to the tribunal of popular opinion, the answers of Peter Galle were published, with disparaging comments by Olaus Petri.

While thus undermining the claims of ecclesiastical authority, the King was also making insidious attacks upon the property of the Church. He systematically billeted his troops upon the monasteries; he left no means untried to get a hold upon their internal affairs; he sought out legal pretexts for reclaiming lands given to them by his ancestors. The property of the Bishops suffered in like manner, and especially that of the richest of them, the aged Brask, whom the King seems to have despoiled with special malice or policy. Archbishop Joannes Magni suffered even worse things. Injudicious letters which he had written to ecclesiastics abroad subjected him to a charge of conspiracy, on which he was arrested and imprisoned. The King allowed him to leave Sweden in the autumn of 1526, ostensibly on an embassy to Poland; but it was really a banishment, from which he never returned. He took up his abode at Danzig and was soon afterwards confirmed by the Pope and consecrated with the barren title of Archbishop of Upsala. And thus at length the way was prepared for further encroachment. By the terms of the summons, the Diet of Vesterås was to discuss questions of faith, and especially the relations between Sweden and the Papacy.

The Diet met on June 24, 1527. There were present four Bishops, four canons, fifteen lay members of the *Riksråd*, one hundred and twenty-nine nobles, thirty-two burgesses, fourteen deputies of the miners, and one hundred and four of the peasants. For the first time in Swedish history the Bishops were degraded from their place of honour next the King and were ranked below the senators. Smarting under the affront, they held a secret meeting before the session of the following day, at which, instigated by Brask, they signed a set of protests, a copy of which was found fifteen years afterwards under the floor of the cathedral, against anything that might be done in the direction of Lutheranism or contrary to the authority of the Pope. When the Diet again met the Chancellor arose in Gustavus' name, reviewed the events of his reign, and urged the necessity for a larger revenue, plainly pointing to the ecclesiastical property as the only source from which it might be obtained. Brask replied on behalf of the Bishops, saying that they

could not help the state of the kingdom; that they would do all in
their power to put down abuses, but that, being directed by the Pope
to defend their property, they could not do otherwise. This brought
Gustavus himself to his feet. He enquired whether the members of
the Diet considered this a fair answer. Thure Jönsson, the oldest
amongst them, replied that it was. "Then," said Gustavus, "I will no
longer be your King, and if you can find one who will please you better
I shall be glad. Pay me for my property in the kingdom, and return
what I have expended in your service; and then I solemnly protest
that I will never return to this degenerate and thankless native land of
mine." With this outburst he strode from the hall and left them
to discuss at their leisure. He knew what the result must be; he
had made Sweden, and it could not do without him. They had all
the power in their hands, whilst his only asset was his own personality. But it was enough; and after three days the members of the
Diet sent to say that they would conform to his wishes in all
things.

Gustavus was now master. The Orders, with the exception of the
clergy, made their proposals for dealing with the crisis. Contrary to all
precedent, these proposals were formulated by the *Riksråd* instead of
being voted on by the whole Diet; but the resulting decree, the famous
Vesterås Recess, was nevertheless put forth in its name. It provided
that all episcopal, capitular, and monastic property which was not
absolutely required (and of this he was the judge) was to be handed
over to the King; all the lands exempt from taxes (*Frälsejord*) which
had been given to the Church since 1454 were to revert to the original
owners; taxable land (*Skattejord*) was to be given up however long it
had been alienated. Preachers were to set forth the pure Word of God
and nothing else, whilst on the religious question in general a disputation was to be held in the presence of the Diet, and a settlement to be
made on it as a basis. The disputation, if held at all, was naturally
of no importance; and the Diet proceeded, on June 24, to pass the
Vesterås Ordinantie, consisting of twenty-two regulations on the subject
of religion. By these, detailed provision was made for the confiscation
of the bulk of the Church property, in accordance with the terms of the
Recess. No dignitaries were to be appointed until their names had
been approved by the King; parish clergy were to be appointed by the
Bishops, subject to removal by the King in case of unfitness; small
parishes might be united where it was desirable, the Gospel was to be
taught in every school, compulsory confession was abolished, monks were
not to be absent from their monasteries without licence from the civil
authority, and so forth. The result of these Ordinances was to give the
King all the power that he could wish for over the Church. Dispirited
and almost heartbroken, the aged Brask before long obtained permission
to visit the island of Gottland, which was part of his diocese, crossed

the Baltic, and joined Archbishop Magni at Danzig. None of his brethren dared to oppose Gustavus' will.

Nor was it only the ecclesiastical order that suffered. In Sweden, unlike Denmark, none but the King gained power through the Reformation. The *Riksråd*, once all-important, was now nothing more than a complaisant royal Council. As leader of a popular movement, Gustavus had triumphed over the nobles, who were now glad to make common cause with the peasants wherever they were aggrieved. It should however be noted that one of the Vesterås Ordinances gave the nobles the right to recover all their property which had been acquired by the churches and convents since the redaction of the year 1454, an important concession. There were revolts from time to time, generally directed in part at any rate against the new ecclesiastical order, as for instance in West Gothland in 1529 under Thure Jönsson, and again on a larger scale in 1542 under Nels Dacke. But they were in general easily put down, and always left Gustavus' power stronger than before. Nor was this all. The inevitable result of the changes which were being made was to put into abeyance rights which formerly belonged to one class or another of the community. These were by degrees seized upon by Gustavus as a kind of extension of his prerogative royal; and before long he was exercising without opposition an authority which no previous King of Sweden had ever possessed. In a Council held at Örebro early in 1540, the chief nobles were made to take an oath acknowledging Gustavus' sons, Johan and Erik, as the legitimate heirs to the kingdom; and the Act of Hereditary Settlement, passed on January 13, 1544, formally recognised hereditary succession in the male line as the rule of the Swedish constitution. Meanwhile the kingdom grew greatly in wealth and importance. Under Gustavus' influence the mines of the north became vast sources of wealth; manufactures grew up everywhere, and commerce was fostered by treaties with England, France, Denmark, and Russia. Before his death, which took place on Michaelmas Day, 1560, he had raised Sweden to a condition of unexampled prosperity, and had prepared the way for the great epoch of the next century.

We now return to the Swedish Church. Although the Ordinances of Vesterås had shorn it of its grandeur and delivered it into Gustavus' hands, they had not abolished its essential character. On January 5, 1528, the Bishops elect of Skara, Strengnäs, and Åbo were consecrated by the Bishop of Vesterås "by command of the King," without the confirmation of the Pope indeed, but with the accustomed rites; and on the following day Gustavus himself was crowned by them "with great pomp" in the Cathedral of Upsala. The monasteries were deprived of most of their property, and many of them ceased to exist at once; but the rest only died away by degrees, until at length there remained but a few nuns in the cloisters of Vadstena, Nadendal, Skenninge, and Skog, who lived on the King's bounty. But no man in all Sweden died for the old faith. A certain number of the clergy were deprived, but the bulk of them still went on ; and their general condition may perhaps be gauged by the fact that in not a few cases they married their former housekeeper or mistress in order to legitimatise the children. The Bishops had lost much of their property, but were still comparatively well off ; for many years the new Archbishop of Upsala, Laurentius Petri (called Nericius), consecrated in 1531, used to support some fifty students in Upsala, and Bishop Skytte of Åbo supported eight abroad.

Gustavus himself did all in his power to prevent changes being forced on a reluctant people. A synod held at Örebro in 1529, under the presidency of Laurentius Andreae, provided that a lesson from the Swedish Bible should be read daily in all cathedrals, and that evangelical preachers should be appointed to carry the new doctrines about the country ; but the King was so careful to preserve the old ceremonies, or such of them as " were not repugnant to God's Word," that he roused no little indignation amongst the more extreme Reformers as having fallen away from the Gospel. In 1528 he issued an ordinance insisting upon the payment of the legal dues of the clergy. Ten years later, when the nobles seemed to have learned too well the lesson which he had given them in the despoiling of churches, he restrained and rebuked those whose religious zeal manifested itself only in the way of destruction. " After this fashion," he said, " every man is a Christian and evangelical." Yet he recognised no limits to his own power : " it behoveth us as a Christian monarch," he wrote to the commons of the northern province, " to appoint ordinances and rules for you ; therefore must ye be obedient to our royal commands, as well in matters spiritual as temporal." In 1540, when Laurentius Andreae and Olaus Petri were put on their trial for treason in not having made known to the King a conspiracy, the existence of which they had learned in confession, the Archbishop was compelled to be their judge. They were condemned to death, and only obtained pardon by the payment of a large fine.

But although Gustavus ever denied that he was setting up a new Church in Sweden, the changes became more pronounced as time went on, both in doctrine and discipline. Olaus Petri was putting forth a continual stream of tracts and pamphlets in Swedish which reflected his own strict Lutheranism, and by degrees they had a considerable effect. The first Swedish service-book, *Een Handbock pää Swensko*, appeared in 1529 ; it was followed in 1530 by a hymn-book, and in 1531 by the first Swedish " Mass-book " (*Ordo Missae Sueticae*), the Eucharistic doctrine of which was the " Consubstantiation " of Luther's earlier days ; all these were many times reprinted in subsequent years, though the use of the Latin service was by no means everywhere abolished. Gustavus himself gradually went further. He repudiated prayers for the dead, and confession ; for instance, he refused on his deathbed to listen to the clergy when they urged him to confess his sins and seek absolution. He seems at one time almost to have contemplated the discontinuance of the episcopal office. In 1539 one George Norman, who had been recommended to him by Melanchthon, was appointed, by a commission not unlike that which had been given by Henry VIII to Cromwell a few years before, to superintend and visit the clergy and churches of Sweden; and a general visitation of the whole kingdom took place under his auspices in 1540. From 1544 the King refused to give the episcopal title to any but the Archbishop of Upsala; the rest he styled Ordinaries. As time went on, the dioceses were divided up into some twelve portions in all, each under its Ordinary. That this division was in itself desirable is likely enough, for the old dioceses were very large and unwieldy. Moreover some at any rate of Gustavus' new Ordinaries were in episcopal orders; *e.g.* when the old diocese of Åbo (Finland) was subdivided into Åbo and Viborg, the two new Ordinaries, Michael Agricola (who had previously been vicar-general of the whole diocese) and Paulus Juusten, were consecrated as Bishops together by Bishop Bothvid of Strengnäs in 1554. Nevertheless the effect of his action was undoubtedly to cast a slight upon the episcopal Order, and had there not been a reaction subsequently it must have been highly prejudicial if not fatal to the continued existence of episcopacy in Sweden.

The nine years of Gustavus' son and successor Erik XIV (1560–9), for some time the suitor of Elizabeth of England, were years of disaster for the Swedish State, and not less so for the Church. He inclined towards Calvinism, and already during his father's lifetime an overture had been made by Calvin towards the Swedish royal House by the joint dedication of a writing to father and son. It was ineffective so far as Gustavus was concerned, but Erik on his accession at once began to show favour towards Calvinists, announced his intention of making Sweden a refuge for distressed Protestants, and used his authority in the Church to bring about the suppression of a few fast days and other observances of the old order. His wasteful extravagance from the first pressed heavily on the State. But the real afflictions arose in the latter part of his reign, when he was engaged in war both at home and abroad, and everything was allowed to fall into neglect; churches fell into ruins, the church plate disappeared, benefices were not filled up, or only by incompetent persons, and the schools ceased to exist. At length in 1569 Erik was dethroned by his brothers, Johan and Karl, to whom their father had left hereditary dukedoms, and who seem to have agreed upon a joint conduct of the government after Erik's deposition; and some years later he was brutally murdered in prison, in pursuance of a vote of the members of the *Riksråd*, both lay and clerical.

The new King, Johan III, was a scholar and a theologian, whose reading of Cassander and other similar divines led him to lay all possible stress upon the ancient order of the Swedish Church, whilst his love for his consort, Catharine, the sister of Sigismund II of Poland, who was a Roman Catholic, inclined him to seek a reconciliation with the Pope, if it could be obtained on reasonable terms.   Under his influence a new Church order (*Kyrko-ordning*) was drawn up by the aged Archbishop Laurentius Petri and put forth by authority, which became the basis of the practice which prevails at the present day. Care is taken for the education and examination of the clergy, though the use by them of books of Homilies, such as the *Postilla* of Olaus Petri, is permitted.   Latin psalms and prayers may still be used, and confession, excommunication, and public penance are provided for.   The Bishop is elected by the clergy and others having competent knowledge, and consecrated in due course.   The people choose their minister and present him to the Bishop, who either ordains him or another in his place ; but it is to be noticed that the same form of service is to be used whether the person so "consecrated" is previously a layman or a minister from another charge.   There are also assistant clergy or chaplains (*Kapellaner*) in the larger parishes.   Before long the King was able to make further changes.   The old Archbishop died in October, 1573 ; in June of the following year "the principal divines" were convened for the election of a successor, and "the votes of the great majority" were given to his son-in-law, Laurentius Petri Gothus, who was a student of the Fathers, and in many ways likeminded with the King.

In December the Archbishop elect was confirmed by the King after giving his assent to a series of seventeen articles which approved of the restoration of the convents, prayers for the dead, and the veneration of saints ; and on July 15, 1575, he was consecrated "according to the complete Catholic use," with mitre, crosier, ring, and chrism, which were also used by the new Archbishop in future consecrations of his suffragans.   A royal ordinance presently restored to the Archbishop that jurisdiction over his suffragans which had almost ceased to exist under Gustavus ; and another gave the Archbishop and Chapter of Upsala a voice in all elections of Bishops.   Other changes were made of the same general character, and some of the old convents were reopened. In 1576 a more important step was taken : a new liturgy on the lines of the reformed Roman Missal, the so-called "Red Book of Sweden" (*Röda Boken*), was published ; it was fathered by the Archbishop in a preface, but was really the work of the King and his secretary, Peter Fechen.   It was adopted, after considerable opposition (in which the Bishops of Linkœping and Strengnäs took part) at the Diet of 1577 ; and the King did his best to force it upon the whole Church.   But he was never able to compel all the country clergy to use it ; and his brother Karl, the Duke of Suthermanland (afterwards Charles IX), the ablest by far of the "brood of King Gustavus," not only refused to adopt it, but made himself the champion of the *Kyrko-ordning* of 1571 and of all who suffered for their fidelity to it.   The result during

Johan's lifetime was estrangement, and very nearly civil war, between the brothers; after his death it led to the triumph of Lutheranism at the Upsala *möte*.

All this time the King was carrying on negotiations with the Papacy. So early as 1572 Cardinal Stanislaus Hosius was writing hopefully of his conversion. In 1576 two Jesuits from Louvain, Florentius Feyt and Laurentius the Norwegian, appeared at Stockholm in the guise of evangelical preachers. They were instructed to proceed with great caution. The Cardinal gave directions that the last-named was to extol faith and depreciate works without faith, to preach Christ as the only mediator, and His cross as the only means of salvation; " and thereupon," he proceeded, " let them show that nothing else has been preached in the papal Church." We know from their own account that at the King's bidding they concealed their real condition and were taken for Lutherans; and the clergy were compelled to receive their instruction, which was carried on in the spirit of Hosius' directions. In the same year the King sent messengers to Rome to negotiate for the restoration of the papal authority in Sweden. It soon became evident that he was asking for conditions which were not likely to be granted; he demanded, amongst other things, the concession of the Cup to the laity, the partial use of Swedish in the liturgy, the surrender of clerical exemptions, toleration of the marriage of the clergy (though with a preference for celibacy), and the condonation of all that had been done in the past.

The time was past for such concessions, although hopes of something of the kind were held out more than once by Cardinal Hosius in his letters. In 1577 however the Jesuit Antony Possevin was sent to the north, with a commission as Legate to the Emperor, and instructions to use all his influence with King Johan. He made his appearance in the following year; and so great was the impression which he produced upon the King that after a few interviews, as we are told in his reports, Johan declared his willingness to make the Tridentine profession of faith without waiting to see what concessions the Pope might be willing to make towards Sweden. He accordingly did so, made his confession and was absolved (penance being imposed upon him for the murder of his brother, for which he had always felt the deepest remorse), and received the Communion in the Roman manner. This year, then, marks the zenith of the papal influence. About the same time Bishop Martin Olafsson of Linkœping, who had always been opposed to the direction in which things were moving in the Swedish Church, was deposed and degraded for calling the Pope antichrist. Luther's Catechism, which had been used in the schools for some years, was made to give place to that of Canisius; many Jesuits were admitted into the country, on one pretext or another, and large numbers of Swedish boys were sent abroad to be educated in their seminaries; above all, the primatial see was kept vacant for four years after the death of Laurentius Petri Gothus in 1579, in the hope that it might next be filled by an Archbishop of the Roman obedience.

This hope was doomed to be disappointed, for the proposed surrender proved to be less attractive on a nearer view. The King's plans in religion were closely bound up with political schemes which had for their object the obtaining for himself the Duchies of Bari and Rossani in right of his wife, whose mother was a Sforza ; and these had just received a check. Gregory XIII declined to make the concessions which Johan thought that he had been led to expect ; and on further consideration he found himself too honestly convinced of the essential soundness of the position of the Swedish Church to be content to give up all that had been won already. The last shreds of the influence of the Romanising party disappeared entirely after the death of Queen Catharine in 1584 ; the Jesuits and their *fautores* were once more expelled ; and Johan, after turning his thoughts for a moment towards the orthodox east, settled down to the work of consolidating the Swedish Church as he found it.

Not long afterwards, however, the question was reopened, and in a more acute form, by the death of Johan III on November 17, 1592. The crown fell to his son Sigismund, who had been elected King of Poland in 1586, and who was a convinced Roman Catholic. With the consent of the *Riksråd*, his uncle Duke Charles at once assumed the government in his name ; and together they resolved to make provision for the maintenance of Protestantism before the new King arrived. The *Råd* was anxious that the matter should be dealt with by certain members of their own body in conjunction with the delegates of the clergy ; but Charles had made his brother promise two years before that a general assembly (*Kyrko-möte*) should be held, and he assented to the demand of the clergy that it should take place now. Accordingly a synod was convened which was attended by deputies both clerical and lay from all parts of the kingdom, though Finland was but sparsely represented. There were present, in addition to the members of the *Riksråd*, four Bishops (most of the sees were vacant, and were filled whilst the Synod was still in session), over three hundred clergy, and nearly as many nobles and representatives of the citizens, miners, and peasants. The famous " *Upsala-möte* " was opened on February 25, 1593, Nicolaus Bothniensis, one of the professors of theology at Upsala, being chosen as speaker. The assembly first laid down the rule of Scripture as the basis of all doctrine. Then it sought a doctrinal standard ; and the obvious one was the Augsburg Confession, which had already been commonly accepted in Sweden, though it had never been definitely adopted by the Swedish Church. The articles were now gone through one by one, after which it was solemnly received as the confession of the Swedish Church. Luther's Catechism was again made the basis for instruction in religion ; the use of the " Red Book " was abolished, and Laurentius Petri's Church Ordinance once more became the standard of worship, subject however to a certain amount of pruning in the matter of ritual.　After this the Synod proceeded to the details of practical reform.

The Upsala *möte* may be considered the coping-stone of the Swedish Reformation.　Sigismund came to the throne with the knowledge that his new kingdom had made a definite stand from which there could be no withdrawal; and although many efforts were made during his reign on behalf of Roman Catholicism, first for concurrent establishment, and then for bare toleration, the issue was never for a moment doubtful. The Swedish Church was definitely committed to Lutheranism; the clergy continued to be an estate of the realm down to the middle of the nineteenth century; and separation from the national communion was so severely punished that until modern days organised dissent was practically unknown.　The endeavours of Charles IX, the most learned of the royal brothers, to widen the doctrinal basis of the Swedish Church, were on the whole unsuccessful.　But it was not only in Sweden that the *möte* had far-reaching consequences.　The definite adhesion of Sweden to the Augsburg Confession gave strength to the cause of Protestantism everywhere: it opened the way for the Protestant League of the North in the following century.

NOTE ON THE REFORMATION IN POLAND

The Reformation in Poland, although its influence on general European history in the period treated in this volume is comparatively slight, has some features of special interest. It pursued its course for nearly half-a-century without material hindrance either from the national government or the authorities of the Church. During this era its difficulties arose principally from the dissensions of the Reformers, from the independence of the nobility, the ignorance and apathy of the oppressed peasantry, and the want of sympathy between the country and the towns, where the German element was strong, and between the burghers and the nobles. Thus the evolution of a national Reformed Church was impossible; the Reform movement never obtained any vital hold on the mass of the people; and no united opposition could be offered to the forces of the Counter-Reformation, when at length they began to act. On the other hand the lack of organisation, of combination, and of national and ecclesiastical control, left the way free for the most hazardous and audacious speculations. Every man's intellect was a law to himself, and heresy assumed its most exorbitant forms.

The conditions of the Church in Poland called for reform not less than elsewhere. The Bishops were enormously wealthy; and the character of the episcopate was not likely to be improved by the measures of 1505, and 1523, which were intended to exclude all but nobles from the bishoprics. The right of the King to nominate to bishoprics was practically recognised. In 1459 a memorable attack was made upon the administration of the Polish Church by John Ostrorog, a man not only of the highest rank, but of great learning. His indictment, made before the Diet, foreshadows the general demand for a reform of the Church, though nothing is said about doctrine. The excessive authority of the Pope, the immunity of the clergy from public burdens and public control, the exactions of the Papacy, the expenses of litigation before the Curia, indulgences, simony, and the requirement of fees for spiritual offices, the unworthiness and ignorance of monks and clergy, the encouragement of idleness, are all put forward with no sparing hand. Owing to·the privileges of the Polish nobility the power of the ecclesiastical Courts was less in Poland than elsewhere, and excommunication was openly set at defiance. On the side of doctrine Hussite influence, continually spreading in Poland during the fifteenth century, prepared the ground; and the fact that nearly a half of the subjects of the Polish Crown, the Slavonic population of the South and East, professed the faith of the Greek Church, familiarised the Jagellon Kings with divergences in faith, and the people with the existence of other beliefs.

It was not long before the movement initiated by Luther spread to Poland, and it appeared first in Polish Prussia, the western part of the territory of the Teutonic Order, ceded by it in 1466 to King Casimir III. Danzig was the first centre of an active propaganda, and the urban population favoured the new opinions. The ecclesiastical authorities endeavoured to act with firmness, but found their authority insufficient. In 1525 the Reformers captured the town government, and the Reformation was set on foot. But in the following year Sigismund I, then King of Poland and Grand Duke of Lithuania, took forcible measures to suppress the Reform. In this, almost the only energetic step taken by that King against the spread of Reform, he was actuated by political motives. In 1523 Albert of Brandenburg, the last Grand Master of the Teutonic Order, had adopted the Reform, and in 1525 he converted the dominions entrusted to his charge into a hereditary dukedom; and Sigismund feared that the Reforming tendencies of West Prussia might lead the inhabitants into closer political relations with the emancipated master of East Prussia. In spite, however, of Sigismund's temporary success at Danzig, Lutheran opinions continued to spread, and finally triumphed in Polish Prussia.

In Poland itself frequent acts against the new opinions were passed by ecclesiastical synods, in 1527, 1530, 1532, 1542, and 1544. But the Church was powerless in face of the famous Polish privilege, "*neminem captivare nisi jure victum*," and the other immunities of the nobles. The ecclesiastical Courts were regarded with general contempt. The hostility of the Diets was undisguised. In 1538 they forbade the Polish clergy to receive any preferment from the Pope, in 1543 they abolished annates, and in 1544 they subjected the clergy to ordinary taxation. Sigismund I issued an order in 1534 forbidding Polish students to study at foreign universities, but this order was cancelled in 1543; and the inaction of Sigismund proclaims either his impotence or his lack of zeal. His son, Sigismund II Augustus, who succeeded in 1548, was probably rather friendly than indifferent. In any case the power of the King was little; and individual nobles took what line they pleased without reference to King or Church.

In these circumstances not only did Lutheran views spread freely but other heresies appeared. A society was formed at Cracow, under the influence of Francisco Lismanini, which not only ventilated the opinions of the more orthodox Reformers, but also cast doubt upon the doctrine of the Trinity. In 1548 the Reformation in Poland received a great impulse by the expulsion from Bohemia of the Bohemian Brethren, a sect which received a definite organisation about 1456, and had survived through many vicissitudes, preserving many of the more advanced Hussite opinions. Luther, at first hostile to their views, afterwards became reconciled, and established a spiritual communion with them. Ferdinand, after other repressive measures had failed, expelled them from his territories; and on their way towards Prussia they found temporary hospitality in Posen, where they were entertained by Andreas Gorka, the Castellan of Posen. The Bishop of Posen, however, before long procured their expulsion; they passed into Prussia, leaving behind, however, many converts; and their congregations afterwards evangelised many districts of Posen and of Great Poland.

The reign of Sigismund Augustus (1548–72) saw the Polish Reformation at its height. The Synod of Piotrkow in 1552, at which Stanislaus Hosius, the Bishop of Ermland, first took a prominent part as a defender of the Church, initiated a vigorous campaign against the Reform; but although the clergy procured the martyrdom of a poor priest, they found themselves helpless against the nobles. The Diet of 1552 left to the clergy the power of judging heresy, but deprived them of the authority to inflict any civil or political penalty. In the same year a Polish Reformer, Modrzewski, laid before the King a remarkable and moderate scheme of national ecclesiastical reform; but there was no authority capable of carrying it out. In 1556 licence assumed the form of law, and the principle of *cujus regio* was carried to its extreme consequence, when the Diet enacted that every nobleman could introduce into his own house any form of worship at his pleasure, provided that it was in conformity with the Scriptures. The King at this time also demanded from Pope Paul IV in the name of the Diet the concession of mass in the vernacular, communion in both kinds, the marriage of priests, the abolition of annates, and a National Council for Reform and the union of sects. He received in the following year a stinging reprimand from the fiery Pontiff for an offence in which he was little more than a passive agent.

The Reformation seemed to be triumphant. But excessive liberty was a source of weakness. The Bohemian brethren, indeed, formed a durable union with the Genevan Churches in Poland in 1555. The former were most powerful in Posen and Great Poland, the latter in Little Poland and Lithuania. But the Lutherans were a persistent obstacle to union. It was hoped that the return of John Laski (à Lasco) to his native land in 1556 might put an end to divisions. This member of a noble Polish house had listened to the voice of Zwingli and Erasmus in his youth, and afterwards had renounced his prospects of high preferment in his own Church in order to preach reform. His self-denying labours in East Friesland had been crowned with success, and as head of the community of foreign Reformers in London he had won a reputation beyond the Channel. His gentle nature, and the moderate character of his opinions, which, although they were nearest to those of Calvin and Zwingli, were calculated to give the least possible offence to the Lutherans, raised great hopes of him as a mediator. But he died in 1560, having effected nothing.

Protestant dissensions continued, and the Protestant cause was further discredited by the activity of the anti-Trinitarians. Lismanini had openly denied the Trinity, and Bernardino Ochino in 1564 found many hearers. He was expelled, however, very shortly. The Unitarians had their centre at Pinczow, near Cracow, and among their leaders were first Stancari and Lismanini, and afterwards Georgio Biandrata, and Peter Gonesius, a Pole. Even in the face of this double danger, from their own advanced wing and from the Catholic side, the Protestants failed to achieve unity. At length at the synod of Sandomir, 1570, mutual toleration rather than union was arranged between the Lutherans on the one hand, and the united Church of Genevans and Bohemians on the other. Thus the critical time of the death of Sigismund Augustus in 1572 found the Protestant sects widely spread in the Polish dominions, enjoying virtual toleration, but probably not very deeply rooted in the Polish people, compromised by advanced freethinkers, and barely concealing their mutual antagonism.

Meanwhile dangers were arising. The direct efforts of Stanislaus Hosius, the mission of Lippomani in 1555, and that of Commendoni in 1563, did little to check the Reformed opinions. But from the introduction of the Jesuits into Poland at the suggestion of Cardinal Hosius in 1564, and from the transfer into their hands of the institutions of higher education founded by him in Poland, dates the beginning of a more insidious and effective opposition, which was destined in a period beyond our present scope to attain complete success.

This brief note may serve to show the position of the new religions in Poland down to the death of Sigismund Augustus. But the name of Socinus is so closely linked with the religious history of that country and with that of the *dissidentes de religione* (the appellation given in Poland in 1573 to the adherents of the Reformation, though afterwards extended in its significance), that a word must be said about the two well-known teachers of that name. Lelio Sozzini was a native of Siena, born in 1525. Attracted early by the writings of Luther, he made himself suspected at home, and travelled widely throughout Europe, coming into contact with all the leading Reformers. He visited Poland twice, and doubtless found kindred spirits there; he probably influenced Lismanini; but although the audacity of his opinions and the free expression of his doubts seem to have caused him to be regarded with suspicion by more orthodox Reformers, he does not appear to have actually denied the doctrine of the Trinity. He died in 1562. His nephew, Fausto Sozzini, passed the line. He also was born at Siena in 1539. He came to Poland in 1579, after the anti-Trinitarian opinions had long been developed there. Under the protection of the Transylvanian Prince, Stephen Báthory, the sect had flourished, and had acquired in the town of Racow its own school, church, and printing-press. Sozzini speedily won great influence, and was able to influence the doctrines of the Unitarians. Eventually the sect received his name, and was known as Socinian.

The distinctive doctrine of the Socinians was the denial of the doctrine of the Trinity, the teaching of One God. They recognised divinity in the Father alone, and denied it to the Son and the Holy Ghost. They reverenced Christ as the Messiah, as a teacher and a reformer, but as a human being. They believed nevertheless in His supernatural birth, in His miracles, His resurrection, His ascension. They believed that He received revelations from the Father. They followed also the Bible as their guide and standard ; giving it their own interpretation, which differed from that of the Protestants and of the Fathers of Nicaea. They rejected the Augustinian doctrine of original sin, and believed that salvation was to be obtained by conscientious following of Christ's teaching, and virtuous living. They rejected therefore also the doctrine of the Atonement. Baptism was for them only the symbol of admission into the Christian communion, and the Lord's Supper a mere memorial. This remarkable sect had its origin in the active brains of speculative Italians, its favourable ground for growth in the religious liberty or anarchy of Poland, but it received its definite organisation, its tenets, and its name from Fausto Sozzini.

CHAPTER XVIII

THE CHURCH AND REFORM

THE necessity of reform and of a spiritual regeneration of Catholicism had been acknowledged again and again at the opening of the sixteenth century by men of high position in the Church. Time after time it was admitted by the Sacred College, and at each Conclave the whole body of Cardinals pledged themselves to reform. Commissions were appointed but nothing came of them ; and the Fifth Lateran Council (1512–17), instead of reforming the evils that had resulted from excessive centralisation, did little more than lay down the "*plenitudo potestatis*" of the papal monarchy with an insistency that had hitherto found expression only in the pages of curialist writers.

The vested interests of the officials of the Roman Court were in fact too strong for the forces working for reform ; and the measures which might have obviated the schism and nipped the revolution in the bud were not taken until it was too late. The opponents of reform had the strength of a group of men working together with a definite knowledge of what they wanted to defend. The Catholic reformers on the other hand were scattered, voices in the desert, with no means of common action. Nor, when opportunities occurred to them, were they for long agreed as to the particular lines reform should take. The seeds of the later divisions among the Catholic reformers existed from the very first, and the course of events soon led to those differences becoming acute. For men desired reform from very different motives. The ascetic temperament saw nothing but the moral abuses and the corruption of the clergy ; the humanist desired a greater freedom of thought, and a certain toleration of divergences of opinion which was abhorrent to the doctrinal reformer. The latter shared with the humanist the wish for a reconstruction of the traditional dogma, but wished to see the line between orthodoxy and heterodoxy drawn with no uncertain hand. Ultimately, two great parties evolved themselves among the Catholic reformers : the one desired conciliation and the discovery of a common ground on which the old and the new ideas might be harmonised ; the other, while sharing with the former party its indignation at the moral corruption of the Church, yet parted company with it with regard to the reform of doctrine. The supremacy of St Thomas and of the great scholastics must be preserved, and the whole body of dogma which the Middle Ages had evolved must be retained. Concession of any kind was not to be heard of ; and this party believed that a further increase of the powers of the Papacy and of the centralisation of authority was the surest safeguard of the Church. The former party wished for a real Catholic reformation ; the latter succeeded in reducing a movement which started with so great a promise to little more than a counter-reformation. It will be our purpose in this chapter to sketch the steps by which this was brought about, and all real reform, such as might have conciliated nascent Protestantism and preserved the unity of the Western Church, was made impossible.

The aspirations of scattered individuals for reform first found a nucleus and an organisation in the "Oratory of Divine Love," founded at Rome towards the end of the Pontificate of Leo X. This famous society numbered among its members some of the most learned prelates and upright laymen who were connected with the Court of Rome in that day. They met for prayer and meditation in the little church of Santi Silvestro e Dorotea in Trastevere and discussed means for the purification of the Church. Almost every tendency of thought and temperament among the Catholic reformers was to be found there. Caraffa and Sadoleto, Gaetano da Thiene and Giberti were alike members. The ascetic and the humanist, the practical and the doctrinal reformer met together and worked in harmony. Their numbers were some fifty or sixty in all. In the last years of the Pagan Renaissance, when its weaker elements were coming to the surface, and when decadence rather than a new interest in life was becoming its keynote, there was thus growing in numbers and influence a party full of promise for the future history of the Church. A stern and almost Puritan moral ideal was combined with a belief that there was no essential antagonism between faith and culture, between profane learning and Christian knowledge. As the great medieval theologians and scholastics had interpreted Christianity to their age, and had harmonised the divergent elements in the knowledge of their time, so now in the Oratory of Divine Love the feeling found expression that the work had to be done afresh, and that the new revelation given to men by the Renaissance must be incorporated into the system of Christian thought.

Nor was it only the desire for a closer alliance between Christianity and humanism which bound many of these men together. Augustine had always been a force in the medieval Church, and the Augustinian elements in its theology were ever again asserting themselves and claiming supremacy. The attraction of Augustine felt so strongly by Luther was not felt only by him. The end of the fifteenth and the beginning of the sixteenth centuries were marked by a renewed study of St Augustine in many quarters, and by a consequent revival of the Pauline ideas of Justification in different forms. As Reginald Pole said in one of his letters, the jewel which the Church had so long kept half concealed was again brought to light. This trend of thought found expression in the writings of Thomas de Vio, Cardinal Cajetan, and for some time was looked on with favour in the highest quarters of the Church. That section of the Oratory of Divine Love which wished to spiritualise theology and to deepen the bases of the Christian life found ample support in the accepted theology of the day.

Venice was the home from which came many of the thinkers of this type in the Oratory of Divine Love. After the Sack of Rome in 1527 its members were scattered; but in a short time many of them met again at Venice, where they found new recruits. The Senator Gasparo Contarini and Gregorio Cortese, Abbot of San Georgio Maggiore, were the most influential of the new members. Giberti had become Bishop of Verona in 1524, and his household became a new centre for the reforming movement. His administration of his diocese set an example to other prelates; and his reform of his clergy served in many ways as a model to the Fathers at Trent, though he himself did not live to take any active part in that assembly. At Padua Reginald Pole spent many years, and though he was only a layman his manner of life and conduct of his household were not unworthy to be compared with those of Giberti. The University of Padua numbered then among its teachers some of the most eminent scholars of the day, and it was one of the centres of the Christian Renaissance. Modena also was one of the strongholds of the Catholic reformers; Giovanni Morone, who afterwards with difficulty escaped the charge of heresy, was its Bishop. Sadoleto, Bishop of Carpentras, Gregorio Cortese, and other leaders of the movement either were Modenese or had been connected with Modena. The union of scholarship and holiness of life with zeal for practical reform, as exemplified in these men, is rare in the history of the Church.

The movement for reform from within thus inaugurated in Italy did not become a power in official circles in Rome until the pontificate of Paul III. The paper reforms of the Fifth Lateran remained a dead letter, while the good intentions of Adrian VI came to nothing. His reign, nevertheless, will ever be memorable from his confession that the source of the poison which was corrupting the whole Church was in the papal Court, nay even in the Pontiffs themselves. Ignorant of the world, ignorant of the forces at work in Rome itself, Adrian was helpless. If he had had any measure of success, his reforms would have been of a moral and practical kind alone. Having lived most of his life in cloisters, he knew little of the change that had come over human thought. St Thomas was his master, and he did not wish to go beyond the work of the greatest of medieval thinkers. Adrian was a precursor of Caraffa and the later Counter-Reformation, rather than of the peace-loving Contarini and the learned Giberti.

Clement VII, of the House of Medici, was well-meaning and wished to remove the worst abuses in the Church. The hell through which the Papacy passed during his pontificate was indeed paved with good intentions, but they all came to nothing. The cares of the temporal power and the interests of his family left little time for the reformation of society. Still in 1524 the Roman Congregation was set up to reform the clergy; but in the troublous years which followed, leading up to the Sack of Rome, little could be done. Giberti, who with Nicholas Schomberg, the Cardinal of Capua, appears to have influenced Clement's policy in those early years of his reign, had little time to spare from secular affairs; and it was not until he finally retired to his Bishopric of Verona that he obtained an opportunity of playing the part of a reformer. Thus, while the Teutonic lands were rapidly falling away from the Church, nothing was done in Rome itself to heal the abuses which all men acknowledged to be crying for reform.

There was one remedy for the Church's evils which was a nightmare to Clement. A reform of the Church by a free General Council was a cry which grew in intensity and sprang up from many quarters as Clement's vacillating reign dragged on its way. Luther had appealed from the Pope to a free General Council; and the appeal was echoed in the German Diets. Charles himself took up the idea; but, as it soon came to be seen that what Charles meant by a General Council was very different from that desired by the Protestants, the enthusiasm for it soon cooled down in Germany; and the idea of a National Council for the settlement of the affairs of religion took its place. At times, when it was a useful weapon to be used against the Pope, Charles also gave the idea of a National Council his support; but he sincerely desired the convocation of an Ecumenical Council, and he fell back on the alternative only when the conduct of the Papacy forced his hands. General Councils had ominous memories for the Papacy since the days of Pisa, Constance, and Basel; and Clement no doubt felt that the government of the Church during his pontificate would not stand the ordeal of a public examination. General Councils were apt to get out of hand, and no one could foresee whither they might ultimately lead. Clement succeeded in putting off the evil day at the price of letting events in Germany take their own course.

With Clement's successor, Alessandro Farnese, who took the title of Paul III (1534), a new era began; and at last the party of Catholic reformers found their opportunity. One of the first acts of the new Pope was to confer a Cardinal's hat upon Gasparo Contarini; and soon after Caraffa, Sadoleto, and Pole also received the sacred purple. The leaders among the Catholic reformers were summoned to Rome. On January 30, 1536, a Bull was read in the Consistory for the reform of many of the papal offices, but it was not published; and in the summer of the same year Paul appointed a commission of nine to report on the reforms that were needful. The nine members of the commission were Contarini, Caraffa, Sadoleto, Giberti, Pole, Aleander, Federigo Fregoso, Gregorio Cortese, and the Master of the Sacred Palace, Tommaso Badia. Their report presented in 1537 is the well-known *Consilium delectorum cardinalium et aliorum praelatorum de emendanda ecclesia*. The great principle to which they return again and again is that laws ought not to be dispensed with save for grave cause, and that even then no money should be taken for dispensation. To the system of money payments they trace the chief evils of the Roman Court. Everything could be obtained for money, however hurtful it might be to the general welfare of the Church. The report does not confine itself to the evils at the fountain-head. The whole Church was infected with corruption. Unfit persons were habitually ordained and admitted to benefices. Pensions and charges were imposed upon the revenues of benefices which made it impossible for the holder to live an honest life. Expectatives and reservations had a demoralising effect. Residence was generally neglected by the Bishops and clergy; and exemptions from the authority of the Ordinary enabled leaders of scandalous lives to persist in their wickedness. The regular clergy were no better than the seculars. Scandals were frequent in the religious Houses; and the privileges of the Orders enabled unfit persons to hear confessions. The Cardinals were as bad as the Bishops with regard to residence, and accumulated offices in their persons. Indulgences were excessive in number, and superstitious practices were too often encouraged. Much evil had followed from the granting of marriage dispensations; and absolutions for the sin of simony could be obtained for a mere song. In Rome itself the services were slovenly conducted and the whole priesthood was sordid. Loose women were openly received even in the houses of Cardinals. Unbelief grew apace, and unnecessary disputations on trivial points disturbed the faith of the vulgar. It was the duty of the Mother and Mistress of all Churches to lead the way in the amending of these evils.

Simultaneously with the appointment of this remarkable commission for reform Paul III published a Bull (May 29, 1536), summoning a General Council to meet at Mantua in May, 1537; and a Bull of Reformation was published in September, 1536. But the renewal of war prevented the Council from assembling, and its meeting was deferred. Meanwhile little was done to carry out the proposals of the reform commission. It was decided on the suggestion of the Cardinal of Capua, Nicholas Schomberg, not to publish the report, as it revealed so many grave scandals in connexion with the Holy See. The document was however privately printed in Rome, and by some means a copy reached Germany. It was republished there with scoffing comments. This incident shows that there was little chance of any papal attempts at reform being regarded in Germany as seriously intended. A beginning was indeed made at Rome. The offices of the Datary, the Chancery, and the Penitentiary were overhauled ; and a report signed by Contarini, Caraffa, Aleander, and Badia — the "*Consilium quattuor delectorum a Paulo III super Reformatione sanctae Romanae Ecclesiae*"—was in the autumn of 1537 presented to the Pope.

But in reality little seems to have been done. The General Council never met at Mantua. The Duke did not desire its presence in his territory ; and the war between Charles and Francis made it practically impossible. The Council was then summoned to meet at Vicenza on May 1, 1538, but it again had to be postponed. It soon became clear that the Pope's zeal for reform was rapidly waning. Contarini did his best to stir him up to action. In his "*Epistola de potestate Pontificis in usu clavium*" and in his "*De potestate Pontificis in compositionibus*" he emphasised the propositions that the Papacy was a sacred charge, and that its powers were to be used for the good of the Church and not to its destruction. In all Contarini's writings the conception of the Papacy as a monarchy and not a tyranny appears. It is a monarchy over freemen, and its powers are to be used according to the light of reason. Though the Catholic reformers held strongly to the divine mission of the Papacy in the Church, they distinguished carefully between the legitimate and the illegitimate exercise of its authority. Freely the Papacy had received, freely it should give. The whole official system of the Curia with its fees and extortions had become a scandal. An iniquitous traffic in sacred things had grown up. Contarini appealed to the Pope to root out effectively this canker, which was destroying the spiritual life of the Church. In November, 1538, Contarini travelled with Paul III to Ostia, and they discussed his writings. "Our good old man," as Contarini calls him in a letter to Pole, made him sit by his side, and talked with him about the reform of the *compositiones*. The Pope informed him that he had read his treatise, and spoke to him with such Christian feeling that his hopes were thus awakened anew at the moment when he was about to give way to despair.

Sarpi doubts the sincerity of Paul III with regard to reform. He believes that the Pope took up various projects of reform merely as an excuse to prove that a Council was unnecessary. But Sarpi's prejudice always blinds him to any good action on the part of a Pope ; and there is little doubt that Paul was in earnest in wishing to remove the graver abuses of the papal Court. But he was an old man when he ascended the papal throne, and his energy did not increase with years ; moreover, he was not a zealot, possessed with one overmastering idea. The interests of his family, his own personal comfort, and the dignity of the Holy See, were to him things that were not to be lightly risked in the carrying out of any scheme of reform.

Nothing came immediately of his talk with Contarini in the autumn of 1538; but in the spring of 1540 a fresh, and, as it appeared, a more energetic beginning of reform was made in Rome. In April Giberti was summoned from his diocese to give the Sacred College the benefit of his experience; and commissions were appointed for carrying out reforms in the Apostolic Chamber, the Rota, the Chancery, and the Penitentiary. The hopes with which the pontificate had begun were fully revived. Giovanni Morone, the papal Nuncio in Germany, had again and again in his letters pressed upon the Pope the necessity of a Council and of energetic measures of reform, if the Church was to be saved in Germany. Morone's instructions ordered him to be as conciliatory as possible; and it seemed that moderate men on both sides might arrange an understanding. The proposal of Faber, the Bishop of Vienna, to condemn as heretical a series of propositions selected from Lutheran writers, was disapproved of by the Pope. The failure so far of the attempts to assemble a General Council made Charles fall back on a series of national conferences, in which endeavours were made to find some common terms of agreement that might serve as a basis for the action of the Ecumenical Council when it should meet.

It was in pursuance of this policy that the famous Religious Colloquy took place at Ratisbon in April, 1541, after preliminary meetings at Hagenau (June, 1540) and at Worms (November, 1540). The detailed story of the negotiations belongs to the history of Germany; but the discussions which took place are of interest to us as showing the extent of the reconstruction of the Church system to which the most liberal of the Catholic reformers were prepared to consent. Agreement was arrived at on the fundamental articles of Original Sin, Free Will, and Justification. With regard to the last, a neutral formula was arrived at midway between the Lutheran doctrine and that formulated later at Trent. Justification was two-fold, and depended both on "inherent" and on "imputed" righteousness. It was attained by faith; but that faith must be living and active. The marriage of priests might be permitted but not encouraged, as also communion in both kinds. On the general doctrine of the Sacraments, and especially on the doctrine of the Eucharist, agreement was found more difficult; and when the papal prerogatives came on for discussion a clear divergence of opinion showed itself. It was clear that, after concessions on both sides, a considerable gulf still remained between them. Moreover, even if the peacemakers could come to terms, there were still Luther and the Pope to reckon with. Luther was suspicious, even unduly suspicious, of all papal advances; and he refused to believe in the sincerity of proposals in which his old adversary Eck had a share. The Pope, on the other hand, unhesitatingly rejected any ambiguous definition of the papal prerogative and of the doctrine of the Sacraments; and the agreement on Justification was viewed with suspicion in Rome, and only tolerated after much explanation. It was clear that no final settlement could be carried at the conference, which was accordingly brought to an end by the Emperor at the beginning of June, 1541.

Something at any rate had been gained, and the beginnings of a peaceful solution had been made. That complete success should have been attained at Ratisbon was probably impossible from the first. The exigencies of the political situation at the time made it the interest of the enemies of Charles to prevent a settlement of the religious difficulties, which it was feared would strengthen his hands. Moreover it was clear that the Catholic reformers were no longer as united as they had been; and their influence over the Pope was evidently lessening. Caraffa was drifting apart from his colleagues, and was rapidly becoming the leader of a party whose spirit was very different from that of the gracious idealists with whom he had been associated. The future of Catholicism lay in the balance; and the next few years would determine for centuries the attitude of the Roman Church towards the modern world, its politics, and its thought. It may be that when the Colloquy of Ratisbon took place it was already too late to save the unity of the Church in Germany. But to contemporaries even that did not seem quite hopeless. It was difficult for men living in the midst of the drama to realise how far the world had moved from its old orbit and how few of the old landmarks remained. To declare dogmatically, however, that the attempt at compromise made at Ratisbon was doomed to failure from the first is to assume that Protestantism and Catholicism had already taken up the definite positions which they reached at the end of the century. In the case of Catholicism, however, it was only after a struggle, the issue of which was long doubtful, that its attitude was definitely determined.

The revival of religious life combined with a strict adherence to the old scholastic dogma — the feeling, as Carnesecchi put it, that men had the Catholic religion, and only desired that it should be better preached — revealed itself first in an awakening of the old religious Orders and the formation of others to meet new needs. The numerous exemptions from episcopal jurisdiction possessed by the old Orders had given rise to many grave abuses, and contributed to the slackening of their spiritual life. Spain, the home of religious orthodoxy united with religious zeal, led the way in reform. The achievement of national unity at the end of the fifteenth century brought with it a revival of the Spanish Church. The State used the Church for its own purposes, and the royal authority became all powerful. The Spanish hierarchy, though always fervently Catholic, was never ultramontane. Papal interference was carefully limited; and, with the aid of the revived Inquisition, Ximenes reformed the Spanish Church. The religious Orders were brought under control; and the morals of the Spanish clergy soon compared favourably with those of the rest of Christendom. A revival of Scholasticism in its Thomist form took place, of which the great Dominican Melchior Cano became later the chief exponent. Stress was laid upon the divine right of the episcopate. Bishops were not merely curates of the Pope. The nobler sides of medieval Christianity were again displayed to the world by the Spanish Church. The darker side, the horrors of the Inquisition, the intellectual intolerance and narrow outlook on life, the deficient sense of human freedom and the rights of conscience, were there also; but in a narrower sphere the seeds were being sown of one of the greatest religious revivals the world has seen. The line which events took in Spain could not fail in time to react upon the Catholic reform movement in Italy; and that reaction became more and more powerful. The inspiration of the movement in Italy was at first indigenous; but in time the gloomy fanaticism of Spain overshadowed it and crushed out its more humane elements.

But in its beginnings the movement was a spontaneous expression of the single desire to make the Catholic religion once more a reality. With many it took the form of a restoration of the primitive austerity of the older Orders. Gregorio Cortese recalled to its ideal the Italian Benedictine Congregation, reorganised in 1504, and impressed upon it its duty of supporting the Church by its learning. The Camaldolese, an offshoot of the Benedictines founded by St Romuald in the eleventh century, were reformed by Paolo Giustiniani, a member of a noble Venetian family. A number of these monks under his direction led an ascetic life at Massaccio, between Ancona and Camerino. After his death in 1528 Monte Corone became the centre of the new Congregation; and the Order spread rapidly throughout Southern Europe. The old monastic Orders, however, only set an example which, powerful for good though it was, went but a little way in restoring Catholicism among the people. It was reserved for the Franciscans and for new religious societies to bring about a revival of popular religion. In 1526 Matteo de' Bassi was authorised by Clement VII to found a reformed branch of Franciscans, pledged to revive the simple rule of their founder. They came to be known as Capuchins from their garb. Simple and superstitious, they appealed to the populace; and they became the spiritual guides and counsellors of the people. Religion was vulgarised in their hands, and their influence was not altogether for good. Some of them embraced Protestant ideas; and for a time the Order was viewed with some suspicion. But to the Capuchins more than perhaps to any other organisation does the Roman Church owe the preservation of the mass of the Italian people in her fold.

The older Orders of monks and friars were, however, unequal by themselves to achieving the regeneration of Catholicism. The secular clergy in many parts had fallen into a lower state of degradation than the regulars; and it was one of the chief concerns of the Oratory of

Divine Love to bring the parish priests to a sense of their high calling. Two of the members of the Oratory, Gaetano da Thiene and Giovanni Pietro Caraffa, took the first active steps to effect this reformation. Gaetano da Thiene, of an ancient family of Vicenza, was one of the *pronotari participanti* at the papal Court under Julius II. The life, however, became distasteful to him, and he accordingly resigned his post and took orders. He was one of the earliest members of the Oratory. After a short time he left Rome and worked in Vicenza and Venice, preaching to the people and doing good works. His experience there taught him that the weakness of the Church was largely due to the inefficiency and corruption of the parochial clergy. Accordingly, in 1523, he returned to Rome with the idea of founding a society to remedy this evil. There he again met Caraffa, who at once fell in with his views; and the two worked together to achieve this end. The Canons Regular of St Augustine may have suggested to Gaetano da Thiene the Order which they obtained the permission of Clement VII to found in 1524.

The new society was to consist of ordinary secular clergy bound together by the three monastic vows. They were to be, in short, secular priests with the vows of monks. The reformation of the clergy and a life of contemplation were to be the objects of the society.

The new society is important, not so much on account of its own work among the secular clergy as for the example it set. It always remained small in numbers, and its membership came to be confined to the nobility. Though the original conception was due to Gaetano da Thiene, yet it was from Caraffa that the society took its name. It became known as the Order of Theatines after his see of Chieti (Theate). It was no doubt largely due to his administrative ability and power of organisation that the society was a success. It found many imitators. A similar society of regular clerks was founded at Somasca in the Milanese, 1528, by Girolamo Miani, son of a Venetian senator ; and at Milan the order of Barnabites was established about 1530 by three noble ecclesiastics, Zaccaria, Ferrari, and Morigia. The Barnabites were extremely successful in their labours ; and their society carried into practice far and wide the scheme which Gaetano da Thiene had been the first to conceive for the improvement of the secular clergy.

Quietly and unostentatiously, with little active assistance from the papal Court, the regeneration of Catholicism in Italy was thus begun. Caraffa was the guiding genius in the work, so far as a movement which was so wide can be connected with a single man ; and it was pregnant with importance for the future that he was growing more and more estranged from the liberal Catholic reformers, with whom he had at one time worked in the Oratory of Divine Love. The path which Contarini and his friends were indicating, greater freedom in discipline, reduction of papal prerogative, and a considerable restatement of the traditional dogma, meant a break with the past which, when its full import dawned upon them, shocked Caraffa and those who clung to medieval Christianity. The Ratisbon proposals of 1541 opened their eyes, and the parting of the ways came. The group of Catholic reformers split in two; and the division paralysed for a time the work which had been begun with the *Consilium de emendanda ecclesia*. Until it was clear that a reform of morals would not entail any surrender of medieval theology and of the medieval system of Church government, Caraffa and his friends made impossible any general scheme of reform. The new Orders, the Theatines, the Barnabites, and the Capuchins, were restoring Catholicism rapidly on the old lines. Their work went steadily on, and meanwhile it was enough to wait. They were doing the work as Caraffa, and not as Contarini, wanted it to be done. The progress made, however, was not as rapid as might have been wished, until two agencies appeared upon the scene which became the most potent of the forces that regenerated Catholicism, and breathed into it a militant spirit, making all conciliation impossible. The Inquisition — the Holy Office for the Universal Church — and the Society of Jesus were the new organisations which achieved the work.

The Inquisition which was set up in Rome in 1542 by the Bull *Licet initio* was not new, but the adaptation of an old organisation to the changed conditions of the times. The tendency to persecute appeared in the Church in very early days, but its lawfulness was always challenged; and it was not until the eleventh and twelfth centuries that any deliberate attempt was made to persecute systematically. A wave of heresy then passed over western Europe. Dualism and Manichaeism, always prevalent in the East, obtained a firm footing in the West; and the south of France became their stronghold. The Church became alarmed at the spread of ideas which not only were subversive of Christian faith but threatened the foundations of society and morals. The crusading spirit was diverted from the infidel to the heretic. The Albigensian crusade achieved its purpose. But something more was needed than an occasional holy war upon heresy. The work was taken in hand at first by the new episcopal Courts, which were beginning to administer the recently codified Canon Law in every diocese. But their action was spasmodic; and in the thirteenth century their efforts were reinforced by a papal Inquisition entrusted to the Dominican and Franciscan Orders. It was regulated by the papal Legates and its authority was enforced by provincial Councils. The Papacy however never had complete control of it; and side by side with it the old episcopal Inquisition went on. The episcopate viewed the papal Inquisition with jealousy, and in the fourteenth century succeeded to some extent in limiting its powers. In the fifteenth century its work was done and its activity ceased. It had stamped out heresy in Central

Europe at an awful expenditure of human life and at the cost of a complete perversion of the spirit of Christianity.

At the moment however when it was about to disappear Spain asked for its introduction into that country. The problem of the Moors and the Jews prompted the request; and on November 1, 1477, Sixtus IV authorised Ferdinand and Isabella to set up the Inquisition in their States. The Papacy consented with reluctance; and both Sixtus IV and Innocent VIII reserved a right of appeal to the Holy See. But they were both obliged to give way; and by a brief of August 23, 1497, Alexander VI finally abandoned the claim.

The Spanish Inquisition thus, though founded by Rome, did not remain under its direct control. The Spanish monarchy was responsible for it and used it as an instrument of State, though at times the terrific engine which it had created got beyond its control. The thoroughness with which Torquemada did his work achieved its object; and when Ximenes became Chief Inquisitor in 1507 the fierceness of persecution to some extent relaxed. It was this third or Spanish form of the Inquisition the success of which suggested to Caraffa the setting up of an Inquisition in Rome to supervise the whole Church. The idea was warmly supported by Ignatius Loyola; and accordingly Paul III, by a Bull of July 21, 1542, set up the Holy Office of the Universal Church. Six Cardinals were appointed commissioners, and were given powers as Inquisitors in matters of faith on both sides of the Alps. The Papacy thus provided itself with a centralised machinery, which enabled it to supervise the measures taken for checking the spread of the new opinions. Pius IV and Pius V extended the powers of the Inquisition, and its organisation reached its most developed form under Sixtus V, who by the Bull *Immensa* remodelled it along with the other Roman congregations. The number of Cardinals composing it was increased to twelve; and there were in addition a Commissary, an Assessor, and a body of Consultors, who were chosen from among canonists and theologians. Besides these officials, there were numerous Qualificators who gave their opinion on questions submitted to them. There were also an advocate charged with the defence of accused persons, and other subordinates. The Roman Inquisition not only proceeded against any persons directly delated to it, but also heard appeals from the sentences of Courts of the Inquisition in other localities. Inquisitors were in addition sent by it to any place where they appeared to be needed.

Though the sphere of active work of the Roman Inquisition was confined to Italy, it achieved the purpose, not only of stamping out Protestantism in the peninsula, but of bringing back the old intolerant spirit into the government of the Church. Conciliation and confessions of failure could not go hand in hand with the Inquisition. The failure of Contarini at Ratisbon in 1541, followed by the establishment of the Inquisition in 1542, marks the active beginning of the Counter-Reformation in its narrower sense. A restoration of Catholicism by violence and irresistible force was beginning, which was driving the party of conciliation from the field and rendering all their endeavours useless. The proposals of the peacemakers were belied by the actions of the Inquisition.

The Society of Jesus was the second of the two great organisations which rose up to save the tottering Church. What the papal Inquisition did for Italy the Society of Jesus did for the Catholic Church throughout the world. Where force could not be used, persuasion and the subtler forms of influence were possible; and in the Society of Jesus the most powerful missionary organisation the world has ever seen was placed at the disposal of the Papacy. With rapidity little short of marvellous the Society spread not only throughout Europe but to China and the Indies, and became one of the chief powers in the counsels of the Church. Jesuit Fathers moulded to a considerable extent the dogmatic decrees at Trent. The emergence of the Papacy from the ordeal of the Council, with its prerogative increased rather than diminished, was largely due to their efforts.

Don Inigo Lopez de Recalde, their founder, was born in 1491 at the castle of Loyola in Guipuzcoa. He served as a page at the Court of Ferdinand of Aragon, and his youth and early manhood were devoted to the profession of arms. A severe wound which he received at the siege of Pampeluna in 1521 lamed him for life. During a long and painful period of convalescence there fell into his hands several books dealing with the life of Christ and the heroic deeds of the Saints. So deep an impression was made upon his mind that he determined to devote himself entirely to the service of God and transfer his allegiance from an earthly to a heavenly army. Restored to health early in 1522, he set out as a knight errant of Christ and the Virgin. We hear of him first at Montserrat at a shrine of the Virgin famous throughout Spain. But his stay here was short, and we next find him at Manresa not far from Montserrat. At Manresa, according to the traditional story, Ignatius had his celebrated vision lasting for eight days, in which the plan of his society was revealed to him and the method which he worked out in his *Spiritual Exercises*. There is reason to believe, however, that the evolution of his great idea was a very gradual process, and that he owed more to others than his disciples have been usually willing to admit. At any rate we know for certain that he left Manresa early in 1523 as a pilgrim for the Holy Land. He had already conceived the idea of founding a great society for the service of the Church. But its exact nature was not yet at all clear in his mind. Ignatius had little knowledge of the great world and its needs. To a Spaniard war with the infidel was an obvious idea; and it is not surprising that the reconquest of Jerusalem should occur to him at the first as the most laudable object for his society. His stay at Jerusalem was not, however, very successful. A reckless enthusiast might cause trouble amidst a Mohammedan population; and Ignatius was refused permission to remain in Jerusalem and returned to Venice in 1524.

But the long journey had left its mark on his mind. He perceived his ignorance of the world and his lack of education, and he determined to do his best to remedy these defects. From 1524 to 1528 he studied at the Universities of Barcelona, Alcalà, and Salamanca; and in 1528 he proceeded to the University of Paris. It has been suggested that fear of the Inquisition prompted him to this step; for twice, once at Alcalà and once at Salamanca, he had fallen under its suspicion and narrowly escaped condemnation. At Paris Ignatius proceeded more cautiously; and the seven years of his stay there mark the crisis of his life when the visionary and enthusiast developed into an organiser and leader of men. Patiently and quietly, accepting no rebuff, he gathered round him one by one a little band whom he had infected with his enthusiasm. Pierre Lefèvre, a Savoyard, was his first disciple. Through him he obtained an influence over Francis Xavier, the future Apostle of the Indies, though he was no easy conquest. Diego (Jacobus) Laynez and Alfonso Salmeron, both Spaniards, were the next converts; and Nicholas Bobadilla and Simon Rodriguez soon followed. On August 15, 1534, the seven of them heard mass and received the communion in the church at Montmartre and made a vow of poverty and chastity. They also solemnly bound themselves to go to Jerusalem for the glory of God when they had finished their courses at the University; but, if it was found impossible to do so within a year, they agreed to throw themselves at the feet of the Holy Father and place themselves absolutely at his disposal.

Accordingly in 1537 they left Paris and went to Venice with the object of reaching the Holy Land. On the eve of their leaving Paris Lefèvre had gained three fresh recruits, Claude le Jay, Jean Codure, and Pasquier-Brouet; when Ignatius, who had meanwhile visited Spain, rejoined his companions, the little band had thus increased to ten. They, however, found it impossible to proceed to Jerusalem in consequence of the war with the Turks, and therefore, in accordance with their vow, determined to offer their services to the Pope. It was at Venice that Caraffa and Ignatius met, and it is probable that it was Caraffa's influence which brought home to Ignatius that there was more important work for him and his disciples nearer home. The infidel was at the time less of a danger to the Church than the heretic; and, just as in the middle ages the transition from a crusade against the one to a crusade against the other was easy, so now it was not difficult to persuade Ignatius that his true mission was the extirpation of Protestantism and the expulsion of half-hearted brethren.

Caraffa would have wished Ignatius and his disciples to unite themselves to his favourite Order of Theatines, but to this Ignatius would in no way consent. He felt his own peculiar mission vividly, and what were to be the characteristic features of his Institute were rapidly taking shape in his mind. Though displeased by the refusal of Ignatius to conform to his wishes, Caraffa none the less gave him every encouragement. Caraffa's later dislike of the Society when he was Pope was due to deeper causes than Ignatius' refusal to throw in his lot with him. The diplomatic skill which had marked Ignatius ever since he left Spain in 1528 displayed itself in the caution with which he approached the Holy See. Accompanied by Lefèvre and Laynez, he determined to visit Rome, leaving his other companions to carry on in northern Italy the work of preaching and teaching and the gathering of fresh disciples, which they had begun in Venice. He felt it was necessary to survey the ground at Rome before attempting to settle there. On his journey Ignatius had a vision in a little church not far from Rome, which shows that the worldly wisdom which he had acquired had not dimmed his sense of a divine mission. God appeared to him in this wayside sanctuary, and he heard a voice saying, "*Ego vobis Romae propitius ero.*"

It was October, 1539, when the three enthusiasts reached Rome. Reform was in the air ; and, though, as we have seen, little was done to carry out the suggestions of the *Consilium de emendanda ecclesia*, yet Paul III was ready to give every encouragement to any scheme for the improvement of the Church which did not call for any great self-denial on the part of the Papacy itself. Ignatius and his companions were accordingly favourably received and authorised to preach a reform of manners in Rome. The door thus being opened, Ignatius felt that the time had come to summon his other disciples to join him. At Easter, 1538, the little band were again united ; and the work which they had begun in northern Italy was extended to Rome. Contarini, as well as Caraffa, welcomed new allies and became their protector. It only remained for Ignatius and his friends to draw up a definite Rule and to obtain confirmation from the Pope.

A supplication was accordingly drawn up indicating the objects and constitution of their proposed Society. Their petition was referred to a committee of three Cardinals, with Guidiccioni at its head, who at first reported unfavourably on the scheme. The needs of the day required the reform or suppression of existing religious Orders rather than the creation of new. Ignatius was however not discouraged. He worked on ; and at length on September 27, 1540, the opposition was overcome, and by the Bull *Regimini militantis ecclesiae* the Society of Jesus was founded. The Bull contained a recitation of the petition of Ignatius and his companions ; and it is the only certain authority in our possession from which we can learn the nature of his plan in its early form. The first thing which strikes the reader is that, while the objects of the Society are clearly indicated, its constitution is only vaguely outlined.

Its members are to bear arms in the service of Christ and of the Roman Pontiff, His Vicar, to whom they are to take a special vow of obedience. They are to be the militia of the Holy See, devoting themselves to its service whenever it may direct. As preachers and directors of consciences they are to work for the propagation of the faith, and above all by means of the education of the young. They are to take the vows of poverty and chastity, and obedience to the General whom they set over themselves, in all things which concern the observance of their Rule.

The power granted to the General is unprecedented in its extent. The right of command belongs to him entirely. He is to decide for each his vocation and define his work. This is the only indication in the Bull of the elaborate hierarchy of degrees which appears in the later constitution of the Society. At the same time this apparently absolute power granted to the General is limited by the fact that in certain cases he is to take the advice of his council, which is to consist, in important matters, of the greater part of the Society, while in affairs of less moment those members who happen to be in his immediate neighbourhood alone need be consulted. Here, and in the insistence on a period of probation before admission to the Society, there is an apparent approximation to the constitutions of the older religious Orders, in which, however much stress might be laid on the duty of obedience to authority, that authority was always bound to act in a canonical and constitutional way. If then the scheme laid before Paul III contained the germ from which the matured constitution of the Society was to grow, yet there were also present in it elements which disguised the extent to which the Society was a new departure. The language of Ignatius' petition is not inconsistent in its main features with the future constitution of the Society, but it did not necessarily imply it. The unique nature of the new organisation was not fully realised by the officials of the Roman Court. The limitation of the number of members to sixty, which was inserted in the Bull, may however show that they did not intend it to grow to unmanageable size until its tendencies revealed themselves more clearly.

On April 4, 1541, six out of the original ten members of the Society, who were then in Rome — Ignatius, Laynez, Salmeron, Le Jay, Pasquier-Brouet, and Codure — met to elect their General. The four who were absent with the exception of Bobadilla had sent their votes in writing. Ignatius was unanimously elected. He, however, refused the honour ; but he was again elected on April 7. At last on April 17 he gave way ; and on April 22 he received the vows of his companions at the church of San Paolo *fuori le mura*. Thus began the generalate of Ignatius, which lasted until his death on July 31, 1556. The fame of the new Order soon spread throughout the Catholic world, and many fresh members were admitted to its ranks. A second Bull (*Injunctum nobis*) was obtained from Paul III, dated March 14, 1543, which repealed the clause of the former Bull limiting the number of members to sixty. Meanwhile Ignatius continued to work at the Constitutions; and the experience which he gained during the first years of the Society's existence no doubt unconsciously modified his scheme for its government. The great increase in the number of members — an increase which he himself did not altogether welcome — with the consequent mixture of heterogeneous elements in the Society, made it advisable to strengthen the authority of the General and to weaken still further those checks on his power which appear in the petition of 1540. In no other way could the unity of action of the Society be preserved. Judging from the part played after the death of Ignatius by Laynez, it is extremely probable that this development was largely due to his influence.

However this may be, the change undoubtedly took place; and by a Bull of Paul III of October 18, 1549 (*Licet debitum pastoralis officii*), and by a Bull of Julius III of July 21, 1550 (*Exposcit pastoralis officii*), the power of the General's Council was still further limited and other changes were made in the original plan. It is clear from the language of both these Bulls that, though further drafts of the Constitutions had been laid before the Papal authorities, Ignatius had not yet reduced them to their final form. From the Bull of Julius III it is evident that the system of a series of degrees in the Society was already shaping itself, but that the government of the Society had not yet become the system of absolutism it afterwards became.

Julius III (1550–5) was kindly disposed towards Ignatius; and during his pontificate the *Collegium Romanum* and the *Collegium Germanicum* were set up in Rome, to both of which he granted an annual subsidy. His successor Marcellus II, the Cardinal of Santa Croce, had been one of the Legates at Trent. It was due to his influence that Laynez and Salmeron were present at the Council as the theologians of the Pope. With Marcellus the Counter-Reformation ascended the papal throne; and the Jesuits appeared about to become the predominant influence in the Roman Court. But he died three weeks after his election, and was succeeded by Caraffa, who took the title of Paul IV. The new Pope immediately displayed hostility to the Order. A domiciliary visit was paid to the Gesù and a search made for arms. Paul's hostility to Spain made him suspect a body which had such close relations with that country. He, however, employed Laynez in connexion with his schemes for reform; and it was only after the death of Ignatius that he interfered in the internal affairs of the Society.

Laynez was elected Vicar-General on August 3, 1556, to administer the affairs of the Society until the Congregation could assemble to elect a new General, and to approve the Constitutions which Ignatius had left. For various reasons the meeting of the General Congregation seems to have been delayed; and Laynez spent the time in preparing a final edition of the Institute for submission for its approval. Dissensions meanwhile broke out ; Laynez was accused of purposely deferring the meeting of the General Congregation in his own interests. Bobadilla, Rodriguez, and Pasquier-Brouet were the leaders of the opposition. They appealed to the Pope against the arbitrary conduct of the Vicar-General, and requested that the government of the Society during the interregnum might rest with the Council of the Society. The Pope then called upon Laynez to bring before him the Constitutions and rules of the Society. Cardinal Carpi was appointed to enquire into the matter. His report recommended the confirmation of Laynez as Vicar-General, but advised that in future he should be obliged to consult the Council. Laynez, however, managed to obtain from the Pope a second enquiry, which was conducted by Cardinal Ghislieri, the future Pius V. It is not clear what the exact result of this second enquiry was, but Laynez skilfully managed to divide the opposition and paralyse its efforts. At length on June 19, 1558, the General Congregation met ; and July 2 was appointed for the election of the new General. Twenty Fathers were present. Cardinal Pachecho superintended the election by order of the Pope, and Laynez was elected by thirteen votes out of twenty. The assembly then proceeded to approve the Constitutions in the form they were presented to it by Laynez.

Laynez had apparently won a great triumph. He had quelled the opposition to his authority. He had persuaded the assembly to accept the Latin version by Polanco of Ignatius' Institute, by which the absolute power of the General was secured. But he had reckoned without the Pope. When Paul IV heard that the General Congregation had confirmed the Constitutions of the Society without consulting him and were about to adjourn, he sent Cardinal Pachecho to demand the insertion of two alterations in the Rule. In the first place, the Jesuits were to be bound to recite the offices of the Church in choir as other religious Orders were bound to do ; and in the second place, the office of General was to be for three years only and not for life. Paul IV evidently feared the power which the Constitutions of the Society would give to an able man to wield as he thought fit. The Society might become an *imperium in imperio*. The "black Pope" might become a dangerous power behind the throne. If we read the story in the light of the later history of the Society, this is not an improbable interpretation of the action of Paul IV.

Laynez saw there was nothing to do but submit. The General Congregation bowed to the wishes of the Holy Father and dispersed. The two alterations of the Rule were not incorporated in it, but are printed as an appendix to the edition published at Rome in December, 1558. Laynez could do nothing but wait for better times. They were not long in coming. On August 18, 1559, Paul IV died and was succeeded by Pius IV. who did not share his predecessor's dislike of the Order. Laynez seized a favourable opportunity of bringing before the Society the question whether a mere informal order of a Pope was binding on them ; but they considered it better to bring the matter directly before Pius IV, who revoked the order of his predecessor so far as that was necessary. The Papacy thus gave way in its first struggle with the Society which was to be so often more a master than a servant.

It has been necessary to describe at considerable length the early history of the government of the Society, in order to show how gradually it revealed its true nature to the world, and that absolutism did not triumph without considerable opposition in the Society itself. The new institution, however, from its very beginning, was the expression of the principle of blind obedience to authority. Other Orders had inculcated it as a virtue ; but none had provided so searching a discipline by which complete ascendancy could be attained over its disciples. Moreover its purpose was not merely to produce Christian humility and the spirit of self-denial in the individual. It was to make each member a ready instrument for the purposes of the Society in its warfare with the world. A practical object was always the end in view — the triumph of the Church over hostile forces, the conquest of the hosts of Satan whatever form they might assume. A perpetual warfare was to be waged, and success could only be obtained by faithful obedience to orders. The theory of this discipline is developed in the *Spiritual Exercises* of St Ignatius, a work of genius in devotional literature. Though it owes its form to a considerable extent to the *Exercitatorio de la vida espiritual* of Dom Garcia de Cisneros, the Benedictine Abbot of Montserrat, published in 1500, which Ignatius no doubt found in use at the convent at Montserrat during his stay there, and to the writings of mystics such as Gerard Zerbold of Zutphen and Mauburnus (Johannes Momboir), members of the Brotherhood of the Common Life, which he probably met with during his stay in Paris, yet it is no mere compilation. The spirit which breathes through its pages differs from that which distinguishes most mystical writings, in that the absorption of the soul in God is not to be the end of action but the source of inspiration for further work. The moral paralysis of pantheism, the danger of all mystics, is avoided. According to the plan of the work the meditations are divided into four main divisions or weeks. In the first period the course of the meditations is conducted so as to produce in the neophyte a kind of hypnotism, a passive state in which he will be ready to receive the impressions that it is desired to make upon him. In the second week the glories of the Heavenly King and the privileges of His service are set before the disciple. The armies of Christ and Satan are contrasted, and the demands that God makes upon men are set forth. The third and fourth weeks are devoted to meditation upon the sacred story, the life and passion of Christ, and the enormity of human sin ; and finally the eternal joys of heaven are set before the disciple. To gain them he must give up liberty and the freedom of thinking for himself. Absolute obedience to the bride of Christ, the Church, its doctrines and its life, is the only way of salvation.

Such was the ideal which Ignatius set before the world in the *Spiritual Exercises;* and its spirit was faithfully reproduced in his Society. The *Spiritual Exercises* became the Bible of the Order and moulded its religious life. The novice on admission was trained in its method. He lost his personality to find it again only in the Society. He himself was but raw material for the Society to mould as it would. All his faculties were to be developed, but the initiative was never left to him. The life of the Society was a life of mutual supervision and subordination. That there were diversities of gifts was fully recognised, but no man might be the judge of his own capabilities. The Society, through its General and those appointed by him, apportioned to each his work. The novices were distinguished according as they were selected for the priesthood or for secular duties ; while those whose vocation was not yet clear formed a separate class called "indifferents." After a novitiate of two years, promotion was given to the grade of "scholastics." Those who belonged to this class spent some five years in the study of arts, and then acted themselves as teachers of junior classes for a similar period. The study of theology followed for four or five years ; and then admission might be given to the rank of spiritual coadjutors. Others however were confined to the rank of temporal coadjutors. They were employed in the service of the Society and ministered to its needs, and may be compared to the lay-brethren of other Orders. The great majority of members of the Society never passed beyond the rank of spiritual coadjutor. They took part in all the missionary work of the Society, in preaching and teaching. The heads of its Colleges and Residences were taken from this class ; but they had no share in the government of the Society, which was confined to the "Professed of the Four Vows," who were the Society in the strictest sense of the word. Besides the three ordinary vows, they took one of special allegiance to the Pope, undertaking to go whithersoever he might order. The higher offices of the Society were confined to them. Their number was always small in comparison with the total membership of the Society; and at the death of Ignatius they only numbered thirty-five. There was also a small class called the "Professed of the Three Vows," which only differed from that of the spiritual coadjutors in that the vows were taken in a more solemn way. It was reserved for those who were admitted into the Society for exceptional purposes.

At the head of this elaborate hierarchy stood the General. His power was absolute so far as the ordinary affairs of the Society were concerned ; but he could not alter its constitution except with the consent of the General Congregation. An intricate system of checks and counter-checks guarded against any part of the huge machine getting beyond his control, a system to which to some extent he also was subject. Six assistants were appointed to keep a watch upon him, and the possibility of his deposition was provided for. Espionage and delation permeated the whole Society. Absolute as his authority was, the General felt that in the Society there was a great impersonal force behind him, which prevented him from departing from the spirit of the founder.

Admirably fitted as such an organisation was, with its combination of adaptability and stability, to carry on the work of the Society with the least possible friction, yet it was inevitable that the influx of able men into the Society should lead to a variety of ideas. The intended unity of thought as well as action could only be partially enforced, and the abler minds could not be made to think alike. A considerable Spanish opposition arose in the Society, which criticised what it thought to be certain evil tendencies in the body. Mariana wrote a work on the defects of the Order; and the theory of morals, which Pascal criticised, did not become prevalent in the Society without a struggle. But in its first and golden age such division as there was did not weaken to any appreciable extent its unity of action, and it offered an unbroken front to the enemies of the Church.

The spread of the Society's organisation and the ubiquity of its members in the first years of its existence were remarkable. The Latin countries, Italy, Spain, and Portugal, were soon covered with a network of its institutions; and Jesuit Fathers became an influence in the counsels of Princes. North of the Alps progress was less rapid. In Southern Germany and Austria a foothold was obtained; but it was not until after the final dissolution of the Council of Trent that much progress was made there. In France considerable opposition had to be overcome before the Society could obtain an entry at all; and its afterwards famous College of Clermont long lived a precarious existence. Candid critics in the Church were not wanting. Melchior Cano called the Jesuits the precursors of Antichrist; and St Carlo Borromeo in his later years viewed with suspicion the power and tendencies of the Society. Great as their importance became, almost immediately after their foundation, in the councils of the Church, their missionary influence, at any rate outside the Latin countries, is commonly antedated. Their educational system, which was a great advance on anything which had gone before, was only gradually developed; and by means of it their greatest services to the Church were rendered. During the years in which the Council of Trent sat, and in those immediately preceding, it was the Inquisition which was the most potent weapon in the hands of the Papacy. The Jesuits rendered yeoman service at the Council itself, and their day came when it was brought to a successful conclusion.

Such were the forces at work in the Church when at length circumstances allowed the long deferred Council to meet. The Christian Renaissance, with its ideal of the unity of faith and reason and its attempt to find a place within the Church for all that was best in the achievements of the human mind, its philosophy, its science, and its art, was rapidly being eclipsed by a new spirit, which claimed for Church authority complete control, and gave little scope to human freedom and self-realisation. The sacrifice of the intellect rather than its consecration was demanded. Mankind was to remain in bondage to the dead hand of the past. The progress that was being rapidly made in human knowledge was to be ignored. Catholicism was never to go beyond its medieval exponents. Conciliation and compromise with the new views was consequently treason, and " No surrender " was the cry.

Paul III stood aloof and looked on as the new power grew in strength and made itself felt in the Church. The last of the Renaissance Popes, he was liberal in his sympathies, but he never gave his whole confidence to any party. The reformed and tolerant Catholicism, which seemed about to prevail in the early years of his reign, found itself only partially supported, if not abandoned, and others were allowed to frustrate its efforts. Contarini, on his return to Italy after the Colloquy of Ratisbon, was rewarded with the government of Bologna, but his influence was gone. His death occurred soon after, on August 24, 1542, and he was spared the further disillusionment which the Council would have inevitably brought to him. He was one of the noblest figures in an age of great men, and the blessing of the peacemaker was his. Giberti survived him little more than a year, dying on December 30, 1543. The loss of Contarini and Giberti was an irreparable blow to the party of conciliation. Sadoleto, Pole, and Morone survived ; but none of them had the force of character to fight a losing cause ; and Pole and Morone ended their days in trying to vindicate their orthodoxy, the one by playing the part of a persecutor in England, the other by winding up the Council in the papal interest. For the time, however, Viterbo, of which Pole was governor, became the centre of the remnants of that little band which had first found a common bond in the Oratory of Divine Love. Everything now depended on the coming Council, and there was nothing but to await events.

Though the Colloquy of Ratisbon had failed to achieve any permanent result, yet the Emperor did not altogether despair of conciliation. The varying circumstances of the political situation from time to time affected his attitude towards the Lutherans ; but he appears to have had a genuine desire all along for a thorough reformation of abuses in the Church by a General Council, from which the Roman Court itself was not to be exempt. Paul III, on the other hand, had little desire for a Council, at which it was clear, after the events at Ratisbon, that the papal prerogative was likely to be severely handled. It was impossible for him, however, to resist the demands of the Emperor altogether ; and, after an interview between them at Lucca, Paul III at length again agreed to summon a Council. Accordingly on May 22, 1542, a Bull was published summoning a General Council to meet at Trent on November 1, 1542. Trent was selected as the place of assembly, with the hope of satisfying the German demand that the Council should meet on German territory. Though the population of Trent was mainly Italian, it was within the Empire and under the protection of Charles' brother Ferdinand. At the same time it was easy of access to the Italian Bishops, and was not so far distant as to be beyond the Pope's control. It was an ecclesiastical principality under its Bishop, Christofero Madruzzo, Cardinal of Trent.

In August, 1542, Parisio, Morone, and Pole, the Legates appointed to open the Council, started for Trent; and the Council was duly opened on November 1. There were, however, only a few Italian prelates present; and, as no more arrived, by a Bull of July 6, 1543, the Pope again adjourned the Council. The war between Charles and Francis I again made the Council impossible; and at the Diet of Speier in 1544 it was agreed that all proceedings against the Lutherans should be stayed until a free and general Council could be held in Germany. Charles also promised to hold a Diet in which the religious questions should again be discussed and if possible arranged. The Lutherans were privately assured that an endeavour should be made to frame a scheme of comprehension, and that the Pope should not be allowed to stand in the way.

The proceedings at Speier seriously alarmed the Pope; and on August 5, 1544, he addressed a strong letter of remonstrance to the Emperor. The sin of Eli would be his, he wrote, if he did not lift up his voice against the unwarranted interference in the affairs of religion by the Emperor and the Diet. Toleration was pernicious, and the attempt to regulate the affairs of the Church in a national assembly largely composed of laymen unheard of. He was himself desirous of a reformation, and had declared this often by promising a Council; and it was the Emperor himself who, through the war, was hindering the one means which could restore the peace of Christendom. The Pope now saw that it was necessary for him to take active steps if the control of the situation was not to pass out of his hands. Unless something was done, Charles might be driven to follow the example of Henry VIII, and the German Church might fall away from the Holy See. The Council must be held in order to satisfy Charles, but it must be conducted with quite other objects than those contemplated by him. The formulation of doctrine should be its chief business. The old traditional doctrine of the Church must be laid down afresh so as to make all conciliation of the Protestants impossible. All discussion of the papal prerogatives must be avoided; and the reform of practical abuses must take quite a secondary place. Having enunciated the Church's doctrine, the Council might leave to the Holy Father the carrying out of such reforms as were necessary.

The Council in fact was to be used as an agent of the Counter-Reformation and as another means to the defeat of Protestantism.

All the resources of a skilful and patient diplomacy were now devoted to this end. A Bull was published on September 17, 1544, summoning the Council to meet on March 14, 1545; and Cardinal Alessandro Farnese was sent to Germany to come, if possible, to an understanding with the Emperor. On September 18, 1544, the Treaty of Crépy was signed, and it was no longer so essential to Charles to keep on good terms with the Lutherans. The Emperor and the Papacy soon began to draw nearer to one another. Charles refused to confirm the rights of the Lutherans without regard to the proceedings of the Council, but at the same time he proceeded with the greatest caution. He did not feel strong enough as yet to provoke a general contest with German Protestantism. The Turkish danger was again imminent, and the Imperial treasury was empty. It thus came about that, when at length the Papacy was willing to proceed actively with the Council, the Emperor on the other hand wished to defer it for a time, as it seemed likely to drive the Lutherans to desperation. Charles accordingly at the Diet of Worms in 1545 allowed the religious question to be again discussed, and proposed another colloquy of the theologians. Until the Diet was concluded he requested the Pope to defer the opening of the Council. Paul III vigorously protested against what was nothing short of an insult to the Council; and the negotiations proceeded. Charles even went so far as to propose the transference of the Council to a really German town, from Trent which was only German in name, and the Pope replied by threatening to translate it to Rome or Bologna. Charles then saw that further concession was necessary, as he could not afford to risk the hostility of the whole of Germany, which this transfer would inevitably provoke. In October, 1545, accordingly, after the conclusion of the Diet of Worms, he requested the Pope to open the Council as quickly as possible at Trent; and informed him that the religious negotiations at the Diet were not seriously intended, and that their only purpose was to deceive the Protestants until his military preparations were ready and he should be able to crush them.

The negotiations that led up to the opening of the Council thus ended in a triumph for the Papacy; and the Protestants had little to expect from a Council which began under such auspices. Their only hope lay in a conflict of interests between the Emperor and the Pope, and these Powers now appeared in close alliance. Their agreement was not however so close as it appeared, and the Papacy felt that only the first step had been gained. Charles, even when in alliance with the Pope, never intended the Council to content itself with a solemn publication of Catholic dogmas to the world. A reform of the Church in head and members was necessary, even if the wishes of the Protestants were to be ignored. Charles never had any intention of merely playing the papal game. The exigencies of the political situation would determine the extent of the concessions he would make to the Papacy ; and Paul III felt that it was no easy task which still lay before him.

Paul III deemed it unwise to preside in person at the Council. An old man of nearly eighty, the prospect of the journey and a lengthy sojourn at Trent was alone sufficient to deter him from the idea ; besides which it was better for the Papacy to avoid being directly involved in the struggle of parties which was inevitable at the Council. He accordingly appointed three Legates to preside over its meetings and to conduct the business. They were to keep in close communication with Rome, and no important matter was to be decided until he had been consulted. His choice fell upon Giovanni Maria del Monte, Marcello Cervini, Cardinal of Santa Croce, and Reginald Pole. Del Monte and Cervini were entirely devoted to the papal interest. The former was hasty and impatient, a worldly Cardinal of the unreformed papal Court. Cervini represented the party of Caraffa and the new Catholicism, intolerant, narrow, and uncompromising, but keenly anxious for the removal of moral abuses in the Church. Cervini, moreover, was a diplomatist of the first order ; and it was due to him that the numerous rocks and shoals on which the Papacy stood in danger of being wrecked during the Council were skilfully avoided. He prevented many a scene, which the haughtiness of del Monte had provoked, from becoming serious ; and none knew better how to pour oil on troubled waters. Pole was little more than a cipher from the beginning. His academic mind was helpless amidst the play of living forces in which he found himself ; and he had to acquiesce in the policy of his colleagues who had the Papacy behind them. His nomination as Legate was only intended to give the appearance of conciliation to the papal policy, and he felt himself helpless from the first. He spoke several times in favour of moderation, but soon lost heart. His ill health provided him with a convenient pretext to withdraw later from a scene in which he was doomed to be a failure. Great as was his intellectual ability, he had none of the qualities of a leader ; and he was unequal to playing the part that Contarini might have played in the Council.

On March 13, 1545, the Legates made their solemn entry into Trent. They had the vaguest instructions, and could do nothing but wait, while the negotiations mentioned above went on between Charles and the Pope. At length, when a favourable juncture seemed to have arrived, the Pope ordered them to open the Council on December 13, 1545, and bade a number of Italian Bishops make their way to Trent. The attendance at the opening ceremony was but meagre. Besides the Legates and Cardinal Madruzzo, the Bishop of Trent, only four Archbishops, twenty Bishops, and five Generals of Orders, with a small number of theologians, were present. Of the Bishops, five were Spanish and two French ; and Sweden, England, and Ireland were represented by one Bishop each.

Cardinal Madruzzo was the only prelate who in any sense could be said to represent the Empire ; and the rest were Italians.

The first three sessions were spent in making the necessary arrangements for the business of the Council. A division of opinion at once arose as to the exact title to be used. The proposal of the Legates, "*Sacrosancta Tridentina synodus in Spiritu sancto legitime congregata in ea praesidentibus tribus apostolicae sedis legatis,*" was not satisfactory to a portion of the Council ; and it was proposed to add the words "*universalem ecclesiam repraesentans.*" The intention of the amendment was to express the superiority of the Council even to the Pope, and to revive the memories of Constance and Basel. The Legates expressed their dislike of it to the Pope on these grounds, though in public they resisted it merely as being unnecessary ; and they succeeded in obtaining the rejection of the proposal. A question of more practical importance followed as to the right of voting. At Constance voting had been by nations ; and Abbots and theologians, as well as Bishops and Generals of Orders, were allowed to vote. The Bishops were, however, very jealous of their privileges ; and it was decided to confine the power of voting to Bishops and heads of religious Orders. The claim of absent Bishops to vote by proxy was rejected by the Legates by order of the Pope. Only Bishops "*in partibus*" might represent their diocesans. This was a great victory for the curial party. In the absence of voting by nations, it ensured a preponderant influence to the Italian Bishops, who were mostly blind adherents to the Papacy. Many of them were very poor and were in fact dependent upon the Legates for their daily bread. The papal pensions and the hope of being rewarded with lucrative offices kept them loyal to the Curia, the interests of which were largely their own.

It was from the Spanish Bishops on the other hand that the Legates had most to fear. Charles had issued peremptory orders for them to attend the Council ; and they became the backbone of the opposition to the pretensions of the Curia. The work of Ximenes had borne good fruit ; and the Spanish Bishops were the most learned and the ablest among the members of the Council. Their orthodoxy was unimpeachable, they had no sympathy with the wishes of the moderate party for conciliation in doctrine, but equally with them they were determined to maintain the supremacy of the Council to the Pope, and to remove the abuses of the papal Court. So alarmed were the Legates by their arrival and by the prospects of an increase in their number, that they wrote to the Pope urgently requesting that ten or twelve capable Italian Bishops of proved fidelity might be sent to the Council to resist them.

The divergence between the interests of the Curia with its Italian supporters and the foreign Fathers was plainly revealed when the order of business came to be determined. In his instructions to the Legates Paul III clearly laid down that reform was only a secondary and less important cause of the convocation of the Council. Its principal work was to be the definition of dogma. It was for this latter purpose that Paul III had consented to summon the Council. By proclaiming anew the old dogmas reconciliation with the Protestants would be rendered impossible; and before any reforms hostile to the papal interests could be undertaken it would probably be possible to bring the Council to an end. The Emperor and the Spanish Bishops, together with the few moderate and independent men among the Italians, had however no intention of meekly submitting to the indefinite postponement of the consideration of reform. When the Church had been purified, then the time would come for the discussion of questions of doctrine. Led by Cardinal Madruzzo, who represented the imperial views, they insisted on reform being taken in hand at once. The Legates were placed in a very difficult position and were afraid of risking an open defeat. Feeling ran so high in the Council, that an open revolt was likely if they insisted on beginning with the discussion of doctrine alone. They accordingly, at the suggestion of Thomas Campeggio, the Bishop of Feltre, proposed a compromise, that doctrine and reform should be treated at the same time by the separate commissions, and should come before the Council in alternation; and for this proposal, in spite of the opposition of Cardinal Madruzzo, they obtained a majority on January 22, 1546. The compromise was a partial defeat to the curial party and revealed the strength of the opposition. The Pope was furious and called upon the Legates to get the decision rescinded. The Legates, however, pointed out that this was impossible; and the Pope accordingly acquiesced with a bad grace. He, however, prohibited the discussion of any plan for the reform of the Roman Court until it had been first referred to him. As a consolation the Legates reminded the Pope that they could always lengthen the discussion on the dogmas, so as to receive his opinion on the questions of reform that were under consideration at the same time.

The details of the procedure of the Council were arranged with less difficulty. The whole Synod was divided into three classes, and the work of preparation was distributed between them. A preliminary discussion of each question, after it had been prepared by the theologians and canonists, was to take place in the special congregation to which it was allotted. The matter was then to be further discussed in a General Congregation of the whole Synod; and if approved it was to be promulgated in a solemn session of the Council. The rules of procedure being thus settled, the dogmatic discussions were opened at the Fourth Session, which began on April 8, 1546.

The rule of Faith was first considered. The Nicene Creed including the *filioque* had been reaffirmed in the Third Session with the significant description " *symbolum fidei quo sancta* Romana *ecclesia utitur.*" The sources of knowledge of religious truth were now examined; and Scripture and tradition were set side by side as having equal authority. Tradition was defined as "*traditio Christi*" and " *traditio apostolorum (Spiritu Sancto dictante*)." The Church alone had the right to expound Scripture ; but silence was maintained as to the relations of the Pope and the Church in the matter. The traditional Canon of Scripture was accepted ; and the Vulgate was declared the authoritative text, which no one was to presume to reject.

It was not to be expected that these definitions would be accepted without opposition. Nacchianti, Bishop of Chioggia, maintained that Scripture was the sole rule of faith ; but he found only six supporters. Others proposed to distinguish between apostolic traditions and tradition in general, but they also met with defeat. The declaration that the text of the Vulgate was infallible was out of harmony with the knowledge of the time, and met with criticism in the papal household itself. The enthusiasm of the theologians at Trent, mostly Dominicans, for medieval theology was almost too zealous to please the Roman Court. The Pope could not help feeling a certain displeasure at the Council coming to a decision on such fundamental points without consulting the Holy See. He directed the Legates to have the decrees of the Fourth Session examined anew ; but, on their protesting, he gave way and abandoned the idea of dictating directly to the Council, on condition that its decrees should always be submitted for his approbation before being published.

In accordance with the order of business agreed upon, reform was next taken in hand ; and a discussion began upon a difficult point of discipline, the question as to the rules for preaching and catechising. This raised the contentious question of the relation of the Bishops to the regular clergy. Stormy scenes took place, and reverend prelates gave one another the lie. The Bishops of Fiesole and Chioggia were the most offensive to the Legates, on account of their plain speaking, and their recall from the Council was requested of the Pope. A considerable number of Bishops demanded that there should be no exemptions from episcopal control. The discussions soon passed to wider issues. It was claimed that the residence of Bishops in their dioceses was "*jure divino*," and that the Pope therefore possessed no power of dispensing with it. The Legates, however, succeeded in keeping to the question immediately before them ; and it was finally decided that, while the regulars were to be allowed to preach in the churches of their own Order without episcopal permission, they were to be prohibited from doing so in other churches without the licence of the Ordinary.

Original Sin was the next subject of discussion ; and this led on to the thorny paths of Free Will and Justification. The Emperor endeavoured to defer the discussion on these speculative points ; but the Pope was determined to obtain definitions which would make the breach with the Protestants irreparable. The Legates again (June 2, 1546) requested that more Italian Bishops might be sent to the Council to cope with the opposition ; and the consideration of the nature of Justification was entered upon. A Neapolitan, Thomas de San Felicio, Bishop of La Cava,

and a few theologians, maintained the doctrine of Justification by Faith
alone, but their views could obtain no hearing; and a scene ensued
in which San Felicio and a Greek Bishop fell upon one another, and
the latter's beard was torn out in handfuls. The discussion then confined
itself to the mediating view which Contarini had advocated in his
Tractatus de Justificatione. Pighius, Pflug, and Gropper had maintained
a similar position in Germany; and it had the adherence of some of the
ablest Catholic intellects, both north and south of the Alps. Seripando,
the General of the Augustinians, was the chief champion in the Council
of this view. Seripando in many respects resembled Sadoleto. The
best elements of humanism and Christianity were united in him; and
the position he took up on this doctrine was in harmony with the
traditions of the Augustinian Order. He distinguished between an
"inherent" and an "imputed" righteousness; and the "inherent" only
justified because of the "imputed"; the one was needed to complete
the other. In the imputed righteousness of Christ alone, however, lay
our final hope. The inherent righteousness, the righteousness of works,
was by itself of no avail.

It was in this discussion that Laynez and Salmeron, the two Jesuits
who had been brought to the Council by Cervini as the Pope's theologians, first played a prominent part in the debates of the assembly.
Ignatius was of opinion that the Council was not of very high importance; but he wished his Society to receive favourable notice there.
Laynez and Salmeron had received very careful instructions as to their
behaviour in the Council. They were to use every opportunity for
preaching and carrying on pastoral work. Dogmatics, however, were to
be avoided in the pulpit, and no excessive asceticism that might be
repellent was to be practised. The *Spiritual Exercises* were to be
introduced whenever an occasion offered itself. In the meetings of the
Council they were to speak with moderation and avoid giving offence;
but they were to oppose anything approaching to the new views. Every
night they were to meet and discuss their joint plans of action with Le Jay.

The politic instructions of Ignatius, which Laynez and Salmeron
faithfully carried out, were eminently successful. The Jesuits were
exempted from the general prohibition of preaching during the Council,
and soon obtained considerable influence with the Spanish Bishops.
They came to be known as the great advocates of purity of dogma and
scholasticism in the Council; and their importance rapidly increased.
When Ignatius wished to recall Laynez, Cervini wrote to say that he
was indispensable. With regard to the conflicting claims of the Papacy
and the Bishops, Ignatius wished the Jesuits to play the *rôle* of mediator;
but this position was soon abandoned, and they became the scientific
supporters of the Roman claims. Their skill in patristic and scholastic
quotation was remarkable, and they read to the Council what were whole
treatises rather than speeches.

Laynez especially devoted himself to the great question of Justification. While admitting the distinction between "inherent" and "imputed" righteousness, he maintained that the "imputed" righteousness became involved in the "inherent." The merits of Christ were imparted to man through faith; and we must rely on the merits of Christ not because they complete but because they produce our own. The efficacy of works was thus implied. Seripando had maintained that we must rely on the "imputed" righteousness: the righteousness of Christ was alone true and sufficient, and it was our faith in that which ultimately justified us. Such a view made reconciliation with the Protestants not impossible, while that of Laynez brought all hopes of agreement to an end.

In his speech against Seripando, Laynez pointed out with great skill the weakness of mediating theology; and the superficial clearness of his logic appealed to the assembled Fathers. The moderate party, though unable to persuade the Council of their views, were yet able to obtain a decree on the subject sufficiently ambiguous to allow the possibility of the development of Jansenism in the future. The formula, however, made reconciliation with the Protestants impossible; and the Papacy and the Jesuits thus obtained their object. Pole exhorted the Council not to reject any opinion simply because it was held by Luther, but his voice had little weight. Seripando was left to lead the moderates; and Pole left the Council at the end of June, his health breaking down, and retired to Padua. In August the Pope requested him to return to Trent, but he excused himself; and in October he was definitely relieved of his functions. Meanwhile the decrees of the Fifth Session were solemnly published on June 17, 1546; and Paul III approved and ratified by a brief the decrees with regard to preaching. Only the Bishop of Fiesole protested against this indirect claim of the Pope that the decrees of the Council required his assent and confirmation.

Though the Legates had successfully steered their way through the discussions on the most fundamental points of doctrine, they still feared the determination of the Emperor and the Spanish Bishops to carry out a thorough reform. To prevent this they endeavoured to procure the translation of the Council to an Italian town where it would be more completely under their control. Madruzzo, who was the energetic advocate of the Emperor's ideas on the subject of reform, had several acrimonious conflicts with the irritable del Monte; and the situation again became strained. Cardinal Pachecho went so far as to accuse the Legates of falsifying the votes. The charge was groundless, but it is an indication how high feeling ran. The Emperor peremptorily refused to consent to the translation of the Council; and the Legates had to content themselves with endeavouring to obtain the solemn publication of the decrees on Justification. A further rampart against the Protestants in the form of doctrinal decrees upon the Sacraments was also prepared;

and, while the Emperor endeavoured to prevent further definition of doctrine, the Legates did all they could to hasten it on. Fearing to press the Emperor too far, Cervini, diplomatic as ever, proposed a compromise. The publication of the decrees on Justification was to be delayed, if the Emperor would consent to the suspension of the Council for six months and to all disciplinary reform being left to the Pope. The Emperor however rejected the proposal at once; and the Legates then, on December 29, 1546, persuaded the Council to agree to the publication of the decrees on Justification at the Sixth Session on January 13, 1547. This was accordingly done; and the decrees were confirmed by the Pope, who, as a concession to the Council in return for the adjournment of the question of the residence of Bishops, proceeded to publish a Bull requiring Cardinals holding bishoprics in plurality to resign them within a certain date. So far as it was carried out, the Bull was little more than a dead letter, as they reserved to themselves many pensions and charges upon the revenues of the sees which they resigned.

Rapid progress was made meanwhile with the decrees on the Sacraments, while that on the residence of Bishops was again delayed. The view that residence was "*jure divino*," and therefore not dispensable by the Pope, was again insisted on by the Spanish Bishops; and Carranza wrote a special treatise on the subject. But the servile Italian majority was continually increasing; and, when the independent Bishop of Fiesole maintained that the Episcopate possessed all spiritual powers in itself and that Bishops were not simply the delegates of the Pope, the manuscript of his speech was demanded, in order that he might be proceeded against for derogating from the authority of the Holy See. This was however too much for the Council; and such a storm ensued that his manuscript was returned to him. The Legates however succeeded in avoiding any mention of the Cardinals in the decree on residence, and no reference was made to the question whether it was "*jure divino*" or not. Residence was simply declared necessary, and power was given to Bishops to visit all the churches of their diocese, including the Cathedral Chapter. The whole decree was, however, limited by the prescription that it was not to diminish in any way the authority of the Holy See. In this form it was solemnly published at the Seventh Session on March 5, 1547, together with decrees on the Sacraments in general, and on baptism and confirmation.

While affairs were thus proceeding in the Council, the Emperor was obtaining a series of successes in Germany which alarmed the Pope. Paul III had no desire to see Charles too powerful, and was afraid that he might come in person to Italy and insist on far-reaching reforms. He therefore determined to authorise the Legates to transfer the Council to Bologna. The translation was not, however, to be carried out on the sole authority of the Legates, but they were to endeavour to obtain a vote of the Council approving of it. A convenient pretext was found in the fact that there had been a few cases of plague in Trent; and, on the ground that the health of the Fathers was endangered, at the Eighth public Session (March 11, 1547) the Council by 38 votes to 14, with 4 abstentions, decided to adjourn to Bologna. Cardinal Pachecho and the Spanish Bishops however remained at Trent and awaited the Emperor's orders.

Charles was exceedingly angry when he heard the news. He refused in any way to recognise the translation of the Council; and the Spanish Bishops were prohibited from quitting Trent on any pretext whatsoever. They were, however, to refrain from any conciliar act which might provoke a schism. The course of European politics during the next two years has been narrated elsewhere. Charles remained firm. His political difficulties did not diminish, but the mission of Cardinal Sfondrato did not move him, and Paul III was disappointed of his hopes from France. The Diet of Augsburg recognised the prelates at Trent as the true Council; and the Emperor attempted to settle the religious affairs of the nation by the *Interim* until a General Council acceptable to him should meet. Nothing remained for Paul III but to bow to the inevitable; and on September 17, 1549, he formally suspended the Council of Bologna. The Pope made a show of himself undertaking the reform of the Church, and appointed a commission of Cardinals for the purpose; but before his real intentions in the matter could become clear he died (November 10, 1549).

The Cardinal del Monte came out of the conclave as Julius III on February 7, 1550. Reginald Pole was nearly elected, but Caraffa reminded the Conclave of his Lutheran tendencies at the Council, and succeeded in turning the scale against him. Cervini was the candidate of the party of reaction; but the Imperialists regarded him as their most dangerous enemy at Trent and secured his exclusion. Del Monte, though he had been not less hostile to the interests of the Emperor, might be gained over; and events justified to some extent their anticipations. The new Pope was utterly selfish. He only desired to enjoy the Papacy in peace, and he was quite willing to acquiesce in the Emperor's wishes, so far as they did not entail any loss of power to the Holy See. He at once agreed to the return of the Council to Trent, and on November 14, 1550, published a Bull summoning it to meet on May 1, 1551. In return for a guarantee from the Emperor that the papal authority should remain intact, he even consented to leave it an open question whether the preceding decisions of the Council were binding and to grant the Lutherans a hearing.

The new Pontificate seemed to be opening under the most favourable auspices. Reform was again entered upon at Rome. A commission of six Cardinals was appointed to consider the conditions of appointment to benefices, and another commission to reform the procedure of Conclaves. Difficulties, however, soon arose. Henry II of France wished the Pope to join a league against the Emperor, and, when he declined, refused to recognise the coming Council. The German Bishops, and still more the Protestants, despaired of any good result from another papal assembly, and showed no eagerness to attend. The Spaniards likewise were reluctant to take a long journey which would probably be fruitless. Only some forty prelates were present at Trent when the Council was reopened on May 1, 1551. Cardinal Marcello Crescenzio, together with two Bishops, Pighino, Archbishop of Siponto, and Lippomano, Bishop of Verona, were the papal representatives. The two Bishops, with the title of Nuncios, were to assist Crescenzio, who alone exercised the legatine authority.

The choice of presidents did not augur well for the success of the Assembly. Crescenzio was a blind adherent of the Papacy, and obstinate to boot; and his assistants were equally attached to the curial party. They well understood that it was their business to proceed further with the emphatic restatement of the old dogma in the interests of the Papacy, which had been so successfully begun. The Papacy had no more intention of conciliation in doctrine than it had during the Sessions held under Paul III. The second meeting at Trent was thus, from the beginning, doomed to failure so far as the Protestants were concerned, as the first had been. The Emperor and the Pope were no more in real agreement than before. The meagre attendance at the opening left no alternative to the Council but to adjourn; and September 1 was accordingly fixed for the first (Twelfth) public Session. By that time the Electors of Mainz and Trier had arrived, together with a few other German and Spanish Bishops. It was agreed to take up the work at the point at which it had been dropped in the previous assembly of the Council; and in this manner all its previous decisions were tacitly confirmed. In such circumstances it was little good attempting to persuade the Protestants to send representatives to the Council; but nevertheless the Emperor persevered in the attempt.

The doctrine of the Eucharist was the first subject entered upon by the Council. Laynez and Salmeron, who again appeared in the Council as the Pope's theologians, and with a greater influence than ever, strongly opposed any concession to Protestant views in the matter, even in points of discipline, such as communion in both kinds. The Jesuits had a considerable share in drawing up the decrees and adopted a purely conservative attitude. The German prelates, however, and a few others advocated strongly a concession with regard to the cup. Finally, at the request of the representative of the Emperor, the matter was deferred until the Protestants should arrive. Meanwhile the discussion on reform was resumed. The abuse of the right of appeal to the Pope from the episcopal Courts was prohibited, and the procedure of the Courts regulated. Decrees to this effect, together with the decisions on the Eucharist, omitting those on communion in both kinds, were promulgated at the Thirteenth public Session, which was held on October 11, 1551. A safe-conduct was also granted to the Protestants who should attend the Council, though not until after much negotiation as to its exact wording.

The Legate began now to grow anxious as to the course affairs would take on the arrival of the Protestants, and tried to hasten the deliberations of the Council. At the general Congregation on November 5, Crescenzio proposed that the Fathers, in order to save time, should simply accept or reject the articles that the theologians had prepared. The proposal was, however, rejected by a bare majority. As the two Jesuits were now the most influential among the theologians, the success of the Legate's proposal would have meant that they would have practically dictated the decrees of the Council.

The Sacraments of Penance and of Extreme Unction were next discussed, together with thirteen further decrees on reform. Many minor grievances were removed, but burning questions were skilfully avoided. The conclusions arrived at were promulgated at the Fourteenth public Session, held on November 25, 1551. At length, in January, 1552, some Protestant delegates arrived in Trent, representing the Duke of Württemberg, the Elector Maurice of Saxony, and a few of the south German towns. The Legate opposed their admission to the public Congregation unless they first accepted all the conclusions of the Council; but the representatives of the Emperor finally overcame the opposition of the Legate, and the delegates were allowed to address the general Congregation on January 24, 1552. The only result was to reveal how wide was the gulf between the Council and the Protestants. Nevertheless, at the Fifteenth public Session on January 25, 1552, it was decided to adjourn the next public Session until March 19, 1552, in order to enable other Protestants to arrive; and another and more explicit safe-conduct was granted to them. The theological discussions meanwhile continued, but nothing was done. It was obvious that the situation was hopeless. In February many of the Bishops departed. In March the Protestant delegates also left; and finally, on the news of the rapid advance of Maurice of Saxony, the Council was suspended on April 28, 1552.

The Peace of Passau (1552) and its confirmation at the Diet of Augsburg (1555) marked the failure of the Emperor's policy. The unity of the Church was definitely broken. The two Confessions were compelled to tolerate one another in their respective spheres; and all attempts at conciliation and compromise were abandoned. So far as the Papacy was concerned, the Council passed away as a bad dream. Julius III determined to risk no more experiments; and the remainder of his pontificate was spent in beautifying his villa near the *Porta del Popolo*, the *Villa di Papa Giulio*, which is his chief memorial. On his death on March 24, 1555, Cervini at last ascended the papal throne as Marcellus II.

He was the first true Pope of the Counter-Reformation, of blameless life and untarnished orthodoxy, and zealous for reform. A friend of the Jesuits, he was at the same time tactful and diplomatic; and he well understood the maxim that on occasions more prudence and less piety was better than more piety and less prudence. But Marcellus II only survived his election three weeks, and was succeeded by the uncompromising Caraffa, who took the title of Paul IV. The Counter-Reformation was now master.

The new reign began in earnest with reform. The Papacy itself would purify the Church and needed no Council to assist it. A Bull was published announcing that the first care of the new Pontiff would be the reform of the universal Church and of the Roman Court. Congregations were appointed to carry out this announcement. Edict after edict was issued for the reform of convents; and the whole method of appointment to clerical offices was overhauled. But what no one could have anticipated happened. Reform and the Catholic reaction were sacrificed to what Paul IV thought were the political interests of the Holy See. He had ever been a hater of Spain, and he now made it his object to free the Papacy from its thraldom. His unworthy nephews attained an ascendancy over him by playing upon the anti-Spanish mania of the old man. The purification of the Church sank into the background.

But the failure of his nephews to achieve the object dearest to his heart opened his eyes towards the end of the year 1558; and, when Cardinal Pachecho had the courage at the session of the Inquisition on January 9, 1559, to reply to Paul's excited cries of "Reform! Reform!" "Holy Father, reform must first of all begin among ourselves," the Pope was convicted of sin. His nephews were banished, and reform of the whole administration in Church and State was again begun. A large remission of taxation had marked Paul's accession, and the burdens of the people were now still further lightened. The *Dataria*, on which all the schemes of reform under Paul III had been shattered, was taken in hand once more, and with a considerable measure of success. The removal of vexatious taxation and of the toll on good works was pressed forward. At the beginning of the reign Ignatius and Laynez had been consulted; and Paul IV realised from the example of their Society that freedom of spiritual services was the road to success. He saw that the whole system of fees levied on every possible occasion was utterly bad. Marriage dispensations, a very profitable source of revenue, he would have none of. Officials must not live by Court fees, nor should their offices be bought and sold, or performed by a deputy who had to make his own profit. In short, the object of Paul's reforms was to substitute direct for indirect taxation. The levying of tenths was approved; and the people were to be taught that it was their duty to give directly towards the support of the Holy See. At the same time Paul IV recognised that too many of the rights of the Bishops had been absorbed by Rome; and in this way many of his reforms anticipated the ordinances made later in the last Sessions of the Council of Trent.

An equal zeal for purity of doctrine and for purity of life was shown by the energetic old man. The Inquisition exercised its powers with the utmost vigour, and even Cardinals were not spared. Morone was imprisoned; and the suppression of liberal Catholicism as well as Protestant opinions was now definitely taken in hand. The Inquisition and the Index suppressed the slightest tendency to diverge from medieval theology. The spirit of Ignatius and his Society had now taken possession of the Church.

Paul IV, however, died on August 18, 1559; and an immediate reaction set in in Rome. The severity of his measures had made him many enemies; and even among those in favour of reform there was a considerable number who had no wish that it should be the arbitrary work of the Pope. All the Cardinals accordingly, before entering the Conclave, bound themselves to summon anew the General Council in the case of their being elected; and on December 26, 1559, Giovanni Angelo de' Medici (Medicino) was elected Pope. He was a Milanese, of middle-class origin, and unconnected with the great Florentine family. Learned and kindly and of exemplary life, he was better acquainted with the times in which he lived than his predecessor had been. He wished to live at peace with all men, and to win the support of the Catholic monarchs for the Holy See. At the same time, he had no intention of suffering any diminution of the papal prerogative. Before his accession he had expressed himself in favour of concessions in discipline, such as the practice of communion in both kinds; and he believed that by this means a Council might heal the divisions of the Catholic world without endangering the rights of the Holy See. Events showed that it was not so easy to confine the issues to such narrow lines; but at the opening of his reign Pius IV looked forward to a Council with no misgiving.

The Emperor Ferdinand and Francis II of France greeted with approval the proposals of the Pope to hold a Council. But they at once proceeded to name conditions which were received with little favour at Rome. Complete freedom must be given to the Council. It must be held in a German town, and it should work above all for the reconciliation of the Protestants. In view of these proposals, Pius IV, chiefly under the influence of his nephew Carlo Borromeo, Secretary of State, drew back from the idea of a Council. The Pope, in his turn, made impossible conditions, and considered the question of carrying out the necessary reforms by means of Congregations of Cardinals. Events in France, however, compelled the Pope to proceed with the proposed Council. The States-General at Orleans (January 10, 1561) ordered the French Bishops to meet on January 20, 1561, to prepare for a National Council if the announcement which had been made of a General Council were not carried out. A papal Bull had been issued on November 29, 1560, summoning a Council to Trent for April 6, 1561; and Pius hastened to assure the

French of the seriousness of his intentions. The French national synod was accordingly abandoned ; and Trent was accepted as the place of meeting. Before the assembly could meet there was, however, another difficulty to be settled. The Emperor and the French government wished for an explicit declaration that the Council was a new assembly, and not merely a continuation of the previous Sessions at Trent as Philip II and the Spanish Church insisted. The sympathies of the Pope were with Philip ; but it was necessary not to offend the Emperor and the French. Accordingly the question was left in doubt, and no definite pronouncement was made on the matter.

Meanwhile the preparations for the Council went on. The Pope instructed his Nuncios to invite all Christian Princes to the Council, whether schismatic or not. The Protestant Powers, however, had little confidence in the proposed assembly ; and it soon became clear that the Council would be confined to the nations still in communion with the See of Rome. Ferdinand, however, and the French government had no intention of allowing the Council simply to register the wishes of the Curia. Both Powers wished for concessions which might unite to the Church the moderate Protestants and disaffected Catholics in their dominions. The reforms which they desired are enumerated in the instructions given to the French ambassadors at the Council, and in the *Libel of Reformation* which the Emperor caused to be drawn up. The Mass in the vulgar tongue, revision of the service books, communion in both kinds, the marriage of priests, reform of the Curia and a reduction in the number of Cardinals, the enforcement of residence on ecclesiastics, the abolition of the whole system of dispensations and exemptions, and a limitation of the power of excommunication, were among the chief points demanded. The whole Church system was in fact to be revised, and the share of the Papacy in its government to be reduced. Bavaria supported most of these demands ; and in fact nearly all Catholics north of the Alps desired a radical reform of the Church.

Philip II and the Spanish Bishops, on the other hand, wished for no alteration in the ritual and practice of the Church ; but they equally desired a thorough reform of the Curia and a diminution of the papal authority. At the same time they wished it to be distinctly declared that the assembly was a continuation of the previous Council, and that an effectual bar should be thus provided against any advances towards Protestantism. The Spanish Bishops were opposed, even more strongly than the papal Court, to any alteration in the discipline and practice of the Church. The division among the Catholic Powers gave the Papacy a means of which it was quick to avail itself. The history of the third meeting of the Council of Trent is mainly the story of the skilful diplomacy with which the Papacy played off one nation against another and succeeded in bringing all efforts for radical reform to naught. The task was not difficult, as there was little co-operation among the Powers even in the pursuit of objects which they had in common ; and the Council ended in strengthening rather than weakening the papal grip upon the Church. The Papacy supported by the Italian episcopate defied the Christian world.

No less than five Legates were appointed to preside over the Council. At their head was placed Ercole di Gonzaga, Cardinal of Mantua, brother of the Duke, a man of conciliatory disposition ; and he had for his colleagues Girolamo Seripando, the former General of the Augustinians, who had played a prominent part in the earlier Sessions, Luigi Simonetta, and Jacopo Puteo, both of them canonists of renown, and Stanislaus Hosius, who had worked hard against heresy in Poland. The last-named three were firmly devoted to the papal interests. Puteo, however, soon fell ill, and his place was taken by Cardinal Marc d'Altemps, Bishop of Constance, a young man of little experience. Ludovico Madruzzo, nephew of Cardinal Madruzzo, had succeeded his uncle in the bishopric of Trent, and received the Legates on their arrival on April 16, 1561.

The Bishops, however, arrived but slowly, and summer and autumn went by. At length the Pope could wait no longer, and fixed the first (Seventeenth) Session for January 18, 1562. There were then assembled for the opening of the Council five Cardinals, three Patriarchs, eleven Archbishops, ninety Bishops, four Generals of Orders, and four Abbots. The first business undertaken by the Council was the question of an Index of Prohibited Books. It was decided to revise the Index issued by Paul IV ; and a commission of eighteen prelates was appointed for the purpose. A safe-conduct was then granted to any Protestants who might come to the Council in the same terms as that granted under Julius III. But this was nothing more than a formality, as there was not the least prospect that any would attend. It was, however, necessary to satisfy the Emperor so far. Although the numbers present at the opening of the Council were greater than they had ever been in any of the earlier Sessions at Trent or Bologna, the assembly was purely a gathering of the Catholic world. There was no longer even the possibility, which had existed at an earlier date, of a frank meeting of the Protestants and a consideration of their objections. The Papacy had defeated the attempt before, and mutual distrust now made it hopeless. The interest of the third meeting of the Council lies in the effort made by certain elements in Catholicism to readjust the balance of forces in the government of the Church, and to satisfy the needs of Catholics north of the Alps.

The cleft between the parties revealed itself at the very beginning of the Council. The Legates inserted in the decree concerning the opening of the Council the words "*proponentibus legatis ac praesidentibus*." Against this the Spanish Bishops, led by Guerrero, Archbishop of Granada, protested. Its object was to diminish the ind power of the Council apart from the Pope, by taking away i initiative. Any proposals hurtful to the Papacy and the Curia would thus be barred. Philip II through his ambassadors supported the objections of the Spanish Bishops to the clause. The Legates however explained the words away, and the opposition had not the courage to bring the matter to the vote. The situation at first was not very promising for the opposition. A little group of Spanish Bishops, led by a determined man, the Archbishop of Granada, stood face to face with an overwhelming number of Italian prelates, the great majority of whom were devoted to or dependent upon the Curia. A few northern Bishops and a few independent Italians supported them, but they were not certain of the help even of all the Spaniards. Some of these, chief of whom was the Bishop of Salamanca, had already been won over by the Curia. Behind the Spanish Bishops, however, were the Catholic Powers. All alike were determined to maintain the liberty of the Council to declare its supremacy over the Pope, and to free the Church from the curial despotism. There was, however, no harmony of action and a singular lack of co-operation among them, even for the objects which they had in common. Moreover their efforts were ultimately paralysed by the fact that, while the Emperor and France desired the Council to start entirely afresh and to make concessions in Church ritual and practice which would meet the needs of their respective countries, Spain, on the other hand, was determined that the Council should be considered a continuation of the old, and develop the old dogma and practice on the traditional lines. The skilled intriguers of the Curia found a promising field for their work.

The second (Eighteenth) public Session was held on February 26, 1562. The resolutions with regard to the Index and the safe-conduct to the Protestants were then published. The Congregations, meanwhile, proceeded with their work ; and doctrine and reform were taken in hand together as before. The decrees on the Eucharist were taken up at the point where they had been left in 1552. Communion in both kinds, and the communion of children, remained to be considered. The articles of reform dealt with diocesan and parochial administration; and the question of the residence of Bishops was again raised. Simonetta endeavoured to avoid a declaration on the subject ; but to this the Council would not consent ; and on March 11, 1562, its discussion was begun by the general Congregation. The Council was unanimous as to the necessity of residence ; the only disagreement was as to its being "*jure divino*" or merely "*lege ecclesiasticâ*." This indirectly raised the question of the limits of papal authority ; and the controversy soon became heated. The Legates were not agreed as to the attitude they should adopt. Simonetta opposed any concession on the subject, while the Cardinal of Mantua and Seripando hesitated. At length, on April 20, the Legates put the question to the vote. 66 voted for the divine nature of the obligation of residence, while 71 either rejected it absolutely or voted for remitting the question to the Pope. The result was not altogether pleasing to the Curial party. Only a minority had voted for a direct negative on the subject. Simonetta wrote secret letters to Rome, accusing his colleagues of betraying the interests of the Holy See by precipitately putting the matter to the vote. The whole Council was now in a state of confusion. The Cardinal of Mantua and Seripando ceased to feel sure of their ground. The papal letters to the Legates changed their tone. Borromeo urged Simonetta to oppose any action of his colleagues which would be hurtful to the interests of the Holy See. The recall of the Cardinal of Mantua was seriously considered at Rome. Everything stood still while frequent letters were exchanged between the Legates and Rome. The French ambassador profanely remarked that the Council was not free, as the Holy Spirit came to Trent in the courier's bag from Rome.

To add to the difficulties of the Legates, on June 2 a despatch arrived from Rome ordering the Council to be definitely declared a continuation. Philip II had insisted on this, and the Pope had had to give way. But, no sooner had the news arrived, than the French and Imperial ambassadors declared that they and the prelates of their respective countries would take no further part in the Council if this were done. There was nothing for the Legates to do but to temporise, in spite of the distinct orders of the Pope; and on June 6 the Twentieth Session was held, merely to be prorogued. Meanwhile, the general Congregation continued the discussion of the decrees on the Eucharist; and here the question of communion in both kinds caused further trouble. A cross division of parties arose, Spain and Italy against France and Germany. The Imperial ambassadors allowed themselves to be outwitted by the Legates. The consideration of Ferdinand's *Libel of Reformation* was deferred; and the Council occupied itself with matters of purely secondary importance. The Legates knew well how to follow Borromeo's advice and to gain " *il beneficio del tempo.*"

Pius IV meanwhile hesitated. He gave way to the Legates on the point of the continuation and left the logic of facts to demonstrate its reality. He mollified Philip as best he could. With regard to the obligation of residence nothing was done. After the vote of April 20 the Legates had referred it to the Pope, and rumours reached Trent that Pius had declared it to be "*jure divino*," but this was not confirmed. The Curia came to no decision. It was unwise to run counter to the opinion of the great majority of the Catholic world in the matter, and the question was left in suspense. To show the zeal of the Papacy three Bulls were published at the end of May reforming the Apostolic Chamber, the Penitentiary, and the Chancery; and meanwhile the Council marked time.

So hopeless did the situation appear that the Pope even contemplated the transference of the Council to an Italian town and a complete breach with the non-Italian nations. So strong an opposition, however, showed itself to the mere suggestion that the idea had to be abandoned; and other means were adopted to bring the Council to a more reasonable frame of mind. Carlo Visconti, afterwards Bishop of Ventimiglia, the Pope's confidential agent at Trent, worked unceasingly to increase the papal influence in the Council. The old methods were pursued with the Italian Episcopate. When a Bishop arrived at Trent, Visconti consulted with the Legates as to whether he should receive payment for his services or not. Those who could not be reached by pensions were not always proof against the hope of promotion in the Church. When these methods failed, threats were sometimes effective. The few independent Bishops underwent the most outrageous provocations and too easily lost heart. They gave up the struggle before it was half begun. The papal diplomacy was completely successful; and Philip was persuaded to order the Spanish Bishops to let the question of the divine obligation of residence drop for a while. Pius made matters smoother by taking the hint from Visconti to treat the Cardinal of Mantua with more consideration, and flattered many of the Bishops of the opposition with complimentary letters. Simonetta was warned not to show excessive zeal, and he and the Cardinal of Mantua were publicly reconciled.

The Twenty-first public Session was at length held on July 21, 1562, and the decrees on the Eucharist and on reform were solemnly published, the questions of the possibility of granting the chalice and the nature of the obligation of residence being skilfully avoided. The Council went on to discuss the doctrine of the Mass; and further decrees dealing with reform were drawn up. The Imperial ambassadors, who throughout the Council displayed little tact, pressed on the Legates an immediate consideration of the Emperor's demands for the use of the chalice in Germany. The Pope all along had not felt strongly on the point; and so persistent was the German demand that he was prepared to accede to it. The Spanish and Italian opposition to the concession was, however, very strong, and Laynez threw all his influence into the scale against it. He read a lengthy theological treatise on the subject, and influenced many votes. In these circumstances it would have been wise for the Emperor to proceed cautiously and not run the risk of an open defeat. The ambassadors, however, thought otherwise; and on August 22 the Cardinal of Mantua submitted the Emperor's proposal to the Council. The voting took place on September 6, when 29 voted in the affirmative simply; 31 in the affirmative with the proviso that the matter should be referred to the Pope; 19 were in favour of its being granted in Hungary and Bohemia alone; 38 rejected it absolutely; 10 did the same but desired to leave the definite decision to the Pope; 24 were in favour of its being left to the Pope without the Council expressing an opinion; and 14 thought the matter not yet ripe for decision. It was a discouraging result for the Imperial ambassadors, but they made one more effort and moved a decree recommending to the Pope the request of the Emperor. This was, however, rejected by 79 to 69. The Cardinal of Mantua, however, came to the rescue, to avoid a breach with the Emperor, and on September 16 moved to refer the matter simply to the Pope, without any expression of opinion on the part of the Council. Simonetta gave his support to this proposal, and it was carried by 98 votes to 38. The Emperor thus at the best could get nothing from the Council, and was referred back to the Pope. At the Twenty-second public Session, which took place on the following day (September 17, 1562), the decrees on the Mass and a series of minor reforms were approved; but even then 31 Bishops voted against any reference of the question of the chalice to the Pope.

The Council then took up the discussion of the Sacrament of Orders. Though there was little disagreement as to the nature of the grace conferred in ordination, yet the question of the relations of the various members of the hierarchy to one another and to the Pope was likely to cause difficulty, and troubled waters were soon again entered upon. The French and Imperial ambassadors protested against any further definition of dogmas, and demanded that the Council should await the arrival of the French and German Bishops who were on their way. A thorough reform of the Church might then be entered upon. They further complained of the haste in which proceedings were conducted. The Legates only communicated the decrees on reform to the Bishops two days before the general Congregations, and it was impossible to examine them properly in that time. The Legates returned an evasive answer, and the discussions on the Sacrament of Orders were proceeded with. The papal legion was strengthened by the arrival of more Italian Bishops; and at the same time several of the more independent prelates left Trent. The Spaniards felt that it was necessary to assert themselves again; and on November 3 the Archbishop of Granada propounded the view that Bishops were the Vicars of Christ by the divine law under His chief Vicar the Bishop of Rome. This raised the whole question of the Pope's supremacy, and an angry debate ensued. The Bishop of Segovia went so far as to say that the supremacy of the Bishop of Rome was unknown to the primitive Church. Laynez again made himself the chief advocate of the papal prerogative and displayed a violent hostility to the Episcopate. In the midst of these discussions the Cardinal of Lorraine arrived with twelve French Bishops and three Abbots on November 13, 1562. The attitude which he would adopt was eagerly awaited by both parties. On November 23 the Cardinal appeared in the assembly and in a speech made similar demands to those made by the Emperor in the *Libel of Reformation*, and a little later declared himself in favour of the divine right of the Episcopate. On January 2, 1563, the French demands were formally presented to the Legates. The articles were thirty-four in number and embraced most of the proposals previously demanded by the Emperor. They suffered the same fate as his and were simply forwarded to Rome for consideration.

It was now obvious to all that the Papacy had no intention of carrying out any reforms of importance. The papal policy was clearly expressed in a letter of Borromeo to the Legates, in which he informed them that they must keep two objects in sight, that of strengthening the papal power over the Council, and that of procuring its speedy dissolution. To this intent the Legates endeavoured to have the Pope described as "*rector universalis ecclesiae*" in the canon dealing with the Episcopate; but owing to the opposition of the Cardinal of Lorraine they failed. The interminable discussions continued; month after month passed by and nothing was done. At the beginning of February Ferdinand had moved to Innsbruck with the object of being nearer the scene of affairs. The Legates thereupon sent Commendone to see him and endeavour to come to some understanding. His embassy, however, had little success and he soon returned to Trent.

All turned now upon the action of France and the Emperor. On February 12, 1563, the Cardinal of Lorraine journeyed to Innsbruck to confer with Ferdinand; and there he found assembled with the Emperor, Maximilian, King of the Romans, Albert V, Duke of Bavaria, and the Archbishop of Salzburg. The Cardinal, in a memorandum which he presented to the Emperor, attributed the barren result of the Council to the fact that only matters which had been approved of at Rome were allowed to be decided at Trent. The overwhelming majority of Italian Bishops, and the fact that the right of initiative rested with the Legates alone, prevented any real reform. As a remedy the Cardinal suggested that the Ambassadors should have the right of making proposals directly to the Council, and that a larger number of non-Italian Bishops should be sent for to counterbalance the Italian majority. Above all, the Emperor should come in person to Trent and exercise his influence upon the Council.

Ferdinand, however, saw little hope in these proposals. It was a practical impossibility to find any other non-Italian Bishops who would go to Trent; and his own presence would give the papal party an opportunity of raising the cry that the Council was not free. To attempt to give the Ambassadors a right of initiative in the Council would only lead to the breaking up of the assembly. The Emperor was, in fact, fast losing hope of obtaining any good from the Council. The failure to obtain the concession of the chalice from the Council in September, 1562, was a great disappointment to him; and the slow progress that the Council had made since that time filled him with despair. At the beginning of March, 1563, he turned to the Pope instead of to the Council, in the hope of persuading him to bring about some effective reforms. The Pope threw all the blame for the delay upon the Council, and especially upon the Spanish Bishops for raising theoretic and useless questions. In this way one country could be played off against another. The Papacy perceived, however, that Ferdinand's confidence in the Council was much shaken, and determined to send a Cardinal to Innsbruck to endeavour to alienate him from it still further.

Meanwhile at Trent still further delay was caused by the death of two of the Legates. The Cardinal of Mantua died on March 2, and Cardinal Seripando on March 17, 1563. Cardinal d'Altemps had returned to Rome some time previously ; and Simonetta and Hosius did not care to act alone. They accordingly wrote to the Pope asking that two new Legates might be sent. The papal choice fell upon Morone and Navagero. The former was now a devoted servant of the Papacy and had re-established his reputation for orthodoxy. He was, however, very acceptable to the Emperor, and the moderate party still had some hopes of him. Navagero, on the other hand, was an open adherent of the curial party. The new Legates arrived at Trent on April 13, 1563. Morone, after an introductory discourse to the assembled Fathers, at once set out for Innsbruck. The Jesuit Father, Canisius, was with the Emperor and acted as the agent of the Roman Court in the Imperial entourage. This remarkable man, the first German Jesuit, was perhaps the ablest of the leaders of the Catholic reaction in Germany. Alike at Cologne, where he withstood the influence of the Archbishop Hermann von Wied, and at Ingolstadt, where in 1550 he became Rector of the University, he turned back the advancing tide of Protestantism. In 1552 Ferdinand, then King of the Romans, had summoned him to Vienna, and Canisius soon obtained considerable influence over him. At Ferdinand's request Canisius drew up a Catechism, which was translated into many languages and from which thousands were instructed in the rudiments of the Catholic faith. His *Summa Doctrinae Christianae* became the text-book of Catholic teachers and preachers throughout Germany. When Ignatius set up a Province of his Society in Upper Germany, it was only natural that he should place Canisius at its head. Directly Canisius heard of the arrival of Morone at Trent he sent urgent messages to him to come to Innsbruck as soon as possible. France and Spain had not yet agreed upon active co-operation with the Emperor; but with so many objects in common an agreement as to a course of action might occur at any moment. Canisius skilfully prepared the way for Morone. He pointed out to Ferdinand that by an amicable arrangement with the Holy Father he might obtain more than he would ever get from the Council. Ferdinand began to waver. His previous policy had ended in failure. Philip had been unmoved by his warning that reform of the rites and ceremonies of the Church, and not only of its discipline, was necessary to preserve Germany to the Church. By means of the Council he had achieved nothing. Morone now arrived with the definite offer of the concession of the chalice directly the Council should be terminated; and Ferdinand was won over. He agreed to give the Legates his support, and declared himself content with the minor reforms that the Legates proposed to put before the Council. The Papacy had thus gained the first step. It remained to come to terms with the Cardinal of Lorraine and Philip II.

Morone returned to Trent on May 27, and the discussions on the Sacrament of Orders were actively resumed. It was finally decided to avoid all mention of the disputed points as to the direct divine origin of episcopal authority and whether residence was "*jure divino*" or not. The decrees in this ambiguous form were published at the Twenty-third public Session on July 15, 1563. The difficulties of the Legates were, however, not yet over. Philip sent to the Council a new ambassador, the Count de Luna, who was instructed to demand anew the suppression of the formula "*proponentibus legatis*," and pressed forward the formulation of doctrine and a thorough reform of discipline. But the Emperor gave his support to the Legates, and the situation remained unchanged. National feeling now ran very high, and a dispute as to precedence between the French and Spanish ambassadors nearly brought the Council to an end. The state of tension is well illustrated by the interjection of a member of the Curialist party after a French prelate had denounced the abuses of the Roman Court : "*a scabie Hispana incidimus in morbum Gallicum.*"

Meanwhile efforts were being made to draw the Cardinal of Lorraine over to the papal party. A man of little sincerity, able and ambitious, he considered his own interests alone. After the death of his brother, the Duc de Guise, and the conclusion of the Treaty of Amboise, his position was not very secure at home ; and in those circumstances the friendship of the Holy See was not to be despised. The papal diplomacy began its work early in the year 1563 ; and by the end of June the Cardinal was won over. Through his influence the French government agreed in August to the Council being brought to an end on the terms which the Emperor had accepted. The French Bishops meekly followed the lead of the Cardinal and ceased to oppose the policy of the Legates. The Spaniards alone remained, and agreement with them was not so easy. They were the puritans of the Council. Political expediency had no meaning to them. As they could not be bought, the only thing for the Papacy to do was to outmanœuvre them.

Direct appeals to Philip II, to consent to the Council being brought to an end failed ; so there was for the time nothing to be done but to allow the Council to occupy itself in matters which were comparatively of little importance. The Sacrament of Matrimony was discussed and its nature defined. The marriage of priests was forbidden without any opposition, though the Imperial ambassadors made a feeble protest. The question of clandestine marriages gave some trouble. They had admittedly given rise to great abuses, but the view that the Sacraments were *ipso facto* operative (*ex opere operato*), drove many of the prelates to advocate their recognition. Finally, however, they were, by 133 votes to 59, declared invalid. The work of reform was also continued. The Legates brought forward a series of decrees for the reform of the morals and discipline of the clergy. They involved the abandonment by the Curia of many valuable privileges, but at the same time they entrenched upon the rights of the State. To ecclesiastical tribunals powers were assigned which no government could afford to tolerate; the rights of patrons were interfered with; and immunities of the clergy, which had long been abandoned in practice, were again claimed. The Catholic Powers for once united in their protests, and the more extravagant claims were withdrawn in consequence. The conduct of the Cardinal of Lorraine in this matter shows how completely he had thrown in his lot with the Holy See. He had visited Rome in September, and his head was completely turned by the flattery which he received. He went so far as to advise the French government to submit to some of the extravagant claims put forth on behalf of the clergy; but his advice was not followed. The Council now resolved itself into chaos. The control of the Legates became little more than nominal. Pius himself had consented to a reform of the Cardinals being included in the general reform of the clergy; but the Italian Episcopate were not willing to see what they regarded as the privileges of their nation swept away. They succeeded in reducing the proposed reforms of the Sacred College to a mere shadow. The French ambassadors withdrew to Venice, hopeless of any good coming out of such an assembly. The firmness of the Spanish Bishops, however, prevented the scheme of reform being completely nullified by reservations and exceptions; and on November 11, 1563, the Twenty-fourth public Session was held, and the decree on matrimony and twenty-one out of the forty-two decrees on reform proposed by the Legates were promulgated, the remaining decrees being deferred to a later Session.

Everything was now subordinated to bringing the Council to an end. The Papacy ordered the Legates to withdraw the proposals which infringed the rights of the State; and canons dealing with the remaining matters under discussion were drawn up with feverish haste. Purgatory, the Invocation of Saints, and Indulgences were hastily defined; and twenty more decrees of reformation were prepared. The Spanish ambassador and the Spanish Bishops maintained their protests to the end, but with no avail. A rumour that the Pope was dying hastened matters still faster. The Twenty-fifth Session was opened on December 3, 1563; and on December 4 the Council was brought to an end amid the acclamations of the assembled Fathers. 255 members of the Council signed its decrees, the four Legates, Cardinal Madruzzo and the Cardinal of Lorraine, 3 Patriarchs, 25 Archbishops, 168 Bishops, 7 Abbots, 7 Generals of Orders, and 39 who were absent represented by their proctors.

With the close of the Council of Trent the determination of the principles which were to regulate the reorganisation of the Catholic Church was completed. There followed, under the direction of the Papacy, an application and working out in detail of those principles, which was a task of many years; but the struggle was over and the battle won. Medieval theology had been emphatically restated. The scission of Christendom into two halves, each going its own way regardless of the other, was definitely confirmed. The spirit of dogmatic certainty, which drew its chief nourishment from Spanish soil and of which the Society of Jesus was the clearest expression, was to be the predominating influence for the future in the Church. Her doctrine was now completely articulated for the first time. Matters which the medieval Church had left to the speculations of the Schools were now authoritatively settled; and the Church was provided with a logical presentation of her position, definitely marking it off from all other circles of ideas. The issues had been put before the world, and it remained for Catholicism and Protestantism to fight the battle to the bitter end.

Though the triumph of the Counter-Reformation thus enabled the Church to present a united front as against Protestantism, it is not true that all opposition to the prevailing tendencies within the Church had been silenced. Many of the dogmatic decrees of Trent were as such a compromise. The great decree on Justification preserved room in the Church for those Augustinian ideas which the Church had never been completely able to assimilate, and which found subsequent expression in Jansenism. Great as was the influence of the Jesuits at Trent, they did not succeed in winning a complete triumph for their theology. This was not, however, of so great consequence as might appear; for all particular dogmas were beginning to sink into the background, compared with the one great principle that the use and wont of the Roman Church is law, and that to the Pope alone appertains the right to expound the teaching of the Church. The complete expression of this principle was impossible at Trent; the hostile elements were too strong; but the way was laid open. The papal supremacy over the Church received a new extension as the result of the work of the Council. The confirmation of the Pope was acknowledged to be necessary for the validation of its decrees. The supreme power in the universal Church was admitted to rest in the Roman Pontiffs. They were the Vicars of Christ on earth. The attempt to enunciate the direct divine authority of the episcopate was frustrated. The *Vaticanum* was only the logical outcome of certain elements in the *Tridentinum*.

The decrees on reformation successfully removed the worst abuses which had brought the Church and the clergy into contempt. The authority of the Bishops over their clergy, both secular and regular, was considerably strengthened; and means were provided for the removal of evil livers and the incompetent. The parochial clergy were compelled to preach; and the whole discipline of the Church was improved. The practical reform, however, that was most far-reaching in its results was probably the establishment of seminaries for the education of the clergy in each diocese. This measure provided the Church with an adequate supply of trained men for its service, and removed the reproach which had formerly rested on the clerical state. At the same time it made the clergy a body more distinct from the laity than they had ever been before. It narrowed the interests of the clergy, and made them to a considerable extent the blind instruments of their superiors. Together with the system of celibacy, it separated the clergy from the ordinary social life of the people, and accentuated the division between the Church and the modern world.

The Council left to the Papacy the right of interpreting its decrees; and Pius IV hastened to enunciate this principle in the Bull *Benedictus Deus* (January 26, 1564), which confirmed its proceedings. No prelate was to publish any gloss upon the decrees of the Council or venture to interpret them without papal authorisation. In 1588 Sixtus V set up a special Congregation of the Council of Trent, to supervise the carrying out of its decisions. Meanwhile the Papacy anxiously endeavoured to persuade the Catholic Powers to accept in their entirety the decrees of the Council; but with the decrees on doctrine governments did not concern themselves. They were accepted throughout the Catholic Church, but with the decrees on discipline it was different. Even in the modified form which they received after the protests of the ambassadors, they infringed many ancient rights of the secular power in various countries, rights which it was not likely would be easily abandoned. In the end the decrees on discipline were only accepted in their entirety by the Emperor Ferdinand for his hereditary dominions, by Portugal, and by the King of Poland. France and the Empire never accepted them, while Spain and Venice received them with a reservation of their own rights which had practically the same effect. There were limits beyond which no modern State could allow the papal claims to go.

The tasks which the Council had left to the Pope were actively taken in hand. The Breviary and the Missal were revised, and a new edition of the *Corpus Juris Canonici* was published. A purification of Church music was begun. A commission of eight Cardinals was appointed on August 2, 1564; and in Palestrina a genius arose who became the founder of modern Church music. His famous *Missa di Papa Marcello*, performed before the commission on April 28, 1565, subordinated the music to the words, and substituted a dignified and masterly simplicity for the florid and decadent style which had hitherto characterised ecclesiastical music in Rome. The most important task left to the Papacy was however the preparation of an Index of Prohibited Books. So early as 1479 Sixtus IV had empowered the University of Cologne to inflict penalties on printers, purchasers, and readers of heretical books.

This was confirmed and extended by the Bull *Inter multiplices* of Alexander VI in 1501. At the fifth Lateran Leo X in 1515 authorised the Master of the Sacred Palace to act as censor in Rome and the papal States; and the Inquisition in 1543 began to regard the censorship as one of its functions. The first lists of prohibited books were however drawn up in 1546 and 1550 at Louvain, in 1549 at Cologne, and by the Sorbonne between 1544 and 1551. The first papal Index was that of Paul IV, which was published in 1559. It was arranged alphabetically, but under each letter came three categories. The first class consisted of the heresiarchs, all of whose writings were prohibited. This was a mere list of names. The second class consisted of writers, some of whose productions, which were enumerated, tended to heresy, impiety, magic, or immorality. The third class consisted of writings, chiefly anonymous, which were unwholesome in doctrine. The Index of Paul IV met with much opposition; and Naples, Milan, Florence, and Venice refused to print or enforce it. Pius IV modified it in 1561 by allowing the use of non-Catholic editions of the Fathers and other inoffensive writings to licensed readers, provided comments by heretics of the first class had been previously erased. No *Index Expurgatorius*, however, as distinguished from an *Index Librorum Prohibitorum*, was ever published officially at Rome. The harder work of pointing out particular passages which must be deleted was only undertaken in Spain. The Papacy contented itself with prohibiting books altogether or with a "*donec corrigatur*," of which nothing came.

The *Index Librorum Prohibitorum* of Paul IV was however condemned at Trent as a bad piece of work; and a commission was appointed to revise it. Ten rules to be observed were drawn up, but the work itself was left to the Papacy. The new Index was published by the Papacy in March, 1564, and is known as the Tridentine Index. The Index of Paul IV was improved, and some of its worst blunders removed. It was accepted by Portugal, Belgium, Bavaria, and parts of Italy. In 1571 Pius V set up a special Congregation of the Index distinct from the Inquisition; and in 1588 this body was empowered by Sixtus V to undertake further revision of the Index. Twenty-two new rules took the place of the ten laid down at Trent; and this new Index was published in 1590. Shortly after its publication, however, Sixtus V died; and Clement VIII restored the Tridentine rules and issued another Index in 1596. The materials collected for the Index of 1590 were used, though the Spanish Index of Quiroga published in 1584 was one of the chief sources. The Index of 1596 remained the standard, though additions were made to it, until the middle of the eighteenth century.

So far as the southern nations were concerned the Index achieved its work. The peoples who continued to adhere to the Catholic Church were cut off from the culture and science of the North, and a serious blow was dealt to human progress. It was impossible for such measures to succeed ultimately; but for a time at any rate they were a serious hindrance to the advance of knowledge. The learned Jesuit Canisius, in a striking letter written to the Duke of Bavaria in 1581, printed in Reusch's great history of the Index, pointed out the futility of such measures. Repression by Edicts and Indexes could never succeed; construction was needed as well as destruction, and good authors must be provided to take the place of bad. A revival of Catholic scholarship, such as Canisius advocated, marked the close of the sixteenth century, a revival in which his own Order played a prominent part. Rome became again a centre of Christian learning; and the *Annals* of Baronius were worthy to stand by the *Centuries of Magdeburg*. New editions of the Fathers were prepared. In 1587 appeared the Roman edition of the Septuagint, and both Sixtus V and Clement VIII endeavoured to improve the text of the Vulgate. Historical scholarship ceased to be the monopoly of one party. The Jesuits were the equals in learning of their adversaries and their educational system was immeasurably superior. Protestantism in Germany was torn asunder by petty feuds; and by sheer force of superior ability and unremitting labour Catholicism was restored, first in the Rhine lands and then on the Danube. The story of this work, the success of which drove Protestantism to desperation and assisted to provoke the Thirty Years' War, is beyond our scope. It is sufficient to notice here that it was the fruit of that new Catholicism which emerged triumphant from the Council of Trent. Saintliness of life and the beauty of holiness were again exhibited to the world in a Carlo Borromeo and a Filippo Neri; while Protestantism was too often sinking into a time-serving Erastianism or developing an arid scholasticism of its own which quenched the springs of religious life.

Increased centralisation in government and strict definition of dogma made Catholicism after Trent a far more powerful fighting force than it had ever been before, but it was only at the price of drawing in its borders and limiting its sympathies. There is a curious likeness in essence, though in forms of expression they are poles asunder, between Puritanism in England and the movement of which Caraffa and Ignatius are the typical representatives in the Roman Church. Both alike subordinate the wider interests of humanity to the supposed requirements of religious faith. The sacred was rigidly marked off from the profane; and the culture of the world and its wisdom were banned and avoided as evil in themselves. The world was given up as hopeless, and the attempt to separate its evil from its good was abandoned. The work which Clement of Alexandria and Origen had begun for the ancient Church, and Thomas Aquinas and the great Schoolmen had achieved for the Church of the Middle Ages, was not done anew for the modern world. The true Renaissance was not absorbed into the circle of ecclesiastical ideas; and the medieval conception of Catholicity was limited rather than widened. The modern world, if not actually hostile to the Church, grew up apart from it and by its side rather than under its influence. The kingdom of intellectual unity — which Raffaelle had depicted for Julius II on the walls of the Vatican — was not realised. The leaders of the Christian Renaissance had not the moral enthusiasm or the force of character necessary for the task. As the gentle Andrewes and the gracious Falkland had to give way before the sterner enthusiasm and the narrow pedantry of Laud, which in its turn fell before a more single-minded but still narrower creed, so Contarini and his associates abdicated the leadership to Ignatius and Caraffa. Neither Pole nor Morone had the spirit of martyrdom; and freedom could not triumph without its roll of martyrs. It was left to the sects in the future to vindicate the rights of conscience, and to extort by force from without what liberal church-men had failed to achieve within the Church. There was a touch of the dilettante spirit in the aristocratic circles of the Catholic reformers in Italy at the opening of the sixteenth century which paralysed their efforts and enervated their moral fibre. The movement was too academic to influence the world effectively. Some of its members fell into the sins which they themselves had denounced, and like Cortese ended their lives in joining in the hunt for benefices. The rest contented themselves with a lower ideal as best they could, and stood helplessly aside. The Church was reformed and underwent a moral regeneration; but religious and intellectual freedom were left further off than ever. The issues at stake were, however, made clear, and the parties in the great struggle were definitely marked out. A *modus vivendi* between authority and liberty could not be found. Neither would tolerate the other, and Europe was doomed to be the battlefield of the contending principles. The sword alone could be the arbiter.

CHAPTER XIX

TENDENCIES OF EUROPEAN THOUGHT IN THE AGE OF THE REFORMATION

WHEN the sixteenth century opens, the West, with the exception of Italy, is still medieval, distinguished by a superficial uniformity of mind, thinking ideas which it has ceased to believe and using a learned tongue which it can hardly be said to understand. When the century closes, the West, with the possible exception of Italy, now fallen as far to the rear as she once stood in the van, has become modern; its States have developed what we may term a personal consciousness and an individual character, have created a vernacular literature and a native art, and have faced new problems which they seek by the help of their new tongues to state and to solve. In Spain, the land of ancestral and undying pride, the humours of a decayed chivalry have been embodied in a tale which moves to laughter without ever provoking to contempt. In Portugal the navigators have created afresh the epic feeling; a new Iliad has been begotten, where swifter ships plough a vaster sea than was known to the ancient Greeks, where braver heroes than Agamemnon do battle against a mightier Troy, while travellers fare to remoter and stranger lands than those visited by Odysseus. In France, where the passion for unity is beginning to work like madness in the brain, Rabelais speaks in his mother tongue the praises of the new learning; Montaigne makes it the vehicle of the new temper and its cultured doubt; Clement Marot uses it to sing the Psalms of the ancient Hebrew race; John Calvin to defend and commend his strenuous faith; while Descartes, born in this century though writing in the next, states his method, defines his problem, and determines the evolution of modern philosophy, in the language of the people as well as in that of the learned. In England the century began in literary poverty, but it ended in the unapproached wealth of the Elizabethan age. In Germany, where the main intellectual interest was theological and confessional, Martin Luther gave the people hymns that often sound like echoes of the Hebrew Psalter; Kepler, listening to the music which nature reserves for the devout ear, discovered the unity which moves through her apparent disorder; and Jakob Boehme, though but a cobbler, had visions of higher mysteries than the proud can see. The Netherlands proved

690

their heroism in their struggle for independence, and their love of knowledge in the tolerant reasonableness that made them a home for the persecuted of all lands. In Scotland William Dunbar, Gawin Douglas, and David Lindsay shed lustre upon the early decades of the century, while in its later years Reformers like Knox and scholars like Andrew Melville trained up a people who had imagination enough to love and achieve liberty without neglecting letters. The thought which at once effected and reflected so immense a revolution can be here traced only in the broadest outlines.

We are met at the threshold by a two-fold difficulty — one which concerns the included thought, and another which concerns the thought excluded. The sixteenth century is great in religion rather than philo- sophy, and stands in remarkable contrast to its immediate successor, which is great in philosophy rather than religion. With the latter, the great modern intellectual systems may be said to begin; and to it belong such names as Bacon and Descartes, Hobbes and Locke, Spinoza and Leibniz, Gassendi and Malebranche. But without the earlier century the later would have been without its problems and therefore without its thinkers. The pre-eminence of the one in religion involved the pre-eminence of the other in thought; for what exercises the spirit tends to emancipate speculation and raises issues that reason must discuss and resolve before it can be at peace with itself and its world. Hence the thought whose course we have to follow is thought in transition, deal- ing with the old questions, yet waking to the new, quickened by what is behind to enquire into what is within and foreshadow what is before. But, while the thought that is to concern us may thus be described as moving in the realm of our ultimate religious ideas, the thought that is not to concern us moves in the realm of political and social theory. The two realms touch, indeed, and even interpenetrate; yet they are distinct. The ideal of human society is a religious ideal; but it is a consequence or a combination of religious ideas rather than one of the ideas themselves. Hence, though certain of the most potent thinkers of the sixteenth century occupied themselves with the constitution and order of human society, with the actual or ideal State both in itself and in relation to the actual or ideal Church, yet they must here be rigorously excluded, and our view confined to the thought that had to do with the religious interpretation of man and his Universe.

It is customary to distinguish the Renaissance, as the revival of letters, from the Reformation as the revival of religion. But the distinction is neither formally correct nor materially exact. The Renaissance was not necessarily secular and classical — it might be, and often was, both religious and Christian; nor was the Reformation essentially religious and moral — it might be and often was political and secular. Of the two revivals the one is indeed in point of time the elder; but the elder is not so much a cause as simply an antecedent of the younger. Both revivals were literary and interpretative, both were imitative and re-creative; but they differed in spirit, and they differed also in province and in results. There was a revival of letters which could not possibly become a reformation of religion, and there was a revival which necessarily involved such a reformation; and the two revivals must be distinguished if the consequences are to be understood.

The roots of the difference may be found, partly, in the minds that studied the literatures, and partly in the literatures they studied, though even here the qualities, the interests, and the motives of the minds only stand the more clearly revealed. The difference is better expressed by a racial than by a temporal distinction; the term "race," indeed, as here used does not denote a unity of blood, which can seldom if ever exist, but unities of language, inheritance, association, and ideas. In this sense, the Catholic South was in speech, in custom, in social temper, in political and municipal institutions distinctly Latin; and for similar reasons the Protestant North may be termed Teutonic. Now of these two the Latin race was in thought the more secular, while the Teutonic was the more religious; but as regards custom and institutions the Latin peoples were the more conservative, while the Teutonic were the more inclined to radical change. And this is a difference which their respective histories may in some measure explain. The Latin race, especially in Italy, was the heir of the Roman Empire, still a vivid memory and a living influence; its monuments survived, its paganism had not utterly perished; its gods were still named in popular speech; customs which it had sanctioned and dreams which it had begotten persisted, having refused, as it were, to undergo Christian baptism. Italy was to the Latins as much a holy land as Palestine had been to the Crusaders, with graves and relics and shrines lying in every valley and looking out from every hill; and these appealed all the more to the imagination since ecclesiastical Rome was a reality and imperial Rome a memory and a dream. The Eternal City was like a desolate widow who yet tarried and yearned for the return of the Caesar who had been her spouse.

And if Rome lived in the dust of her ancient roads and the ruins of her temples, the Italian peoples and States seemed singularly suggestive of Greece. Their republics and tyrants, their civic life and military adventurers, their rich cities with their colonies and commerce, their rapid changes of fortune, their swift oscillations from freedom to bondage and from bondage back to freedom, their love of art and of letters, their mutual jealousies and ambitions, were Greek rather than Roman; indeed at certain moments they might almost make us feel as if ancient Greece had risen from the dead and come to live upon the Italian soil. Here then the Renaissance could not but be classical: not the product of some accident like the capture of a city or the fall of an ancient dynasty, but the inevitable outcome of minds quickened by the Italian air and made creative by the vision of a vast inheritance. The Teutonic mind, on the contrary, had no classical world behind it; its pagan past was remote, dark, infertile, without art or literature, or philosophy, or history, or any dream of a universal empire which had once held sway over civilised man. In a word, its conscious life, its social being, its struggles for empire and towards civilisation, its chivalry, its crusades, its mental problems and educational processes, all stood rooted in the Christian religion. Behind this the memory of men did not go, and into the darkness beyond the eye could as little penetrate as the vision of the man can trace the growth of knowledge in his own infant mind.

Now these differing conditions made it as natural that the Teutonic Renaissance should concern itself with the early Christian ideal as that the Latin should with the ancient classical literature; and, where they touched religion, that the one should be more occupied with its intellectual side and the other with its institutional; for where the Roman Empire had lived the Roman Church now governed. The literature which the Teutonic mind mainly loved and studied and edited was patristic and Christian; but the literature which the Latin mind chiefly cultivated was classical and pagan. The Latin taught the Teuton how to read, to edit, and to handle ancient books; but nature taught both of them the logic that binds together letters and life. As a consequence, the Latin Renaissance became an attempt to think again the thoughts, and live again the life, embalmed in the literature of Greece and Rome; while the German Renaissance became an attempt to reincarnate the apostolical mind. The Latin tendency was towards classical Naturalism, but the Teutonic tendency was towards the ideals of the Scriptures, both Hebrew and Greek. Among the Latins almost every philosophical system of antiquity reappeared, though in an instructively inverted order; but among the Teutons the field was occupied by theologies based on Augustine and Paul, while philosophy began as an interpretation, not of literary thought or societies, but of man, individual and social, as he had lived and was living.

Hence, in the region of belief the Latins were the more critical and the Teutons the more positive. The thought which the Latins studied was that of a world into which Christ had not entered, though it was one in which Caesar had reigned; but the thought which the Teutons cultivated had Christ as its source and God as its supreme object. The Latin Renaissance thus produced two most dissimilar yet cognate phenomena: intellectual systems affecting mainly the notion of Deity, and Orders like the Society of Jesus, organised for the work of conservation and reaction. On the other hand, the parallel phenomena produced by the Teutonic Renaissance were attempts either to revive the religion of the apostolic literature, or to found the Protestant Churches and States. What concerns us here is the new thought, and not the new organisations; and these preliminary distinctions and discussions will enable us to set the Latin, or Classical Renaissance, in its true relation to the Teutonic or religious.

We begin with the most obvious of the influences exercised by the Revival of Letters upon the thought of the sixteenth century, viz., those concerned with grammar and what it signified, and with language as the creation and the interpreter of thought. It has often been said that the Church preserved the knowledge of Latin as a living tongue; but Lorenzo Valla (1406–57) would have said, if the tongue were still alive it were better dead. As a grammarian Valla held grammar to be higher than dialectic, for it took as many years to learn as dialectic took months; and he may be said to have discovered literary and historical criticism by executing with its help judgment on three famous documents, viz., the Vulgate, which he condemned as faulty in style and incorrect in translation; the Donation of Constantine, which he proved by its anachronisms to be late and false and forged; and the Apostolic Symbol, whose terms and clauses he showed could not be of apostolic origin. His criticism of these documents (we omit all reference to that of the pseudo-Dionysius) was prophetic and more potent in a later generation than in his own. Erasmus published in 1505 the *Annotationes* on the Vulgate, and in a dedication which served as a preface he compared Valla as a grammarian and Nicolas of Lyra as a theologian; and he argued from the errors which had been proved to exist in the version which the Church had in a sense canonised by use, in a way that was at once an apology and a call for his own edition of the Greek New Testament nine years before it appeared. In 1517 a copy of the *De Donatione Constantini Magni* came into the hands of Ulrich von Hutten, who published it, and with his usual careless audacity dedicated it to the Pope, whom he straightway proceeded to denounce as a usurper and robber. Later this was sent to Luther just as he was meditating his *De Captivitate Babylonica Ecclesiae;* and it strengthened his trust in the German people, confirmed him in the belief that the Pope was Antichrist, and fortified him for the daring deed of burning the Pope's Bull. The criticism of the Apostles' Creed indicated a method of discussing dogma which only needed to be applied to become a theory of development capable of dissolving the vast systems of the traditional schools. We need not be surprised that Calvin speaks of Valla as "an acute and judicious man, and an instrument of the Divine Will."

The Italian mind was simple in spite of all its subtle complexity, and in the Renaissance it was like the explorer who set out to find a new way to India and found a new world instead. It had no more typical son than Giovanni Pico della Mirandola. He was—if we are to believe his nephew and biographer—chivalrous, beautiful, radiant, a man it was impossible to see without loving, an artist who loved art, a thinker who delighted in thought, a seeker whose passion it was to find the truth, and who would gladly have sold all he possessed to buy it. Born in 1463, he studied Canon Law at Bologna; then, first at Padua, and later at Paris, he cultivated philosophy. When only twenty-one he returned to Italy and read Plato in Florence under Ficino; three years later he travelled to Rome, where he drew up nine hundred theses, philosophical and theological, which he offered to discuss with the scholars of all lands, promising, if they came, to bear the cost of their journey. But heresy was discovered in some of the theses, and the disputation was prohibited. Later he devoted himself to a contemplative life, renounced the world, divided his goods between his nephew and the poor, saying that, once he had finished the studies which he had undertaken, he should wander barefoot round the world in order that he might preach Christ. He was a mystic; nature was to him a parable, history was an allegory, and every sensuous thing an emblem of the Divine. He magnified man, though he distrusted self; and as he believed that truth came only by revelation he felt bound to seek it from those who had thus received it from God. Hence he searched for truth, successively in Aristotle, in Plato, in Plotinus, and in the pseudo-Dionysius, who seemed to many, even after Valla had written, the source of the highest and purest truth. But as Pico said, philosophy seeks truth, theology finds it, but religion possesses it; and the truth which religion possesses is God's. Man can best discover it in the place where God has been pleased to set it.

Now, in his quest for truth and its purest sources, Pico heard of the Cabbala, and conceived it to be the depository of the most ancient wisdom, the tradition of the aboriginal revelation granted to man. And just then John Reuchlin, German mystic and scholar, found Pico. He was older in years but younger in mind. He had studied philology in Paris, law in Orleans, and he had lectured on Greek in Tübingen; he was then on his second visit to Italy, with all the mystic in him alive and unsatisfied. The God whom he wanted, the logic of the Schools could not give him; by their help he might transcend created existence, though even then what they led him to was only the boundless sea of negation. In Aristotle the impossible, in Plato the incredible, was emphasised; but in the region of spirit things were necessary which thought found impossible or reason pronounced incredible. The Neo-Pythagorean School saved Reuchlin from the tyranny of the syllogism and restored his faith. In this mood he came to Pico, and to his mood the Cabbala appealed; its philosophy was a symbolical theology which invested words and numbers, letters and names, things and persons, with a divine sense. But Reuchlin was more than a mystic with a passion for fantastic mysteries; he was also a scholar; and the idea that there were truths locked up in Hebrew, the tongue which God Himself had spoken at the Creation and which He had then given to man, compelled him to learn the language that he might read the thought in the words of

Deity. So he put himself to school under a Jewish physician, acquired enough Hebrew to pursue his studies independently, and, as a result, published in 1506 his *De Rudimentis Hebraicis*. He himself named this book a *monumentum aere perennius*, and history has justified the name. It helped to define and determine the religious tendencies in Teutonic humanism, to change the fanciful mysticism that had begotten the book into a spirit at once historical, critical, and sane. It practically made the Hebrew Scriptures Christian, an original text which could be used as a Court of appeal for the correction of the translation and of the canon which the usage of the Church had accepted and endorsed. Knowledge of the language thus made the interpretation of the Old Testament more historical and more ethical; it could now be read as little through the Gnosticism of the Cabbala as through the Roman associations of the Vulgate.

The event which took the Old Testament out of the hand of phantasy turned it into an instrument of reform; for if it is doubtful whether Protestantism could have arisen without the knowledge of the Old Testament, it is certain that without it the Reformed Church could not have assumed the shape it took. In all this, of course, specific dangers might lie for the scholar who could no longer freely use the allegorism of Alexandria to convey the New Testament into the most impossible places of the Old, and who was therefore tempted to reverse the process and employ the language and spirit of the Old Testament in the interpretation of the New. But these dangers were still in the future; for the present it will be enough to recall the story, told in an earlier volume, of the controversy between Reuchlin and Pfefferkorn, and of the burning of Reuchlin's books by the Inquisition. In consequence of this unjust treatment, the humanists addressed a series of letters, at once eulogistic and apologetic, to Reuchlin, which were published in 1514 under the title *Epistolae clarorum Virorum*. (The second edition in 1519 substituted " *illustrium* " for " *clarorum*.")

This book suggested to one of the younger and brighter humanists, John Jäger — better known as Crotus Rubeanus, Luther's " *Crotus noster suavissimus*," a professor at Erfurt — a series of imaginary epistles written by vagrant students in the execrable dog-Latin of the Schools, to Ortwinus Gratius, otherwise Ortwin de Graes, professor of *belles lettres* at Cologne, a man whom Luther in his most emphatic and plain-spoken style described as " *poetistam asinum, lupum rapacem, si non potius crocodilum*." The *Epistolae*, while describing the experiences or adventures of their supposed authors, — and it is here where the characters so humorously reveal themselves — praise Gratius as well as the divines and divinity of the Schools, and censure the "*poetae seculares* " or "*juristae*" who had eulogised Reuchlin. In their composition various scholars collaborated, notably Ulrich von Hutten, then ablaze with the enthusiasm for Germany and the passion against Rome which made the

strife a joy to his soul. " The prison is broken," he cried, " the captive
is free and will return no more to bondage." " O century when studies
bloom and spirits awake, it is happiness to live in thee ! "

Strauss thought the *Epistolae* a supreme work of art, named them
" *eine weltgeschichtliche Satire*," and placed them alongside *Don Quixote*,
since they were pervaded by so excellent a humour as to be higher and
better than any merely satirical production. There is here ground for
ample and radical differences, but on one point there is none—the success
of the satire. It deceived the very elect ; the friars who were satirised
saw the truth of the portrait and did not feel its shame, even though
the men of serious mind, who could not be deceived, were offended.
Erasmus did not love it ; nor did Luther, who said " *Votum probo, opus
non probo*," and named the author " *einen Hanswurst*" ; but it made
the Schoolmen ridiculous, and while they were laughed at Reuchlin was
applauded. He died in 1522, six years after the *Epistolae* had appeared
—the same year in which Luther published his New Testament—
sorrowing over the lapse from the Church and from letters of his young
kinsman, Melanchthon, and over the coming revolution which yet had
in him a plain prophet and a main cause.

In 1516, two years after the first volume of the *Epistolae*, Erasmus'
Novum Instrumentum appeared. The man himself we need neither discuss
nor describe. He was a humanist, that is, his main interest was literature ;
but his humanism was German ; that is, the literature which mainly inter-
ested him was religious. In an age of great editors he was the most
famous ; but he was not a thinker, nor a man who could seize or be seized
by large ideas and turn them into living and creative forces. His greatest
editorial achievements were connected not with the classics, where his
haste and his agility of mind made him often a faithless guide, but with
the New Testament and the Fathers of the Church. Religion he loved
for the sake of letters rather than letters for the sake of religion. He
had a quick eye, a sharp pen, a fine humour, and could hold up to man
and society a mirror which showed them as they were. He was fastidious
and disliked discomfort, yet he could make it picturesque and amusing.
His letters are like a crowded stage on which his time lives for ever ; and
we can hear and see even as his ear heard and as his eye saw. We are,
indeed, never allowed to forget that he is a rather too self-conscious
spectator ; and that while all around him men differ and he is a main
cause of their differences, yet there is nothing he more desires than to
be left alone to live as untroubled as if he had no mind. He is " so
thin-skinned that a fly would draw blood " ; yet, or possibly therefore, he
is a good hater, especially of the ignorant mob, the obtuse and vulgar
men who could not see or feel the satire within the compliment or the
irony hidden in an ambiguous phrase.

He is one of the men whose unconscious revelations of himself have
a nameless charm ; we see him as a student whose very circumstances

remind him of his origin, *ortus a scorto* as his enemies said, impecunious, forced into an Order he did not love, thirsting for a knowledge hard to obtain, seeking it at home or in Paris, where life is fast while his clerical guardian is suspicious and his own temper self-indulgent. Then we are touched by the early struggles of a scholar who loved learning and good living, and neither liked nor acquiesced in the poverty which seemed his destined lot, though we may be offended by his complaints, which are too frequent to be dignified, and his appeals for help, which are too urgent to be compatible with self-respect as we understand it. His pictures of our gracious and spacious England, loved because it is so kind to the stranger — the seclusion and erudition of Oxford, the repose and learned activity of Cambridge, the regal Henry, the magnificent Wolsey, the devout Colet, the genial More, the statesmanlike yet thoughtful Warham, who can rule the Church and yet remember the scholars who serve it, — are of a sort which pleases the reader and which he loves to read. And if he desires first-hand knowledge of the manners and morals of a picturesque day, the miseries of the sea and the comforts of the shore, or the discomforts of continental travel with its strange bedfellows, crowded inns, dirty linen, and unsavoury food; or of the dignified society and refined art of living to be then found in the great Italian cities; or of Rome and Roman society under Julius II, where a warlike Pontiff and cultured Cardinals, the spirit of the Borgia and the temper of the Renaissance, make the capital of Christendom an epitome of the world; or of the hopes, the disappointments, and the sorrows of an editor with a zeal for letters and a passion for praise, who negotiates now with mean and now with open-handed publishers, and stands between three publics, one sympathetic and appreciative, a second suspicious and sore and critical, fearful lest he go too far, and a third exacting and insatiable, determined to compel him to go much further than he wishes; or of the Reforming men and movements, the strange and tempestuous Luther, the audacious and restless Hutten, the moderate and scholarly Pirkheimer, the conciliatory and reasonable Melanchthon, the heroic and magnanimous Zwingli, the learned and large-minded Œcolampadius, — then he will find this knowledge superabundantly in this vivid and entertaining correspondence.

Yet, if we would know Erasmus, he must be studied in his more serious works, as well as in his letters. There we shall find the clergy of all grades from the friar and the parish priest to the Pope, the superstitions and ceremonies, the pilgrimages and fastings, the distinctions in dress and food, the worship of relics and of Saints, — pilloried and satirised and killed, at least so far as ridicule can kill. And his lighter moods express his graver mind; and unless this mind be known there is no person in history to whom we shall find it harder to be just. He is a proud and a strong man, when questions are at issue for which he supremely cares; but he will seem to us indifferent or vain or weak where the question is one for which he did not care, however much we may wish he had. And, curiously, where his strength as well as his weakness most appears is in his edition of the New Testament. The inaccuracies of his text, the few and the poor authorities he consulted, the haste of the editor, the hurry of the publisher, the carelessness of the printer, and the facility with which he inserted in the third and later editions a text like 1 *John* v. 7, which he had omitted in the first and second, are all instances of weakness familiar even to the unlearned.

But the sagacity — which saw in the Epistle to the Hebrews a work instinct with the spirit but without the style of Paul, which doubted whether John the Apostle were the author of the Apocalypse, which discerned in Luke the Greek of a writer skilled in literature, which perceived in the Gospels quotations from a memory which could be at fault, or which inferred textual errors even where the authorities were agreed — is characteristic of the honest scholar and indicative of the courageous man. What is still more significant, is the deliberate way in which as an editor and exegete he repeats the views and reaffirms the arguments of his more occasional works. Stunica charged him with the impiety of casting doubt on the claims and the authority of the Roman See and of denying the primacy of Peter. The Church, Erasmus said, was the congregation of all men throughout the whole world who agreed in the faith of the Gospel. As to the Lord's Supper, he saw neither good nor use in a body imperceptible to the senses; and he found no place in Scripture which said that the Apostles had consecrated bread and wine into the body and blood of the Lord. Heathenism of life and Judaism of worship had come upon the Church from the neglect of the Gospel. Ceremonies were positive laws made by Bishops or Councils, Popes or Orders which could not supersede the laws of nature or of God. The priest who wore a lay habit or let his hair grow was punished; but if he became a debauchee he might yet remain a pillar of the Church.

These were brave things for a man so timid as Erasmus and so desirous of standing well with the authorities of the Church to say; and in saying them he was governed by this historical idea: — things unknown to the New Testament were unnecessary to the Christian religion; what contradicted the mind of Christ or hindered the realisation of His ends was injurious to His Church. This idea determined the attitude of Erasmus both to Rome and to Protestantism. He, indeed, honestly believed that where Lutheranism reigned there literature perished; and that to restore the knowledge of the New Testament was to bring back the mind of Christ, who was the one teacher God had appointed, and therefore the sole and supreme authority in His Church. Hence, his difference from Luther was as inevitable as his difference from Rome, and more absolute, for in the one case he differed from a man, in the other from a system. It has often been said that his *De libero arbitrio* enabled him to express his difference from Luther without expressing his agreement with Rome, or recanting "his earlier criticism of ecclesiastical abuses." This judgment is both prejudiced and unjust. It is indeed certain that the book was written in the desire to dissociate himself from Luther, as well as in response to the appeal to write something against the new heresy; but it is no less certain that the book expressed a point on which Luther's scholasticism offended the humanism of Erasmus. The saying "*liberum arbitrium esse nomen inane*" seemed to him an "*aenigma absurdum*," and for this reason—it was unknown to the New Testament and the Apostolic Church. It might be Augustinian, it certainly was scholastic; but it was neither Biblical nor primitive. Erasmus, in short, wrote as a Greek and not as a Latin theologian, as a Classical scholar and not as a Western divine. He could not have selected a point more characteristic of his own position. He would have the Christian religion known through its creative literature; he would not have it identified with the philosophy or theology of any school.

So far we have been occupied with the formal rather than the material side of thought; now we must consider the latter, or thought in its objective expression as at once evolved, governed, and served by the critical method.

We begin with the Latin Renaissance. Its thought grew out of the study of Classical literature, though it reversed rather than followed the sequences of the Classical mind. The one began where the other ended, in an eclectic Neo-Platonism, or a multitude of borrowed principles reduced by a speculation, more or less arbitrary, to a reasoned unity which was yet superficial; but it ended where the other began, in attempts to interpret the nature within which man lived, with a view to the better interpretation of man. Though the order of evolution was inverted, it was yet in the circumstances the only order possible. For the mind which the voice of literature awakened could only respond to a voice which was articulate and intelligible. The mind was old in speculation, though its problems were new, and its age was reflected in the solutions it successively attempted or accepted. It had been educated in schools where theology reigned while Aristotle governed; and it revolted from the governing minister out of loyalty to the reigning sovereign, whose authority extended over regions of too infinite variety to be administered by his narrow and rigid methods.

The literature which enlarged the outlook changed the mind; it could not think as it had thought before or believe as it had believed concerning the darkness and error of pagan antiquity. The light which dwelt in ancient philosophy broke upon it like an unexpected sunrise, which it saw with eyes that had been accustomed to a grey and creeping dawn. And this means, that Classical thought was seized at the point where it stood nearest to living experience, and yet formed the most expressive contrast to it. This point was where philosophy had done its best to become a religion, and had tried out of its school to make a Church. Hence, the new mind in the first flush of its awaking turned from its ancient master, Aristotle, and threw itself into the arms of the Neo-Platonists. Gemistos Plethon, who took part in the Council of Florence, 1439, was intellectually the most potent of the Greeks who helped in the Renaissance. He regarded Aristotle as a westernised Mohammedan rather than as a Greek, a man who had indeed once lived on the Hellenic soil, but who had become an alien in race and an enemy in religion, speaking in the Latin schools ideas which he owed to a Moorish interpreter. So Plethon expounded to the awakening West Plato as the Neo-Platonists understood him, "the Attic Moses," the transmitter of a golden tradition which the secular Aristotle had tried to break and which ran back through Pythagoras to Zoroaster on the one hand and Abraham on the other. His philosophy was at once monotheistic and polytheistic; God was one and infinite, but He acted by means of ideas or spirits, or minor deities who filled the space between us and Him. As first and final cause He ordered all things for the best, and left no room for chance or accident. Providence was necessity and fate providence, the world in all its parts and life in all its elements were vehicles of a divine purpose. The soul of man was immortal; the doctrine of reminiscence proved that it had lived before birth and so could live after death.

Plethon emphasised in every possible way the differences between Plato and Aristotle, refusing to allow them to be reduced to a mere question of terminology. This teaching lifted men above the arid syllogisms of the schools, enriched their view of themselves and nature, of God and history, and gave reality to the ancient saying "*ex oriente lux.*" For it came more as a religion than as a philosophy; even the apparatus of worship was mimicked; ceremonies were instituted, holy or feast days were observed; celebrities became saints, before the bust of Plato a taper was ceremoniously burned. The neophytes underwent a species of conversion; Marsilio Ficino (1433–99) was said to have been called in his youth to be a physician of souls, and designated as the translator of the two great masters, Plato and Plotinus. Man was conceived as like unto God, and was named divine; his destiny was to seek eternal union with the God from whom he came. That God was the archetype of the universe, its unmoved mover and orderer, the ground of all our reasoning, the light of all our seeing. He knew the world from within when He knew Himself, for creation was only the expression of the divine thought, God as it were speaking with Himself, and man overhearing His speech.

The circle of those devoted to the study of this philosophy contained the most distinguished scholars of the day. Besides Ficino there stood his friends or converts, Angelo Poliziano, though his fame is mainly philological; Cristoforo Landino, the exponent of Horace, of Virgil, and of Dante, who has given us a picture of Florentine society which recalls Plato's *Symposium;* Girolamo Benivieni, the poet who sang in praise of Platonic love ; the architect, painter and man of letters, Leo Battista Alberti ; Pico della Mirandola, of whose faith and fame and achievements we have already spoken; and above all the men of the Medicean House who founded the so-called Platonic Academy of Florence. This was rather a Society than a School, not an equipped and organised college, but an association of like-minded men who cultivated philosophy and professed to live according to the philosophy they cultivated. It added lustre to the reign of the Medici, helped to define its character, to fix upon it name and distinction. Under Cosmo and his son Piero, and especially under his grandson Lorenzo, it became the centre and sum and even source of Florentine culture. But the patronage of the House proved fatal to the thought for which the Academy stood ; with the House it rose, lived in its smile, fell in its fall. Yet it did not fall before it had accomplished things that could not die. It revealed the world which the Church had extinguished and the Schoolmen superseded ; it raised the reason that could speculate concerning truth above the authority that would legislate in its behalf ; it taught men to believe that the truth lived in the soul rather than in books, that nature was beautiful and man was good, and that truth existed before Church or Councils and stood outside them both, and that man attains to the larger humanity by the study of that literature in which the truth adapted to his nature is best expressed. These were indeed notable contributions to the thought of the century.

But though Plato lived in the New Academy, Aristotle still reigned in the older Schools. He had been too efficient an instrument in education to be easily pushed aside; but the thought which is to shape living mind must not itself be dead. Hence the men, who were by birth as well as by discipline Aristotelians, set themselves to rejuvenate the ancient Master and change his obsolete speech into the language of the day. Three tendencies at once showed themselves, one which interpreted Aristotle in the sense and manner of Averroes ; a second which construed him by the help of the Greek commentators, especially Alexander of Aphrodisia ; and a third which laboured to reconcile him with Plato, some of the last-named going to Aristotle for their physics, but to Plato for their metaphysics. It soon became evident that the philosophical questions involved theology and raised issues affecting certain dogmas of the Church. These issues were more sharply defined in the Aristotelian than in the Neo-Platonic Schools and seriously alarmed the Church. How this was and with what reason, Pomponazzi (1462–1524) — Peretto, or little Peter, as he was affectionately named — will help us to understand.

Reverence for Aristotle had become in him a second nature ; and though he writes poor Latin and knows no Greek, and is, as he said, in comparison with his master but an insect beside an elephant, yet he desires to serve truth by interpreting his philosophy. He frankly emphasised its opposition to faith; and narrowly escaped being burned for his pains, though his books were not so fortunate. He said: "The thinker, who inquires into the divine mysteries, is like Proteus. In face of consequences he neither hungers nor thirsts, eats or sleeps; the Inquisition persecutes him as a heretic; the multitude mocks him as a fool." Doubt is native to him, and like Descartes he doubts that he may know; but, unlike Descartes, his doubt is more critical than speculative, more literary than philosophical. And if he has a doubt to express he dearly loves to express it in another name than his own, or shield himself behind some noted authority. Religions he conceives as laws instituted by lawgivers, like Christ or Mohammed, for the regulation of life. They are governed in their coming and going, in their bloom and decay, by time and space; and their horoscope can be cast just as if they were mortal beings. Christianity is proved true by its miracles, which are not impossible, though they have now ceased to happen and fictitious marvels have taken their place. Since religions are laws, they must promise to reward the righteous and threaten to punish the wicked; and as conduct rather than knowledge is their end they may use parables and myths, which, of course, need not be true. Man is like the ass which must be beaten that it may carry its burden; to teach him deep mysteries would be but to waste our breath. Nor are we to esteem him too highly or exhort him to become godlike, for how can man resemble a God whom he cannot know? As it is impossible to have natural grounds for a supernatural faith we must be content to hold it without reason, though it may be a gift of grace. If religion be moral then man must be free. And though his freedom may be incapable of rational proof yet it is a matter of conscious experience. This, indeed, may seem incompatible with Providence, which Aristotle conceived as general rather than particular, though we conceive it as a general made up of all particulars; but where philosophy is blind revelation may see, and it is better to trust it than to walk in darkness. The God who governs has created, and creation was willed in eternity, but happens in time, for Aristotle's idea of an eternal creation is sophistical. As the workman loves his handiwork so God loves all His creatures and wills their good. He has given to every being, not perhaps the absolutely best, but the best for it and for the universe, viewed in their complementary and reciprocal relations. For men supplement each other; what seems in and by itself a defect may become an excellency when seen from the standpoint of the collective whole. Man lives in humanity, humanity within nature, nature in God; and we ought to know all together before we judge any separately.

This is what would be called to-day a system of philosophical agnosticism, where man's ignorance becomes a plea, if not a reason for faith ; but what it signified to Pomponazzi we shall best understand by turning to his famous treatise on the Immortality of the Soul. The treatise is at once an attempt at the historical interpretation of Aristotle and a serious independent discussion. It is practically concerned with the question : How did Aristotle conceive immortality, as personal or as collective ? It is as little soluble by the natural reason as the cognate question whether the world is eternal or created ; in each case the problem as to the beginning holds the key of the problem as to the end. The Aristotelian Schoolmen had argued that the capacity of the soul to think the eternal and will the universal implied its immortality. But what is the soul ? We cannot define it as thought percipient of the universal reason, for there can be no thought without ideas and no ideas without sense. The soul which lives within nature must develop according to natural law and in obedience to it. Now, we never find soul without body; and hence we must ask : how are these related ? Not as mover and moved, else their proper analogies would be the ox and the waggon it draws, but as matter and form, *i.e.* without the body the soul could not be, for only through the body does man take his place in nature and realise his rational activity. Hence the human soul cannot exist without the human body, and must therefore be liable to the same mortality. And this conclusion is worked out in connexion with the moral doctrine that man is bound to act from love of virtue and horror of vice, and not from any hope of reward or fear of punishment, and so to act as to make all nature the better for his action. Reason, then, must conclude that the soul is mortal ; but religion comes to our aid, and by teaching us to believe in the resurrection of the body resolves our doubts. Of this doctrine philosophy knows nothing, and so we can hold it only as an article of faith. This is in effect all Pomponazzi can teach us ; religion and reason occupy opposite camps ; neither can hold intercourse with the other. The truths of religion are the contradictions of the reason ; the processes of the reason cannot serve the cause of religion. The new scholasticism was a philosophy of reasoned ignorance where the cardinal verities of religion were the inconceivabilities of thought.

But here certain new forces which seriously affected the course and the development of Latin thought must be referred to and analysed. The ecclesiastical situation began to change, and the temper of the Renaissance changed with it. Thought had revived without conscious antagonism to the Church, though with the clear sense of opposition to the Schools and their methods. Churchmen had been forward in cultivating the new spirit, had encouraged and studied its literature, appreciated and promoted its art. But the Reformation, with its attendant incidents, made the Church suspicious of movements which might contain the seeds of revolt, while the Renaissance, always sensitive to outer conditions, lost its spontaneity, becoming self-conscious and critical. Italy after 1525 became what the Moorish wars had made Spain, sullen in temper and jealous in disposition; she imitated Spanish methods and developed the Inquisition; in Rome, once careless and happy, the Holy Office was founded.

One of the earliest fruits of this change of feeling was the revival of Scholasticism and the increased influence of the Spanish mind upon the Italian. This revived Scholasticism, which was bred mainly in two Orders, both of Spanish origin, the Dominican and the Jesuit, and introduced by them into schools and universities, pulpits and Courts, learning and literature, was used to prove the necessity of the Church to religion, of the Pope to the Church, and of all three to society and the State. It had the learning which the Renaissance created, but was without its knowledge of antiquity, its sympathy with it, or its belief in finding there virtue and truth. Its purpose was indeed quite specific: to prove not that the Church was the mother of culture or mistress of art, but that she was the sole possessor of truth, the one authority by which it could be defined, authenticated, and guaranteed. The line of defence was bold: the Church was the creation of God, its government His express design, its rulers instituted by His immediate act. Secular rulers were but mediate creatures of God, appointed through the people and responsible to them; but spiritual rulers were His immediate creation and responsible to Him alone. And since the Church was the sole custodian of truth, it was not permissible to seek it without her or outside her; to profess to have found it independently was to be heretical; to obey what had been so found was to fall into the deadliest schism. The argument may have been narrow, but it was clear and strenuous; it may not have converted opponents, but it convinced friends. The Church became conscious of her mission; she was the guardian of thought, the guide of mind. She alone could judge what was truth and what error, what men ought to do or ought not to know. And as she believed so she acted, with results that are broadly written upon the face of history. The new Scholastics converted their own Church from the Catholicity which encouraged the Renaissance to the Romanism which suppressed its thought.

This, then, is what we have now to see; and so we resume our discussion of the thought which, as it faced the second quarter of the sixteenth century, began to feel the creeping shadow of the future. The change came slowly — for mind loves a violent catastrophe as little as nature — still it came and was marked by the rise of physical in succession to metaphysical speculation. The Neo-Platonic school had tended to a mystical and allegorical conception of the world, which implied a doctrine of the divine immanence and looked towards Pantheism. The Aristotelians, on the other hand, emphasised the ideas of cause and Creator, conceived the universe as manufactured and limited, and God as transcendent, the two being correlated in the manner of the later deism. The one school was inclined to read nature through Deity, the other Deity through nature; but in each case nature took its meaning from the temper and fundamental postulates of the school. The traditional ideas were Aristotelian; the universe was geocentric; its main fact was the opposition of heaven and earth, with the involved antithesis of the higher or celestial element, and the four lower elements, earth, air, fire, water, all movement being explained from their attempts to effect a change of place.

This theory could not satisfy men who believed in a philosophy of immanence; and efforts were soon made to dislodge it. One of the earliest and most notable of these stands associated with the name of Bernardino Telesio (1508–80). He was a devout son of the Church as well as a zealous student of nature, and he disliked Aristotle for two reasons: first, because his philosophy knows neither piety nor a Creator; and, secondly, because he tried to interpret nature without questioning herself. Telesio's fundamental principle was this: nature must be explained in her own terms according to the method of experience and by the instrument of the senses. He conceived matter as a substance incapable of increase or decrease, more or less passive, yet susceptible of being acted upon by two forces, heat and cold, which, as causes, respectively, of expansion and contraction, produce all motion and all change. The heavens are the home of heat, and the earth of cold; and the constant effort of heat to illumine the dark and quicken the cold issue in a conflict whence come all the movement and variety of nature. The whole proceeds according to immanent laws and without the intervention of God. Nature is self-contained and self-sufficient; which however did not mean that she is without intelligence; on the contrary, there is a soul in things; each supplements and serves the other; mind lives in each, and works through the whole. Bacon saw in Telesio a return to Parmenides; others have seen in him an anticipation of Kant; others again have construed his principle "*non ratione sed sensu*" as if he were the first of modern empiricists, the forerunner of the sensuous philosophy, both English and French. In all these views there is a measure of truth. He clothed his doctrines in a guise more or less mythical; he could best conceive natural forces as personal, and he was never so ideal as when he meant to be most realistic. But he intended to be true to his principle, to construe nature not through metaphysics or theology, but from herself alone. It is this that makes him so significant in the history of thought, anticipating so much of what Bacon achieved, and places him, in spite of his crude and allegorical nomenclature, amid the forefathers of modern physics.

The speculations of Telesio did not stand alone; they were characteristic of his race and time. Italy, during what remained of the century, seemed to forsake philosophy for science, but the science she cultivated was only disguised philosophy. A distinguished contemporary, a critic and a Platonist, was Francesco Patrizzi (1529–97), who agreed with the Telesian physics, but differed in his metaphysics : arguing that, as both the corporeal and spiritual light emanated from one source, each was the kin and correlate of the other, the effects being reduced to unity by the unity of the cause. Another and younger contemporary, who loved to think and speak of himself as Telesio's disciple, though he only saw the master after death, was Tommaso Campanella (1568–1639). His career has something of the tragedy which belongs to another and even more distinguished contemporary, Galileo Galilei (1564–1642), for whom he wrote while suffering imprisonment a noble though unsuccessful Apology. Like Galilei, Campanella lived after Copernicus, and was attracted by his sublimer and vaster view of the universe; and, like Copernicus, he was accused of heresy in consequence, spending, partly on account of his religious and partly on account of his political views, twenty-seven years of his life in prison. He was at first, and he probably remained, in spite of all the persecutions he endured, a faithful Catholic. While he followed Telesio, he was yet a most independent disciple. His science evolved into a philosophy of existence, whose highest truth is the Deity, and whose fixed first principle is the thought, the "*Notio abdita innata*," which is man. He was praised by Leibniz as one who soared to heaven, in contrast to Hobbes, who grovelled upon the earth. Then as Telesio anticipated Bacon, Campanella anticipated Descartes. Though he does not use the formula he holds the principle of the "*cogito ergo sum.*" Both are rooted in Augustine, who said : "As for me, the most certain of all things is that I exist. Even if thou deniest this and sayest that I deceive myself, yet thou dost confess that I am, for if I do not live how could I deceive myself?" One of the strangest things in connexion with the Catholic Campanella is the State, as described by him in his *Civitas Solis*. It is an echo of the Platonic Republic, without private property or family, with sexual intercourse publicly regulated and children owned and educated by the State, without a priesthood or public and positive religion, with philosophers as rulers and work-men as the true nobility. It was a noble dream, and shows how little physical speculation had killed ethical passion ; the best interpreted earth was empty till it was made the home of happy and contented men.

Giordano Bruno (1548–1600) is of all the thinkers of the Latin Renaissance the most modern ; in him science becomes philosophical, and philosophy speaks the language of science, confronts, defines, and enlarges its problems. As a man he is passionate, explosive, impetuous, vain, intolerant, and indomitable ; and where these qualities are allowed freely to mix and express themselves it is very difficult indeed to be just. He himself says that "if the first button of one's coat is wrongly buttoned all the rest will be crooked" ; and the event which set his whole life awry happened when, as a lad of sixteen, he entered the Dominican Order. He early thought himself into heresy, and in his nature were fires which "all the snows of Caucasus" could not quench. In the effort to unfrock himself he became a wanderer, tried Rome, roamed over Northern Italy, crossed the Alps, and settled at Geneva, where he found neither the discipline nor the doctrine of the Reformed Church to his mind. He then emigrated to Toulouse, where he studied the New Astronomy, tried to be at home and to teach the fanatical Catholics of southern France in a city where the Inquisition had an ancient history. He next moved to Paris, where he attempted to instruct the doctors of the Sorbonne and to make his peace with the Church; and, failing, he crossed to England, where he lived for a while, wrote and published in London, and at Oxford claimed with much literary extravagance the right to lecture. To his Italian soul England was an uncongenial clime; he praised Elizabeth, as the Inquisition remembered later to his hurt; but he despised the barbarians over whom she ruled, and the ostentatious wealth and intellectual impotence of Oxford in her day.

From England he wandered back to France and thence to Germany, where he lectured at Wittenberg and eulogised Luther, who had "like a modern Hercules fought with Cerberus and his triple crown." He was elected to a professorship at Helmstedt; which he soon forsook for Frankfort. But the home-sickness which would not be denied was on him, and he turned back to Italy where bloomed the culture which was to him the finest flower of humanity, where dwelt the men who moved him to love and not to hate, whose speech and thought threw over him a spell he could not resist. He was denounced to the Inquisition; spent eight years in prison, first in Venice and then in Rome; and, finally, on February 17, 1600, he was sent to the stake. Caspar Scioppius, a German who had passed from the Protestant to the Roman Church, and who loved neither Bruno nor his views, tells us that when the prisoner heard his sentence he only said, "You who condemn me perhaps hear the judgment with greater fear than myself." And he adds that at the stake Bruno put aside a crucifix which was held out to him, and so entered heaven proclaiming how the Romans dealt with "blasphemous and godless men." A modern admirer sees, in the eyes uplifted to the blue, a spirit that would have no dark image stand between him and the living God.

It is customary now to describe Bruno's system as a form of pantheism. The term was not known then, or indeed for more than a hundred years after his death, which means that the idea is as modern as the term. Bruno was roundly named, just as Spinoza was later, an atheist, for men thought it was all one to identify God with nature and to deny His independent existence. The systems were indeed radically unlike; for while the one was a theophantism or apotheosis of nature, the other was an akosmism or a naturalisation of God : in other words, Bruno started with nature and ended with Deity, but Spinoza began with Deity, his *causa sui, substantia*, or *ens absolute infinitum*, and reasoned down to nature. The antecedents of the one system were classical and philosophical but those of the other Semitic and religious. The historical factors of Bruno's thought were two, ancient or Neo-Platonic, and modern or scientific. His system, if system it can be called, may be described as an attempt to state and to articulate the ideas inherited by him in the terms of the universe which Copernicus had revealed.

He conceived this universe as infinite, and so rejected the ancient scholastic idea of a limited nature with its distinctions and divisions of place, its here and there, its above and below, its cycles and epicycles. But the universe, which has no centre and therefore no circumference, has yet a unity for consciousness, and wherever consciousness is its unity appears. And this unity signifies that order reigns in the universe ; that its phenomena are connected ; that individual things are yet not insulated ; and this coherence implies that all are animated by a common life and moved by a common cause. And this cause must be as infinite as the universe ; for an infinite effect can proceed only from an infinite cause, and such a cause can be worthily expressed only in such an effect. But there is no room for two infinities to exist at the same moment in the same place ; and so the effect must be simply the body of the cause, the cause the soul of the effect. Hence the cause is immanent, not transcendent ; matter is animated, the pregnant mother who bears and brings forth all forms and varieties of being. And the soul which animates matter and energises the whole is God ; He is the *natura naturans*, Who is not above and not outside, but within and through, all things. He is the monad of monads, the spirit of spirits, carried so within that we cannot think ourselves without thinking Him.

There are, indeed, other expressions in Bruno ; God is described as "the supersubstantial substance," as "the supernatural first principle," exalted far above nature, which is only a shadow of divine truth, speaking to us in parables. And this is possible, because in every single thing the whole is manifested, just as one picture reveals the artist's power and promise. But these things signify that he refused to conceive God as a mere physical force or material energy, and held, on the contrary, that He must be interpreted in the terms of mind or spirit. He hates, indeed, the notion that nature is an accident, or the result of voluntary action ; and he labours to represent it as a necessity, seeking by a theory of emanation or instinctive action to reconcile the notions of necessity and God. Yet he does not conceive the best as already attained. Everything in nature strives to become better ; everywhere instinct feels after the good, though higher than instinct is that which it seeks to become, ⋯ional action that wills the best. Thought rises, like sense and ⋯wer to higher forms. Heroic love, which desires the

intuition of the truth, drives us ever upwards, that we may attain the
perfect rest where understanding and will are unified.

Bruno's speculations were those of a poet as well as a philosopher;
and were in various ways prophetic. His death by fire at Rome signified
that Italy had neither the wit nor the will to understand men of his
kind; that for her the Renaissance had run its course, so that men must
pursue its problems elsewhere in the hope of a more satisfactory solution.
Descartes' "*de omnibus dubitandum est*" was but the negative expression
of Bruno's positive effort after emancipation from authority, the freedom
without which thought can accomplish nothing. Spinoza's *substantia*, with
its twin attributes of thought and extension on the one hand, and Leibniz'
monadology on the other, carried into more perfect forms the quest on
which he had embarked. But to us he has an even higher significance;
he is the leader of the noble army of thinkers who have tried at once to
justify and to develop into a completer system of the universe the dreams
and the doctrines of modern science. It is this which makes him the fit
close of the movement, which began by waking the old world from its
grave and ended by saluting the birth of the thought that made the
whole world new.

We have not as yet approached the French Renaissance, which
has indeed an interest and character of its own. It was, while less
philosophical, more strictly educational, literary, and juristic than the
Italian; and may be described as both Teutonic and Latin in origin:
It entered the north and penetrated as far as Paris with the *Adagia* of
Erasmus, published in 1500; but it reached the south from Italy,
crossing the Alps with the gentlemen of France who accompanied their
Kings on those incursions which had, as Montaigne tells us, so fateful
an influence on the French morals and mind. Correspondent to this
difference in origin was a difference in spirit and in the field of activity.
In the north the Renaissance made its home in the schools, and worked
for the improvement of the education, the amelioration of the laws, and
the reform of religion, as names like Bude, Pierre de la Ramée, and
Beza, may help us to realise; but in the south it was more personal
and less localised, its learning was nearer akin to culture than to education, and it loved literature more than philosophy. Hence the forms it
assumed in France can hardly be said to call for separate discussion here.
Especially is this true of its more northern form; a better case might be
made out for the southern. To it belong the great names of Rabelais
and Montaigne; but their place is in a history of literature rather than
of thought, though both affected the course of the latter too profoundly
to be left unmentioned here.

Coleridge has said that Rabelais was "among the deepest as well as
boldest thinkers of his age"; that the rough stick he used yet "contained a rod of gold"; and that a treatise could be written "in praise of

the moral elevation of his work which would make the Church stare and
the conventicle groan, and yet would be the truth, and nothing but the
truth." These may seem hard sayings, utterly incredible if portions of
his work are alone regarded, but accurate enough if the purpose and
drift of his teaching as a whole be considered. It has been well said
that the confession of faith of the *curé* of Meudon has far more moral
reality than that which Rousseau puts into the mouth of his Savoyard
vicar. He believes that the universe needs no other governor than its
Creator, whose word guides the whole and determines the nature, pro-
perties, and condition of each several thing. Pascal's famous definition
of Deity, "a circle whose centre is everywhere and whose circumference
is nowhere," is but an echo from Rabelais. And he can, with the wisest
of the ancients and the best of the moderns, speak of the "great Soul
of the universe which quickens all things." La Bruyère described his
work as "a chimera; it has the face of a beautiful woman, but the tail
of a serpent." Yet surely the man who had to wear the mask of a
buffoon that he might preach the wisdom of truth and love to his age,
well deserves the epigram which Beza wrote in his honour:

> " *Qui sic nugatur, tractantem ut seria vincat,*
>   *Seria cum faciet dic, rogo, quantus erit ?* "

Montaigne is of all Frenchmen most thoroughly a son of the
Renaissance. He loves books, especially the solid and sensible and
well-flavoured books written in the ancient classic tongues, the men who
made and those who read them, and he loved to study man. He says:
"*Je suis moy mesme la matière de mon livre.*" And he does not understand himself in any little or narrow sense, but rather as the epitome
and mirror of mankind. The world in which he lived was not friendly
to the freedom of thought which was expressed in affirmative speech or
creative conduct, and so he learned to be silent — or sceptical. He had
seen men hate each other, willingly burn or be burned, out of love to
God; and he was moved by pity to moralise on the behaviour of those
who were so positive where they could not know, and so little understood the God in whom they professed to believe that they never saw
what the love of Him bound them to be and to do. The man that he
studied and described was not abstract but concrete man, with all his
foibles and failings, limited in his nature but infinite in his views,
differing without ceasing from his fellows, and not always able to agree
with himself. And man, so conceived, dwells amid mystery, has it
within him, and confronts it without. Custom may guide him, but
not reason; for reason builds on arguments, whose every position
depends on another, in a series infinitely regressive. "*Les hommes
sont tourmentés par les opinions qu'ils ont des choses, non par les choses
mesmes.*" Where man is so ignorant he ought not to be dogmatic;
where truth is what all seek and no one can be sure that he finds,

i.e. where it is nothing but a mere probability, it is a folly to spill human blood for it.

God is unknown even in religion; as many as the nations of men so many are the forms under which He is worshipped. And when they try to conceive and name Him, they degrade Him to their own level. God is made in the image of man rather than man in the image of God; to the Ethiopian He is black, to the Greek He is white, and lithe and graceful; to the brute He would be bestial and to the triangle triangular. Man, then, is so surrounded with contradictions that he cannot say what is or is not true. Wisdom was with Sextus Empiricus when he said: "παντὶ λόγῳ λόγος ἴσος ἀντικεῖται. *Il n'y a nulle raison qui n'en ait une contraire, dit le plus sage parti des philosophes.*" Where man so doubts he is too paralysed to fight or to affirm. Montaigne's sympathies might be with those who worked and suffered for a new heaven and a new earth; but his egoism inclined to the conventional and followed the consuetudinary. Prevost-Paradol termed him "*une perpétuelle leçon de tempérance et de modération.*" But this is a lesson which men of culture may read contentedly; while those who struggle to live or to make life worth living will hardly find in it the Gospel they need.

We turn now to the Teutonic Renaissance. Like the Latin, it began as a revolt against the sovereignty of Aristotle; but, unlike the Latin, its literary antecedents were patristic and Biblical rather than classical. They were, indeed, so far as patristic, specifically Augustinian, and, so far as Biblical, Pauline. With Augustine, the underlying philosophy was Neo-Platonic, with a tendency to theosophy and mysticism; with Paul, the theology involved a philosophy of human nature and human history. This does not mean that other Fathers or other Scriptures were ignored, but rather that Paul was interpreted through Augustine, and Christ through Paul. This fundamental difference involved two others. In the first place, a more religious and more democratic temper; the religious being seen in the attempt to realise the new ideals, and the democratic in the strenuous and combatant spirit by which alone this could be accomplished. The thought which lived in the Schools could not resist the authority that spoke in the name of the Church and was enforced by the penalties of the State; but the thought which interpreted God to the conscience was one that bowed to no authority lower than His. In the second place, Teutonic was more theological than Latin thought. The categories, which the past had formulated for the interpretation of being, it declined to accept; and so it had to discover and define those which it meant to use in their stead. The God with whom it started was not an abstract and isolated but a living and related Deity; and man it conceived *sub specie aeternitatis*, as a being whom God had made and ruled. The very limitation of its field was an enlargement of its scope; its primary *datum* was the Eternal God, and its secondary was the created universe, especially the man who bore the image of his Maker. This man was no mere individual or insulated unit, but a race — a connected, coherent, organic unity. The human being was local, but human nature was universal; before the individual could be, the whole must exist; and so man must be interpreted in terms of mankind rather than mankind in the terms of the single and local man. And this signified that in character, as well as in nature, the race was a unity; the past made the present, the heir became as his inheritance; and so any change in man had to be effected by the Maker and not by those He had made. And here Augustine pointed the way to the goal which Paul had reached: the will of God had never ceased to be active, for it was infinite; and it could not cease to be gracious, for it was holy and perfect; therefore, from this will, since man's nature was by his corporate being and his inevitable inheritance evil, all the good he could ever be or achieve must come.

This fundamental idea was common to the types most characteristic of the Teutonic Renaissance. It was expressed in Luther's *Servum Arbitrium*, in Zwingli's *Providentia Actuosa*, in Calvin's *Decretum Absolutum*. These all signified that the sole causality of good belonged to God, that grace was of the essence of His will, and that where He so willed, man could not but be saved, and, where He did not so will, no amelioration of state was possible. But this must not be interpreted to mean that man had been created and constituted of God for darkness rather than light; on the contrary, these thinkers all agree in affirming a universal light of nature, *i.e.* ideas implanted in us by the Creator, or, as Melanchthon phrased it, "*Notitiae nobiscum nascentes divinitus sparsae in mentibus nostris.*" In this position they were more influenced by Paul than by Augustine; with the Apostle, they argued that the moral law had been written in the heart before it was printed on tables of stone, and that without the one the other could neither possess authority nor be understood. But they also argued that knowledge without obedience was insufficient; and therefore they held God's will to be needed to enable man both to will and to do the good. But their differences of statement and standpoint were as instructive as their agreements. When Luther affirmed the absolute bondage of the will and Calvin the absolute decree of God, the one looked at the matter as a question of man's need, the other as a question of God's power; and so they agreed in idea though they differed in standpoint. Yet the difference proved to be more radical than the agreement. And so, when Zwingli said "he would rather share the eternal lot of a Socrates or a Seneca than that of the Pope," he meant that God willed good to men who were outside the Church or the covenants, without willing the means which both Luther and Calvin conceived to be necessary to salvation. It is through such differences as these that the types and tendencies of Teutonic thought must be conceived and explained.

Luther's Article of a Standing or Failing Church, Justification by Faith alone, is the positive side of the idea which is negatively expressed as the bondage of the will ; and the idea in both its positive and negative forms implies a philosophy of existence which may be stated as a question thus: How is God, as the source of all good, related to man as the seat and servant of evil ?　God and man, good as identical with God and evil as inseparable from man, are recognised, and the problem is: how is the good to overcome the evil ? The man who frames the problem is a mystic ; God is the supreme desire and delight of his soul ; and he conceives sin as a sort of inverted capacity for God, the dust which has stifled a thirst and turned it into an infinite misery.　Now, Luther has two forms under which he conceives God's relation to man, a juristic denoted by the term "justification," and a vital denoted by the term "faith." "Justification " is the acquittal of the guilty : "faith is nothing else than the true life realised in God." The one term thus describes the universe as ethically governed, while the other describes man as capable of participating in the eternal life ; and the two together mean that he can realise his happiness or his end only as he shares the life of God and lives in harmony with His law.　The philosophy here implied is large and sublime, though its intrinsic worth may be hidden by the crudity of its earliest forms.　The Lutheran doctrine of the *communicatio idiomatum* attempts, for example, to establish a kind of equation between the ideas of God and man.　The person of Christ is a symbol of humanity ; in it man can so participate as to share its perfections and dignity.　Christ's humanity is capable of deity ; God lives in Him now openly, now cryptically, but ever really ; and His humanity so penetrates the Deity as to touch Him with a feeling of our infirmities and make Him participant in our lot as we are in His life.

This is the very root and essence of German mysticism, which gives to the German hymns their beauty and their pathos, which inspired the speculations of Brenz and Chemnitz, and which later determined Schelling's doctrine of "indifference" or the "identity of subject and object," and Hegel's "absolute idealism." If we read Boehme from this point of view, how splendid his dreams and how reasonable his very extravagances become ! We are not surprised to hear him speak of the necessity of antitheses to all being, and especially to the life and thought of God, of evil being as necessary as good, or wrath as essential as love in God, who is the fundament of hell as well as of heaven, both the everlasting No, and the eternal Yes.　He dwells in nature as the soul dwells in the body ; there is no point in the body where the soul is not, no spot in space and no atom in nature where we can say, "God is not here."　The man who is His image, who is holy as He is holy, good as He is good, is of no other matter than God.　This may be Pantheism, but it is not rational and reasoned like Bruno's ; it is emotional and like a thing of imagination all compact.　It is born of the love that

loses the sense of personal distinctness and identity in the joy, not of
absolute possession, but of being possessed. Boehme says that the processes of nature conceal God, but the spirit of man reveals Him ; and how
can it reveal a God it does not know ? But the spirit that has never
seen and touched Deity has never known Him or been so one with Him
as to know Him as he knows himself. Here lives the very soul of Luther
and the essence of all his thought. Boehme's friend and biographer
describes him as a little man of mean aspect, thin voice, snub nose, but
eyes blue as heaven, bright and gleaming like the windows of Solomon's
temple. And he lived in harmony with lines which he wrote with his
own toil-stained hand :

> *" Wem Zeit ist wie Ewigkeit*
> *Und Ewigkeit wie Zeit,*
> *Der ist befreit*
> *Von allem Streit."*

Of course, such a change as Luther instituted could not but powerfully affect the minds of men. But certain concomitants must not be
set down as effects ; and the Peasants' War had its causes in centuries
of German history, though among its occasions must be reckoned the
ideas which the Reformation had thrown as it were into the air. But
quite otherwise was it with the Anabaptist movement. While it sprang
up and flourished in provinces and cities where Zwingli was potent
as well as in places more expressly Lutheran, yet it belonged more
specifically to the Lutheran than to the Reformed Church. To discuss
its causes and forms would carry us far beyond our available space. It is
enough to say : the principle of parity which it emphasised was more
antagonistic to the one Church than to the other. Luther created his
Church by the help of Princes ; Calvin founded his on the goodwill of
the people. The system that claimed fullest freedom for the individual
could find less fault with the latter than with the former. And it is
significant that the heresies which troubled the Lutherans were largely
political and social, while those that afflicted the Reformed were mainly
intellectual and moral. In nothing is the character of a Society more
revealed than in the heresies to which it is most liable.

Zwingli and Calvin alike conceived God under the category of will,
and construed man and history through it. Both held faith to be a consequence of, rather than a condition for, election ; man believed because
God had so decreed, and into His will every step in their upward or
downward progress was resolved. Now, this emphasis on the will of God
necessarily threw into prominence the ideas of God and will, with the
result that the main varieties of opinion in the Reformed Church
concerned these two ideas. If the will of God was the supreme and sole
causality in all human affairs, and if the will always was as the nature
was, it became a matter of primary consequence to know what kind of
being God was, and what His nature and character. This question was

early and potently raised, and in a most significant quarter. Zanchius, himself an Italian, who so emphasised the will of God as to anticipate Spinoza and represent God as the only free Being in nature and the sole cause in history, wrote in 1565 to Bullinger warning him against being too easy in the matter of credentials of orthodoxy, as he had many heretical compatriots. "*Hispanus (Servetus) gallinas peperit; Italia fovet ova; nos jam pipientes pullos audimus.*" And it is curious that the attempts to find a simpler conception of God than Calvin's, or to modify his notion of the will by the notion of the Deity whose will it was, came mainly from men of Latin stock. Servetus was the son of a Spanish father and a French mother; Lelio and Fausto Sozzini, uncle and nephew, the one the father of the doctrine, the other of the sect, which respectively bear their name, were Italians, as were also Bernardino Ochino, who wrote a once famous book concerning the freedom and bondage of the will, "*the Labyrinth,*" in which he argued that man ought to act as if he were free, but when he did good he was to give all the glory to God as if he were necessitated, and Celio Secondo Curione, who desired to enlarge the number of the elect till it should comprehend Cicero as well as Paul; while Sebastian Castellio, who is described by some contemporaries as French, though by others as Italian — as a matter of fact he was born in a Savoyard village not far from Geneva — argued that as God is good His will must be the same, and if all had happened according to it there could have been no sin. These views may be regarded as the recrudescence of the Latin Renaissance in the Reformed Church, and are marked as attempts to bring in a humaner and sweeter conception of God. They failed, possibly because of the severity and efficiency of the Reformed legislation, or possibly because they did not reckon with the Augustinian sense of sin, or most probably for reasons which were both political and intellectual. It is indeed strange, that positions so strongly rational and so well and powerfully argued should not have been maintained and crystallised into important religious societies; but as Boehme helps us to see, the man who knows himself to be evil expects and appreciates wrath as well as mercy in God. This may be the reason why the attempts made by some of the finest minds in the sixteenth century to soften the severer ideas of Deity seemed to their contemporaries heresies, and seem to the student of history ineffective failures.

The problem was soon attacked from another side. The field in which the will of God was exercised was the soul of man. That will concerned, therefore, him and his acts; if these acts were done because God had so determined, then two consequences followed: the acts would show the quality of the will, and the man would not be consciously free, would know himself an instrument rather than an agent. The criticism from these points of view was mainly northern; those who urged it did so in the interests of man and morality. In Calvin's own lifetime the doctrine of foreordination, or of the operation of the Divine will in its relation to human affairs, was assailed by two men — Albert Pighius, a Catholic from the Netherlands, and Jérome Hermes Bolsec, a Parisian, an unfrocked Carmelite monk, who had turned physician, and had for a time been closely attached to Calvin. The former argued that if God was the absolute cause of all events and acts, then to Him we owed, not only the goodness of the good, but the wickedness of the wicked ; the second, that if faith is made the consequence rather than the condition of election, then God must be charged with partiality. But towards the end of the century a more serious movement took place. The question of the Divine will had exercised the Reformed theologians, especially as criticism had compelled them to consider it in relation to sin as well as to salvation, *i.e.* both as to the causation of the state from which man was to be saved, and as to his deliverance from it. Certain of the more vigorous Reformed divines, including Beza himself, said that the decree in date precedes the Fall, for what was first in the Divine intention is last in execution ; the first thing was the decree to save, but if man is to be saved he must first be lost ; hence the Fall is decreed as a consequence of the decreed Salvation. But the milder divines said that the decree of God takes the existence of sin for granted, deals with man as fallen, and elects or rejects him for reasons we cannot perceive, though it clearly knows and regards. The former were known by the name of supralapsarians, and the latter by the name of sublapsarians. In the seventeenth century an acute and effective criticism was directed against both forms of the belief, which, although it falls beyond our scope, must receive passing notice here. Jacobus Arminius (Jakob Herman), a Dutch preacher and professor, declined to recognise the doctrine as either Scriptural or rational. He held that it made God the author of sin, that it restricted His grace, that it left the multitudes outside without hope, that it condemned multitudes for believing the truth, viz. that for them no salvation was either intended or provided in Christ, and it gave an absolutely false security to those who believed themselves to be the elect of God. The criticism was too rational to be cogent, for it was, as it were, an assertion of the rights of man over against the sovereignty of God. And it involved the men who pursued it in the political controversies and conflicts of the time. The Arminians were most successful when the argument proceeded on principles supplied by the conscience and the consciousness of man ; and the Calvinists when they argued from the majesty and the might of God. But if the Arminians were dialectically victors, they were politically vanquished. The men who organised authority in Holland proved stronger than those who pleaded and suffered for freedom.

There are still large fields of thought to be traversed before we can do even approximate justice to the mind of Protestantism ; but our space is exhausted. All we can now do is to drop a hint as to what was intended ; we should have wished to sketch the Renaissance that followed the Reformation as fully as the literary Revival which preceded it. Theodore Beza is a man whose fame as a Genevan legislator and divine has eclipsed his name as a scholar and educator ; but it ought not to be forgotten that he was an elegant humanist before he became a convinced reformer and his most fruitful work was done in the provinces of sacred learning and exegesis. The Estiennes, Robert and Henry, are potent names in the history of Greek and Roman letters ; they accomplished much for the languages and the literatures which they loved ; — Robert, in particular, standing out as a devoted friend of religion and of science, for both of which he made immense sacrifices. Our *textus receptus* and its division into verses are witnesses to his zeal. Joseph Scaliger and Isaac Casaubon had the merit of awakening the envy, which was but inverted admiration, and the supple hate, which was like the regret of the forsaken, of the society whose mission it was to roll back the advancing tide of the freer thought that had come to quicken interest in letters ; while Gerard Jan Vossius construed the classical mythology through religion, and both through Old Testament history in a way that contributed to form comparative science in the regions of thought, religion, and language. Protestant scholars had a larger and more realistic way of looking at classical problems than the men of the earlier Renaissance, and by its dissociation from polity and custom Teutonic thought, even while it seems narrower in scope, is yet far wider in outlook and interest than Latin. It goes into a more distant past, and rises to higher altitudes. It came as a revolt, but it grew into a development ; it continued free from the authority that would have suppressed it, and used its freedom to achieve results which the more fettered Latin mind panted after in vain. France continued in the seventeenth century the literary activity of Italy in the sixteenth ; but speculation loves freedom, and refused to live where it could not be free. The events, which emancipated England from monotonous uniformity in religion, set the problems that have been the main factors in her historical development, and the chief causes of her philosophical activity and her literary greatness. Modern thought is the achievement of Northern and Central Europe, but it is the possession of universal man.

CHAPTERS I, II, AND III

MEDICEAN ROME, AND HABSBURG AND VALOIS

BIBLIOGRAPHIES

Armstrong, E., Charles V. 2 vols. London. 1902.

Franklin, A. Les Sources de l'Histoire de France. Paris. 1877.

Langlois, C. V., and Stein, H. Les Archives de l'Histoire de France. Paris. 1893.

Manno, A. Bibliografia storica della monarchia de Savoia. Turin. 1884 etc.

Mazzatinti, G. Gli archivi della Storia d' Italia. Rocca S. Casciano. 1897–8. (In progress.)

Monod, G. Bibliographie de l'Histoire de France. Paris. 1888.

Pastor, L. Geschichte der Päpste. Vol. III. Freiburg i. B. 1895. Translated by F. I. Antrobus. Vols. V and VI. London. 1891.

Pirenne, H. Bibliographie de l'histoire de Belgique. 2nd ed. Brussels. 1902.

PUBLISHED DOCUMENTS

Albèri, E. Relazioni degli Ambasciatori Veneti. Series I, 1, 2, 3, 4, 6. Series II, 1, 2, 5. Florence. 1846–62.

Boislisle, A. M. de. Chambre des Comptes de Paris. Pièces justificatives pour servir à l'histoire des premiers présidents. 1506–1791. Paris. 1893.

Charles V.

    Bradford, W. Correspondence of the Emperor Charles V and his ambassadors ... from ... Vienna. Edited by W. Bradford. London. 1850.

    Casanova, E. Lettere di Carlo V a Clemente VII. 1527–33. Florence. 1893.

    Döllinger, J. J. Beiträge zur politischen, kirchlichen, und Kultur-Geschichte. Vols. I, II. Ratisbon. 1862.

    Gachard, P. Correspondance de Charles Quint et d'Adrian VI. Brussels. 1859.

    Kervyn de Lettenhove. Commentaires de Charles Quint. A revision of a Portuguese translation of the Spanish original. Brussels. 1862.

    Lanz, K. Correspondenz des Kaisers Karl V. Aus dem königlichen Archiv und der Bibliothèque de Bourgogne zu Brüssel. Leipzig. 1844–6.

    —— Staatspapiere zur Gesch. Karls V. Aus der Bibl. de Bourgogne. Stuttgart. 1845.

    —— Aktenstücke zur Gesch. Karls V. Aus dem k. k. Hof- und Staatsarchiv zu Wien. Monumenta Habsburgica. Part II.

Clement VII. La politica di Clemente VII, fino al sacco di Roma. Secondo i documenti Vaticani. Rome. 1884.

Collection des documents inédits de l'Histoire de France.

XXXVI.   Négociations de la France avec la Toscane. Edd. G. Canestrini and A. Desjardins. Vols. II, III. 1861–9.

XLIV.   Négociations diplomatiques entre la France et l'Autriche durant les trente premières années du XVIᵉ Siècle. Ed. le Glay. 2 vols. 1845.

XLVI.   Captivité du roi François I. Ed. A. Champollion-Figeac. 1847.

XLVII.   Négociations de la France dans le Levant. Ed. E. Charrière. Vols. I, II. 1848.

XLVIII.   Relations des Ambassadeurs Vénitiens sur les affaires de France au XVIᵉ Siècle. Ed. N. Tommaseo. 2 vols. 1838.

XLIX.   Papiers d'État du Cardinal de Granvelle. Ed. Ch. Weiss. Vols. I–V. 1841–3.

Lettres de Catherine de Médicis. Ed. H. la Ferrière. Vol. I (1533–63). 1880.

Diane de Poitiers (Diane de Brezé, Duchesse de Valentinois). Lettres inédites de Diane de Poitiers, publiées avec une introduction et des notes par G. Guiffrey. Paris. 1866.

Documenti ispano-genovesi dell' Archivio di Simancas. Ed. M. Spinola etc. Atti della Società Ligure di Storia patria. Vol. VIII, Fasc. 1, 2.

Farnese, Cardinal. Lettere scritte a nome del Card. Farnese. Ed. A. Caro. 3 vols. (IV–VI of Opere). Milan. 1807.

Francis I. Catalogue des Actes de François I. 7 vols. Paris. Imprimerie nationale. 1887–96.

Fredericq, P. Corpus documentorum inquisitionis haereticae pravitatis Neerlandicae. Ghent. 5 vols., to Dec. 1528. 1889–1903.

Guiffrey, G. Procès criminel de Jehan de Poitiers, seigneur de Saint Vallier. 1867.

Laemmer, H. Monumenta Vaticana historiam ecclesiasticam saeculi XVI, illustrantia. Freiburg i. B. 1861.

Laurent, C., and Lamure, J. Recueil des ordonnances des Pays Bas, 2ᵉ Série. 1506–1700. Brussels. 1898.

Leonis X, P. M., Regesta. Ed. Card. Hergenröther. Freiburg i. B. 1884–5.

Loaysa, G. de. Cartas al Emperador Carlos V . . . 1530–2 por su Confesor. Edited by G. Heine. Berlin. 1848. German translation published separately.

Marguerite d'Angoulême. Lettres de Marguerite d'A. reine de Navarre. Published by A. Génin. Société de l'Histoire de France. 1841–2.

Molini, G. Documenti di Storia Italiana. 1522–30. 2 vols. Florence. 1836–7.

Morone, G. Ricordi inediti di G. Morone, Gran Cancelliere dell' ultimo Duca di Milano . . . pubblicati del C. Tullio Dandolo . . . Milan. 1855.

Pacheco, J. F., and Cardinas, F. de. Coleccion de documentos inéditos relativos al descubrimento y colonizacion de las posesiones españolas en America y Oceania. Madrid. 1864.

Pellicier, G. Correspondance politique de Guillaume Pellicier, ambassadeur de France à Venise. Ed. A. Jausserat-Radel. Commission des Archives historiques. Paris. 1899.

Pieper, A. Die päpstlichen Legaten und Nuntien in Deutschland, Frankreich und Spanien, 1550–9. Münster. 1897.

Ribler, G. Lettres et Mémoires d'Estat. Paris. 1666.

Saige, G. Documents historiques relatifs à la principauté de Monaco. 1891.

Serristori, A. Legazioni di A. Serristori, ambasciadore di Cosimo I, a Carlo Quinto e in corti di Roma. Ed. L. Canestrini. Florence. 1853.

Virz, C. Akten über die diplomatischen Beziehungen der römischen Kurie zu der Schweiz, 1512–52. Basel. 1895.

For State Papers published in England *see Bibliographies of Chapters XIII.–XVI.*

CONTEMPORARY HISTORIES, CHRONICLES, MEMOIRS, ETC.

Bardi, A. Carlo V e l' assedio di Firenze (1528–30). Arch. Stor. Ital. 1898.

Barrillon, J. Journal de Jean Barrillon, secrétaire du Chancelier Duprat, 1515–21. Ed. P. de Vaissière for Société de l'hist. de France, 1897.

Belcarius, F. Historia Gallica, 1461–1581. Venice. 1581.

Bembo, P. (Cardinal). Opere. 4 vols. Venice. 1729. In Collezione dei Classici Italiani. Vols. 55–66. Milan. 1808–12.

Bodin, J. Les six livres de la République. Paris. 1583.

Boyin, F. de, Baron du Villars. Mémoires sur les guerres de Piedmont. Paris. 1607. Michaud et Poujoulat, x. Petitot, xxxiii–vii.

Brantôme, P. de Bourdeille, Sʳ de. Edited by L. Lalanne. Soc. de l'Hist. de France. Paris. 1864–82.

Carloix, V. Mémoires de la Vie de François de Scepeaux, Sire de Vieilleville, 1527–71. 5 vols. Paris. 1757. Also in Petitot, xxvi–xxviii.

Casa, G. Della. Opere, i, ii. Venice. 1752.

Castiglione, B. Il libro del Cortegiano. Venice. 1528, etc.

Cellini, Benvenuto. Vita, da lui medesimo scritta. Naples. 1730. Rome. 1901, etc. Translated by T. Roscoe. London. 1822. By J. A. Symonds. London. 1888, etc.

Cimber, L. et Danjou, F. Archives curieuses de l'histoire de France. 1ᵉ série. Paris. 1835.
    III. Brief discours du siège de Metz.
        Le discours de la prinse de Calais.
        Histoire particulière de la Cour du roy Henry II (by Claude de l'Aubespine).
        Le siège et prinse de Thionville.

Cini, C. B. Vita del Signor Cosimo de' Medici. Florence. 1611.

Clementis VII Epistolae per Sadoletum scriptae. Ed. P. Balan. Monumenta saeculi xvi historiam illustrantia. Innsbruck. 1885.

Coligny, G. de. Siège de Saint Quentin. Michaud, viii. Petitot, xl.

Cronique du roi Francoys premier. Ed. G. Guiffrey for Soc. de l'hist. de France. Paris. 1860.

Du Bellay, M. and G. Mémoires 1513–52. Michaud et Poujoulat, v.

Ferronus, A. Pauli Aemilii historiae continuatio usq. ad an. 1547. Paris. 1550.

Giustiniani, A. Annali della Repubblica di Genova. Genoa. 1537. Ed. V. Canepa. 2 vols. Genoa. 1854.

Gosellini, G. Compendio storico della guerra di Parma et del Piedmonte, 1548–73. In Misc. di Storia Ital. xvii. Turin. 1878.

Grassis, Paris de. Il Diario di Leone X. Ed. M. Armellini. Rome. 1884.

Guicciardini, F. Opere inedite. Ed. Canestrini. 10 vols. Florence. 1856–67.

—— Storia d' Italia. 4 vols. Milan. 1889.

Guise, F. de. Mémoires. Michaud et Poujoulat, vi. Paris. 1839.

Journal d'un bourgeois de Paris sous le règne de François I, 1515–36. Edited by M. L. C. Lalanne for the Soc. de l'hist. de France. Paris. 1854.

Jovius, P. Historiarum sui temporis libri xiv. 1494–1547. Florence. 1550–2.

—— Vita Leonis decimi. Florence. 1548, etc.

La Mothe Fénelon, B. de Salignac, Marquis de. Le voyage du Roy (Henri II, de France) aux pays bas de l'Empereur en l'an MDLIII. Paris. 1554.

—— Le Siège de Metz en l'an 1552. Paris. 1553. Ed. F. M. Chabert. Metz. 1856. Michaud, viii. Petitot, xxxix, xl.

Louise de Savoie. Journal. 1476–1522. Michaud et Poujoulat, v.

Mameranus, N. Commentarius de ultima Caroli V expeditione, 1544, adversus Gallos suscepta. In S. A. Würdtweiss, Subsidia diplomatica. No. 305. x. Heidelberg. 1772–80.

Montluc, B. de. Commentaires et lettres, 1521–76. Michaud, vii. Ed. A. de Ruble, for Soc. Hist. France. 5 vols. Paris. 1864–72.

Nardi, J. Le Historie della citta di Fiorenza, 1494–1531. Ed. A. Gelli. 2 vols. Florence. 1858.

Navagero, A. Il viaggio fatto in Spagna et in Francia con la descrizione etc. Venice. 1563.

Paradin, G. Histoire de notre temps, 1515–56. Lyons. 1558.

Pierragues, A. D. Giornali del Principe d' Orange nelle Guerre d' Italia, 1526–30. Florence. 1898.

Pitti, J. Istoria Fiorentina. Archivio Storico Ital. Vol. i. Florence. 1842.

Quentin, E. Journal du Siège de Péronne, 1536. From MS. of Me Jean Dehaussy. Péronne. 1897.

Rabutin, F. de. Commentaires des dernières guerres dans la Gaule Belgique. Paris. 1555–9. Michaud, vii. Petitot, xxxvii–ix.

Reisner, A. Historia Herrn Georgs und Herrn Caspars von Frundsberg. Frankfort. 1572.

Relation des troubles de Gand sous Charles Quint. Ed. L. P. Gachard. Collection de Chroniques belges. 1846.

Rochechouart, G. de. Mémoires, 1497–1565. Michaud et Poujoulat, viii.

Ruscelli, G. etc. Lettere di Principi. Venice. 3 vols. 1564— .

Salazar, P. de. Coronica del nostro emperador Carlos V. Sevila. 1552.

Sandoval, P. de. Historia del emperador Carlos V. 2 vols. Pampeluna. 1618–24 etc.

San Quentin, la batalla de. In Coleccion de Documentos inéditos para la historia de España. ix. Madrid. 1846.

Saulx-Tavanes, Gaspard de. Mémoires, 1530–73. Michaud, viii. Petitot, xxvi–viii.

Scheurl, Chr. Geschichtbuch der Christenheit von 1511–1521. J. C. F. Knaake, in Jahrbücher d. deutschen Reiches und der Kirche im Zeitalter der Reformation. Leipzig. 1872.

Sepulveda, J. G. de. De rebus gestis Caroli V libri xxx. Madrid. 1780.

Sleidanus, J. De statu religionis et reipublicae Carolo V Caesare. Augsburg. 1555. Ed. J. G. Böhmer. 3 vols. Frankfort. 1785.

Ulloa, A. Vita del gran Capitano Don F. Gonzaga nella quale . . . si descrivono le guerre d' Italia, e d' altri paesi, 1525–57. Venice. 1563.

—— La vita dell' Imperatore Carlo V e le cose occorse, 1500–60. Venice. 1560.

Varchi, B. Istoria delle guerre della Republica Fiorentina accorse nel tempo che la Casa de' Medici s' impadroni del governo. 2 vols. Leyden. 1720.

Vettori, F. Sommario della storia d' Italia dal 1511–27. Archivio storico Italiano. Appendice. Vol. vi. 1842.

GENERAL HISTORY OF THE PERIOD

Armstrong, E. Charles the Fifth. 2 vols. London. 1902.

Baumgarten, H. Karl der Fünfte. 3 vols. (to 1539). Stuttgart. 1885–92.

Leva, G. di. Storia documentata di Carlo V. 5 vols.

Maurenbrecher, W. Karl V und die deutschen Protestanten, 1545–55. Düsseldorf. 1865.

Mignet, F. A. M. Rivalité de François I et de Charles Quint. 2 vols. Second edition. Paris. 1875.

Raumer, F. L. G. von. Geschichte Europas seit dem Ende des fünfzehnten Jahrhunderts. Leipzig. 1832–50.

Robertson, W. History of the reign of Charles V. London. 1769.

SECONDARY WORKS AND SPECIAL TREATISES

FRANCE WITH LORRAINE

Bacon, J. Life and times of Francis I. London. 1829.

Belleval, R., Marquis de. Les fils de Henri II. La cour, la ville et la société de leur temps. Paris. 1898.

Claudin, A. Histoire de l'imprimerie en France aux 15e et 16e siècles. Vol. I. Paris. 1900.

Dupuy, A. Réunion de la Bretagne avec la France. 2nd vol. 1880.

Duvernoy, E. Politique des ducs de Lorraine dans leurs rapports avec la France et l'Autriche de 1477–1545. Nancy. 1893.

Faguet, E. Seizième Siècle. Études littéraires. Paris. 1894.

Fitte, S. Das staatsrechtliche Verhältniss des Herzogthums Lothringen zum deutschen Reich seit 1542. Strassburg. 1891.

Gaillard, G. H. Histoire de François I, Roi de France. 7 vols. Paris. 1766–9.

Griessdorf, H. C. J. Der Zug Kaisers Karl V gegen Metz. Hallische Abhandlungen zur neueren Geschichte. XXVI. 1891.

Hamy, P. A. François I et Henry VIII à Boulogne 1532. Paris. 1898.

Hanotaux, G. Études historiques sur le XVIe et le XVIIe siècle en France. Paris. 1886.

Issleib, S. Moritz v. Sachsen gegen Karl V bis zum Kriegzuge 1552. N. Archiv für Sächs. Gesch. VI. 1885.

Jacqueton, G. Le Trésor de l'Épargne sous François I. Revue Historique. Paris. 1894.

—— La politique extérieure de Louise de Savoie. Chalon sur Saône, 1892. Bibliothèque de l'École pratique des hautes Études. Fasc. 88.

La Ferrière, Comte de. Le XVIe Siècle et les Valois d'après les documents inédits du Brit. Mus. et du Record Office. Paris. 1879.

Lavisse, E. Histoire de France. Vol. V. Part I. Paris. 1902–3.

Madelin, L. Les premières applications du Concordat de 1516. Mélanges de l'École Française de Rome. Vol. XVII. 1897.

Martin, H. Histoire de France. Vols. VII, VIII. Fourth edition. Paris. 1878.

Michelet, J. Histoire de France. Vols. X, XI. Paris. 1855–56.

Paillard, C., and Hérelle. L'invasion Allemande en 1544. Paris. 1884.

Petit de Julleville, L. Histoire de la langue et de la littérature française. Vol. III. Paris. 1897.

Pimodan, G., Marquis de. La réunion de Toul à la France. Paris. 1880.

Pouy, L. E. F. La Bataille de Saint Quentin (1557) d'après le récit de Paré. Saint Quentin. 1875.

Rahlenbeck, C. H. Metz et Thionville sous Charles V. Brussels. 1881.

Ranke, L. von. Französische Geschichte, vorn. im 16. u. 17. Jahrh. Vol. I. Stuttgart. 1852–61. Vol. VIII of Sämmtliche Werke. Leipzig. 1874, etc. Translated by M. A. Garvey. Vol. I. London. 1852.

Rott, E. Histoire de la représentation française en Suisse. Paris. 1900.

Roy, M. Le Ban et l'Arrière-ban du bailliage de Sens au XVIe siècle. Sens. 1885.

Ruble, A. de. Le traité de Cateau Cambrésis, Paris. 1889.

Scherer, H. Der Raub der drei Bisthümer Metz, Toul, und Verdun, 1552. Hist. Taschenbuch 866. 1842.

Schlomka, E. Die politischen Beziehungen zwischen Kurfürst Moritz und Heinrich II von Frankreich von 1550 bis zum Vertrag von Chambord, 15 Jan. 1552. 1884.

Sismondi, Simonde de. Histoire des Français. Vols. XVI, XVII, XVIII. Paris. 1834.

Spont, A. Semblançay. La bourgeoisie financière au début du 16ᵉ siècle. Pari 1895.

—— Marignan et l'organisation militaire sous François I. Revue des Quest. Hi toriques, July 1899.

Teulet, J. B. A. T. Relations politiques de la France et de l'Espagne avec l'Écosse xvıᵉ siècle. Bordeaux and Paris. 1862.

Trefftz, J. Kursachsen und Frankreich, 1552–6. Leipzig. 1891.

Vachez, A. Histoire de l'acquisition des terres nobles par les roturiers dans l provinces de Lyonnais, Forez et Beaujolais du xıııᵉ au xvıᵉ siècles. Lyons. 189

Weill, G. Les théories sur le pouvoir royal en France pendant les guerres de religio Paris. 1892.

Zeller, J. La diplomatie française vers le milieu du xvıᵉ siècle, d'après la correspo dance de Guillaume Pellicier. 1881.

ROME AND THE MEDICI

Balan, P. Clemente VII e l' Italia de' suoi tempi. Milan. 1887.

Brosch, M. Geschichte des Kirchenstaates. 2 vols. Hamburg. 1880–2.

Creighton, M. (Bishop). History of the Papacy during the period of the Reformatio Vol. VI. London. 1882.

Feà, C. Notizie intorno Raffaele, etc. e paragone relativamente dei meriti di Giulio e Leone X sul loro secolo. Rome. 1822.

Gnoli, D. Roma e i Papi nel seicento. In La Vita Italiana nel seicento. Mila 1895.

—— Descriptio urbis o Censimento della popolazione di Roma c. 1522. Archivi della Soc. Romana di Santa Patria. Vol. 17. Rome. 1894.

Hellwig, W. Die politischen Beziehungen Clements VII zu Karl V im Jahre 15' Leipzig. 1889.

Höfler, C. von. Papst Adrian VI. 1522–3. Vienna. 1880.

—— Wahl und Thronbesteigung des letzten deutschen Papstes, Adrian VI, 15² Vienna. 1872.

Müntz, E. Les arts à la cour des Papes pendant le xvᵉ et le xvıᵉ siècle. 3rd pa Bibliothèque des Écoles françaises d'Athènes et de Rome. Fasc. xxvııı.

—— Les antiquités de la ville de Rome aux 14ᵉ, 15ᵉ, et 16ᵉ siècles. Paris. 1886.

—— Les historiens et les critiques de Raphael. Paris. 1883.

—— Les collections d'antiques formées par les Médicis au xvı siècle. Académie d Inscriptions et Belles Lettres. Histoire et Mémoires. Vol. 35.

Nitti, F. S. Documenti ed osservazioni riguardanti la politica di Leone X. Archiv della Soc. Rom. di Santa Patria. Vol. 16.

—— Leone X e la sua politica secondo documenti e carteggi inediti. Florenc 1892.

Ranke, L. von. Die römischen Päpste. Vols. xxxvıı–xxxıx of Sämmtliche Werk Leipzig. 1894, etc. English translation by Mrs. Austin. 3rd ed. 2 vol 1847.

Renazzi, F. M. Storia dell' Università di Roma. 4 vols. Rome. 1803–6.

Roscoe, W. Life and Pontificate of Leo X. 4 vols. Liverpool. 1805. 5th editio London. 1846.

Sugenheim, S. Entstehung und Ausbildung des Kirchenstaates. Leipzig. 1854.

Villa, A. R. Memorias para la historia del asalto y saques de Roma. Madrid. 1895

ITALY, SICILY, AND SAVOY

Baguenault de Puchesse. Négociations de Henri II avec le Duc de Ferrare (1555–7 Le Mans. 1869.

Baschet, A. La diplomatie vénitienne au xvıᵉ siècle. Paris. 1862.

Beloch, J. Bevölkerungsgeschichte der Republik Venedigs.

Canale, M. G. Storia della Republica di Genova, 1528–50. Genoa. 1874.

Celli, L. Ordinanze militari d. Repubblica Veneta nel secolo XVI. Rome. 1894.

Cipolla, C. Storia delle Signorie Italiane — 1530. Milan. 1881.

Claparède, T. Hist. de la Réformation en Savoie. Geneva. 1893.

Costanzo, A. di. Historia del Regno di Napoli. Aquila. 1581. Also in Collezione de' classici Italiani. Vols. 119–21.

Creighton, M. (Bishop). History of the Papacy, etc. Vols. V, VI.

Crespi, L. A. Il senato di Milano. Ricerche intorno alla costituzione del stato di Milano al tempo di dominazione Spagnuola.

Ferrari, G. Histoire des révolutions d'Italie. Vol. 4. Paris. 1858.

Grethen, R. Die politischen Beziehungen Clements VII zu Karl V. Hanover. 1887.

Guicciardini, L. Il Sacco di Roma. Paris. 1644.

La Lumia, I. La Sicilia sotto Carlo V. 1862.

Livi, G. La Corsica e Cosimo I de' Medici. Florence. 1885.

Loiseleur et Baguenault de Puchesse. L'expédition du Duc de Guise à Naples. Paris. 1876.

Perrens, F. T. Histoire de Florence depuis la domination des Medici. Vol. 3. Paris. 1890. Translated by H. Lynch. London. 1892.

Professione, A. Della Battaglia di Pavia al sacco di Roma. Rome. 1890.

Randi, C. La guerra di sette anni sotto Clemente VII. Arch. della Soc. Rom. di Storia Patria VI, 3 and 4.

Reumont, A. von. Beiträge zur italienischen Geschichte. 6 vols. Berlin. 1853–7.

—— Geschichte der Stadt Rom. 3 vols. Berlin. 1867–70.

Ricotti, E. Storia della Monarchia Piemontese. Vol. I. Florence. 1862.

Romanin, S. Storia documentata di Venezia. Vol. VI. Venice. 1856.

Rossi, A. Francesco Guicciardini e il governo fiorentino, 1527–40. 2 vols. Bologna. 1899.

Segre, A. Una questione fra Carlo III Duca di Savoia et Don Ferrante Gonzaga, 1550. Torino. 1896.

—— La Marina Sabauda ai tempi di Emanuele Filiberto. Rome. 1898.

Sozzini, A. Sienese war. Archivio Storico Italiano. II. Florence. 1842.

Symonds, J. A. Renaissance in Italy. 7 vols. London. 1875–86.

Villa, A. Rodriguez. Italia desde la batalla de Pavia hasta el saco de Roma. In Curiosidades de la historia de España. Madrid. 1885.

—— La Reina Doña Juana la Loca. Madrid. 1892.

LOW COUNTRIES AND BURGUNDY

Alexandre, P. Hist. du Conseil privé dans les anciens Pays-Bas. Brussels. 1895.

Asch van Wijck, H. W., and others. De Slag bij St Quentin. Utrecht. 1891.

Biographie Nationale de Belgique. 16 vols. (to Pepyn). Brussels. 1866.

Blok, P. J. Geschiedenis van het Niederlandische Volk. Vol. II. Bk V. Groningen. 1892 etc. Translated (in abbreviated form) by Ruth Putnam. New York and London. Vol. II. 1899.

Borman, C. de. Les Échevins de la souveraine justice de Liège. Liège. 1900.

Fredericq, P. De Nederlanden onder Keizer Karl. Ghent. Willems-Fonds Academy. 1885 etc.

—— Geschiedenis der Inquisitie in de Nederlanden tot aan hare herinrichting onder Keizer Karl V, 1025–1520. 2 vols. Ghent. 1892–7.

Gachard, L. P. Collection des voyages des souverains des Pays-Bas. Vol. IV. Brussels. Commission roy. d'Hist. 1874 etc.

—— Trois années de l'histoire de Charles V d'après l'ambassadeur vénitien Navagero. Brussels. 1865.

Gomart. Siège et Bataille de St Quentin (1557). Saint Quentin. 1859.

Heidrich, P.   Der geldrische Erbfolgestreit, 1537–43.   In Beiträge z. deutschen Territorial- und Städtegeschichte. Kassel, 1895.

Henne, A.   Histoire du règne de Charles-Quint en Belgique.   10 vols.   Brussels. 1858–60.

—— Histoire de la Belgique sous le règne de Charles-Quint.   4 vols.   Brussels. 1865.

Hove, A. van. Étude sur les conflits de juridiction dans le diocèse de Liège à l'époque d'Erard de la Marck. Louvain. 1900.

Juste, V.   Charles V et Marguerite d'Autriche.   Brussels.   1859.

Lamure, E.   Le grand Conseil des ducs de Bourgogne de la maison de Valois. Brussels.   1900.

Picardie, La guerre de 1557 en.   Société académique de Saint Quentin.   Saint Quentin. 1896.

Rachfahl, F.   Trennung der Niederländer vom deutschen Reiche.   Westdeutsche Zeitschrift. Vol. XIX, pt 2.   1900.

Reiffenberg, F. A. F. T., Baron de.   Histoire de l'Ordre de la Toison d'Or.   Brussels. 1850.

SPAIN

Bonn, M. J.   Spaniens Niedergang während der Preis-Revolution des 16ten Jahrhunderts.   In Brentano und Lotz, Münchner Volkswirthschaftliche Studien. 1896.

Cappa, R.   Estudios críticos acerca la Dominacion Española en America.   2nd edition. Madrid.   1888 etc.

Häbler, K.   Die wirthschaftliche Blüte Spaniens im 16ten Jahrhundert und ihr Verfall. In Jastrow; Historische Untersuchungen, Heft 1.   Berlin.   1888.

—— Die Geschichte der Fuggerschen Handlung in Spanien.   Weimar.   1895.

Helps, Sir A.   The Spanish Conquest in America.   4 vols.   London.   1855–61.

Lea, H. C.   The Moriscos of Spain.   London.   1901.

—— Chapters from the Religious History of Spain connected with the Inquisition. Philadelphia.   1890.

Loubens, M. J. G.   Essais sur l'administration de la Castille au XVIᵉ siècle.   Paris. 1860.

Ranke, L.   Spanien unter Karl V, Philipp II, und Philipp III.   Vol. XXXIII of Sämmtliche Werke.   Leipzig.   1874, etc.

BIOGRAPHY

Bouchot, H.   Catherine de Médicis.   Paris.   1899.

Cantini, L.   Vita di Cosimo de' Medici.   Florence.   1805.

Darmesteter, A. M. J.   Margaret of Angoulême, Queen of Navarre.   London. 1886.

Decrue, F.   Anne de Montmorency, Grand Maître et Connétable de France. à la cour . . . de François I.   Paris.   1885.

—— Anne de Montmorency, Connétable et pair de France, sous Henri II.   Paris. 1889.

Du Prat, A. T., Marquis.   Vie d'Antoine Duprat.   Paris.   1857.

Dupré-Lasale, E.   Michel de l'Hôpital avant son élévation au poste de Chancelier de France.   Paris.   1898.

Fabroni, A.   Magni Cosmi Medicei Vita.   2 vols.   Pisa.   1789–98.

Gachard, L. P.   Retraite et Mort de Charles Quint au Monastère de Yuste.   Acad. Imp. et Royale.   Brussels.   1854–5.

Juste, T.   Vie de Marie de Hongrie.   Brussels.   1855.

La Mure, J. M. de. Histoire des Ducs de Bourbon, en forme d'annales sur preuves authentiques. 4 vols. Paris. 1860-97.

Lefranc, A. Marguerite de Navarre et le platonisme de la Renaissance. Bibliothèque de l'École des Chartes. Vols. LVIII, LIX. 1897-8.

Marillac, O. de. Vie du Connétable de Bourbon. Paris. 1836.

Moeller, C. Éléonore d'Autriche et de Bourgogne, reine de France. Paris. 1895.

Petit, E. Andrea Doria. Paris. 1887.

Robert, U. Philibert de Chalon, Prince d'Orange, 1502-30. Boletin de la R. Acad. de la Historia. July to September. Madrid. 1901.

Vaissière, P. de. Charles de Marillac, ambassadeur et homme politique . . . 1510-60. Paris. 1896.

Stirling-Maxwell, Sir W. The Cloister Life of the Emperor Charles V. London. 1852 etc.

Zanoni, E. Vita pubblica di Fr. Guicciardini. Bologna. 1896.

MISCELLANEOUS

Burckhardt, J. Die Cultur der Renaissance in Italien. Basel. 1860. 8th edition. 2 vols. Leipzig. 1901. Translated by S. G. Middlemore. London. 1878.

Cat, E. De Caroli Quinti in Africa Rebus Gestis. 1891.

Cerezeda, M. G. Tratado de las Campañas . . . de los ejércitos del Emperador Cárlos V desde 1521 hasta 1545. Sociedad de Bibliófilos Españoles. Madrid. 1873-6.

Ehrenberg, R. Das Zeitalter der Fugger. Geldkapital und Kreditverkehr im 16ten Jahrhundert. Jena. 1895.

Gebhart, E. Les origines de la Renaissance en Italie. Paris. 1879.

—— Études méridionales. Paris. 1887.

Geymüller, H. Baron von. Geschichte der Baukunst der Renaissance in Frankreich. 2 vols. Darmstadt. 1896-9.

Gossart, E. Charles Quint et Philippe II. Étude sur les origines de la prépondérance politique de l'Espagne en Europe. Mémoires de l'Académie Royale. Brussels. 1896.

—— Notes pour servir à l'histoire de Charles Quint. Brussels. 1897.

Gonse, L. La Sculpture Française depuis le XIVᵉ siècle. Paris. 1895.

Höfler, C. A. C. von. Karls I Wahl zum Römischen König. Sitzungsberichte der Wiener Academie. 1873.

Kraus, F. X. Geschichte der Christlichen Kunst. Vol. II. Freiburg i. B. 1897.

La Vita Italiana nel seicento. Conferenze tenute nel 1894. Milan. 1895.

Müntz, E. Histoire de l'Art pendant la Renaissance. Paris. 1888– .

Niel, P. J. G. Portraits des personnages français les plus illustres du XVIᵉ siècle. Reproduits 1848-56 avec notices. 2 vols. Paris. 1848.

Palustre, L. L'Architecture de la Renaissance. Paris. 1892.

Rösler, R. Die Kaiserswahl Karls V. Vienna. 1868.

Turba, G. Ueber den Zug Kaiser Karls V gegen Algier. Vienna. 1890.

For Medicean Rome *see also Bibliography of Chapters* XII *and* XVII, *for* Habsburg and Valois *Bibliographies of Chapters* V-IX.

CHAPTER IV

LUTHER

(I) GERMAN SOCIAL LIFE AND POPULAR AND FAMILY RELIGION IN THE LAST DECADES OF THE 15TH AND IN THE EARLIER DECADES OF THE 16TH CENTURIES.

(A) CONTEMPORARY

Barack, K. A. Zimmerische Chronik. 4 vols. 2nd ed. Freiburg i. B. 1881-2.
Chroniken der deutschen Städte. 29 vols. Leipzig. In progress.
Gess, F. Die Klostervisitationen des Herzogs Georg von Sachsen, nach ungedruckten Quellen dargestellt. Leipzig. 1888.
Grimm, J. Weisthümer. 7 vols. (Vols. v–vii, edited by R. Schroeder.) Göttingen. 1840-2, 1866, 1869, 1878.
Häbler, K. Das Wallfahrtsbuch des Hermann Kunig von Vach, und die Pilgerreisen der Deutschen nach Santiago de Compostella. Drucke und Holzschnitte des 15 und 16 Jahrhunderts, No. 1. Strassburg. 1899.
Hasak, V. Die letzte Rose oder Erklärung des Vaterunser nach Marcus von Weida (1501) und Münzinger von Ulm (c. 1470). Ratisbon. 1883.
Hätzerlin, Clara. Liederbuch. Edited by C. Haltaus. Quedlinburg. 1840.
Liliencron, R. v. Die historischen Volkslieder der Deutschen vom dreizehnten bis zum sechszehnten Jahrhundert. 3 vols. and appendix. Leipzig. 1865-9.
Lorenzi, Ph. de. Geilers von Keysersberg ausgewählte Schriften. Trier. 1881.
Munzenberger, J. Frankfurter und Magdeburger Beichtbüchlein. Mainz. 1883.
Sachs, Hans. Fastnachtspiele. Neudrucke deutscher Literaturwerke, Nos. 26, 27, 31, 32, 39, 40, 42, 43, 51, 52, 60, 63, 64. Halle.
Thausing, M. Dürers Briefe, Tagebücher und Reime. Vienna. 1872.
Wackernagel, Ph. Das deutsche Kirchenlied von der ältesten Zeit bis zum Anfang des 17 Jahrhunderts. Leipzig. 1865.
Weller, E. Repertorium typographicum. Die deutsche Literatur im ersten Viertel des 16ten Jahrhunderts (with two supplements). Nördlingen. 1864, 1874, 1885.
Zarncke, F. Sebastian Brants Narrenschiff. Leipzig. 1854.

(B) SECONDARY

Binder, F. Charitas Pirkheimer, Aebtissin von St Clara zu Nürnberg. Freiburg i. B. 1893.
Binz, C. Dr Johann Weyer, der erste Bekämpfer des Hexenwahns. Bonn. 1885-8.
Brück, H. Der religiöse Unterricht für Jugend und Volk in Deutschland in der zweiten Hälfte des fünfzehnten Jahrhunderts. Mainz. 1876.
Cruel, R. Geschichte der deutschen Predigt im Mittelalter. Detwold. 1879.
Dacheux, L. Jean Geiler de Keysersberg. Paris and Strassburg. 1876.
Eye, A. von. Leben und Wirken Albrecht Dürers. 2nd ed. Nürnberg. 1868.
Falk, F. Die Druckkunst im Dienste der Kirche, zunächst in Deutschland bis zum Jahre 1520. Vereinschrift der Görresgesellschaft. Cologne. 1879.
—— Die deutsche Messauslegungen von der Mitte des 15 Jahrhunderts bis zum Jahre 1525. Vereinschrift der Görresgesellschaft. Cologne. 1889.

Falk, F. Die deutschen Sterbebüchlein von der ältesten Zeit des Buchdrucks bis zum Jahre 1520. Vereinschrift der Görresgesellschaft. Cologne. 1890.

Flathe, L. Geschichte der Vorläufer der Reformation. 2 vols. Leipzig. 1835.

Freytag, G. Bilder aus der deutschen Vergangenheit. Vol. ii, Pt ii. Aus dem Jahrhundert der Reformation. New ed. Leipzig, 1899. (An earlier edition was translated by Mrs Malcolm. London. 1862.)

Friedrich, J. Astrologie und Reformation, oder die Astrologen als Prediger der Reformation und Urheber des Bauernkriegs. Munich. 1864.

Gothein, E. Politische und religiöse Volksbewegungen vor der Reformation. Breslau. 1878.

Hagen, C. Deutschlands literarische und religiöse Verhältnisse im Reformationszeitalter. 3 vols. 2nd ed. Frankfort. 1868.

Hansen, J. Zauberwahn, Inquisition und Hexenprozess etc. Histor. Bibliothek xii. Munich and Leipzig. 1900.

Hasak, V. Der christliche Glaube des deutschen Volkes beim Schluss des Mittelalters dargestellt in deutschen Sprachdenkmälern. Ratisbon. 1868.

—— Dr M. Luther und die religiöse Literatur seiner Zeit bis zum Jahre 1520. Ratisbon. 1881.

Höfler, C. A. C. von. Denkwürdigkeiten der Charitas Pirckheimer. Quellensamml. z. fränk. Gesch., Vol. iv. 1852.

Kaweran, G. Caspar Güttel. Halle. 1882.

Keller, W. Die Reformation und die aelteren Reformationsparteien. Leipzig. 1885.

Krebs, J. Zur Geschichte der Heiligenthumsfahrten. Cologne. 1881.

Kriegk, G. L. Deutsches Bürgerthum im Mittelalter. Frankfort. 1868, 1871.

Leitschuh, F. Albrecht Dürer's Tagebuch der Reise in die Niederlande. Leipzig. 1884.

Lichtenberg, R., Freiherr v. Ueber den Humor bei den deutschen Kupferstechern und Holzschnittkünstlern des 16 Jahrhunderts. Strassburg. 1897.

Lorenz, J. Volkserziehung und Volksunterricht im späteren Mittelalter. Paderborn and Münster. 1887.

Schuchardt, Chr. Lucas Cranachs, des aelteren, Leben und Werke. 2 vols. Leipzig. 1851–70.

Schulz, Alwin. Deutsches Leben im 14ten und 15ten Jahrhundert. Prague, Vienna, Leipzig. 1892.

Schwaumkell, E. Der Cultus der heiligen Anna am Ausgange des Mittelalters. Freiburg. 1893.

Scott, W. B. Albert Dürer, his Life and Works. London. 1869.

Uhlhorn, G. Die christliche Liebesthätigkeit im Mittelalter. Stuttgart. 1887. Cf. Zeitschrift für Kirchengeschichte, iv, pp. 44 ff.

Ullmann, C. Reformatoren vor der Reformation. 2nd ed. 2 vols. Gotha. 1866. Transl. by R. Menzies. 2 vols. Edinburgh. 1855.

Walther, W. Die deutsche Bibelübersetzung des Mittelalters. Brunswick. 1889.

Wilken, E. Geschichte der geistlichen Spiele in Deutschland. Göttingen. 1872.

Zur Geschichte des Klerus. Allgemeine Zeitung. Oct. 28, 1873.

(II) MYSTICISM AND HUMANISM IN THEIR RELATION TO LUTHER

(A) CONTEMPORARY

Becker, D. J. Chronica eines fahrenden Schülers oder Wanderbüchlein des Johannes Butzbach. Ratisbon. 1869.

Bocking, E. Ulrici Hutteni Opera. 5 vols. Leipzig. 1871. A supplement contains, Epistolae obscurorum virorum cum notis illustrantibus adversariisque scriptis. 2 vols. Leipzig. 1864, 1869.

Boos, H. Thomas und Felix Platter. Leipzig. 1876.

Gillert, K. Der Briefwechsel des Konrad Mutianus. Halle. 1890.

Muther, T. Die Wittenberger Universitäts- und Facultätsstatuten vom Jahre 1508. Halle. 1867.

Theologia deutsch. Critical edition by Fr. Pfeiffer. 4th ed. Gütersloh. 1900.

(B) Secondary

Delprat, C. H. Verhandeling over de Broederschap van Gerard Groote. Arnhem. 1856.

Drummond, R. B. Erasmus. 2 vols. London. 1873.

Geiger, L. Renaissance und Humanismus in Italien und Deutschland. Berlin. 1882.

Grube, K. Gerard Groot und seine Stiftungen. Vereinschrift der Görresgesellschaft. Cologne. 1883.

Hering, H. Die Mystik Luthers im Zusammenhange seiner Theologie. Leipzig. 1879.

Kämmel, H. K. Geschichte des deutschen Schulwesens im Uebergange vom Mittelalter zur Neuzeit. Leipzig. 1892.

Kampschulte, F. W. Die Universität Erfurt in ihrem Verhältniss zu dem Humanismus und der Reformation. Aus den Quellen dargestellt. 2 vols. Trier. 1856, 1860.

Krause, C. Helius Eobanus Hessus, sein Leben und seine Werke. 2 vols. Gotha. 1879.

Muther, T. Aus dem Universitäts- und Gelehrtenleben im Zeitalter der Reformation. Erlangen. 1866.

Nichols, F. M. The Epistles of Erasmus from his earliest letters to his fifty-first year arranged in order of time. London. 1901.

Preger, W. Geschichte der deutschen Mystik im Mittelalter. 3 vols. (unfinished). Leipzig. 1874, 1881, 1893.

—— Beiträge zur Geschichte der religiösen Bewegung in den Niederlanden in der 2ten Hälfte des 14ten Jahrhunderts. Munich. 1894.

Pröhle, H. A. Andreas Proles, Vicarius der Augustiner, ein Zeuge der Wahrheit kurz vor Luther. Gotha. 1857.

Reindell, W. Luther, Crotus, and Hutten. Marburg. 1890.

Riederer, J. B. Nachrichten zur Kirchen- Gelehrten- und Büchergeschichte. 4 vols. Altdorf. 1764—8.

Roth, F. Willibald Pirkheimer. Halle. 1887.

Schwarz, B. Jakob Wimpheling, der Altmeister des deutschen Schulwesens. Gotha. 1875.

Schwertzell, G. Helius Eobanus Hessus. Halle. 1874.

Strauss, D. F. Ulrich von Hutten. 2 vols. 2nd ed. Leipzig. 1874. Translated and slightly abridged by Mrs George Sturge. London. 1874.

Wiskowatoff, P. v. Jacob Wimpheling. Berlin. 1867.

(III) LIVES OF LUTHER AND ORIGINAL SOURCES FOR INCIDENTS IN HIS CAREER

(A) Contemporary

Cochlaeus, J. Commentarius de actis et scriptis M. Lutheri ... ab anno 1517 usque ad annum 1537. St Victor prope Moguntiam. 1549.

Cruciger, Caspar. Tabulae chronologicae actorum M. Lutheri. Wittenberg. 1553.

Faber, K. Dr M. Luthers Briefe an Allbrecht, Herzog in Preussen. Königsberg. 1811.

Förstemann, C. E. Neues Urkundenbuch zur Geschichte der evangelischen Kirchen- reformation. Vol. I (all published). Hamburg. 1842.

Kolde, Th. Analecta Lutherana. Gotha. 1883.

Leib, Killian. Annales von 1503–1523. (Vols. VII and IX of von Aretin's Beiträge zur Geschichte und Literatur.) Munich. 1803–6.

Loesche, G. Analecta Lutherana et Melanchthoniana. Tischreden Luthers und Aus- sprüche Melanchthons. Gotha. 1892.

Löscher, V. E. Vollständige Reformations-Acta und Documenta. 3 vols. Leipzig. 1720–9.

Luther, Martin. Werke. Kritische Gesammtausgabe. Weimar. 1883 etc. (Twenty volumes have been published.)

Mathesius, J. Historien von . . . Martini Lutheri Anfang, Lere, Leben, und Sterben. Nürnberg. 1570. Critical edition by G. Loesche. Prague. 1896.

Melanchthon, P. Historia de vita et actis Lutheri. Wittenberg. 1545. (To be found in Vol. VI of the Corpus Reformatorum.)

Myconius, Fr. Historia Reformationis, 1517–42. Edited by E. S. Cyprian. Leipzig. 1718.

Ratzeberger, M. MS. Geschichte über Luther und seine Zeit. Edited by Ch. G. Neudecker. Jena. 1850.

Seidemann, J. K. A Lauterbach's Tagebuch . . . die Hauptquelle der Tischreden Luthers. Dresden. 1872.

Selneccer, N. Historia . . . D. M. Lutheri. Leipzig. 1575.

Wrampelmeyer, H. Tagebuch über Dr Martin Luther, geführt von Dr Conrad Cordatus (1537). Halle. 1885.

(B) Secondary

Berger, A. E. Martin Luther in kulturgeschichtlicher Darstellung. 2 vols. Berlin. 1895.

Enders, L. Dr Martin Luthers Briefwechsel. 5 vols. Frankfort and Stuttgart. 1884–93.

Kolde, Th. Martin Luther. Eine Biographie. 2 vols. Gotha. 1884, 1893.

Köstlin, J. Martin Luther, sein Leben und seine Schriften. 2 vols. 1875.

Lang, H. Martin Luther. Ein religiöses Charakterbild. Berlin. 1870.

Lenz, M. Martin Luther. Festschrift zum 10. Nov. 1883. Berlin. 1883.

Lindsay, T. M. Luther and the German Reformation. Edinburgh. 1900.

Seckendorf, V. L. Commentarius . . . de Lutheranismo. Frankfort. 1692.

Seidemann, J. K. Erläuterungen zur Reformationsgeschichte. Dresden. 1872.

Treitschke, H. von. Luther und die deutsche Nation. Preussische Jahrbücher. November. 1883.

(IV) LUTHER'S LIFE UP TO THE BEGINNING OF THE INDULGENCE CONTROVERSY

(A) Contemporary

Constitutiones Fratrum Heremitarum Sancti Augustini. Nürnberg. 1504.

Kessler, J. Sabbata. Chronik der Jahre 1523–1539. Edited by Egli and Schoch. St Gallen. 1902.

(B) Secondary

Buchwald, G. Zur Wittemberg Stadt- und Universitätsgeschichte in der Reformationszeit. Leipzig. 1893.

Elze, Th. Luthers Reise nach Rom. Berlin. 1899.

Hausrath, A. M. Luthers Romfahrt, nach einem gleichzeitigen Pilgerbuche. Berlin. 1894.

Jürgens, C. Luther von seiner Geburt bis zum Ablassstreit. 3 vols. Leipzig. 1846, 1847.

Keller, L. Johann von Staupitz. Leipzig. 1883.

Kohler, K. F. Luthers Reisen und ihre Bedeutung für das Werk der Reformation. Eisenach. 1873.

Kolde, Th. Die deutschen Augustiner-Congregationen und Johann v. Staupitz. Gotha. 1879.

—— Friedrich der Weise und die Anfänge der Reformation mit archivalischen Beilagen. Erlangen. 1881.

Köstlin, J. Geschichtliche Untersuchungen über Luthers Leben vor dem Ablassstreit. Theologische Studien und Kritiken for 1871, pp. 7–54. Gotha. 1871.

Krumhaar, K. Die Grafschaft Mansfeld im Reformationszeitalter. Eisleben. 1845.

Oergel, G. Vom jungen Luther. Erfurt. 1899.

Paulus, N. Der Augustiner Bartholomaeus Arnold von Usingen, Luthers Lehrer und Gegner. In Strassburger theologische Studien, Vol. i, Pt iii. Strassburg and Freiburg. 1893.

Richard, A. V. Licht und Schatten. Ein Beitrag zur Culturgeschichte von Sachsen und Thuringen im xvi Jahrhundert. Leipzig. 1861.

(V) THE INDULGENCE CONTROVERSY

(A) Contemporary

Kapp, J. E. Sammlung einiger zum päpstlichen Ablass, überhaupt . . . aber zu der . . . zwischen D. Martin Luther und Johann Tetzel hiervongeführten Streitigkeit, gehörigen Schriften, mit Einleitungen und Anmerkungen versehen. Leipzig. 1721.

—— Kleine Nachlese einiger . . . zur Erläuterung der Reformationsgeschichte nützlicher Urkunden. (Four parts.) Leipzig. 1727–33.

Mirabilia Romae. Nürnberg. 1491. (A critical edition by G. Parthey. Berlin. 1869.)

(B) Secondary

Beringer, F. (Soc. Jes.). Der Ablass, sein Wesen und Gebrauch. 12th ed. Paderborn, 1898.

Bouvier, J. B. Treatise on Indulgences (translated by F. Oakley). London. 1848.

Bratke, E. Luthers 95 Theses und ihre dogmenhistorischen Voraussetzungen. Göttingen. 1884.

Brieger, Th. Das Wesen des Ablasses am Ausgange des Mittelalters, untersucht mit Rücksicht auf Luthers Theses. Leipzig. 1897.

Dieckhoff, A. W. Der Ablassstreit dogmengeschichtlich dargestellt. Gotha. 1886.

Gröne, V. Tetzel und Luther. 2nd ed. Soest. 1860.

Köhler, W. Dokumente zum Ablassstreit von 1517. Tübingen and Leipzig. 1902.

Körner, F. Tezel der Ablassprediger. Mit bes. Rücksicht auf kathol. Anschauungen. Frankenberg. 1880.

Lea, H. C. A History of Auricular Confession and Indulgences in the Latin Church. 3 vols. Philadelphia. 1896.

May, J. Der Kurfürst Cardinal und Erzbischof Albrecht II von Mainz und Magdeburg und seine Zeit. 2 vols. München. 1865, 1875.

(VI) FROM THE INDULGENCE CONTROVERSY TO THE DIET OF WORMS

(A) CONTEMPORARY

Balan, P. Monumenta Reformationis Lutheranae ex tabulis S. Sedis secretis 1521–5. Ratisbon. 1883–4.

Brewer, J. S. Letters and Papers, foreign and domestic, of the reign of Henry VIII. Vol. III. London, 1870.

Brieger, T. Aleander und Luther, 1521. Die vervollständigten Aleander-Depeschen nebst Untersuchungen über den Wormser Reichstag. Pt I. Gotha. 1894.

Kalkoff, P. Die Depeschen des Nuntius Aleander. 2nd ed. Halle. 1897.

Laemmer, H. Monumenta Vaticana historiam ecclesiasticam saeculi XVI illustrantia. Freiburg. 1861.

—— Meletematum Romanorum Mantissa. Regensburg. 1875.

Murner, T. An den grossmächtigsten und durchlauchtigsten Adel deutscher Nation (1520), edited by Ernst Voss. (No. 153 of Neudrucke deutscher Literaturwerke des XVI und XVII Jahrhunderts.) Halle. 1899.

Wace and Buchheim. Luther's Primary Works. 2nd ed. London. 1896.

(B) SECONDARY

Albert, R. Aus welchen Gründen disputirte Johann Eck gegen Luther in Leipzig 1519? Zeitschrift für die historische Theologie. XLIII, pp. 332–441. Gotha. 1873.

Baur, A. Deutschland in den Jahren 1517–1525 getrachtet im Lichte gleichzeitiger anonymer und pseudonymer deutscher Volks- und Flugschriften. Ulm. 1872.

Beard, C. Martin Luther and the Reformation in Germany until the close of the Diet of Worms. London. 1889.

Bezold, F. v. Geschichte der deutschen Reformation. Berlin. 1890.

Creighton, M. (Bishop). A History of the Papacy. Vol. VI. 2nd ed. London. 1897.

Döllinger, J. J. Die Reformation, ihre innere Entwickelung. 3 vols. Ratisbon. 1846–8.

Friedrich, J. Der Reichstag zu Worms, 1521. Nach den Briefen Aleanders. Munich. 1871.

Gebhardt, B. Die Gravamina der deutschen Nation. 2nd ed. Breslau. 1895.

Hausrath, A. Aleander und Luther auf dem Reichstage zu Worms. Berlin. 1897.

Jacoby, H. Die Liturgik der Reformatoren. Vol. I. Introduction — Liturgik Luthers. Gotha. 1871.

Janssen, J. Geschichte des deutschen Volkes seit dem Ausgang des Mittelalters. Vol. II. 18th ed. Freiburg i. B. 1897.

Kolde, T. Luther und der Reichstag zu Worms 1521. Schriften des Vereins für Reformationsgeschichte. No. 1. Halle. 1883.

Kuczýnski, A. Thesaurus libellorum historiam Reformatorum illustrantium (Verzeichniss einer Sammlung von nahezu 3000 Flugschriften Luthers und seiner Zeitgenossen). Leipzig. 1870.

Maurenbrecher, W. Studien und Skizzen zur Geschichte der Reformationszeit. Leipzig. 1874.

Ranke, L. v. Deutsche Geschichte im Zeitalter der Reformation. Vols. II, III. 6th ed. Leipzig. 1881, 1882.

Seidemann, J. K. Die Leipziger Disputation im Jahre 1519. Dresden. 1843.

Schade, O. Satiren und Pasquille aus der Reformationszeit. 3 vols. Hanover. 1850–8.

Thomas, G. M. Martin Luther und die Reformationsbewegung in Deutschland 1520–1525. In Auszügen aus Marino Sanuto's Diarien. Ansbach. 1883.

Ulmann, H. Franz von Sickingen. Leipzig. 1872.

Wiedemann, T. Johann Eck. Ratisbon. 1865.

See also Bibliography of Chapters V–VIII.

CHAPTERS V–VIII

GERMANY, 1521–1555

I. MANUSCRIPTS

The materials for the history of Germany during the Reformation are probably more extensive, more scattered, and more difficult of description in brief than those for the history of any other country in Europe; for whereas other States had as a rule one central government, one chancery, and one foreign office, Germany had many. There are not only the imperial archives, the domestic and foreign correspondence of Charles V and of the German *Reich*, but every important Prince had his own domestic correspondence and his correspondence with other German Princes as well as with foreign Powers; and thus there is no one repository of materials for German history as in London, Paris, or Simancas. Even the correspondence of Charles V is divided between Vienna, Brussels, and Simancas, while the despatches of foreign representatives at Charles V's Court and at the Imperial Diets must be sought principally in Rome, Paris, Venice, and London.

Next in importance to the Emperor's correspondence are the records of the Diets, of which the most complete series is that preserved at Frankfort (cf. Jung, R., Das historische Archiv der Stadt Frankfurt am Main, Frankfort, 1896, pp. 50, 51). These relate mainly to the internal affairs of the Empire; but the archives of the Electors and of other Princes such as the Landgrave of Hesse and the Dukes of Bavaria are important for foreign as well as for domestic history. Of these archives the chief are those of Austria at Vienna and Innsbruck, Ernestine Saxony at Weimar, Albertine Saxony at Dresden, Hesse at Marburg, Brandenburg at Berlin, the Palatinate at Heidelberg, Bavaria at Munich, Cleves at Düsseldorf, Brunswick at Wolfenbüttel, and of the spiritual electors of Mainz, Cologne, and Trier at their respective metropolitan cities.

Scarcely inferior in interest are the archives of some of the imperial cities. The 'Stadtarchiv' sometimes contains not merely bulky materials for municipal and local history, but chronicles relating the political and religious events of the day, and occasionally political correspondence of substantial value (cf. Jung *ut supra*; the mere list of classes of documents at Frankfort occupies a hundred folio pages). The political correspondence of Strassburg, for instance, is of the highest importance; while the records of smaller cities often become of prime value for events of more than local importance. Those of Mühlhausen throw much light on the history of the Peasants' War in Thuringia, those of Münster are the principal source for our knowledge of the Anabaptist rising, and those of Lübeck for the '*Grafenfehde*,' while it was on the records of Ulm that Ranke based his account of Charles V's negotiations in the winter of 1546–7. An indication of the contents of these national and local archives is given in C. A. H. Burkhardt's admirable Hand- und Adressbuch der deutschen Archive (2 pts. Leipzig, 1887).

The publication of these vast masses of material is being energetically pursued by State-governments, universities, voluntary associations, and individual scholars. There are royal and ducal historical commissions like that of Saxony and that of Baden; directions of State archives such as the Prussian; university bodies, the most active of which, the Bavarian Akademie der Wissenschaften, has published or is publishing the Allgemeine deutsche Biographie, the Jahrbücher der deutschen Geschichte, the Reichstagsakten, the Briefe und Akten zur Geschichte des xvi Jahrhunderts, the Chroniken der deutschen Städte, the Forschungen zur deutschen Geschichte and annual 'Sitzungsberichte'; voluntary associations of a theologico-historical character, such as the Görresgesellschaft zur Pflege der Wissenschaft im katholischen Deutschland, and the Verein für Reformationsgeschichte, or with a local purpose like the Verein für Oberhessische Geschichte, or the Historische Verein für Niedersachsen. Nearly every State, and many districts and cities, have associations for the publication of their records. There are some two hundred periodical publications in Germany devoted to historical research; and practically every historical dissertation for a doctorate in German universities is based upon the study of some portion of unpublished material. The fullest guide to these current works is the annual bibliography appearing in the Historische Vierteljahrsschrift (ed. G. Seeliger, Leipzig). Elaborate surveys of the historical output for each year are contained in Berner's Jahresberichte der Geschichtswissenschaften (Berlin, xxv Bde, 1878–1902); concise ones in the Mittellungen a. d. histor. Litteratur (edited for the Histor. Gesellsch. in Berlin by Dr F. Hirsch); while the more important articles in German periodicals are generally noticed in the Historische Zeitschrift and the English Historical Review. A slight but useful index is supplied by F. Förster's Kritischer Wegweiser durch die neuere deutsche historische Literatur, Berlin, 1900. The best general bibliography is Dahlmann-Waitz, Quellenkunde der deutschen Geschichte, 6th ed. by E. Steindorff, 1894. There are also separate bibliographies of the history of many of the chief German states.

II. PRINTED AUTHORITIES FOR THE WHOLE PERIOD 1521–1555

A. DOCUMENTS

(1) *Relating to general history*

Albéri, E. Le Relazioni degli Ambasciatori Veneti al Senato durante il secolo decimosesto. 15 vols. Florence. 1839–62. 3rd Ser.

Bradford, W. Correspondence of Charles V. London. 1850.

Döllinger, J. J. I. Documente zur Geschichte Karls V. In Beiträge zur politischen, kirchlichen und Cultur-Gesch. des xvi Jahr. Vol. 1. Ratisbon. 1862.

Fiedler, J. Relationen Venetianischer Botschafter über Deutschland und Oesterreich im 16 Jahrh. Fontes Rerum Austriacarum. Vol. xxx. Vienna. 1870.

Förstemann, C. G. Neues Urkundenbuch zur Geschichte der evangelischen Kirchenreformation. Hamburg. 1842.

Gachard, L. P. Relations des ambassadeurs vénétiens sur Charles V. Brussels. 1856.

Goldast, Melchior. Collectio Constitutionum Imperialium. Frankfort. Vols. I and II. 1713.

Harpprecht, G. N. von. Staatsarchiv des kayserlichen Kammergerichts. 5 pts. Frankfort. 1757–69. Ulm. 1785–9.

Klüpfel, K. Urkunden zur Geschichte des schwäbischen Bundes 1488–1533. Stuttgart. 1846–53.

Koch, C. G. Neue und vollständige Sammlung der Reichsabschiede. 4 pts. Frankfort. 1747.

Krafft, Carl. Briefe und Dokumente aus Zeit der Reformation im 16 Jahrh. Elberfeld. 1876.

Laemmer, H. Monumenta Vaticana. Freiburg i. B. 1861.

—— Analecta Romana. Schaffhausen. 1864.

Lanz, K. Correspondenz des Kaisers Karl V. 3 vols. Leipzig. 1844–6.

—— Aktenstücke und Briefe zur Gesch. Karls V. Mon. Habsb. Pt I. Vienna. 1854.

—— Staatspapiere zur Geschichte Karls V. Stuttgart. 1845.

Le Glay, E. Négotiations diplomatiques entre France et l'Autriche. Coll. de Documents Inédits. Paris. 2 vols. 1845.

Lenz, M. Briefwechsel Philipps von Hessen mit Butzer. Leipzig. 3 vols. 1880–91.

Letters and Papers, Foreign and Domestic, of the Reign of Henry VIII. Vols. III and IV, ed. J. S. Brewer. Vols. v–xix, ed. J. Gairdner. 1519–44. London. 1860–1903.

Löscher, V. E. Vollständige Reformations-acta und Documenta. 3 vols. Leipzig. 1720–8.

Lünig, J. C. Das deutsche Reichsarchiv. 24 vols. Leipzig. 1713–22.

Monumenta Habsburgica. 1473–1576. 2 vols. Kaiserl. Akad. der Wissensch. Vienna. 1853–7.

Neudecker, Chr. G. Merkwürdige Aktenstücke aus dem Zeitalter der Reformation. 2 Abth. Nürnberg. 1838.

—— Urkunden aus der Reformationszeit. Cassel. 1836.

Raumer, F. L. G. von. Briefe aus Paris zur Erläuterung der Gesch. des 16 und 17 Jahrh. 2 parts. Leipzig. 1831.

Reichstagsakten unter Karl V herausgegeben durch die Münchener historische Kommission. Vol. I, ed. A. Kluckhohn. 1893. Vols. II–III, ed. A. Wrede. Gotha. 1896, 1901.

Spanish State Papers, Calendar of. Ed. Bergenroth. Vols. I–II. Ed. Gayangos. Vols. III–VII. London. 1862–1899.

State Papers published by the Record Commission. 11 vols. London. 1830–1852.

Turba, G. Venetianische Depeschen vom Kaiserhofe. Dispacci di Germania. Vols. I–II. Hist. Komm. d. k. Akad. d. Wissens. Vienna. 1889, 1892.

Venetian State Papers, Calendar of. Ed. Rawdon Brown. Vols. III–VI. London. 1864–1884.

(ii) *The religious leaders and their writings*

(a) Luther and the Lutherans

The published volumes of the correspondence and works of Luther and his colleagues are far too numerous to be set out in detail. None of the various editions of Luther's works is completely satisfactory, the best being the Erlangen edition 1826–1879; an excellent edition by F. Knaake and others is however in course of publication (Weimar, 1883 sqq. 20 vols.). See also Burkhardt, Luthers Briefwechsel, 1866; Kolde. Analecta Lutherana, 1883; the Letters, ed. de Wette and Seidemann, 6 vols., 1825–58; Förstemann and Bindseil's editions of the Table-talk (Tischreden, 4 vols., 1844–8, and in Latin, 3 vols., 1863). The great 'Corpus Reformatorum' (ed. C. G. Bretschneider and H. E. Bindseil, Halle, 1834–1900, 89 vols.) consists chiefly of the works of Melanchthon and Calvin. See also Bugenhagen's Briefwechsel, ed. Vogt, Stettin, 1888; A. L. Herminjard's Correspondances des Reformateurs dans les Pays de la langue française (10 vols., Geneva, 1866 etc.); and the works of Justus Jonas (ed. Kawerau, Halle, 1884–5), Sebastian Lotzer (ed. A. Goetze, Lei~   ⁻⁰⁰2), Friedrich Myconius, John and Stephen Agricola, Ambrose Blaurer, Jo˙   ⁻olfgang Capito, Carlstadt,

A. Corvinus, Andreas Osiander, J. Honterus (Vienna, 1898), Urbanus Rhegius, and Schnepf. (Cf. Hagenbach's Leben und ausgewählte Schriften der Väter der reformirten Kirche, 10 pts, Elberfeld, 1857–62.)

(*See also Bibliography of Chap. IV.*)

(b)   The Humanists

The writings of Erasmus continue to be of value until his death in 1536; there is no satisfactory edition of his works, that of Le Clerc (Leyden, 10 vols., 1703–6) being the one generally used (cf. bibliogr. note in Emerton's Erasmus, 1899, pp. xxiii–vi). See also Beatus Rhenanus, Briefwechsel, ed. Horawitz and Hartfelder (Leipzig, 1886; cf. A. Horawitz, Des Beatus Rhenanus literarische Thätigkeit 1530–47, Leipzig, 1873; and id., Die Bibliothek und Correspondenz des Beatus Rhenanus, Vienna, 1874); Ulrich Zasius, Epistolae, ed. Riegger, Ulm, 1774 (cf. R. Stintzing, Ulrich Zasius, Basel, 1857). For other Humanists consult: Fr. Roth, Willibald Pirkheimer, Halle, 1887; C. Krause, Helius Eobanus Hessus, 2 vols., Gotha, 1879; and Burkhardt-Biedermann, T., Bonifacius Amerbach und die Reformation, Basel, 1894; J. von Aschbach, Die Wiener Universität und ihre Humanisten, Vienna, 1877; K. Hartfelder and F. von Bezold on Konrad Celtes, Historische Zeitschrift for 1882 and 1883; A. Horawitz, Caspar Bruschius, Leipzig, 1875.

(c)   The Catholics

Of the works by Catholic writers of the time the most important are those of Cochlaeus, Thomas Murner, Johann Eck, Emser, Karl von Miltitz, Alexander Hegius, J. A. Faber, Gropper, Pflug, and Johann Dietenberger (cf. W. Friedensburg, Beiträge zur Briefwechsel der katholischen gelehrten Deutschlands im Reformationszeitalter, in Zeitschr. für Kirchengeschichte 1897–1902).

(d)   The Zwinglians

Zwingli's works are noticed in the bibliography to Chap. X. The works of his successor, Heinrich Bullinger, and of Oecolampadius, Caspar Hedio, Theodore Bibliander, Leo Jud, Oswald Myconius, Joachim von Watt (Vadianus), should also be consulted.

B.   Contemporary Chronicles, Correspondences, Histories, and Memoirs

Bullinger, Heinrich.   Reformationsgeschichte.   Edd. Hottinger and Vögeli.   Frauenfeld.   6 vols.   1838–40.

Charles V.   Commentaries.   Ed. Kervyn de Lettenhove.   Brussels.   1862.   (Cf. O. Waltz, Die Denkwürdigkeiten Kaiser Karls V.   Bonn.   1901.)

Cochlaeus [verè Dobneck], Johann.   Comment. de scriptis et actis Lutheri.   1517–1546.   Mainz.   1549.   Republ. as 'Historia.'   Paris.   1565.

Cruciger, Caspar.   Tabulae chronologicae actorum M. Lutheri.   Wittenberg.   1553.

Fabricius, Henricus.   Kurtze Chronick 1500–1568.   Ed. L. Surius.   Cologne.   1568.

Flugschriften aus der Reformationszeit.   19 parts.   Halle.   1895–1902.

Franck, Sebastian.   Chronica.   3 parts.   Strassburg.   1531.   (Later editions with additions, 1536, 1555, 1585; cf. C. A. Hase, Sebastian Franck, der Schwärmgeist, Leipzig, 1869 ; H. Bischof, Seb. Franck und deutsche Geschichtschreibung, 1857; and H. Oncken, Sebastian Franck als Historiker in Hist. Zeitschr. LXXXII, 385–435.)

Freher, Marquard. Germanicarum rerum scriptores. 3 vols. Frankfort. 1600–11.

Herberstein, Siegmund von. Selbstbiographie 1486–1553 (Fontes Rerum Austr. 1, 67–396).

Kessler, Johann. Sabbata. Ed. Goetsinger. St Gall. 1870. Also edited by Egli and Schoch. St Gall. 1902.

Königstein, W. Tagebuch, 1520–48. Ed. G. E. Steitz. Frankfort. 1876.

Lauterbach, A. Tagebuch. Ed. Seidemann. Dresden. 1872.

Leib, Killian. Annales, 1502–23. Ed. Aretin, Beyträge vii, ix (Munich, 1803–6), and 1524–48 in Döllinger, Beiträge ii (Ratisbon, 1863).

Lenz, M. Briefwechsel Landgraf Philipps d. Grossen von Hessen mit Bucer. Publicationen aus den Preuss. Archiven. Berlin. 1880 etc.

Mathesius, J. Ausgewählte Werke. Ed. G. Loesche. Prague. 1896–8.

Melanchthon, Philip. Historia de vita et actis Lutheri. Wittenberg. 1546.

Mencke, J. B. Scriptores rerum Germanicarum praecipue Saxonicarum. Leipzig. 3 vols. 1728–30.

Myconius, Friedrich. Historia Reformationis. 1517–42. Ed. E. S. Cyprian. Leipzig. 1718.

Prinsen, J. Collectanea van Gerardus Geldenhauer Noviomagus. Amsterdam. 1901.

Ratzeberger, M. Handschriftliche Geschichte über Luther und seine Zeit. Ed. Neudecker. Jena. 1850.

Scheurl, Chr. Briefbuch, 1505–40. Ed. E. von Soden and Knaake. Potsdam. 2 vols. 1867–72.

Scultetus, Abr. Annales (to 1536). In von der Hardt's Historia Literaria. Frankfort. 1717.

Seckendorf, Veit Ludwig. Comment. Hist. de Lutheranismo. Frankfort. 1692.

Senckenberg, H. C. Sammlung von ungedruckt und raren Schriften zu Erläuterung der Rechte und Geschichte von Teutschland. 4 parts. Frankfort. 1745–51.

Sleidan [verè Philippson], Johann. Comment. de statu religionis Carlo V Caesare. Strassburg. 1555. (Cf. F. W. Weise, Über die Quellen der Comment. Sleidans, Halle, 1879; Baumgarten, Ueber Sleidans Leben und Briefwechsel, Strassburg, 1878, and Sleidans Briefwechsel, Strassburg, 1881; Th. Paur, Sleidans Kommentäre über die Regierungszeit Karls V, Leipzig, 1843; and Winckelmann, Sleidan und seine Kommentäre, Zeitschr. für Gesch. des Oberrheins, N. F. xiv, 565–606.)

Spalatin [verè Burckard, Georg]. Annales Reformationis (to 1543). Leipzig. 1768.
—— Chronikon, 1513–1526. In Mencke, Vol. ii.
—— Hist. Nachlass und Briefe. Ed. C. G. Neudecker. Jena. 1851. (Cf. Drews, 'Spalatiniana' in Zeitschr. für Kirchen-Gesch. xix–xx, and O. Clemen, Spalatiniana in Beiträge ii, 138–42.)

Struve, B. G. Corpus Historiae Germanicae. 2 vols. Jena. 1730.
—— Rerum Germanicarum Scriptores. 3 vols. Strassburg. 1717.

Surius, Laur. Comment. brevis rerum gestarum 1500–1574. Cologne. 1568. [In answer to Sleidan.]

Waltz, O. Flersheimer Chronik. Leipzig. 1874.

C. Secondary Authorities

(i) *General histories and biographies of Charles V*

Armstrong, E. The Emperor Charles V. 2 vols. London. 1902.

Baumgarten, H. Geschichte Karls V (to 1539). 3 vols. 1885–92.

Bezold, F. von. Geschichte der deutschen Reformation. Berlin. 1890.

Datt, Johann Philipp. Volumen rerum Germanicarum novum, sive de pace imperii publica (a history of the Swabian League). Ulm. 1698.

Egelhaaf, G. Deutsche Geschichte im Zeitalter der Reformation. 2nd ed. Berlin, 1885.

—— Deutsche Gesch. im XVI Jahrh. bis zum 1555. Bibliothek deutscher Gesch. Stuttgart. 2 Bde. 1889–92.

Fischer, K. Gesch. der auswärtigen Politik und Diplomatie im Reformationszeitalter. Gotha. 1874.

Häusser, L. Gesch. des Zeitalters der Reformation. Ed. Oncken. 1868. Engl. tr. 1885.

Janssen, J. Geschichte des deutschen Volkes seit dem Ausgang des Mittelalters. Vols. III–VI. Ed. L. Pastor. Freiburg i. B. 1897. (Cf. Erläuterungen und Ergänzungen zu Janssen's Geschichte, ed. L. Pastor, Freiburg i. B., 1898 etc. and Janssen's An meine Kritiker, Freiburg, 1883.) English translation by M. A. Mitchell and A. M. Christie. 6 vols. London. 1896–1903.

Krebs, K. Beiträge und Urkunden zur deutschen Geschichte im Zeitalter der Ref. Leipzig. 1895.

Lamprecht, K. Deutsche Geschichte. Vol. V. Berlin. 1894–5. (Cf. the criticisms of H. Oncken, H. Delbrück, and M. Lenz, and Lamprecht's reply in Zwei Streitschriften, Berlin, 1897.)

Menzel, C. A. Neuere Geschichte der Deutschen. Breslau. 12 vols. 1826–48.

Namèche, A. J. L'Empereur Charles V. 5 tom. Louvain. 1889.

Nitzsch, K. W. Geschichte des deutschen Volkes bis zum Augsburger Religionsfrieden. 3 vols. 2nd ed. Leipzig. 1883–5, 1892.

Pichot, A. Charles Quint, Chronique de sa vie. Paris. 1854.

Ranke, Leopold von. Deutsche Geschichte im Zeitalter der Reformation. 6 vols. 6th ed. Leipzig. 1882. Vols. I–III of Sämmtliche Werke. Leipzig. 1874, etc.

Robertson, William. History of the Reign of the Emperor Charles V. London. 3 vols. 1770. 10th ed. 1802. Latest ed. London. 1887.

Vandenesse, J. Journal des voyages de Charles Quint. Ed. Gachard. Brussels. 1874.

Zeller, J. Hist. d'Allemagne. Vol. V. Paris. 1891.

The Allgemeine deutsche Biographie (46 Bde, Leipzig, 1875–1902) and Herzog's Realencyklopädie für Protestantische Theologie und Kirche (2nd ed. 18 Bde, Leipzig, 1877, etc.) are both indispensable works of reference, the articles being usually careful monographs written by specialists and enriched by useful bibliographical notes. Compare also numerous contributions by Baumgarten, J. Roth, Kawerau, Kolde, and other scholars to the 'Schriften des Vereins für Reformationsgeschichte' (1883–1903).

(ii) *Works on Religious History*

Alzog, G. Handbuch der allgemeinen Kirchengeschichte. 10th ed., by F. X. Kraus. Vol. II. Mainz. 1882.

Baum, J. W. Capito und Butzer. Väter der Reformirten Kirche. Elberfeld. 1860.

Baumgarten, H. Jakob Sturm. Strassburg. 1876.

Bayer, G. Johannes Brenz. Stuttgart. 1899.

Bubucke, H. Wilhelm Gnaphaeus, ein Lehrer, aus dem Reformationszeitalter. Emden. 1875.

Bugenhagen, Joannes. Lives of, by L. W. Graepp (Gütersloh, 1897), H. Hering (Halle, 1889), C. A. T. Vogt (Elberfeld, 1867).

Carrière, M. Die Philosophische Weltanschauung der Reformationszeit in ihren Beziehungen zur Gegenwart. 2 vols. Leipzig. 1887.

Döllinger, J. J. I. Beiträge zur politischen, kirchlichen, und Cultur-Geschichte. 2 vols. Ratisbon. 1862–3.

—— Die Reformation. 3 vols. Ratisbon. 1846–8.

Erichson, A. Martin Butzer. Strassburg. 1891.

Fabricius, J. A. Centifolium Lutheranum. Hamburg. 1728–30.

Fuessli, J. C. Carlstadts Lebensgeschichte. Frankfort. 1776.

Gerdes, D. Scrinium Antiquarium . . . ad hist. Ref. eccl. spectant. 8 vols. Groningen. 1749–65.

Gulick, W. von. Johann Gropper und seine Thätigkeit in Köln bis 1540. Münster. 1902.

Hase, C. A. Kirchengeschichte. Leipzig. 11th ed. 1886.

Hartmann, Julius. Leben und ausgewählte Schriften der Väter der lutheranischen Kirche. 5 pts. Elberfeld. 1861–70.

—— E. Schnepff, der Reformator in Schwaben etc. Tübingen. 1870.

—— and Jaeger, C. Johann Brenz. 2 vols. Hamburg. 1840–2.

Haussleiter, J. Melanchthon-Kompendium. Greifswald. 1902.

Heppe, H. L. J. Dogmatik des deutschen Protestantismus im 16 Jahrh. 3 vols. Gotha. 1857.

—— Geschichte der lutherischen Concordienformel und Concordie. 2 vols. Marburg. 1857–9.

Jacoby, H. Die Liturgik der Reformatoren. Gotha. 1871 etc.

Jaeger, C. F. Andreas Bodenstein von Carlstadt. Stuttgart. 1856.

Jäger, C. Mittheilungen zur schwäbischen und frankischen Reformationsgeschichte. Stuttgart. 1828.

Jarcke, C. E. Studien und Skizzen zur Geschichte der Reformation. Schaffhausen. 1846.

Kawerau, W. Thomas Murner. Halle. 1890–1.

—— G. Johann Agricola von Eisleben. Berlin. 1881.

—— Hieronymus Emser. Halle. 1896.

Keil, F. S. Luthers Lebensumstände. 4 pts. Leipzig. 1764.

Keim, C. T. Ambrose Blaurer, der schwäbische Reformator. Stuttgart. 1860.

Keller, L. Die Reformation und die älteren Reformparteien. Leipzig. 1885.

Kolde, Th. Beiträge zur Reformationsgeschichte, in Kirchengeschichtliche Studien. 1888 etc.

—— Andreas Althamer, der Humanist und Reformator in Brandenburg-Ansbach. Erlangen. 1895.

Kurtz, J. H. Lehrbuch der Kirchengeschichte. 11th ed. Leipzig. 1890.

Kügelgen, C. W. Luthers Auffassung von der Gottheit Christi. Leipzig. 1901.

—— Rechtfertigungslehre des Johs. Brenz. Leipzig. 1898.

Lemmens, Leonhard. Augustin von Alfeld. Freiburg. 1897.

Liessem, H. J. Groppers Leben und Wirken. Cologne. 1876.

Luther, Martin. Lives of, by Th. Kolde, 2 vols., 1884–93; J. Köstlin, 2 vols., Elberfeld, 1875, 5th ed. 1902; Kuhn, 3 vols., Paris, 1883; M. Lenz, 3rd ed., Berlin, 1897; Plitt and Petersen, Leipzig, 1883; H. E. Jacobs, New York, 1898; P. M. Rade, 3 vols., Tübingen, 1901.

Marheinecke, Ph. Geschichte der teutschen Reformation. 4 vols. Berlin. 1831–4.

Maurenbrecher, W. Geschichte der katholischen Reformation. Nördlingen. 1880.

—— Studien und Skizzen zur Geschichte der Reformationszeit. Leipzig. 1874.

Melanchthon (verè Schwarzerd), Philip. Lives of, by G. Ellinger (Berlin, 1902); J. W. Richard (New York, 1898); R. Schaefer (Gütersloh, 1897); and Schmidt (Elberfeld, 1861).

Moeller, W. Andreas Osiander. Elberfeld. 1870.

—— Reformation und Gegenreformation. Freiburg. 1899.

—— History of the Christian Church. Vol. iii, trs. J. H. Freese. London. 1900.

Mosen, P. E. Hieronymus Emser. Leipzig. 1890.

Müller, Karl. Kirchengeschichte. Vol. ii. Tübingen. 1902.

Neudecker, C. G. Gesch. der deutschen Reformation von 1517–1532. Leipzig. 1843.

—— Neue Beiträge zur Gesch. der Ref. 2 vols. Leipzig. 1841.

—— Gesch. des evangelischen Protestantismus in Deutschland. 2 pts. Leipzig. 1844.

Pastor, Ludwig. Die kirchlichen Reunionsbestrebungen während der Regierung Karls V. Freiburg i. B. 1879.

—— Geschichte der Päpste. 2nd ed. Freiburg. 1888 etc. Engl. transl. by Antrobus. London. 1891 etc.

Paulus, N. Die Strassburger Reformatoren und die Gewissensfreiheit. Strassburg. 1895.

—— Der Augustinermönch Johannes Hoffmeister. Freiburg. 1891.

Postina, A. Eberhard Billick. Freiburg. 1901.

Pressel, Th. Ambrosius Blaurers des Schwäbischen Reformators Leben und Schriften. Stuttgart. 1861.

—— Anecdota Brentiana. Tübingen. 1868.

Schäfer, E. Luther als Kirchenhistoriker. Gütersloh. 1897.

—— W. Galerie der Reformatoren. 5 vols. Meissen. 1838–43.

Scheel, O. Luthers Stellung zur heiligen Schrift. Tübingen. 1902.

Schlegel, J. K. T. Kirchen- und Reformationsgeschichte von Norddeutschland und den Hannover'schen Staaten. 3 vols. Hanover. 1828–32.

Schmidt, G. L. Justus Menius, der Reformator Thüringens. 2 vols. Gotha. 1867.

Schott, Th. Luther und die deutsche Bibel. 2nd ed. Stuttgart. 1883.

—— Briefwechsel zwischen Christoph, Herzog von Würtemberg und P. P. Vergerius. Stuttgart, Literarischer Verein, 1843 etc. Vol. cxxiv.

Seidemann, J. K. Beiträge zur Reformationsgeschichte. 2 vols. Dresden. 1846–8.

—— Erläuterungen zur Reformationsgeschichte. Dresden. 1872.

—— Karl von Miltitz. Dresden. 1844.

Seitz, O. Die Theologie d. Urbanus Rhegius, speziell sein Verhältnis zu Luther und Zwingli. Gotha. 1898.

Soden, F. von. Beiträge zur Gesch. der Reformation und der Sitten jener Zeit. Nürnberg. 1855.

Spahn, M. Joh. Cochläus. Berlin. 1897. (Cf. Th. Kolde in Realencyklop. für Prot. Theologie, iv, 194–200.)

Thomas, G. M. M. Luther und die Reformationsbewegung in Deutschland 1520–32. Ansbach. 1883.

Vogel, E. G. Bibliotheca biographica Lutherana. Halle. 1851.

Wedewer, H. G. Joannes Dietenberger. Freiburg. 1888.

Wiedemann, Th. Johann Eck. Ratisbon. 1865.

(iii) *Literature and Art*

Erhard, H. A. Geschichte des Wiederaufblühens wissenschaftlicher Bildung. 3 vols. Magdeburg. 1827–32.

Geiger, L. Renaissance und Humanismus in Deutschland. Berlin. 1882.

Hagen, C. Deutschlands literarische und relig. Verhältnisse im Reformationszeitalter. 3 vols. Frankfort. 1868.

Heller, J. Lucas Cranach's Leben und Werke. 2nd ed. Nürnberg. 1854.

Holstein, H. Die Reformation im Spiegelbilde der dramatischen Litteratur des 16 Jahrh. Halle. 1886.

Kawerau, W. Hans Sachs und die Reformation. Halle. 1889.

Kuczýnski, A. Thesaurus libellorum historiam Reformatorum illustrantium. Leipzig. 1870.

Müller, J. Luthers reformatorische Verdienste um Schule und Unterricht. Berlin. 1903.

Schade, O. Satiren und Pasquillen aus der Reformationszeit. 3 vols. Hanover. 1856–8.

Schuchardt, C. Lukas Cranachs Leben und Werke. 2 vols. Leipzig. 1851.

Schmidt, C. Histoire littéraire de l'Alsace. Paris. 2 vols. 1879.
—— La Vie et les Travaux de Jean Sturm. Strassburg. 1855.
Schweitzer, Ch. Étude sur Hans Sachs. Nancy. 1887.
Strobel, G. T. Beyträge zur Litteratur besonders des xvi Jahrh. 2 vols. Nürnberg. 1784–7.
—— Neue Beyträge. 5 vols. Nürnberg. 1790–4.
Thausing, M. Dürers Briefe, Tagebücher und Reime. Wien. 1872. 2nd ed. 1884.
Von der Hardt, Hermann. Historia Literaria Reformationis. Leipzig. 5 pts. 1717.
Zucker, M. Dürer's Stellung zur Reformation. Erlangen. 1886.

See also works on the universities of Erfurt (by Kampschulte, 2 vols., Trier, 1856–60); Heidelberg (by J. F. Hautz, 2 vols., Mannheim, 1862–4); Marburg (by K. W. Justi, Marburg, 1827); Königsberg (by M. Töppen, Königsberg, 1844); Jena (by J. C. E. Schwarz, Jena, 1858); Tübingen (by R. von Mohl, Tübingen, 1871, and Klüpfel, Leipzig, 1877), and Wittenberg (by F. L. C. von Medem, Anclam, 1867, and G. Buchwald, Leipzig, 1893), and the Geschichte der Wissenschaften in Deutschland.

(iv) *Sociology, Economics, and Geography*

Barthold, F. W. Geschichte der deutschen Städte und des deutschen Bürgerthums. 4 pts. Leipzig. 1850–3.
Ehrenberg, R. Das Zeitalter der Fugger. 2 vols. Jena. 1896. (Cf. die Stellung der Fugger zum Kirchenstreite des xvi Jahrh. in Hist. Vierteljahrsschr. 1898, 473– 510.)
Erhardt, P. Die nationalökonomischen Ansichten der Reformatoren. Theol. Studien und Kritiken. Hamburg. 1880–1.
Fischer, K. Deutschlands öffentliche Meinung im Reformationszeitalter und in der Gegenwart. Berlin. 1895.
Heller, V. Die Handelswege Inner-Deutschlands. N. Archiv für Sächs. Gesch. Vol. v.
Hentzner, Paul. Itinerarium Germaniae.... Nürnberg. 1612.
Hering, H. Ueber die Liebesthätigkeit der deutschen Reformation. (To 1529.) In Theol. Studien und Kritiken. Hamburg. 1883–5.
Kaser, K. Politische und soziale Bewegungen im deutschen Bürgerthum zu Beginn des 16 Jahrh. Stuttgart. 1899.
Kawerau, W. Die Reformation und die Ehe. Halle. 1892.
Liliencron, R. von. Deutsches Leben im Volkslied um 1530. Stuttgart. 1886.
Munster, Sebastian. Cosmographia. Basel. 1545.
Nobbe, H. Die Regelung der Armenpflege im 16 Jahrh. Zeitschr. für Kirchen- gesch. x.
Richter, P. E. Bibliotheca geographica Germaniae. Leipzig. 1896.
Riggenbach, B. Das Armenwesen der Reformation. Basel. 1883.
Schmoller, G. Zur Gesch. der national-ökonomischen Ansichten in Deutschland während der Reformationsperiode. Zeitschr. für d. Ges. Staatswiss. Vol. xvi.
Stern, A. Die Socialisten der Reformationszeit. Berlin. 1883.
Sugenheim, S. Frankreichs Einfluss auf Deutschland. 2 vols. Stuttgart. 1845–56.
Voigt, J. Fürstenleben und Fürstensitte. Raumer's Hist. Taschenbuch, 1835.
Werner, J. Die soziale Frage im Zeitalter der Reformation. 1889. In Weber's Sammlung theologischer und socialer Reden und Abhandlungen. Mühlheim. 1888 etc.

See also Schmoller's Staats- und sozialwissenschaftliche Forschungen, 18 vols. Leipzig, 1878 etc.; and the Zeitschrift für sozial- und wirthschaftliche Geschichte. Freiburg, 1893-1903.

(v) *Constitutional History*

Beiträge zur Geschichte des römischen Rechts in Deutschland. Stuttgart. 1896 etc.

Below, G. von. Territorium und Stadt. Historische Bibliothek. 1900.

Boehmer, J. H. Meditationes in constitutionem criminalem Carolinam. Halle. 1770.

—— Jus Ecclesiasticum Protestantium. 5 vols. Halle. 1720–63.

Brunner, H. Forschungen zur Geschichte des deutschen Reichs. Stuttgart. 1894.

Eichhorn, C. F. Deutsche Staats- und Rechtsgeschichte. 4 pts. Göttingen. 1821–3.

Furstenwerth, L. Die Verfassungsänderungen in den Reichsstädten zur Zeit Karls V. Göttingen. 1893.

Gierke, Otto. Untersuchungen zur deutschen Staats- und Rechtsgeschichte. Breslau. 1878–99.

Goldast, Melchior. Monarchia S. Romani Imperii. 2 vols. Frankfort. 1611–14.

—— Politische Reichshändel. Frankfort. 1614.

Holtzendorff, F. Encyklopädie der Rechtswissenschaft. 2 vols. Leipzig. 1870–1.

Laband, P. Das Staatsrecht des deutschen Reiches. 4th ed. Tübingen. 1901.

Lünig, J. C. Thesaurus juris der Grafen und Herren des heilig. römisch. Reichs. Leipzig. 1725.

Moser, J. J. Teutsches Staatsrecht. 50 vols. 1737–54.

Müller, K. E. H. Reichssteuern und Reichsreformationsbestrebungen im xv und xvi Jahrh.

Rachel, Walther. Verwaltungsorganisation und Ämterwesen der Stadt Leipzig bis 1627. Leipzig. 1902.

Rieker, Karl. Staat und Kirch nach lutherischer, reformirter, moderner Anschauung. Hist. Vierteljahrsch. 1898, 370–416.

Schröder, R. Lehrbuch der deutschen Rechtsgeschichte. 3rd ed. Leipzig. 1898.

Stintzing, R. Gesch. der deutschen Rechtswissenschaft. Munich. 1880.

Stobbe, O. Geschichte der deutschen Rechtsquellen. 2 pts. Brunswick. 1860–4.

Turner, S. E. Sketch of the Germanic Constitution. New York. 1888.

D. SEPARATE STATES AND THEIR RULERS

(1) *Secular and territorial States and Districts*

(a) Austria and the Austrian Duchies

Bachmann, A. Lehrbuch der Oesterreichischen Reichsgeschichte. Prague. 1896.

Böhl, E. Beiträge zur Gesch. der Reformation in Oesterreich. Jena. 1902.

Buchholtz, F. B. Gesch. der Regierung Ferdinands I. 9 vols. Vienna. 1831–8.

Fontes rerum Austriacarum. 50 vols. Vienna. 1849–1901. (An index to these 50 vols. was publ. by V. Junk, 1901.)

Gévay, A. Urkunden und Aktenstücke zur Gesch. der Verhältnisse zwischen Oesterreich, Ungarn, und der Pforte 1526–1541. Vienna. 9 pts. 1838–42.

Huber, A. Geschichte Oesterreichs. Vols. iv–v. (Gesch. d. europ. Staaten.) Gotha. 1888.

Krones, F. X. Handbuch der Oesterreich. Gesch. 5 vols. Berlin. 1876–9.

—— Grundriss der Oesterreichischen Geschichte. Vienna. 1882.

Kupelweiser, L. Die Kämpfe Oesterreichs mit d. Osmanen 1526–37. Vienna. 1899.

Loserth, J. Reformation und Gegenreformation in den innerösterreich. Ländern. Stuttgart. 1896–8.

Luschin v. Ebengreuth, A. Österreichische Reichsgeschichte. Bamberg. 1896.

Raupach, B. Evangelische Oesterreich. 6 pts. Hamburg. 1732–44.

Waldau, G. E. Gesch. der Protestanten in Oesterreich, Steyermark, Kärnthen und Krain. 2 pts. 1784.

Wiedemann, Th. Gesch. der Reformation und Gegenreformation im Lande unter der
    Enns. Prague. 1879.
Wolf, A. Gesch. Bilder aus Oesterreich. 2 vols. Leipzig. 1866.

See also the Archiv für Kunde Oesterreichischer Geschichtsquellen, 33 vols.,
Vienna, 1848–65, continued as the Archiv für Oesterreichische Geschichte, 53 vols.,
Vienna, 1865–1903.

(b) Baden

Bossert, G. Beiträge zur badisch-pfälzische Reform-Gesch. Zeitschr. für Gesch. des
    Oberrheins. Vol. XVII. 1902.
Fester, R. Die Religionsmandate des Markgrafen Philipp von Baden 1522–33.
    Zeitschr. für Kirchengesch. Vol. XI.
Jaeger, Carl. Briefe und Bilder aus dem Grossherzogthum Baden. 2 vols. Leipzig.
    1841.
Vierordt, K. F. Gesch. der evangel. Kirche in Baden. 2 vols. Carlsruhe. 1847–56.

See also the Zeitschrift für Gesch. des Oberrheins published by the Badische
histor. Kommission since 1886.

(c) Bavaria

Aretin, C. M. von. Bayerns auswärtige Verhältnisse seit dem Anfang des XVI
    Jahrh. Passau. 1839.
Muffat, C. A. Correspond. und Aktenstücke zur Gesch. der polit. Verhältnisse der
    Herzöge Wilhelm und Ludwig von Baiern 1527–1541. Munich. 1857.
Riezler, S. Geschichte Baierns. Vol. IV. Gotha. 1899. (Gesch. d. europ. Staaten.)
Rudhart, Ignaz. Geschichte der Landstände in Baiern. 2 vols. Munich. 1819.
Sugenheim, S. Bayerns Kirchen- und Volkszustände im XVI Jahrh. Giessen. 1842.
Winter, V. A. Geschichte der evangelischen Lehre in Baiern. 2 pts. Munich.
    1809–10.

See also the Forschungen der königl. bayerischen Akademie der Wissenschaften,
Munich, 1860 etc. (Index to Vols. I–XX publ. by Gustav Buchholz, Göttingen, 1880);
and the Sitzungsberichte der historischen Classe of the Akademie der Wissenschaften,
Munich, 1871–1903.

(d) Bohemia

Bachmann, A. Geschichte Böhmens. Gotha. 1899.
Dačicky, M. Paměti. Ed. A. Rezek. 2 vols. Prague. 1878–80.
Denis, E. Fin de l'indépendance Bohème. Pt. II. Paris. 1890.
Freher, M. Scriptores rerum Bohemicarum. 2 vols. Hanover, 1602.
Gindély, A. Quellen zur Gesch. der Böhmischen Brüder. Fontes Rerum Austr. XIX.
    1857–8.
—— Die böhmischen Landtagsverhandlungen, von 1526 bis auf die Neuzeit. Prague.
    1877 etc.
—— Monumenta Historica Bohemica. 11 pts. Prague. 1865–70.
Gluth, O. Die Wahl Ferdinands I zum König von Böhmen. Mittheil. d. Vereins f. d.
    Gesch. der Deutschen in Böhmen. Prague. 1862 etc. Vol. XV.
Landtagsverhandlungen, D. böhm., u. Landtagsbeschlüsse v. J. 1526 bis auf die
    Neuzeit. Herausg. vom k. böhm. Landesarchiv. Prague.
Palácky, Fr. Geschichte von Böhmen. 5 vols. Prague. 1836–67.
Rezek, A. Gesch. der Regierung Ferdinands I in Böhmen. Prague. 1878.
Rieger, G. C. Die alten und neuen Böhmische Brüder. 3 vols. Zullichau. 1734–9.

See also the publications of the Verein für Geschichte der Deutschen in Böhmen.
Prague. 1862 etc.

(e) Brandenburg and Prussia

Altmann, W. Ausgewählte Urkunden zur brandenburg-preussischen Verfassungs- und Verwaltungsgeschichte. 2 vols. Berlin. 1897.

Baczko, L. A. F. von. Geschichte Preussens. 6 vols. Königsberg. 1792–1800.

Bornhak, C. Geschichte des preussischen Verwaltungsrechts. 3 vols. Berlin. 1884–8.

Droysen, J. G. Gesch. der preussischen Politik. 5 vols. Berlin. 1855–86.

Hartknoch, A. C. Preussische Kirchenhistoria. Frankfort. 1686.

Heidemann, J. Die Reformation in der Mark Brandenburg. Berlin. 1889.

Preussischen Geschichtschreiber, Die, des XVI und XVII Jahrh. Verein für die Gesch. des Preussens. Leipzig. 1876.

Ranke, L. von. Zwölf Bücher preussischer Geschichte. 5 vols. Leipzig. 1874.

Spieker, Ch. W. Kirchen- und Reformationsgeschichte der Mark Brandenburg. Berlin. 1839.

Stölzel, A. Brandenburg-Preussens Rechtsverwaltung und Rechtsverfassung. 2 vols. Berlin. 1888.

Tschakert, P. Urkundenbuch zur Reformationsgeschichte des Herzogthums Preussen. 3 vols. Leipzig. 1890.

Voigt, J. Briefwechsel der Gelehrten mit Herzog Albrecht von Preussen. Königsberg. 1841.

See also the Zeitschrift für preussische Geschichte und Landeskunde, the Hohenzollern Forschungen and the publications of the Verein für die Geschichte des Preussens.

(f) Brunswick

Havemann, H. Geschichte von Braunschweig-Lüneburg. 3 vols. Göttingen. 1853–7.

Heinemann, O. Geschichte von Braunschweig und Hannover. Gotha. 1882.

Hüne, A. Geschichte von Hannover und Braunschweig. 2 pts. Hanover. 1824–30.

Koldewey, F. Beiträge zur Kirchen- und Schulgeschichte des Herzogtums Braunschweig. Wolfenbüttel. 1888.

Lentz, C. G. H. Braunschweigs Kirchenreformation. Leipzig. 1828.

Spittler, L. T. Geschichte von Calenberg. 2 vols. Göttingen. 1786.

Stüve, J. E. Beschreibung und Geschichte d. Hochstifts und Fürstenthums Osnabrück. Osnabrück. 1789.

Vaterländisches Archiv für hannoverisch-braunschw. Geschichte. Edd. Spilcker and Brönnenberg. Lüneburg. 1830–3.

Wrede, A. Die Einführung der Reformation im lüneburgischen Lande. Göttingen. 1887.

—— Ernst der Bekenner, Herzog von Braunschweig. Halle. 1888.

See also the Zeitschrift des historischen Vereins für Niedersachsen. Hanover.

(g) Cleves-Jülich-Berg

Below, G. von. Landtagsakten von Jülich-Berg. Vol. I. 1400–1562. Düsseldorf. 1895.

Koch, H. H. Die Reformation in Jülich. 2 vols. Frankfort. 1883.

See also the Zeitschrift des Bergischen Geschichtsvereins. Bonn. 1863 etc.

(h) Elsass

Rathberger, J. Elsässische Reformationsgeschichte. 2 pts. Strassburg. 1885.

Röhrich, T. W. Geschichte der Reformation in Elsass. 3 pts. Strassburg. 1830–2.

(i)　Franconia

Lith, J. W. von der.　Erläuterung der fränkischen Reformationshistorie.　Schwabach. 1733.

Stein, F.　Geschichte Frankens.　2 vols.　Schweinfurt.　1885–6.

(j)　Hesse

Ackermann, C. A.　Bibliotheca Hessiaca.　10 pts.　Cassel.　1884–99.

Glagau, Hans.　Anna von Hessen.　Marburg.　1899.

Hassencamp, F. W.　Hessische Kirchengeschichte im Zeitalter der Reformation. 2 vols.　Marburg.　1852–5.

Hessische Landtagsakten.　Hist. Komm. für Hesse und Waldeck.　Marburg.　1901.

Koehler, W.　Hessische Kirchenverfassung im Zeitalter der Reformation.　Giessen. 1894.

Lanze, Wigand.　Hessische Chronik.　Zeitschr. des Vereins für Hessische Geschichte. Cassel.　1837.

Muenscher, F.　Geschichte von Hessen.　Marburg.　1894.

Paetel, G.　Die Organisation des hessischen Heeres unter Philipp dem Grossmüthigen. Berlin.　1897.

Rommel, Ch. von.　Philipp der Grossmüthige.　3 vols.　Giessen.　1830.

—— Geschichte von Hessen.　10 vols.　Marburg and Cassel.　1820–1858.

See also the Mittheilungen des Oberhessischen Vereins für Geschichte, esp. Neue Folge xi, 1–30.

(k)　Holstein

Waitz, G.　Schleswig-Holsteins Geschichte.　2 vols.　Göttingen.　1852.

(l)　Hungary

Bel, M.　Adparatus ad historiam Hungariae.　2 pts.　Posen.　1735–46.

—— Compendium Hungariae Geographicum.　Posen.　1753.

Csuday, Eugen.　Die Geschichte der Ungarn.　Ed. Marvai.　Berlin.　2 vols.　1899. (Cf. Hist. Vierteljahrschrift, 1903, i, 91 sqq.)

Engel, J. C.　Monumenta Ungrica.　Vienna.　1809.

Fessler, I. A.　Die Geschichte der Ungarn.　10 vols.　Leipzig.　1815–25.　[The best edition, by E. Klein, is not in the British Museum.]

Horváth, M.　Geschichte Ungarns.　2 vols.　Pesth.　1863.

Istváni, N.　Regni Hungarici historiae lib. xxxiv.　Vienna.　1758.

Katona, István.　Hist. critica primorum Hungariae Ducum.　Hist. regum stirpis Austriacae.　22 vols.　Buda.　1778–1810.

Pray, G. S. J.　Epistolae Procerum regni Hungariae (to 1531).　Vienna.　1806.

Smolka, S.　Ferdinands I Bemühungen um die Krone von Ungarn.　Archiv für Oesterr. Gesch.　Vienna.　1848.　Vol. vii.

Verancsics, A.　De rebus gestis Joannis [Zapolya] Regis Hungariae (in M. G. Kovachich's Scriptores Rerum Hung., Buda, 1798, Vol. II, pp. 39 etc.).

See also the Monumenta Hungariae Historica in course of publication by the Magyar Tudomanvos Akadémia.　Pesth.　1857 etc.

(m)　Mecklenburg

Beltz, R.　Mecklenburgische Geschichte in Einzeldarstellungen.　Berlin.　1899 etc.

Rudloff, F. A.　Mecklenburgische Geschichte.　3 pts.　Schwerin.　1780–1822.

Schnell, H. Mecklenburg im Zeitalter der Reformation. Berlin. 1900.

Schreiber, H. Johann Albrecht I, Herzog von Mecklenburg. Schrift. des Vereins für Ref. Gesch. 1899.

Schröder, D. Kirchenhistorie des evangelischen Mecklenburgs. 2 pts. Rostock. 1788.

Stein, F. Herzog Magnus von Mecklenburg, Bischof von Schwerin. Schwerin. 1899.

Von Lützow, C. E. Geschichte Mecklenburgs. 3 pts. Berlin. 1827–35.

(n) Oldenburg

See Jahrbuch für Geschichte des Herzogthums Oldenburg. 7 vols.

(o) The Palatinate

Alting, H. Historia Ecclesiae Palatinae. In Monumenta Pietatis. Pt I. Frankfort. 1701.

Gothein, E. Die Landstände der Kurpfalz. Zeitschr. für Gesch. des Oberrheins. N. F. Vol. III.

Häusser, L. Gesch. der rheinischen Pfalz. 2 vols. Heidelberg. 1845.

Jung, H. In Beiträge Bayer. Kirchengeschichte. Vol. I. [Catalogue of materials for the eccles. history of the Palatinate.]

Leodius, Hubertus Thomas. Annal. de vita Frederici El. Palatini lib. XIV. Frankfort. 1624. (Cf. Hasenclever, Die Schmalkaldener, 1901, pp. 242–7.)

Lippert, F. Reformation in Kirche, Sitte, und Schule der Oberpfalz. Freiburg. 1897.

Remling, F. X. Das Reformationswerk in der Pfalz. Mannheim. 1846.

See also the Zeitschrift für Geschichte des Oberrheins, and Gesellschaft für rheinische Geschichtskunde.

(p) Pomerania

Barthold, F. W. Geschichte von Rügen und Pommern. 4 pts. Hamburg. 1839–45.

Berckmann, Joannes. Stralsundische Chronik. In Mohnike and Zober's Stralsundische Chroniken. Pt I. Stralsund. 1883.

Kantzow, Th. Chronik von Pommern: ed. Böhmer, Stettin 1835 and again in 1896–7.

Medem, F. L. B. von. Geschichte der Einführung der evangel. Lehre in Pommern. Greifswald. 1837.

Ripke, J. N. Die Einführung der Reformation in den baltischen Provinzen. Riga. 1883.

(q) Saxony

Becker, J. Kurfürst Johann und seine Beziehungen zu Luther 1520–8. Leipzig. 1890.

Böttiger, C. W. Gesch. des Kurstaates und Königr. Sachsen. 2nd ed. Heeren and Ukert's series. Hamburg. 1867.

Buchholtz, G. Bibliothek der sächs. Geschichte. Leipzig. 1902 etc.

Burckhardt, C. A. Ernestinische Landtagsakten 1487–1532. Thüringische Geschichtsquellen. N. F. Vol. V. Jena. 1902.

Glafey, A. F. Geschichte des Chur- und Fürstlichen Hauses zu Sachsen. 4th ed. Nürnberg. 1753.

Seidemann, J. K. Die Reformationszeit in Sachsen 1517–1539. Dresden. 1846.

Wachsmuth, E. W. G. Niedersächsische Geschichte. Berlin. 1863.

Welck, H. Georg der Bärtige, Herzog von Sachsen. Brunswick. 1900.

See also the Archiv and Neues Archiv für Sächsische Geschichte; the Geschichtsquellen der Provinz Sachsen, Magdeburg, 28 vols.; the Geschichtsquellen der Provinz

Sachsen und angrenzenden Gebiete, **xxx** vols., Halle; and the **Publications of the** Sächsische Kommission für Geschichte, which has in preparation the **Akten und Briefe** des Herzogs Georg, the Pol. Corresp. of Maurice, a **bibliography of Saxon history by** Hautzsch, and Akten zur Geschichte des Bauernkrieges.

(r) Silesia

Biermann, G. Geschichte des Protestantismus in Oesterreichisch-Schlesien. **Prague.** 1897.

Soffner, J. Gesch. der Reformation in Schlesien. Breslau. 1887.

Wachter, F. Schlesien unter Ferdinand 1524-64. Zeitschr. des Vereins für Gesch. Schlesiens. Vol. **xix.** Breslau. 1856 etc.

(s) Swabia

Baumann, F. L. Forschungen zur schwäbischen Geschichte. Kempten. **1898.**

Keim, C. Schwäbische Reformationsgeschichte. Tübingen. 1855.

Pfister, J. C. Geschichte von Schwaben. 5 vols. Stuttgart. 1803–1827.

See also the Zeitschrift des historischen Vereins für Schwaben und Neuburg.

(t) Württemberg

Ernst, V. Briefwechsel des Herzogs Christoph. 2 vols. Stuttgart. **1899–1901.**

Hartmann, J. Württembergische Kirchengeschichte. Stuttgart. 1893.

—— Geschichte der Reformation in Württemberg. Stuttgart. 1835.

Heyd, L. F. Ulrich, Herzog zu Württemberg. 3 vols. Tübingen. 1841–4.

—— W. Bibliographie der württembergischen Geschichte. 2 vols. **Stuttgart.** 1897.

Kugler, B. Herzog Ulrich von Württemberg. Stuttgart. 1865.

—— Christoph, Herzog zu Württemberg. 2 vols. Stuttgart. 1868–72.

Pfister, J. C. Herzog Christoph zu Württemberg. 2 pts. Tübingen. 1819–20.

Sattler, C. F. Gesch. des Herzogthums Württemberg. 5 pts. Ulm. 1764–8.

Schäfer, D. Württembergische Geschichtsquellen. Stuttgart. Vols. 1–11. **1894–5.**

Schmid, J. C., and Pfister, J. C. Denkwürdigkeiten der Württemberg. und Schwäbischen Reformationsgeschichte. 2 vols. Tübingen. 1817.

Schneider, E. Württembergische Geschichte. Stuttgart. 1896.

—— Württembergische Reformationsgeschichte. Stuttgart. 1887.

Stälin, P. F. von. Gesch. Wirtembergs. Vol. **iv.** Stuttgart. 1873.

See also the Württembergische Vierteljahrshefte für Landesgeschichte and the Zeitschrift of the Verein für das Württembergische Franken.

(ii) *Ecclesiastical States*

Augsburg. Braun, P. L. Geschichte der Bischöfe von Augsburg. 4 vols. **Augs**burg. 1813–15.

Steichele, A. Das Bisthum Augsburg. Augsburg. 1861 etc.

Bamberg. Erhard, O. Die Reformation in Bamberg 1522–1556. Erlangen. 1898.

Heller, Joseph. Reformationsgeschichte des ehemaligen Bisthums **Bamberg.** Bamberg. 1825.

Looshorn, J. Die Geschichte des Bisthums Bamberg. Munich. 1886 etc. Vol. **iv.**

Cologne. Ennen, L. Gesch. der Ref. im Bereiche der alten Erzdiöcese Köln. Cologne. 1849.

Ley, C. A. Die Kölnische Kirchengeschichte. Cologne. 1882.

Meyer, C. Köln im Zeitalter der Reformation. 1892. (Sammlung wiss. Vorträge, N. F. Ser. **vii,** No. 153.)

Halberstadt. Langenbeck, W. Gesch. der Ref. des Stiftes. Göttingen. 1886.

Mainz. Gudenus, V. F. Codex diplomaticus Moguntinus. Göttingen. 1743–68.
 Hennes, J. Albrecht von Brandenburg, Erzbischof von Mainz. Mainz. 1858.
 May, J. Der Kurfürst, Kardinal, und Erzbischof Albrecht II. 2 vols. Munich.
  1865–75.
 Redlich, P. Kardinal Albrecht von Brandenburg. Mainz. 1900.
Münster. Erhard, H. A. Geschichte Münsters. Münster. 1837.
Salzburg. Schmid, J. Anfang der Reformation im Erzstift Salzburg 1517–25.
 Salzburg. 1899.

 See also the Mittheilungen der Gesellschaft für Salzburg. Landeskunde. 40 vols.

Speier. Remling, F. X. Geschichte der Bischöfe von Speier. 2 vols. Mainz. 1852–4.
 —— Urkundenbuch zur Geschichte der Bischöfe von Speier. 2 vols. Mainz.
  1852–3.
Trier. Die Reformation in Trier. Bonn. 1845.
Würzburg. Ludewig, J. P. Würzburgische Geschichtsschreiber. Frankfort. 1713.
 Braun, C. Gesch. der Heranbildung des Klerus in der Diöcese Würzburg. 2 vols.
 Würzburg. 1889–97.

(iii) *The Cities*

The most important source for the history of German cities is the great series of Chroniken der deutschen Städte, ed. Karl Hegel, xxix vols., Leipzig, 1862–1902, which is still in progress. It comprises at present the Nürnberg 'Chroniken' (5 vols.), Augsburg (5 vols.), Brunswick (2 vols.), Magdeburg (2 vols.), Strassburg (2 vols.), Cologne (3 vols.), Regensburg (1 vol.), Mainz (2 vols.), Lübeck (3 vols.), and the Westphalian and Lower Rhine cities (3 vols.). Besides this series most large German towns have published or are publishing their 'Urkundenbücher,' but this class of document refers generally to a period earlier than the Reformation. The more important towns have also as a rule their 'Gesellschaft,' 'Archiv,' or 'Verein für Geschichte,' and it would require a whole volume to enumerate the various political and constitutional histories of German towns. The following list comprises only histories of the Reformation in some of the more important towns which materially influenced the general course of German history.

Augsburg. Jaeger, C. Gesch. der Stadt Augsburg. Darmstadt. 1837.
 Roth, Fr. Augsburgs Reformationsgeschichte 1517–30. Munich. 1881. Re-ed.
  Augsburg. 1901.
 Von Stetten, Paul. Geschichte der Reichsstadt Augsburg. Augsburg. 1762,
  1788.
 Wolfart, K. Die Augsburger Reformation in 1533–4. Leipzig. 1901.
Colmar. Rocholl, H. Anfänge der Reformation in Colmar. Leipzig. 1875–8.
 —— Die Einführung der Reformation in Colmar. Leipzig. 1876.
Constance. Issel, E. Reformation in Konstanz. Freiburg. 1898.
 Laible, J. Geschichte der Stadt Konstanz. Constance. 1896.
Esslingen. Keim, C. T. Reformationsblätter der Reichstadt Esslingen. Esslingen.
 1860.
Frankfort. Jung, R. Frankfurter Chroniken und annalistische Aufzeichnungen der
  Reformationszeit. Frankfort. 1888.
 Steitz, G. E. Der lutherische Prädikant H. Beyer. Ein Zeitbild aus Frankfurts
  Kirchengeschichte. Frankfort. 1852.
Goslar. Hölscher, H. Gesch. der Reformation in Goslar. Hanover. 1902.
Göttingen. Erdemann, G. Gesch. der Reformation. Göttingen. 1888.
Greifswald. Uckeley, A. Reform-Gesch. der Stadt Greifswald. Greifswald. 1902.

Hamburg. Goos, M. Hamburgs Politik um die Mitte des xvi Jahrh. Hamburg.
        1896.
    Sillem, H. C. W. Die Einführung der Reformation in Hamburg. Verein für
        Ref. Gesch. Halle. 1886.
Hanover. Bahrdt, W. Gesch. der Ref. Hanover. 1891.
Leipzig. Buchwald, G. Reformationsgeschichte der Stadt Leipzig. Leipzig. 1900.
    Seifert, F. Die Reformation in Leipzig. Leipzig. 1883.
Lübeck. Schreiber, H. Die Reformation Lübecks. Halle. 1902.
Lüneburg. Wrede, A. Die Einführung der Reformation in Lüneburg. Göttingen.
        1887.
Magdeburg. Huelsse, F. Die Einführung der Ref. in der Stadt Magdeburg. Magde-
        burg. 1883.
Marburg. Kolbe, W. Die Einführung der Reformation in Marburg. Marburg.
        1871.
Memmingen. Dobel, F. Memmingen im Reformationszeitalter. 5 pts. Memmingen.
        1877–8.
    Unold, J. F. Reformationsgeschichte der Stadt Memmingen. Memmingen. 1817.
Nördlingen. Geyer, C. Die Nördlinger evangelischen Kirchenordnungen des xvi
        Jahrhunderts. Munich. 1896.
Nürnberg. Baader, J. Beiträge zur Kunstgesch. Nürnbergs. Nördlingen. 1860.
    Heide, G. Beiträge zur Gesch. Nürnbergs in der Reformationszeit. Mauren-
        brecher's Taschenbuch, 1892.
    Lüdewig, S. Die Politik Nürnbergs im Zeitalter der Reformation. Göttingen.
        1893.
    Roth, F. Die Einführung der Reformation in Nürnberg. Würzburg. 1885.

    On J. Müllner's ms. Annales of Nürnberg *see* Lochner in Hist. Pol. Blätter lxxiv,
841–865, 901–924.

Ratisbon. Gemeiner, Carl T. Regensburgische Chronik. 4 vols. Ratisbon. 1800–24.
    Geyer, W. Die Einführung der Reformation in Regensburg. Ratisbon. 1892.
Reutlingen. Hartmann, Julius. Matthäus Alber, der Reformator der Reichsstadt
        Reutlingen. Tübingen. 1863.
Strassburg. Baum, A. Magistrat und Reformation in Strassburg bis 1529. Strass-
        burg. 1887.
    Birck, H. Die politische Correspondenz der Stadt Strassburg im Zeitalter d.
        Reformation. Strassburg. 1882 etc.
    Gerbert, C. Gesch. der Strassb. Sektenbewegung 1524–34. Strassburg. 1889.
    Hubert, F. Die Strassburg. Liturg.-Ordnungen im Zeitalter der Ref. Göt-
        tingen. 1900.
    Renouard de Bussière, M. T. Hist. de l'Établissement du Protestantisme à
        Strasbourg. Paris. 1856.
    —— Hist. du Développement du Protestantisme à Strasbourg. 2 vols. Strass-
        burg. 1859.
    Virck, H., and Winckelmann, O. Politische Korresp. der Stadt Strassburg im
        Zeitalter der Ref. Vol. i. Strassburg. 1879. Vol. ii. 1887. Vol. iii.
        1898.
Ulm. Keim, C. T. Die Reformation der Reichsstadt Ulm. Stuttgart. 1851.
Worms. Soldau, Hans. Beiträge zur Gesch. der Stadt Worms. Worms. 1896.

III. MONOGRAPHS, ETC., REFERRING TO SEPARATE CHAPTERS

A. CHAPTER V. NATIONAL OPPOSITION TO ROME

Baader, Joseph. Die Fehde des Thomas von Absberg wider den Schwäbischen Bund. Munich. 1880.

Balan, P. Monumenta Reformationis Lutheranae ex tabulis S. Sedis secretis 1521–5. Ratisbon. 1883–4.

Barge, H. Neue Aktenstücke zur Gesch. d. Wittenberger Unruhen von 1521–2. Zeitschr. für Kirch.-Gesch. xxii, 120–9.

Barthold, F. W. Georg von Frundsberg. Hamburg. 1833.

Baur, A. Deutschland in den Jahren 1517–27. Ulm. 1872.

Bogler, W. Hartmuth von Kronberg. Zeitschr. für Reform-Gesch. no. 57, 1897.

Brasse, Ernst. Die Gesch. des Speierer Nationalkonzils vom Jahre 1524. Halle. 1890.

Bremer, F. P. Franz von Sickingen's Fehde gegen Trier. Strassburg. 1885.

Brieger, Th. Aleander und Luther. Gotha. 1884.

Brückner, A. Zur Gesch. des Reichstags von Worms. Die Verhandlungen über das Regiment. Heidelberg. 1860.

Clemen, O. Beiträge zur Reformationsgeschichte. Aus Büchern und Handschriften der Zwickauer Ratsschulbibliotek. 2 vols. Berlin. 1901–2.

Druffel, A. von. Die Bayrische Politik im Beginne der Reformationszeit 1519–24. Munich. 1885.

Friedensburg, W. Eine ungedruckte Depesche Aleanders (Quellen aus Italienischen Archiv. Vol. i, 1897).

—— Der Regensburger Konvent von 1524. In Hist. Aufsätze dem Andenken an G. Waitz gewidmet. Hanover. 1886.

Friedrich, J. Der Reichstag in Worms, 1521. Munich. 1870.

Gachard, P. Corresp. de Charles V und Adrien VI. Brussels. 1859.

Gebhardt, B. Die hundert Gravamina der deutschen Nation. Breslau. 1884. 2nd ed. 1895.

Haupt, H. Beiträge zur Reformationsgeschichte der Reichsstadt Worms 1523–4. Giessen. 1898.

Hausrath, A. Aleander und Luther. Berlin. 1898.

Höfler, C. A. C. von. Papst Adrian VI. Vienna. 1880.

Hutten, Ulrich von. Schriften. Ed. C. Bocking. Leipzig. 1859–69. Cf. Strauss, D. F. Ulrich von Hutten. 2 pts. Leipzig. 1858. 4th ed. 1878.

Jörg, J. E. Deutschland in der Revolutionsepoche 1522–6. Freiburg. 1851.

Kalkoff, Paul. Die Depeschen des Nuntius Aleander vom Wormser Reichstag. 2nd ed. Halle. 1897.

—— Briefe, Depeschen, und Berichte über Luther. Halle. 1898.

Kawerau, G. Luthers Rückkehr von der Wartburg nach Wittenberg. Halle. 1901.

—— Thomas Murner und die deutsche Reformation. Halle. 1891.

Keller, Ludwig. Aus den Anfangsjahren der Reformation. Monatshefte d. Comenius-Gesellschaft, Berlin, 1899, pp. 176–85.

Kolde, Th. Friedrich der Weise und die Anfänge der Reformation. Erlangen. 1881.

Kraus, V. Das Nürnberger Reichsregiment. Innsbruck. 1883.

Meyer, Chr. Der Wiedertäufer Nikolas Storch. Hohenzollerische Forschungen. Berlin. v, 273–81.

Moser, J. J. Beiträge zur reichsritterschaftlichen Sachen. Nürnberg. 1773–4.

Münch, E. Franz von Sickingens Thaten, Pläne, Freunde und Ausgang. 3 pts. Stuttgart. 1827–9.

Pirckheimer, Charitas. Denkwürdigkeiten. Ed. C. A. C. von Höfler. Bamberg. 1852.

Rathgeber, J. Thomas Murner's Nova Germania. Sybel's Hist. Zeitschr. **1877, 3.**

Redlich, O. Der Reichstag von Nürnberg 1522–3. Leipzig. 1887.

Rettberg, P. Studien zum Verständnis der Politik des Kurfürst. Richard von Trier 1519–26. Greifswald. 1901.

Richter, E. A. Der Reichstag zu Nürnberg 1524. Leipzig. 1888.

Soldan, F. Der Reichstag zu Worms 1521. Worms. 1883.

Thomas, G. M. Luther und die Reformationsbewegung in Deutschland 1520–5. Ansbach. 1883.

Tschakert, Paul. Georg von Polentz, Bischof von Samland. Leipzig. Kirchengesch. Studien. 1888.

Uhlhorn, J. G. W. Die Reformation. Part II. Luther und die Schwärmen. Hanover. 1868.

Ulmann, H. Franz von Sickingen. Leipzig. 1872.

Waltz, O. Der Wormser Reichstag im Jahre 1521. Forschungen z. deutschen Gesch. Vol. VIII. Göttingen.

Weizsäcker, J. Der Versuch eines Nationalkonzils in Speier den 11 Nov. 1524. Sybel's Hist. Zeitschr. LXIV.

Wille, J. Die Uebergabe des Herzogthums Würtemberg an Karl V. Forschungen zur d. Gesch. Vol. XXI.

Wülcker, E., and Virck, H. Des kursächs. Rathes Hans von Planitz Berichte aus dem Reichsregiment in Nürnberg 1521–3. Königl. Sächs. Komm. Leipzig. 1899.

—— Reichstag und Reichsregiment zu Anfang der Reformationszeit. Preuss. Hist. Jahrb. 1884.

Wyneken, C. F. Die Regimentsordnung von 1521 in ihrem Zusammenhange mit dem Churverein. Forschungen zur d. Gesch. Vol. VIII.

B. Chapter VI. Social Revolution and Catholic Reaction

(1) *The Peasants' War*

Baumann, Fr. L. Quellen zur Gesch. des Bauernkrieges in Ober-Schwaben. Stuttgart. 1877.

—— Die Zwölf Artikel der oberschwäbischen Bauern. Kempten. 1896.

—— Akten zur Gesch. des Bauernkrieges aus Oberschwaben. Freiburg. **1881.**

Bax, E. Belfort. The Peasants' War in Germany. London. 1899.

Beger, L. Zur Gesch. des Bauernkriegs nach Urkunden zu Karlsruhe. Forschungen zur deutschen Gesch. Vols. XXI–II. Göttingen. 1862–86.

Bensen, H. M. Gesch. des Bauernkrieges in Ostfranken. Erlangen. 1840.

Berlichingen, Götz von. Lebensbeschreibung. Ed. Schönhuth. Heilbronn. **1858.**

—— Geschichte von, by F. W. Berlichingen-Rossach. Leipzig. 1861.

Cornelius, C. A. Studien zur Geschichte des Bauernkrieges. Munich. 1861.

Cronthal, M. Die Stadt Würzburg im Bauernkriege. Würzburg. 1888.

Czerny, A. Der erste Bauernaufstand in Oberösterreich 1525. Linz. 1882.

Ehrard, O. Der Bauernkrieg in Bamberg. Beitr. Bayer. Kirchengesch. Vol. I. 1896.

Elben, A. Vorderösterreich in 1524. Strassburg. 1889.

Engbert, S. Der Mässinger Bauernhaufe. Eichstätt. 1895.

Falckenheimer, W. Philipp der Grossmüthige im Bauernkriege. Marburg. 1887.

Fischer, E. W. Ueber die sogenannte Reformation Kais. Friedrichs III. Hamburg. 1858.

Friedrich, J. Astrologie und Reformation, oder die Astrologen als Prediger der Reformation und des Bauernkriegs. Munich. 1864.

Friess, Lorenz. Geschichte des Bauernkrieges in Ostfranken. Würzburg. 2 vols. 1876–83.

Götze, A. Die Artikel der Bauern, 1525. Hist. Vierteljahrschrift, 1901, pp. 1–32; 1902, pp. 1–33.

Haegenmüller, J. B. Geschichte der Stadt Kempten. 2 vols. Kempten. 1840–7.

Harer, P. Beschreibung des Bauernkrieges. Halle. 1881. (Cf. P. Sander in Deutsch. Zeitschrift Gesch. Wiss. N. F. 1, 2.)

Hartfelder, C. Bauernkrieg in Südwest Deutschland. Stuttgart. 1884.

Herolt, J. Chronik; in Geschichtsquellen der Stadt Hall. Stuttgart. 1894.

Hoetzsch, Otto. Besitzverteilung und wirtsch.-soziale Gliederung der ländlichen Bevölkerung im 16 Jahrh. Leipziger Studien. Vol. VI. Part 4.

Jäger, C. Gesch. von Heilbronn. 2 vols. Heilbronn. 1828.

—— Markgraf Casimir und der Bauernkrieg. Nürnberg. 1892.

Jordan, R. Zur Gesch. der Stadt Mühlhausen in 1523–5. Mühlhausen. 1901.

Jörg, J. E. Deutschland in der Revolutionsperiode 1522–6. Freiburg. 1851.

Kautsky, Carl. Communism in Central Europe in the time of the Reformation. Engl. trans. London. 1897.

Kluckhohn, A. Ueber das Projekt eines Bauernparlamentes zu Heilbronn. Nachricht. von d. Gesellsch. der Wissensch. zu Göttingen. No. 7. 1893.

Lamprecht, K. Die Entwickelung des rheinischen Bauernstandes. Westdeutsche Zeitschr. für Gesch. Vol. VI.

Lehnert, K. F. Studien zur Gesch. der Zwölf Artikel vom Jahre 1525. Halle. 1894.

Leist, F. Quellenbeiträge zur Gesch. des Bauernaufruhrs in Salzburg. Salzburg. 1888.

Lenz, M. Zur Schlacht bei Frankenhausen. Hist. Zeitschrift. LXIX.

Leodius, H. T. Der Bauernkrieg. In Freher's Scriptores. Vol. III. pp. 239 sqq.

Loserth, J. Die Stadt Waldshut und die vorderösterreichische Regierung in 1523–6. Vienna. 1891.

Lucke, W. Die Entstehung der "15 Bundesgenossen" des Joh. Eberlin von Günzburg. Halle. 1902.

Marquard, M. Kempten und der Bauernkrieg. Allgäuer Geschichtsfreund. XIII. 1–22, 37–45.

Muck, Georg. Geschichte von Kloster Heilsbronn. 3 vols. Nördlingen. 1879–80.

Müller, L. Beiträge zur Gesch. des Bauernkrieges. Zeitschr. des hist. Vereins für Schwaben und Neuburg. Augsburg. 1889–91.

Münzer, Thomas. Aussgetrückte Emplössung des falschen Glaubens. Mühlhausen. 1524. Ed. R. Jordan. Mühlhausen. 1901.

—— Lives of, by O. Merx (includes also Heinrich Pfeiffer), Göttingen, 1889; G. Th. Strobel, Nürnberg, 1795, and J. K. Seidemann, Dresden, 1842.

Nabholz, A. Bauernbewegung in d. Ost-Schweiz 1524–5. Zurich. 1896.

Neumann, R. Zur Gesch. des Bauernkrieges. Frankfort. 1882.

Oechsle, E. F. Beiträge zur Geschichte des Bauernkrieges in den Schwäbisch-Fränkischen Gegenden. Heilbronn. 1844.

Prossl, J. Die Beschwerden d. bischöfl. Bambergischen Unterthanen im Bauernkriege. Munich. 1901.

Rabenlechner, M. M. Der Bauernkrieg in Steiermark. Freiburg. 1901.

Radlkofer, M. Entstehungsgeschichte und Autorschaft der Zwölf Artikeln. Zeitschr. für d. h. Verein für Schwaben. Vol. XVI. 1889.

—— John Eberlin von Günzburg und Hans Jakob Welhe von Leipheim. Nördlingen. 1887.

Reiser, F. Reformation des K. Sigismund. 1876. (Cf. H. Werner in Hist. Vierteljschr. V, 467–86, and C. Koehne in N. Archiv. Vol. XXIII.)

Renouard de Bussière. Hist. de la guerre des paysans. Paris. 2 vols. 1852.

Riezler, S. In Sitzungsberichte der Münchener Akademie, Hist. Classe, 1891, pp. 708 sqq.

Riggenbach, B. Johann Eberlin von Günzburg. Tübingen. 1874.

Ryhiner, H. Chronik des Bauernkrieges. Basler Chroniken, VI, 461–504. 1902.

Sauder, H. Vorarlberg zur Zeit des deutschen Bauernkrieges. Mühlbacher's Mittheilungen. IV. Innsbruck. 1880 etc.

Schmidt, J. H. Die "15 Bundesgenossen" d. Joh. Eberlin von Günzburg. **Leipzig.**
1900.

Schrechenbach, P. F. Luther und der Bauernkrieg. Oldenburg. 1895.

Schreiber, H. Der deutsche Bauernkrieg. 3 vols. Freiburg i. B. 1863–6.

Sepp, J. N. Der bayerische Bauernkrieg. Munich. 1884.

Steitz, G. E. Dr Gerhard Westerburg, der Leiter des Bürgeraufstandes zu **Frank**furt in 1525. Archiv für Frankfurts Gesch. N. F. v, 192 sqq.

Stern, A. Ueber die Zwölf Artikel der Bauern. Leipzig. 1868.

—— Regesten zur Gesch. des Bauernkrieges vornehmlich in der Pfalz. **Zeitschr. für**
Gesch. des Oberrheins. Vol. xxiii. Karlsruhe. 1870.

Stolze, W. Zur Vorgesch. des Bauernkrieges. Staats- und Socialwissenschaft.
Forschungen. Vol. xviii. Pt iv. Leipzig. 1900.

Thomas, Max. Markgraf Kasimir im Bauernkriege. Breslau. 1898. **Gotha.** 1900.

Vogt, W. Die Vorgeschichte des Bauernkrieges. Halle. 1887.

—— Die bayrische Politik im Bauernkriege. Nördlingen. 1883. [Chiefly **against**
Jörg.]

—— Die Korrespondenz des Schwäbischen Bundes-Hauptmanns 1524–7. 4 pts. **Augs**burg. 1879–83.

Wachsmuth, W. Der deutsche Bauernkrieg. Leipzig. 1834.

Waldau, G. E. Materialien zur Gesch. des Bauernkrieges. 3 pts. **Chemnitz.**
1791–4.

Zimmermann, W. Allgemeine Gesch. des Grossen Bauernkrieges. 3 vols. **Stuttgart.**
1841–3. 2nd ed. 1856.

Zöpfl, H. Die Hauptmannschaft des Götz von Berlichingen. Heidelberg. 1850.

(ii)　*Plot and counterplot from 1525 to 1529*

Balan, P. Clementis VII epistolae. (Vol. i of Monumenta saeculi xvi hist. **illustrantia.**
Innsbruck. 1885.)

Beclagung Teutscher nation über die umbillichen beschwerd und bezwingknuss des
Römischen stüls. s. l. 1526.

Casanova, E. Lettere di Carlo V a Clemente VII 1527–33. Florence. 1893.

Ehsess, S. Gesch. der Pack'schen Händel. Freiburg i. B. 1881.

—— Landgraf Philipp von Hessen und Otto von Pack. Freiburg i. B. 1886.

Friedensburg, W. Der Reichstag zu Speier in 1526. Jastrow's Hist. Untersuchungen.
Pt v. Berlin. 1887.

—— Zur Vorgesch. des Gotha-Torgauischen Bündnisses. Marburg. 1884.

—— Beiträge zum Briefwechsel zwischen Herzog Georg von Sachsen und Landgraf Philipp von Hessen. Neues Archiv für Sächs. Gesch. Dresden. 1880 etc.
Bd vi.

Grethen, R. Die politischen Beziehungen Clemens VII zu Karl V 1523–7. Hanover.
1887.

Hellwig, W. Die politischen Beziehungen Clemens VII zu Karl V im Jahre 1526.
Leipzig. 1889.

Joachim, E. Die Politik des letzten Hochmeisters in Preussen, Albrecht von **Branden**burg. Berlin. 1892.

Karstens, W. Sächsisch-Hessische Beziehungen in 1524–6. Kiel. 1886.

Kluckhohn, A. Der Reichstag zu Speier im J. 1526. Sybel's Hist. Zeitsch. **Munich.**
1859 etc. Vol. lvi.

Ney, J. Analekten zur Gesch. des Reichstags zu Speier im J. 1526. **Zeitschr. für**
Kirchengesch. viii, ix, xii. Hamburg. 1888.

Schomburgk, W. Die Pack'schen Händel. Maurenbrecher's Hist. Taschenbuch.
Leipzig. 1882.

Schornbaum, K. Stellung d. Markgraf Kasimir, 1524–7. Erlangen. 1901.

Schornbaum, K. Markgraf Georg und d. Sächsisch-Hessische Bündnissbestrebung von 1528. Beitr. zur bayer. Kirchengesch. VIII 193–212.

Schwarz, H. Landgraf Philipp und die Pack'schen Händel. Leipzig. 1881. (Cf. W. Schomburgk in Maurenbrecher's Taschenbuch. 1882.)

Stoy, St. Erste Bündnisbestrebungen evangelischer Stände. Jena. 1888.

Virck, H. Die Städte und das Bündniss der evangelischen Fürsten 1526–7. Weimar. 1887.

Von der Lith, J. W. Erläuterung der Reformation von 1524 bis 1528. Schwabach. 1733.

(iii) *The organisation of Lutheran Churches*

Berlit, G. Luther, Murner, und d. Kirchenlied des 16 Jahrh. Leipzig. 1899.

Bugenhagen, J. Kirchenordnungen für die Stadt Braunschweig. Wolfenbüttel. 1885.

Burkhardt, C. A. Geschichte der deutschen Kirchen- und Schulvisitationen im Zeitalter der Reformation. Leipzig. 1879 etc.

Cohrs, F. Evangel. Katechismusversuche vor Luthers Enchiridion. 4 vols. Berlin. 1900–1902. (Cf. Beiträge zur bayer. Kirchengeschichte VIII 237–9.)

Fricke, F. Luthers kleiner Katechismus. Göttingen. 1897.

Friedrich, G. Luther und die Kirchenverfassung. Darmstadt. 1894.

Hartmann, Julius. Aelteste katechetische Denkmale der Ev. Kirche, oder die kleinen Katechismen von Brenz, Althammer, Lachmann, und Luther aus den Jahren 1527–9. Stuttgart. 1844.

Hase, C. A. Herzog Albrecht von Preussen und sein Hofprediger [J. Funck]. Leipzig. 1879.

Kästner, A. Die Kinderfragen. Der erste deutsche Katechismus. Leipzig. 1902.

Lambert, François. Lives of, by Baum (Strassburg, 1840), F. W. Hassencamp (Elberfeld, 1860), Stieve (Breslau, 1867) and Louis Ruffet (Paris, 1873).

Planck, G. J. Geschichte der Entstehung, der Veränderungen und der Bildung unseres Protestantischen Lehrbegriffs. 6 vols. Leipzig. 1781–1800.

Richter, A. L. Die evangel. Kirchenordnungen des 16 Jahrh. 2 vols. Weimar. 1846.

Sehling, E. Die evangelischen Kirchenordnungen des 16 Jahrh. Leipzig. 1902.

(iv) *The Protest of* 1529

Jung, A. Geschichte des Reichstags zu Speier in 1529. Strassburg. 1830.

Müller, J. J. Hist. von der evangel. Stände Protestation und Apellation. Jena. 1705.

Ney, J. Geschichte des Reichstages zu Speier in 1529. Hamburg. 1880.

Tittmann, J. A. H. Die Protestation zu Speyer. Leipzig. 1829.

C. CHAPTER VII. THE CONFLICT OF CREEDS AND PARTIES

(i) *The Conference at Marburg and Confession of Augsburg*

Bess, B. Luther in Marburg 1529 (Preuss. Jahrb. CIV 418–31, Berlin, 1901).

Bresch, F. Strasbourg et la querelle sacramentaire. Montauban. 1902.

Brieger, Th. Beiträge zur Gesch. des Augsburg. Reichstages 1530. Zeitschr. für Kircheng. XII. 1891.

—— Die Torgauer Artikel. In Kirchengeschichtliche Studien. Leipzig. 1888.

Bucer, M. Historische Nachricht von dem Gespräch zu Marburg. Simler, Sammlung II, ii, 471 sqq.

Calinich, H. J. R. Luther und die Augsburgische Confession. Leipzig. 1861.

Erichson, A. Das Marburger Religionsgespräch. Strassburg. 1880.

Escher, H. Die Glaubensparteien in der Eidgenossenschaft und ihre Beziehungen zu den deutschen Protestanten 1527–31. Frauenfeld. 1882.

Facius, Moriz. Gesch. des Reichstages zu Augsburg. Leipzig. 1830. (Cf. books on the same subject published the same year by C. Fikenscher and C. Pfaff.)

Ficker, J. Die Konfutation des Augsburg. Bekenntnisses. Leipzig. 1891.

—— Das Konstanzer Bekenntniss. Tübingen. 1902.

—— Aktenstücke zu den Religionsverhandlungen des Reichstages zu Regensburg, 1532. Zeitschr. für K. Gesch. xii.

Förstemann, K. E. Urkundenbuch zu der Gesch. des Reichstags zu Augsburg. 2 vols. Halle. 1833–5.

Greiner. Briefwechsel Konrad Mocks . . . auf dem Reichstag zu Augsburg 1530. Württemb. Viertelj. vi. 52–107, vii. 50–88.

Jaeger, C. Die Augsb. Konfession der vier Städte. Els.-Lothr. Protestantischer liberaler Verein. No. xiv. 1880.

Knaake, J. K. F. Luthers Anteil an der Augsburgischen Confession. Berlin. 1863.

Kolde, Th. Nürnberg und Luther vor dem Reichstag zu Augsburg. Kircheng. Studien. Leipzig. 1888.

Loaysa, G. de. Cartas al Carlos V 1530–2. Ed. G. Heine. Berlin. 1848.

Löscher, V. E. Historia Motuum. Leipzig. 1770.

Meyer, C. La réfutation de la confession d'Augsbourg. Alençon. 1896.

Moriköfer, J. C. Ulrich Zwingli nach den urkundlichen Quellen. 2 pts. Leipzig. 1867–9.

Müller, E. F. K. Die Bekenntnisschriften d. reform. Kirche. Leipzig. 1902.

Paetzold, A. Die Konfutation des Vierstädtebekenntnisses. Leipzig. 1899.

Popowski, F. von. Kritik der handschriftlichen Sammlung des Joh. Faber zu der Gesch. des Augsburg. Reichstags in 1530. Königsberg. 1880.

Rückert, L. J. Luthers Verhältnis zum Augsburgischen Bekenntniss. Jena. 1854.

Salig, C. A. Vollständige Hist. der Augsburg. Confession. 4 pts. Halle. 1730–45.

Schirrmacher, F. W. Briefe und Akten zu der Gesch. des Religionsgespräches zu Marburg und des Reichstages zu Augsburg. Gotha. 1876.

Tschakert, P. Die Augsburgische Konfession. Leipzig. 1901.

—— Die bisher unbekannte Ulmer Handschrift der Augsb. Konfession. Theol. Studien und Kritiken, 1903, pp. 48–70.

Uhlhorn, J. G. W. Die Reformation. Luther und die Schweizer. Hanover. 1868.

Virck, H. Melanchthons politische Stellung auf dem Reichstage zu Augsburg 1530. Zeitschr. für Kirchengeschichte. Vol. ix. 1887.

(ii)　*The Schmalkaldic League*

Meurer, M. Der Tag zu Schmalkalden und die Schmalkaldischen Artikeln. Leipzig. 1837.

Pfender, P. Les articles de Smalkalde. Paris. 1899.

Schmidt, G. Zur Geschichte des Schmalk. Bundes. Forsch. zur Deutschen Gesch. Vol. xxv.

Singer, P. Beziehung des Schmalkald. Bundes zu England. Greifswald. 1901.

Winckelmann, O. Der Schmalkaldische Bund 1530–2 und der Nürnberger Religionsfriede. Strassburg. 1892.

Zangemeister, K. Die Schmalkaldischen Artikel vom Jahre 1537. Heidelberg. 1883.

(iii)　*The Württemberg War of 1534*

Heyd, L. F. Die Schlacht bei Laufen. Stuttgart. 1834.

Wille, J. Philipp der Grossmütige von Hessen und die Restitution Ulrichs von Württemberg 1526–35. Tübingen. 1882.

Wille, J. Analekten zur Gesch. Oberdeutschlands insbesondere Würtembergs 1534–40. Zeitschr. für Gesch. des Oberrheins. Karlsruhe. 1858–68. Vol. xxxvii.

Winckelmann, O. Die Verträge von Kadan und Wien. Brieger's Zeitschr. für Kirchengesch. xi, 212 sqq.

(iv) *The Anabaptists*

Bax, E. Belfort. Rise and Fall of the Anabaptists. London. 1903.

Beck, Josef. Die Geschichtsbücher der Wiedertäufer in Oesterreich-Ungarn. Fontes Rer. Austr. Vol. xliii.

Bullinger, H. Der Wiedertäuferen Ursprung, Furgang, Secten, etc. Zurich. 1560.

Burckhardt, P. Die Basler Täufer. Basel. 1898.

Cornelius, C. A. Berichte der Augenzeugen über das Wiedertäuferreich. Münster. 1853.

—— Geschichte des Münsterischen Aufruhrs. 2 vols. Leipzig. 1855–60.

—— Die Niederländischen Wiedertäufer während der Belagerung Münsters. Munich. 1869.

—— Historische Arbeiten. Leipzig. 1899.

—— Die Eroberung der Stadt Münster. Von Raumer's Taschenbuch, 1872.

Detmer, H. Bilder an den relig. und sozial. Unruhen in Münster. Münster. 1902.

Egli, E. Die Züricher Wiedertäufer. Zurich. 1878.

—— Die St Galler Täufer. Zurich. 1887.

Gresbeck, H. In Geschichtsquellen des Bisthums Münster. Vol. ii. Münster. 1852.

Hase, C. A. Das Reich der Wiedertäufer. Leipzig. 1860.

Heath, R. Anabaptism 1521–36. London. 1895.

Heresbach, Conrad. Historia anabaptistica. Ed. Bouterwek. Elberfeld. 1866.

Hoffmann, Melchior. Prophecey oder weissagung aus heliger schrifft. Basel. 1530?

Hoffmeister, Johann. Dicta Memorabilia. Cologne. 1543.

Jochmus, H. Geschichte der Kirchenref. zu Münster und ihres Untergangs durch die Wiedtäufer. Münster. 1825.

Keller, L. Geschichte der Wiedertäufer und ihres Reichs zu Münster. Münster. 1880.

—— Die Wiederherstellung der Kathol. Kirche nach dem Wiedertäuferunruhen. Sybel's Hist. Zeitschr. xlvii 429 sqq.

—— Hans Denks Protestation und Bekenntniss. Monatschr. d. Comen.-Gesellsch. vii 231–43.

—— Ein Apostel der Wiedertäufer [Hans Denck]. Preuss. Jahrbücher. September, 1882.

Kerssenbroch, Herman. Anabaptistici Furoris . . . hist. narratio. Ed. H. Detmer. Münster. 1899. (Cf. Detmer, Kerssenbroch's Leben und Schriften. Münster. 1900.)

Kirchmair, Georg. Denkwürdigkeiten seiner Zeit 1519–53. Part i. In Fontes Rer. Austriacarum, i 417–534.

—— Das Bäptische Reich. Würtemberg (?). 1563.

Kolde, Th. Zum Prozess des Johann Denk. Leipzig. Kirchengesch. Studien. 1888.

Kripp, J. von. Ein Beitrag zur Gesch. der Wiedertäufer in Tyrol.

Krohn, B. N. Geschichte der Wiedertäufer. Leipzig. 1758.

Linden, F. O. zur. Melchior Hoffmann, ein Prophet der Wiedertäufer. Leipzig. 1885.

Melanchthon, P. Unterricht wider der Lere der Wiederteuffer verteutschet durch Justus Jonas. Wittenberg. 1528.

—— Etliche Propositiones wider der Lehre der Widerteuffer. Wittenberg. 1535.

Menius, Justus. Von dem Geist der Widerteuffer. Wittenberg. 1544.

Neue Zeitung von den Wiedertäufferen und ihrer Sect. Strassburg (?). 1528.

Ottius, J. H. Annales Anabaptistici. Basel. 1572.

Rembert, K. Die Wiedertäufer im Herzogtum Jülich. Berlin. 1899.

Renouard de Bussière, M. T. Les Anabaptistes. Hist. du Lutheranisme, de l'Anabaptisme et du règne de Jean Bockelsohn à Münster. Paris. 1853.

Rheglus, Urbanus. Disputation . . . wider alle Chiliasten. Ed. C. J. H. Fick. Hermannsburg. 1860.

Roth, Fr. Zur Geschichte der Wiedertäufer in Oberschwaben. Zeitschr. d. Vereins für Schwaben, Vols. xxvii–viii, 1901–2.

Rothmann, Bernard. Schriften. Ed. E. W. H. Hochhuth. Gotha. 1857. (Cf. H. Detmer, Beiträge zur Gesch. Bernhard Rothmanns in Monatsbll. d. Comenius-Gesells. ix, 273–300, 1901.)

Tumbült, G. Die Wiedertäufer; die sozial. und relig. Bewegungen zur Zeit der Reformation. Leipzig. 1899.

Winter, V. A. Geschichte der Bairischen Wiedertäufer. Munich. 1809.

(*See also* numerous articles in the Monatshefte d. Comenius-Gesellschaft.)

(v) *Lübeck and the "Grafenfehde"*

Alten, F. von. Graf Christoph von Oldenburg und die Grafenfehde. Hamburg. 1853.

Faulstitch, E. Zur Geschichte Stralsunds in der Zeit der Grafenfehde. Stralsund. 1902.

Gloy, A. Beitr. zur Gesch. der Leibeigenschaft in Holstein. Kiel. 1901.

Handelmann, H. Die letzten Zeiten der Hansischen Uebermacht. Kiel. 1853.

Koppmann, K. Zur Geschichte Dr Joh. Oldendorps. Beitr. zur Gesch. der Stadt Rostock, Vol. iii.

Schäfer, Dietrich. Geschichte von Dänemark. Vol. iv. Gotha. 1893.

Schlözer, K. von. Verfall und Untergang der Hansa. Berlin. 1853.

Waltz, G. Lübeck unter Jürgen Wullenweber und die Europäische Politik. Berlin. 3 vols. 1855–6.

Wurm, C. F. Die politischen Beziehungen Heinrichs VIII zu Marcus Meyer und Jürgen Wullenwever. Hamburg. 1852.

(vi) *Lutherans and Catholics, 1535–44*

Blatter, A. Thätigkeit Melanchthons bei den Unionsversuchen 1539–41. Bern. 1899.

Brandenburg, Erich. Herzog Heinrich der Fromme von Sachsen 1537–41. Dresden. 1896.

—— Polit. Korrespondenz Moritz von Sachsen. Vol. i, to 1543. Leipzig. 1900.

Brieger, Th. G. Gasparo Contarini und das Regensburger Konkordienwerk d. J. 1541. Gotha. 1870.

Bucer, M. Dialogi oder Gesprech von der gemainsame und den Kirchenübungen der Christen. Augsburg. 1535.

Dittrich, F. Nuntiaturbericht Morones 1539–40. Paderborn. 1892.

—— Gasparo Contarini. Braunsberg. 1885.

—— Regesten und Briefe des Kardinals G. Contarini. Braunsberg. 1881.

Druffel, A. von. Ueber den Vertrag zwischen Karl V und dem Papst von Juni 1541. Deutsche Zeitsch. für Gesch. Vol. iii. 1889.

Ettenius, Cornelius. Berichte über die Reise des Legaten Vorstius 1536–7. Ed. Arendt. Raumer's Hist. Taschenbuch, 1839.

Fraustadt, A. Die Einführung der Ref. im Hochstifte Merseburg. Leipzig. 1843.

Friedensburg, W. Zur Gesch. des Wormser Konvents 1541. Zeitschr. für Kirchen-Gesch. Vols. xxi-ii, 1900-1.

—— Nuntiaturberichte aus Deutschland; published by the K. Preuss. hist. Institut in Rome i i 1892 (Despatches of Vergerio 1533-6); i ii 1898 (Despatches of Morone 1536-8); i iii-iv 1893 (Despatches of Aleander 1538-9).

Gachard, L. P. Trois Années de Charles-Quint 1543-6. Brussels. 1865.

Heide, G. Die Verhandlungen des Vizekanzlers Held 1537-8. Hist.-Polit. Blätter für d. kathol. Deutschland. Vol. cii. Munich.

Heppe, H. Urkundliche Beiträge zur Gesch. der Doppelehe des Landgrafs. Niedner's Zeitschr. xxii, 265 sqq.

Hoffmann, E. Naumburg im Zeitalter der Reformation. Leipziger Studien. Vol. vii, Part i, 1901. (Cf. F. Köster, Beiträge in Zeitschr. für Kirchen-Gesch. xxii, 145-59, 278-330.)

Kayser, C. Die reformatorischen Kirchenvisitationem in den welfischen Landen 1542-4. Göttingen. 1897.

Koldewey, F. Heinz von Wolfenbüttel. Halle. 1883.

Meinardus, O. Die Verhandlungen des Schm. Bundes von 14 bis 18 Feb. 1539. Forschungen zur deutschen Geschichte. Göttingen. Vol. xxii.

Meine, F. Die Stellung Joachims II. Lüneburg. 1898.

Moses, R. Die Religionsverhandlungen in Hagenau und Worms, 1540-1. Jena. 1889.

Pastor, L. Correspondenz Contarinis, 1541. Hist. Jahrbuch, 1880.

Schulte, F. X. Luther und die Doppelehe des Landgrafen von Hessen. Paderborn. 1869.

Schwarz, K. Römische Beiträge zu J. Groppers Leben und Wirken. Hist. Jahrbuch der Görresgesellsch. Vol. vii.

Spiess, P. E. Gesch. des kaiserlich. neunjährig. Bundes von 1535-44. Erlangen. 1788.

Traut, H. Kurfürst Joachim II von Brandenburg und der Türkenfeldzug vom Jahre 1542. Gummersbach. 1892.

Vetter, P. Die Religionsverhandlungen auf dem Reichstage zu Regensburg. Jena. 1899.

Weiss, C. Papiers du Cardinal de Granvelle. 4 vols. Paris. 1841-8. (Cf. Correspondance du Cardinal de Granvelle. Brussels. 1897.)

(vii) *The Cleves War*

Crecelius, W. Der geldrische Erbfolgestreit 1538-43. Zeitschr. des Bergischen Geschichtsvereins. Bonn. 1863 etc. Vol. xxiii.

Heidrich, Paul. Der geldrische Erbfolgestreit 1537-43. Cassel. 1895.

D. Chapter VIII. Religious War

(i) *Authorities for the whole or the greater part of chapter*

Brandenburg, E. Moritz von Sachsen. Vol. i. Leipzig. 1898.

Braunsberger, O. B. Petri Canisii epistolae et acta. Vol. i, 1541-56. Freiburg i. B. 1896.

Brunner, S. Korrespondenzen . . . Ferdinands I in kirchlichen Angelegenheiten 1546-59. Studien . . . aus den Benedictiner und Cistercienser Orden. Vol. v.

Calendar of State Papers. Foreign Series, 1547–53. London. 1861.

Cornelius, C. A. Zur Erläuterung d. Politik d. Churf. Moritz von Sachsen. Münchener Histor. Jahrbuch. Munich. 1866.

Dreytwein, Dion. Esslingische Chronik 1548–64. Ed. A. Diehl. Tübingen. 1901.

Druffel, A. von. Briefe und Akten zur Gesch. d. XVI Jahrh. 1546–55. Vols. I–IV, 1873–96. Vol. V. Ed. W. Goetz. 1898.

Häberlin, F. D. Neueste Deutsche Reichsgeschichte vom Anfang des Schmalk. Krieges. 28 vols. Halle. 1774 etc.

Haussleiter, J. Aus der Schule Melanchthons. Theologische Disputationen zu Wittenberg 1546–60. Greifswald. 1897.

Hortleder, Fr. Der römischen Keyser . . . Handlungen und Ausschreiben . . . von den Ursachen des teutschen Krieges . . . 2 pts. Frankfurt. 1617–8. (Cf. M. Ritter in N. Archiv für Sächs. Gesch. Dresden. 1880. Vol. I.)

Issleib, S. Moritz von Sachsen als protestantischer Fürst. Hamburg. 1898.

Langenn, F. A. von. Melchior von Ossa. Leipzig. 1858.

—— Christoph von Carlowitz. Leipzig. 1854.

—— Moritz von Sachsen. 2 vols. Leipzig. 1841.

Massarelli, A. Tagebuch vom Concil zu Trient. Ed. Döllinger. Vol. I. Nördlingen. 1876.

Maurenbrecher, W. Karl V und die deutschen Protestanten 1545–55. Düsseldorf. 1865.

—— Kurfürst Moritz von Sachsen. Studien u. Skizzen z. Gesch. d. Reformationzeit. Leipzig. 1874.

Pieper, A. Päpstliche Legaten und Nuntien in Deutschland . . . Part I, 1550–9. Münster. 1897.

Reichenberger, R. Wolfgang von Salm, Bischof von Passau 1540–1555. Freiburg. 1902.

Ribier, G. Lettres et Memoires d'Estat. Paris. 1666. 2 vols.

Sastrow, Bartholomew. Memoirs. Ed. Mohnike, 3 vols., Greifswald, 1823–4; abridged translation published as Social Germany in Luther's Time. London. 1902.

Sehling, E. Die Kirchengesetzgebung unter Moritz von Sachsen und Georg von Anhalt. Leipzig. 1899. (Cf. E. Brandenburg in Hist. Vierteljahrschr. 1901, pp. 195–237.)

Sturm, Jakob. Life of, by Baumgarten. Strassburg. 1876.

Sturm, John. La vie et travaux, by Ch. Schmidt. Strassburg. 1855.

Trent, Council of. Monumenta Tridentina. Ed. Druffel. Vol. I. Munich. 1899.

—— Diariorum, Actorum, Epistt., Tractatuum nova collectio. Ed. Merkle. Görresgesellschaft. Freiburg i. B. 1901.

Turba, G. Beiträge zur Gesch. der Habsburger 1548–1558 (reprinted from the Archiv für Oester. Gesch. XC). Vienna. 1901.

Voigt, G. Moritz von Sachsen, 1541–7. Leipzig. 1876.

Weiss, Ch. Papiers d'État du Cardinal de Granvelle. 9 vols. Paris. 1841–52.

Wolf, Gustav. Deutsche Gesch. im Zeitalter der Gegenreformation. Vol. I. Berlin. 1898–9.

(11) *The Prelude to War* 1544–6

Brandenburg, E. Die Gefangennahme Herzog Heinrichs durch d. Schmalk. Bund. Leipzig. 1894.

—— Regensburger Vertrag zwischen d. Habsburgern und Moritz. Hist. Zeitschr. LXXX, 1–42.

Bruns, F. Vertreibung Heinrichs von Braunschweig. Marburg. 1889.

Caemmerer, H. von. Das Regensburger Religionsgespräch im Jahre 1546. Berlin. 1901.

Drouven, G. Die Ref. in d. Cölnischen Kirchenprovinz zur Zeit . . . Hermann von Wied. Cologne. 1876.

Druffel, A. von. Karl V und die Römische Kurie 1544–6. Abhandl. d. Münchener Akad., 1877, 1881, 1890.

Friedensburg, W. Am Vorabend des Schmalkaldischen Krieges. Quellen aus Ital. Archiv. 1897, II, 140–51.

—— Die Kriegsvorbereitungen Karls V. Ib. VII, 63–71.

—— Nuntiaturberichte aus Deutschland; published by the K. Preuss. hist. Institut in Rome I viii. (Despatches of Verallo 1545–6.) Gotha. 1898.

Gachard, L. P. Trois Années de Charles Quint 1543–6. Brussels. 1865.

Hasenclever, A. Die Politik der Schmalkaldener vor Ausbruch des Schmalk. Krieges. Berlin. 1901.

Kannengiesser, P. Der Reichstag zu Worms 1544–5. Strassburg. 1891.

—— Die Kapitulation zwischen Karl V und Paul III gegen den Protestanten 1546. Strassburg. 1888.

Paulus, N. Luthers Lebensende, Freiburg, 1898. (Cf. also the references in Janssen's Deutsche Gesch., English transl. VI, 281–2.)

Schmidt, G. Zur Gesch. des Schmalkalder Bundes Dec. 1545–Feb. 1546. Forschungen zur Deutschen Gesch. xxv. 1885.

Springer, J. Beiträge zur Gesch. des Wormser Reichstags 1544–5. Leipzig. 1882.

Ursprung und Ursach gegenwertiger Uffrür. Wittenberg. 1546.

Varrentrapp, C. Hermann von Wied und sein Reformationsversuch in Köln. Leipzig. 1878.

Voigt, G. Moritz von Sachsen 1541–7. Leipzig. 1876.

—— Der Bund mit den Habsburgern 1546. Archiv für Sächs. Ges. N. F. III.

(iii) *The Schmalkaldic War 1546–7*

Avila, Luis de. Comment. de la guerra de Alemania ed. 1858. [Charles V's "Commentaries" dealing with the war are largely based on Avila; Avila's book roused resentment among the German Princes; for a criticism of it attributed to Schartlin see Mencke, Scriptt. 1730, Vol. III.]

Baumgarten, H. Zur Gesch. des Schmalk. Krieges. Sybel's Hist. Zeitschr. Vol. XXXVI. 1876.

Christmann, Curt. Melanchthons Haltung im Schm. Kriege. Berlin. 1902.

Druffel, A. von. Des Viglius von Zwichem Tagebuch des Schmalkald. Donaukrieges. Munich. 1877.

—— Beitrag zur militärischen Würdigung des Schmalkald. Krieges. Munich. 1882.

Etliche kurtze gespräche die jetzige kriegsleuff im Teutschenland belängend. Sine loco. 1546.

Fischer, Karl. Die Stifte Magdeburg und Halberstadt im Schm. Kriege. Berlin. 1895.

Friedensburg, W. Nuntiatur des Verallo 1546–7. Nuntiaturberichte aus Deutschland. Div. I. Vol. IX. 1899.

Holländer, A. Strassburg im Schmalkald. Kriege. Strassburg. 1881.

Issleib, S. Die Wittenberger Kapitulation vom Jahre 1547. Neues Archiv für Sächs. Gesch. 1891.

Jahn, J. G. Geschichte des Schmalkaldischen Krieges. Leipzig. 1837.

Kannengiesser, P. Karl V und Maximilian von Egmont, Graf von Buren. Freiburg i. B. 1895.

Ladurner, P. J. Der Einfall der Schmalkaldener in Tirol. Archiv für Gesch. Tirols. Innsbruck. I, 145 sqq.

Le Mang, R. L. Die Darstellung des Schmalk. Krieges in den Denkwürdigkeiten Karls V. 3 pts. Jena, Leipzig and Dresden. 1890, 1899, 1900.

Lenz, M. Die Kriegsführung der Schmalkaldener gegen Karl V an der Donau. Sybel's Hist. Zeitschr. Vol. xlix. 1883.

—— Die Schlacht von Mühlberg. Gotha. 1879.

Mugnier, F. Faletz et Guerre de Charles-Quint dans l'Allemagne 1546–7. Paris. 1902.

Neue Zeitung des jetzigen Krieges. Sine loco. 1546.

Riezler, S. Die Baierische Politik im Schmalkald. Krieg. Hist. Abhandl. der Baier. Akad. xxi. 1894.

Schärtlin von Burtenbach. Lebensbeschreibung. Frankfort. 1777. (Cf. Th. Herberger, Schärtlin und seine an die Stadt Augsburg geschriebenen Briefe, Augsburg, 1852, and Schönhuth, Leben und Thaten Schertlins, Münster, 1858.)

Stenius, Simon. Versio et Supplicatio . . . descr. belli Schmalkald. In Freher's Scriptt. 1717, vol. iii.

Summarium dess evangelischen, das ist des Schmalkaldischen Kriegs. Anon. Sine loco. 2 pts. 1548.

Tieftrunk, K. Odpor stavův českých proti Ferdinandovi I. (The revolt of the Cech estates against Ferdinand in the spring of 1547.) Prague. 1872.

Voigt, G. Geschichtsschreibung über den Schmalkaldischen Krieg. Leipzig. 1874.

Wenck, W. Die Wittenberger Kapitulation von 1547. Sybel's Hist. Zeitschr. Vol. xx. (Cf. S. Issleib in N. Archiv für Sächs. Gesch. Vol. xii.)

(iv) *Charles V and his victory*

Ascham, Roger. Epistolarum libri quatuor. Oxford. 1703.

—— A Report and Discourse of the affairs of Germany during certain years while the said Roger was there. London. 1570? (Cf. A. Katterfeld, Roger Ascham. Strassburg. 1879.)

Beutel, G. Ueber den Ursprung des Augsburger Interims. Leipzig. 1888.

Bossert, G. Das Interim in Würtemberg. Halle. 1895.

Briefwechsel des Herzogs Christoph von Württemberg 1550–4. Stuttgart. 2 vols. 1899–1901.

Druffel, A. von. Die Sendung des Kardinals Sfondrato an den Hof Karls V 1547–8. Munich. 1892.

Friedberg, E. Agenda. . . . Ein Beitrag zur Gesch. des Interims [in Saxony]. Halle. 1869.

Gossart, E. Charles V et Philippe II. Brussels. 1896.

—— Notes pour servir à l'hist. du règne de Charles V. Brussels. 1897.

Herrmann, F. Das Interim in Hessen. Marburg. 1901.

Horning, W. Briefe von Strassburger Reformatoren u. a. über die Einführung des Interims in Strassburg (1548–54). Strassburg. 1887.

Jacobs, Ed. Johann Meinerzhagen und das Interim. Elberfeld. 1893.

Kupke, G. Nuntiaturen d. Bertano und Camaiani 1550–2. Nuntiaturberichte hrsg. durch d. k. preussischen Institut in Rom. Vol. xii. 1900.

Loserth, J. Die Registratur Erzherzog Maximilians aus den Jahren 1547–1551. Fontes Rerum Austr. xlviii.

Meinardus, O. Der Katzenelnbogische Erbfolgestreit. Wiesbaden. 2 vols. 1898, 1902. [Contains documents etc. about Philip of Hesse's imprisonment, and controverts Turba, Issleib, and Brandenburg.]

Melanchthon, P. Bedencken auffs Interim. s. l. 1548. Eng. transl. London. 1548.

Meyer, Chr. Zur Gesch. des Interim in Brandenburg-Anspach. Hohenzollerische Forschungen vi, 328–46.

—— Der Augsburger Reichstag nach einem fürstlichen Tagebuch. Preuss. Jahrb. 1898, 206–242.

Rachfall, F. Die Trennung der Niederlande vom deutschen Reiche. West-Deutsche Zeitschr. Vol. xix, pt. 2. 1900.

Turba, G. Verhaftung und Gefangenschaft des Landgr. Philipp. Vienna. 1896. (Cf. Meinardus above, S. Issleib, Die Gefangenschaft des Landgr. in N. Archiv für Sächs. Gesch. 1893, vol. xiv, and L. Schädel in Mitt. d. Oberhessischen Gesch. Vereins, Neue Folge, xi, 31–56.)

Waldeck, Wolrad von. Tagebuch während des Reichstages zu Augsburg 1548. Ed. C. L. Tross. Stuttgart. 1861.

Wolf, G. Das Augsburger Interim. Zeitschr. für Gesch. d. Wissensch. N. F. ii, 1.

(v) *The War of Liberation*

Barge, H. Die Verhandlungen zu Linz und zu Passau im Jahre 1552. Stralsund. 1893, 1897.

Des Moustiers-Mérinville. L'évêque de Bayonne, sa vie et correspondance. Limoges. 1895. [Useful for the bishop's negotiations with respect to the treaty of Friedwald.]

Fischer, G. Die persönliche Stellung und polit. Lage Ferdinands vor und während der Passauer Verhandlungen. Königsberg. 1891.

Goetz, W. Die bayerische Politik im ersten Jahrzehnt der Regierung Herzog Albrecht V. Munich. 1896.

Issleib, S. Moritz von Sachsen gegen Karl V bis zum Kriegzuge 1552. N. Arch. für Sächs. Gesch. vol. vi, 1885; the same continued, ibid. vol. vii, 1886.

—— Magdeburgs Belagerung durch Moritz. Ib. vol. v, 1884.

Kanngiesser, R. Der Zug Georgs von Mecklenburg ins Erzstift Magdeburg in 1550. Magdeburg. 1888.

Kiewning, H. Albrechts von Preussen und Markgraf Johanns von Brandenburg Antheil am Fürstenbund gegen Karl V. Königsberg. 1889. (Cf. Altpreuss. Monatsch. xxvi and Forschungen zur Brandenb. Gesch. vol. iv.)

Neumann, R. Die Politik d. Vermittlungspartei in 1552 bis zum Beginn der Verhandlungen zu Passau. Greifswald. 1896.

Radlkofer, M. Der Zug Kurf. Moritz 1552. Zeitschr. des hist. Vereins für Schwaben. Vol. xvii. 1890.

Scherer, H. Der Raub der drei Bisthümer in 1552. Raumer's Hist. Taschenbuch. 1842.

Schirrmacher, F. W. Johann Albrecht I, Herzog von Mecklenburg. 2 pts. Wismar. 1885.

Schlomka, E. Die polit. Beziehungen zwischen Moritz und Heinrich II 1550–2. Halle. 1884.

Schönherr, D. Gesammte Schriften. Ed. M. Mayr. 2 vols. Innsbruck. 1899–1902.

Voigt, J. Der Fürstenbund gegen Karl V. Raumer's Hist. Taschenbuch. 1857.

Von dem Kriege vor Magdeburg. In Chroniken der deutschen Städte, vol. xxvii, pt. v. Leipzig. 1899.

Warnecke, A. Die diplomatische Thätigkeit des Lazarus von Schwendi. Göttingen. 1890.

Wenck, W. Albertiner und Ernestiner nach d. Wittenberg. Kapitulation. Archiv für Sächs. Gesch. Vol. viii.

—— Kurfürst Moritz und Herzog August. Ib. vol. ix.

—— Kurfürst Moritz und die Ernestiner in 1551-2. Forschungen zur deutschen Gesch. Vol. xii.

Witter, J. Die Beziehung und der Verkehr des Kurf. Moritz mit König Ferdinand 1547–52. Jena. 1886.

(vi) *From the Treaty of Passau to the Peace of Augsburg*

Brandi, K. Der Augsburger Religionsfriede. Munich. 1896.

Chabert, F. M. Journal du siège de Metz. Metz. 1857.

Druffel, A. Beiträge zur Reichsgeschichte 1553-5, ed. K. Brandi. Munich. 1896.

Ernst, V. Die Entstehung der Executionsordnung von 1555. Württemb. Viertelj. x. 1-110.

Griessdorf, H. C. J. Der Zug Karls V gegen Metz. Halle. 1891.

Holländer, A. Strassburg im französischen Kriege 1552. Strassburg. 1888.

Isslelb, S. Von Passau bis Sievershausen. N. Archiv für Sächs. Gesch. Vol. viii. 1887.

Joel, F. August von Sachsen bis zur Erlangung d. Kurwürde. N. Archiv für Sächs. Gesch. Vol. xix, 1898.

Meyer, Chr. Zur Gesch. d. markgräfl. Krieges 1553-4. Hohenzollerische Forschungen v, 298-368, vi, 52-107.

Ritter, M. Der Augsburger Religionsfriede. Raumer's Hist. Taschenbuch. 1882.

Spieler, Ch. W. Geschichte des Augsburger Religionsfriedens. Schleiz. 1854.

Trefftz, J. Kursachsen und Frankreich 1552-6. Leipzig. 1891.

Voigt, J. Markgraf Albrecht Alcibiades. 2 vols. Berlin. 1852.

Schwabe, L. Kursachsen und die Verhandlungen über den Augsburger Religionsfrieden. N. Archiv für Sächs. Gesch. Dresden. Vol. x.

Wolf, G. Der Augsburger Religionsfriede. Stuttgart. 1890.

CHAPTER IX

THE REFORMATION IN FRANCE

I. ORIGINAL DOCUMENTS

Albéri, E. Le relazioni degli ambasciadori Veneti. I^{ra} serie. I–IV. Florence. 1839–60.

Argentré, C. du Plessis de (Bishop of Tulle). Collectio judiciorum de novis erroribus. I, II. Paris. 1728.

Aymon, T. Tous les synodes nationaux des églises réformées de France. I. The Hague. 1710. (Contains also letters of Cardinal Santa Croce.)

Becker, P. A. Marguerite, duchesse d'Alençon, et Guillaume Briçonnet, évêque de Meaux, d'après leur correspondance manuscrite (1521–24). Bulletin de la Société de l'Histoire du protestantisme français. Ed. N. Weiss. XLIX. Paris. 1900. (Subsequently cited as Bull. prot. franç.)

Bourrilly, V. L. François Ier et les Protestants. Les essais de concorde en 1535. Bull. prot. franç. XLIX. Paris. 1900.

—— Jean Sleidan et le Cardinal du Bellay. Ib. L. 1901.

—— Lazare de Baïf et le Landgrave de Hesse. Ib.

Bulæus, C. E. Historia universitatis Parisiensis. VI. Paris. 1673.

Calendar of State Papers. Foreign series. I–VI. London. 1861–6; Venetian. II–VII, ib. 1867–90; Letters and Papers of Henry VIII. III–XVI, ib. 1867–98. (For further particulars see Bibliographies to Chaps. XIII–XVI.)

Calvin, J. Opera, ed. G. Baum, E. Cunitz and E. Reuss. XI–XIX. (Letters.) Brunswick. 1873–9.

Castelnau, M. de. Mémoires. Ed. J. le Laboureur. I. Brussels. 1731.

Catalogue des actes de François Ier. I–VII. Paris. 1887–96. (To be completed in 10 volumes, the last three containing a bibliography and indices.)

Cimber, L, et Daujon, F. Archives Curieuses. 1e série. Paris. 1835. IV. Histoire du tumulte d'Amboise.

Collection des documents inédits. Lettres de Catherine de Medicis. Ed. H. de la Ferrière. I. 1880. Négociations du règne de François II. Ed. A. L. Paris. 1841. Perrenot, A., Card. de Granvelle. Papiers d'État. Ed. C. Weiss. III–VI. 1842–6.

Condé. Mémoires de Condé. I–III. The Hague. 1743.

Crespin, J. Histoire des Martyrs. Ed. D. Benoist (from the edition of 1619). I, II. Toulouse. 1885–7.

Delisle, L. Notice sur un registre des procès-verbaux de la faculté de théologie de Paris pendant les années 1503–1533. Paris. 1899. [The MS. of this register, which formerly belonged to the Duc de la Trémoïlle, is now in the Bib. nationale.]

Durand de Maillane, P. T. Les libertés de l'église gallicane. 5 vols. Lyons. 1771.

Este, Ippolito de (Cardinal of Ferrara). Négociations. Paris. 1658.

Herminjard, A. L. Correspondance des Réformateurs dans les pays de langue française. 9 vols. published, reaching to the year 1544. Geneva and Paris. 1866-97.

Isambert, F. A. Recueil général des anciennes lois françaises. xii–xiv. Paris. 1828-9. (This will be superseded for the reign of Francis I by the Ordonnances des Rois de France. Vol. i (1515, 1516) published 1902.)

Layard, Sir A. H. Despatches of Michele Suriano and Marcantonio Barbaro, Venetian Ambassadors at the Court of France, 1560–1563. Publications of the Huguenot Society of London. Lymington. 1891.

L'Hospital, Michel de. Œuvres. Ed. P. J. S. Duféy de l'Yvonne. i, ii. Paris. 1824.

Ribier, G. Lettres et Mémoires d'Estat. i. Paris. 1666.

Weiss, N. La chambre ardente. Paris. 1889.

II. HISTORIES, MEMOIRS, AND OTHER NARRATIVES WHOLLY OR IN PART CONTEMPORARY

Haton, Claude. Mémoires. Ed. F. Bourquelot. Coll. des doc. inéd. i. Paris. 1857.

Histoire Ecclésiastique des églises réformées au royaume de France. (A compilation edited under the direction of Beza. Antwerp. 1580. Ed. G. Baum and E. Cunitz. 3 vols. Paris. 1883-9.)

Journal d'un bourgeois de Paris sous le règne de François premier. Ed. L. Lalanne for the Soc. de l'hist. de France. Paris. 1854.

Languet, Hubert. Epistolae secretae. Part ii. Halle. 1699.

[La Place, P. de.] Commentaires de l'Estat de la Religion et Republique sous les Rois Henry et François seconds, et Charles neufieme. 1565. Reprinted in the Panthéon littéraire. Ed. J. A. C. Buchon. Paris. 1836.

Pasquier, Estienne. Lettres. Book iv. Paris. 1586.

[Regnier de la Planche, L.] Histoire de l'Estat de France sous le règne de François II. 1576. Ed. E. Mennechet. 2 vols. Paris. 1836.

Rœmond, Florimond de. L'histoire de la naissance, progrès et décadence de l'hérésie de ce siècle. Book vii. Paris. 1605.

Santa Croce, P. (Cardinal). De civilibus Galliae dissensionibus. In Martène et Durand, Vet. Script. et Monum. amplissima collectio. v. 1426–75. Paris. 1729.

Saulx-Tavannes, Gaspard de. Mémoires. [At the château de Sully. 1617.] Michaud et l'Poujoulat. viii. Petitot. xxvi–xxviii.

Serres, Jean de. Commentarii de statu religionis et reipublicae in regno Galliae. Part i. [Geneva.] 1571.

Thou, J. A. de. Historiae sui temporis. i, ii. Bks i–xxix. Paris. 1604-6. Ed. S. Buckley. London. 1733.

III. LATER WORKS

A. GENERAL HISTORIES OF FRENCH PROTESTANTISM

In order of publication

Aubigné, Théodore Agrippa de. Histoire Universelle. Books i, ii. Maillé. 1616. Ed. A. de Ruble for the Soc. de l'hist. de France. i. Paris. 1886.

Soldan, W. G. Geschichte des Protestantismus in Frankreich bis zum Tode Karls IX. i. Leipzig. 1855.

Polenz, G. von. Geschichte des französischen Calvinismus. i. Gotha. 1857.

Lutteroth, H. La réformation en France pendant la première période. Paris. 1859.

Baird, H. M. History of the rise of the Huguenots of France. i. New York. 1879. London. 1880.

B. Ecclesiastical Histories

Gerdes, D. Introductio in historiam Evangelii seculo XVI passim per Europam renovati doctrinaeque Reformationis. I–IV. Groningen. 1744–52.

Guettée, l'Abbé. Histoire de l'Église de France. VIII, IX. Paris. 1856.

Hottinger, J. H. Historiae ecclesiasticae Novi Testimenti Euneas. VII. 713 ff. Hanover. 1665.

Lichtenberger, F. L. Encyclopédie des Sciences religieuses. 13 vols. Paris. 1877–82.

Pallavicini, Sforza. Istoria del concilio di Trento. Ed. F. A. Zaccaria. I, II. Rome. 1833.

Raynaldus, O. Annales Ecclesiastici. Ed. A. Theiner. XXXI–XXXIV. Bar-le-Duc and Paris. 1877–79.

C. Histories of Protestantism in Particular Cities and Provinces

Arnaud, E. Histoire des Protestants de Dauphiné. I. Paris. 1876.

—— Histoire des Protestants de Provence, du Comtat Venaissin et de la principauté d'Orange. 2 vols. Paris. 1884.

Coquerel, A. fils. Précis de l'histoire de l'église réformée de Paris, 1572–1594. Paris. 1862.

Corbière, P. Histoire de l'église réformée de Montpellier. Montpellier and Paris. 1861.

Dieterlen, H. Le synode général de Paris, 1559. Paris. 1873.

Floquet, A. Histoire du Parlement de Normandie. II. Rouen. 1840.

Gaullieur, E. Histoire de la réforme à Bordeaux et dans le ressort du Parlement de Guienne. I. Paris. 1884.

Hauser, H. La réforme en Auvergne. Bull. prot. franç. XLVII, XLVIII. 1898, 1899.

Leroux, A. Histoire de la réforme dans la Marche et le Limousin. Limoges. 1888.

Lièvre, A. Histoire des Protestants du Poitou. I. Paris. 1856.

Montarde, E. Étude historique sur la réforme à Lyon. Geneva. 1881.

Naef, F. La réforme en Bourgogne. Paris. 1901.

Puech, A. La Rénaissance et la Réformation à Nismes. Nimes. 1893.

Robert-Labarthe, U. de. Histoire du Protestantisme dans le Haut Languedoc. 2 vols. Paris. 1895–6.

Rossier, L. Histoire des Protestants de Picardie. Paris. 1861.

Vaurigand, B. Essai sur l'histoire des églises réformées de Bretagne, 1535–1808. I. Paris. 1870.

Viénot, J. Histoire de la réforme dans le pays de Montbéliard, 1524–1573. I. Montbéliard. 1900.

See for the bibliography of this section the sale-catalogue of the library of Henri Bordier, nos. 277–354, Paris, 1889, and, for recent works, H. Hauser in Rev. hist. XXVI. 85 ff., 1901.

D. Biographies

Atkinson, C. T. Michel de l'Hospital. London. 1900.

Baird, H. M. Theodore Beza. New York. 1899.

Baum, J. W. Theodor Beza. 2 vols. Leipzig. 1843–52.

Bersier, E. Coligny avant les guerres de religion. Paris. 1884.

Bouillé, R. de. Histoire des Ducs de Guise. I, II. Paris. 1849.

Buisson, F. Sébastien Castellion. I. Paris. 1892.

Decrue, F. Anne de Montmorency. 2 vols. Paris. 1885 and 1889.

Delaborde, J. Gaspard de Coligny. I. Paris. 1879.

Doumergue, E. Jean Calvin. I, II. Lausanne. 1899, 1903.

Forneron, H. Les Ducs de Guise. I. Paris. 1877.

Graf, K. H. Jacobus Faber Stapulensis. Zeitschrift für die historische Theologie. Hamburg and Gotha. 1852.

Guillemin, J. J. Le Cardinal de Lorraine. Paris. 1847.

Haag, Eugène and Émile. La France Protestante. 10 vols. Paris. 1846–58. 2nd ed. Ed. H. Bordier. 6 vols. (to GAS) published. Paris. 1877–88.

Lefranc, A. La jeunesse de Calvin. Paris. 1888.

Marcks, E. Gaspard von Coligny. Stuttgart. 1892.

Pinvert, L. Lazare Baif. Paris. 1900.

Ruble, A. de. Antoine de Bourbon et Jeanne d'Albret. 2 vols. Paris. 1881–2.

Schmidt, C. Gérard Roussel. Strassburg. 1845.

E. MISCELLANEOUS

Bourrilly, V. L. Les préliminaires des guerres de religion. Bull. prot. franç. XLV. 1896.

Bower, H. M. The fourteen of Meaux. London. 1894.

Hauser, H. La propagation de la Réforme en France. Revue des cours et conférences. Paris. 1894.

—— La Renaissance et la Réforme en France, 1512–52. Revue historique. LXIV. Paris. 1897.

—— The French Reformation and the French People in the Sixteenth Century. American Historical Review. IV. New York. 1899.

Klipffel, H. Le colloque de Poissy. Paris and Metz. 1867.

Lefranc, A. Les idées religieuses de Marguerite de Navarre, d'après son œuvre poétique. Paris. 1898.

—— Un nouveau registre de la faculté de théologie de Paris au XVIᵉ siècle. Bull. prot. franç. 1902.

Madelin, L. Les premières applications du Concordat de 1516 d'après les dossiers du Château Saint-Ange. École française de Rome. Mélanges d'archéologie et d'histoire. XVII. Paris. 1887.

Mignet, F. Lettres de Jean Calvin. Journal des Savants. 1856, 1858, 1859. Paris.

Paillard, C. Additions critiques à l'histoire de la conjuration d'Amboise. Rev. hist. XIV. Paris. 1880.

Philippson, M. Westeuropa im Zeitalter von Philipp II, Elizabeth und Heinrich IV. Oncken's Allgemeine Geschichte. III, 2, pp. 1–113. Berlin. 1882.

Picot, G. Histoire des États Généraux. II. Paris. 1872.

Ranke, L. von. Französische Geschichte, vornehmlich in 16ᵗᵉⁿ und 17ᵗᵉⁿ Jahrhundert. I. Stuttgart and Tübingen. 1852. Vol. VIII of Sämmtliche Werke. Berlin. 1874 etc.

Roget, A. Histoire de Genève. I–VI. Geneva. 1870–81.

Rolland, R. Le dernier procès de Berquin. École française de Rome. Mélanges. XII. Paris. 1892.

Ruble, A. de. Le colloque de Poissy. Mémoires de la Société de l'hist. de Paris et de l'Île de France. XVI. Paris. 1889.

Schmidt, C. Die Unions-Versuche Franz I. Zeitschr. für die historische Theologie. Leipzig. 1850.

Sthyr, H. V. (Bishop). Lutheranerne i Frankrig i Aarene 1524–26. Copenhagen. 1879.

Numerous short notices, besides the longer articles cited above, will be found in the Bulletin de la Société de l'histoire du protestantisme français; ed. Weiss. Paris.

CHAPTER X

THE HELVETIC REFORMATION

I

A. BIBLIOGRAPHIES

Brandstetter, J. L. Repertorium über die in Zeit- und Sammelschriften der Jahre 1812–1890 enthaltenen Aufsätze und Mittheilungen schweizergeschichtlichen Inhaltes. Basel. 1892.

Finsler, G. Zwingli-Bibliographie. Zurich. 1897.

> An appendix to the above by the same author, in Zwingliana, 1902, No. 1 (pp. 287–90), brings it up to date.

—— Bibliographie der schweizerisch-reformierten Kirchen. Vol. I. Die deutschen Kantone. In Bibliographie der schweizerischen Landeskunde. 1896.

Haller, G. E. von. Verzeichniss der Bücher und Schriften betreffend die Reformationsgeschichte, mitgetheilt von C. Siegwart-Müller, in Archiv für die schweizerische Reformationsgeschichte, vol. I (1868), following Haller's Bibliothek der schweizer. Geschichte, 1785 etc.; after Haller's death in 1786 the collection was continued, and completed up to 1871, by R. P. Gall-Morel in Archiv f. d. schw. Reform. Gesch., vol III (Freiburg, 1876), pp. 1 ff.

Mülinen, J. E. F. von. Prodromus einer schweiz. Historiographie. Bern. 1874.

Sinner, L. von. Bibliographie der Schweizergeschichte. Bern. 1851.

Strickler, J. Neuer Versuch eines Litteratur-Verzeichnisses zur schweiz. Reformationsgeschichte enthaltend die zeitgenössische Litteratur, 1521–1532. In Actensammlung, etc., ed. by Strickler. Vol. v, pt 2.

Wyss, G. v. Geschichte der Historiographie in der Schweiz. Zurich. 1894.

References should also be made to Anzeiger für schweizerische Geschichte: herausgegeben von der Allgemeinen geschichtsforschenden Gesellschaft der Schweiz (Bern) for continuations. A useful English sketch of the literature for the general history of Switzerland is given in Vincent, Government in Switzerland (New York, 1900), pp. 341–360. R. Stähelin has published accounts of Swiss Reformation historical works in Brieger's Zeitschrift f. Kirchengeschichte: for 1875–78 in vol III (1879), pp. 547 ff.: for 1879–82 in vol. VI (1884), pp. 429 ff.

B. GUIDES TO MS. MATERIAL

Erichson. Zwingli-Autographen in Elsass. Ibid. 1886, pp. 111–114.

Escher, H. Verzeichniss der Zwingli-Autographen aus der Stadtbibliothek und der Kantonsbibliothek in Zürich. Ibid. 1885, pp. 217 ff.

Archiv für schweiz. Reformationsgeschichte, I, II, III, contain much information on single groups. Escher's Glaubensparteien is largely based on unpublished MSS.

Mohr, T. von. Regesten der Archive der schweiz. Eidgenossenschaft auf Anordnung der schweiz. Geschichtlichen Gesellschaft. (Vol. ı contains Einsiedeln, Canton Bern before the Reformation, Rapperschwyl, Abbey of Pfäffers, etc., by various writers.)

Rott, E. Inventaire sommaire de documents relatifs à l'Histoire de la Suisse conservés dans les Archives et Bibliothèques de Paris, et spécialement de la Correspondance échangée entre les Ambassadeurs de France aux Ligues et leur gouvernement, 1440–1700. [Part ı is for 1444–1610, and Part v contains the Index.]

Schweizer, P. Verzeichniss der Zwingli-Autographen aus dem Staatsarchiv in Zürich. In Theologische Zeitschrift aus der Schweiz, ed. Meili, 1885, pp. 196 ff. with note on p. 232. Zurich.

Stähelin, R. Zwingli-Autographen in Basel. Ibid. 1886, pp. 53–54.

The MSS. have been largely worked over and printed, especially those for Zwingli's life. The Civic and Cantonal libraries are mostly catalogued. For foreign, diplomatic, and theological relations other libraries, although largely worked, have still material: e.g. Marburg, Stuttgart, Strassburg, and Innsbruck.

II

A. EDITIONS OF WORKS

Huldrici Zwinglii Opera: Schuler and Schulthess. 8 vols. Zurich. 1828–42. Supplement by Schulthess and Marthaler. Zurich. 1861.

A new edition by Dr Emil Egli and Dr Georg Finsler is in preparation, to be published at Berlin, under the patronage of the Zwingli-Verein in Zurich.

The fundamental edition was that of Froschauer, edited by Rudolph Gualter. 1544–5: the vernacular works were translated into Latin.

A useful hand-book, arranged by subjects, is Huldreich Zwingli's Sämmtliche Schriften in Auszuge, von L. Usteri und S. Vögelin. Zurich. 1819–20. 2 vols.

For single works see the Bibliography by Finsler (*above*).

III

CHRONICLES, DOCUMENTS, AND LETTERS

A. General Chronicles

Anshelm, V. Berner Chronik vom Anfang der Stadt Bern bis 1526. 6 vols. Bern. 1825–33. Also Bern, 1884.

Bullinger, H. Reformationsgeschichte. Edited by Hottinger and Vögeli. Frauenfeld. 1838–40.

Edlibach, G., mit Einleitung von J. M. Usteri. Mitteilung der antiquarischen Gesellschaft in Zürich. Vol. ıv. Zürich. 1846.

Kessler. Sabbata. Chronik der Jahre 1523–39: von Ernst Götzinger. St Gallen, 1866–8. Mitteilungen z. vaterländischen Geschichte. St Gallen. hist. Verein. Vols. v–x. A new edition with commentary is announced by Egli and Schoch.

Myconius, O. Vita Huldrici Zwinglii ab Oswaldo Myconio conscripta. (The best edition is in Neander's Vitae Quatuor Reformatorum. Berlin. 1841.)

Salat, Johann. Chronik der schweizerischen Reformation von deren Anfängen bis A.D. 1534. In Archiv für schweizerische Reformationsgeschichte. Vol. I. Solothurn. 1868.

Sicher. Die Chronik Fridolin Sichers. Edited by E. Götzinger in the St Gallen Mittell. zur vaterländischen Geschichte xx. Neue Folge, x. St Gallen. 1885.

Tschudi, V. Chronik der Reformationsjahre 1521–1533, von I. Strickler. Separatausgabe (No. xxiv) des Glarner hist. Jahrbuchs. Bern. 1889. Also in Archiv für Schw. Gesch. Vol. ix, pp. 322–447.

Wyss. Die Chronik des Bernhard Wyss, von Georg Finsler. Basel. 1901. In Quellen zur schweizerischen Reformationsgeschichte unter Leitung von Dr E. Egli.

See also Verzeichniss in the Index Volume (Vol. v, pt 2) of Strickler's Actensammlung.

B. DOCUMENTS

General

Egli, E. Actensammlung zur Geschichte der Züricher Reformation, 1519–33. Zurich. 1879.

Füsslin, J. K. Beyträge zur Erläuterung der Kirchen Reformationsgeschichte des Schweizerlandes. 5 pts. Zurich. 1741–55. See especially the article on Conrad Hofmann.

Gisi, W. Actenstücke zur Schweizergeschichte der Jahre 1521–1522 (contains French documents). Archiv für Schw. Gesch. Vol. xv, pp. 285–318.

Simler, J. J. Sammlung alter und neuer Urkunden zur Beleuch. der Kirchengeschichte, vornehmlich des Schweizerlandes. 2 vols. Zurich. 1759–63.

Strickler, J. Eidgenoss. Abschiede. Vol. iv, 1 *a* (1521–28), Brugg, 1873 and 1 *b* (1529–33), Zurich, 1876.

—— Actensammlung zur schweizerischen Reformationsgeschichte in den Jahren 1521–32. 5 vols. Zurich. 1877–1884.

C. CHRONICLES, DOCUMENTS, ETC.

Special points and subjects

Bannwart, P. (edited by). Denkschrift der Priorin und Schwestern in St Catharinathal über ihre Erlebnisse während der Reformationszeit. Archiv für schw. Ref. iii, pp. 99–116.

Basel. Chronik des Karthäuser-Klosters in Klein-Basel, 1401–1532. In Basler Chroniken, vol. i (edited by W. Vischer und A. Stern). Leipzig. 1887.

Bernoulli, A. (edited by). Die Anonyme Chronik der Mailänderkriege (1507–16). In Basler Chroniken, vol. vi, pp. 463 f. Leipzig. 1902.

Blösch, E. (edited by). Eine neue Quelle zur Gesch. der Berner Disput. In Theolog. Zeitschrift aus der Schweiz, 1891, pp. 157 ff.

Bucer, M. Historische Nachricht von dem Gespräch zu Marburg zwischen Luthern und Zwinglin. In Simler, Sammlung, etc. Vol. ii, pt ii, pp. 471 sqq.

Collin, R. Summa colloquii Marpurgensis. In Hospinian, Historia Sacramentaria (*see below*, Theological section), or in Zwingli, Opera (edd. Schuler und Schulthess), iv, pp. 173 ff.

Cysat, Renward. Luzern's Geheimbuch verfasst von Stadtschreiber R. Cysat. Edited by Scherer-Boccard. Archiv für schw. Ref. iii, pp. 117–176.

Egli, E. Documente und Abhandlungen zur Geschichte Zwinglis und seiner Zeit. Printed in Analecta Reformatoria i, pp. 1–24. Zurich. 1899.

Egli, E. On Zwingli's notes concerning the Bernese Disputation in Staatsarchiv, Zurich. Analecta Reformatoria I, pp. 37–44.

Faber, J. (Bishop). Report of the Disputation of Jan. 29, 1523, to the Innsbruck government. In Katholische Schweizerblätter, Series 11 (1895), No. II, pp. 183 ff. Edited by J. G. Mayer. Lucerne. 1895.

Gall-Morel, R. P. Urkunden zur Geschichte Zwinglis aus dem Stiftsarchiv Einsiedeln. ASRG. I, pp. 787 ff.

Hedio. Reisebericht (to Marburg). Edited by Erichson in Zeitschrift für Kirchengeschichte, IV, pp. 420 ff.

Küssenberg, H. Chronik (for Baden, 1522 onwards). Edited by Huber in Archiv für schw. Ref. III, pp. 411 ff.

Landolt. Urkunden zur Reformationsgeschichte des Städtchens Stein-am-Rhein. 1523–8. In Archiv für schw. Ref. III, pp. 624–630.

Lavater. Verantwortung betreffend seinen Oberbefehl bei Kappel. Edited by Egli in Anal. Reform. I, pp. 150–164.

Ryff, F. Chronik, 1514–41. In Basler Chroniken, vol. I, edited by Vischer und Stern. Leipzig. 1887.

Ryhiner, H. Chronik des Bauernkrieges, 1525. In Basler Chroniken, vol. VI, edited by A. Bernoulli, pp. 463 ff. Leipzig. 1902.

Scherer-Boccard. Acten zum Christlichen Bündniss zwischen Ferdinand und den V Orten (1525–29). Aus dem Luzerner Staatsarchiv. Archiv für schw. Ref. III, pp. 555–598.

—— Preliminaracten zu einem Schutzbündniss zwischen Papst Clement VII, Kaiser Karl V, und den V Katholischen Orten. Archiv für schw. Ref. II, pp. 546–557.

—— 135 päpstliche Schreiben an Tagsatzungen, Orte, etc., grossentheils aus dem XVI Jahrhundert. Archiv für schw. Ref. II, pp. 1–97.
[*See also* Cysat.]

Schirrmacher. Briefe und Acten zur Geschichte des Religionsgespräches zu Marburg 1523 und des Reichstages zu Augsburg 1530 nach den Handschriften des Joh. Aurifaber. Gotha. 1876.

D. Letters

See also Finsler's Bibliographie, pp. 171–2; and Zwingli's Letters in vols. VII and VIII of Opera.

Arbenz, E. Die Vadianische Briefsammlung. In Mitt. zur vaterländischen Geschichte XXIV, 4, pp. 80 ff., XXV, XXVII, and XXVIII, pp. 1 ff. St Gallen. 1890.

Egli, J. E. Unpublished letters from the Augsburg Reichstag (Aug. and Sept. 1530). In Analecta Reformatoria I, pp. 45–60. Zurich. 1899.

Fechter. Achtzehn ungedruckte Briefe von Ulrich Zwingli und Albertus Durerius an B. Rhenanus. In Archiv für schw. Geschichte, vol. X, pp. 185 ff. Zurich. 1885.

Friedensburg, W. Beiträge zum Briefwechsel der katholischen Gelehrten Deutschlands im Reformationszeitalter. Zeitschr. für Kirchengesch. Vol. XX, pp. 59–95 and 242–259 for letters of Bishop Faber. 1899–1900.

Füsslin, J. K. Epistolae ab Ecclesiae Helveticae reformatoribus vel ad eos scriptae. Zurich. 1742.

Herminjard, A. L. Correspondance des Réformateurs dans les pays de langue française (especially vol. II). 8 vols. Geneva, Basel, Lyons, Paris. 1866–93.

Lenz, M. Zwingli und Landgraf Philip. In Zeitschr. für Kirchengesch. 1879, vol. III, pp. 28 ff., 220 ff., 429 ff.

Liebenau, T. von. Briefe über die Disputation in Baden. Aus dem Luzerner Staatsarchiv. Archiv für schw. Ref. 1869, I, pp. 798 ff.

Scherer-Boccard, T. von. Schreiben Franz I von Frankreich an Orte der Eidgenossenschaft. Aus dem Staatsarchiv von Luzern. Archiv für schw. Ref. III,
pp. 631–640.

Stähelin, R. Briefe aus der Reformationszeit. Basel. 1887.

Troll, J. K. Three Letters to the Council at Winterthur. Printed in Neujahrsbl.
v. d. Bürgerbibliothek zu Winterthur, XI 6, VI 1, V 16. Winterthur. 1844.

Virck, H., and Winckelmann, O. Politische Correspondenz der Stadt Strassburg im
Zeitalter der Reformation. Strassburg. I. 1882. II. 1887.

Wartmann, H. Fünf Briefe H. Zwinglis an Joachim von Watt aus dem Stadtarchiv von St Gallen. Mittell. zur vaterländ. Geschichte III, pp. 210–216.
1866. St Gallen.

IV

A. BIOGRAPHIES

(In order of importance)

Stähelin, R. Huldreich Zwingli. Sein Leben und Wirken nach den Quellen
dargestellt. 2 vols. Basel. 1895–97.

Mörikofer, J. C. Ulrich Zwingli nach den urkundlichen Quellen. 2 vols. Leipzig.
1867–69.

Christoffel, R. Huldreich Zwingli, Leben und ausgewählte Schriften. Elberfeld.
1857. The biography translated into English by Cochran. Edinburgh. 1858.

Jackson, S. M. Huldreich Zwingli, 1484–1531. New York and London. 1901.

Also: Stähelin in Herzog-Plitt, Real-Encyclopädie: Hoff in Lichtenberger's
Encyclopédie des Sciences religieuses, 1882, vol. XII, pp. 521 ff.: Egli in Allg.
Deutsche Biographie.

B. BIOGRAPHICAL STUDIES AND ARTICLES

See also Finsler's Bibliographie, pp. 169–172

Christen, E. Zwingli avant la Réforme de Zurich. Geneva. 1899.

Egli, E. Zwingli und die Ostschweizerischen Anhänger der Lutherischen Abendmahlslehre. In Anal. Reform. I, pp. 61 ff.

—— Zwingli und die Synoden, besonders in der Ost-Schweiz. In Anal. Reform. I,
pp. 80 ff.

—— Zwinglis Stellung zum Kirchenbann und dessen Verteidigung durch die
St Galler. In Anal. Reform. I, pp. 99 ff.

—— Zwingli in Wien. Theolog. Zeitschrift aus d. Schweiz. Zurich. Vol. I,
1884, p. 92.

—— Die Namensform Zwingling. Theolog. Zeitschrift aus d. Schweiz. Vol. I,
1884, p. 185.

Erichson, A. Zwinglis Tod und dessen Beurtheilung durch Zeitgenossen. Strassburg. 1883.

Ghinzoni. Ulrico Zwinglio e Francesco II Sforza. Boll. Stor. della Svizzera
Italiana XV, 1893, pp. 9 ff. Bellinzona.

Heer, G. Zwingli als Pfarrer von Glarus. Zurich. 1884.

Kind, Paul. Ulrich Zwingli und Franz II Sforza. Theolog. Zeitschrift aus d.
Schweiz. 1896, pp. 131–9.

Nitz, C. A. Ulrich Zwingli. Gotha. 1884.

Odinger, Th. Ein Idyll Rudolf Gualter's über Zwinglis Tod. Theolog. Zeitschrift
aus d. Schweiz. 1891, pp. 54–59.

Oechsli, **W.** Zwingli als politischer Theoretiker. In Turicensia, pp. 87–113. Zurich. 1891.

Reber, B. Zwinglis politisches Wirken bis zur Schlacht von Pavia. Beiträge zur vaterländ. Geschichte. Vol. v, 1854, pp. 245 ff.

Schweizer, A. Zwinglis Bedeutung neben Luther. Zurich. 1884.

Stähelin, R. Huldreich Zwingli und sein Reformationswerk. Halle. 1883.

—— Zwingli als Prediger. Theolog. Zeitschr. aus d. Schweiz. 1887, pp. 12 ff.

Steck, R. Zwingli in Basel. Theolog. Zeitschrift aus d. Schweiz. Vol. i, 1884, pp. 185–187.

Usteri, L. Initia Zwinglii. Studien und Kritiken, Jahrg. 58, 1885, pp. 607–672, und Jahrg. 59, 1886, pp. 95–159: also separately printed.

—— Zu Zwinglis Elenchus. Zeitschr. für Kirchengesch. Vol. xi. 1889–90, pp. 161–165. (See also Baur, Zeitschr. für Kirchengesch. x, 1889, pp. 330–344.)

Werder, J. Zwingli als politischer Reformator. Beiträge zur vaterländischen Geschichte, Neue Folge. Vol. i, pp. 263 ff. Basel. 1882.

For various details reference should be made to Zwingliana, Zurich, 1897 etc., ed. Egli.

C. HISTORIES

a. GENERAL

Beard, C. The Reformation of the 16th century in its relation to modern thought and knowledge. London. 1883.

Hagenbach, K. R. Kirchengeschichte von der ältesten Zeit bis zum 19 Jahrhundert. Vol. iii. Geschichte der Reformation vorzüglich in Deutschland und der Schweiz. 4th ed. Leipzig. 1870. Translated into English by Evelina Moore. 2 vols. Edinburgh. 1878–79.

Hergenröther, J. A. G. Concilien-Geschichte (Vol. ix of Hefele). Freiburg i. B. 1890.

Janssen, J., and Pastor, L. Geschichte des deutschen Volkes seit dem Ausgang des Mittelalters. Freiburg i. B. 1899. Especially vol. iii, pp. 92–264; also, An meine Kritiker (Freiburg i. B. 1891); and, Ein zweites Wort an meine Kritiker (Freiburg i. B. 1895).

Möller, W., and Kawerau, G. Lehrbuch der Kirchengeschichte. Vol. iii, Reformation und Gegenreformation. Freiburg i. B. and Leipzig. 1894. Translated into English by J. H. Freese. London and New York. 1900.

Ranke, L. v. Deutsche Geschichte im Zeitalter der Reformation. Especially iii, pp. 40–72, 232–269. Vol. iv of Sämmtliche Werke. Leipzig. 1874 etc.

Schaff, P. History of the Christian Church. Modern Christianity. The German Reformation, A.D. 1517–1530 (Divisions I and II). Edinburgh. 1888.

b. CONSTITUTIONAL, ECONOMIC, ETC.

Blumer, J. J. Rechtsgeschichte der Schweiz. Demokratien. (For Uri, Schwyz, Unterwalden, Glarus, Zug, and Appenzell.) Vol. i, to 1531. Vol. ii, to 1798. St Gallen. 1850 and 1858.

Bluntschli, J. C. Geschichte des Schweizerischen Bundesrechtes von dem ersten ewigen Bunde bis auf die Gegenwart. Vol. i, to p. 343. Vol. ii, documents, to page 276. Stuttgart. 1875.

Dändliker, K. Die Berichterstattungen und Anfragen der Zürcher Regierung an die Landschaft in der Zeit vor der Reformation. Jahrbuch für schw. Gesch. Vol. xxi, pp. 38–70.

—— Zürcher Volksanfragen von 1521 bis 1798. Jahrbuch für schw. Gesch. Vol. xxiii, pp. 147 f.

Dubs, A. Das öffentliche Recht der Schweiz. Eidgenossenschaft. I, II. 2nd edition. Zurich. 1878.

Erhardt. Die national-ökonomischen Ansichten der Reformatoren. Zweiter Art. Huldreich Zwingli. Theolog. Stud. u. Kritik. 1881, I, pp. 106 ff.

Fechter, D. A. Basels Anstalten zur Unterstützung der Armen und Kranken während des Mittelalters. Beiträge zur vat. Geschichte, IV, 185.

Moses. Federal Government of Switzerland. Oakland, California. 1889.

Riggenbach. Das Armenwesen der Reformation. Basel. 1883.

Strickler, J. Grundzinse, Frohndienste und Zehnten, oder Bilder aus der Geschichte des bäuerlichen Grundbesitzes. Zeitschr. f. Schweiz. Statistik. 1874. 2.

Vincent, J. M. Government in Switzerland. New York and London. 1900.

c. LOCAL, ETC.

Baden, R. Die Reformation und ihr Einfluss auf das Zürcherische Recht. Theolog. Zeitschrift aus d. Schweiz. 1902 (I), pp. 9-20.

Baur, A. Zur Vorgeschichte der Disputation von Baden. Zeitschr. für Kirchengesch. Vol. XXI, pp. 91-111. 1900-1.

Blösch, E. Der Kardinal Schinner. Akademischer Vortrag. 1890.

—— Geschichte der schweizerisch-reformierten Kirchen. Vols. I and II. Bern. 1899.

—— Die Vorreformation in Bern. Jahrbuch für schw. Gesch. Vol. IX. 1884.

Brieger. Ueber einen angeblich neuen Bericht über das Marburger Religionsgespräch. In Zeitschr. für Kirchengesch. I, pp. 628-638.

Büchtold, J. Hans Salat. Sein Leben und seine Schriften. Basel. 1876.

—— Nicklaus Manuel. In vol. II of the Bibliothek älterer Schriftwerke der deutschen Schweiz und ihrer Grenzgebiete. Frauenfeld. 1876.

Camenisch, C. Carlo Borromeo und die Gegenreformation im Veltlin. Chur. 1901.

Clemen, O. Hinne Rode. Zeitschr. für Kirchengesch. Vol. XVIII, pp. 346-372 and note 639-640. 1897-8.

Coolidge, W. A. B. The Republic of Gersau. English Hist. Review IV, pp. 481 f.

Dierauer, J. Geschichte der schweizerischen Eidgenossenschaft. Vol. II, to 1510. Gotha. 1892.

Dändliker, K. Komtur Schmidt von Küssnacht. In Züricher Taschenbuch. 1897.

—— Geschichte der Schweiz. 3 vols. Zurich. 1884.

—— A short history of Switzerland, translated by Salisbury. London. 1899.

Egli, E. Zürcherische Kirchenpolitik von Waldmann bis Zwingli. Jahrbuch für schw. Gesch. Vol. XXI, pp. 1-34.

—— Die Züricher Wiedertäufer zur Reformationszeit. Zurich. 1878.

—— Die Schlacht von Cappel, 1531. Mit zwei Plänen und einem Anhange ungedruckter Quellen. Zurich. 1873.

—— Das Religionspräch zu Marburg. Theolog. Zeitschrift aus der Schweiz. Vol. I, 1884, pp. 5-30. Zurich.

Ernest, Ulrich. Geschichte des Zürchischen Schulwesens bis gegen Ende des 16 Jahrhunderts. Zurich. 1879.

Escher, H. Die Glaubensparteien in der Eidgenossenschaft und ihre Beziehungen zum Ausland : vornehmlich zum Hause Habsburg und zu den deutschen Protestanten. Frauenfeld. 1882. [Of first-rate importance.]

—— Die Verhältnisse der freien Gotteshausleute. Archiv f. sch. Geschichte. Vol. VI, pp. 3-29. 1849. Zurich.

Fiali. Reformation und Gegenreformation in den freien Ämtern. Archiv für schw. Ref. pp. 529 ff.

Gisi, W. Antheil der Eidgenossen an der europäischen Politik in den Jahren 1512 bis 1516. Schaffhausen. 1866.

Gisi, W. Der Antheil der Eidgenossen an der europäischen Politik während der Jahre 1517 bis 1521. Archiv f. sch. Geschichte. Vol. XVII, pp. 63–132. 1871. Zurich.

Götzinger, E. Zwei Kalender vom Jahre 1527. Schaffhausen. 1865.

Grüneisen, E. Nicklaus Manuel. Stuttgart. 1837.

Herzog, J. J. Christoph von Uttenheim, Bischof von Basel zur Zeit der Reformation. Beiträge. Vol. I, 1839, pp. 33–93 (with note on p. 305). Basel.

Hidber, B. Renward Cysat, der Stadtschreiber zu Luzern. Archiv f. schw. Geschichte. Vol. XIII, pp. 161–224 and XX, pp. 3–88.

Horawitz, A. Johann Heigerlin (gen. Faber), Bischof von Wien. Vienna. 1884.

Huber, A. Die Waldstätte bis zur festen Begründung ihrer Eidgenossenschaft. Innsbruck. 1861.

Hyrvoix. François Ier et la première guerre de religion en Suisse 1529–1531, d'après la correspondance diplomatique. In Revue des Questions historiques, April, 1902, pp. 465–537.

Jecklin, F. Blaurock. In Jahresbericht XXI der histor.-antiq.-Gesellschaft von Graubünden. 1891. pp. 1 f.

Kawerau, W. Thomas Murner und die deutsche Reformation. Halle. 1891.

Kesselring. Interpolirte Zwingli Briefe. Theolog. Zeitschrift aus d. Schweiz. Vol. I, 1884. Zurich.

Kluckhohn. Urkundliche Beiträge zur Geschichte der kirchlichen Zustände; insbesondere des sittlichen Lebens der katholischen Geistliche in der Diöcese Konstanz während des XVI Jahrhunderts. Zeitschr. für Kirch. Vol. XVI, 1896–7, pp. 590–625.

Lichtenhahn, K. Die Secularisation der Klöster und Stifte Basels. Beiträge. Vol. I, pp. 94–109.

Loserth. Die Stadt Waldshut und die vorder-österr. Regierung, 1523–1526. In Arch. f. öst. Ges. 77, pp. 1 ff.

Lüthi, E. Die Bernische Politik in den Kappelerkriegen. Bern. 1880.

Marmor, W. Die Beziehungen der Stadt Constanz zu der Eidgenossenschaft während des Mittelalters; 1259–1520. Archiv f. schw. Geschichte. Vol. XVIII, pp. 111–189. 1873. Zurich.

Mayer, J. G. Das Konzil von Trient und die Gegenreformation in der Schweiz. Vol. I. Stanz. 1901.

—— Das Stift Rheinau und die Reformation. Jahrbuch für schw. Gesch. Vol. XXVI, pp. 295–312.

Meyer von Knonau. Aus der schweiz. Geschichte in der Zeit der Reformation und Gegenreformation. Die Eidgenossenschaft gegenüber dem deutschen Bauernkrieg von 1526. Hist. Zeitschrift, 1878, I.

Meyer, D. Die Reformation der deutschen Schweiz im Gewande der dramatischen Dichtung. Theolog. Zeitschrift aus d. Schweiz. 1892, pp. 121–128 and 163–176.

Mezger, J. J. Geschichte der deutschen Bibelübersetzungen in der schw. reform. Kirche. Basel. 1876.

Nitsche, R. Geschichte der Wiedertäufer in der Schweiz zur Reformationszeit. Einsiedeln. 1885.

Oechsli, W. Zwingli als politischer Theoretiker. In Turicensia, pp. 87–113. Zurich. 1891.

—— Das eidgenoss. Glaubensconcordat von 1525. Jb. f. Sch. Ges. XIV, pp. 263 ff.

—— Die Anfänge des Glaubens-konfliktes zwischen Zürich und den Eidgenossen 1521–1524. Winterthur. 1883.

Oper, L. Die Stadt Basel und ihr Bischof. Beiträge. Vol. IV (1850), pp. **229 ff.**

Pastor, L. Die kirchlichen Reunionsbestrebungen während der Regierung Karls V. aus den Quellen dargestellt. Freiburg i. B. 1879.

Pestalozzi, C. Heinrich Bullinger. Leben und ausgewählte Schriften. Elberfeld. 1858.

Riggenbach, E. J. Der Kirchengesang in Basel seit der Reformation. In Beiträge, vol. IX (1870), Basel, pp. 327 ff. Also note on same in vol. X (1875), p. 365.

Rilliet, A.   Les Origines de la Confédération Suisse.   Histoire et Légende.   Geneva. 1869.

Rockholz, E. L.   Tel und Gessler.   Heilbronn.   1877.

Rohrer, F.   Das christliche Bürgerrecht.   Lucerne.   1876.

—— Das sogenannte Waldmannische Concordat.   Jahrbuch f. Schw. Geschichte. Vol. iv, pp. 1 ff. 1879 (with criticism by Stähelin, Zeitschr. für Kirchengesch. 1884, pp. 429 ff.).

Rott, E.   Histoire de la représentation diplomatique de la France auprès des cantons suisses, de leurs alliés, et de leurs confédérés.   2 vols.   Vol. i (1430–1559). Bern.   1900.

Ruchat, A.   Histoire de la Réformation de la Suisse, edited by Vulliemin.   7 vols. Paris and Lausanne.   1835–8.

Salzberger, G.   Beiträge zur Toggenburgischen evangelischen Kirchengeschichte. Mitteil. zur vaterländische Geschichte.   iii, pp. 16 ff.   1866.   St Gallen.

Sarasin, A.   Versuch einer Geschichte des Basler Münsters.   In Beiträge, vol. i (1839), pp. 1–32.

Schaffroth, J. G.   Der Reformator Niklaus Manuel von Bern.   Basel.   1885.

Schiss.   Die Beziehungen Graubündens zur Eidgenossenschaft besonders zu Zürich im xvi Jahrhundert.   Jahrbuch für schw. Gesch.   Vol. xxvii, pp. 29 f.

Schreiber, H.   Heinrich Loriti Glareanus.   Freiburg.   1837.

Schultz, Emil.   Reformation und Gegenreformation in den freien Aemtern.   Basel. 1899.

Schweizer, P.   Die Behandlung der Zürcherischen Klostergüter in d. Reformationszeit.   In Theolog. Zeitschrift aus der Schw. (ed. Meili).   Vol. ii (1885), pp. 161 ff. Zurich.

Seitz, O.   Die Stellung des Urbanus Rhegius im Abendmahlsstreite.   ZKG.   Vol. xix, pp. 293–329.   1898–9.

Stähelin, R.   Die reformatorische Wirksamkeit. . . . Vadians.   Beiträge, Neue Folge, i (1882), pp. 191–262.

Stehlin, K.   Ueber die diplomatischen Verbindungen Englands mit der Schweiz im 16 und 17 Jahrhundert.   Beiträge.   Vol. vii (1860), pp. 45 f.

Vetter, F.   Die Reformation von Stadt und Kloster Stein-am-Rhein.   Jahrbuch für schw. Gesch.   Vol. ix, 1884, pp. 213–261.

Vischer, W.   Die Sage von der Befreiung der Waldstätte.   Leipzig.   1867.

Vögelin, S.   Das alte Zürich.   Zurich.   1878.

Vuilleumier, H. V.   L'Église du pays de Vaud au temps de la Réformation.   Lausanne, 1902.

Vulliemin, L.   Histoire de la Confédération Suisse.   2 vols.   Lausanne.   1879.

Waldburger, A.   Rheinau und die Reformation.   Jahrbuch für schw. Gesch.   Vol. xxv, pp. 81–362.

Weber, H.   Geschichte des Kirchengesangs in der deutschen reformirten Schweiz seit der Reformation.   Zurich.   1878.

Wyss, G. von.   Ueber d. Geschichte d. drei Lande, 1215–1301.   Zurich.   1858.

d. Theological

[*See also* Stähelin, Christoffel and Mörikofer in Biographies; *also* Corpus Reformatorum, Breitschneider, vol. xxvi.]

Baur, Aug.   Zwinglis Theologie, ihr Werden und ihr System.   2 vols.   Halle. 1885–89.

Daniel, H. A.   Codex Liturgicus (especially vol. iii).   4 vols.   Leipzig.   1847–53.

Dieckhoff, A. W.   Die Evangelische Abendmahlslehre im Reformationszeitalter.   i [all that has appeared].   Göttingen.   1854.

Dilthey, W. In Archiv für Geschichte der Philosophie, vol. v, 1892, pp. 367 ff.:
    vol. vi, 1893, pp. 119 ff., pp. 523 ff.
—— Die Glaubenslehre der Reformatoren. In Preuss. Jahrbücher, 1894, i, 70.
Engelhardt, E. Die innere Genesis und der Zusammenhang der Marburger, Schwa-
    bacher und Torgauer Artikel, sowie der Augsburger Confession. In Zeitschrift
    für hist. Theologie, 1865, pp. 519–529.
Frank, F. H. R. Die Theologie der Concordienformel. 4 vols. Erlangen. 1858–65.
Gottschick, J. Hus', Luther's und Zwingli's Lehre von der Kirche. Zeitschr. für
    Kirchengesch. viii (1886–7), pp. 345–394 and 543–616.
Harnack, A. Dogmengeschichte, Pt ii, Bk iii, Chap. iv. In English Translation:
    vol. vi, pp. 168 ff. London. 1899.
Heitz. Ueber den Taufritus der reformirten Kirche der Schweiz. Theolog Zeitschrift
    aus d. Schweiz. Vol. iii. 1886, pp. 158–167.
Hospinianus, R. Historia Sacramentaria. 2 vols. Geneva. 1681. (Vol. ii, De ori-
    gine et progressu controversiae sacramentariae, reaches to 1612.)
Hundeshagen, K. B. Die Konflikte des Zwinglianismus, Lutherthums und Calvinismus
    in den Bernischen Landkirchen, 1522–1558, nach meist ungedruckten Quellen
    dargestellt. Bern. 1842.
—— Beiträge zur Kirchenverfassungsgeschichte und Kirchenpolitik, insbesondere des
    Protestantismus. Wiesbaden. Vol. i. 1864.
Kügelgen, E. W. von. Die Ethik Huldreich Zwinglis. Leipzig. 1902.
Loofs, F. Leitfaden zum Studium der Dogmengeschichte. 3rd ed. Halle. 1893.
Löscher, V. E. Historia Motuum (between Lutherans and Reformed). 1st edition.
    1723–24; 2nd edition, by J. R. Kiesling. Leipzig und Schwabach. 1770.
Müller, E. F. K. Die Bekenntnisschriften der reformierten Kirche—in authentischen
    Texten, pp. 1–100. Leipzig. 1903.
Niemeyer, H. A. Collectio Confessionum in ecclesiis reformatis publicatarum.
    Leipzig. 1840.
Richter, Aem. L. Die evangelischen Kirchenordnungen des sechzehnten Jahrhunderts.
    Urkunden und Regesten zur Geschichte des Rechts und der Verfassung der evan-
    gelischen Kirche in Deutschland, pp. 21 ff. and 134 ff. 2 vols. Weimar. 1846.
Richter, L. Geschichte der evangelischen Kirchenverfassung in Deutschland (pp. 148–
    166). Leipzig. 1851.
Schaff, Ph. Bibliotheca Symbolica. New York. 1877.
Schmid, H. Der Kampf der Lutherischen Kirche um Luthers Lehre vom Abendmahl
    im Reformationszeitalter. Leipzig. 1868.
Schweizer, A. Die protestantischen Centraldogmen in ihrer Entwicklung innerhalb
    der reformierten Kirche. Zurich. 1854–6.
Sigwart, C. Ul. Zwingli, der Charakter seiner Theologie mit besonderer Rücksicht
    auf Picus von Mirandola. Stuttgart and Hamburg. 1855.
Stahl, F. J. Die Lutherische Kirche und die Union. Berlin. 1860.
Thomasius-Seeberg. Dogmengeschichte des Mittelalters und der Neuzeit. Vol. ii,
    pp. 395–421 and 520–637. Erlangen and Leipzig. 1889.

(See also Bibliographies to Chapters V–VIII, and to Chapter XI.)

CHAPTER XI

CALVIN

I. BIBLIOGRAPHIES

Catalogus operum Calvini. Ioannis Calvini Opera quae supersunt omnia. Vol. LIX, pp. 462–512.

Catalogus operum quae sunt de Calvino. Ioannis Calvini Opera quae supersunt omnia. Vol. LIX, pp. 517–586.

Haag, Eug. et Em. La France protestante.... Tome III, pp. 143–162. Paris. 1852.

Herzog-Plitt, J. J. Realencyklopädie für protestantische Theologie und Kirche. Vol. III, pp. 77–79. Leipzig. 1878. Ibid. 3rd ed., edited by Hauck. Vol. III, pp. 654, 655. Leipzig. 1897.

Rilliet, A. Bibliographie de la vie de Calvin. Paris. 1864.

Schaff, Ph. History of the Christian Church, vol. VII, pp. 228–231. New York. 1892. Edinburgh. 1893.

Senebier, J. Auteurs à consulter sur la vie de Calvin. Histoire littéraire de Genève, pp. 260–265. Geneva. 1786.

II. ORIGINAL AUTHORITIES

Calvini, Ioannis, Opera quae supersunt omnia. LIX vols. Corpus Reformatorum. Vols. XXIX–LXXVII. Brunswick and Berlin. 1869–97.

Works of Calvin published by the Calvin Translation Society. Edinburgh. 1843–55.

Bonnet, J. Lettres françaises de Jean Calvin. 2 vols. Paris. 1854. Translation: Letters of John Calvin. I, II, by Constable. Edinburgh. 1855. III, IV, by Gilchrist. Philadelphia. 1858.

Herminjard, A.-L. Correspondance des Réformateurs dans les pays de langue française. 9 vols. Basel, Geneva, Lyons. 1866–97.

III. BIOGRAPHIES

A. GENERAL

Adam, Melchior. Vita Calvini. In Vitae theologorum, pp. 63–113. Frankfort. 1618.

Alexander, W. Lindsay. Calvin. Encyclopaedia Britannica, edd. VIII and IX.

Audin, V. Histoire de la vie, des ouvrages et des doctrines de Calvin. 1st ed. Paris. 1841. Later ed. 1873. Translation: Gill, Life of Calvin. London. 1850.

Bayle, P. Calvin. Dictionnaire historique et critique. Vol I. Rotterdam. 1696.

Beza, Th. Vita Calvini. Corpus Reformatorum, XLIX. 1879. Translation: Beveridge, Calvin's Tracts, vol. I. Transl. Soc. Edinburgh, 1844.

Bèze, Th. de. Discours contenant en brief l'histoire et mort de Maistre Jean Calvin. Geneva. 1564. And in the Corpus Reform., *ut supra*.

Bungener, F. Calvin, sa vie, son œuvre, et ses écrits. Paris. 1862–3. Translated into English, German, and Dutch in 1863, and in 1877 into Danish.

Dardier, Ch. Calvin le réformateur. Encyclopédie des sciences religieuses, II, 529–545. Paris. 1877.

Diehl, K. v. J. Kalvin, Teolog i Reformator (Zwiastun Ewangeliczny). Warsaw, 1864–5.

Doumergue, E. Jean Calvin. Les hommes et les choses de son temps. Lausanne. Vol. I, La jeunesse. 1899. Vol II, Les premiers Essais. 1902. [This work is still incomplete; vol. II ends with Calvin's return to Geneva.]

Dyer, T. H. The life of John Calvin. London. 1849.

Funk. Calvin. Wetzer und Welte: Kirchenlexikon, II, 1728–44. Freiburg. 1883.

Goguel, G. Le réformateur de la France et de Genève, Jean Calvin. Toul. 1863.

Guizot, F. P. G. La vie de quatre grands chrétiens: Calvin, pp. 149–376. Paris. 1873. Translation: London. 1881.

Haag, E. Vie de Calvin, à l'usage des écoles protestantes. Paris. 1840.

—— E. C. La France protestante, III, 109–162. Paris. 1852.

Henry, P. Das Leben Calvins. 3 vols. Hamburg. 1835–44. Translation: Stebbing. Life and Times of Calvin. 2 vols. London. 1849.

Herzog, J. J. Calvin. Realencyklopädie für prot. Theologie und Kirche. Leipzig. 1st ed. 1854, 2nd ed. 1878.

Mackenzie, J. Memoirs of the life and writings of John Calvin. London. 1818.

Stähelin, E. Calvins Leben und ausgewählte Schriften. Elberfeld. 1863.

—— R. Calvin. Realencyklopädie für prot. Theologie und Kirche, III, 654–683. 3rd ed. Leipzig. 1897.

B. SPECIAL PERIODS

1. *Youth and Conversion*

Couard-Lys, E. Documents inédits relatifs à Calvin. Bull. du comité des travaux historiques et scientifiques, Section d'hist. et de philologie, pp. 7–13. Paris. 1884.

Dalton, H. Calvins Bekehrung. Deutsche evang. Blätter. Halle. 1893.

Desmay, J. Remarques sur la vie de Jean Calvin, hérésiarque, tirées des Registres de Noyon. Rouen. 1621–57. Archives curieuses de l'histoire de France, V, pp. 387–398. Paris. 1835.

Lang, A. Die Bekehrung Johannes Calvins. Studien zur Geschichte der Theologie und Kirche. Vol. II. Pt I. Leipzig. 1897.

Lecoultre, H. La conversion de Calvin. Rev. de théol. et de philosophie, pp. 5–30. Lausanne. 1890.

Lefranc, A. La Jeunesse de Calvin. Paris. 1888.

Levasseur, J. Annales de l'église cathédrale de Noyon. Paris. 1633.

2. *Calvin in Geneva*

Bolsec, Hier. Histoire de la Vie, Mœurs, Actes, Constance et Mort de Jean Calvin jadis ministre de Genève. Lyons. 1577. A Latin version was published at Cologne, 1580. The book has often been republished [though its animus is too marked to allow of its being trusted]; a later edition with introduction and notes is by L. F. Chastel. Lyons. 1875.

Cornelius, C. V. Historische Arbeiten, vornehmlich zur Reformationszeit. Leipzig. 1899.

Galiffe, J. A. Matériaux pour l'histoire de Genève. 2 vols. Geneva. 1829.

Kampschulte, F. W. Johann Calvin, seine Kirche und sein Staat in Genf. Vol. I. 1869. Vol. II. Leipzig. 1899.

Pierson, A. Studiën over J. K. Amsterdam. 1881. (De Omwenteling te Genève voor K., pp. 17–57. K.'s Geloofsverandering, pp. 58–109. K. in de eerste helft van 1536, pp. 243–256.) Nieuwe Studiën. Amsterdam. 1883. Kalvin en Caroli, pp. 17–89. Kalvin's Nederlaag in 1538, pp. 90–149.

—— Studiën over J. K. 1540–2. Ser. III. Amsterdam. 1891. (K. naar Genève Teruggeroepen, pp. 1–42. K. en de troebelen te Neuchâtel, pp. 43–83. De eerste maanden te Genève, pp. 84–122. Caroli naar de Nederlaag, pp. 123–184.)

Roget, A. Histoire du peuple de Genève depuis la Réforme jusqu'à l'Escalade. Geneva. 1870–83.

3. *Death*

F. V. La Mort de Calvin. La Croix. Paris. 1864.

Zahn, A. Die beiden letzten Lebensjahre von Calvin. Leipzig. 1895.

4. *Private life*

Bonnet, J. Idelette de Bure. Bull. 1856, pp. 638–646. Étrennes chrétiennes. Geneva, 1857, pp. 104–123. Récits du 16e siècle, Paris, 1864, pp. 75–100.

—— Les amitiés de Calvin. Bull. 1864, pp. 89–96. —Ibid. 1869, pp. 257–268, 449–462. Récits du 16e siècle, Paris, 1864, pp. 101–175, 319–352.

Gaberel, J. La vie intime de Calvin. Souvenirs religieux, pp. 273–293. Toul. 1865.

Galiffe, J. A. Notices généalogiques sur les familles Génevoises. pp. 106–113. Geneva. 1836.

Hausrath, A. Calvins Verheirathung. Leipzig. 1883.

Lang, A. Das häusliche Leben Johann Calvins. Beilage zur Allg. Zeitung, nos. 137, 138, 140, 142. Munich. 1893.

Ollier, D. Le mariage de Calvin. Rev. chrétienne, 1892, II, pp. 210–226.

C. Thought and Theology

Baur, F. C. Christliche Dogmengeschichte. Vol. III. Leipzig. 1867.

—— Die christliche Lehre von der Dreieinigkeit und Menschwerdung Gottes. . . . Vol. III. Tübingen. 1843.

Bonnet, J. Le traité De Clementia. Rev. chrét. 1857, pp. 219–22.

Cunningham, W. The reformers and the theology of the Reformation, pp. 292–525. Edinburgh. 1862.

Gass, W. Geschichte der prot. Dogmatik, I. pp. 99–124. 1854.

Köstlin, J. Calvins Institutio nach Form und Inhalt in ihrer geschichtlichen Entwicklung. Studien und Kritiken, pp. 7–62, 410–486. Gotha. 1868.

Lecoultre, H. Calvin d'après son commentaire sur le De Clementia. Rev. de théol. et de phil., pp. 51–77. Lausanne. 1891.

Loofs, Friedrich. Die lehrhafte Auffassung des evangelischen Christentums durch Calvin. Dogmengeschichte, pp. 390–401.

Rilliet, A. Introduction hist. au Catéchisme et à la confession de fois, 1537. Le premier catéchisme de Calvin, I–XCVIII. Paris. 1878.

Rougemont, H. de. L'Inst. chrét. de Calvin dans sa rédaction primitive. Le Chrétien évangélique, pp. 77–83. Lausanne. 1886.

Schneckenburger, M. Vergleichende Vorstellung des lutherischen und ref. Lehr-
    begriffs. 2 vols. Stuttgart. 1855.
Schweizer, A. Die prot. Centraldogmen in ihrer Entwicklung innerhalb der ref.
    Kirche. I, pp. 150-249 *et passim.* Zurich. 1854.

IV. HISTORY OF THE SIXTEENTH CENTURY IN RELATION
TO CALVIN

Baird, H. M. History of the rise of the Huguenots. 2 vols. London. 1880.
Bez, G. Les luttes religieuses en France et Calvin d'après sa correspondance. Tool.
    1887.
Histoire Ecclésiastique des Églises Réformées au Royaume de France. 1580. Later
    ed., by Baum and Cunitz. 3 vols. 1883-9.
Merle d'Aubigné, J. H. Histoire de la réformation en Europe au temps de Calvin.
    Paris. 1863-78. Translation. History of the Reformation in Europe in the time
    of Calvin. London. 1863-.
Polenz, C. von. Geschichte des französischen Calvinismus. Gotha. I. 1857. II.
    1859.
Puaux, F. Histoire de la réformation française. Paris. 1857-9.

See also previous section (Biographies, General).

V. CALVIN AND HERESY

Brunnemann, K. M. Servetus. Eine aktenmässige Darstellung des 1553 in Genf
    gegen ihn geführten Criminalprozesses. Berlin. 1865.
Buisson, F. Sébastien Castellion, sa vie et son œuvre. 2 vols. Paris. 1892.
Cologny, L. L'antitrinitairisme à Genève. Geneva. 1873.
Dardier, C. Michel Servet d'après ses plus recents biographes. Revue historique.
    XI. Paris. 1879.
Florimond de Raemond. L'histoire de la naissance, progrez et décadence de l'hérésie.
    Paris. 1605.
Rilliet, A. Relation du procès criminel intenté à Genève en 1553 contre Servet.
    Mém. et documents de la société d'histoire et d'archéologie de Genève, pp. 1-160.
    Geneva. 1844.
Tolliu, H. Charakterbild M. Servets. Berlin. 1876.
—— Servet über Predigt, Taufe und Abendmahl. Theologische Studien und Kriti-
    ken. Gotha. 1881.
Willis, R. Servetus and Calvin. London. 1877.

VI. CALVIN AS EDUCATOR

Borgeaud, Ch. Calvin Fondateur de l'Académie de Genève. Paris. 1897.
Damagnez, A. Influence de Calvin sur l'instruction. Montauban. 1886. This is a
    very meritorious example of the *theses* published at Montauban. Those dealing
    with Calvin are an immense multitude, and may be said to cover the whole field
    of his thought and activity.
Heiz, J. Calvin's Thätigkeit für die Schule. Zeitschrift für praktische Theol.
    Frankfort. 1889.
Schenck, J. C. Johann Calvin's Verdienste auf dem Gebiete der Erziehung und des
    Unterrichts. Frankfort. 1863.

VII. CALVIN AS STATESMAN

Biesterveld, P. Calvin gewaardeerd in sijne politieke beginselen. Tijdschrift voor geref. Theol. Kampen, 1900, pp. 272–276.
Choisy, E. La théocratie à Genève au temps de Calvin. Geneva. 1897.
Hundeshagen, K. B. Ueber den Einfluss des Calvinismus auf die Idee vom Staat und staatsbürgerlicher Freiheit. Bern. 1842.
Merle d'Aubigné. Jean Calvin, un des fondateurs dès libertés modernes. Paris. 1868.
Tissot, F. Les relations entre l'Église et l'État à Genève au temps de Calvin. Lausanne. 1874.
Weber, G. Geschichtliche Darstellung des Calvinismus im Verhältniss zum Staat in Genf und Frankreich. Heidelberg. 1836.

VIII. COMPARATIVE ESTIMATES

Beard, C. The Reformation of the 16th century. London. 1883.
Gaberel, J. Calvin et Rousseau. Geneva. 1878.
Viguet, C. O. Étude sur le caractère distinctif de Calvin. Geneva. 1864.

IX. GENERAL CHURCH HISTORY

Baur, F. C. Geschichte der christlichen Kirche. Vol. IV. Tübingen. 1863.
Fisher, G. P. The Reformation. London. 1873.
Gieseler, J. C. L. Lehrbuch der Kirchengeschichte. Bonn. 1855.
Hardwick, C. A history of the Christian Church during the Reformation. London. 1873.
Hase, K. A. Kirchengeschichte. Leipzig. 1886.
Häusser, L. The period of the Reformation. 2 vols. London. 1873.
Kurtz, J. H. Church History. Transl. by J. Macpherson. Vol. II. London. 1890.
Möller, W. Kirchengeschichte. Vol. III. Freiburg i. B. 1894.
Rothe, Richard. Kirchengeschichte. Heidelberg. 1875.

X. CALVIN AND FRENCH LITERATURE

Gérusez, E. Histoire de la littérature française. Paris. 1872.
——— Histoire de l'éloquence politique et religieuse en France, pp. 192–285. 1837.
Nisard, D. Histoire de la littérature française. Paris. 1844.
Petit de Julleville, L. Histoire de la langue et de la littérature française (pp. 319–354, Théologiens et prédicateurs). Paris. 1897.
Sayous, A. Études littéraires sur les écrivains français de la Réformation. Paris. 1841.

CHAPTER XII

THE CATHOLIC SOUTH

MANUSCRIPTS

Pietro Speziali de Gratia Dei is still in MS. in the St Mark's Library at Venice.

Many letters and papers of Renée are in the Turin archives, at Rome, Florence, and Modena.

Carnesecchi's process is in the Archives of Trinity College, Dublin, and Caracciolo's Life of Pius IV, in many transcripts, at Rome (Barberini), Naples, and London (Brit. Mus. Harl.).

The process of Carranza is in the Library of the Real Academia de la Historia at Madrid.

The documents of the Inquisition at Udine, Modena, Naples, Palermo, and elsewhere have not yet been entirely used for historical purposes.

PUBLISHED DOCUMENTS

Artigny, A. G. de. Nouveaux Mémoires d'histoire. Paris. 1749. Vol. II. [The process against Serveto at Vienne.]

Beccadelli, L. Monumenti. Ed. G. Morandi. 3 vols. Bologna. 1797, 1799, 1804.

Bembo, P. (Card.). Opere. Ed. Morelli. 12 vols. Milan. 1808-10.

Biblioteca della Riforma Italiana. 1883 f.

Boehmer, E. Epistolae quaedam Joannis Sturmii et Hispanorum qui Argentorati degerunt. 1872.

Cabré, A. Cartas de San Ignacio de Loyola. Madrid. 1874 etc.

Caracciolo, A. De vita Pauli IV collectanea historica. Cologne. 1612.

Castelvetro, L. Opere, colla vita dell' autore scritta dal L. A. Muratori. Bern. 1727.

Contarini, G. Regesten u. Briefe des Cardinals C. Ed. F. Dittrich. Braunsberg. 1881.

—— Opera. Paris. 1571.

Crespin, J. Histoire des Martyrs persécutés et mis à mort pour la vérité de l'Évangile. 1585. New edition. Toulouse. 1885.

Documentos ineditos para la historia de España. Vols. V, X, XI, XL, LXVIII. 1842 etc.

Doellinger, I. von. Beiträge zur Geschichte. Vol. I. Ratisbon. 1862.

Enzinas, F. de (Dryander). Epistolae quinquaginta. In Kahnis's Zeitschrift für die historische Theologie, 1870, pp. 387 ff. Leipzig.

—— Mémoires. Ed. Campan. 2 vols. Brussels. 1862-3. German translation with notes by E. Boehmer. Bonn. 1893.

Fazy, H. Procès de Valentin Gentilis et de Nicolas Gallo. In Mémoires de l'Institut national Génevois. Vol. XIV. Geneva. 1878.

Ferrero, E., and Müller, G. Carteggio di Vittoria Colonna. Turin. 1889.

Fontana, B. Documenti Vaticani contro l' eresia luterana in Italia. Archivio della R. Soc. Rom. di Storia Patria. Vol xv. Rome. 1892.

Friedensburg, W. Nuntiaturen des Vergerio. Gotha. 1892.

—— Nuntiaturen des Morone. Gotha. 1892.

Frizzi, A. Memorie per la storia di Ferrara. Ed. Laderchi. Vol. iv. Ferrara. 1848.

Galiffe, J. B. G. Le Réfuge italien de Genève aux xvie et xviie Siècles. 1881.

Gar, T. Relazioni della Corte di Roma. E. Albéri, Relazioni degli ambasciatori Veneti, Ser. ii, vols. iii, iv. Florence. 1846, 1857.

Gibbings, R. Trial and Martyrdom of P. Carnesecchi. Dublin. 1856.

—— The Roman Index Expurgatorius. Dublin. 1837.

Graziani, A. M. Vita Commendoni Cardinalis. Paris. 1669.

Henriques, G. J. C. [W. J. C. Henry]. Ineditos Goesianos. Vol. ii. (O processo na Inquisição.) Lisbon. 1899.

Herminjard, A. L. Correspondance des Réformateurs. Esp. vols. iv, vii. Geneva. 1878, 1886.

Kausler, E., and Schott, T. Briefwechsel zwischen Chr. Herzog von Württemberg und P. P. Vergerius. Stuttgart. 1875.

Laemmer, H. Monumenta Vaticana. Freiburg in Breisgau. 1861.

Leva, G. de. Eretici di Cittadella. Atti dell' Instituto Veneto, pp. 679–772. Venice. 1872–3.

Loaysa, G. de. Briefe an Kaiser Karl V. Ed. G. Heine. [Spanish text and German translation published separately.] Berlin. 1848.

Miscellanea di Storia Italiana. Vols. vi, x, xv. 1869 etc.

Noltenius, G. L. Vita Olympiae Moratae. Ed. J. G. V. Hesse. Frankfort on the Oder. 1775.

Paleario, A. Opera. Ed. F. A. Hallbauer. Jena. 1728.

Pastor, L. Correspondenz des Cardinals Contarini. In Historisches Jahrbuch i. 1880.

Philip II. Correspondance sur les affaires des Pays Bas. Ed. L. P. Gachard. Vols. i, ii. Brussels. 1848.

Pole, R. (Card.). Epistolae. Ed. A. M. Quirini. 5 vols. Brescia. 1744-45-48-52.

Rebello da Silva, L. A. Corpo Diplomatico Portuguez. Vols. ii.–v. Lisbon. 1865–68–70–74.

Reformistas antiguos españoles. 20 vols. (A description by Wilkens in Brieger's Zeitschrift für Kirchengeschichte ix 341. Gotha. 1847–80.)

Reusch, F. H. Die Indices librorum prohibitorum des sechszehnten Jahrhunderts. Stuttgart. 1887.

Reyna, Cassiodoro de. Epistolae xiii. Ed. Boehmer. In Kahnis, Zeitschrift für die historische Theologie xl, 285 ff. Leipzig.

Ribadeneira, P. de. Vida del P. Ignacio de Loyola, etc. Madrid. 1594.

Rilliet, J. H. A. Relation du procès intenté à Genève en 1553 contre Michel Servet. 1844. Reprinted in Calvin's Works. viii. 1870.

Sadoleto, J. Opera. 4 vols. Venice. 1737-8.

Sanuto, M. Diarii. Venice. 1879 etc.

Sepulveda, J. G. de. Opera. 4 vols. Madrid. 1780.

Serristori, A. Legazioni. Florence. 1853.

State Papers, Calendar of Venetian. v. Ed. by Rawdon Brown. London. 1873.

Valdés, A. de. Litterae xl ineditae. Ed. E. Boehmer. In Homenaje a Menéndez y Pelayo. Ed. by Juan Valera. Vol. i. Madrid. 1899.

—— J. de. Tradaitos. Ed. E. Boehmer. Bonn. 1880. And other tracts of Valdés edited by Boehmer.

Vergerio, P. P. Opera. Tübingen. 1563.

Wiffen, B. B. Life and writings of Juan Valdés, with a translation of his CX. Considerations by J. T. Betts. London. 1865.

PRINCIPAL HISTORIES

Boehmer, E. Bibliotheca Wiffeniana, Spanish Reformers of two Centuries from 1520. 2 vols. published. Strassburg and London. 1874, 1883.
Cantù, C. Gli Eretici d' Italia. 3 vols. Turin. 1865-7.
Carvalho, A. Herculano de. Historia da Origem e do Estabelecimento da Inquisição em Portugal. 3 vols. Lisbon. 1864, 1867, 1872.
Castro, A. de. Historia de los Protestantes españoles. Cadiz. 1851. Eng. translation by T. Parker. London. 1851.
Comba, E. I nostri Protestanti. 2 vols. published. Florence. 1881, 1897.
Gerdes, D. Specimen Italiae Reformatae. Leyden. 1765.
Leva, G. de. Storia Documentata di Carlo V. Vol. III. Venice. 1867.
Llorente, J. A. Histoire critique de l'Inquisition d'Espagne. 4 vols. Paris. 1818.
McCrie, T. History of the Reformation in Italy. Edinburgh. 1827. New edition, 1855.
—— History of the Reformation in Spain. Edinburgh. 1829. New edition, 1855.
Menéndez y Pelayo, M. Historia de los Heterodoxos Españoles. 3 vols. Madrid. 1880-2.
Philippson, M. Zeitalter von Philipp II. und Elizabeth. 2 vols. Berlin. 1882-3.
—— La Contre-Révolution religieuse du XVIe siècle. 1884.
Schäfer, E. Beiträge zur Geschichte des spanischen Protestantismus und der Inquisition. 3 vols. Gütersloh. 1902.
Wilkens, C. A. Geschichte des spanischen Protestantismus. Gütersloh. 1888.

SPECIAL TREATISES

(Many of the following books contain documents previously unpublished.)

Agostini, A. Pietro Carnesecchi e il Movimento Valdesiano. Florence. 1899.
Amabili, L. Il santo Officio della Inquisizione in Napoli. 2 vols. Città di Castello. 1892.
Amante, B. Giulia Gonzaga. Bologna. 1896.
Antonio, N. Bibliotheca Hispana Nova. 2 vols. Madrid. 1783-8.
Barros y Sousa, M. F. de. *See* Santarem.
Battistella, A. Il s. Officio e la Riforma in Friuli. (With documents.) Udine. 1895.
Benrath, K. Über die Quellen der italienischen Reformations-Geschichte. Bonn. 1876.
—— Bernardino Ochino von Siena. Leipzig. 1875. New Edition. 1892. English translation without the documents. London. 1876.
—— Geschichte der Reformation in Venedig. Halle. 1887.
—— Julia Gonzaga. Halle. 1900.
Bernino, D. Istoria di tutte l' Eresie. IV. Venice. 1745.
Bertolotti, A. Martiri del libero pensiero. 1891.
Bock, F. S. Historia Antitrinitariorum. Vol. II. Königsberg and Leipzig. 1784.
Boehmer, E. Franzisca Hernandez und Frai Franzisco Ortiz. Leipzig. 1865.
Bonnet, J. Vie d'Olympia Morata. 3rd ed. Paris. 1856.
Boverio da Saluzzo, Z. Annali de' Fratri minori Cappucini. Venice. 1643.
Braun, W. Cardinal Gasparo Contarini. 1903.
Bruni, L. Cosimo I. de' Medici e il processo d' eresia del Carnesecchi. Turin. 1891.
Caballero, F. A. Vida de Melchor Cano. Madrid. 1871.
—— Juan y Alfonso Valdés. Madrid. 1875.
Cantù, C. Storia degli Italiani. Vol. X. 1876.

Cantù, C. Italiani illustri. Vol. II. Milan. 1879.

Carrasco, M. Alfonso et Juan de Valdés. Geneva. 1880.

Cecchetti, B. La republica di Venezia e la corte di Roma. 2 vols. Venice. 1874.

Christ, E. Spanische Glaubenshelden. Basel. 1886.

Coligny, L. L'antitrinitarianisme à Genève au temps de Calvin. 1873.

Cuccoli, E. M. Antonio Flaminio. Bologna. 1897.

Davari, S. Cenni storici intorno al Tribunale della Inquisizione in Mantova. Archivio Storico Lombardo VI. Milan. 1879.

Dittrich, F. Gasparo Contarini. Braunsberg. 1885.

Doumergue, E. Jean Calvin. Vol. II. Lausanne. 1903.

Droin, M. Histoire de la Réformation en Espagne. 2 vols. Lausanne and Paris. 1880.

Elze, Th. Geschichte der protestantischen Bewegungen in Venedig. Bielefeld. 1883.

Feliciangeli, B. Notizie sulla Caterina Cibo. Camerino. 1891.

Ferrai, E. Studi Storici, pp. 88–173. 1892.

Fontana, B. Renata di Francia. 3 vols. (Vol. II. Documents.) Rome. 1889–99.

Gerdes, D. Scrinium Antiquarium sive Miscellanea Groningana. 8 vols. Bremen. 1749–65.

Hoefler, C. von. Papst Adrian VI. Vienna. 1880.

Hoermann, A. Francisco de Enzinas und sein Kreis. 1902.

Hubert, F. Vergerio's publizistische Thätigkeit. Göttingen. 1893.

Jahrbücher für protestantische Theologie. III. Hase on Carnesecchi and Altieri. IV. Benrath on Caraffa, etc. Leipzig. 1877–78.

Jensen, O. Gio. Pietro Caraffa og de religiöse Strömninger i Italien paa hans Tid. Copenhagen. 1880.

Lafuente, M. Historia general de España. Vol. XIII. Madrid. 1854.

La Fuente, V. de. Historia Eclesiastica de España. Vol. V, pp. 205–266. Madrid. 1874.

La Mantia, V. Origine e Vicende dell' Inquisizione in Sicilia. 1886.

Lassalle, J. La Réforme en Espagne au XVIe siècle. Paris. 1883.

Laugwitz, H. Bartholomäus Carranza. Kempten. 1870.

Linde, A. van der. Michael Servet, een brandoffer der gereformeerde inquisitie. Groningen. 1891.

Lüben, W. Gaetano di Tiene. 1883.

Maurenbrecher, W. Studien und Skizzen zur Geschichte der Reformationszeit. Leipzig. 1874.

—— Geschichte der katholischen Reformation. Vol. I. Nördlingen. 1880.

Mossolin, B. Giangiorgio Trissino. 1878.

Muratori, L. A. Delle Antichità Estensi ed Italiane. 2 vols. Modena. 1717–40.

Ploncher, A. Della vita e delle opere di Ludovico Castelvetro. 1879.

Porta, P. D. R. de. Historia reformationis ecclesiarum Raeticarum. 3 vols. Chur. 1771, 1776, 1786.

Ranke, L. von. Die römischen Päpste. I. Vol. XXXVII of Sämmtliche Werke, Leipzig, 1874 etc.

Reumont, A. von. Vittoria Colonna. Freiburg i. B. 1881. Italian translation by Müller and Ferrero, with additions by the Author. Turin. 1883.

Reusch, F. H. Luis de León. Bonn. 1873.

—— Der Index der verbotenen Bücher. Vol. I. Bonn. 1885.

Roberti, G. B. Notizie storico-critiche della vita de Francesco Negri. 1839.

Rodocanachi, E. Renée de France, in G. Guenard's Conférences de la Société d'études italiennes. Paris. 1895, 1896.

Rodrigo, F. J. G. Historia de la Inquisicion. II. Madrid. 1877.

Rosi, M. La Riforma religiosa in Liguria. Atti della Società ligure di Storia Patria. XXIV. Genoa. 1894.

Sandonnini, T. Ludovico Castelvetro. Bologna. 1882.

Santarem, M. F. de Barros, y Sousa, Visc. de, and others. Quadro Elementar das Relações Politicas de Portugal. Vols. X, XI, XII. Paris and Lisbon. 1866, 1869, 1874.

Schellhorn, J. G. Amoenitates Literariae. 14 vols. Frankfort and Leipzig. 1725-31.
—— Amoen. Historiae ecclesiasticae et litterariae. 2 vols. **Frankfort and Leipzig.** 1737-8.
—— De Consilio de emendanda Ecclesia. Zurich. 1748.
—— Ergötzlichkeiten aus der Kirchenhistorie und Literatur. 3 vols. Ulm and Leipzig. 1761-4.
Schiess, T. Rhetia, von F. Niger aus Bassano. [With biographical notice of Negri.] Chur. 1897.
Schmidt, C. Peter Martyr Vermigli. Elberfeld. 1858.
Sclopis, F. Le Cardinal Jean Morone. 1869.
Sixt, C. H. Petrus Paulus Vergerius. Brunswick. 1855. Later edition with additions. 1871.
Ticknor, G. History of Spanish Literature. 3 vols. 4th ed. Boston, Mass. 1872.
Tiraboschi, G. Biblioteca Modenese. 6 vols. Modena. 1781-6.
—— Storia della Litteratura Italiana. vii. Milan. 1822.
Tollin, H. Das Lehrsystem M. Servets. 3 vols. Gütersloh. 1876-8-9.
Trechsel, F. Die protestantischen Antitrinitarier. 2 vols. Heidelberg. 1839-44.
Vasconcellos, J. de. Damião de Goes. Oporto. 1897.
Vecchiato, E. L' Inquisizione sacra a Venezia. 1891.
Young, M. Life and Times of Aonio Paleario. 2 vols. London. 1860.

See also Articles, etc., in

> La Ciudad de Dios. Valladolid. 1887 ff.
> Revista de España. Madrid. 1868-1896.
> Rivista Cristiana. Florence. 1873-1887.
> Brieger's Zeitschrift für Kirchengeschichte. Gotha. 1876 ff.
> Wetzer-Welte, Kirchenlexicon. Ed. F. Kaulen. Freiburg i. B. 1886 ff.
> Raumer's Historisches Taschenbuch. Leipzig. 1882.
> Archivio Storico Italiano. xv, xvi. Florence. 1856-57.
> Herzog-Hauck, Real-Encyklopädie für protestantische Theologie. Leipzig. 1877 f.

(See also Bibliography of Chapter XVIII.)

CHAPTER XIII

HENRY VIII

UNPUBLISHED MATERIAL

There is but little unpublished matter of historical value connected with the reign of Henry VIII except State papers in English and foreign Archives; and of these full notices will be found in the Calendars published for the Master of the Rolls, with specific references to the sources. Of the collections in foreign countries the most important are: —

At Paris. Archives du Ministère des Affaires Étrangères. *See below under* Published Documents, Kaulek, J., *and* Lefèvre-Pontalis, G.

At Simancas. Archivo General. Transcripts by Bergenroth are in the British Museum, Add. MSS. 28572–28595.

At Venice, Milan, etc. *See* Calendars, Venetian, *under* Published Documents.

At Rome. Vatican Archives and other Transcripts are in the Public Record Office. Notices of the documents will be found, each under its date, in the Calendar of Letters and Papers. *See also* Laemmer, H.; Theiner, A.; and Ehses, S., *under* Published Documents.

At Vienna. Transcripts of the Archives relating to England are in the Public Record Office, and notices of each separate document will be found under date in the Letters and Papers, and also in the Spanish Calendar.

ENGLAND

EARLY CHRONICLES AND HISTORIES

General

Chronicle of the Grey Friars of London. Ed. by J. G. Nichols. Camden Soc. 1859.

Chronicle of Calais. Ed. by J. G. Nichols. Camden Society. London. 1846.

Chronicle (Spanish) of King Henry VIII. Translated by M. A. S. Hume. London. 1889. [A strange, confused account by a Spaniard who was in England in the end of the reign.]

Fabyan, Robert. Chronicles. Ed. by Ellis. 1811.

Hall, E. Chronicle. London. 1548. Reprinted, 1809.

Herbert, Edward, Lord, of Cherbury. Life and Reign of Henry VIII. London. 1649 etc. (May be consulted in Kennett's Complete History of England. Vol. II. 1706.)

Holinshed, R. Chronicles. Vols. II and III. London. 1587.

London Chronicle in the times of Henry VII and Henry VIII. Ed. C. Hopper. Camden Miscellany. Vol. IV. 1859.

Stow, J. Chronicle. London. 1615.

Wriothesley, C. Chronicle. Vol. I. Ed. W. D. Hamilton. Camden Soc. 1875.

Special

Cavendish, G. Life of Wolsey. Kelmscott ed. 1898.

Chauncy, M. Historia aliquot Martyrum. Ed. V. M. Doreau. London. 1888.

Foxe, J. Acts and Monuments. Townsend's ed. Vols. IV, V. 1846.

—— Narratives of the Reformation. Ed. J. G. Nichols. Camden Soc. 1859.

Harpsfield, N. Treatise of the pretended Divorce between Henry VIII and Catherine of Aragon. Ed. N. Pocock. Camden Soc. 1878.

More, Cresacre. Life and death of Sir Thomas More. Ed. J. Hunter. London. 1828.

Ortroy, Van (Bollandist). Vie du bienheureux Martyr, Jean Fisher. Brussels. 1893.

Roper, W. Life of Sir T. More. Paris. 1626. Chiswick. 1817.

Sanders, N. Historia Schismatis Anglicani. Cologne. 1628.

—— —— Translation by D. Lewis. London. 1877.

Stapleton, T. Tres Thomae. (Sir T. More being one.) Cologne. 1612.

PUBLISHED DOCUMENTS

Actenstücke und Briefe zur Geschichte Kaiser Karls V. Monumenta Habsburgica. (Kaiserliche Akademie der Wissenschaften.) Vienna. 1853, 1857.

Baga de Secretis, Calendar of. Third Report of Dep. Keeper of the Public Records. App. II, 234–268.

Bradford, William. Correspondence of Charles V and his Ambassadors at the Courts of England and France. London. 1850.

Calendars, Rolls Series :—

    Letters and Papers, Henry VIII. Vols. III and following. Edd. J. S. Brewer, James Gairdner, R. H. Brodie. 1867 etc.

    Spanish State Papers. Vols. II and following. Edd. G. A. Bergenroth and P. de Gayangos. 1866 etc.

    Venetian. Vols. III–V. Ed. Rawdon Brown. 1869–73.

    Carew MSS. (1515–74). Edd. J. S. Brewer and W. Buller. 1867. [Vowell's Life of Sir Peter Carew, printed at the end of the Introduction, contains at pp. lxxx, lxxxi an account of the loss of *the Mary Rose*.]

Collier, J. P. Trevelyan Papers. Pts I and II. Camden Soc. 1857, 1863.

Dasent, J. R. Acts of the Privy Council. New Series. Vol. I. Rolls Series. 1890.

Ehses, S. Römische Dokumente zur Geschichte der Ehescheidung Heinrichs VIII von England, 1527–1534. Paderborn. 1893.

Ellis, Sir H. Original Letters. Three Series. 1824–46.

Erasmi Epistolae. London. 1642. Another edition, by Leclerc, published at Leyden. 1703. — [The Epistles of Erasmus, translated and arranged in order of time by F. M. Nichols — only comes down, at least at present, to the accession of Henry VIII; but is of great value to the student.]

Excerpta Historica. 1831. pp. 260–5, 290–2.

Gee, H., and Hardy, W. H. Documents illustrative of English Church History. London. 1896.

Hales, J. A Discourse of the Commonweal of this realm of England. 1549. Ed. by E. Lamond. Cambridge. 1893.

Hamy's Entrevue. *See next Section.*

Haynes, S. State Papers, 1542-70. London. 1740.

Henry VIII's Love Letters to Anne Boleyn. Published by Hearne, App. to Robert of Avesbury, 347-361, and in the Harleian Miscellany, vol. III, 47-60; also by Editor of the *Historia Britonum* [W. Gunn] in the Pamphleteer, vol. XXI, 346-8 and vol. XXII, 114-123, with some valuable additional documents. They have also been published at Paris by Crapelet in an 8º volume, with the addition of a contemporary French poem containing a life of Anne Boleyn written a fortnight after her execution.

Historical MSS. Commission:— Calendar of the MSS. of the Marquis of Salisbury. Pt I. 1883.

Jessopp, A. Monastic Visitations in the Diocese of Norwich. Camden Soc. 1888.

Kaulek, J. Correspondance politique de MM. de Castillon et de Marillac. Paris. 1885.

Laemmer, H. Monumenta Vaticana. Freiburg i. B. 1861.

Lanz, Karl. Correspondenz des Kaisers Karl V. Vols. I, II. Leipzig. 1844-5.

Leach, A. F. Visitations of Southwell. Camden Soc. 1891.

Lefèvre-Pontalis, G. Correspondance politique d'Odet de Selve. Commission des Archives Diplomatiques. Paris. 1888.

Merriman, R. B. Life and letters of Thomas Cromwell. 2 vols. Oxford. 1902. [The collection of letters includes all those known to have been written by Cromwell.]

Nichols, J. G. Inventories of the Household Stuff of Henry Fitzroy Duke of Richmond, and of Katherine Princess Dowager. Camden Miscellany. Vol. III. 1885.

Nicolas, Sir N. H. Proceedings and Ordinances of the Privy Council. Record Commission. Vol. VII.

Pocock, N. Records of the Reformation. 2 vols. Oxford. 1870.

Pole, Cardinal R. Epistolæ. Ed. Quirini. Brixen. 1744-57.

Rutland Papers. Ed. Jerdan. Camden Soc. 1842.

Rymer, T. Fœdera. Vols. XIV, XV. 1st ed.

Scotland. The late Expedicion in Scotlande . . . under the Erle of Hertforde, 1544. Printed by Reynold Wolfe, 1544. Reprinted by John Graham Dalzell in Fragments of Scottish History. Edinburgh. 1798.

State Papers, Henry VIII. 11 vols. Published by the Government. 1830-52. Vol. I (in two Parts) contains Domestic State Papers; vols. II, III, Irish; vols. IV, V, Scotch; vols. VI-XI, Foreign.

Statute of the Realm. Vol. III. 1817.

Theiner, A. Vetera Monumenta Hibernorum et Scotorum historiam illustrantia. Romæ. 1864.

Turnbull, W. B. Account of Monastic Treasures confiscated at the Dissolution. By Sir John Williams, master and treasurer of the jewels to Henry VIII. Abbotsford Club. Edinburgh. 1836.

Wilkins, D. Concilia. Vol. III. 1737.

Wright, T. Suppression of the Monasteries. Camden Soc. 1843.

See also Collections in the Church Histories of Burnet, Collier, and Dodd.

PRINCIPAL MODERN HISTORIES

So much new light has been thrown upon this period, that all previous general histories of England, such as those of Hume, Rapin, Lingard, and Froude, require very material correction as well as enlargement. The same is also the case with the most familiar Church Histories, viz. those of Burnet, Collier, and Dodd, though their collections of documents are of great value. The following works may be named as embodying some of the results of recent research : —

Brewer, J. S. The Reign of Henry VIII. 2 vols. London. 1884.

Clowes, W. L. The Royal Navy. Vol. I. London. 1897.

Dixon, R. W. History of the Church of England. Vols. I, II. London. 1878, 1881.

Doreau, V. M. Henri VIII et les Martyrs de la Chartreuse de Londres. Paris. 1890.

Du Boys, A. Catherine d'Aragon et les Origines du Schisme Anglican. Geneva. 1880. Translation by C. M. Yonge. 2 vols. London. 1881.

Friedmann, P. Anne Boleyn. 2 vols. 1884.

Gairdner, James. The English Church in the Sixteenth Century. 1902.

Gasquet, F. A. Henry VIII and the English Monasteries. 2 vols. London. 1888. Revised popular edition in one volume. London. 1899.

Green, M. A. E. Lives of the Princesses of England. Vols. IV and V. London. 1849–55.

Hamy, A. Entrevue de François Premier avec Henry VIII à Boulogne sur Mer en 1532. Paris. 1898. With valuable collection of documents.

Hendriks, L. The London Charter-house. London. 1889.

Merriman, R. B. Life and Letters of Thomas Cromwell. 2 vols. Oxford. 1902.

Pollard, A. F. Henry VIII. London. 1902. [With valuable engravings from contemporary pictures.]

Ranke, L. von. Englische Geschichte, vornehmlich im sechzehnten und siebzehnten Jahrhundert. Vol. I. Vol. XIV of Sämmtliche Werke. Berlin. 1874 etc.

—— A History of England (translation of the preceding). Vol. I. Oxford. 1875.

Strickland, A. Lives of the Queens of England. Vol. II. London. 1854.

Stubbs, W. (Bishop). Seventeen Lectures on the Study of Medieval and Modern History. Lectures XI, XII. Oxford. 1887. 1900.

Auxiliary Information

Anderson, C. The Annals of the English Bible. 2 vols. London. 1845.

Armstrong, E. Charles V. London. 1902.

Ashley, W. J. Introduction to English Economic History. London. 1892.

Bapst, E. Deux Gentilshommes-Poètes de la Cour de Henri VIII. Paris. 1891.

Bridgett, T. E. Lives of Fisher (1888) and More (1891).

Busch, W. Cardinal Wolsey und die englisch-kaiserliche Allianz, 1522–5. Bonn. 1886.

—— Der Ursprung der Ehescheidung König Heinrichs VIII. von England. Historisches Taschenbuch, Sechste Folge, VIII, 271–327.

—— Der Sturz des Cardinals Wolsey. Historisches Taschenbuch, Sechste Folge, IX, 39–114.

Creighton, M. (Bishop). Cardinal Wolsey. Twelve English Statesmen Series. London. 1888.

Cunningham, W. Growth of English Industry and Commerce. Cambridge. 1896.

Du Bellay, Martin. Mémoires. Michaud et Poujoulat. V.

Early English Text Society's Publications : — England in the Reign of Henry VIII. 1871, 1878.

—— Four Supplications. 1871.

English Historical Review. XI, 673–702. XII, 1–16. 237–253. London. 1896–7.

Furnivall, F. J. Ballads from MSS. Ballad Society. 1868–72.

Gasquet, F. A. The Eve of the Reformation. London. 1900.

Gratianus, Orthuinus. Fasciculus Rerum expetendarum et fugiendarum. Cum Appendice operâ Edwardi Brown. London. 1690.

Jacqueton, G. La Politique extérieure de Louise de Savoie. Paris. 1892.

Jusserand, J. A. A. F. English Wayfaring Life in the Middle Ages. Translated by L. Toulmin Smith. London. 1892.

Leadam, I. S. The Domesday of Inclosures, 1517–8. Royal Hist. Soc. London. 1897. Comp. Royal Hist. Society's Transactions, N.S. VI, 167; VII, 127; VIII, 251 and XIV, 231–303.

Mignet, F. A. M. Rivalité de François I et de Charles Quint. Paris. 1875.

Mullinger, J. B. The University of Cambridge. Vols. I and II. Cambridge. 1873, 1884.

Oppenheim, M. A History of the Administration of the Royal Navy and of Merchant Shipping in relation to the Navy. 1506–1660. London. 1897.

Pauli, R. Aufsätze zur Englischen Geschichte. Leipzig. 1869.

—— —— Neue Folge. Leipzig. 1883.

—— Drei volkswirthschaftliche Denkschriften aus der Zeit Heinrichs VIII. Göttingen. 1878. In vol. XXIII of Abhandlung der Königlichen Gesellschaft der Wissenschaften zu Göttingen.

Rogers, J. E. T. The History of Agriculture and Prices. Vol. IV. Oxford. 1882.

Royal Historical Society's Publications (*see also* Leadam, I. S.) :—
  Transactions, Old Series. IV, 260. Memoir of Geo. Wishart. By Ch. Rogers. VIII, 242. Henry VIII's 'Assertio Septem Sacramentorum.' By J. M. Brown.
  —— New Series. VI, 167. The Inquisition of 1517; also VIII, 127 and VIII, 251. By I. S. Leadam. VII, 21. Notes on the Family of Betoun. By H. E. Malden. IX, 167. The Tudors and the Currency. By C. W. C. Oman. XIII, 75. The Fall of Cardinal Wolsey. By J. Gairdner. XIV, 231. The Inquisitions of Depopulation in 1517. By E. F. Gay (in answer to Leadam).

Russell, F. W. Kett's Rebellion in Norfolk. London. 1859.

Schanz, G. Die Handelsbeziehungen zwischen England und den Niederlanden, 1485–1547. Würzburg. 1879.

Seebohm, F. The Oxford Reformers of 1498. John Colet, Erasmus, Thomas More. 3rd ed. London. 1896.

Shaw, W. A. History of Currency. London. 1895.

Skelton, J. Poetical Works. Ed. A. Dyce. 2 vols. London. 1843.

Strype, John. 'Memorials of Cranmer' and 'Ecclesiastical Memorials,' valuable chiefly for their documents.

Trollope, E. On Anne Askew, in Associated Architectural Societies' Report, VI, 117–134.

Westcott, B. F. (Bishop). History of the English Bible. London. 1868.

Wood, Ant. à. Hist. and Antiquities of the University of Oxford. Vol. II. Oxford. 1796.

SCOTLAND

See Bibliography in Brown, P. H. History of Scotland. Vol. I. Cambridge. 1899.

PUBLISHED DOCUMENTS

Bannatyne Miscellany. Vol. I. Edin.

Exchequer Rolls of Scotland. Vols. XV–XVIII. Ed. by G. P. McNeill. Register House Series.

Hamilton Papers. 2 vols. Ed. by J. Bain. Register House Series.

Register of the Privy Council of Scotland. Vol. I. Ed. by J. H. Burton. Register House Series.

Ruddimann, T. Epistolæ Jacobi Quarti, Jacobi Quinti et Mariæ, Regum Scotorum. Edin. 1722–4.

State Papers. *See above.* [Vols. IV and V relate to Scotland.]

Teulet, A. Papiers d'État . . . relatifs à l'histoire de l'Écosse. Bannatyne Club. Vol. I. Paris. [1851.]

—— Relations politiques de la France et de l'Espagne avec l'Écosse au 16ᵐᵉ siècle. Paris and Bordeaux. 1862. [Virtually identical in its contents with the preceding.]

Theiner, A. *See above*, England, Published Documents.

The late Expedicion in Scotlande. *See above*, ibid.

HISTORIES

Bapst, E. Les Mariages de Jaques V. Paris. 1889.

Brown, P. Hume. History of Scotland. Vols. I, II. Cambridge. 1899, 1902.

Buchanan, G. Rerum Scoticarum Historia. Edinburgh. 1582 etc.

—— —— Translation by Aikman. 4 vols. Glasgow. 1827.

Diurnal of Occurrents. Bannatyne Club. Edinburgh. 1833.

Green, M. A. E. Lives of the Princesses of England. Vol. IV.

Holinshed, R. Chronicles. Vol. I. London. 1587.

Herkless, J. Cardinal Beaton. Edin. 1891.

Knox, John. Works. Vol. I. History of the Reformation. Ed. by D. Laing. Bannatyne Club. Edinburgh. 1846.

Lesley, J. History of Scotland. Edin. 1830.

Pinkerton, J. History of Scotland. London. 1797.

Strickland, A. Lives of the Queens of Scotland. Vols. I, II. Edin. 1850–1.

Tytler, P. F. History of Scotland. Eadie's edition. Vol. II. Glasgow. [1873–7.]

Wright, Thomas. History of Scotland. 3 vols. London and New York. 1856.

IRELAND

PUBLISHED DOCUMENTS

Calendar of the State Papers relating to Ireland. Ed. H. C. Hamilton. Vol. I. 1860.

Calendar of the Carew MSS. at Lambeth. Ed. J. S. Brewer and W. Bullen. Vol. I. 1867.

State Papers, Henry VIII. *See above.* [Vols. II and III relate to Ireland.]

HISTORIES

Annals of the Four Masters. Ed. J. O'Donovan. Vol. III. Dublin. 1848.

Bagwell, R. Ireland under the Tudors. Vol. I. 1885.

Holinshed, R. Chronicles. Vol. I. London. 1587.

Richey, A. G. A short History of the Irish People. Dublin. 1887.

Wright, Thomas. History of Ireland. 2 vols. London. 1854.

CHAPTER XIV

THE REFORMATION UNDER EDWARD VI

MANUSCRIPTS

A. State Papers

The Domestic State Papers of the reign of Edward VI in the Record Office are comparatively scanty, there being only nineteen volumes in the regular series, and seven volumes of Addenda (consisting chiefly of documents relating to Scotland and the Borders). The Foreign State Papers include an imperfect series of despatches from English representatives abroad, transcripts of despatches from foreign ambassadors resident in England, and a series entitled the Calais Papers. Many were transcribed with a view to a new edition of Rymer's Foedera, and a list of them is printed in vol. III, pp. xxxiv-liii, of Hardy's Syllabus, 1885. There are also five volumes of State Papers relating to Scotland. For other diplomatic correspondence, see type-written Lists of Transcripts in the Record Office; and Reports 33, 36, 39, 42-7 of the Deputy Keeper of Records.

The State Papers at the British Museum are numerous, but, not as a rule being arranged according to subject, they are difficult to consult; there are, however, Bergenroth's Transcripts of Simancas Papers (Add. MSS. 28595-7) and a series of Scottish State Papers known as the Hamilton Papers (Add. MSS. 32091, 32647-8, 32654, and 32657). Other single volumes of great value are scattered throughout the Cotton, Harley, Lansdowne, Royal, Stowe, and Additional Collections, and the only guide to them is to be found in the various MS. Class Catalogues kept in the MSS. Department at the Museum. Some of the more important volumes are Edward VI's Journal (Cotton MS. Nero C. x), the Privy Council's Warrant Book (Royal MS. 18 C. xxiv), Starkey's collection of letters and papers (Harley MS. 353), and the documents relating to Somerset's agrarian policy (Lansdowne MS. 238).

The Privy Council's Register is at the Privy Council Office in Whitehall; the Inner Temple Library possesses a valuable collection of State Papers entitled the Petyt MSS.; the Talbot Papers in the College of Arms contain some six thousand public and private letters dating from the sixteenth century; the Marquis of Salisbury's collection at Hatfield includes some three hundred documents relating to the reign, and isolated State Papers are to be found in many other private libraries.

B. Miscellaneous MSS.

Besides State Papers, the Record Office contains a vast mass of materials to which the historian must have occasional recourse. Such are the Patent and Close Rolls, the records of the Star Chamber, the Admiralty Courts and Court of Requests, the Courts of Augmentations, First Fruits and Tenths, and the Baga de Secretis, which contains records of the state trials (cf. J. Scargill-Bird's Guide to the Record Office, 2nd ed. 1896). Acts of Parliament not printed in the Statutes at Large may be found in the Rolls of Parliament at the Record Office, but Acts not entered on the Roll and not printed in the Statutes at Large must be sought at the Parliament Office. The Society of Antiquaries possesses an interesting collection of MS. Proclamations.

C. Ecclesiastical Documents

The most important unpublished sources are the episcopal registers, particularly those of the Archbishop of Canterbury and the Bishop of London. The Records of Convocation were destroyed at the Fire of London, but a collection of Synodalia, 1547–1580, exists in Brit. Mus. Egerton MS. 2350. In the British Museum the Lansdowne Collection is particularly rich in ecclesiastical MSS.; volumes 335, 388, 389, 819, and 1045 contain some of Foxe the martyrologist's papers, and others are extant in Harley MSS. 416–426 and 590. The Royal Collection has other ecclesiastical documents of interest, particularly the report (Royal MS. 17 B xxxix) of the debate in the Lords on the first Act of Uniformity, the earliest report of a parliamentary debate extant (cf. also MS. Class Catalogue, 'Church History,' in Brit. Museum Department of MSS.). Corpus Christi College, Cambridge, has a valuable collection of Cranmer's papers bequeathed by Archbishop Parker (cf. Nasmith's Catalogus, 1777). There are also some MSS. of importance at Lambeth (see H. J. Todd's Catalogue, 1812).

CONTEMPORARY PRINTED AUTHORITIES

1. Calendars

The Calendar of Domestic State Papers (ed. Lemon, 1856) is inadequate, but the Addenda for Edward VI's reign (ed. M. A. E. Green, and appended 1870 to the Domestic Calendar for 1601–3) is more satisfactory. The Foreign Calendar (ed. Turnbull, 1861) is also adequate. The Scottish Calendar (ed. Thorpe, 1858) is superseded, so far as Edward VI's reign is concerned, by the Calendar of Scottish State Papers (ed. Bain, Edinburgh, 1898), and the Venetian Calendar (ed. Rawdon Brown, 1873) contains little of importance except Barbaro's Relation (pp. 338–362). The Hamilton Papers have been printed in full by the Lord Clerk Register of Scotland (2 vols., ed. Bain, Edinburgh, 1890).

2. Other Collections of State Papers

Correspondance Politique d'Odet de Selve. 1546–9. French Foreign Office. **Paris.** 1888.

Ribier, G. Lettres et Mémoires d'Estat. Paris. 2 vols. 1666.

Teulet, A. Relations Politiques de la France et de l'Espagne avec l'Écosse. **5 vols.** Paris. 1862.

—— Papiers d'État relatifs à l'histoire de l'Écosse au xvie siècle. **Bannatyne Club.** 3 vols. Edinburgh. 1851–60.

Vertot, l'Abbé. Ambassades des Noailles en Angleterre. 5 vols. Leyden. **1763.**

Weiss, C. Papiers d'État du Cardinal de Granvelle. Coll. de doc. Inédits. **9 vols.** Paris. 1841–52.

A few documents relating to the period are also printed in the Hardwicke Papers, edited by the 2nd Earl of Hardwicke, 2 vols., London, 1778; and the Sadlier State Papers, edited by A. Clifford, 2 vols., Edinburgh, 1809.

3. Collections of Private Letters and Papers

Ellis, Sir H. Original Letters. (From the British Museum.) 11 vols. London. 1824–1846.

Haynes, S. Burghley State Papers. London. 1740.

Kempe, A. J. Loseley MSS. (Selections from Papers at Loseley Park, Guildford.) London. 1835.

Lodge, E. Illustrations of British History, etc. (Letters in the College of Arms.) 2nd ed. 3 vols. London. 1838.

Pocock, N. Troubles connected with the First Book of Common Prayer. (Papers selected from the Petyt MSS.) Camden Soc. London. 1884.

Reports and Appendices to Reports of the Historical MSS. Commission. (These are too numerous to be mentioned in detail; the most important is the Calendar of Lord Salisbury's MSS. The Papers at Longleat are inadequately represented in the Report, but some of the more interesting are printed in the Wilts Archæological Magazine, vols. xv, xvi; compare also 1st Rep. App., p. 42, 2nd Rep. App., pp. 41, 45, 151, 152.)

4. Parliamentary and Official

Acts of the Privy Council. Ed. J. R. Dasent. Vols. ii–iv. London. 1890–2.

Dumont, J. Corps Universel Diplomatique. 8 vols. The Hague. 1725.

Journals of the House of Commons. Vol. i. London, n. d.

Journals of the House of Lords. Vol. i. London, n. d.

Official Return of Members of Parliament. 4 pts. London. 1878–1891. [These are the only lists of members extant, but they are very incomplete in the 16th century.]

Proclamations. London. 1550. (A collected volume of Proclamations. 1547–1550.)

Rymer, T. Foedera. Original ed. 1704–1717. 17 vols.

Statutes of the Realm. Record Commission. Vol. iv, Pt 1. 1819.

See also the Reports of the Deputy-Keeper of Records; esp. Appendix to Rep. iv, summarising the contents of the Baga de Secretis, and Lists and Indexes issued by the Record Office.

5. Contemporary Chronicles, Tracts, etc.

Chronicle of Queen Jane and Queen Mary. London. Camden Soc. 1850.

Cooper, T. Epitome of Chronicles.[1] London. 1560.

Grafton, R. Chronicle. London. 1568. New ed. 2 vols. London. 1809.

Greyfriars' Chronicle. Camden Soc. London. 1852.

Hoby, Sir T. Travels and Life, 1547–64. Camden Soc. Miscellany, vol. x, 1902.

Literary Remains of Edward VI. Roxburghe Club. Ed. J. G. Nichols. 2 vols. London. 1857. [Contains all the extant writings of the young King and prints many other illustrative documents. Edward VI's statements must always be received with caution, but these two volumes are the most valuable of all printed collections for the history of the reign.]

Machyn, H. Diary. Camden Soc. London. 1847.

Narratives of the Reformation. Camden Soc. London. 1860.

Ponet, Bishop. Treatise of Politicke Power. 1556. Other editions, 1639 and 1642.

Smith, Sir T. De Republica Anglorum. London. 1583. The only adequate contemporary account of the English constitution.

Spanish Chronicle of Henry VIII. Ed. M. A. S. Hume. London. 1889. [Untrustworthy.]

Wriothesley, C. Chronicle. Camden Soc. 2 vols. London. 1875.

6. Ecclesiastical

Bucer, M. Scripta Anglicana. Basel. 1577.

Cardwell, E. Documentary Annals of the Reformed Church of England. 2 vols. Oxford. 1844.

Foxe, J. Acts and Monuments. 8 vols. Ed. G. Townsend. London. 1843–9. [Contains a vast number of facts and documents, and its errors are certainly not greater than in similar works.]

Knox, John. Works. Bannatyne Club. 6 vols. Edinburgh. 1846–64. [Especially the Admonition to the Professors of the Truth in England.]

Pole, R. Epistolae. 5 vols. Brescia. 1744–57.

Sleidan. [Philippson, Jean.] Commentarii, Strassburg, 1555, and History of the Reformation from 1517 to 1556. Ed. 1689.

Sparrow, A. Collection of Articles, Injunctions, and Canons. London. 1661.

Wilkins, David. Concilia. London. 1737. 4 vols.

Zurich Letters and Original Letters. Parker Soc. 4 vols. 1845–7.

See also the works of Cranmer, Coverdale, Hooper, Latimer, Bale, Bradford, Bullinger, Becon, Hutchinson, Ridley (all published by the Parker Society). A similar Corpus of the works of Roman Catholic divines is needed. The most important contemporary statements of the Roman Catholic case are Gardiner's Explanation and Assertion of the True Catholic Faith, 1551, and Confutatio Cavillationum, Paris, 1552; Tunstall's De Veritate, Paris, 1554; and (Bishop) Thomas Watson's Wholesome and Catholic Doctrine (London, 1558, re-ed. by T. E. Bridgett, London, 1876).

7. Social and Economic

Ballads from MSS. Ballad Society. Ed. F. J. Furnivall. London. 1868.

Brynkelow, H. Complaynt of Roderick Mors. Early English Text Society. 1874.

Crowley, R. Works. Early English Text Society. 1872.

Discourse of the Commonweal. Ed. E. Lamond. Cambridge. 1893.

Four Supplications of the Commons. Early English Text Society. 1871.

Lever, Thomas. Sermons. Ed. E. Arber. London. 1871.

Starkey, Thomas. England under Henry VIII. Early English Text Soc. 1871.

Tusser, T. Hundred Points of Husbandry. London. 1557.

Wilson, T. Discourse upon Usury. London. 1572.

8. Relations with Scotland

Berteville, Sir J. Recit de l'Expédition en Écosse (1547). Bannatyne Club. 1825.

Patten, W. Expedition into Scotland. In Tudor Tracts. Ed. A. F. Pollard. Arber's English Garner. 1903.

The Complaynt of Scotland, Epitome of the King of England's Title to the Sovereignty of Scotland, Henryson's Godly and Golden Book, and Somerset's Epistle to the Nobility of Scotland, are all edited for the Early English Text Soc. 1872.

SECONDARY AUTHORITIES

A. General

Carte, T. History of England. 4 vols. London. 1747–55. Oxford. 6 vols. 1851.

Froude, J. A. History of England. 12 vols. London. 1856–1870. [The only History which has made adequate use of the foreign correspondence of the reign.]

Hayward, Sir J. Life and Reign of Edward VI. London. 1630.
Holinshed, Raphael. Chronicles. 3 vols. London. 1577.
Lingard, J. History of England. 8 vols. London. 1819–1830.
Pollard, A. F. England under Protector Somerset. 1900. (With bibliography.)
Rapin de Thoyras, Paul. Histoire d'Angleterre. 13 vols. The Hague. 1724–36.
Speed, J. History of Great Britain. London. 1611.
Stow, J. Annals. London. 1631.
Turner, S. Modern History of England. 2 vols. London. 1826, 1829.
Tytler, P. F. England in the Reigns of Edward VI and Mary. 2 vols. London. 1839.
    [Important for the documents printed in it.]

B. ECCLESIASTICAL

Blunt, J. H. The Reformation of the Church in England. London. Vol. II. 1896.
Burnet, G. History of the Reformation. 3 vols. London. 1679, 1715. Ed. Pocock.
    7 vols. Oxford. 1865. [The latter is an excellent edition, containing much new
    matter and Wharton's Specimen of Errors; originally published in 1693 under the
    pseudonym 'Anthony Harmer.']
Collier, Jeremy. Ecclesiastical History. Ed. Lathbury. 9 vols. London. 1852.
Dixon, R. W. History of the Church of England. Vols. II and III. 2nd ed. London.
    1893.
Dodd, C. Church History. Ed. Tierney. 5 vols. London. 1839–1843.
Fuller, T. Church History. London. 1655. Ed. J. S. Brewer. 6 vols. Oxford.
    1845.
Gairdner, J. The English Church from 1509 to 1558. London. 1902. (With biblio-
    graphical notes.)
Heylyn, P. Ecclesia Restaurata. London. 1661. Ed. Robertson. 2 vols. London.
    1849.
Maitland, S. R. Essays on the Reformation. London. 1899.
Sanders, N. De Origine ac Progressu Schismatis. Cologne. 1585. Transl. Lewis.
    London. 1877.
Soames, H. History of the Reformation. 4 vols. London. 1826–8.
Spelman, Sir H. History of Sacrilege. London. 1698.
Strype, J. Ecclesiastical Memorials and Life of Cranmer. London. (In Oxford edit.
    26 vols. 1820 sqq.) [An indispensable authority.]

SPECIAL SUBJECTS

A. CONSTITUTIONAL HISTORY

Atterbury, F. (Bishop). Rights and Privileges of an English Convocation. 2nd ed.
    London. 1701.
Bailey, A. Succession to the English Crown. London. 1879.
Child, G. W. Church and State under the Tudors. London. 1890.
Cobbett, W. State Trials. Vol. I. London. 1809.
—— Parliamentary History. London. 1806.
Dicey, A. V. The Privy Council. Oxford. 1860.
Gibson, E. Synodus Anglicana. Ed. E. Cardwell. Oxford. 1854.
Harbin, George. The Hereditary Right of the Crown of England. [Erroneously
    ascribed to Hilkiah Bedford.] London. 1713.
Lathbury, T. History of the Convocation of the Church of England. 2nd ed. London.
    1853.

Leadam, I. S. The Star Chamber. Selden Soc. 1904.
—— The Court of Requests. Selden Soc. 1898.
Makower, F. Constitutional History of the Church of England. (Engl. transl.) London. 1895.
Meyer, A. O. Die englische Diplomatie in Deutschland zur Zeit Eduards VI. Breslau. 1900.
Oppenheim, M. History of the Administration of the Navy. London. 1896.
Porritt, E. The Unreformed House of Commons. 2 vols. Cambridge. 1903.
Report of the Royal Commission on Ecclesiastical Courts. London. 2 vols. 1883.
Scofield, C. L. The Star Chamber. Chicago. 1900. (Cf. 'Calendar of Star Chamber Proceedings' in Dep.-Keeper of Records' 49th Rep.; and 'List of Star Chamber Proceedings,' 1485–1558, in R. O. 'Lists and Indexes,' vol. XIII, 1902.
Stanford, Sir W. Exposition of the King's Prerogative. London. 1567.

B. Social and Economic

Ashley, W. J. English Economic History. (With bibliography.) Vol. I, pt. 2. 1893.
Cheyney, E. P. Social Changes in England in the 16th Century. Philadelphia, Pa. 1895. (With bibliography.)
Cobbett, W. Protestant Reformation. London. 2 pts. 1824, 1827. Ed. F. A. Gasquet. 1896.
Cunningham, W. Growth of English Industry and Commerce. 3rd ed. Cambridge. 1896–1903.
Dowell, S. History of Taxation. 2nd ed. 4 vols. London. 1888.
Leadam, I. S. Domesday of Enclosures. Royal Hist. Soc. 2 vols. London. 1897.
Prothero, R. E. Pioneers and Progress of English Farming. London. 1888.
Rogers, T. History of Agriculture and Prices in England. Vols. III, IV. Oxford. 1882.
Russell, F. W. Kett's Rebellion. London. 1859. [Prints many documents.]
Smith, J. Memoirs of Wool. 2 vols. 1747.

C. The English Bible, Church Services and Ornaments

Anderson, C. Annals of the Bible. 2 vols. London. 1845.
Certificates of Chantry Commissioners. Surtees Soc. Vol. XCI. Durham. 1894.
Cotton, H. Editions of the Bible in England, 1505–1850. Oxford. 1852.
Dore, J. R. Old English Bibles. 2nd ed. London. 1888.
Gasquet, F. A., and Bishop, E. Edward VI and the Book of Common Prayer. London. 1890. [A most valuable book.]
Grove, Sir G. Dictionary of Music. 4 vols. London. 1878–1889.
Inventories of Church Goods. Surtees Society. Vol. XCVII. Durham. 1897.
Julian, J. Dictionary of Hymnology. London. 1892.
Lancashire Chantries. Ed. F. R. Raines. Chetham Society. Manchester. 1862.
Liturgies of Edward VI. Parker Society. Ed. J. Ketley. Cambridge. 1844.
Mély, F. de, and Bishop, E. Bibliographie Générale des Inventaires Imprimés. 3 vols. Paris. 1892–5.
Micklethwaite, J. T. The Ornaments of the Rubric. Alcuin Club Tracts. London. 1897.
Nightingale, J. E. Church Plate of Dorset, 1889, and of Wilts, 1891. Salisbury.
North, T. Church Bells of Leicestershire, 1876; of Northamptonshire, 1878; Rutland. 1880; Lincolnshire, 1882. — Leicester. Bedfordshire, 1883; Hertfordshire, 1887. — London.
Parker, J. The First Prayer-Book of Edward VI. Oxford. 1877.
Peacock, E. English Church Furniture in Lincolnshire. 1866.

Procter, F., and Frere, W. H. New History of the Book of Common Prayer. London. 1901.

Pullan, L. History of the Book of Common Prayer. London. 1900.

Somerset Chantries. Ed. E. Green. Somerset Record Soc. London. 1888.

Todd, H. J. Observations on the Metrical Versions of the Psalms by Sternhold, Hopkins, and others. London. 1822.

Trollope, A. Church Plate of Leicestershire. Leicester. 1890.

D. BIOGRAPHY

Cranmer, Archbishop. Lives of, by H. J. Todd (2 vols. 1831), C. W. Le Bas (2 vols. 1833), Dean Hook in Lives of the Archbishops of Canterbury (12 vols. 1860–76), and A. F. Pollard (1904).

Dictionary of National Biography. 66 vols. London. 1885–1901.

Hennessy, G. Novum Repertorium Eccl. Londin. London. 1898.

Le Neve, J. Fasti Eccl. Anglicanae. Ed. Sir T. D. Hardy. 3 vols. Oxford. 1854.

Nares, E. Memoirs of Lord Burleigh. Vol. I. London. 1828.

Newcourt, R. Repertorium Eccl. Londin. Parochiale. 2 vols. London. 1708, 1710.

Stubbs, W. (Bishop). Reg. Sacrum Anglicanum. 2nd ed. Oxford. 1897.

Wordsworth, C. Ecclesiastical Biography. 4th ed. 4 vols. London. 1853.

E. DEBASEMENT OF THE COINAGE

Hawkins, E. Silver Coins of England. London. 1887.

Oman, C. W. C. In Trans. Royal Hist. Soc. New Ser. Vol. IX. London. 1895.

Ruding, R. Annals of the Coinage. 3rd ed. Ed. Akerman. 3 vols. London. 1840.

F. EDUCATION AND THE UNIVERSITIES

Carlisle, N. Endowed Grammar Schools. 2 vols. London. 1818.

Cooper, C. H. Athenae Cantab. 2 vols. Cambridge. 1858–61.

—— Annals of Cambridge. 4 vols. Cambridge. 1842–52.

Leach, A. F. English Schools at the Reformation. Westminster. 1896.

Mullinger, J. B. History of the University of Cambridge. Vol. II. Cambridge. 1884.

Wood, A. Athenae Oxonienses. Ed. Bliss. 4 vols. London. 1813–1820.

—— Hist. et Antiquitates Univ. Oxon. Ed. Gutch. 2 vols. Oxford. 1791–6.

—— Colleges and Halls of Oxford, with the 'Fasti Oxon.' Ed. Gutch. Oxford. 1790.

G. TOPOGRAPHY

Camden, W. Britannia. London. 1586. Ed. Gibson and Gough. 3 vols. London. 1789.

Leland, J. Itinerary. Ed. Hearne. 9 vols. Oxford. 1770.

Norden, Saxton, and Speed's maps. Published 1600–1620. Among the Cotton Charters in the British Museum MSS. Department are a number of unpublished contemporary maps, plans, sketches of fortifications in England and abroad, e.g. Boulogne, Calais, etc., which are necessary for a clear understanding of military operations. Published contemporary maps are very scarce. Cf. J. P. Anderson, British Topography, London, 1881.

Stow, J. Survey of London. 1598. Ed. Strype. 2 vols. London. 1720.

CHAPTER XV

PHILIP AND MARY

(Chiefly supplementary to Bibliography for Chapter XIV, the authorities being, in many cases, the same)

MANUSCRIPTS

A. State Papers and Correspondence

The Domestic State Papers of Mary's reign preserved in the Record Office are comprised in fourteen volumes for England, with eight volumes of Addenda; two volumes for Ireland and part of one for Scotland. Of the transcripts of Papers at Simancas by G. A. Bergenroth at the British Museum only a small portion (Add. MSS. 28597, ff. 110–221) relate to the reign of Mary.

B. Calendars of State Papers and Correspondence

I. *Domestic*

1. Calendar of State Papers of the Reigns of Edward VI, Mary, Elizabeth, ed. by R. Lemon. 1856. 2. *Foreign.* Calendar of State Papers of the Reign of Mary, ed. by William B. Turnbull. 1861. [This volume contains errors in the assigned dates, corrections of which are given in A. O. Meyer, Die Englische Diplomatie in Deutschland, etc., pp. 109–111.] 3. Calendar of State Papers and Manuscripts relating to English Affairs in the Archives of Venice and other Libraries in Northern Italy. Edited by Rawdon Brown, vol. v (1534–1554); vol. vi (1554–1558). Catalogue des Manuscrits Français. Tome 1ᵉʳ, Ancien Fonds. Paris. 1868. Nos. 2846, 2933, 5113, 5127. Letters and Memorials of State in the Reign of Queen Mary, etc. Translated from the Originals at Penshurst in Kent. By Arthur Collins. 2 vols. 1746.

II. *Other Collections*

1. Calendar of the MSS. belonging to the Marquis of Salisbury, preserved at Hatfield House, published by the Historical MSS. Commission. Pt 1, pp. 93–94; No. 375 (where for 1551 read 1553) supplies facts relating to Mary's movements subsequent to Edward's death; see also pp. 123, 125. Pt 2, pp. 85, 146, 241, 243, 269, 288, 291–293, 332, 345 [useful generally for precedents established in Mary's reign]. 2. Calendar of MSS. belonging to the Corporation of Reading: Ein Kurtze anzeygung der ding, so sich in Engellandt zwischen den Königlichen Majestaten, König und Königin und dem Cardinal Polum verloffen haben [1554]. xiii. 284–295. 3. Calendar of MSS. belonging to Sir Richard Sutton, pp. 66–67, 89–92.

C. Diplomatic

1. Commendone, I. F. Lettere, in Miscellanea di Storia Italiana. Vol. VI. 1865.
2. Michiel, Giovanni, Les Dépêches de, Ambassadeur de Venise en Angleterre pendant les années de 1554 à 1557, dechiffrées et publiées d'après les documents conservés aux archives nationales de Venise, par P. Friedmann. Venice, 1869. [In Italian; Friedmann's discovery of the key to the cipher was a memorable achievement. The letters addressed to the Senate of Venice are of the highest interest, although, unfortunately, those for 1554 are lost; they include his 'Report of England' made in 1557 (a description decried by Froude but praised by Rawdon Brown), to be found in English in Ellis, Original Letters (2nd series), vol. II; also in Venetian Calendar, vol. VI, pt 2, 1043–1085.] 3. Navagero, Card. M. Bernardo, Relazione alla Ser^ma Rep^ca di Venezia tornando di Roma Ambasciatore appresso del Pontefice Paolo IV. 1858.
4. Noailles, Ambassades de Messieurs de, en Angleterre. Ed. l'Abbé Vertot. 5 tomes, Leyden. 1763. Of these letters the originals are partly preserved in Brussels and partly no longer to be found. Transcripts however are in the Bibliothèque Nationale in Paris as follows: Archives des affaires étrangères, mémoires et documents, fonds divers, 14 (Angleterre, 12), 1553–1557. Copie du journal des voyages de François de Noailles en Angleterre, pendant l'ambassade de son frère Antoine de Noailles. Extraits et analyses des documents de la Correspondance politique d'Angleterre pendant les ambassades d'Antoine de Noailles (mai 1553–mai 1556), Gilles de Noailles (mai–nov. 1556), François de Noailles (oct. 1556–juill. 1557), par de Valincourt. 15 (Angleterre, 13), 1556–1560. Recueil de copies de documents relatifs à l'Écosse: lettres des ambassadeurs de France en Angleterre, etc. According to P. Friedmann, not more than a fourth part of the Noailles correspondence is included in the volumes published by the Abbé de Vertot. [Thirty volumes of the correspondence of this celebrated family of diplomatists, formerly preserved in the library of the Louvre, were burnt in 1871. See Louis Paris, Les Papiers des Noailles de la Bibliothèque du Louvre. Paris. 1875.]
5. Renard, Simon, Letters to and from the Emperor Charles V. Printed in Papiers d'État du Cardinal de Granvelle. Vols. III and IV. Publiés sous la direction de M. Ch. Weiss. Paris. Imprimerie Royale. 1841. The originals are in the public library at Besançon. Of these, some of which are not included in the volumes edited by Weiss, a complete enumeration is given by M. A. Caston in Catalogue Générale des Manuscrits des Bibliothèques publiques de France, *Départements*, vol. XXXIII. The letters included by Weiss are distinguished by a W. Other correspondence of Renard and Jean Schyfre was formerly preserved in the Archives du Royaume de Belgique in Brussels, but has partly disappeared. Transcripts of the portion 20 Feb. 1553 to 15 June 1554 are, however, in the Record Office Transcripts (Sect. II, vols. CXLV, CXLVI), and were used both by Tytler and Froude.

D. Collections of Private Letters

Copia d' una Lettera d' Angleterra, nella quale narra l' entrata dell' Card. Polo in Inghilterra per la conversione di quella Isola alla Fede Catholica. Milan. 1554.

Poli Epistolae. 5 vols. Brescia. 1744–57.

E. Contemporary Chronicles, Tracts, etc.

Accession (the) of Queen Mary: being the contemporary Narrative of Antonio de Guaras, a Spanish Merchant resident in London. Edited with an Introduction, Translation, Notes, and an Appendix of Documents, including a contemporary Ballad in Fac-simile, by R. Garnett. London. 1892.

Annales, or A General Chronicle of England. Begun by John Stow and augmented with Matters forraigne and domestique, ancient and moderne, unto the end of the present yeere 1631. By Edmund Howes, Gent. London. 1631.

Chronicle of the Grey Friars. Edited by J. G. Nichols. Camden Society. 1852.

Chronicle of Queen Jane and of Two Years of Queen Mary and especially of the Rebellion of Sir Thomas Wyat, written by a Resident in the Tower of London. Ed. by J. G. Nichols. Camden Society. 1850. [The 'Resident' was probably one Rowland Lea.]

Florebellus, Ant., Mutinensis, ad Philippum et Mariam reges de restituta in Anglia Religione Oratio. Lovanii. 1555. [Floribelli was bishop of Lavello.]

Guidus, Ant. Oratio in funere Mariae Brittaniae Reginae ad Cardinales Regumque Rerumpublicarum Legatos Romae habita VIII ante Idus Mart. 1559. Romae, ex Officina Salviana, 1559.

Grafton, Ri. Chronicle at large and meere History of the Affayres of Englande. Ed. Sir H. Ellis. London. 1809.

Gray, G. J. General Index to Hazlitt's Handbook of Bibliographical Collections (London, 1893), pp. 494 and 597.

Journey of the Queen's Ambassadors to Rome, anno 1555. Hardwicke State Papers. Vol. I.

The Primer in Latin and English (after the Use of Sarum) with many godlye and devoute Prayers. . . . Where unto is added a playne and godlye treatise concerning the Masse. John Waylande. London. 1555.

Proctor, Jo., Historie of Wyates Rebellion. Printed in Grosse's Antiquarian Repertory, III, 65-115. London. 1808. [The narrative of a strong Romanist.]

Rosso, Giuglio Baviglio. I successi d' Inghilterra dopo la morte di Odoardo VI fino alla giunta in quel regno di Don Filippo d' Austria, princ. di Spagna. Ferrara. 1560. [The Venetian edition of 1558 (which is that used by Froude) is mutilated and does not bear the writer's name.]

BIOGRAPHIES

Beccadelli, Ludovico. The Life of Cardinal Reginald Pole, written originally in Italian, translated into English with Notes critical and historical. By B. Pye. London. 1776. [Beccadelli, or Beccatelli, was Pole's secretary.]

Carew, Sir Peter, Life of, by John Hooker (or Vowell). Edited by Sir John Maclean. London. 1857.

Dormer, Jane. Duchess of Feria, Life of [by Henry Clifford, her Secretary]. Edited by Estcourt and Stevenson. London. 1887.

Hoby, Sir Thos. Travel and Life of (1547-1564), written by himself. Camden Miscellany. Vol. x.

EDUCATION

1. Letter of Queen Mary to the bishopp of Winchester, chancellor of our University of Cambridge, 20 Aug. 1553. 2. Mere, J., Queen Mary's Visitation [of the University of Cambridge], Nov. 1556. 3. Ordinationes Reginaldi Poli pro Regimine Universitatis, item pro Directione et salubri Regimine Collegiorum, Aularum seu Domorum ejusdem Universitatis Cantabr. 21 Nov. 1557. The foregoing all in Lamb, J., Collection of Letters, Statutes and other Documents from the MS. Library of Corpus Christi College. London. 1838.

SECONDARY AUTHORITIES

GENERAL

Armstrong, E. The Emperor Charles V. 2 vols. London. 1902.

Brosch, M. Geschichte von England. Vol. vi. Gotha. 1890.

Castelnau, Mich., de Mauvissière. Mémoires. Ed. J. le Laboureur. Brussels. 1731.

Druffel, A. von. Briefe und Akten zur Gesch. des 16 Jahrhunderts. 4 vols. 1873–96 (vol. iv).

Forneron, H. Histoire de Philippe II. 2 vols. Paris. 1881.

Friedmann, P. New Facts in the History of Mary, Queen of England. Macmillan's Mag. xix, 1–12.

Griffet, H. Nouveaux éclaircissements sur l'histoire de Marie, reine d'Angleterre. Paris. 1776.

Henne, Alexandre. Histoire du règne de Charles-Quint en Belgique. 4 vols. Brussels. 1866.

Heylyn, Jo. Examen Historicum, or Discovery and Examination of the Mistakes, Falsities and Defects in some Modern Histories. London. 1659.

Motley, J. L. Rise of the Dutch Republic. Vol. i. London. 1855.

Ranke, L. von. Die römischen Päpste. Vol. i. Vol. xxxvii of Sämmtliche Werke. Leipzig. 1874 etc.

Relations politiques des Pays-Bas et de l'Angleterre sous le règne de Philippe II, publiées par M. le Baron de Lettenhove. 10 vols. Vol. i: Depuis l'Abdication de Charles-Quint jusqu'au Départ de Philippe II pour l'Espagne (25 Oct. 1555— 24 Aout 1559). Brussels. 1882.

Stone, J. M. History of Mary I, Queen of England. London. 1901.

Wiesener, L. The Youth of Queen Elizabeth (1533–1558). 2 vols. English Translation. London. 1879.

Zimmermann, A. Marie die Katholische. Freiburg i. B. 1890.

BIOGRAPHICAL

Duruy, G. Le Cardinal Carlo Caraffa. Paris. 1882.

Freeman, E. A. Cardinal Pole. Essays, 4th Series. (First published in Sat. Rev. 1869.)

Graziani, Ant. Maria, bishop of Amelia. De Vita I. F. Commendoria, Cardinalis, Libri iv. Paris. 1669. French translation by Fléchier. Paris. 1694.

Hook, W. F. (Dean). Lives of Cranmer and Pole in Archbishops of Canterbury. N. S. Vols. ii, iii. London. 1868, 1869.

Hume, M. A. S. Visit of Philip II (1554). English Hist. Review. 1892.

Lee, F. G. Reginald Pole, Cardinal Archbishop of Canterbury. London. 1888.

Madden, Sir F. Privy Purse Expenses of Princess Mary, with Memoir and Notes. London. 1831.

Phillips, Thos. History of the Life of Cardinal Pole. Oxford. 1764.

Pope, Sir Thos. Life of, by Thomas Wharton. London. 1772. (See also Life in D. N. B. and English Hist. Review, xi, 282–.)

Zimmermann, A. Kardinal Pole, sein Leben und seine Schriften. Ratisbon. 1893.

SPECIAL SUBJECTS

Creighton, C. History of Epidemics in Britain. Cambridge. 1891.

Leadam, I. S. Narrative of the Pursuit of the English Refugees in Germany under Queen Mary. Trans. of Royal Historical Society. 1896.

Verney Family, Letters and Papers of the, edited by J. Bruce. Camden Society. 1853. [Important for the Dudley Conspiracy.]

CHAPTER XVI

THE ANGLICAN SETTLEMENT AND THE SCOTTISH REFORMATION

The chief bibliographical works concerning this period of British history are (1) J. Scott's Bibliography of Works relating to Mary Queen of Scots, 1544–1700 (printed for the Edinburgh Bibliographical Soc., 1896), and (2) H. M. Dexter's Congregationalism (for which see below under II. B.). Catalogues of early printed books in the great libraries give some assistance.

The principal manuscript materials in England that have not yet been printed or adequately abstracted in Calendars are the State Papers, Domestic, at the Record Office. There are a few volumes at the British Museum containing State Papers, to which the class catalogue in the MS. Room serves as a guide. The Parker MSS. at Corpus Christi Coll. Camb. have been much used by historians and publishers of documents, but a full calendar is a desideratum.

I. GENERAL HISTORY OF ENGLAND AND SCOTLAND

A. RECORDS, STATE PAPERS, AND LETTERS

Acts of the Parliament of Scotland (Official ed.). Vol. II. 1814.

Acts of the [English] Privy Council, vol. VII (1558–70). London. 1893.

Anderson, J. Collections relating to the History of Mary Queen of Scots. Edinburgh. 1727–8.

Beale, R. Argument touching the validity of the marriage of Charles Brandon. In MS. Camb. Univ., Dd. iii. 85. [See Dict. Nat. Biog. IV, 6.]

Birrel, R. Diary. Fragments of Scotch History, ed. J. G. Dalyell. Edinburgh. 1798.

Browne, A., and Bacon, N. Tracts on the Succession to the Crown. In Booth, N., The Right of Succession to the Crown. 1723.

Castelnau, M. de. Mémoires. Ed. J. le Laboureur, Bruxelles, 1731. (1st ed. Paris, 1660.)

Correspondencia de Felipe II. Documentos inéditos para la Historia de España, ed. Navarrete and others. Vol. LXXXVII. Madrid. 1886.

Dewes, Simonds. Journal of the Parliaments of Queen Elizabeth. London. 1682.

Diurnal of Remarkable Occurrents. Bannatyne Club. 1833.

Doleman, R. [i.e. Parsons, R.]. A Conference about the next Succession to the Crown. [St Omer.] 1594.

Dyson, H. Queene Elizabeth's Proclamations, 1618. (Brit. Mus. Grenv. 6463.)

Egerton Papers. Camden Soc. London. 1840.

Ellis, H. Original Letters, 1st Ser., vol. II; 2nd Ser., vol. II; 3rd Ser., vol. III. London. 1824–46.

Exchequer Rolls of Scotland. Vols. xviii, xix. Edinburgh. 1898.

Ferrière, H. de la. Lettres de Catherine de Médicis. Vol. i. Paris. 1880.

Forbes, P. Full View of the Public Transactions in the Reign of Elizabeth. 2 vols. London. 1740–1.

Froude, J. A. Spanish Transcripts. Brit. Mus. MS. Addit. 26056.

Gachard, L. P. Correspondance de Marguerite d'Autriche. Vol. i. Brussels. 1867.

—— Correspondance de Philippe II. Vols. i, ii. Brussels. 1848–61.

Gonsalez, T. Documents from Simancas. Transl. S. Hall. London. 1865.

Hales, J. Declaration of the Succession of the Crown, 1563. In [Harbin, G.] Hereditary Right of the Crown. London. 1713.

Hamilton MSS. Eleventh Rep. of Hist. MSS. Com. App. vi. London. 1887.

Hamilton Papers. Vols. i, ii. Edinburgh. 1890–2.

Hardwicke, Philip, Earl of. Miscellaneous State Papers. Vol. i. London. 1778.

Haynes, S. Burghley State Papers. London. 1740.

Journal of the House of Commons (Official ed.). Vol. i, no date.

Journal of the House of Lords (Official ed.). Vol. i, no date.

Keith, R. History of the Affairs of Church and State in Scotland. Spottiswoode Soc. Edinburgh. 1844. (1st ed. Edinburgh, 1734.)

Kervyn de Lettenhove. Relations politiques des Pays-Bas et de l'Angleterre. Vols. i–iii. Brussels. 1882–3.

Labanoff, A. Lettres inédites de Marie Stuart. Paris. 1839.

—— Lettres, instructions et mémoires de Marie Stuart. London. 1844.

Languet, Hubert. Epistolae. Halle. 1699.

Leicester's Commonwealth. [London.] 1641. (Erroneously attributed to Parsons the Jesuit. For its history see Dict. Nat. Biog. xvi, 121.]

Members of Parliament, Returns. Part i. Blue book, 1878.

Nuntiaturberichte aus Deutschland, 1560–72. Hist. Com. d. Akad. d. Wissensch. Vienna. 1897.

Paris, L. Négotiations . . . relatives au règne de François II. Paris. 1841.

Pollen, J. H. Papal Negotiations with Mary Queen of Scots. Scot. Hist. Soc. Edinburgh. 1901.

Prothero, G. W. Select Statutes and other Constitutional Documents. London. 1894.

Register of the Great Seal of Scotland (1546–80). Edinburgh. 1886.

Register of the Privy Council of Scotland. Vol. i (1545–69). Edinburgh. 1877.

'Roman Transcripts.' MS. at Record Office. [Copies made in various Roman Archives.]

Rutland Manuscripts. Hist. MSS. Com. Rep. xii, App. 4. London. 1888.

Rymer, T. Foedera. Vol. xv. London. 1713.

State Papers. Borders of England and Scotland. Calendar. Vol. i. Edinburgh. 1894.

State Papers, Domestic. MS. at Record Office. [The published Calendar, Vols. i and vii, merely indicates the nature of the documents.]

State Papers, Foreign. Elizabeth. Calendar. Vols. i–vi. London. 1863–9.

State Papers. Hatfield or Cecil MSS. Calendar. Vol. i. London. 1883, repr. 1895.

State Papers of Sir Ralph Sadler, ed. Clifford. Edinburgh. 1809.

State Papers. Scotland and Mary Queen of Scots. Calendar. Vol. i. Edinburgh. 1898.

State Papers, Spanish (1558–67). Calendar. London. 1892.

State Papers, Venetian. Calendar. Vol. viii. London. 1890.

Statutes of the Realm (Official ed.). Vol. iv. 1819. [The original Acts of Parliament preserved in the Parliament Office sometimes supply a little additional information.]

Stevenson, J. Selections from manuscripts relating to Mary Queen of Scots. Maitland Club. Edinburgh. 1837.

Teulet, A. Papiers d'état . . . relatifs à l'histoire de l'Écosse. Bannatyne Club. Paris. 1851.

—— Relations politiques de la France et de l'Espagne avec l'Écosse. Paris. 1862.

Turba, G. Venetianische Depeschen vom Kaiserhofe. Vol. iii. Vienna. 1895.
Strickland, A. Letters of Mary Queen of Scots. London. 1842.
Weiss, C. Papiers d'état du Cardinal Granvelle. Vols. iv–vi. Paris. 1843–6.
Wright, T. Queen Elizabeth and her Times. London. 1838.

B. CHRONICLES AND EARLY HISTORIES

Beaugué, J. de. L'histoire de la Guerre d'Escosse. Maitland Club. Edinburgh. 1830. Another edition, Bordeaux, 1862.
Brantôme. Œuvres complètes. Ed. L. Lalanne. Paris. 1864–82.
Buchanan, George. Rerum Scoticarum Historia. Edinburgh. 1583.
Burghley, Life of. In F. Peck, Desiderata Curiosa. London. 1779. (1st ed. in 1732.)
Camden, W. Annales. London. 1615.
Complaynt, the, of Scotlande, 1549. Early Eng. Text Soc. London. 1872.
Conaeus, G. Vita Mariae Stuartae. Würzburg and Rome. 1624.
Condé, Mémoires de. The Hague. 1743.
Hayward, J. Annals of Queen Elizabeth. Camden Soc. London. 1840.
Herries, Lord. Historical Memoirs. Abbotsford Club. Edinburgh. 1836.
Hollinshed, R. Chronicle. London. 1586–7. [As to the rare first edition, see Dict. Nat. Biog. xxvii, 131.]
Jebb, S. De vita et rebus gestis Mariae ... quae scriptis tradidere auctores sedecim. London. 1725.
[Lesley, J.] A defence of the Honour of ... Marie, Queene of Scotland. London. 1569. [See Scott, Bibliography, pp. 20, 23.]
Lesley, J. De origine ... Scotorum. Romae. 1578.
—— History of Scotland. Scot. Text Soc. Edinburgh. 1888.
Lyndsay of Pitscottie. Historie of Scotland. Scot. Text Soc. Edinburgh. 1899.
Machyn's Diary. Camden Soc. London. 1844. [See Eng. Hist. Rev. xi, 282.]
Maitland, J. Narrative of the Principal Acts of the Regency. Edinburgh. 1822.
Melville, James. Memoirs. Bannatyne Club. Edinburgh. 1827. (Maitland Club.) Edinburgh. 1833. (1st. ed. 1683.)
Naunton, R. Fragmenta Regalia. London. 1641. [For the various editions, see Dict. Nat. Biog. xl, 128.]
Nichols, J. Progresses of Queen Elizabeth. London. 1823. Vol. i. p. 60 : Coronation Service.]
Stow, J. Annales of England. London. 1605. (1st ed. 1592.)
—— Memoranda. Three Fifteenth Century Chronicles. Camden Soc. London. 1880.
Wriothesley, C. Chronicle. Camden Soc. London. 1875.

C. MODERN WORKS

Beesley, E. S. Queen Elizabeth. London. 1892.
Bekker, E. Beiträge zur englischen Geschichte im Zeitalter Elisabeths. Giessen. 1887. Elisabeth und Leicester. Giessen. 1890.
Brosch, M. Habsburgische Vermälungspläne mit Elisabeth. Mitth. d. Instituts für österreich. Geschichtsforschung. x, 121. Innsbruck. 1889.
Brown, P. Hume. History of Scotland. Vols. i, ii. Cambridge. 1899–1902.
Brugmans, H. Engeland en de Nederlanden, 1558–67. Groningen. 1892.
Burton, J. H. History of Scotland. Ed. 2. Edinburgh. 1873.
Chalmers, G. Life of Mary Queen of Scots. London. 1818.
Creighton, M. (Bishop). Queen Elizabeth. London. 1896.
Cunningham, W. Growth of English Industry and Cambridge, 1903, pp. 127–137. [The recoinage

Duruy, G. Le Cardinal Carlo Caraffa. Paris. 1882.

Fleming, D. Hay. Mary Queen of Scots from her birth until her flight into England. London. 1897.

Forneron, H. Les ducs de Guise et leur époque. Paris. 1877.

—— Histoire de Philippe II. Paris. 1881.

Froude, J. A. History of England. Reign of Elizabeth. London. 1864.

Gairdner, J. The Death of Amy Robsart. Eng. Hist. Rev. i, 235; xiii, 83.

Hallam, H. Constitutional History of England. London. 1832.

Henderson, T. F. Lives of Mary Stuart, Douglas (Lady Margaret), Hamilton (James, 3rd Earl of Arran), Maitland (William), Stewart (Lord James), Stewart (Matthew, Earl of Lennox), in Dict. Nat. Biog.

Hosack, J. Mary Queen of Scots and her Accusers. Ed. 2. Edinburgh. 1870.

Hume, M. A. The Courtships of Queen Elizabeth. London. 1896.

—— The great Lord Burghley. London. 1898.

Lang, A. History of Scotland. Vols. i, ii. Edinburgh. 1900–2.

—— Scandal about Queen Elizabeth. [Amy Robsart.] Blackwood's Magazine, cliii, 209. Edinburgh. 1893.

Lee, S. L. Life of Robert Dudley. In Dict. Nat. Biog. xvi, 112 [for death of Lady Robert, with bibliography].

Lingard, J. History of England. Ed. 6. London. 1854.

Marcks, E. Königin Elisabeth. Bielefeld. 1897.

Mathieson, W. L. Politics and Religion in Scotland. Glasgow. 1902.

Maurenbrecher, W. Beiträge zur Geschichte Maximilians II. Hist. Zeitschrift, vol. xxxii (1874), pp. 221, 277.

Mignet, F. A. M. Histoire de Marie Stuart. Ed. 6. Paris. 1885.

Müller, T. Das Konklave Pius IV. Gotha. 1889.

Nares, E. Memoirs of Lord Burghley. London. 1823–38.

Paillard, C. La conjuration d'Amboise. Revue historique. Vol. xiv (1880), pp. 61, 311.

Philippson, M. La contra-révolution religieuse. Bruxelles. 1884.

—— Histoire du règne de Marie Stuart. Paris. 1891–2.

Pollen, J. H. Papers published in 'The Month,' 1900–2, and in Dublin Review, Jan. 1903.

Rait, R. S. The Scottish Parliament. London. 1901.

—— Relations between England and Scotland. London. 1901.

Ranke, L. v. Englische Geschichte. Vol. xiv of Sämmtliche Werke. Berlin. 1874 etc.

Reimann, E. Der Streit zwischen Papstthum und Kaiserthum im Jahre 1558. Forschungen zur deutschen Geschichte. Vol. v, p. 291. Göttingen. 1865.

Ritter, M. Deutsche Geschichte im Zeitalter der Gegenreformation. Vol. i. Stuttgart. 1889.

Rogers, J. E. T. History of Agriculture and Prices. Vol. iv, pp. 197 ff. [The recoinage of 1561.] Oxford. 1882.

Ruble, A. de. Antoine de Bourbon et Jeanne d'Albret. Paris. 1881–2.

—— Le traité de Cateau-Cambrésis. Paris. 1889.

—— La première jeunesse de Marie Stuart. Paris. 1891.

Rye, W. The Murder of Amy Robsart. London. 1885.

Schlossberger, A. Verhandlungen über die beabsichtigte Vermählung des Erzherzogs Karl mit der Königin Elizabeth. Forschungen zur deutschen Geschichte. Vol. v, p. 1. Göttingen. 1865.

Skelton, J. Maitland of Lethington. Ed. 2. Edinburgh. 1894.

Storm, G. Maria Stuart. Uebersetzt von P. Wittmann. Munich. 1896.

Swinburne, A. C. Mary Queen of Scots. Encyclop. Britan. Vol. xv. Edinburgh. 1883.

Tait, J. Life of Mary of Guise in Dict. Nat. Biog.

Tytler, P. F. History of Scotland. London. 1876.

Voss, W. Die Verhandlungen Pius IV mit den katholischen Mächten. Leipzig. 1887.

Wertheimer, E. Heirathsverhandlungen zwischen Elizabeth und Erzherzog Karl. Hist. Zeitschrift. Vol. xl (1878), p. 385.

Wiesener, L. The Youth of Queen Elizabeth. Engl. Transl. London. 1879.

Wolf, G. Zur Geschichte der deutschen Protestanten, 1555–9. Berlin. 1888.

II. ECCLESIASTICAL AFFAIRS OF ENGLAND AND SCOTLAND

A. Primary Materials

Bateson, M. A collection of Original Letters from the Bishops to the Privy Council, 1564. Camden Miscellany. Vol. ix. London. 1893.

Book of the Universal Kirk. Vol. i. Bannatyne Club. Edinburgh. 1839.

Beza, T. Tractatus pius . . . de vera excommunicatione. London. 1590.

Bucholtz, F. B. v. Geschichte der Regierung Ferdinand des Ersten. Vienna. 1831–8. Vol. ix, pp. 699–702.

Bullarium Romanum. Luxemb. 1727. Vol. i, p. 840. [Bull of 15 Feb. 1559.] Vol. ii, p. 324. [Bull deposing Elizabeth.]

Bullinger, H. Bullae papisticae . . . contra . . . Angliae Reginam Elizabetham . . . defensio. London. 1571.

Calderwood, D. History of the Kirk of Scotland. Woodrow Soc. Edinburgh. 1842–9. (1st ed. 1678.)

[Calvin's Letters.] Thesaurus Epistolicus Calvinianus. Brunswick. 1872–9. (Corpus Reformatorum, ed. Baum, Cunitz, Reuss. Vols. xxxviii–xlviii.)

Cardwell, E. Documentary Annals of the Church of England. Oxford. 1839.

—— History of Conferences. Oxford. 1840.

—— Synodalia. Oxford. 1842.

Catholic Tractates of the Sixteenth Century. Ed. T. G. Law. Scot. Text Soc. Edinburgh. 1901.

[Clerke, B.] Fidelis servi subdito infideli responsio. London. 1573.

Coke, Sir E. Fourth Institute, 324 ff. [Headship of Church and High Commission.] London. 1797. (1st ed. 1644.)

Confession (The), of the faythe and doctrine beleued and professed by the Protestantes of the Realm of Scotlande. London. 1561.

Dyer, Sir J. Reports, fo. 234, plac. 15. London. 1632. [Bonner's case: see also Curia Regis Rolls, no. 1212, Roll 13 at Record Office.]

Erastus, T. Explicatio gravissimae quaestionis, utrum excommunicatio, etc. Pesclavii [= London]. 1589.

Forbes-Leith, W. Narratives of Scottish Catholics. Edinburgh. 1885.

Fox, J. Acts and Monuments. London. 1844–9. [For early editions, see Dict. Nat. Biog., vol. xx, p. 147.]

Gude and Godlie Ballatis. Ed. A. F. Mitchell. Scot. Text Soc. Edinburgh. 1897.

Heppe, H. The Reformers of England and Germany. Engl. Transl. London. 1859.

Hessels, J. H. Ecclesiae Londino-Batavae Archivum. Vol. i. Cambridge. 1887.

Hospinianus, R. Concordia discors. Geneva. 1678.

Jewel, J. Works. Parker Soc. Cambridge. 1845–50.

Kausler, E. v., und Schott, T. Briefwechsel zwischen Cristoph, Herzog v. Württemberg, und P. P. Vergerius. Tübingen. 1875.

Knox, J. Works. Ed. D. Laing. Edinburgh. 1846–55; and for Bannatyne Club. Edinburgh. 1855–64.

Law, T. G. Abp. Hamilton's Catechism. Oxford. 1884.

Le Plat, J. Monumentorum ad historiam Concilii Tridentini . . . Collectio. Vol. vi, pp. 272–3. Lovanii. 1781–7.

Liturgies set forth in the Reign of Elizabeth. Ed. Clay. Parker Soc. Cambridge. 1847.

Lyndsay, Sir David. Poetical Works. Ed. Laing. Edinburgh. 1879.

Morus, H. Historia Provinciae Anglicanae Societatis Jesu. St Omer. 1660.

Müller, E. F. Karl. Die Bekenntnisschriften der reformierten Kirche. Leipzig. 1903.

Nowell, A. Sermon before Parliament. MS. Caius Coll. 64.

Pallavicino, S. Vera Concilii Tridentini Historia. Antwerp. 1670. Vol. II, p. 531.

Parker, M. Correspondence. Parker Soc. Cambridge. 1853.

Parker Society's Publications. General Index. Cambridge. 1855.

Reformatio Legum, ed. Cardwell. Oxford. 1850.

Ribier, G. Lettres et mémoires. Paris. 1677. Vol. II, p. 776.

Robertson, J. Statuta Ecclesiae Scotticanae. Bannatyne Club. Edinburgh. 1866.

Sanders, N. MS. Report to Cardinal Morone of the change of religion in England. Copy among 'Roman Transcripts' at the Record Office.

—— De visibili Monarchia Ecclesiae. Louvain. 1571.

—— De origine . . . Schismatis Anglicani. Edited and continued by E. Rishton. Cologne. 1585.

Saravia, H. De diversis gradibus ministrorum. London. 1590.

Sarpi, P. Histoire du Concile de Trente. Transl. P. F. le Courayer. Amsterdam. 1736. Vol. II, p. 52.

Schaff, P. The Creeds of the Evangelical Protestant Churches. London. 1877.

Schickler, F. de. Les églises de refuge en Angleterre. Paris. 1892.

Scott, Hew. Fasti Ecclesiae Scoticanae. Edinburgh. 1866–71.

Sickel, T. Zur Geschichte des Concils von Trient. Vienna. 1872.

Somers Tracts. Ed. by Sir W. Scott. Vol. I, pp. 61–85, 163–174, 189–208. London. 1809.

Sparrow, A. A collection of Articles, Injunctions, etc. London. 1675.

Spottiswoode, J. History of the Church and State of Scotland. Spottiswoode Soc. Edinburgh. 1851. (1st ed. London, 1655.)

Strype, J. Annals of the Reformation. Oxford. 1824.

—— Lives of Parker, Grindal, Whitgift, Cheke, Smith, Aylmer. Oxford. 1820–2. [For earlier editions, see Dict. Nat. Biog. LV, 69.]

Whitgift, J. Works. Parker Soc. Cambridge. 1851–3.

[Whittingham, W.] A Brief Discours off the Troubles begonne at Franckford. 1575. Reprinted, 1846.

—— Life of, in Camden Miscellany. Vol. VI. London. 1870.

Wilkins, D. Concilia. Vol. IV. London. 1737.

Winzet, N. Certain Tractates. Scot. Text Soc. Edinburgh. 1888–90.

Zürich Letters (Epistolae Tigurinae). Two Series. Parker Soc. Cambridge. 1842–5.

Controversial Tracts. The titles of the most important may be found in Dict. Nat. Biog. In the first years of the reign the chief Anglican apologists are John Jewel and Alexander Nowell. For the Roman side see the lives of Henry Cole, Thomas Dorman, Thomas Harding, James Harpsfield, Nicolas Harpsfield, Alban Langdale, John Rastell, Thomas Stapleton: also of William Allen, Robert Parsons, Nicholas Sanders. The first stages of the Puritan development are to be found rather in letters, episcopal injunctions, etc., than in tracts. But see the lives of Matthew Parker and other Elizabethan bishops of the first generation; also those of Thomas Cartwright, Anthony Gilby, John Fox, Christopher Goodman, Laurence Humphrey, Thomas Lever, Thomas Sampson, and William Whittingham.

B. Modern Works

Bailey, T. J. Ordinum Sacrorum in Ecclesia Anglicana Defensio. London. 1870.

Bellesheim, A. History of the Catholic Church of Scotland. Trans. O. H. Blair. Edinburgh. 1887.

Benrath, K. Bernardino Ochino. Leipzig. 1875.

Bonnard, A. Thomas Eraste. Lausanne. 1894.

Bridgett, T. E. Blunders and Forgeries. London. 1890. [Ware's forgeries.]
—— and Knox, T. F. The true story of the Catholic Hierarchy. London.
    1889.
Brown, P. Hume. John Knox. London. 1895.
—— George Buchanan. Edinburgh. 1890.
Burnet, G. History of the Reformation. Ed. Pocock. Oxford. 1865. (1st ed.
    1678–1714.)
Churton, R. Life of Alexander Nowell. Oxford. 1809.
Collier, J. Ecclesiastical History. Ed. Barham. London. 1840–1. (1st ed.
    1708–14.)
Creighton, M. (Bishop). The Excommunication of Queen Elizabeth. Eng. Hist.
    Rev. vii, 81.
Cunningham, J. The Church History of Scotland. Edinburgh. 1882.
Denny, E., and Lacey, T. A. De Hierarchia Anglicana. London. 1895. Supple-
    mentum. Romae. 1896.
Dexter, H. M. Congregationalism as seen in its Literature. New York. 1880.
    [Valuable bibliography.]
Dimock, N. Dangerous Deceits. London. 1895.
—— Vox Liturgiae Anglicanae. London. 1897.
Dixon, R. W. History of the Church of England. London. 1878–1902.
Dodd, C. Church History of England. Ed. Tierney. London. 1839–43.
Dorner, I. A. Geschichte der protestantischen Theologie. Munich. 1867.
Dugdale, H. G. Life of Edmund Geste. London. 1840.
Estcourt, E. E. The Question of Anglican Ordinations. London. 1873.
Figgis, J. N. Erastus and Erastianism. Journ. of Theol. Studies, ii, 66. London.
    1901.
Forbes-Leith, J. La révolution religieuse en Angleterre. Revue des quest. hist,
    lviii, 456. Paris. 1895.
Fuller, T. The Church History of Britain. Ed. Brewer. Oxford. 1845. (1st ed.
    1655.)
Gee, H. The Elizabethan Clergy. Oxford. 1898.
—— The Elizabethan Prayer-Book and Ornaments. London. 1902.
Gibson, E. C. S. The Thirty-Nine Articles. Ed. 2. London. 1898.
Grub, G. Ecclesiastical History of Scotland. Edinburgh. 1861.
Hardwick, C. History of the Articles of Religion. Cambridge. 1859.
Heylin, P. Ecclesia Restaurata. Ed. Robertson. Cambridge. 1849. (1st ed. 1661.)
Jacobs, H. E. The Lutheran Movement in England. Philadelphia. 1891.
Kluckhohn, A. Friedrich der Fromme. Nördlingen. 1879.
Kugler, B. Christoph, Herzog zu Wirtemberg. Stuttgart. 1868.
Kurtz, J. H. Church History. Engl. Transl. London. 1888.
Lamb, J. Historical Account of the Thirty-Nine Articles. Cambridge. 1829.
Laurence, R. Bampton Lectures for 1804. Ed. 3. Oxford. 1838.
Lechler, G. V. Geschichte der Presbyterial- und Synodalverfassung. 1854.
Lee, F. G. The Church under Elizabeth. London. 1892.
Lorimer, P. Life of Patrick Hamilton. Edinburgh. 1857.
—— John Knox and the Church of England. London. 1875.
M‘Crie, T. Life of Knox. Ed. Crichton. Edinburgh. 1840. (1st ed. 1812.)
MacColl, M. Lawlessness, Sacerdotalism, and Ritualism. Ed. 3. London. 1875.
—— The Reformation Settlement. Ed. 10. London. 1901.
Mackay, Æ. Lives of Hamilton (Patrick), Knox (John), Lindsay (David), in Dict. Nat.
    Biog.
Maitland, F. W. Elizabethan Gleanings. Eng. Hist. Rev. xv, 120, 324, 530, 757.
Maxwell, A. The History of Old Dundee. Edinburgh. 1891, pp. 81 ff. [George
    Wishart.]
Micklethwaite, J. T. The Ornaments of the Rubric. Alcuin Club Tracts. London.
    1897.
Mitchell, A. F. The Scottish Reformation. Edinburgh. 1900.

Mullinger, J. B. History of the University of Cambridge from the Royal Injunctions of 1535. Cambridge. 1884.

Neal, D. History of the Puritans. London. 1754.

Parker, J. The Ornaments Rubrick. Oxford. 1881.

—— Did Queen Elizabeth take other order? Oxford. 1878.

Perry, G. G. History of the English Church. Second Period. Ed. 6. London. 1900.

—— T. W. The Declaration on Kneeling. London. 1863.

Pestalozzi, C. Heinrich Bullinger. Elberfeld. 1858.

Pocock, N. The Reformation Settlement of the English Church. Eng. Hist. Rev. I, 677.

—— Condition of Morals and Religious Belief in the Reign of Edward VI. Eng. Hist. Rev. x, 417.

Preger, W. Matthias Flacius Illyricus Erlangen. 1859. [Adiaphorist controversy.]

Proctor, F. History of the Book of Common Prayer. Ed. W. H. Frere. London. 1902.

Pullan, L. History of the Book of Common Prayer. Ed. 3. London. 1901.

Rigg, J. M. Life of Bernardino Ochino in Dict. Nat. Biog.

Ruble, A. de. Le colloque de Poissy. Paris. 1889.

Sage, Bp J. Works. Spottiswoode Soc. Edinburgh. 1844-6.

Schaff, P. History of the Creeds of Christendom. London. 1877.

Shaw, W. A. Elizabethan Presbyterianism. Eng. Hist. Rev. III, 655.

Simpson, R. Edmund Campion. London. 1896.

[Simpson, R. (?)]. Parpaglia's Mission to Elizabeth. North British Review. London. (1870.) Vol. LII, p. 366.

Stephen, W. History of the Scottish Church. Edinburgh. 1894-6.

Swainson, C. A. In the Advertisements of 1566 was order taken, etc.? Cambridge. 1880.

—— An Essay on the History of Article XXIX. Cambridge. 1856.

Tomlinson, J. T. The Prayer Book, Articles, and Homilies. London. 1897.

Waddington, J. Congregational History, 1200-1567. London. 1869.

Arguments and judgments in various modern lawsuits: see Digests to 'The Law Reports' under 'Ecclesiastical Law': especially Sheppard *v.* Bennett (3 A. and E. 167; 4 P. C. 371); Hebbert *v.* Purchas (3 P. C. 605); (Ridsdale *v.* Clifton 2 P. D. 276); Read *v.* Bp of Lincoln (1891 P. 9; 1892 A. C. 644).

NOTE

Of the books mentioned under this last head some may be considered as classical. Others have been selected out of a vast number as recent representatives of the various parties and schools which comment on the religious changes made in the period (1558-63) treated in Chapter XVI.

CHAPTER XVII

THE SCANDINAVIAN NORTH

PUBLISHED DOCUMENTS

Aarsberetninger fra det [Danske] K. Geheime-Archivet. Edd. C. F. Wegener etc. Copenhagen. 1855 f.

Aktstykker til Nordens Historie i Grevefeldens Tid. Ed. C. Paludan-Müller. 2 vols. Odense. 1852–3.

Allen, C. F. Briefe og Aktstykker til Oplysning af Christiern II og Frederik I's Historie. I. Copenhagen. 1854.

Altes und Neues von Gelehrten Sachen aus Dännemark. 3 vols. Copenhagen and Leipzig. 1768.

Andersson, A. Skrifter från Reformationstiden. (Skrifter utgifna af Svenska Litteratursällskapet.) Upsala. 1889 f.

Bang, A. C. Den Norske Kirkes symbolske Böger. Christiania. 1889.

Brask, J. Epistolae. (Handlingar rörande Sveriges Historia XIII–XVIII.) Stockholm. 1861 f.

Bugenhagen, J. Briefswechsel. Ed. O. Vogt. Stettin. 1888.

Bullarium Romano-Sueo-Gothicum. Ed. Magnus a Celse. Stockholm. 1782.

Christiern II's Arkiv. Handlingar rörande Severin Norby. Ed. N. J. Ekdahl. 4 vols. Stockholm. 1835–42.

Dänische Bibliothek (ed. Herbö Langebek and Moeller). Vols. I–IX. Copenhagen and Leipzig. 1738–43.

Danske Magazin. 6 vols. Copenhagen. 1745–52. — Nye Danske Magazin. 6 vols. 1794–1836. — Danske Magazin. Ser. III. 6 vols. 1843–60. — Ditto. Ser. IV. 1861 f.

Danske Samlinger. Ed. C. Bruun etc. Series I, vols. I–VI. 1865–71; ditto, Series II. Copenhagen. 1871 f.

Diplomatarium Dalecarlicum. Ed. C. G. Kröningssvärd and J. Liden. 4 vols. Stockholm. 1842–53.

Eliae, Paul. Danske Skrifter. Ed. C. G. Secher. Copenhagen. 1855.

—— Historiske Optegnelsesbog. Ed. A. Heise. 2 parts. 1890–1.

—— Chronicon Skibyense. Scriptores rerum Danicarum. I. Ed. Rœrdam.

Fant, E. M. Acta et litterae ad historiam Reformationis in Suecia. Upsala. 1807.

Fryxell, A. Handlingar rörande Sveriges Historia, ur Utrikes Arkiver. 9 vols. Stockholm. 1836–43.

Gustaf I's Registratur. (Handlingar rörande Sveriges Historia.) Ed. by I. I. Nordström. 10 vols. Stockholm. 1861–87.

Handlingar rörande Skandinaviens Historia. Stockholm. 1816 f. *Passim*.

Hildebrand, E. Svenska Riksdagsakter. Stockholm. 1887 etc.

Historika Handlingar. Kongliga Samfundet för Utgivande af Handskrifter rörande Skandinaviens Historia. 11 vols. Stockholm. 1861–79.

Hosius, S. Opera. 2 vols. Cologne. 1584.

Kalkar, C. H. Aktstykker henhörende til Danmarks Historie i Reformationstiden. Odense. 1845.

Krag, N., and Stephanius, S. Den Konge Christian III's Historie. Edd. Suhm and Gram. 2 vols. and suppl. Copenhagen. 1776–8–9.

Kyrko-Ordningar och Förslag dertill före 1686. i. Handlingar rörande Sveriges Historia. ii, ii. Stockholm. 1872.

Laurensen, P. Malmœbogen. Ed. H. F. Rœrdam. Copenhagen. 1868.

—— En stakket Undervisning. Ed. H. F. Rœrdam. Copenhagen. 1890.

Lindblom, J. A. Linköping Bibliotheks Handlingar. 2 vols. Linköping. 1793–5.

Meddelelser fra det norske Rigsarchiv. Christiania. 1870 etc.

Münter, F. Aktstykker vedkommende Kong Christian og Dronning Dorotheas Kroning af Bugenhagen. Copenhagen. 1831.

Norske Rigsregistranter. Christiania. 1861 etc.

Ordinatio ecclesiastica Regnorum Daniae. Ed. J. Bugenhagen. Copenhagen. 1537.

Palladius, Peder. Visitatsbog. Ed. A. C. L. Heiberg. Copenhagen. 1867.

Pedersen, Chr. Danske Skrifter. 5 vols. Ed. C. J. Brandt and R. T. Fenger. Copenhagen. 1850–5.

Petri, Olaus. Svenska Krönika. Ed. G. E. Klemming. Stockholm. 1860. [A revised version by his brother Laurentius in Scriptores rerum Suecicarum. ii. Upsala. 1828.]

—— Postilla. Stockholm. 1857.

Pontoppidan, E. Annales Ecclesiae Danicae. ii, iii. Copenhagen. 1744–7.

Regesta Diplomatica Historiae Danicae. i. Copenhagen. 1847.

Rœrdam, Holgar F. Monumenta Historiae Danicae. Vols. i, ii. Copenhagen. 1873–5.

Sacchinus, Juvencius and Cordara, Historiae Societatis Jesu (for Possevin's reports). Antwerp. 1620 f.

Samling af Christian den Tredies Breve til Reformateurs (in Aarsberetninger fra det K. Geheime-Archivet, i). Copenhagen. 1855.

Schumacher, And. Gelehrter Männer Briefe an die Könige in Dännemark. 3 vols. Copenhagen and Leipzig. 1758–9.

Scriptores Rerum Suecicarum. Vols. i and ii. Ed. E. M. Fant etc. Upsala. 1818–28. Vol. iii. Ed. C. Annerstedt. Upsala. 1871.

Svenska Riksdagsakter. Ed. E. Hildebrand and Oskar Alin. Stockholm. 1887 f.

Swart, P. Gustaf I's Krönika. Ed. G. E. Klemming. Stockholm. 1870.

Tausen, H. Smaaskrifter. Ed. H. F. Rœrdam. Copenhagen. 1870.

Theiner, A. Schweden und seine Stellung zum heiligen Stuhl. 2 vols. Augsburg. 1838–9. Fr. transl. by J. Cohen. Paris. 1842.

Thyselius, P. E. Handlingar til Sveriges Kyrkohistoria under K. Gustaf I. Örebro. 1839–41.

Troil, U. von. Skrifter och Handlingar til Uplysning i Svenska Kyrko och Reformations Historien. 5 pts. Upsala. 1790–1.

PRINCIPAL HISTORIES

Alin, O. Sveriges Nydaningstid 1521–1611. Stockholm. 1878.

Allen, C. F. De tre nordiske Rigers Historie 1497–1536. iii, iv, v. Copenhagen. 1867–70–72.

—— Haandbog i Fäderlandets Historie.. Copenhagen. 1870. (French tr. by E. Beauvois, with good bibliography. 2 vols. Copenhagen. 1878.)

Anjou, L. A. Svenska Kyrkoreformationens Historia. 3 vols. Upsala. 1851. Eng. tr. by H. Mason. 1859.

Bang, A. C. Den Norske Kirkes Historie i det sextende Aarhundrede. Christiania. 1901.

Barfod, F. Danmarks Historie fra 1319 til 1670. 6 vols. Copenhagen. 1885–93.

Cornelius, C. A. Svenska Kyrkans Historia efter Reformationen. Vol. I. Upsala. 1886.

Dahlmann, F. C. Geschichte von Dänemark. III. Gesch. d. europ. Staaten. Hamburg. 1843.

Danmarks Riges Historie. Vol. III (1481–1588). By A. Heise. Copenhagen.

Geijer, E. G. Geschichte Schwedens. I, II. Hamburg. 1832–4. Eng. tr. by J. H. Turner. London. 1845.

Helveg, L. N. Den Danske Kirkes Historie. 5 vols. Copenhagen. 1870.

Jensen, H. N. A. Schleswig-Holsteinische Kirchengeschichte. Ed. A. L. J. Michelsen. III. Kiel. 1877.

Keyser, J. R. Den Norske Kirkes Historie under Katholicismen. 2 vols. Christiania. 1856–8.

Lau, G. J. T. Geschichte der Reformation in Schleswig-Holstein. Hamburg. 1867.

Münter, F. Kirchengeschichte von Dänemark und Norwegen. 3 vols. Leipzig. 1823–33.

Paludan-Müller, C. De förste Konger af den Oldenborgske Slegt. Copenhagen. 1874.

Schäfer, D. Geschichte von Dänemark. IV. Gesch. d. europ. Staaten. Gotha. 1893.

Waltz, G. Schleswig-Holsteins Geschichte. 2 vols. Göttingen. 1851.

Weidling, J. Schwedische Geschichte im Zeitalter der Reformation. Gotha. 1882.

SPECIAL TREATISES

(Many of the books in this list contain documents previously unpublished)

Baazius, J. *sen.* Inventarium Ecclesiae Sueo-Gothorum. Linköping. 1642.

Bang, A. C. Den Norske Kirkes Geistlighed i Reformations-aarhundredet. Christiania. 1897 f.

—— Dokumenter og Studier vedrœrende den lutherske Katekismus' Historie i Nordens Kirke. 2 vols. Christiania. 1893–9.

Brandt, C. J. Om Lunde-Kanniken Christiern Pedersen og hans Skrifter. Copenhagen. 1882.

Butler, C. M. The Reformation in Sweden. New York. 1884.

Clauss, C. H. Christian der Dritte. Dessau. 1859.

Engelstoft, C. T. Reformantes et Catholici tempore quo sacra emendata sunt in Dania concertantes. Copenhagen. 1836.

—— De Confutatione Latina quae Apologiae concionatorum evang. anno 1530 traditae apposita est commentatio. Copenhagen. 1847.

Faut, E. M. De successione canonica episcoporum Sueciae. Upsala. 1790.

Flaux, A. de. La Suède au XVIme siècle. Paris. 1861.

Gustavus Vasa, the History of. With extr. from his corr. London. 1852. [Contains a short bibliography.]

Gerdes, D. Historia Reformationis. III. Groningen and Bremen. 1749.

Gfrörer, A. F. Gustav Adolph. Ed. 2. Stuttgart. 1845.

Gieseler, J. C. L. Lehrbuch der Kirchengeschichte. III. Bonn. 1853.

Gramm, J. Dissert. de Reformatione in Dania. In Scriptorum a Societate Hafniensi editorum III. Copenhagen. 1747.

Hammerich, F. Danmark under Adelsvälden, 1523–1660. 4 vols. Copenhagen. 1854–9.

Handelmann, H. Die letzten Zeiten der hanseatischen Uebermacht in Norden. Kiel. 1853.

Hering, H. Doktor Pomeranus, Johannes Bugenhagen. Schriften des Vereins für Reformationsgeschichte. vi 22. Halle. 1888.

Knudsen, H. Joachim Rœnnow. Copenhagen. 1840.

Königsfeldt, J. P. F. De katholske Biskopper i Danmark. Historiske Aarböger. Ed. C. Molbech. iii. Copenhagen. 1851.

Magni, O. Historia de gentibus septentrionalibus. Rome. 1555.

[Mason, A. J.] The Loss of the Succession in Denmark. Church Quarterly Review, xxxii. London. 1891.

Messenius, J. Scondia Illustrata. Ed. J. Peringskjold. 15 vols. Stockholm. 1700-5.

Molbech, C. Historiske Aarböger. 3 vols. Copenhagen. 1845-51.

Müller, P. E. Vita Lagonis Urne. 2 pts. Copenhagen. 1831-3.

Münter, B. Symbolae ad illustrandum Bugenhagii in Dania Commorationem. Copenhagen. 1836.

—— Den Danske Reformationshistorie. 2 vols. Copenhagen. 1802.

Nicholson, A. Apostolical Succession in the Church of Sweden. 2 pts. London. 1880-7.

Nissen, R. T. Den Nordiske Kirkes Historie. Christiania. 1875.

Norlin, T. Svenska Kyrkans Historia efter Reformationen. 2 vols. Stockholm. 1864-71.

Paludan-Müller, C. Grevens Feide. 2 vols. Copenhagen. 1853-4.

—— Jens Andersen Beldenak. Odense. 1837.

Reuterdahl, H. Svenska Kyrkans Historia. 4 vols. Lund. 1838-66.

Römer, R. C. H. Specimen historico-theologicum de Gustauo I. Utrecht. 1840.

Rördam, H. F. Mester Jœrgen Jensen Sadolin. Odense. 1866.

Schmitt, L. Die Verteidigung der katholischen Kirche in Dänemark. Paderborn. 1899.

—— Der Karmeliter Paulus Heliä. Stimmen aus Maria-Laach, No. 60. Freiburg i. B. 1893.

—— Johann Tausen. Görresgesellschaft. Bonn. 1894.

Sjögren, O. Gustaf Wasa. Stockholm. 1896 f.

Thyselius, P. E. Bidrag till Svenska Kyrkans Historia. Upsala. 1851 etc.

Vogt, K. A. T. Johannes Bugenhagen Pomeranus. Elberfeld. 1867.

Waltz, G. Lübeck unter J. Wullenwever u. d. Europ. Politik. 3 vols. Berlin. 1855.

Watson, P. B. The Swedish Revolution under Gustavus Vasa. Cambridge, Mass. 1889.

Willson, T. B. History of Church and State in Norway. London. 1903.

Yssel de Schepper, G. A. Lotgevallen van Christiern II en Isabella van Oostenrijk. Zwolle. 1870.

See also Articles etc. in

Annaler for nordisk Oldkyndighed (Copenhagen).

Colonial Church Chronicle. 1861.

Historisk Tidsskrift (Christiania).

Historisk Tidsskrift (Copenhagen).

Kirkehistoriske Samlinger *and* Nye Kirkehistoriske Samlinger. 1847 seqq.

Norske Magazin.

Skandinavisk Museum *and* Skandinaviske Litteratur-Selskabs Skrifter. Copenhagen. 1798-1832.

Theologisk Tidsskrift.

Videnskabernes Selskabs Skrifter *og* Afhandlinger (Copenhagen).

Zeitschrift für historische Theologie xi; xvii (Reformation in Sweden); xx (Reformation in Iceland).

Zeitschrift für Kirchengeschichte. viii, xiii.

CHAPTER XVIII

THE CHURCH AND REFORM

*Some of the material for the following bibliography was collected by **Lord Acton**, and the note on Manuscripts is in his own words*

I. MANUSCRIPTS

The archives of the Council of Trent are dispersed in many places. At the Vatican, they occupy 151 volumes. From these, mainly, the Authentic Acts will be edited by the directors of the Historische Jahrbuch; and Sickel is preparing to publish the Correspondence between Rome and the Legates during the later period.

The Farnese papers are at Naples, the Borromeo papers in the Ambrosian Library; the Altemps papers at Sesto Calende. There are 12 volumes of Commendone at Città di Castello, and 42 volumes of Cervini, the most valuable of all, at Florence; while the letters of Cardinal Pole have to be brought together from at least eight public collections. Beyond the diplomacy of the Catholic States, the Record Office contains more than is indicated in the Calendars.

Most of Pallavicini's sources are accounted for. Part of Sarpi's are reported to have been lost in a fire; but his chief authority for the last years is preserved in the Gonzaga Archives at Mantua.

Information as to manuscript materials, the present limit, and the direction of research, is given by some of the writers mentioned; by Koellner, Theiner, Calenzio, Druffel, Sickel; by Finazzi, in the Miscellanea di Storia Italiana; Cigogna, Inscrizioni Veneziane; and Valentinelli, Regesten zur Deutschen Geschichte aus den Handschriften der Marcusbibliothek (Abhandlungen der Historischen Classe der Bayrischen Akademie, 1866).

Transcripts, made from time to time for learned men, are preserved at Paris, Naples, Venice, Bergamo, Trent, at the British Museum and the Bodleian. Among these are the letters of the papal agent, Visconti, and the diaries of the Secretary Massarelli.

II. AUTHORITIES, AND COLLECTIONS OF DOCUMENTS, MAINLY CONTEMPORARY

Balan, P. Clementis VII Epistolae. Monumenta seculi xvi hist. illustrantia, vol. i. Innsbruck. 1885.

Baluze, S. Miscellanea, ed. Mansi, iii, iv. 4 vols. Lucca. 1764.

Bartholomaeus de Martyribus, F. Opera. II 423–456. Rome. 1735.

Beccadelli, L. Monumenti. Ed. G. Morandi. 2 vols. Bologna. 1797–1804.

Braunsberger, O. B. Petri Canisii Epistolae et Acta. Vol. I. 1541–56. Freiburg i. B. 1896.

Bucholtz, F. B. von. Geschichte Ferdinand des Ersten. 9 vols. Vienna. 1838.

Calenzio, G. Documenti inediti e nuovi lavori letterarii sul Concilio di Trento. Rome. 1874.

Carayon, A. Documents inédits concernant la compagnie de Jésus. 23 vols. Poitiers. 1863–86.

Caro, Annibale. Delle Lettere del Commendatore, scritte a nome del Card. Alessandro Farnese. 3 vols. Milan. 1807.

—— Prose Inedite. Ed. G. Cugnoni. Imola. 1872.

Carraciolo, A. De vita Pauli IV. Cologne. 1612.

Castelnau, M. de. Mémoires. Ed. Le Laboureur. 3 vols. Brussels. 1731.

Cerasoli, F. Alcuni documenti inediti relativi al Concilio di Trento. In Archivio Storico Italiano, serie 5, vol. VIII. pp. 289–295. Florence. 1891.

Cimber, M. L., and F. Danjou. Archives Curieuses, VI. 1–170. Paris. 1835.

Coleccion de Documentos ineditos para la Historia de España, vol. IX. Madrid. 1846. (Doc. relativos al concilio de Trento.)

Commendone, J. F. Lettere. In Miscellanea di Storia Italiana, VI. pp. 1–240. (Regia Deputazion di Storia Patria.) Turin. 1869.

Concilium Tridentinum. Diariorum, Actorum, Epistularum, Tractatuum Nova Collectio; edidit Societas Goerresiana. Diariorum Pars Prima. Herculis Severoli Commentarius, Angeli Masserelli Diaria I–IV. Ed. Sebastianus Merkle. Freiburg i. B. 1901.

Condé, Mémoires du Prince de. 6 vols. 1743–45. Michaud, VI.

Constitutiones Societatis Jesu. Rome. 1558.

Contarini, G. Opera. Paris. 1571.

Cortese, G. Epistolarum Familiarium Liber. Venice. 1573.

Cyprianus, E. S. Tabularium Ecclesiae Romanae, saeculi XVI. Frankfort. 1731.

Della Casa, Giovanni. Opere, II. 6 vols. Naples. 1733.

Döllinger, J. J. von. Ungedruckte Berichte und Tagebücher zur Geschichte des Concils von Trient. 2 vols. Nördlingen. 1876.

—— Beiträge zur Politischen, Kirchlichen, und Culturgeschichte der sechs letzten Jahrhunderte. Vols. I, III. Ratisbon. 1862–82.

Druffel, A. von. Beiträge zur Reichsgeschichte. In Briefe und Akten zur Gesch. des sechzehnten Jahrhunderts. (Bavarian Academy.) 4 vols. Munich. 1873–96.

—— and K. Brandi. Monumenta Tridentina. Beiträge zur Geschichte des Concils von Trient. Vol. I. 1546–7. Munich. 1899.

Ehses, S. Eine Denkschrift aus dem Jahre 1530 über Berufung eines allgemeinen Conzils. In Römische Quartalschrift. pp. 473–492. 1894.

Fiedler, J. Relationen Venetianischer Botschaften über Deutschland und Oesterreich im 16ten Jahrhunderte. Fontes Rerum Austriacarum, Diplom. et Acta, XXX. Vienna. 1870.

Friedensburg, W. Nuntiaturberichte aus Deutschland. 1533–9. 4 vols. Gotha. 1892–3.

Giberti, J. M. Opera. Edd. P. and H. Ballerini. Verona. 1740.

Granvelle, Card de. Papiers d'État. Ed. C. Weiss. III–VII. Collection des documents inédits de l'Histoire de France. 1842–9.

Gratianus, A. M. De Scriptis invita Minerva, cum adnotationibus H. Lagomarsini. 2 vols. Florence. 1745–6.

—— De Vita J. F. Commendoni Cardinalis. Libri IV. Paris. 1669.

Grisar, H. Iacobi Lainez Disputationes Tridentinae. 2 vols. Innsbruck. 1886.

Historiae Societatis Jesu pars prima sive Ignatius auctore Nicolao Orlandino. Pars secunda sive Lainius. Pars tertia sive Borgia. Pars quarta sive Everardus auctore F. Sacchino. Pars quinta sive Claudius, tomus prior auctore F. Sacchino. Pars quinta, tomus posterior, ab anno Christi 1591 ad 1616 auctore

J. Juvencio. Pars sexta complectens res gestas sub M. Vitelleschio, tomus prior ab anno Christi 1616 auctore J. C. Cordara. Tomus secundus ab anno Christi 1625 ad annum 1632. Antwerp and Rome. 1620–1750.

Hosius, S. Epistolae ad Diversos. In Opera II. Cologne. 1584.

—— Epistolae. 2 vols. Vols. IV and IX. In Acta Historica. Edd. F. Hipler and V. Zakrzewski. Cracow. 1879 and 1888.

Hugo, C. L. Sacrae antiquitatis Monumenta Historica, Dogmatica, Diplomatica. I. 215–426. Étival. 1725.

Imago primi seculi Societatis Jesu a Provincia Flandro-Belgica ejusdem Societatis representata. Antwerp. 1640.

Instructions et Lettres des Rois tres-chrestiens et de leurs ambassadeurs et autres Actes concernant le Concile de Trent. Paris. 1654.

Laemmer, H. Analecta Romana. Schaffhausen. 1857–67.

—— Monumenta Vaticana historiam ecclesiasticam seculi XVI illustrantia. Freiburg i. B. 1861.

Le Plat, J. Monumentorum ad Historiam Concilii Tridentini potissimum illustrandum spectantium amplissima collectio. 7 vols. Louvain. 1781–7.

L'Europe Savante, IX 63–241. The Hague. 1719. Le Courayer's selection from Visconti's letters for 1562.

Loyola, Ignacio de. Cartas. Madrid. 1874–7.

Maffei, G. P. De vita et moribus Loyolae. Cologne etc. 1585.

Mansi, J. D. Conciliorum Supplementum, v. Venice. 1751.

Martene, E., and Durand, U. Amplissima Collectio, VIII. 1022–1445. Paris. 1733.

Milledonne, A. Journal de Concile de Trente. Ed. A. Baschet. Paris. 1870.

Monumenta historica Societatis Jesu nunc primum edita a Patribus ejusdem Societatis. Madrid. 1894 etc.

Morone, G. Legazione. In Brieger's Zeitschrift für Kirchengeschichte, III 654. Gotha. 1879.

Paleotto, G. Acta Concilii Tridentini, 1562–3. Ed. J. Mendham. 1842.

Paris, L. Négociations, lettres et pièces diverses relatives au règne de François II. In Collection de documents inédits sur l'histoire de France. 1841.

Pastor, L. Correspondenz Contarinis, 1541. 1880.

Planck, G. J. Anecdota ad Historiam concilii Tridentini pertinentia. Göttingen. 1791–1818.

Pogiani, J. Epistolae. Ed. H. Lagomarsini, S. J. 4 vols. Rome. 1762–8.

Pole, R. Epistolae, et aliorum ad ipsum. Ed. A. M. Quirini. 5 vols. Brescia. 1744–57.

Relazioni della corte di Roma. Ed. T. Gar. I, II. In E. Alberi, Relaz. degli Amb. Venet. Ser. II. Vols. III and IV. Florence. 1846 and 1857.

Ribadeneyra, P. Vida del P. Ignacio de Loyola. Madrid. 1594.

—— Vita Jac. Laynes, Alphonsi item Salmeronis. Cologne. 1604.

—— Vita Ignatii Loiolae qui religionem clericorum societatis Jesu instituit. 8vo. Antwerp. 1587.

Ribier, G. Lettres et Mémoires d'Estat, II. Blois. 1666.

Ruscelli, G. Lettere di Principi. Venice. 1574.

Sadoleto, J. Epistolarum Libri Sexdecim. Lyons. 1560.

Sala, A. Documenti circa la Vita e le Gesta di San Carlo Borromeo. III. 3 vols. Milan. 1861.

Santa Croce, Cardinal P. Lettres. Ed. J. Aymon, in "Tous les synodes nationaux des églises réformées de France auxquels on a joint les mandemens royaux et plusieurs lettres politiques sur ces matières synodales." (Cinquante lettres anecdotes écrites au Cardinal Borromeo par le Cardinal de St Croix.) The Hague. 1710.

—— Vita e Nunziature, in Miscellanea di Storia Italiana, v. pp. 477–1173. (Regia Deputazion di Storia Patria.) Turin. 1868.

Schelhorn, J. G. Amoenitates Historiae Ecclesiasticae. 2 vols. Frankfort and Leipzig. 1737 and 1738.

Serristori, A. Legazioni. Ed. Gius. Canestrini. Florence. 1853.

Sickel, Th. Analecta Juris Pontificii. 1872.

—— Das Reformations-Libell Ferdinands I, in Archiv für österreichische Geschichte, xlv. (Kaiserliche Akademie der Wissenschaften.) Vienna. 1871.

—— Die Geschäfts-ordnung des Concils von Trient. Vienna. 1871.

—— Zur Geschichte des Concils von Trient, 1559–63. Vienna. 1872.

Silva, L. A. Rebello da, and J. da Silva Mendes Seal. Corpo Diplomatico Portuguez, vi–x. (Academia das Sciencias de Lisboa.) 1862–91.

Sleidan, J. Briefwechsel. Ed. H. Baumgarten. Strassburg. 1881.

Tejada y Ramiro, Juan. Coleccion de Canones de la Iglesia Española, iv. 541–886. 5 vols. Madrid. 1849–55.

Theiner, A. Acta genuina Concilii Tridentini. 2 vols. Zagrabr. 1875.

Truchsess, O. Vier ungedruckte Gutachten des Cardinals Otto Truchsess über die Lage der kath. Kirche in Deutschland. Ed. W. E. Schwarz. Römische Quartalschrift, pp. 25–43. 1890.

—— Ein Schreiben des Cardinals Otto von Augsburg über das Koncil von Trient. Ed. Knöpfler. Historisches Jahrbuch, x. p. 555. Munich. 1889.

—— Litterae a Truchsesso annis 1560 et 1561 datae ad Hosium. Ed. A. Weber. Ratisbon. 1892.

Turba, G. Venetianische Depeschen vom Kaiserhofe, ii, iii. Vienna. 1892–5.

Vargas, F. de, and de Malvenda, P. Lettres et Mémoires de, et de quelques Evêques d'Espagne touchant le Concile de Trente. Ed. M. Levassor. Amsterdam. 1699.

Vergerio, P. P. Briefwechsel. Edd. Kausler und Schott. Bibliotek des Literarischen Vereins. Vol. cxxiv. Stuttgart. 1875.

Villanueva, J. L. and J. Viage Literario á las Iglesias de España, con algunas observaciones. Vol. xx (1851). 22 vols. Madrid and Valencia. 1803–52.

—— J. L. Vida Literaria. ii. 409–470. 2 vols. London. 1825.

Vio, Tommaso de, Cardinal Cajetan. Opuscula Omnia. Rome. 1570.

Visconti, C. Lettres Anecdotes, 1563. Ed. J. Aymon. 2 vols. Amsterdam. 1719.

Zebrzydowski, Andreas de V. (Bishop of Cracow). Epistolae, vols. i, ii. In Acta Historica res gestas Poloniae illustrantia. i. Cracow. 1878.

III. PRINCIPAL HISTORIES

Baguenault de Puchesse, F. Histoire du Concile de Trente. 8vo. Paris. 1870.

Becchetti, F. A. Istoria degli ultimi quattro secoli della Chiesa, ix, x. 12 vols. 4to. Rome. 1795–6.

Calenzio, G. Esame Critico-letterario delle opere riguardanti la Storia del Concilio di Trento. Rome and Turin. 1869.

—— Saggio di Storia del Concilio di Trento sotto Paolo III. Rome. 1869.

Ellies Dupin, L. Hist. de l'Eglise du xvie siècle. Paris. 1701–13.

Froude, J. A. Lectures on the Council of Trent. London. 1896.

Janssen, J. Geschichte des Deutschen Volkes, vols. iii, iv. Freiburg i. B. 1876 etc.

Laemmer, H. Zur Kirchengeschichte des sechzehnten und siebenzehnten Jahrhunderts. Leipzig. 1863.

Leva, G. de. Storia Documentata di Carlo V, vols. iv, v. Venice. 1881, 1894.

Maurenbrecher, W. Das Concil von Trient. Raumer's Historisches Taschenbuch. Leipzig. 1886, 1888, 1890.

—— Geschichte der katholischen Reformation. Nördlingen. 1880.

Maynier, L. Études sur le Concile de Trente. Paris. 1874.

Mendham, J. Memoirs of the Council of Trent. London. 1834–46. A copy prepared for a second ed. in the Incorporated Law Society's Library.

Pallavicini, Sforza. Istoria del Concilio di Trento 1656. Ed. F. A. Zaccaria, 4 vols. Rome. 1833. With additions, but omitting controversy, 3 vols. 1846.

⌐Philippson, M. La Contre-Révolution religieuse du xvie siècle. Brussels. 1884.

—— Westeuropa im Zeitalter von Philipp II, Elizabeth und Heinrich IV, I. 71–184. (Oncken, Allgemeine Geschichte, etc.) Berlin. 1882.

Prat, J. M. Histoire du Concile de Trente. 3 vols. Brussels. 1854.

Ranke, L. von. Die Römischen Päbste, I. Berlin. 1834. Werke, xxxvii. Leipzig. 1878.

Raynaldus, O. Annales Ecclesiastici (ed. Mansi, xiii, xiv, xv). Lucca. 1755–6.

Salig, C. A. Vollständige Historie des Tridentischen Conciliums. 3 vols. 4to. Halle. 1741–5.

Sarpi, Paolo. Istoria del Concilio Tridentino. (Pietro Soave Polano.) London. 1619. French translation with notes by P. Le Courayer. 2 vols. London, 1736, and 3 vols. London, 1751.

⌐Ward, A. W. The Counter Reformation. Epochs of Church History. London. 1889.

Wessenberg, I. H. von. Die grossen Kirchenversammlungen. iii, iv. Constance. 1840.

IV. TREATISES ON SPECIAL SUBJECTS

Baini, G. Memorie storico-critiche della vita e delle opere di Giovanni Pierluigi da Palestrina. 2 vols. Rome. 1828.

Baumgarten, H. Geschichte Karls V. Vol. iii. 3 vols. Stuttgart. 1885–92.

—— Über Sleidans Leben und Briefwechsel. Strassburg. 1878.

Bernabei, N. Vita del Cardinale Giovanni Morone vescovo di Modena, e biografie dei Cardinali Modenesi. Modena. 1885.

Braun, W. Cardinal Gasparo Contarini. 1903.

Braunsberger, O. Entstehung und erste Entwickelung der Katechismen des sel. Petrus Canisius. Freiburg i. B. 1893.

Brosch, M. Geschichte des Kirchenstaates. Gotha. 1880.

Cantù, C. Gli Eretici d' Italia, discorsi storici. Vol. ii. 3 vols. Turin. 1865–67.

—— Italiani Illustri, ii. 3 vols. Milan. 1879.

Carayon, A. Bibliographie Historique de la Compagnie de Jésus. Paris. 1864.

Cecchetti, B. La Republica di Venezia e la Corte di Roma nei rapporti della Religione, ii. 25–66. Venice. 1874.

Cossio, A. Il Cardinale Gaetano e la Riforma. Cividale. 1902.

Crétinau-Joly, J. Histoire religieuse politique et littéraire de la Compagnie de Jésus. 6 vols. Paris and Lyons. 1845–6.

Dittrich, F. Gasparo Contarini. Braunsberg. 1883.

Druffel, A. von. Ueber den Vertrag zwischen Kaiser und Papst von Juni 1541. Deutsche Zeitschr. für Gesch. iii. Freiburg i. B. and Leipzig. 1889.

—— L. v. Nogarola. In Sitzungsberichte der Bayr. Akademie, Hist. Classe, 426–456. 1875.

—— Entgegnung auf Maurenbrechers Antikritik. In Historische Zeitschrift, xviii. 128–170. Munich. 1867.

—— Die Sendung des Cardinals Sfondrato an den Hof Karls 1547–48. Abhandlungen der Hist. Classe der k. Bayer. Akad. Wiss. xx. 1893.

—— Karl V und die Römische Curie 1544–46. Vier Abhandlungen der Bayr. Akademie, Hist. Classe. 1877–91.

Duruy, G. Le Cardinal Carlo Caraffa. Paris. 1882.

Eichhorn, A. Der Ermländische Bischof und Cardinal S. Hosius. 2 vols. Königsberg. 1854–5.

Friedensburg, W. Beiträge zur Briefwechsel der katholischen Gelehrten Deutschlands im Reformationszeitalter. In Zeitschrift für Kirchengeschichte. 1897–1902.

Gieseler, J. C. L. Lehrbuch der Kirchengeschichte, iii, 2, pp. 505–569. Bonn. 1853.

Gothein, E. Ignatius von Loyola und die Gegenreformation, pp. 468–520. Halle. 1895.

Guillemin, J. J. Le Cardinal de Lorraine. Paris. 1847.

Harnack, A. Lehrbuch der Dogmengeschichte, iii. 588–617. Berlin. 1890. Engl Trans. Vol. vii, pp. 1–115. London. 1899.

Hefele, C. J. Der Cardinal Ximenes. Tübingen. 1851. Trans. London. 1860.

Hinschius, P. Kirchenrecht, iii. 430–451. 1883. 8vo. Berlin. 1869 etc.

Hoffman, P. E. F. Die Jesuiten. 2 vols. Mannheim. 1871.

Huber, J. N. Der Jesuiten-Orden nach seiner Verfassung und Doctrin, Wirksamkeit und Geschichte characterisirt. Berlin. 1873.

Jenkins, R. C. Pre-Tridentine Doctrine. London. 1891.

—— The Judgment of Thomas de Vio. Canterbury. 1858.

Koellner, W. H. D. E. Symbolik, ii. 7–140. Hamburg. 1844.

Laemmer, H. Die vortridentinisch-katholische Theologie des Reformationszeitalters aus den Quellen dargestellt. Berlin. 1858.

Lafuente, M. Historia general de España, vols. xii, xiii. Madrid. 1853–4.

Lavallée, J. Histoire des Inquisitions religieuses d'Italie et d'Espagne et de Portugal, depuis leur origine jusqu'à la conquête de l'Espagne. 2 vols. Paris. 1809.

Lea, H. C. A History of the Inquisition of the Middle Ages. 3 vols. London. 1888.

—— Chapters from the Religious History of Spain connected with the Inquisition. Philadelphia. 1890.

Limborch, P. van. Hist. Inquisitionis. Amsterdam. 1692.

Llorente, J. L. Historia critica de la Inquisicion de España. 10 vols. Madrid. 1822.

—— J. A. Anales de la Inquisicion de España. 2 vols. Madrid. 1812–13.

Lüber, W. Gaetano da Thiene. 1883.

Maurenbrecher, W. Karl V und die Deutschen Protestanten. Düsseldorf. 1865.

Mendham, J. The Literary Policy of the Church of Rome. London. 1830.

Moses, R. Die Religionsverhandlungen in Hagenau und Worms. 1889.

Müller, H. Les Origines de la Compagnie de Jésus, Ignace et Lainez. Paris. 1898.

Neue Beiträge zur Gesch. des Conzils von Trient. Sybel's Hist. Zeitschr. 1877. Pt i.

Oehler, G. F. Lehrbuch der Symbolik, pp. 88–107. Stuttgart. 1891.

Pastor, L. Die kirchlichen Reunionsbestrebungen, während der Regierung Karls V. Freiburg i. B. 1879.

Pieper, A. Die Päpstlichen Legaten und Nuntien in Deutschland Frankreich und Spanien seit der Mitte des sechzehnten Jahrhunderts. i. Münster. 1897.

Raderus, M. De vita Petri Canisii de Societate Jesu, Sociorum e Germania primi. Libri tres. Munich. 1614.

Reimann, E. Zur Geschichte des Concils von Trient. In Sybel's Hist. Zeitschr. xxx 24. Munich. 1873.

—— in Forschungen zur Deutschen Geschichte, vi, vii, viii. Göttingen. 1866, 7, 8.

Reumont, A. von. Vittoria Colonna. Freiburg i. B. 1881.

Reusch, F. H. Der Index der Verbotenen Bücher. Bonn. 1885.

Ritschl, A. Die Christliche Lehre von der Rechtfertigung und Versöhnung. Vol. i. Geschichte der Lehre. Bonn. 1889.

Sala, A. Biografia di S. Carlo Borromeo. Milan. 1858.

Sclopis, F. Le Cardinal Jean Morone, 1869. In Séances et travaux de l'Académie des sciences morales et politiques (Institut Impérial de France). Vols. xc and xci. Paris. 1869–70.

Serry, J. H. Historia Congregationum de auxiliis gratiae. Venice. 1740.

Sickel, Th. Römische Berichte, 1895–6. In Sitzungsberichte der Phil. Hist. Classe der k. Akademie der Wissenschaften. Vienna. Vol. 133, 1895; vol. 135, 1896; vol. 141, 1899; vol. 143. 1901; and vol. 144, 1902.

Sommervogel, C.   Bibliothèque de la Compagnie de Jésus.   Brussels and Paris. 1890 etc.

Vetter, J. P.   Die Religionsverhandlungen auf dem Reichstage zu Regensburg.   1899.

Watrigant, H.   La Genèse des Exercices de saint Ignace de Loyola.   In Études publiées par des pères de la Compagnie de Jésus. May 20, July 20, October 20. Paris. 1897.

Zur Geschichte des Concils von Trient. In Sybel's Hist. Zeitschr. 1896. No. 3.

(See also Bibliography to Chapter XII.)

CHAPTER XIX

TENDENCIES OF EUROPEAN THOUGHT IN THE AGE OF THE REFORMATION

I. ORIGINAL AUTHORITIES

Acta et scripta Synodalia Dordracena. . . . Erdervik. 1620. [This book was so hastily printed that the text is often confused and incorrect; certain copies were issued without any date on the title page. It is the Remonstrant version of the Synod's proceedings.]

Acta Synodi nationalis . . . auctoritate . . . foederati Belgii provinciarum. . . . Dordrecht. 1620. [The official and authoritative documents of the Reformed Church.]

Arminius, J. Opera theologica. Leyden. 1629.

—— The Works of. Transl. by James Nichols. 2 vols. London. 1825–8. Vol. III. Transl. by William Nichols, the son. London. 1875.

Bacon, Francis. For what he calls the "philosophia pastoralis" of Telesio, see De principiis atque originibus. Gruter's ed., 1653, pp. 208 ff. Spalding's ed. 1859, vol. III, pp. 65 ff. Eng. transl. vol. V, pp. 466 ff.

Bellarmine, Card. Disputationes de Controversiis Christianae Fidei adversus hujus Temporis Haereticos. Ingolstadt. 1587–90. In Opera Omnia. Vols. I–IV. Cologne. 1617.

Boehme, Jacob. Theosophische Schriften. 9 vols. Amsterdam. 1682. Die Werke Boehmes. Ed. Schiebler. 6 vols. Leipzig. 1831–46.

Bruno, Giordano. Opere raccolte e pubblicate da Adolfo Wagner. 2 vols. Leipzig. 1830.

—— Opera Latina. 2 vols. Naples. 1879.

—— Scripta Latina (Gfrörer). Stuttgart. 1836.

Chemnitius, D. M. Examen concilii Tridentini. . . . Geneva. 1641.

Episcopius, Simon. Opera theologica. 2 vols. Amsterdam. 1650, 1665.

Epistolae Clarorum Virorum . . . ad Joannem Reuchlin. 1514.

Epistolae Obscurorum Virorum. Pt I, 3rd ed. 1516, with 41 epistles and 7 in the appendix. — Pt II, 1517, with 62 epistles, 8 being added in an appendix to a second ed. Finally in an ed. publ. 1556 a late Ep. was added, which Böcking describes as "rustice obscena."

Erasmus, Desiderius. Opera. 8 vols. Basel. 1540. 10 vols. Leyden. 1703–6.

—— Novum Instrumentum. Basel. 1516.

Ficino, Marsilio. De Religione Christiana et Fidei Pietate. Florence. 1478.

—— Theologia Platonica de Animorum Immortalitate. Florence. 1482.

—— Opera. Paris. 1641. The edition of his Translations, Venice, 1517, also contains in the dedications and the prefaces matter which is important for his views.

Gemistos Plethon. De virtutibus. Basel. 1552.

—— De Platonicae atque Aristotelicae Philosophiae differentia. Basel. 1574.

Gomarus, Franciscus. Opera theologica omnia. Amsterdam. 1664.

Grotius, Hugo. Opera omnia theologica. 4 vols. Amsterdam. 1679.

Hutten, Ulrich von. Opera omnia. Böcking. 5 vols. With two supplementary vols. Leipzig. 1859–69.

—— Die Deutschen Schriften. Ed. J. Szamatolski. 1891.

—— Gespräche ... übersetzt ... von D. F. Strauss. Leipzig. 1860.

Montaigne, M. de. Essais. 1580–8.

Pico della Mirandola. Pici utriusque Opera. Vol. i. Basel. 1573. Vol. ii. 1601. [The two Picos are the uncle and nephew, John and John Francis.]

Pomponazzi, P. De animae immortalitate. Leyden. 1534.

—— De Incantationibus. Basel. 1556.

—— De Fato, libero Arbitrio, etc. Basel. 1567.

—— Opera. Basel. 1567.

Rabelais, François. Hippocratis et Galeni libri aliquot. Lyons. 1532.

—— Œuvres de Rabelais avec les Remarques de Le Duchat et de La Monnoye. 5 vols. Amsterdam. 1711.

—— Œuvres de Rabelais, ed. variorum ... avec un commentaire historique et philologique, par Esmangart et E. Johanneau. 8 vols. 1823.

—— The whole works of ..., Or the Lives, Heroic Deeds and Sayings of Gargantua and Pantagruel. Done out of French by Sir Thomas Urchard, Knight, M. Motteux and others. 2 vols. London. 1708.

Reuchlin, J. De verbo mirifico. Basel. 1494.

—— De rudimentis hebraicis. 1506. Of the three books i and ii were a lexicon, iii a grammar; published first at Pforzheim, later at Basel at the author's own cost. [The publisher lamented that the book had no sale.] An enlarged edition under supervision of Sebastian Münster appeared at Basel, 1537.

—— De arte predicandi. 1508.

—— De arte cabbalistica. 1516.

Servetus, M. De Trinitatis Erroribus. Libri vii. 1531.

—— Christianismi Restitutio.... 1553.

Socinus, F. De Jesu Christo Servatore. 1594.

—— De sacrae scripturae Auctoritate. Assertiones theologicae de trino et uno Deo. De statu primi hominis ante lapsum. Tractatus de ecclesia. Tractatus de justificatione. These treatises were published in a volume of Opuscula, printed at Cracow, 1611.

—— Opera Omnia. In vols. i and ii of Bibliotheca Fratrum Polonorum. 1656.

Telesio, B. De rerum natura juxta propria principia. Naples. 1586. This is the date of the completed work; books i and ii were published in 1565 at Rome.

Valla, Laurentius. In latinam N.T. interpretationem ex collatione graecor. exemplarium adnotationes. (Ed. Erasmus.) 1505. [The work was dedicated to Christopher Fischer the apostolical protonotary.]

—— Declamatio de falso credita et ementita Constantini M. donatione, cum ipsa hac donatione. Written 1440. Cf. Hutteni Opera i, pp. 18 ff. English translation with Hutten's preface about 1534. French translation, with historical dissertation, 1879.

—— Elegantiarum Lat. Ling. Paris. 1471. [This work has been frequently republished: in the 15th century alone, no fewer than 12 editions appeared.]

—— De Voluptate ac Vero Bono, with its continuation or appendix "De libero Arbitrio." 1483.

—— Opera. Basel. 1540–3. [The edition however is not quite complete.]

Zanchius, H. Omnia opera theologica. 3 vols. Geneva. 1619.

II. BIOGRAPHIES OF REPRESENTATIVE THINKERS

Adamson, R. Giordano Bruno. In The Development of Modern Philosophy, vol. II. Edinburgh. 1903.

Baird, H. M. Theodore Beza. New York. 1899.

Baum, J. W. Theodor Beza, nach handschriftlichen Quellen dargestellt. Leipzig. 1843–52.

Berti, D. Giordano Bruno, sua vita e sua dottrina. Turin. 1868. New edition, 1880.

Christie, R. C. Étienne Dolet, the Martyr of the Renaissance. London. 1880. New edition, revised and corrected, 1899.

Douen, O. Clément Marot et le Psaultier Huguenot. 2 vols. Paris. 1878–9.

Drummond, R. B. Erasmus, his Life and Character as shewn in his Correspondence and Works. 2 vols. London. 1873.

Fiorentino, F. Bernardino Telesio. 2 vols. Florence. 1872.

—— Pietro Pompanazzi. Florence. 1868.

Firth, I. Life of Giordano Bruno. London. 1887.

Geiger, L. Johann Reuchlin; sein Leben und seine Werke. Leipzig. 1871. (See also Geiger's edition of Reuchlin's Briefwechsel. Tübingen. 1875.)

Jortin, J. Life of Erasmus. 2 vols. London. 1758–60.

Levi, D. Giordano Bruno, o La Religione del Pensiero. Turin. 1887.

McIntyre, J. L. Giordano Bruno. London. 1903.

Mayerhoff. Johann Reuchlin. Berlin. 1830.

Monrad, G. (Bishop of Lolland and Falster). L. Valla. Die erste Kontroverse über d. Ursprung d. apostol. Glaubensbekenntnisses. Transl. from the Danish by A. Michelsen. Gotha. 1881.

Schlosser, F. C. Theodor de Beza und Peter Martyr Vermigli. Heidelberg. 1809.

Strauss, D. F. Ulrich von Hutten. Bonn. 1877.

Tocco, F. Le Opere Latine di Giordano Bruno esposte e confrontate con le Italiane. Florence. 1889. See also: Le Opere Inedite di G. B. Naples. 1891.

Wolf, M. von. Lorenzo Valla. Sein Leben und seine Werke. Leipzig. 1893.

III. HERESIES

Anabaptists

Bax, E. Belfort. Rise and fall of the Anabaptists. London. 1903.

Blaupot ten Cate, S. Geschiedenis der Doopgezinden. Leeuwarden. 1839–47.

Bouterwek, C. W. Zur Litteratur und Geschichte der Wiedertäufer. Bonn. 1864.

Cornelius, C. A. Geschichte des Münsterischen Aufruhrs. 2 vols. Leipzig. 1850–60.

—— Historische Arbeiten, Essays II and III. Leipzig. 1899.

Erkbam, H. W. Geschichte der protest. Sekten im Zeitalter der Reform. Hamburg. 1848.

Geschichtsbücher der Wiedertäufer in Oestreich-Ungarn. Ed. by Dr J. Beck. Vienna. 1883.

Heberle, Th. St. und Kr. 1851, pp. 121–194; 1855, pp. 817–890.

History of Anabaptists of High and Low Germany. (Anon.) 1642.

Keller, Ludwig. Geschichte der Wiedertäufer. Münster. 1880.

Loserth, J. Wiedertäufer in Mähren. Archiv für Oesterr. Geschichte. Vol. LXXXI, pp. 135 ff. Vienna. 1894.

—— Balthasar Hubmayer. Brunn. 1893.

—— Die Stadt Waldshut und die Oesterreich. Regierung 1523–6. (Archiv für Oesterr. Geschichte. Vol. LXXVII, p. 1.) Vienna. 1891.

Menno, Simons. Werke. Amsterdam. 1581.
Ottii Annales anabapt. Basel. 1672.
Seidemann, J. C. Thomas Münzer. Dresden and Leipzig. 1842.
Sweetser Buwage. The anabaptists of the 16th century. Papers of Amer. Soc. of Ch. Hist. III.

Socinians

Fock, O. Der Socinianismus. Kiel. 1847.
Krasinski, Count V. Historical Sketch of the Rise, Progress, and Decline of the Reformation in Poland. Engl. transl. 2 vols. London. 1838.
Rees, T. The Racovian catechism. . . . London. 1818.
Tollin, H. Das Lehrsystem Michael Servets genetisch dargestellt. Gütersloh. 1876–78. (Tollin has most exhaustively discussed Servetus and almost every question connected with him. His articles extending over many years are to be found in many German historical and theological reviews and periodicals; notably in the St. u. Kr. Zeitschr. für Wissensch. Theologie, and the Jahrb. für Protestant. Theologie.)
Willis, R. Servetus and Calvin. . . . London. 1877.

Miscellaneous

Arnold, G. Kirchen und Ketzer-Historie. 4 vols. Frankfort am Main. 1699.
Cantù, C. Gli Eretici d' Italia. 3 vols. Turin. 1865-7.
Harnack, A. Dogmengeschichte. Vol. 3. Third Book. 1890. Translation by W. McGilchrist. Vol. VII. London. 1899.

IV. GENERAL

Baur, F. C. Die christliche Lehre von der Dreieinigkeit und Menschwerdung Gottes. 3rd vol. Tübingen. 1843.
Buhle, J. G. Geschichte der neuern Philosophie. Göttingen. 1800.
Bruckerus, Jacobus. Historia critica philosophiae. 4 vols. Leipzig. 1743.
Carriere. M. Die philosophische Weltanschauung der Reformationszeit. Stuttgart. 1847.
Döllinger, J. J. von. Die Reformation. . . . 3 vols. Regensburg. 1851.
Hegel, G. W. F. Geschichte der Philosophie. 3 vols. Berlin. 1836.
Höffding, H. History of modern philosophy. Vol. I. London. 1900.
Lavallée, J. Histoire des Inquisitions Religieuses. 2 vols. Paris. 1808.
Llorente, J. A. Historia critica de la Inquisicion de España. Madrid. Translated by A. Pellier. 2nd ed. 1818. Histoire Critique de l'Inquisition d'Espagne. 4 vols. Paris. 1818.
McCrie, T. History of the Reformation in Italy. Edinburgh. 1827. New ed. 1856.
Philippson, M. La Contre-Révolution Religieuse au XVI Siècle. Brussels. 1884.
Ritter, H. Geschichte der christlichen Philosophie. Hamburg. 1850.
—— Die christliche Philosophie. . . . Göttingen. 1859.
Schultze, F. Geschichte der Philosophie der Renaissance. Jena. 1874.
Tozer, H. F. A Byzantine Reformer. Journal of Hellenic Studies, 1886, pp. 353–380.
Zeller, E. Geschichte der deutschen Philosophie. Munich. 1875.

(See also the Bibliographies to Chapters XVI and XVII of Vol. I.)

CHRONOLOGICAL TABLE

OF

LEADING EVENTS

1503 Death of Alexander VI. Accession of Julius II.
1508 Luther goes to Wittenberg.
1509 Accession of Henry VIII in England.
1511 Synod of Pisa.
1512 Opening of the Fifth Lateran Council.
1513 Death of Julius II. Accession of Giovanni de' Medici as Leo X.
—— Accession of Christian II in Denmark, Norway, and Sweden.
1515 Death of Louis XII of France. Accession of Francis I.
—— Battle of Marignano (September 13).
1516 French Concordat with Leo X.
—— Death of Ferdinand of Aragon.
—— Treaty of Noyon.
1517 Close of the Fifth Lateran Council.
—— Charles V goes to Spain.
—— Publication of Luther's Theses (November).
1518 Luther before the Cardinal-Legate at Augsburg.
—— Zwingli, people's priest at Zurich.
1519 Death of the Emperor Maximilian (January 19).
—— Election of Charles to the Empire (June).
1520 Luther excommunicated.
—— Publication of Luther's *Appeal to the Christian Nobility*.
—— Charles V in England (May). Field of Cloth of Gold (June).
—— Coronation of Charles V at Aachen (October).
—— Christian crowned King of Sweden (November).
—— The Stockholm Bath of Blood.
—— Straits of Magellan passed.
1521 Rising of Gustaf Eriksson (Gustavus Vasa) in Dalecarlia.
—— Defeat of the *Comuneros* at Villalar (April 24).
—— Diet of Worms. Luther placed under the Ban of the Empire.
—— Treaty of Bruges (August). Albany in Scotland.
—— Outbreak of war. Occupation of Milan by the forces of Charles and Leo X
       (November).
—— Death of Leo X (December 1).
1522 Election of Adrian Dedel as Adrian VI.
—— Luther returns to Wittenberg.
—— Battle of the Bicocca (April).
—— Charles V in England. Treaty of Windsor (June).

1522 Charles V in Spain.
—— The Knights' War in Germany.
—— Conquest of Mexico completed.
—— Capitulation of Rhodes to the Turks (December).
1523 First public disputation at Zurich.
—— Flight of Christian II from Denmark.
—— Rule of Frederick I (of Holstein) in Denmark and Norway.
—— Gustavus Vasa King in Sweden.
—— Defection of the Constable of Bourbon.
—— Bonnivet in Italy.
—— Suffolk and van Buren in Picardy.
—— Death of Adrian VI (September 14).
—— Election of Giulio de' Medici as Clement VII.
1524 Retreat of Bonnivet.
—— Albany leaves Scotland for the last time.
—— Beginnings of the Peasants' Rising in Germany (June).
—— Invasion of France. Siege of Marseilles.
—— Francis crosses the Alps.
—— Foundation of the Theatine Order.
1525 Battle of Pavia (February 24).
—— Treaties of the Moor (August).
—— Conspiracy of Girolamo Morone.
—— Prussia becomes a secular duchy.
1526 Treaty of Madrid (January).
—— Marriage of Charles V with Isabella of Portugal.
—— League of Cognac (May).
—— Diet and Recess of Speier.
—— Battle of Mohács (August).
—— Raid of the Colonna on Rome (September).
—— Ferdinand elected King of Bohemia and of Hungary.
—— The Reformation begins in Denmark.
1527 Alliance of Henry VIII and Francis I.
—— Sack of Rome (May 6).
—— Diet of Vesterås in Sweden. Vesterås Recess.
—— Invasion of Italy by Lautrec.
1528 France and England declare war on the Emperor (January).
—— Siege of Naples by Lautrec.
—— Defection of Andrea Doria.
—— Campeggio in England.
1529 Diet of Speier. The "Protest."
—— Execution of Berquin.
—— Civil War in Switzerland. First Peace of Kappel.
—— Treaty of Barcelona (June 29).
—— Charles V in Italy.
—— Peace of Cambray (August 5).
—— Siege of Vienna by the Turks.
—— Conference of Marburg.
—— Fall of Wolsey.
1530 Conference at Bologna (Charles V and Clement VII).
—— Last imperial coronation by the Pope.
—— Charles V in Germany. Diet of Augsburg. Confession of Augsburg.
—— Capture of Florence (August).

1530 Revolt against the Bishop at Geneva.
—— Death of Margaret of Savoy (December).
1531 Ferdinand elected King of the Romans.
—— Maria of Hungary Regent of the Netherlands.
—— Henry VIII Supreme Head of the Church in England.
—— Marriage of Catharine de' Medici with Henry of France (October).
—— Battle of Kappel and death of Zwingli (October).
—— League of Schmalkalden.
1532 Inquisition first established at Lisbon.
—— Annates abolished in England.
—— Alliance of France and England.
—— Turkish invasion repelled.
—— Religious Peace of Nürnberg (July).
—— Charles in Italy.
—— Second Conference at Bologna (December).
—— Conquest of Peru.
1533 English Act in restraint of Appeals to Rome.
—— Wullenwever Burgomaster of Lübeck.
—— Marriage of Henry VIII and Anne Boleyn (May).
—— Catholic League of Halle.
—— Address of Cop. Flight of Calvin.
—— Death of Frederick I of Denmark. Disputed succession.
1534 Anabaptist rising at Münster.
—— Duke Ulrich recovers Württemberg.
—— Peace of Cadan (June).
—— The *Grafenfehde*.
—— Foundation of the Society of Jesus by Ignatius Loyola.
—— Death of Clement VII (September).
—— Accession of Alessandro Farnese as Paul III.
—— The Placards at Paris.
—— English Act against Papal Dispensations, &c.
1535 English Act of Supremacy.
—— Expedition of Tunis.
—— Charles V in Sicily and Naples.
—— Death of Francesco Sforza (November).
1536 First Helvetic Confession.
—— Treaty of Francis with Solyman.
—— Third War between Francis I and Charles V. Savoy occupied by the French (March).
—— Calvin at Ferrara.
—— Publication of the *Christianae Religionis Institutio*.
—— Wittenberg Concord.
—— Calvin at Geneva.
—— Invasion of Provence by Charles V.
—— Smaller monasteries dissolved in England. The Ten Articles.
—— Christian III established on the throne of Denmark and Norway.
1537 Murder of Alessandro de' Medici. Succession of Cosimo I in Florence.
—— *Consilium delectorum Cardinalium de emendanda Ecclesia*.
1538 Calvin expelled from Geneva.
—— Truce of Nice between Charles V and Francis I (June).
—— Catholic League of Nürnberg (June).
—— Death of Charles of Gelders.

1539 Tumult of Ghent.
— William succeeds to Cleves-Jülich.
— Joachim II of Brandenburg becomes a Protestant.
— Death of Duke George of Saxony.
— Monasteries suppressed in England. Act of the Six Articles.
1540 Marriage and divorce of Anne of Cleves.
— Venice makes peace with the Turks.
— Reduction of Ghent (February).
— Investiture of Philip with Milan.
— Edict of Fontainebleau.
— Death of John Zapolya.
— The Jesuit order approved by Paul III.
1541 Religious Colloquy of Ratisbon.
— Solyman takes Buda (September).
— Expedition against Algiers (October).
— Calvin returns to Geneva.
1542 Fourth War between Charles and Francis I.
— John Frederick of Saxony and Philip of Hesse overrun Brunswick.
— Death of James V of Scotland (December).
— The Inquisition established at Rome.
1543 Barbarossa in the Western Mediterranean.
— Expedition of Charles against the Duke of Cleves.
— Conquest of Gelders.
1544 Diet of Speier.
— Battle of Ceresole (April).
— Sieges of Boulogne and St Dizier.
— Peace of Crépy (September).
1545 Massacre of the Waldenses of Provence (April).
— Opening of the Council of Trent (December).
1546 Death of Luther (February).
— Peace between France and England.
— Diet of Ratisbon.
— Alliance of Charles V with Maurice of Saxony.
— League of Charles V with Paul III.
— The Schmalkaldic War.
— Execution of the Fourteen of Meaux.
1547 Death of Henry VIII (January). Accession of Edward VI.
— Somerset Protector.
— Death of Francis I (March). Accession of Henry II.
— The Council removes from Trent to Bologna (March).
— Battle of Mühlberg (April). Maurice Elector of Saxony.
— Murder of Pierluigi Farnese (September).
— Diet of Augsburg (September).
— Battle of Pinkie.
— Establishment of *La Chambre Ardente*.
— Inquisition finally established at Lisbon.
1548 Betrothal of Mary Stewart to the Dauphin Francis.
— The Augsburg *Interim* proclaimed (May).
— First Prayer-Book of Edward VI.
1549 *Consensus Tigurinus*.
— War between England and France.
— Battle of Dussindale.

1549 Fall of Somerset. Rule of Warwick (Northumberland) in England.
—— Council of Bologna suspended.
—— Death of Paul III.
1550 Election of Giovanni Maria del Monte as Julius III.
—— Peace between England and France. Boulogne restored to France.
—— Maurice of Saxony undertakes to execute the ban against Magdeburg.
1551 War in the Parmesan.
—— The Council reopened at Trent.
—— Capture of Tripoli by the Turks.
—— War in Savoy (September).
—— Capitulation of Magdeburg (November).
1552 Treaty of Chambord (January).
—— Second Act of Uniformity and Second Book of Common Prayer.
—— Invasion of Lorraine by France (March). Occupation of the three bishoprics.
—— Flight of Charles V before Maurice of Saxony (May).
—— Suspension of the Council of Trent.
—— Conference at Passau. Treaty of Passau.
—— Siege of Metz (October—December).
1553 League of Heidelberg.
—— Capture of Terouanne (June).
—— Battle of Sievershausen (July). Death of Maurice of Saxony.
—— Death of Edward VI of England (July). Lady Jane Grey proclaimed.
—— Accession of Mary Tudor.
1554 Rising of Sir Thomas Wyatt.
—— Expulsion of Albrecht Alcibiades from Germany.
—— Marriage of Philip of Spain and Mary Tudor (July).
1555 Diet of Augsburg. Religious Peace of Augsburg (September).
—— Death of Julius III (March). Giovanni Pietro Caraffa elected as Paul IV.
—— Fall of Siena (April).
—— Abdication of Charles V at Brussels.
1556 Truce of Vaucelles.
—— War between Paul IV, supported by France, and Philip II, in Italy.
—— The Duc de Guise in Italy (December).
1557 England declares war on France.
—— Battle of St Quentin (August).
—— Paul IV makes peace with Philip II (September).
1558 Capture of Calais (January).
—— Marriage of Mary Stewart and the Dauphin Francis.
—— Laynez elected General of the Jesuit Order.
—— Battle of Gravelines (July).
—— Death of Mary Tudor (November). Accession of Elizabeth.
1559 Death of Christian III of Denmark (January).
—— Acts of Supremacy and Uniformity in England.
—— Treaty of Cateau-Cambrésis (April).
—— John Knox in Scotland. The Lords of the Congregation in arms.
—— Protestant Synod at Paris.
—— Death of Henry II of France (July). Accession of Francis II.
—— Death of Paul IV (August).
—— Election of Giovanni Angelo de' Medici as Pius IV.
1560 Death of Gustavus Vasa of Sweden.
—— Tumult of Amboise (February—March).
—— Michel de l'Hôpital Chancellor of France.

1560 Edict of Romorantin (May).
—— Treaty of Edinburgh (July).
—— Reforming Parliament at Edinburgh (August).
—— Arrest of Condé (October).
—— Death of Francis II of France.   Accession of Charles IX.
—— French Estates at Orleans.
1561 French Estates at Pontoise.
—— Mary Stewart in Scotland (August).
—— Colloquy of Poissy (September).
1562 The Council reopens at Trent.
—— Opening of the Religious Wars in France.
—— Treaty of Hampton Court (September).
1563 The Thirty-nine Articles.
—— Close of the Council of Trent.
1564 Bull *Benedictus Deus*.
—— Death of Calvin (May).

INDEX

Printed in the United States
102636LV00003B/147/A